Buick

Oldsmobile
Pontiac
Full-size Models
Automotive
Repair
Manual

by Ken Freund
and John H Haynes
Member of the Guild of Motoring Writers

Models covered:

Buick: LeSabre, Estate, Electra and Limited

Oldsmobile: Delta 88, Royale and Brougham, Custom Cruiser, Ninety-Eight Luxury, Regency and Brougham

Pontiac: Catalina, Grandville, Brougham, Bonneville and Parisienne

1970 through 1990

Does not include diesel engine and related information or front-wheel drive models

(1U3 – 1551)

ABCDE
FGHIJ
KLM

Haynes Publishing Group
Sparkford Nr Yeovil
Somerset BA22 7JJ England

Haynes North America, Inc
861 Lawrence Drive
Newbury Park
California 91320 USA

Acknowledgements

We are grateful for the help and cooperation of the General Motors Corporation for assistance with technical information, certain illustrations and vehicle photos, and the Champion Spark Plug Company, who supplied the illustrations of various spark plug conditions. Technical writers who contributed to this project include Larry Warren, Mike Stubblefield and Bob Henderson.

A book in the **Haynes Automotive Repair Manual Series**

Printed in the USA

ISBN 1 85010 663 0

Library of Congress Catalog Card Number 90-81414

Contents

1981 Pontiac Bonneville 4-door sedan

About this manual

Its purpose

The purpose of this manual is to help you get the best value from your vehicle. It can do so in several ways. It can help you decide what work must be done, even if you choose to have it done by a dealer service department or a repair shop; it provides information and procedures for routine maintenance and servicing; and it offers diagnostic and repair procedures to follow when trouble occurs.

It is hoped that you will use the manual to tackle the work yourself. For many simpler jobs, doing it yourself may be quicker than arranging an appointment to get the vehicle into a shop and making the trips to leave it and pick it up. More importantly, a lot of money can be saved by avoiding the expense the shop must pass on to you to cover its labor and overhead costs. An added benefit is the sense of satisfaction and accomplishment that you feel after having done the job yourself.

Using the manual

The manual is divided into Chapters. Each Chapter is divided into numbered Sections, which are headed in bold type between horizontal lines. Each Section consists of consecutively numbered paragraphs.

At the beginning of each numbered section you will be referred to any illustrations which apply to the procedures in that section. The reference numbers used in illustration captions pinpoint the pertinent Section and the Step within that section. That is, illustration 3.2 means the illustration refers to Section 3 and Step (or paragraph) 2 within that Section.

Procedures, once described in the text, are not normally repeated. When it is necessary to refer to another Chapter, the reference will be given as Chapter and Section number i.e. Chapter 1/16). Cross references given without use of the word "Chapter" apply to Sections and/or paragraphs in the same Chapter. For example, "see Section 8" means in the same Chapter.

Reference to the left or right side of the vehicle is based on the assumption that one is sitting in the driver's seat, facing forward.

Even though extreme care has been taken during the preparation of this manual, neither the publisher nor the author can accept responsibility for any errors in, or omissions from, the information given.

NOTE

A **Note** provides information necessary to properly complete a procedure or information which will make the steps to be followed easier to understand.

CAUTION

A **Caution** indicates a special procedure or special steps which must be taken in the course of completing the procedure in which the **Caution** is found which are necessary to avoid damage to the assembly being worked on.

WARNING

A **Warning** indicates a special procedure or special steps which must be taken in the course of completing the procedure in which the **Warning** is found which are necessary to avoid injury to the person performing the procedure.

Introduction to the Buick, Oldsmobile, Pontiac full-size, rear-wheel drive models

The full-size General Motors models covered in this manual are of conventional front engine/rear-wheel drive layout.

A variety of General Motors-built V8 and V6 engine were installed in these models over their long production run. The engine drives the rear wheels through either a manual or an automatic transmission via a driveshaft and solid rear axle.

These vehicles are available in a variety of body styles, including two-door coupe, four-door sedan and four-door station wagon models.

Front suspension is independent, using coil springs, with power assisted steering available on later models. Leaf-type springs or coil springs with trailing arms are used in the rear supension, depending on year and model.

Earlier models use drum brakes on all four wheels, while later models feature disc-type brakes at the front and drums at the rear. Some later models are equipped with four-wheel disc brakes. Power assist was available on most models.

Vehicle identification numbers

Modifications are a continuing and unpublicized process in vehicle manufacturing. Since spare parts manuals and lists are compiled on a numerical basis, the individual vehicle numbers are essential to correctly identify the component required.

Vehicle Identification Number (VIN)

This very important identification number is stamped on a plate attached to the left side cowling just inside the windshield on the driver's side of the vehicle (see illustration). The VIN also appears on the Vehicle Certificate of Title and Registration. It contains information such as where and when the vehicle was manufactured, the model year and the body style.

Body identification plate

The body identification plate is located in the engine compartment on the upper surface of the radiator shroud or support on most models

(see illustration). Like the VIN it contains valuable information about the manufacture of the vehicle, as well as information on the options with which it is equipped. This plate is especially useful for matching the color and type of paint for repair work.

Engine identification number

Because of the wide variety of engines with which these models were equipped from all of the General Motors divisions over the many years of manufacture, engine identification numbers can be found in a variety of locations (see illustrations).

Transmission number

The identification numbers can be found in various locations, depending on model and year of manufacture and model transmission (see illustration).

The Vehicle Identification Number (VIN) is visible from outside the vehicle through the driver's side windshield

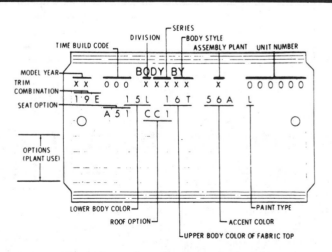

The body number plate is usually found on the radiator support

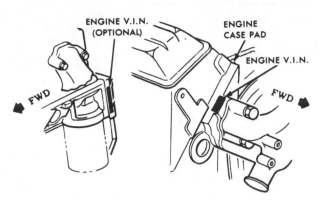

ENGINE V.I.N. (OPTIONAL)

ENGINE CASE PAD

ENGINE V.I.N.

FWD

FWD

Typical Chevrolet engine code number locations

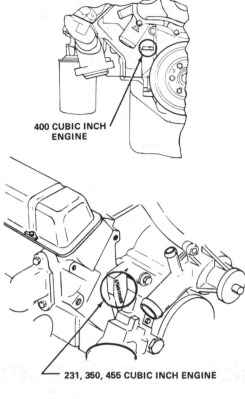

400 CUBIC INCH ENGINE

231, 350, 455 CUBIC INCH ENGINE

Typical Buick engine number locations

ENGINE UNIT NUMBER LABEL

ENGINE CODE LABEL

Oldsmobile engine number locations

ENGINE CODE LOCATION VIN CODES U AND L ENGINES

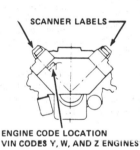

SCANNER LABELS

ENGINE CODE LOCATION VIN CODES Y, W, AND Z ENGINES

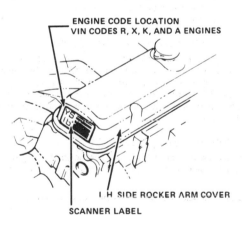

ENGINE CODE LOCATION VIN CODES R, X, K, AND A ENGINES

L H SIDE ROCKER ARM COVER

SCANNER LABEL

Pontiac engine number locations

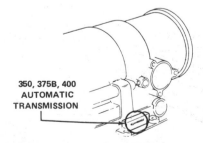

STAMP VEHICLE IDENTIFICATION NUMBER CONSISTING OF THE FIGURE 2 FOLLOWED BY THE LAST 8 DIGITS OF CAR SERIAL NUMBER.

Manual transmission number location

350, 375B, 400 AUTOMATIC TRANSMISSION

On Turbo-Hydra-Matic 350/375/400 transmissions, the identification and serial numbers are usually found stamped on the right side of the housing

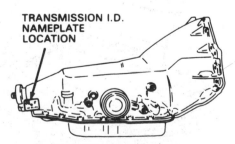

TRANSMISSION I.D. NAMEPLATE LOCATION

Turbo-Hydra-Matic 200 automatic transmission number location

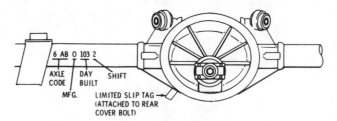

**Typical rear axle and differential information
and number locations**

Rear axle number

Information pertaining to the rear axle and differential can be found stamped on the front surface of the right side axle housing tube on most models and on a tag attached to one of the cover bolts on most models **(see illustration)**. Some models also have final drive ratio and build date information stamped on the flange adjacent to the cover **(see illustration)**.

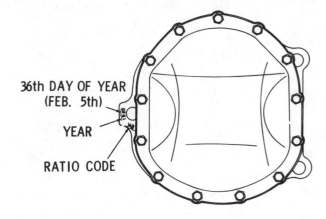

**On some models, rear axle information is stamped on the
right-hand housing flange**

Buying parts

Replacement parts are available from many sources, which generally fall into one of two categories – authorized dealer parts departments and independent retail auto parts stores. Our advice concerning these parts is as follows:

Retail auto parts stores: Good auto parts stores will stock frequently needed components which wear out relatively fast, such as clutch components, exhaust systems, brake parts, tune-up parts, etc. These stores often supply new or reconditioned parts on an exchange basis, which can save a considerable amount of money. Discount auto parts stores are often very good places to buy materials and parts needed for general vehicle maintenance such as oil, grease, filters, spark plugs, belts, touch-up paint, bulbs, etc. They also usually sell tools and general accessories, have convenient hours, charge lower prices and can often be found not far from home.

Authorized dealer parts department: This is the best source for parts which are unique to the vehicle and not generally available elsewhere (such as major engine parts, transmission parts, trim pieces, etc.).

Warranty information: If the vehicle is still covered under warranty, be sure that any replacement parts purchased – regardless of the source – do not invalidate the warranty!

To be sure of obtaining the correct parts, have engine and chassis numbers available and, if possible, take the old parts along for positive identification.

Maintenance techniques, tools and working facilities

Maintenance techniques

There are a number of techniques involved in maintenance and repair that will be referred to throughout this manual. Application of these techniques will enable the home mechanic to be more efficient, better organized and capable of performing the various tasks properly, which will ensure that the repair job is thorough and complete.

Fasteners

Fasteners are nuts, bolts, studs and screws used to hold two or more parts together. There are a few things to keep in mind when working with fasteners. Almost all of them use a locking device of some type, either a lockwasher, locknut, locking tab or thread adhesive. All threaded fasteners should be clean and straight, with undamaged threads and undamaged corners on the hex head where the wrench fits. Develop the habit of replacing all damaged nuts and bolts with new ones. Special locknuts with nylon or fiber inserts can only be used once. If they are removed, they lose their locking ability and must be replaced with new ones.

Rusted nuts and bolts should be treated with a penetrating fluid to ease removal and prevent breakage. Some mechanics use turpentine in a spout-type oil can, which works quite well. After applying the rust penetrant, let it work for a few minutes before trying to loosen the nut or bolt. Badly rusted fasteners may have to be chiseled or sawed off or removed with a special nut breaker, available at tool stores.

If a bolt or stud breaks off in an assembly, it can be drilled and removed with a special tool commonly available for this purpose. Most automotive machine shops can perform this task, as well as other repair procedures, such as the repair of threaded holes that have been stripped out.

Flat washers and lockwashers, when removed from an assembly, should always be replaced exactly as removed. Replace any damaged washers with new ones. Never use a lockwasher on any soft metal surface (such as aluminum), thin sheet metal or plastic.

Fastener sizes

For a number of reasons, automobile manufacturers are making wider and wider use of metric fasteners. Therefore, it is important to be able to tell the difference between standard (sometimes called U.S. or SAE) and metric hardware, since they cannot be interchanged.

All bolts, whether standard or metric, are sized according to diameter, thread pitch and length. For example, a standard 1/2 — 13 x 1 bolt is 1/2 inch in diameter, has 13 threads per inch and is 1 inch long. An M12 — 1.75 x 25 metric bolt is 12 mm in diameter, has a thread pitch of 1.75 mm (the distance between threads) and is 25 mm long. The two bolts are nearly identical, and easily confused, but they are not interchangeable.

In addition to the differences in diameter, thread pitch and length, metric and standard bolts can also be distinguished by examining the bolt heads. To begin with, the distance across the flats on a standard bolt head is measured in inches, while the same dimension on a metric bolt is sized in millimeters (the same is true for nuts). As a result, a

standard wrench should not be used on a metric bolt and a metric wrench should not be used on a standard bolt. Also, most standard bolts have slashes radiating out from the center of the head to denote the grade or strength of the bolt, which is an indication of the amount of torque that can be applied to it. The greater the number of slashes, the greater the strength of the bolt. Grades 0 through 5 are commonly used on automobiles. Metric bolts have a property class (grade) number, rather than a slash, molded into their heads to indicate bolt strength. In this case, the higher the number, the stronger the bolt. Property class numbers 8.8, 9.8 and 10.9 are commonly used on automobiles.

Strength markings can also be used to distinguish standard hex nuts from metric hex nuts. Many standard nuts have dots stamped into one side, while metric nuts are marked with a number. The greater the number of dots, or the higher the number, the greater the strength of the nut.

Metric studs are also marked on their ends according to property class (grade). Larger studs are numbered (the same as metric bolts),

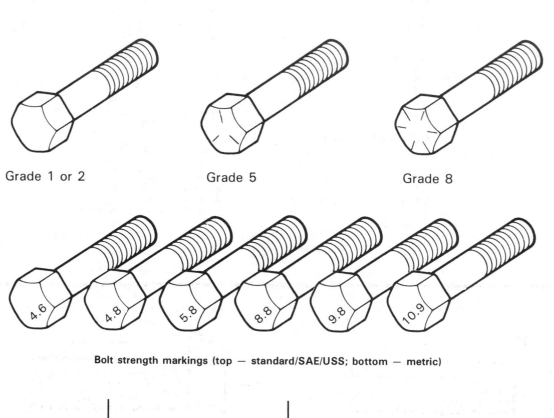

Grade 1 or 2   Grade 5   Grade 8

Bolt strength markings (top — standard/SAE/USS; bottom — metric)

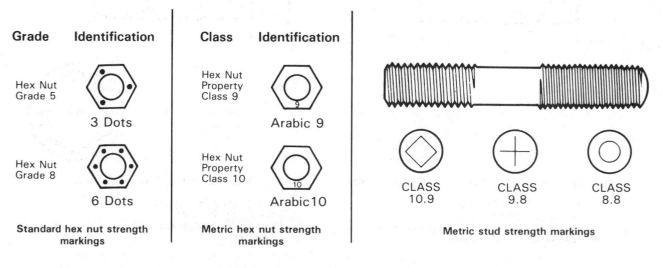

Grade	Identification	Class	Identification
Hex Nut Grade 5	3 Dots	Hex Nut Property Class 9	Arabic 9
Hex Nut Grade 8	6 Dots	Hex Nut Property Class 10	Arabic 10

CLASS 10.9   CLASS 9.8   CLASS 8.8

Standard hex nut strength markings   Metric hex nut strength markings   Metric stud strength markings

while smaller studs carry a geometric code to denote grade.

It should be noted that many fasteners, especially Grades 0 through 2, have no distinguishing marks on them. When such is the case, the only way to determine whether it is standard or metric is to measure the thread pitch or compare it to a known fastener of the same size.

Standard fasteners are often referred to as SAE, as opposed to metric. However, it should be noted that SAE technically refers to a non-metric *fine thread* fastener only. Coarse thread non-metric fasteners are referred to as USS sizes.

Since fasteners of the same size (both standard and metric) may have different strength ratings, be sure to reinstall any bolts, studs or nuts removed from your vehicle in their original locations. Also, when replacing a fastener with a new one, make sure that the new one has a strength rating equal to or greater than the original.

Tightening sequences and procedures

Most threaded fasteners should be tightened to a specific torque value (torque is the twisting force applied to a threaded component such as a nut or bolt). Overtightening the fastener can weaken it and cause it to break, while undertightening can cause it to eventually come loose. Bolts, screws and studs, depending on the material they are made of and their thread diameters, have specific torque values, many of which are noted in the Specifications at the beginning of each Chapter. Be sure to follow the torque recommendations closely. For fasteners not assigned a specific torque, a general torque value chart is presented here as a guide. These torque values are for dry (unlubricated) fasteners threaded into steel or cast iron (not aluminum). As was previously mentioned, the size and grade of a fastener determine the amount of torque that can safely be applied to it. The figures listed here are approximate

Metric thread sizes	Ft-lb	Nm/m
M-6	6 to 9	9 to 12
M-8	14 to 21	19 to 28
M-10	28 to 40	38 to 54
M-12	50 to 71	68 to 96
M-14	80 to 140	109 to 154

Pipe thread sizes	Ft-lb	Nm/m
1/8	5 to 8	7 to 10
1/4	12 to 18	17 to 24
3/8	22 to 33	30 to 44
1/2	25 to 35	34 to 47

U.S. thread sizes	Ft-lb	Nm/m
1/4 — 20	6 to 9	9 to 12
5/16 — 18	12 to 18	17 to 24
5/16 — 24	14 to 20	19 to 27
3/8 — 16	22 to 32	30 to 43
3/8 — 24	27 to 38	37 to 51
7/16 — 14	40 to 55	55 to 74
7/16 — 20	40 to 60	55 to 81
1/2 — 13	55 to 80	75 to 108

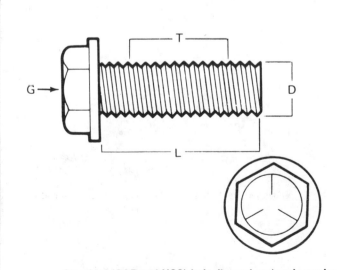

Standard (SAE and USS) bolt dimensions/grade marks

G Grade marks (bolt strength)
L Length (in inches)
T Thread pitch (number of threads per inch)
D Nominal diameter (in inches)

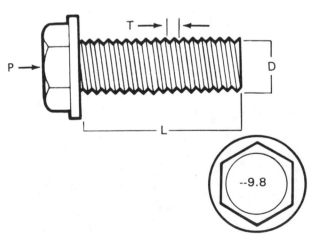

Metric bolt dimensions/grade marks

P Property class (bolt strength)
L Length (in millimeters)
T Thread pitch (distance between threads in millimeters)
D Diameter

for Grade 2 and Grade 3 fasteners. Higher grades can tolerate higher torque values.

Fasteners laid out in a pattern, such as cylinder head bolts, oil pan bolts, differential cover bolts, etc., must be loosened or tightened in sequence to avoid warping the component. This sequence will normally be shown in the appropriate Chapter. If a specific pattern is not given, the following procedures can be used to prevent warping.

Initially, the bolts or nuts should be assembled finger-tight only. Next, they should be tightened one full turn each, in a criss-cross or diagonal pattern. After each one has been tightened one full turn, return to the first one and tighten them all one-half turn, following the same pattern. Finally, tighten each of them one-quarter turn at a time until each fastener has been tightened to the proper torque. To loosen and remove the fasteners, the procedure would be reversed.

Component disassembly

Component disassembly should be done with care and purpose to help ensure that the parts go back together properly. Always keep track of the sequence in which parts are removed. Make note of special characteristics or marks on parts that can be installed more than one way, such as a grooved thrust washer on a shaft. It is a good idea to lay the disassembled parts out on a clean surface in the order that they were removed. It may also be helpful to make sketches or take instant photos of components before removal.

When removing fasteners from a component, keep track of their locations. Sometimes threading a bolt back in a part, or putting the washers and nut back on a stud, can prevent mix-ups later. If nuts and bolts cannot be returned to their original locations, they should be kept in a compartmented box or a series of small boxes. A cupcake or muffin tin is ideal for this purpose, since each cavity can hold the bolts and nuts from a particular area (i.e. oil pan bolts, valve cover bolts, engine mount bolts, etc.). A pan of this type is especially helpful when working on assemblies with very small parts, such as the carburetor, alternator, valve train or interior dash and trim pieces. The cavities can be marked with paint or tape to identify the contents.

Whenever wiring looms, harnesses or connectors are separated, it is a good idea to identify the two halves with numbered pieces of masking tape so they can be easily reconnected.

Gasket sealing surfaces

Throughout any vehicle, gaskets are used to seal the mating surfaces between two parts and keep lubricants, fluids, vacuum or pressure contained in an assembly.

Many times these gaskets are coated with a liquid or paste-type gasket sealing compound before assembly. Age, heat and pressure can sometimes cause the two parts to stick together so tightly that they are very difficult to separate. Often, the assembly can be loosened by striking it with a soft-face hammer near the mating surfaces. A regular hammer can be used if a block of wood is placed between the hammer and the part. Do not hammer on cast parts or parts that could be easily damaged. With any particularly stubborn part, always recheck to make sure that every fastener has been removed.

Avoid using a screwdriver or bar to pry apart an assembly, as they can easily mar the gasket sealing surfaces of the parts, which must remain smooth. If prying is absolutely necessary, use an old broom handle, but keep in mind that extra clean up will be necessary if the wood splinters.

After the parts are separated, the old gasket must be carefully scraped off and the gasket surfaces cleaned. Stubborn gasket material can be soaked with rust penetrant or treated with a special chemical to soften it so it can be easily scraped off. A scraper can be fashioned from a piece of copper tubing by flattening and sharpening one end. Copper is recommended because it is usually softer than the surfaces to be scraped, which reduces the chance of gouging the part. Some gaskets can be removed with a wire brush, but regardless of the method used, the mating surfaces must be left clean and smooth. If for some reason the gasket surface is gouged, then a gasket sealer thick enough to fill scratches will have to be used during reassembly of the components. For most applications, a non-drying (or semi-drying) gasket sealer should be used.

Hose removal tips

Warning: *If the vehicle is equipped with air conditioning, do not disconnect any of the A/C hoses without first having the system depressurized by a dealer service department or an air conditioning specialist.*

Hose removal precautions closely parallel gasket removal precautions. Avoid scratching or gouging the surface that the hose mates against or the connection may leak. This is especially true for radiator hoses. Because of various chemical reactions, the rubber in hoses can bond itself to the metal spigot that the hose fits over. To remove a hose, first loosen the hose clamps that secure it to the spigot. Then, with slip-joint pliers, grab the hose at the clamp and rotate it around the spigot. Work it back and forth until it is completely free, then pull it off. Silicone or other lubricants will ease removal if they can be applied between the hose and the outside of the spigot. Apply the same lubricant to the inside of the hose and the outside of the spigot to simplify installation.

As a last resort (and if the hose is to be replaced with a new one anyway), the rubber can be slit with a knife and the hose peeled from the spigot. If this must be done, be careful that the metal connection is not damaged.

If a hose clamp is broken or damaged, do not reuse it. Wire-type clamps usually weaken with age, so it is a good idea to replace them with screw-type clamps whenever a hose is removed.

Tools

A selection of good tools is a basic requirement for anyone who plans to maintain and repair his or her own vehicle. For the owner who has few tools, the initial investment might seem high, but when compared to the spiraling costs of professional auto maintenance and repair, it is a wise one.

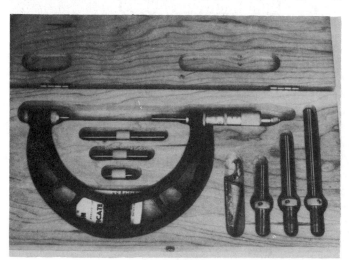

Micrometer set

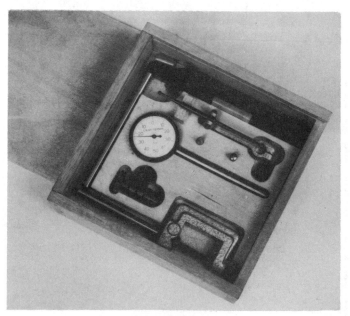

Dial indicator set

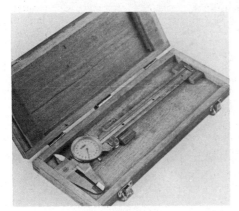

Dial caliper

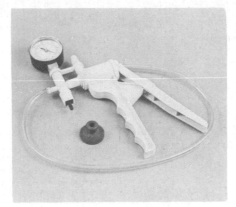

Hand-operated vacuum pump

Timing light

Compression gauge with spark plug hole adapter

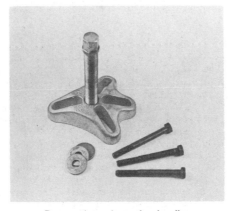

Damper/steering wheel puller

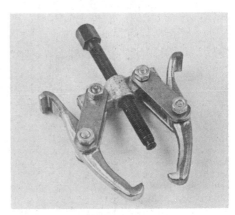

General purpose puller

Hydraulic lifter removal tool

Valve spring compressor

Valve spring compressor

Ridge reamer

Piston ring groove cleaning tool

Ring removal/installation tool

Ring compressor

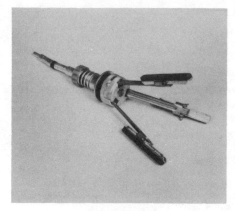

Cylinder hone

Brake hold-down spring tool

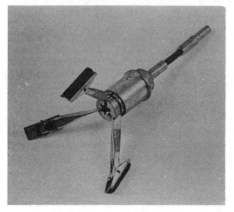

Brake cylinder hone

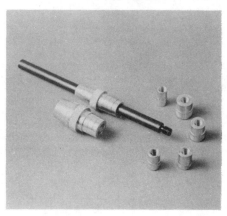

Clutch plate alignment tool

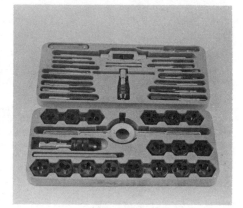

Tap and die set

To help the owner decide which tools are needed to perform the tasks detailed in this manual, the following tool lists are offered: *Maintenance and minor repair, Repair/overhaul* and *Special*.

The newcomer to practical mechanics should start off with the maintenance and minor repair tool kit, which is adequate for the simpler jobs performed on a vehicle. Then, as confidence and experience grow, the owner can tackle more difficult tasks, buying additional tools as they are needed. Eventually the basic kit will be expanded into the repair and overhaul tool set. Over a period of time, the experienced do-it-yourselfer will assemble a tool set complete enough for most repair and overhaul procedures and will add tools from the special category when it is felt that the expense is justified by the frequency of use.

Maintenance and minor repair tool kit

The tools in this list should be considered the minimum required for performance of routine maintenance, servicing and minor repair work. We recommend the purchase of combination wrenches (box-end and open-end combined in one wrench). While more expensive than open end wrenches, they offer the advantages of both types of wrench.

Combination wrench set (1/4-inch to 1 inch or 6 mm to 19 mm)
Adjustable wrench, 8 inch
Spark plug wrench with rubber insert
Spark plug gap adjusting tool
Feeler gauge set
Brake bleeder wrench
Standard screwdriver (5/16-inch x 6 inch)
Phillips screwdriver (No. 2 x 6 inch)
Combination pliers — 6 inch
Hacksaw and assortment of blades
Tire pressure gauge
Grease gun
Oil can
Fine emery cloth
Wire brush

Battery post and cable cleaning tool
Oil filter wrench
Funnel (medium size)
Safety goggles
Jackstands (2)
Drain pan

Note: *If basic tune-ups are going to be part of routine maintenance, it will be necessary to purchase a good quality stroboscopic timing light and combination tachometer/dwell meter. Although they are included in the list of special tools, it is mentioned here because they are absolutely necessary for tuning most vehicles properly.*

Repair and overhaul tool set

These tools are essential for anyone who plans to perform major repairs and are in addition to those in the maintenance and minor repair tool kit. Included is a comprehensive set of sockets which, though expensive, are invaluable because of their versatility, especially when various extensions and drives are available. We recommend the 1/2-inch drive over the 3/8-inch drive. Although the larger drive is bulky and more expensive, it has the capacity of accepting a very wide range of large sockets. Ideally, however, the mechanic should have a 3/8-inch drive set and a 1/2-inch drive set.

Socket set(s)
Reversible ratchet
Extension — 10 inch
Universal joint
Torque wrench (same size drive as sockets)
Ball peen hammer — 8 ounce
Soft-face hammer (plastic/rubber)
Standard screwdriver (1/4-inch x 6 inch)
Standard screwdriver (stubby — 5/16-inch)
Phillips screwdriver (No. 3 x 8 inch)
Phillips screwdriver (stubby — No. 2)

Pliers — vise grip
Pliers — lineman's
Pliers — needle nose
Pliers — snap-ring (internal and external)
Cold chisel — 1/2-inch
Scribe
Scraper (made from flattened copper tubing)
Centerpunch
Pin punches (1/16, 1/8, 3/16-inch)
Steel rule/straightedge — 12 inch
Allen wrench set (1/8 to 3/8-inch or 4 mm to 10 mm)
A selection of files
Wire brush (large)
Jackstands (second set)
Jack (scissor or hydraulic type)

Note: *Another tool which is often useful is an electric drill motor with a chuck capacity of 3/8-inch and a set of good quality drill bits.*

Special tools

The tools in this list include those which are not used regularly, are expensive to buy, or which need to be used in accordance with their manufacturer's instructions. Unless these tools will be used frequently, it is not very economical to purchase many of them. A consideration would be to split the cost and use between yourself and a friend or friends. In addition, most of these tools can be obtained from a tool rental shop on a temporary basis.

This list primarily contains only those tools and instruments widely available to the public, and not those special tools produced by the vehicle manufacturer for distribution to dealer service departments. Occasionally, references to the manufacturer's special tools are inluded in the text of this manual. Generally, an alternative method of doing the job without the special tool is offered. However, sometimes there is no alternative to their use. Where this is the case, and the tool cannot be purchased or borrowed, the work should be turned over to the dealer service department or an automotive repair shop.

Valve spring compressor
Piston ring groove cleaning tool
Piston ring compressor
Piston ring installation tool
Cylinder compression gauge
Cylinder ridge reamer
Cylinder surfacing hone
Cylinder bore gauge
Micrometers and/or dial calipers
Hydraulic lifter removal tool
Balljoint separator
Universal-type puller
Impact screwdriver
Dial indicator set
Stroboscopic timing light (inductive pick-up)
Hand operated vacuum/pressure pump
Tachometer/dwell meter
Universal electrical multimeter
Cable hoist
Brake spring removal and installation tools
Floor jack

Buying tools

For the do-it-yourselfer who is just starting to get involved in vehicle maintenance and repair, there are a number of options available when purchasing tools. If maintenance and minor repair is the extent of the work to be done, the purchase of individual tools is satisfactory. If, on the other hand, extensive work is planned, it would be a good idea to purchase a modest tool set from one of the large retail chain stores. A set can usually be bought at a substantial savings over the individual tool prices, and they often come with a tool box. As additional tools are needed, add-on sets, individual tools and a larger tool box can be purchased to expand the tool selection. Building a tool set gradually allows the cost of the tools to be spread over a longer period of time and gives the mechanic the freedom to choose only those tools that will actually be used.

Tool stores will often be the only source of some of the special tools that are needed, but regardless of where tools are bought, try to avoid cheap ones, especially when buying screwdrivers and sockets, because they won't last very long. The expense involved in replacing cheap tools will eventually be greater than the initial cost of quality tools.

Care and maintenance of tools

Good tools are expensive, so it makes sense to treat them with respect. Keep them clean and in usable condition and store them properly when not in use. Always wipe off any dirt, grease or metal chips before putting them away. Never leave tools lying around in the work area. Upon completion of a job, always check closely under the hood for tools that may have been left there so they won't get lost during a test drive.

Some tools, such as screwdrivers, pliers, wrenches and sockets, can be hung on a panel mounted on the garage or workshop wall, while others should be kept in a tool box or tray. Measuring instruments, gauges, meters, etc. must be carefully stored where they cannot be damaged by weather or impact from other tools.

When tools are used with care and stored properly, they will last a very long time. Even with the best of care, though, tools will wear out if used frequently. When a tool is damaged or worn out, replace it. Subsequent jobs will be safer and more enjoyable if you do.

Working facilities

Not to be overlooked when discussing tools is the workshop. If anything more than routine maintenance is to be carried out, some sort of suitable work area is essential.

It is understood, and appreciated, that many home mechanics do not have a good workshop or garage available, and end up removing an engine or doing major repairs outside. It is recommended, however, that the overhaul or repair be completed under the cover of a roof.

A clean, flat workbench or table of comfortable working height is an absolute necessity. The workbench should be equipped with a vise that has a jaw opening of at least four inches.

As mentioned previously, some clean, dry storage space is also required for tools, as well as the lubricants, fluids, cleaning solvents, etc. which will soon become necessary.

Sometimes waste oil and fluids, drained from the engine or cooling system during normal maintenance or repairs, present a disposal problem. To avoid pouring them on the ground or into a sewage system, pour the used fluids into large containers, seal them with caps and take them to an authorized disposal site or recycling center. Plastic jugs, such as old antifreeze containers, are ideal for this purpose.

Always keep a supply of old newspapers and clean rags available. Old towels are excellent for mopping up spills. Many mechanics use rolls of paper towels for most work because they are readily available and disposable. To help keep the area under the vehicle clean, a large cardboard box can be cut open and flattened to protect the garage or shop floor.

Whenever working over a painted surface, such as when leaning over a fender to service something under the hood, always cover it with an old blanket or bedspread to protect the finish. Vinyl covered pads, made especially for this purpose, are available at auto parts stores.

Booster battery (jump) starting

Certain precautions must be observed when using a booster battery to start a vehicle.
  a) Before connecting the booster battery, make sure the ignition switch is in the Off position.
  b) Turn off the lights, heater and other electrical loads.
  c) Your eyes should be shielded. Safety goggles are a good idea.
  d) Make sure the booster battery is the same voltage as the dead one in the vehicle.
  e) The two vehicles MUST NOT TOUCH each other!
  f) Make sure the transmission is in Neutral (manual) or Park (automatic).
  g) If the booster battery is not a maintenance-free type, remove the vent caps and lay a cloth over the vent holes.

Connect the red jumper cable to the *positive* (+) terminals of each battery.

Connect one end of the black jumper cable to the *negative* (−) terminal of the booster battery. The other end of this cable should be connected to a good ground on the vehicle to be started, such as a bolt or bracket on the engine block (see illustration). Use caution to ensure that the cable will not come into contact with the fan, drivebelts or other moving parts of the engine.

Start the engine using the booster battery, then, with the engine running at idle speed, disconnect the jumper cables in the reverse order of connection.

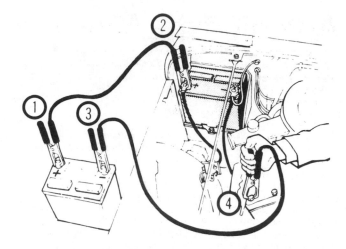

Make the booster battery cable connections in the numerical order shown (note that the negative cable of the booster battery is NOT attached to the negative terminal of the dead battery)

Jacking and towing

Jacking

The jack supplied with the vehicle should only be used for raising the vehicle when changing a tire or placing jackstands under the frame. **Warning:** *Never work under the vehicle or start the engine while this jack is being used as the only means of support.*

The vehicle should be on level ground with the wheels blocked and the transmission in Park (automatic) or Reverse (manual). If the wheel is being replaced, loosen the wheel nuts one-half turn and leave them in place until the wheel is raised off the ground. Refer to Chapter 1 for information related to removing and installing the tire.

Place the jack in the slot in the bumper (early models) or under the vehicle jack locations (later models) in the indicated position (see illustrations). Operate the jack with a slow, smooth motion until the wheel is raised off the ground.

Lower the vehicle, remove the jack and tighten the nuts (if loosened or removed) in a criss-cross sequence.

Towing

Vehicles can be towed with all four wheels on the ground, provided that speeds do not exceed 35 mph and the distance is not over 50 miles, otherwise transmission damage can result.

Towing equipment specifically designed for this purpose should be used and should be attached to the main structural members of the vehicle, not the bumper or brackets.

Safety is a major consideration when towing, and all applicable state and local laws must be obeyed. A safety chain system must be used for all towing.

While towing, the parking brake should be released and the transmission must be in Neutral. The steering must be unlocked (ignition switch in the Off position). Remember that power steering and power brakes will not work with the engine off.

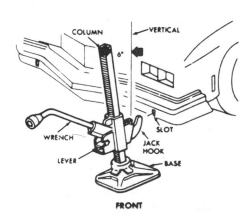

On earlier models, a bumper jack is used to raise the vehicle

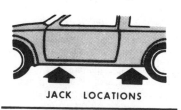

Later model jacking details

Automotive chemicals and lubricants

A number of automotive chemicals and lubricants are available for use during vehicle maintenance and repair. They include a wide variety of products ranging from cleaning solvents and degreasers to lubricants and protective sprays for rubber, plastic and vinyl.

Cleaners

Carburetor cleaner and choke cleaner is a strong solvent for gum, varnish and carbon. Most carburetor cleaners leave a dry-type lubricant film which will not harden or gum up. Because of this film it is not recommended for use on electrical components.

Brake system cleaner is used to remove grease and brake fluid from the brake system where clean surfaces are absolutely necessary. It leaves no residue and often eliminates brake squeal caused by contaminants.

Electrical cleaner removes oxidation, corrosion and carbon deposits from electrical contacts, restoring full current flow. It can also be used to clean spark plugs, carburetor jets, voltage regulators and other parts where an oil-free surface is desired.

Demoisturants remove water and moisture from electrical components such as alternators, voltage regulators, electrical connectors and fuse blocks. It is non-conductive, non-corrosive and non-flammable.

Degreasers are heavy-duty solvents used to remove grease from the outside of the engine and from chassis components. They can be sprayed or brushed on, and, depending on the type, are rinsed off either with water or solvent.

Lubricants

Motor oil is the lubricant formulated for use in engines. It normally contains a wide variety of additives to prevent corrosion and reduce foaming and wear. Motor oil comes in various weights (viscosity ratings) from 5 to 80. The recommended weight of the oil depends on the season, temperature and the demands on the engine. Light oil is used in cold climates and under light load conditions. Heavy oil is used in hot climates and where high loads are encountered. Multi-viscosity oils are designed to have characteristics of both light and heavy oils and are available in a number of weights from 5W-20 to 20W-50.

Gear oil is designed to be used in differentials, manual transaxles and other areas where high-temperature lubrication is required.

Chassis and wheel bearing grease is a heavy grease used where increased loads and friction are encountered, such as for wheel bearings, balljoints, tie rod ends and universal joints.

High temperature wheel bearing grease is designed to withstand the extreme temperatures encountered by wheel bearings in disc brake equipped vehicles. It usually contains molybdenun disulfide (moly), which is a dry-type lubricant.

White grease is a heavy grease for metal to metal applications where water is a problem. White grease stays soft under both low and high temperatures (usually from −100°F to +190°F), and will not wash off or dilute in the presence of water.

Assembly lube is a special extreme pressure lubricant, usually containing moly, used to lubricate high-load parts such as main and rod bearings and cam lobes for initial start-up of a new engine. The assembly lube lubricates the parts without being squeezed out or washed away until the engine oiling system begins to function.

Silicone lubricants are used to protect rubber, plastic, vinyl and nylon parts.

Graphite lubricants are used where oils cannot be used due to contamination problems, such as in locks. The dry graphite will lubricate metal parts while remaining uncontaminated by dirt, water, oil or acids. It is electrically conductive and will not foul electrical contacts in locks such as the ignition switch.

Moly penetrants loosen and lubricate frozen, rusted and corroded fasteners and prevent future rusting or freezing.

Heat-sink grease is a special electrically non-conductive grease that is used for mounting HEI ignition modules where it is essential that heat be transferred away from the module.

Sealants

RTV sealant is one of the most widely used gasket compounds. Made from silicone, RTV is air curing, it seals, bonds, waterproofs, fills surface irregularities, remains flexible, doesn't shrink, is relatively easy to remove, and is used as a supplementary sealer with almost all low and medium temperature gaskets.

Anaerobic sealant is much like RTV in that it can be used either to seal gaskets or to form gaskets by itself. It remains flexible, is solvent resistant and fills surface imperfections. The difference between an anaerobic sealant and an RTV-type sealant is in the curing. RTV cures when exposed to air, while an anaerobic sealant cures only in the absence of air. This means that an anaerobic sealant cures only after the assembly of parts, sealing them together.

Thread and pipe sealant is used for sealing hydraulic and pneumatic fittings and vacuum lines. It is usually made from a teflon compound, and comes in a spray, a paint-on liquid and as a wrap-around tape.

Chemicals

Anti-seize compound prevents seizing, galling, cold welding, rust and corrosion in fasteners. High temperature anti-seize, usually made with copper and graphite lubricants, is used for exhaust system and manifold bolts.

Anaerobic locking compounds are used to keep fasteners from vibrating or working loose, and cure only after installation, in the absence of air. Medium strength locking compound is used for small nuts, bolts and screws that you expect to be removing later. High strength locking compound is for large nuts, bolts and studs which you don't intend to be removing on a regular basis.

Oil additives range from viscosity index improvers to chemical treatments that claim to reduce internal engine friction. It should be noted that most oil manufacturers caution against using additives with their oils.

Gas additives perform several functions, depending on their chemical makeup. They usually contain solvents that help dissolve gum and varnish that build up on carburetor and intake parts. They also serve to break down carbon deposits that form on the inside surfaces of the combustion chambers. Some additives contain upper cylinder lubricants for valves and piston rings, and others chemicals to remove condensation from the gas tank.

Miscellaneous

Brake fluid is specially formulated hydraulic fluid that can withstand the heat and pressure encountered in brake systems. Care must be taken that this fluid does not come in contact with painted surfaces or plastics. An opened container should always be resealed to prevent contamination by water or dirt.

Weatherstrip adhesive is used to bond weatherstripping around doors, windows and trunk lids. It is sometimes used to attach trim pieces.

Undercoating is a petroleum-based tar-like substance that is designed to protect metal surfaces on the underside of the vehicle from corrosion. It also acts as a sound-deadening agent by insulating the bottom of the vehicle.

Waxes and polishes are used to help protect painted and plated surfaces from the weather. Different types of paint may require the use of different types of wax and polish. Some polishes utilize a chemical or abrasive cleaner to help remove the top layer of oxidized (dull) paint on older vehicles. In recent years many non-wax polishes that contain a wide variety of chemicals such as polymers and silicones have been introduced. These non-wax polishes are usually easier to apply and last longer than conventional waxes and polishes.

Safety first!

Regardless of how enthusiastic you may be about getting on with the job at hand, take the time to ensure that your safety is not jeopardized. A moment's lack of attention can result in an accident, as can failure to observe certain simple safety precautions. The possibility of an accident will always exist, and the following points should not be considered a comprehensive list of all dangers. Rather, they are intended to make you aware of the risks and to encourage a safety conscious approach to all work you carry out on your vehicle.

Essential DOs and DON'Ts

DON'T rely on a jack when working under the vehicle. Always use approved jackstands to support the weight of the vehicle and place them under the recommended lift or support points.

DON'T attempt to loosen extremely tight fasteners (i.e. wheel lug nuts) while the vehicle is on a jack — it may fall.

DON'T start the engine without first making sure that the transmission is in Neutral (or Park where applicable) and the parking brake is set.

DON'T remove the radiator cap from a hot cooling system — let it cool or cover it with a cloth and release the pressure gradually.

DON'T attempt to drain the engine oil until you are sure it has cooled to the point that it will not burn you.

DON'T touch any part of the engine or exhaust system until it has cooled sufficiently to avoid burns.

DON'T siphon toxic liquids such as gasoline, antifreeze and brake fluid by mouth, or allow them to remain on your skin.

DON'T inhale brake lining dust — it is potentially hazardous (see *Asbestos* below)

DON'T allow spilled oil or grease to remain on the floor — wipe it up before someone slips on it.

DON'T use loose fitting wrenches or other tools which may slip and cause injury.

DON'T push on wrenches when loosening or tightening nuts or bolts. Always try to pull the wrench toward you. If the situation calls for pushing the wrench away, push with an open hand to avoid scraped knuckles if the wrench should slip.

DON'T attempt to lift a heavy component alone — get someone to help you.

DON'T rush or take unsafe shortcuts to finish a job.

DON'T allow children or animals in or around the vehicle while you are working on it.

DO wear eye protection when using power tools such as a drill, sander, bench grinder, etc. and when working under a vehicle.

DO keep loose clothing and long hair well out of the way of moving parts.

DO make sure that any hoist used has a safe working load rating adequate for the job.

DO get someone to check on you periodically when working alone on a vehicle.

DO carry out work in a logical sequence and make sure that everything is correctly assembled and tightened.

DO keep chemicals and fluids tightly capped and out of the reach of children and pets.

DO remember that your vehicle's safety affects that of yourself and others. If in doubt on any point, get professional advice.

Asbestos

Certain friction, insulating, sealing, and other products — such as brake linings, brake bands, clutch linings, torque converters, gaskets, etc. — contain asbestos. *Extreme care must be taken to avoid inhalation of dust from such products since it is hazardous to health.* If in doubt, assume that they *do* contain asbestos.

Fire

Remember at all times that gasoline is highly flammable. Never smoke or have any kind of open flame around when working on a vehicle. But the risk does not end there. A spark caused by an electrical short circuit, by two metal surfaces contacting each other, or even by static electricity built up in your body under certain conditions, can ignite gasoline vapors, which in a confined space are highly explosive. Do not, under any circumstances, use gasoline for cleaning parts. Use an approved safety solvent.

Always disconnect the battery ground (–) cable *at the battery* before working on any part of the fuel system or electrical system. Never risk spilling fuel on a hot engine or exhaust component.

It is strongly recommended that a fire extinguisher suitable for use on fuel and electrical fires be kept handy in the garage or workshop at all times. Never try to extinguish a fuel or electrical fire with water.

Fumes

Certain fumes are highly toxic and can quickly cause unconsciousness and even death if inhaled to any extent. Gasoline vapor falls into this category, as do the vapors from some cleaning solvents. Any draining or pouring of such volatile fluids should be done in a well ventilated area.

When using cleaning fluids and solvents, read the instructions on the container carefully. Never use materials from unmarked containers.

Never run the engine in an enclosed space, such as a garage. Exhaust fumes contain carbon monoxide, which is extremely poisonous. If you need to run the engine, always do so in the open air, or at least have the rear of the vehicle outside the work area.

If you are fortunate enough to have the use of an inspection pit, never drain or pour gasoline and never run the engine while the vehicle is over the pit. The fumes, being heavier than air, will concentrate in the pit with possibly lethal results.

The battery

Never create a spark or allow a bare light bulb near the battery. The battery normally gives off a certain amount of hydrogen gas, which is highly explosive.

Always disconnect the battery ground (–) cable *at the battery* before working on the fuel or electrical systems.

If possible, loosen the filler caps or cover when charging the battery from an external source. Do not charge at an excessive rate or the battery may burst.

Take care when adding water and when carrying a battery. The electrolyte, even when diluted, is very corrosive and should not be allowed to contact clothing or skin.

Always wear eye protection when cleaning the battery to prevent the caustic deposits from entering your eyes.

Household current

When using an electric power tool, inspection light, etc., which operates on household current, always make sure that the tool is correctly connected to its plug and that, where necessary, it is properly grounded. Do not use such items in damp conditions and, again, do not create a spark or apply excessive heat in the vicinity of fuel or fuel vapor.

Secondary ignition system voltage

A severe electric shock can result from touching certain parts of the ignition system (such as the spark plug wires) when the engine is running or being cranked, particularly if components are damp or the insulation is defective. In the case of an electronic ignition system, the secondary system voltage is much higher and could prove fatal.

Conversion factors

Length (distance)

Inches (in)	X 25.4	= Millimetres (mm)	X 0.0394	= Inches (in)
Feet (ft)	X 0.305	= Metres (m)	X 3.281	= Feet (ft)
Miles	X 1.609	= Kilometres (km)	X 0.621	= Miles

Volume (capacity)

Cubic inches (cu in; in³)	X 16.387	= Cubic centimetres (cc; cm³)	X 0.061	= Cubic inches (cu in; in³)
Imperial pints (Imp pt)	X 0.568	= Litres (l)	X 1.76	= Imperial pints (Imp pt)
Imperial quarts (Imp qt)	X 1.137	= Litres (l)	X 0.88	= Imperial quarts (Imp qt)
Imperial quarts (Imp qt)	X 1.201	= US quarts (US qt)	X 0.833	= Imperial quarts (Imp qt)
US quarts (US qt)	X 0.946	= Litres (l)	X 1.057	= US quarts (US qt)
Imperial gallons (Imp gal)	X 4.546	= Litres (l)	X 0.22	= Imperial gallons (Imp gal)
Imperial gallons (Imp gal)	X 1.201	= US gallons (US gal)	X 0.833	= Imperial gallons (Imp gal)
US gallons (US gal)	X 3.785	= Litres (l)	X 0.264	= US gallons (US gal)

Mass (weight)

Ounces (oz)	X 28.35	= Grams (g)	X 0.035	= Ounces (oz)
Pounds (lb)	X 0.454	= Kilograms (kg)	X 2.205	= Pounds (lb)

Force

Ounces-force (ozf; oz)	X 0.278	= Newtons (N)	X 3.6	= Ounces-force (ozf; oz)
Pounds-force (lbf; lb)	X 4.448	= Newtons (N)	X 0.225	= Pounds-force (lbf; lb)
Newtons (N)	X 0.1	= Kilograms-force (kgf; kg)	X 9.81	= Newtons (N)

Pressure

Pounds-force per square inch (psi; lbf/in²; lb/in²)	X 0.070	= Kilograms-force per square centimetre (kgf/cm²; kg/cm²)	X 14.223	= Pounds-force per square inch (psi; lbf/in²; lb/in²)
Pounds-force per square inch (psi; lbf/in²; lb/in²)	X 0.068	= Atmospheres (atm)	X 14.696	= Pounds-force per square inch (psi; lbf/in²; lb/in²)
Pounds-force per square inch (psi; lbf/in²; lb/in²)	X 0.069	= Bars	X 14.5	= Pounds-force per square inch (psi; lbf/in²; lb/in²)
Pounds-force per square inch (psi; lbf/in²; lb/in²)	X 6.895	= Kilopascals (kPa)	X 0.145	= Pounds-force per square inch (psi; lbf/in²; lb/in²)
Kilopascals (kPa)	X 0.01	= Kilograms-force per square centimetre (kgf/cm²; kg/cm²)	X 98.1	= Kilopascals (kPa)
Millibar (mbar)	X 100	= Pascals (Pa)	X 0.01	= Millibar (mbar)
Millibar (mbar)	X 0.0145	= Pounds-force per square inch (psi; lbf/in²; lb/in²)	X 68.947	= Millibar (mbar)
Millibar (mbar)	X 0.75	= Millimetres of mercury (mmHg)	X 1.333	= Millibar (mbar)
Millibar (mbar)	X 0.401	= Inches of water (inH₂O)	X 2.491	= Millibar (mbar)
Millimetres of mercury (mmHg)	X 0.535	= Inches of water (inH₂O)	X 1.868	= Millimetres of mercury (mmHg)
Inches of water (inH₂O)	X 0.036	= Pounds-force per square inch (psi; lbf/in²; lb/in²)	X 27.68	= Inches of water (inH₂O)

Torque (moment of force)

Pounds-force inches (lbf in; lb in)	X 1.152	= Kilograms-force centimetre (kgf cm; kg cm)	X 0.868	= Pounds-force inches (lbf in; lb in)
Pounds-force inches (lbf in; lb in)	X 0.113	= Newton metres (Nm)	X 8.85	= Pounds-force inches (lbf in; lb in)
Pounds-force inches (lbf in; lb In)	X 0.083	= Pounds-force feet (lbf ft; lb ft)	X 12	= Pounds-force inches (lbf in; lb in)
Pounds-force feet (lbf ft; lb ft)	X 0.138	= Kilograms-force metres (kgf m; kg m)	X 7.233	= Pounds-force feet (lbf ft; lb ft)
Pounds-force feet (lbf ft; lb ft)	X 1.356	= Newton metres (Nm)	X 0.738	= Pounds-force feet (lbf ft; lb ft)
Newton metres (Nm)	X 0.102	= Kilograms-force metres (kgf m; kg m)	X 9.804	= Newton metres (Nm)

Power

Horsepower (hp)	X 745.7	= Watts (W)	X 0.0013	= Horsepower (hp)

Velocity (speed)

Miles per hour (miles/hr; mph)	X 1.609	= Kilometres per hour (km/hr; kph)	X 0.621	= Miles per hour (miles/hr; mph)

Fuel consumption*

Miles per gallon, Imperial (mpg)	X 0.354	= Kilometres per litre (km/l)	X 2.825	= Miles per gallon, Imperial (mpg)
Miles per gallon, US (mpg)	X 0.425	= Kilometres per litre (km/l)	X 2.352	= Miles per gallon, US (mpg)

Temperature

Degrees Fahrenheit = (°C x 1.8) + 32

Degrees Celsius (Degrees Centigrade; °C) = (°F - 32) x 0.56

*It is common practice to convert from miles per gallon (mpg) to litres/100 kilometres (l/100km),
where mpg (Imperial) x l/100 km = 282 and mpg (US) x l/100 km = 235

Troubleshooting

Contents

This section provides an easy reference guide to the more common problems which may occur during the operation of your vehicle. These problems and possible causes are grouped under various components or systems, such as Engine, Cooling system, etc., and also refer to the Chapter and/or Section which deals with the problem.

Remember that successful troubleshooting is not a mysterious 'black art' practiced only by professional mechanics. It's simply the result of a bit of knowledge combined with an intelligent, systematic approach to the problem. Always work by a process of elimination, starting with the simplest solution and working through to the most complex — and never overlook the obvious. Anyone can forget to fill the gas tank or leave the lights on overnight, so don't assume that you are above such oversights.

Finally, always get clear in your mind why a problem has occurred and take steps to ensure that it doesn't happen again. If the electrical system fails because of a poor connection, check all other connections in the system to make sure that they don't fail as well. If a particular fuse continues to blow, find out why — don't just go on replacing fuses. Remember, failure of a small component can often be indicative of potential failure or incorrect functioning of a more important component or system.

Engine

1 Engine will not rotate when attempting to start

1 Battery terminal connections loose or corroded. Check the cable terminals at the battery. Tighten the cable or remove corrosion as necessary.
2 Battery discharged or faulty. If the cable connections are clean and tight on the battery posts, turn the key to the On position and switch on the headlights and/or windshield wipers. If they fail to function, the battery is discharged.
3 Automatic transmission not completely engaged in Park or clutch not completely depressed.
4 Broken, loose or disconnected wiring in the starting circuit. Inspect all wiring and connectors at the battery, starter solenoid and ignition switch.
5 Starter motor pinion jammed in flywheel ring gear. If equipped with a manual transmission, place the transmission in gear and rock the vehicle to manually turn the engine. Remove the starter and inspect the pinion and flywheel at earliest convenience.
6 Starter solenoid faulty (Chapter 5).
7 Starter motor faulty (Chapter 5).
8 Ignition switch faulty (Chapter 12).

2 Engine rotates but will not start

1 Fuel tank empty.
2 Battery discharged (engine rotates slowly). Check the operation of electrical components as described in previous Section.
3 Battery terminal connections loose or corroded. See previous Section.
4 Carburetor flooded and/or fuel level in carburetor incorrect. This will usually be accompanied by a strong fuel odor from under the hood. Wait a few minutes, depress the accelerator pedal all the way to the floor and attempt to start the engine.
5 Choke control inoperative (Chapter 4).
6 Fuel not reaching carburetor. With the ignition switch in the Off position, remove the top plate of the air cleaner assembly and observe the top of the carburetor (manually move the choke plate back if necessary). Depress the accelerator pedal and check that fuel spurts into the carburetor. If not, check the fuel filter (Chapter 1), fuel lines and fuel pump (Chapter 4).
7 Fuel pump faulty (Chapter 4).
8 Ignition condenser faulty (1970 through 1974 models).
9 Worn, faulty or incorrectly gapped spark plugs (Chapter 1).
10 Broken, loose or disconnected wiring in the starting circuit (see previous Section).
11 Distributor loose, causing ignition timing to change. Turn the distributor as necessary to start the engine, then set the ignition timing as soon as possible (Chapter 1).
12 Broken, loose or disconnected wires at the ignition coil or faulty coil (Chapter 5).

3 Starter motor operates without rotating engine

1 Starter pinion sticking. Remove the starter (Chapter 5) and inspect.
2 Starter pinion or flywheel teeth worn or broken. Remove the cover at the rear of the engine and inspect.

4 Engine hard to start when cold

1 Battery discharged or low. Check as described in Section 1.
2 Choke control inoperative or out of adjustment (Chapter 4).
3 Carburetor flooded (see Section 2).
4 Fuel supply not reaching the carburetor (see Section 2).
5 Carburetor in need of overhaul (Chapter 4).
6 Distributor rotor carbon tracked and/or damaged (Chapter 1).

5 Engine hard to start when hot

1 Air filter clogged (Chapter 1).
2 Fuel not reaching the carburetor (see Section 2).
3 Corroded electrical leads at the battery (Chapter 1).
4 Bad engine ground (Chapter 12).
5 Starter worn (Chapter 5).
6 EFE (heat riser) sticking in the closed position (Chapter 1).

6 Starter motor noisy or excessively rough in engagement

1 Pinion or flywheel gear teeth worn or broken. Remove the cover at the rear of the engine (if so equipped) and inspect.
2 Starter motor mounting bolts loose or missing.

7 Engine starts but stops immediately

1 Loose or faulty electrical connections at distributor, coil or alternator.
2 Insufficient fuel reaching the carburetor. Disconnect the fuel line. Place a container under the disconnected fuel line and observe the flow of fuel from the line. If little or none at all, check for blockage in the lines and/or replace the fuel pump (Chapter 4).
3 Vacuum leak at the gasket surfaces of the carburetor. Make sure that all mounting bolts/nuts are tightened securely and that all vacuum hoses connected to the carburetor and manifold are positioned properly and in good condition.

8 Engine lopes while idling or idles erratically

1 Vacuum leakage. Check mounting bolts/nuts at the carburetor and intake manifold for tightness. Make sure that all vacuum hoses are connected and in good condition. Use a stethoscope or a length of fuel hose held against your ear to listen for vacuum leaks while the engine is running. A hissing sound will be heard. Check the carburetor/fuel injector and intake manifold gasket surfaces.
2 Leaking EGR valve or plugged PCV valve (see Chapters 1 and 6).
3 Air filter clogged (Chapter 1).
4 Fuel pump not delivering sufficient fuel to the carburetor (see Section 7).
5 Carburetor out of adjustment (Chapter 4).
6 Leaking head gasket. If this is suspected, take the vehicle to a repair shop or dealer where the engine can be pressure checked.
7 Timing chain and/or gears worn (Chapter 2).
8 Camshaft lobes worn (Chapter 2).

9 Engine misses at idle speed

1 Spark plugs worn or not gapped properly (Chapter 1).
2 Faulty spark plug wires (Chapter 1).
3 Choke not operating properly (Chapter 1).
4 Sticking or faulty emissions system components (Chapter 6).
5 Clogged fuel filter and/or foreign matter in fuel. Remove the fuel filter (Chapter 1) and inspect.
6 Vacuum leaks at the intake manifold or at hose connections. Check as described in Section 8.
7 Incorrect idle speed or idle mixture (Chapter 1).

8   Incorrect ignition timing (Chapter 1).
9   Uneven or low cylinder compression. Check compression as described in Chapter 2.
10 Faulty or incorrectly set contact breaker points (1970 through 1974 models) (Chapter 1).

10   Engine misses throughout driving speed range

1   Fuel filter clogged and/or impurities in the fuel system (Chapter 1). Also check fuel output at the carburetor (see Section 7).
2   Faulty or incorrectly gapped spark plugs (Chapter 1).
3   Incorrect ignition timing (Chapter 1).
4   Check for cracked distributor cap, disconnected distributor wires and damaged distributor components (Chapter 1).
5   Leaking spark plug wires (Chapter 1).
6   Faulty emissions system components (Chapter 6).
7   Low or uneven cylinder compression pressures. Remove the spark plugs and test the compression with gauge (Chapter 2).
8   Weak or faulty ignition system (Chapter 5).
9   Vacuum leaks at the carburetor or vacuum hoses (see Section 8).

11   Engine stalls

1   Idle speed incorrect (Chapter 1).
2   Fuel filter clogged and/or water and impurities in the fuel system (Chapter 1).
3   Choke improperly adjusted or sticking (Chapter 4).
4   Distributor components damp or damaged (Chapter 5).
5   Faulty emissions system components (Chapter 6).
6   Faulty or incorrectly gapped spark plugs (Chapter 1). Also check spark plug wires (Chapter 1).
7   Vacuum leak at the carburetor or vacuum hoses. Check as described in Section 8.

12   Engine lacks power

1   Incorrect ignition timing (Chapter 1).
2   Excessive play in distributor shaft. At the same time, check for worn rotor, faulty distributor cap, wires, etc. (Chapters 1 and 5).
3   Faulty or incorrectly gapped spark plugs (Chapter 1).
4   Carburetor not adjusted properly or excessively worn (Chapter 4).
5   Faulty coil (Chapter 5).
6   Brakes binding (Chapter 1).
7   Automatic transmission fluid level incorrect (Chapter 1).
8   Clutch slipping (Chapter 8).
9   Fuel filter clogged and/or impurities in the fuel system (Chapter 1).
10 Emissions control system not functioning properly (Chapter 6).
11 Use of substandard fuel. Fill tank with proper octane fuel.
12 Low or uneven cylinder compression pressures. Test with compression tester, which will detect leaking valves and/or blown head gasket (Chapter 2).

13   Engine backfires

1   Emissions system not functioning properly (Chapter 6).
2   Ignition timing incorrect (Chapter 1).
3   Faulty secondary ignition system (cracked spark plug insulator, faulty plug wires, distributor cap and/or rotor) (Chapters 1 and 5).
4   Carburetor in need of adjustment or worn excessively (Chapter 4).
5   Vacuum leak at the carburetor or vacuum hoses. Check as described in Section 8.
6   Valves sticking (Chapter 2).
7   Crossed plug wires (Chapter 1).

14   Pinging or knocking engine sounds during acceleration or uphill

1   Incorrect grade of fuel. Fill tank with fuel of the proper octane rating.
2   Ignition timing incorrect (Chapter 1).
3   Carburetor in need of adjustment (Chapter 4).
4   Improper spark plugs. Check plug type against Emissions Control Information label located under hood. Also check plugs and wires for damage (Chapter 1).
5   Worn or damaged distributor components (Chapter 5).
6   Faulty emissions system (Chapter 6).
7   Vacuum leak. Check as described in Section 8.

15   Engine diesels (continues to run) after switching off

1   Idle speed too high (Chapter 1).
2   Electrical solenoid at side of carburetor not functioning properly (not all models, see Chapter 4).
3   Ignition timing incorrectly adjusted (Chapter 1).
4   Thermo-controlled air cleaner heat valve not operating properly (Chapter 1).
5   Excessive engine operating temperature. Probable causes of this are malfunctioning thermostat, clogged radiator, faulty water pump (Chapter 3).

Engine electrical system

16   Battery will not hold a charge

1   Alternator drivebelt defective or not adjusted properly (Chapter 1).
2   Electrolyte level low or battery discharged (Chapter 1).
3   Battery terminals loose or corroded (Chapter 1).
4   Alternator not charging properly (Chapter 5).
5   Loose, broken or faulty wiring in the charging circuit (Chapter 5).
6   Short in vehicle wiring causing a continual drain on battery.
7   Battery defective internally.

17   Ignition light fails to go out

1   Fault in alternator or charging circuit (Chapter 5).
2   Alternator drivebelt defective or not properly adjusted (Chapter 1).

18   Ignition light fails to come on when key is turned on

1   Warning light bulb defective (Chapter 12).
2   Alternator faulty (Chapter 5).
3   Fault in the printed circuit, dash wiring or bulb holder (Chapter 12).

19   'Check engine' light comes on

See Chapter 6

Fuel system

20   Excessive fuel consumption

1   Dirty or clogged air filter element (Chapter 1).
2   Incorrectly set ignition timing (Chapter 1).
3   Choke sticking or improperly adjusted (Chapter 1).
4   Emissions system not functioning properly (not all vehicles, see Chapter 6).

5   Carburetor idle speed and/or mixture not adjusted properly (Chapter 1).
6   Carburetor internal parts excessively worn or damaged (Chapter 4).
7   Low tire pressure or incorrect tire size (Chapter 1).

21   Fuel leakage and/or fuel odor

1   Leak in a fuel feed or vent line (Chapter 4).
2   Tank overfilled. Fill only to automatic shut-off.
3   Emissions system clogged or damaged (Chapter 6).
4   Vapor leaks from system lines (Chapter 4).
5   Carburetor internal parts excessively worn or out of adjustment (Chapter 4).

Cooling system

22   Overheating

1   Insufficient coolant in system (Chapter 1).
2   Water pump drivebelt defective or not adjusted properly (Chapter 1).
3   Radiator core blocked or radiator grille dirty and restricted (Chapter 3).
4   Thermostat faulty (Chapter 3).
5   Fan blades broken or cracked (Chapter 3).
6   Radiator cap not maintaining proper pressure. Have cap pressure tested by gas station or repair shop.
7   Ignition timing incorrect (Chapter 1).

23   Overcooling

1   Thermostat faulty (Chapter 3).
2   Inaccurate temperature gauge (Chapter 12)

24   External coolant leakage

1   Deteriorated or damaged hoses or loose clamps. Replace hoses and/or tighten clamps at hose connections (Chapter 1).
2   Water pump seals defective. If this is the case, water will drip from the weep hole in the water pump body (Chapter 3).
3   Leakage from radiator core or header tank. This will require the radiator to be professionally repaired (see Chapter 3 for removal procedures).
4   Engine drain plugs or water jacket core plugs leaking (see Chapter 2).

25   Internal coolant leakage

Note: *Internal coolant leaks can usually be detected by examining the oil. Check the dipstick and inside of the rocker arm cover(s) for water deposits and an oil consistency like that of a milkshake.*
1   Leaking cylinder head gasket. Have the cooling system pressure tested.
2   Cracked cylinder bore or cylinder head. Dismantle engine and inspect (Chapter 2).

26   Coolant loss

1   Too much coolant in system (Chapter 1).
2   Coolant boiling away due to overheating (see Section 22).
3   Internal or external leakage (see Sections 24 and 25).
4   Faulty radiator cap. Have the cap pressure tested.

27   Poor coolant circulation

1   Inoperative water pump. A quick test is to pinch the top radiator hose closed with your hand while the engine is idling, then let it loose. You should feel the surge of coolant if the pump is working properly (Chapter 3).
2   Restriction in cooling system. Drain, flush and refill the system (Chapter 1). If necessary, remove the radiator (Chapter 3) and have it reverse flushed.
3   Water pump drivebelt defective or not adjusted properly (Chapter 1).
4   Thermostat sticking (Chapter 3).

Clutch

28   Fails to release (pedal pressed to the floor — shift lever does not move freely in and out of Reverse)

1   Clutch fork off ball stud. Look under the vehicle, on the left side of transmission.
2   Clutch plate warped or damaged (Chapter 8).

29   Clutch slips (engine speed increases with no increase in vehicle speed)

1   Clutch plate oil soaked or lining worn. Remove clutch (Chapter 8) and inspect.
2   Clutch plate not seated. It may take 30 or 40 normal starts for a new one to seat.
3   Pressure plate worn (Chapter 8).

30   Grabbing (chattering) as clutch is engaged

1   Oil on clutch plate lining. Remove (Chapter 8) and inspect. Correct any leakage source.
2   Worn or loose engine or transmission mounts. These units move slightly when clutch is released. Inspect mounts and bolts.
3   Worn splines on clutch plate hub. Remove clutch components (Chapter 8) and inspect.
4   Warped pressure plate or flywheel. Remove clutch components and inspect.

31   Squeal or rumble with clutch fully engaged (pedal released)

1   Release bearing binding on transmission bearing retainer. Remove clutch components (Chapter 8) and check bearing. Remove any burrs or nicks, clean and relubricate before reinstallation.
2   Weak linkage return spring. Replace the spring.

32   Squeal or rumble with clutch fully disengaged (pedal depressed)

1   Worn, defective or broken release bearing (Chapter 8).
2   Worn or broken pressure plate springs (or diaphragm fingers) (Chapter 8).

33   Clutch pedal stays on floor when disengaged

1   Bind in linkage or release bearing. Inspect linkage or remove clutch components as necessary.
2   Clutch hydraulic cylinder faulty or there is air in the system.

Manual transmission

Note: *All the following references are to Chapter 7, unless noted.*

34 Noisy in Neutral with engine running

1   Input shaft bearing worn.
2   Damaged main drive gear bearing.
3   Worn countershaft bearings.
4   Worn or damaged countershaft end play shims.

35 Noisy in all gears

1   Any of the above causes, and/or:
2   Insufficient lubricant (see checking procedures in Chapter 1).

36 Noisy in one particular gear

1   Worn, damaged or chipped gear teeth for that particular gear.
2   Worn or damaged synchronizer for that particular gear.

37 Slips out of high gear

1   Transmission mounting bolts loose.
2   Shift rods not working freely.
3   Damaged mainshaft pilot bushing.
4   Dirt between transmission case and engine or misalignment of transmission.

38 Difficulty in engaging gears

1   Loose, damaged or out-of-adjustment shift linkage. Make a thorough inspection, replacing parts as necessary.
2   Air in hydraulic system (Chapter 8)

39 Oil leakage

1   Excessive amount of lubricant in transmission (see Chapter 1 for correct checking procedures). Drain lubricant as required.
2   Side cover loose or gasket damaged.
3   Rear oil seal or speedometer oil seal in need of replacement.
4   Clutch hydraulic system leaking (Chapter 8).

Automatic transmission

Note: *Due to the complexity of the automatic transmission, it is difficult for the home mechanic to properly diagnose and service this component. For problems other than the following, the vehicle should be taken to a dealer or reputable repair shop.*

40 General shift mechanism problems

1   Chapter 7 deals with checking and adjusting the shift linkage on automatic transmissions. Common problems which may be attributed to poorly adjusted linkage are:

   Engine starting in gears other than Park or Neutral
   Indicator on shifter pointing to a gear other than the one actually being used
   Vehicle moves when in Park
2   Refer to Chapter 7 to adjust the linkage.

41 Transmission will not downshift with accelerator pedal pressed to the floor

   Chapter 7 deals with adjusting the TV cable to enable the transmission to downshift properly.

42 Transmission slips, shifts roughly, is noisy or has no drive in forward or reverse gears

1   There are many probable causes for the above problems, but the home mechanic should be concerned with only one possibility — fluid level.
2   Before taking the vehicle to a repair shop, check the level and condition of the fluid as described in Chapter 1. Correct fluid level as necessary or change the fluid and filter if needed. If the problem persists, have a professional diagnose the probable cause.
3   Damaged governor seals (1976 through 1980 THM 200 and 1978 through 1987 THM transmission equipped Buick models). A Buick service bulletin was issued for this condition (no. 87-7200-1). Ask your General Motors dealer for assistance.

43 Fluid leakage

1   Automatic transmission fluid is a deep red color. Fluid leaks should not be confused with engine oil, which can easily be blown by air flow to the transmission.
2   To pinpoint a leak, first remove all built-up dirt and grime from around the transmission. Degreasing agents and/or steam cleaning will achieve this. With the underside clean, drive the vehicle at low speeds so air flow will not blow the leak far from its source. Raise the vehicle and determine where the leak is coming from. Common areas of leakage are:
   a) Pan: Tighten mounting bolts and/or replace pan gasket as necessary (see Chapters 1 and 7).
   b) Filler pipe: Replace the rubber seal where pipe enters transmission case.
   c) Transmission oil lines: Tighten connectors where lines enter transmission case and/or replace lines.
   d) Vent pipe: Transmission overfilled and/or water in fluid (see checking procedures, Chapter 1).
   e) Speedometer connector: Replace the O-ring where speedometer cable enters transmission case (Chapter 7).

Driveshaft

44 Oil leak at front of driveshaft

   Defective transmission rear oil seal. See Chapter 7 for replacement procedures. While this is done, check the splined yoke for burrs or a rough condition which may be damaging the seal. Burrs can be removed with crocus cloth or a fine whetstone.

45 Knock or clunk when the transmission is under initial load (just after transmission is put into gear)

1   Loose or disconnected rear suspension components. Check all mounting bolts, nuts and bushings (Chapter 10).
2   Loose driveshaft bolts. Inspect all bolts and nuts and tighten them to the specified torque.
3   Worn or damaged universal joint bearings. Check for wear (Chapter 8).

46 Metallic grating sound consistent with vehicle speed

   Pronounced wear in the universal joint bearings. Check as described in Chapter 8.

47 Vibration

Note: *Before assuming that the driveshaft is at fault, make sure the tires are perfectly balanced and perform the following test.*

1 Install a tachometer inside the vehicle to monitor engine speed as the vehicle is driven. Drive the vehicle and note the engine speed at which the vibration (roughness) is most pronounced. Now shift the transmission to a different gear and bring the engine speed to the same point.
2 If the vibration occurs at the same engine speed (rpm) regardless of which gear the transmission is in, the driveshaft is NOT at fault since the driveshaft speed varies.
3 If the vibration decreases or is eliminated when the transmission is in a different gear at the same engine speed, refer to the following probable causes.
4 Bent or dented driveshaft. Inspect and replace as necessary (Chapter 8).
5 Undercoating or built-up dirt, etc., on the driveshaft. Clean the shaft thoroughly and recheck.
6 Worn universal joint bearings. Remove and inspect (Chapter 8).
7 Driveshaft and/or companion flange out-of-balance. Check for missing weights on the shaft. Remove the driveshaft (Chapter 8) and reinstall 180° from original position, then retest. Have the driveshaft professionally balanced if the problem persists.

Axles

48 Noise

1 Road noise. No corrective procedures available.
2 Tire noise. Inspect the tires and check tire pressures (Chapter 1).
3 Rear wheel bearings loose, worn or damaged (Chapter 8).

49 Vibration

See probable causes under Driveshaft. Proceed under the guidelines listed for the driveshaft. If the problem persists, check the rear wheel bearings by raising the rear of the vehicle and spinning the wheels by hand. Listen for evidence of rough (noisy) bearings. Remove and inspect (Chapter 8).

50 Oil leakage

1 Pinion seal damaged (Chapter 8).
2 Axleshaft oil seals damaged (Chapter 8).
3 Differential inspection cover leaking. Tighten the bolts or replace the gasket as required (Chapters 1 and 8).

Brakes

Note: *Before assuming that a brake problem exists, make sure that the tires are in good condition and inflated properly (see Chapter 1), that the front end alignment is correct and that the vehicle is not loaded with weight in an unequal manner.*

51 Vehicle pulls to one side during braking

1 Defective, damaged or oil contaminated brake pads or shoes on one side. Inspect as described in Chapter 9.
2 Excessive wear of brake shoe or pad material or drum/disc on one side. Inspect and correct as necessary.
3 Loose or disconnected front suspension components. Inspect and tighten all bolts to the specified torque (Chapter 10).
4 Defective drum brake or caliper assembly. Remove the drum or caliper and inspect for a stuck piston or other damage (Chapter 9).

52 Noise (high-pitched squeal with the brakes applied)

Disc brake pads worn out. The noise comes from the wear sensor rubbing against the disc. Replace the pads with new ones immediately (Chapter 9).

53 Excessive brake pedal travel

1 Partial brake system failure. Inspect the entire system (Chapter 9) and correct as required.
2 Insufficient fluid in the master cylinder. Check (Chapter 1), add fluid and bleed the system if necessary (Chapter 9).
3 Brakes not adjusting properly. Make a series of starts and stops with the vehicle is in Reverse. If this does not correct the situation, remove the drums and inspect the self-adjusters (Chapter 9).

54 Brake pedal feels spongy when depressed

1 Air in the hydraulic lines. Bleed the brake system (Chapter 9).
2 Faulty flexible hoses. Inspect all system hoses and lines. Replace parts as necessary.
3 Master cylinder mounting bolts/nuts loose.
4 Master cylinder defective (Chapter 9).

55 Excessive effort required to stop vehicle

1 Power brake booster not operating properly (Chapter 9).
2 Excessively worn linings or pads. Inspect and replace if necessary (Chapters 1 and 9).
3 One or more caliper pistons or wheel cylinders seized or sticking. Inspect and rebuild as required (Chapter 9).
4 Brake linings or pads contaminated with oil or grease. Inspect and replace as required (Chapters 1 and 9).
5 New pads or shoes installed and not yet seated. It will take a while for the new material to seat against the drum (or rotor).

56 Pedal travels to the floor with little resistance

Little or no fluid in the master cylinder reservoir caused by leaking wheel cylinder(s), leaking caliper piston(s), loose, damaged or disconnected brake lines. Inspect the entire system and correct as necessary.

57 Brake pedal pulsates during brake application

1 Wheel bearings not adjusted properly or in need of replacement (Chapter 1).
2 Caliper not sliding properly due to improper installation or obstructions. Remove and inspect (Chapter 9).
3 Rotor or drum defective. Remove the rotor or drum (Chapter 9) and check for excessive lateral runout, out-of-round and parallelism. Have the drum or rotor resurfaced or replace it with a new one.

Suspension and steering systems

58 Vehicle pulls to one side

1 Tire pressures uneven (Chapter 1).
2 Defective tire (Chapter 1).
3 Excessive wear in suspension or steering components (Chapter 10).

4   Front end in need of alignment.
5   Front brakes dragging. Inspect the brakes as described in Chapter 9.

59   Shimmy, shake or vibration

1   Tire or wheel out-of-balance or out-of-round. Have professionally balanced.
2   Loose, worn or out-of-adjustment wheel bearings (Chapters 1 and 8).
3   Shock absorbers and/or suspension components worn or damaged (Chapter 10).

60   Excessive pitching and/or rolling around corners or during braking

1   Defective shock absorbers. Replace as a set (Chapter 10).
2   Broken or weak springs and/or suspension components. Inspect as described in Chapter 10.

61   Excessively stiff steering

1   Lack of fluid in power steering fluid reservoir (Chapter 1).
2   Incorrect tire pressures (Chapter 1).
3   Lack of lubrication at steering joints (Chapter 1).
4   Front end out of alignment.
5   See Section 63.

62   Excessive play in steering

1   Loose front wheel bearings (Chapter 1).
2   Excessive wear in suspension or steering components (Chapter 10).
3   Steering gearbox out of adjustment (Chapter 10).

63   Lack of power assistance

1   Steering pump drivebelt faulty or not adjusted properly (Chapter 1).
2   Fluid level low (Chapter 1).
3   Hoses or lines restricted. Inspect and replace parts as necessary.
4   Air in power steering system. Bleed the system (Chapter 10).

64   Excessive tire wear (not specific to one area)

1   Incorrect tire pressures (Chapter 1).
2   Tires out-of-balance. Have professionally balanced.
3   Wheels damaged. Inspect and replace as necessary.
4   Suspension or steering components excessively worn (Chapter 10).

65   Excessive tire wear on outside edge

1   Inflation pressures incorrect (Chapter 1).
2   Excessive speed in turns.
3   Front end alignment incorrect (excessive toe-in). Have professionally aligned.
4   Suspension arm bent or twisted (Chapter 10).

66   Excessive tire wear on inside edge

1   Inflation pressures incorrect (Chapter 1).
2   Front end alignment incorrect (excessive toe-out). Have professionally aligned.
3   Loose or damaged steering components (Chapter 10).

67   Tire tread worn in one place

1   Tires out-of-balance.
2   Damaged or buckled wheel. Inspect and replace if necessary.
3   Defective tire (Chapter 1).

Chapter 1   Tune-up and routine maintenance

Contents

Specifications

Recommended lubricants and fluids

Engine oil type	API grade SF or SF/CC multigrade and fuel efficient oil
Viscosity	See accompanying chart
Automatic transmission fluid type	Dexron II automatic transmission fluid
Manual transmission fluid type	SAE 80W or 80W-90 GL-5 gear lubricant
Differential fluid type	SAE 80W or 80W-90 GL-5 gear lubricant
Limited slip differential	Add GM limited slip additive to the specified lubricant
Brake fluid type	DOT 3 brake fluid
Power steering system fluid	GM power steering fluid or equivalent
Steering gear fluid type	GM 4673 M or equivalent

Ignition system

Spark plug type and gap	Refer to the tune-up decal in the engine compartment
Ignition timing	Refer to tune-up decal in the engine compartment
Ignition point gap	
New	0.019 in
Used.	0.016 in
Dwell angle	30°

OIL FILTER AC — PF 45

General

Engine firing order

V6 engine	1-6-5-4-3-2
V8 engine	1-8-4-3-6-5-7-2

Clutch

Clutch pedal free play.	1.0 in

Brakes

Disc brake pad lining thickness (minimum)	1/8-in
Drum brake shoe lining thickness (minimum)	1/16-in

Torque specifications

	ft-lb
Automatic transmission pan bolts	12
Carburetor mounting nut/bolt	10 to 15
Differential cover bolt	10 to 20
Spark plug	15
Wheel lug nut	80 to 90

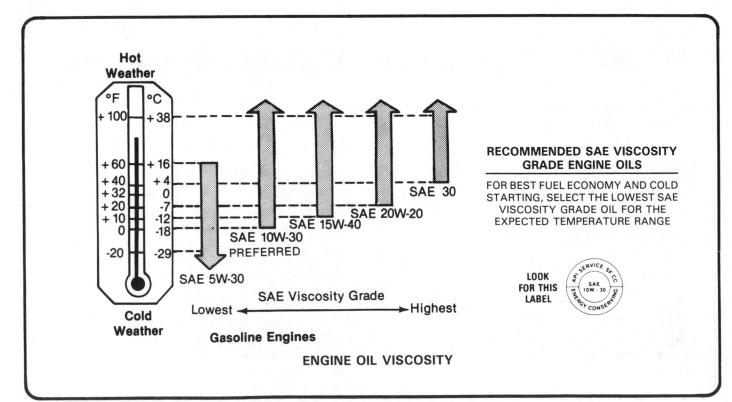

ENGINE OIL VISCOSITY

1 Buick, Oldsmobile, Pontiac full-size RWD maintenance schedule

The following maintenance intervals are based on the assumption that the vehicle owner will be doing the maintenance or service work, as opposed to having a dealer service department do the work. Although the time/mileage intervals are loosely based on factory recommendations, most have been shortened to ensure, for example, that such items as lubricants and fluids are checked/changed at intervals that promote maximum engine/driveline service life. Also, subject to the preference of the individual owner interested in keeping his or her vehicle in peak condition at all times, and with the vehicle's ultimate resale in mind, many of the maintenance procedures may be performed more often than recommended in the following schedule. We encourage such owner initiative.

When the vehicle is new it should be serviced initially by a factory authorized dealer service department to protect the factory warranty. In many cases the initial maintenance check is done at no cost to the owner (check with your dealer service department for more information).

Every 250 miles or weekly, whichever comes first

Check the engine oil level (Section 4)
Check the engine coolant level (Section 4)
Check the windshield washer fluid level (Section 4)
Check the brake and clutch fluid levels (Section 4)
Check the tires and tire pressures (Section 5)

Every 3000 miles or 3 months, whichever comes first

All items listed above plus:
Check the automatic transmission fluid level (Section 6)
Check the power steering fluid level (Section 7)
Check and service the battery (Section 8)
Check the cooling system (Section 9)
Inspect and replace, if necessary, all underhood hoses (Section 10)
Inspect and replace, if necessary, the windshield wiper blades (Section 11)

Every 7500 miles or 12 months whichever comes first

All items listed above plus:
* Change the engine oil and oil filter (Section 12)
Lubricate the chassis components (Section 13)
* Inspect the suspension and steering components (Section 14)
* Inspect the exhaust system (Section 15)
* Check the EFE (heat riser) system (Section 16)
* Check and adjust, if necessary, the clutch pedal free play (Section 17)
* Check the manual transmission lubricant level (Section 18)
* Check the rear axle differential lubricant level (Section 19)

Rotate the tires (Section 20)
* Check the brakes (Section 21)
Inspect the fuel system (Section 22)
Check the carburetor choke operation (Section 23)
Check the carburetor mounting nut torque (Section 24)
Check the throttle linkage (Section 25)
Check the thermostatically-controlled air cleaner (Section 26)
Check the engine drivebelts (Section 27)
Check the seatbelts (Section 28)
Check the starter safety switch (Section 29)

Every 12,000 miles or 15 months, whichever comes first

All items listed above plus:
Replace the ignition contact points and adjust the dwell angle (Section 30)
Check and adjust if necessary the engine idle speed (Section 31)
Replace the fuel filter (Section 32)
Replace the air filter and PCV filter (Section 33)
Check and adjust if necessary the ignition timing (Section 34)

Every 30,000 miles or 24 months, whichever comes first

All items listed above plus:
** Change the automatic transmission fluid (Section 35)
Change the manual transmission lubricant (Section 36)
Change the rear axle differential lubricant (Section 37)
Check and repack the front wheel bearings (Section 38)
Service the cooling system (drain, flush and refill) (Section 39)
Inspect and replace if necessary the PCV valve (Section 40)
Inspect the evaporative emissions control system (Section 41)
Check the EGR system (Section 42)
Replace the spark plugs (Section 43)
Inspect the spark plug wires, distributor cap and rotor (Sections 44 and 45)

* This item is affected by "severe" operating conditions as described below. If your vehicle is operated under severe conditions, perform all maintenance indicated with an asterisk (*) at 3000 mile/3 month intervals. Severe conditions are indicated if you mainly operate your vehicle under one or more of the following:

Operating in dusty areas
Towing a trailer
Idling for extended periods and/or low speed operation
Operating when outside temperatures remain below freezing and when most trips are less than four miles

** If operated under one or more of the following conditions, change the automatic transmission fluid every 12,000 miles:

In heavy city traffic where the outside temperature regularly reaches 90°F (32°C) or higher
In hilly or mountainous terrain
Frequent trailer pulling

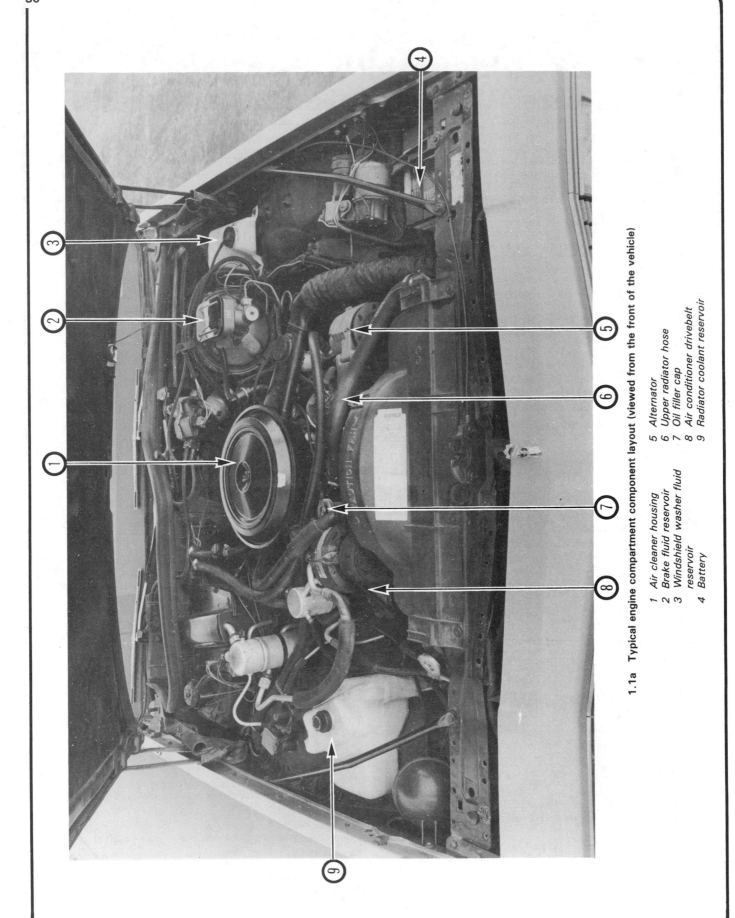

1.1a Typical engine compartment component layout (viewed from the front of the vehicle)

1 Air cleaner housing
2 Brake fluid reservoir
3 Windshield washer fluid
   reservoir
4 Battery
5 Alternator
6 Upper radiator hose
7 Oil filler cap
8 Air conditioner drivebelt
9 Radiator coolant reservoir

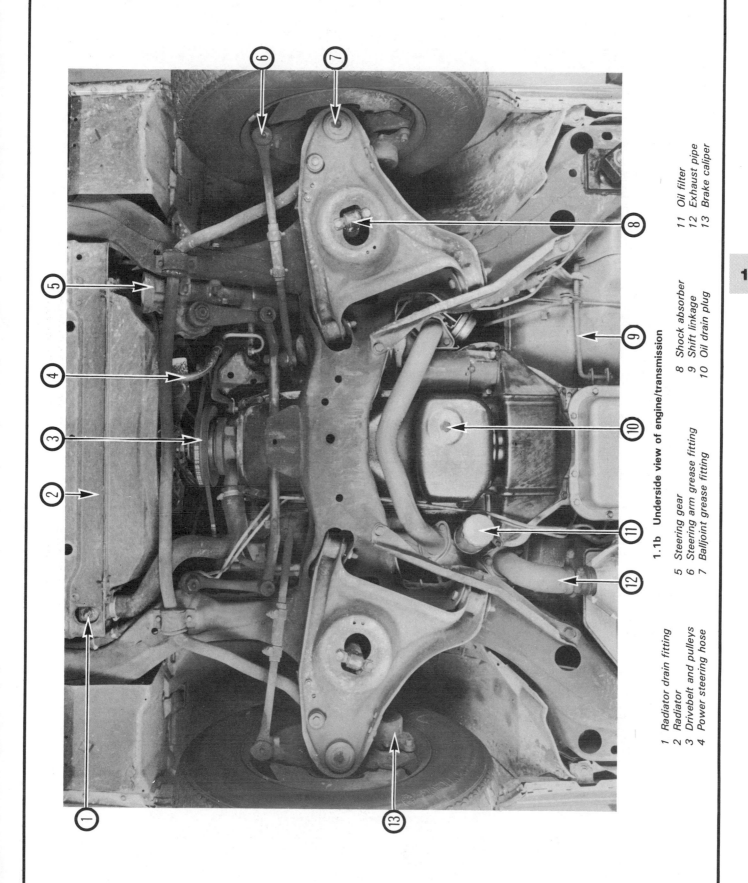

1.1b Underside view of engine/transmission

1 Radiator drain fitting
2 Radiator
3 Drivebelt and pulleys
4 Power steering hose
5 Steering gear
6 Steering arm grease fitting
7 Balljoint grease fitting
8 Shock absorber
9 Shift linkage
10 Oil drain plug
11 Oil filter
12 Exhaust pipe
13 Brake caliper

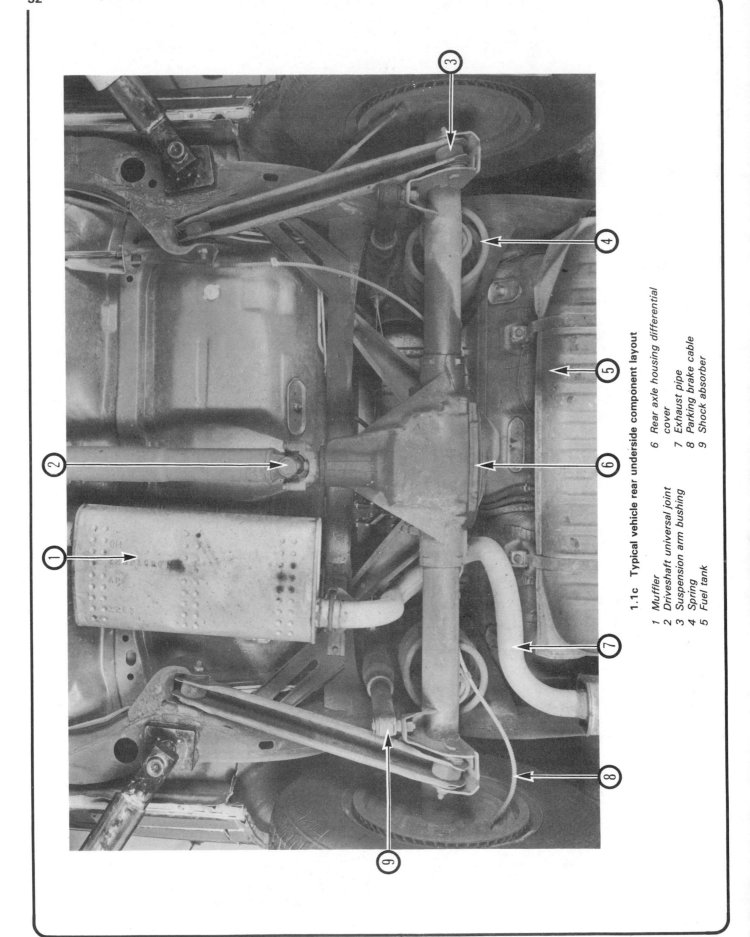

1.1c Typical vehicle rear underside component layout

1 Muffler
2 Driveshaft universal joint
3 Suspension arm bushing
4 Spring
5 Fuel tank
6 Rear axle housing differential cover
7 Exhaust pipe
8 Parking brake cable
9 Shock absorber

2 Introduction

This Chapter is designed to help the home mechanic maintain the Buick, Oldsmobile and Pontiac full-size models with the goals of maximum performance, economy, safety and reliability in mind.

Included is a master maintenance schedule (page 29), followed by procedures dealing specifically with each item on the schedule. Visual checks, adjustments, component replacement and other helpful items are included. Refer to the accompanying illustrations of the engine compartment and the underside of the vehicle for the locations of various components.

Servicing your vehicle in accordance with the mileage/time maintenance schedule and the step-by-step procedures will result in a planned maintenance program that should produce a long and reliable service life. Keep in mind that it is a comprehensive plan, so maintaining some items but not others at the specified intervals will not produce the same results.

As you service your vehicle, you will discover that many of the procedures can — and should — be grouped together because of the nature of the particular procedure you're performing or because of the close proximity of two otherwise unrelated components to one another.

For example, if the vehicle is raised for chassis lubrication, you should inspect the exhaust, suspension, steering and fuel systems while you're under the vehicle. When you're rotating the tires, it makes good sense to check the brakes since the wheels are already removed. Finally, let's suppose you have to borrow or rent a torque wrench. Even if you only need it to tighten the spark plugs, you might as well check the torque of as many critical fasteners as time allows.

The first step in this maintenance program is to prepare yourself before the actual work begins. Read through all the procedures you're planning to do, then gather up all the parts and tools needed. If it looks as if you might run into problems during a particular job, seek advice from a mechanic or an experienced do-it-yourselfer.

3 Tune-up general information

The term *tune-up* is used in this manual to represent a combination of individual operations rather than one specific procedure.

If, from the time the vehicle is new, the routine maintenance schedule is followed closely and frequent checks are made of fluid levels and high wear items, as suggested throughout this manual, the engine will be kept in relatively good running condition and the need for additional work will be minimized.

More likely than not, however, there will be times when the engine is running poorly due to lack of regular maintenance. This is even more likely if a used vehicle, which has not received regular and frequent maintenance checks, is purchased. In such cases, an engine tune-up will be needed outside of the regular routine maintenance intervals.

The first step in any tune-up or diagnostic procedure to help correct a poor running engine is a cylinder compression check. A compression check (see Chapter 2 Part B) will help determine the condition of internal engine components and should be used as a guide for tune-up and repair procedures. If, for instance, a compression check indicates serious internal engine wear, a conventional tune-up will not improve the performance of the engine and would be a waste of time and money. Because of its importance, the compression check should be done by someone with the right equipment and the knowledge to use it properly.

The following procedures are those most often needed to bring a generally poor running engine back into a proper state of tune.

Minor tune-up

Check all engine related fluids (Section 4)
Clean, inspect and test the battery (Section 8)
Check and adjust the drivebelts (Section 27)
Replace the spark plugs (Section 43)
Inspect the distributor cap and rotor (Section 45)
Inspect the spark plug and coil wires (Section 44)
Check and adjust the ignition timing (Section 34)
Check the PCV valve (Section 40)
Check the air and PCV filters (Section 33)
Check the cooling system (Section 9)
Check all underhood hoses (Section 10)

Major tune-up

All items listed under Minor tune-up plus . . .
Check the EGR system (Section 42)
Check the ignition system (Chapter 5)
Check the charging system (Chapter 5)
Check the fuel system (Section 22)
Replace the air and PCV filters (Section 33)
Replace the distributor cap and rotor (Section 45)
Replace the spark plug wires (Section 44)
Replace the ignition points (Section 30)

4 Fluid level checks

Note: *The following are fluid level checks to be done on a 250 mile or weekly basis. Additional fluid level checks can be found in specific maintenance procedures which follow. Regardless of intervals, be alert to fluid leaks under the vehicle which would indicate a fault to be corrected immediately.*

1   Fluids are an essential part of the lubrication, cooling, brake, clutch and windshield washer systems. Because the fluids gradually become depleted and/or contaminated during normal operation of the vehicle, they must be periodically replenished. See *Recommended lubricants and fluids* at the beginning of this Chapter before adding fluid to any of the following components. **Note:** *The vehicle must be on level ground when fluid levels are checked.*

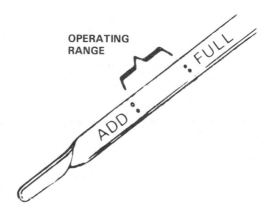

4.4 The engine oil level must be maintained between the marks at all times — it takes one quart of oil to raise the level from the ADD mark to the FULL mark

Engine oil

Refer to illustrations 4.4, 4.6a and 4.6b

2   The engine oil level is checked with a dipstick that extends through a tube and into the oil pan at the bottom of the engine.

3   The oil level should be checked before the vehicle has been driven, or about 15 minutes after the engine has been shut off. If the oil is checked immediately after driving the vehicle, some of the oil will remain in the upper engine components, resulting in an inaccurate reading on the dipstick.

4   Pull the dipstick from the tube and wipe all the oil from the end with a clean rag or paper towel. Insert the clean dipstick all the way back into the tube, then pull it out again. Note the oil at the end of the dipstick. Add oil as necessary to keep the level between the ADD mark and the FULL mark on the dipstick **(see illustration)**.

5   Do not overfill the engine's lubricating system by adding too much oil, since this may result in oil fouled spark plugs, oil leaks or oil seal failures.

4.6a   Oil is added to the engine after removing the twist-off cap (arrow)

6   Oil is added to the engine after removing a twist-off cap **(see illustrations)**. An oil can spout or funnel may help to reduce spills.
7   Checking the oil level is an important preventive maintenance step. A consistently low oil level indicates oil leakage through damaged seals, defective gaskets or past worn rings or valve guides. If the oil looks milky in color or has water droplets in it, the cylinder head gasket(s) may be blown or the head(s) or block may be cracked. The engine should be checked immediately. The condition of the oil should also be checked. Whenever you check the oil level, slide your thumb and index finger up the dipstick before wiping off the oil. If you see small dirt or metal particles clinging to the dipstick, the oil should be changed (Section 12).

Engine coolant

Warning: *Do not allow antifreeze to come in contact with your skin or painted surfaces of the vehicle. Flush contaminated areas immediately with plenty of water. Don't store new coolant or leave old coolant lying around where it's accessible to children or pets — they're attracted by its sweet taste. Ingestion of even a small amount of coolant can be fatal! Wipe up garage floor and drip pan coolant spills immediately. Keep antifreeze containers covered, and repair leaks in your cooling system immediately.*

8   Most vehicles covered by this manual are equipped with a pressurized coolant recovery system. A white plastic coolant reservoir located in the engine compartment is connected by a hose to the radiator filler neck. If the engine overheats, coolant escapes through a valve in the radiator cap and travels through the hose into the reservoir. As the engine cools, the coolant is automatically drawn back into the cooling system to maintain the correct level.
9   If your particular vehicle is not equipped with a coolant recovery system, the level should be checked by removing the radiator cap. However, the cap should not under any circumstances be removed while the system is hot, as escaping stream could cause serious injury. Wait until the engine has completely cooled, then wrap a thick cloth around the cap and turn it to its first stop. If any steam escapes from the cap, allow the engine to cool further. Then remove the cap and check the level in the radiator. It should be about two to three inches below the bottom of the filler neck.
10   The coolant level in the reservoir should be checked regularly. **Warning:** *Do not remove the radiator cap to check the coolant level when the engine is warm.* The level in the reservoir varies with the temperature of the engine. When the engine is cold, the coolant level should be at or slightly above the FULL COLD mark on the reservoir. Once the engine has warmed up, the level should be at or near the FULL HOT mark. If it isn't, allow the engine to cool, then remove the cap from the reservoir and add a 50/50 mixture of ethylene glycol-based antifreeze and water.
11   Drive the vehicle and recheck the coolant level. If only a small amount of coolant is required to bring the system up to the proper level, water can be used. However, repeated additions of water will dilute the antifreeze and water solution. In order to maintain the proper ratio of antifreeze and water, always top up the coolant level with the correct mixture. An empty plastic milk jug or bleach bottle makes an excellent container for mixing coolant. Do not use rust inhibitors or additives.
12   If the coolant level drops consistently, there may be a leak in the system. Inspect the radiator, hoses, filler cap, drain plugs and water pump (see Section 9). If no leaks are noted, have the radiator cap pressure tested by a service station.
13   If you have to remove the radiator cap, wait until the engine has cooled, then wrap a thick cloth around the cap and turn it to the first stop. If coolant or steam escapes, let the engine cool down longer, then remove the cap.
14   Check the condition of the coolant as well. It should be relatively clear. If it's brown or rust colored, the system should be drained, flushed and refilled. Even if the coolant appears to be normal, the corrosion inhibitors wear out, so it must be replaced at the specified intervals.

Windshield washer fluid

15   Fluid for the windshield washer system is located in a plastic reservoir in the engine compartment.
16   In milder climates, plain water can be used in the reservoir, but it should be kept no more than two-thirds full to allow for expansion if the water freezes. In colder climates, use windshield washer system antifreeze, available at any auto parts store, to lower the freezing point of the fluid. Mix the antifreeze with water in accordance with the manufacturer's directions on the container. **Caution:** *Don't use cooling system antifreeze — it will damage the vehicle's paint.*
17   To help prevent icing in cold weather, warm the windshield with the defroster before using the washer.

Battery electrolyte

18   Most vehicles with which this manual is concerned are equipped with a battery which is permanently sealed (except for vent holes) and has no filler caps. Water doesn't have to be added to these batteries at any time. If a maintenance-type battery is installed, the caps on the top of the battery should be removed periodically to check for a low water level. This check is most critical during the warm summer months.

Brake fluid

Refer to illustrations 4.19a, 4.19b and 4.20

19   The brake master cylinder is mounted on the front of the power booster unit in the engine compartment. On earlier models it will be necessary to remove the reservoir cover to check the fluid level **(see illustrations)**.
20   The fluid inside on later models is readily visible. The level should be above the MIN marks on the reservoirs **(see illustration)**. If a low level is indicated, be sure to wipe the top of the reservoir cover with a clean rag to prevent contamination of the brake and/or clutch system before removing the cover.

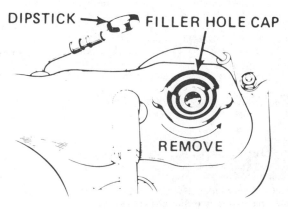

4.6b   On some models, the oil filler cap is located in the rocker cover

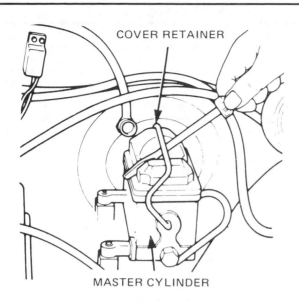

4.19a Early models have a cast iron brake master cylinder with a cover which must be removed to check the fluid level — use a screwdriver to unsnap the retainer

21 When adding fluid, pour it carefully into the reservoir to avoid spilling it onto surrounding painted surfaces. Be sure the specified fluid is used, since mixing different types of brake fluid can cause damage to the system. See *Recommended lubricants and fluids* at the front of this Chapter or your owner's manual. **Warning:** *Brake fluid can harm your eyes and damage painted surfaces, so use extreme caution when handling or pouring it. Do not use brake fluid that has been standing open or is more than one year old. Brake fluid absorbs moisture from the air. Excess moisture can cause a dangerous loss of braking effectiveness.*

22 At this time the fluid and master cylinder can be inspected for contamination. The system should be drained and refilled if deposits, dirt particles or water droplets are seen in the fluid.

23 After filling the reservoir to the proper level, make sure the cover is on tight to prevent fluid leakage.

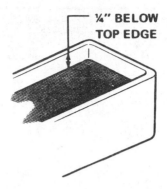

4.19b Early model master cylinder fluid level

24 The brake fluid level in the master cylinder will drop slightly as the pads and the brake shoes at each wheel wear down during normal operation. If the master cylinder requires repeated additions to keep it at the proper level, it's an indication of leakage in the brake system, which should be corrected immediately. Check all brake lines and connections (see Section 21 for more information).

25 If, upon checking the master cylinder fluid level, you discover one or both reservoirs empty or nearly empty, the brake system should be bled (Chapter 9).

5 Tire and tire pressure checks

Refer to illustrations 5.2, 5.3, 5.4a, 5.4b and 5.8

1 Periodic inspection of the tires may spare you the inconvenience of being stranded with a flat tire. It can also provide you with vital information regarding possible problems in the steering and suspension systems before major damage occurs.

2 The original tires on this vehicle are equipped with 1/2-inch side bands that will appear when tread depth reaches 1/16-inch, but they don't appear until the tires are worn out. Tread wear can be monitored with a simple, inexpensive device known as a tread depth indicator (see illustration).

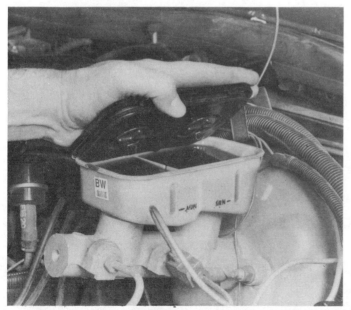

4.20 On late model vehicles, the fluid level inside the brake reservoirs is easily checked by observing the level from outside — fluid can be added to the reservoir after the cover is removed by prying up on the tabs

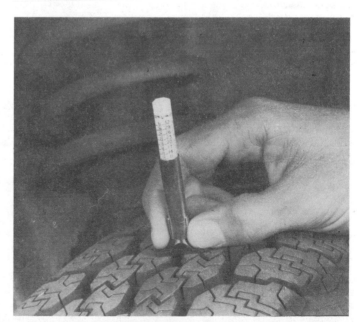

5.2 A tire tread depth indicator should be used to monitor tire wear — they are available at auto parts stores and service stations and cost very little

Condition	Probable cause	Corrective action	Condition	Probable cause	Corrective action
Shoulder wear	• Underinflation (both sides wear) • Incorrect wheel camber (one side wear) • Hard cornering • Lack of rotation	• Measure and adjust pressure. • Repair or replace axle and suspension parts. • Reduce speed. • Rotate tires.	Feathered edge Toe wear	• Incorrect toe	• Adjust toe-in.
Center wear	• Overinflation • Lack of rotation	• Measure and adjust pressure. • Rotate tires.	Uneven wear	• Incorrect camber or caster • Malfunctioning suspension • Unbalanced wheel • Out-of-round brake drum • Lack of rotation	• Repair or replace axle and suspension parts. • Repair or replace suspension parts. • Balance or replace. • Turn or replace. • Rotate tires.

5.3   This chart will help you determine the condition of your tires, the probable cause(s) of abnormal wear and the corrective action necessary

3   Note any abnormal tread wear (see illustration). Tread pattern irregularities such as cupping, flat spots and more wear on one side than the other are indications of front end alignment and/or balance problems. If any of these conditions are noted, take the vehicle to a tire shop or service station to correct the problem.

4   Look closely for cuts, punctures and embedded nails or tacks. Sometimes a tire will hold air pressure for a short time or leak down very slowly after a nail has embedded itself in the tread. If a slow leak persists, check the valve stem core to make sure it's tight (see illustra-

tion). Examine the tread for an object that may have embedded itself in the tire or for a "plug" that may have begun to leak (radial tire punctures are repaired with a plug that's installed in a puncture). If a puncture is suspected, it can be easily verified by spraying a solution of soapy water onto the puncture area (see illustration). The soapy solution will bubble if there's a leak. Unless the puncture is unusually large, a tire shop or service station can usually repair the tire.

5   Carefully inspect the inner sidewall of each tire for evidence of brake fluid leakage. If you see any, inspect the brakes immediately.

5.4a   If a tire loses air on a steady basis, check the valve core first to make sure it's snug (special inexpensive wrenches are commonly available at auto parts stores)

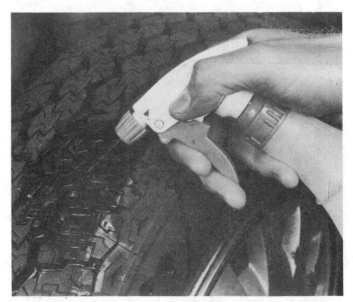

5.4b   If the valve core is tight, raise the corner of the vehicle with the low tire and spray a soapy water solution onto the tread as the tire is turned slowly — slow leaks will cause small bubbles to appear

5.8 To extend the life of your tires, check the air pressure
at least once a week with an accurate gauge
(don't forget the spare!)

6   Correct air pressure adds miles to the lifespan of the tires, improves mileage and enhances overall ride quality. Tire pressure cannot be accurately estimated by looking at a tire, especially if it's a radial. A tire pressure gauge is essential. Keep an accurate gauge in the vehicle. The pressure gauges attached to the nozzles of air hoses at gas stations are often inaccurate.

7   Always check tire pressure when the tires are cold. Cold, in this case, means the vehicle has not been driven over a mile in the three hours preceding a tire pressure check. A pressure rise of four to eight pounds is not uncommon once the tires are warm.

8   Unscrew the valve cap protruding from the wheel or hubcap and push the gauge firmly onto the valve stem (see illustration). Note the reading on the gauge and compare the figure to the recommended tire pressure shown on the placard on the driver's side door pillar. Be sure to reinstall the valve cap to keep dirt and moisture out of the valve stem mechanism. Check all four tires and, if necessary, add enough air to bring them up to the recommended pressure.

9   Don't forget to keep the spare tire inflated to the specified pressure (refer to your owner's manual or the tire sidewall). Note that the pressure recommended for the compact spare is higher than for the tires on the vehicle.

6   Automatic transmission fluid level check

Refer to illustrations 6.3 and 6.6

1   The automatic transmission fluid level should be carefully maintained. Low fluid level can lead to slipping or loss of drive, while overfilling can cause foaming and loss of fluid.

2   With the parking brake set, start the engine, then move the shift lever through all the gear ranges, ending in Park. The fluid level must be checked with the vehicle level and the engine running at idle. **Note:** *Incorrect fluid level readings will result if the vehicle has just been driven at high speeds for an extended period, in hot weather in city traffic, or if it has been pulling a trailer. If any of these conditions apply, wait until the fluid has cooled (about 30 minutes).*

3   With the transmission at normal operating temperature, remove the dipstick from the filler tube (see illustration). The dipstick is located at the rear of the engine compartment on the passenger's side on most models.

4   Carefully touch the fluid at the end of the dipstick to determine if it is cool, warm or hot. Wipe the fluid from the dipstick with a clean rag and push it back into the filler tube until the cap seats.

5   Pull the dipstick out again and note the fluid level.

6   If the fluid feels cool, the level should be about 1/8- to 3/8-inch above the ADD mark (see illustration). If it feels warm, the level should be near the lower part of the operating range. If the fluid is hot, the level should be near the FULL HOT mark. If additional fluid is required, add it directly into the tube using a funnel. It takes about one pint to raise the level from the ADD mark to the FULL HOT mark with a hot

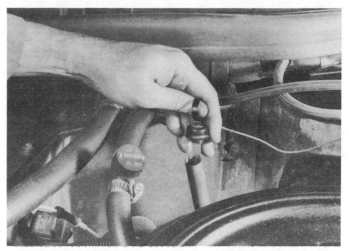

6.3 The automatic transmission dipstick is located at the
rear of the engine compartment, usually on the right side

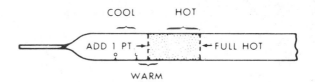

6.6 When checking the automatic transaxle fluid level it is
important to note the fluid temperature

7.2 The power steering pump reservoir (arrow) is located
near the front of the engine

transmission, so add the fluid a little at a time and keep checking the level until it's correct.

7   The condition of the fluid should also be checked along with the level. If the fluid at the end of the dipstick is a dark reddish-brown color, or if it smells burned, it should be changed. If you are in doubt about the condition of the fluid, purchase some new fluid and compare the two for color and smell.

7   Power steering fluid level check

Refer to illustrations 7.2 and 7.6

1   Unlike manual steering, the power steering system relies on fluid which may, over a period of time, require replenishing.

2   The fluid reservoir for the power steering pump is located on the pump body at the front of the engine (see illustration).

3   For the check, the front wheels should be pointed straight ahead and the engine should be off.

4   Use a clean rag to wipe off the reservoir cap and the area around the cap. This will help prevent any foreign matter from entering the reservoir during the check.

5   Twist off the cap and check the temperature of the fluid at the end of the dipstick with your finger.

6   Wipe off the fluid with a clean rag, reinsert the dipstick, then withdraw it and read the fluid level. The level should be at the HOT mark if the fluid is hot to the touch (see illustration). It should be at the COLD mark if the fluid is cool to the touch. Never allow the fluid level to drop below the ADD mark.

7   If additional fluid is required, pour the specified type directly into the reservoir, using a funnel to prevent spills.

8   If the reservoir requires frequent fluid additions, all power steering hoses, hose connections and the power steering pump should be carefully checked for leaks.

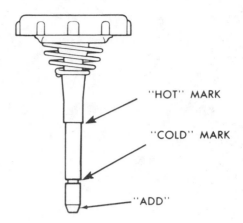

7.6   The markings on the power steering fluid dipstick indicate the safe range

8   Battery check and maintenance

Refer to illustrations 8.1, 8.4 and 8.6

Warning: *Certain precautions must be followed when checking and servicing the battery. Hydrogen gas, which is highly flammable, is always present in the battery cells, so keep lighted tobacco and all other open flames and sparks away from the battery. The electrolyte inside the battery is actually dilute sulfuric acid, which will cause injury if splashed on your skin or in your eyes. It will also ruin clothes and painted surfaces. When removing the battery cables, always detach the negative cable first and hook it up last!*

1   Battery maintenance is an important procedure which will help ensure that you are not stranded because of a dead battery. Several tools are required for this procedure (see illustration).

2   When checking/servicing the battery, always turn the engine and all accessories off.

3   A sealed (sometimes called maintenance-free), side-terminal battery is standard equipment on these vehicles. The cell caps cannot be removed, no electrolyte checks are required and water cannot be added to the cells. However, if a standard top-terminal aftermarket battery has been installed, the following maintenance procedure can be used.

4   Remove the caps and check the electrolyte level in each of the battery cells (see illustration). It must be above the plates. There's

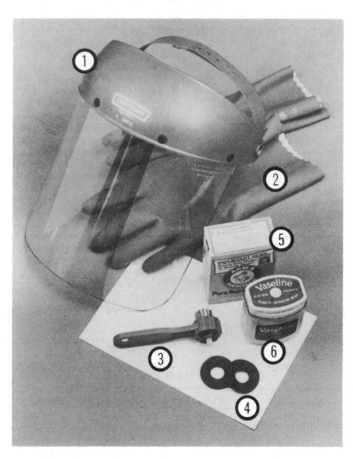

8.1   Tools and materials required for battery maintenance

1   *Face shield/safety goggles* — *When removing corrosion with a brush, the acidic particles can easily fly up into your eyes*

2   *Rubber gloves* — *Another safety item to consider when servicing the battery; remember that's acid inside the battery!*

3   *Battery terminal/ cable cleaner* — *This wire brush cleaning tool will remove all traces of corrosion from the battery and cable*

4   *Treated felt washers* — *Placing one of these on each terminal, directly under the cable end, will help prevent corrosion (be sure to get the correct type for side terminal batteries)*

5   *Baking soda* — *A solution of baking soda and water can be used to neutralize corrosion*

6   *Petroleum jelly* — *A layer of this on the battery terminal bolts will help prevent corrosion*

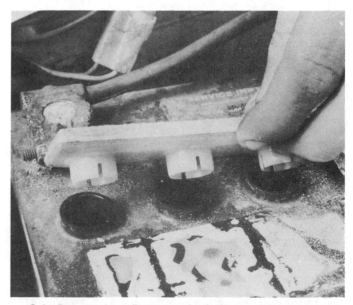

8.4   Remove the cell caps to check the water level in the battery — if the level is low, add distilled water only

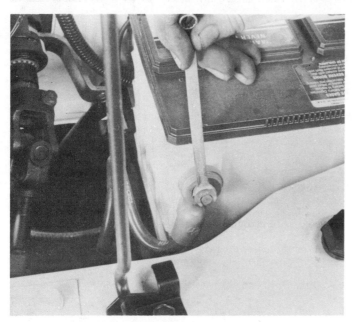

8.6 Make sure the battery terminal bolts are tight

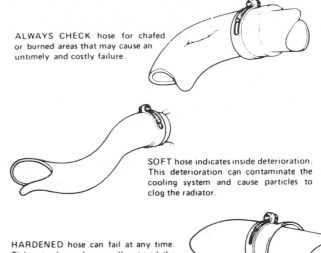

ALWAYS CHECK hose for chafed or burned areas that may cause an untimely and costly failure.

SOFT hose indicates inside deterioration. This deterioration can contaminate the cooling system and cause particles to clog the radiator.

HARDENED hose can fail at any time. Tightening hose clamps will not seal the connection or stop leaks.

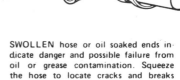

SWOLLEN hose or oil soaked ends indicate danger and possible failure from oil or grease contamination. Squeeze the hose to locate cracks and breaks that cause leaks.

9.4 Cooling system hoses should be carefully inspected to prevent being stranded on the road. Regardless of condition, it is a good idea to replace the cooling hoses with new ones every two years or so

usually a split-ring indicator in each cell to indicate the correct level. If the level is low, add distilled water only, then reinstall the cell caps. **Caution:** *Overfilling the cells may cause electrolyte to spill over during periods of heavy charging, causing corrosion and damage to nearby components.*

5   The external condition of the battery should be checked periodically. Look for damage such as a cracked case.
6   Check the tightness of the battery cable bolts **(see illustration)** to ensure good electrical connections. Inspect the entire length of each cable, looking for cracked or abraded insulation and frayed conductors.
7   If corrosion (visible as white, fluffy deposits) is evident, remove the cables from the terminals, clean them with a battery brush and reinstall them. Corrosion can be kept to a minimum by applying a layer of petroleum jelly or grease to the bolt threads.
8   Make sure the battery carrier is in good condition and the hold-down clamp is tight. If the battery is removed (see Chapter 5 for the removal and installation procedure), make sure that no parts remain in the bottom of the carrier when it's reinstalled. When reinstalling the hold-down clamp, don't overtighten the bolt.
9   Corrosion on the carrier, battery case and surrounding areas can be removed with a solution of water and baking soda. Apply the mixture with a small brush, let it work, then rinse it off with plenty of clean water.
10   Any metal parts of the vehicle damaged by corrosion should be coated with a zinc-based primer, then painted.
11   Additional information on the battery, charging and jump starting can be found in the front of this manual and in Chapter 5.

9   Cooling system check

Refer to illustration 9.4

1   Many major engine failures can be attributed to a faulty cooling system. If the vehicle is equipped with an automatic transmission, the cooling system also cools the transmission fluid and thus plays an important role in prolonging transmission life.
2   The cooling system should be checked with the engine cold. Do this before the vehicle is driven for the day or after it has been shut off for at least three hours.
3   Remove the radiator cap by turning it to the left until it reaches a stop. If you hear a hissing sound (indicating there is still pressure in the system), wait until this stops. Now press down on the cap with the palm of your hand and continue turning to the left until the cap can be removed. Thoroughly clean the cap, inside and out, with clean water. Also clean the filler neck on the radiator. All traces of corrosion should be removed. The coolant inside the radiator should be relatively transparent. If it is rust colored, the system should be drained and re-

filled (Section 39). If the coolant level is not up to the top, add additional antifreeze/coolant mixture (see Section 4).
4   Carefully check the large upper and lower radiator hoses along with the smaller diameter heater hoses which run from the engine to the firewall. On some models the heater return hose runs directly to the radiator. Inspect each hose along its entire length, replacing any hose which is cracked, swollen or shows signs of deterioration. Cracks may become more apparent if the hose is squeezed **(see illustration)**. Regardless of condition, it's a good idea to replace hoses with new ones every two years.
5   Make sure that all hose connections are tight. A leak in the cooling system will usually show up as white or rust colored deposits on the areas adjoining the leak. If wire-type clamps are used at the ends of the hoses, it may be a good idea to replace them with more secure screw-type clamps.
6   Use compressed air or a soft brush to remove bugs, leaves, etc. from the front of the radiator or air conditioning condenser. Be careful not to damage the delicate cooling fins or cut yourself on them.
7   Every other inspection, or at the first indication of cooling system problems, have the cap and system pressure tested. If you don't have a pressure tester, most gas stations and repair shops will do this for a minimal charge.

10   Underhood hose check and replacement

General

1   **Caution:** *Replacement of air conditioning hoses must be left to a dealer service department or air conditioning shop that has the equipment to depressurize the system safely. Never remove air conditioning components or hoses until the system has been depressurized.*
2   High temperatures in the engine compartment can cause the deter-

ioration of the rubber and plastic hoses used for engine, accessory and emission systems operation. Periodic inspection should be made for cracks, loose clamps, material hardening and leaks. Information specific to the cooling system hoses can be found in Section 9.

3   Some, but not all, hoses are secured to the fittings with clamps. Where clamps are used, check to be sure they haven't lost their tension, allowing the hose to leak. If clamps aren't used, make sure the hose has not expanded and/or hardened where it slips over the fitting, allowing it to leak.

Vacuum hoses

4   It's quite common for vacuum hoses, especially those in the emissions system, to be color coded or identified by colored stripes molded into them. Various systems require hoses with different wall thicknesses, collapse resistance and temperature resistance. When replacing hoses, be sure the new ones are made of the same material.

5   Often the only effective way to check a hose is to remove it completely from the vehicle. If more than one hose is removed, be sure to label the hoses and fittings to ensure correct installation.

6   When checking vacuum hoses, be sure to include any plastic T-fittings in the check. Inspect the fittings for cracks and the hose where it fits over the fitting for distortion, which could cause leakage.

7   A small piece of vacuum hose (1/4-inch inside diameter) can be used as a stethoscope to detect vacuum leaks. Hold one end of the hose to your ear and probe around vacuum hoses and fittings, listening for the ''hissing'' sound characteristic of a vacuum leak. **Warning:** *When probing with the vacuum hose stethoscope, be very careful not to come into contact with moving engine components such as the drivebelt, cooling fan, etc.*

Fuel hose

Warning: *There are certain precautions which must be taken when inspecting or servicing fuel system components. Work in a well ventilated area and do not allow open flames (cigarettes, appliance pilot lights, etc.) or bare light bulbs near the work area. Mop up any spills immediately and do not store fuel soaked rags where they could ignite.*

8   Check all rubber fuel lines for deterioration and chafing. Check especially for cracks in areas where the hose bends and just before fittings, such as where a hose attaches to the fuel filter.

9   High quality fuel line, usually identified by the word *Fluroelastomer* printed on the hose, should be used for fuel line replacement. Never, under any circumstances, use unreinforced vacuum line, clear plastic tubing or water hose for fuel lines.

10   Spring-type clamps are commonly used on fuel lines. These clamps often lose their tension over a period of time, and can be ''sprung'' during removal. Replace all spring-type clamps with screw clamps whenever a hose is replaced.

Metal lines

11   Sections of metal line are often used for fuel line between the fuel pump and carburetor. Check carefully to be sure the line has not been bent or crimped and that cracks have not started in the line.

12   If a section of metal fuel line must be replaced, only seamless steel tubing should be used, since copper and aluminum tubing don't have the strength necessary to withstand normal engine vibration.

13   Check the metal brake lines where they enter the master cylinder and brake proportioning unit (if used) for cracks in the lines or loose fittings. Any sign of brake fluid leakage calls for an immediate thorough inspection of the brake system.

---

11   Wiper blade inspection and replacement

Refer to illustration 11.6

1   The windshield wiper and blade assembly should be inspected periodically for damage, loose components and cracked or worn blade elements.

2   Road film can build up on the wiper blades and affect their efficiency, so they should be washed regularly with a mild detergent solution.

3   The action of the wiping mechanism can loosen the bolts, nuts and fasteners, so they should be checked and tightened, as necessary, at the same time the wiper blades are checked.

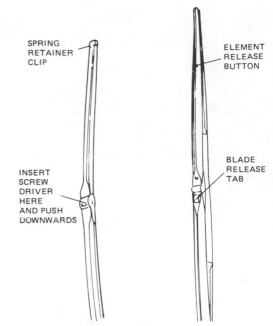

11.6   **The two types of wiper blade elements commonly used on these models**

4   If the wiper blade elements (sometimes called inserts) are cracked, worn or warped, they should be replaced with new ones.

5   Pull the wiper blade/arm assembly away from the glass.

6   Two methods are used to retain the rubber wiper blade element to the blade assembly **(see illustration)**. This 'refill', as it is sometimes called, can be replaced without removing or disassembling the wiper mechanism.

7   One method uses a press-type button, in most cases colored red. Depress the button and then slide the rubber element off of the wiper blade. To install a new element, press the button and slide the new piece into place. Once centered on the blade, it will lock into place.

8   The other method incorporates a spring-type retainer clip at the end of the removable element. When the retainer is pinched together, the element can slide out of the blade assembly. A small pair of pliers can be used to squeeze the retainer. When installing a new element, be certain that the metal insert passes through all of the retaining tabs of the blade assembly.

9   Reinstall the blade assembly on the arm, wet the windshield and check for proper operation.

---

12   Engine oil and filter change

Refer to illustrations 12.3, 12.9, 12.14 and 12.18

1   Frequent oil changes are the most important preventive maintenance procedures that can be done by the home mechanic. As engine oil ages, it becomes diluted and contaminated, which leads to premature engine wear.

2   Although some sources recommend oil filter changes every other oil change, we feel that the minimal cost of an oil filter and the relative ease with which it is installed dictate that a new filter be installed every time the oil is changed.

3   Gather together all necessary tools and materials before beginning this procedure **(see illustration)**.

4   You should have plenty of clean rags and newspapers handy to mop up any spills. Access to the underside of the vehicle is greatly improved if the vehicle can be lifted on a hoist, driven onto ramps or supported by jackstands. **Warning:** *Do not work under a vehicle which is supported only by a bumper, hydraulic or scissors-type jack.*

5   If this is your first oil change, get under the vehicle and familiarize yourself with the locations of the oil drain plug and the oil filter. The engine and exhaust components will be warm during the actual work, so note how they are situated to avoid touching them when working under the vehicle.

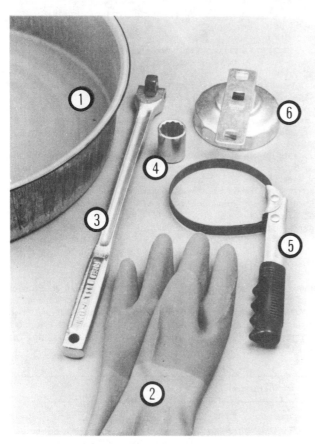

12.3 These tools are required when changing the engine oil and filter

1 **Drain pan** — *It should be fairly shallow in depth, but wide in order to prevent spills*
2 **Rubber gloves** — *When removing the drain plug and filter it is inevitable that you will get oil on your hands (the gloves will prevent burns)*
3 **Breaker bar** — *Sometimes the oil drain plug is pretty tight and a long breaker bar is needed to loosen it*
4 **Socket** — *To be used with the breaker bar or a ratchet (must be the correct size to fit the drain plug)*
5 **Filter wrench** — *This is a metal band-type wrench, which requires clearance around the filter to be effective*
6 **Filter wrench** — *This type fits on the bottom of the filter and can be turned with a ratchet or breaker bar (different size wrenches are available for different types of filters)*

6   Warm the engine to normal operating temperature. If the new oil or any tools are needed, use this warm-up time to gather everything necessary for the job. The correct type of oil for your application can be found in *Recommended lubricants and fluids* at the beginning of this Chapter.

7   With the engine oil warm (warm engine oil will drain better and more built-up sludge will be removed with it), raise and support the vehicle. Make sure it's safely supported!

8   Move all necessary tools, rags and newspapers under the vehicle. Set the drain pan under the drain plug. Keep in mind that the oil will initially flow from the pan with some force; position the pan accordingly.

9   Being careful not to touch any of the hot exhaust components, use a wrench to remove the drain plug near the bottom of the oil pan **(see illustration)**. Depending on how hot the oil is, you may want to wear gloves while unscrewing the plug the final few turns.

10   Allow the old oil to drain into the pan. It may be necessary to move the drain pan as the oil flow slows to a trickle.

11   After all the oil has drained, wipe off the drain plug with a clean rag. Small metal particles may cling to the plug and would immediately contaminate the new oil.

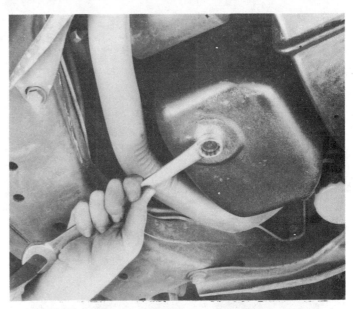

12.9 The oil pan drain plug is located at the bottom of the pan and should be removed with a socket or box-end wrench — DO NOT use an open end wrench as the corners of the bolt can be easily rounded off

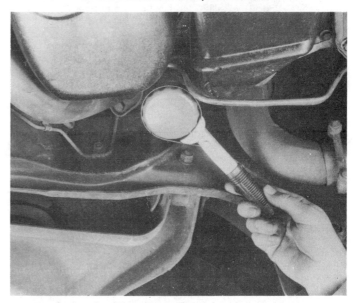

12.14 Use a strap-type oil filter wrench to loosen the filter. Note that the wrench is positioned at the bottom of the filter, where the filter has the most strength. If access makes removal difficult, other types of filter wrenches are available

12   Clean the area around the drain plug opening and reinstall the plug. Tighten the plug securely with the wrench. If a torque wrench is available, use it to tighten the plug.

13   Move the drain pan into position under the oil filter.

14   Use the filter wrench to loosen the oil filter **(see illustration)**. Chain or metal band filter wrenches may distort the filter canister, but it doesn't matter since the filter will be discarded anyway.

15   Completely unscrew the old filter. Be careful; it's full of oil. Empty the oil inside the filter into the drain pan.

16   Compare the old filter with the new one to make sure they're the same type.

17   Use a clean rag to remove all oil, dirt and sludge from the area where the oil filter mounts to the engine. Check the old filter to make sure the rubber gasket isn't stuck to the engine. If the gasket is stuck to the engine (use a flashlight if necessary), remove it.

12.18   Lubricate the oil filter gasket with clean engine oil
before installing the filter on the engine

18   Apply a light coat of clean oil to the rubber gasket on the new oil filter (see illustration).
19   Attach the new filter to the engine, following the tightening directions printed on the filter canister or packing box. Most filter manufacturers recommend against using a filter wrench due to the possibility of overtightening and damage to the seal.
20   Remove all tools, rags, etc. from under the vehicle, being careful not to spill the oil in the drain pan, then lower the vehicle.
21   Move to the engine compartment and locate the oil filler cap.
22   If an oil can spout is used, push the spout into the top of the oil can and pour the fresh oil through the filler opening. A funnel may also be used.
23   Pour four quarts of fresh oil into the engine. Wait a few minutes to allow the oil to drain into the pan, then check the level on the oil dipstick (see Section 4 if necessary). If the oil level is above the ADD mark, start the engine and allow the new oil to circulate.
24   Run the engine for only about a minute and then shut it off. Immediately look under the vehicle and check for leaks at the oil pan drain plug and around the oil filter. If either is leaking, tighten with a bit more force.
25   With the new oil circulated and the filter now completely full, recheck the level on the dipstick and add more oil as necessary.
26   During the first few trips after an oil change, make it a point to check frequently for leaks and proper oil level.
27   The old oil drained from the engine cannot be reused in its present state and should be disposed of. Oil reclamation centers, auto repair shops and gas stations will normally accept the oil, which can be refined and used again. After the oil has cooled it can be drained into a suitable container (capped plastic jugs, topped bottles, milk cartons, etc.) for transport to one of these disposal sites.

13   Chassis lubrication

Refer to illustrations 13.1, 13.2 and 13.6

1   Refer to Recommended lubricants and fluids at the front of this Chapter to obtain the necessary grease, etc. You'll also need a grease gun (see illustration). Occasionally plugs will be installed rather than grease fittings. If so, grease fittings will have to be purchased and installed.
2   Look under the vehicle and see if grease fittings or plugs are installed (see illustration). If there are plugs, remove them and buy grease

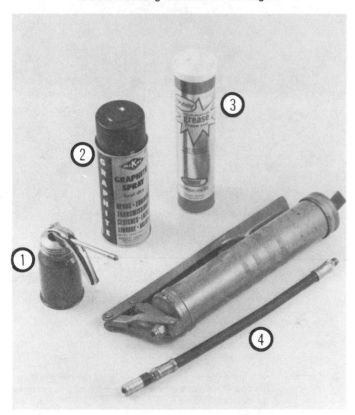

13.1   Materials required for chassis and body lubrication

1   Engine oil — Light engine oil in a can like this can be used for door and hood hinges
2   Graphite spray — Used to lubricate lock cylinders
3   Grease — Grease, in a variety of types and weights, is available for use in a grease gun. Check the Specifications for your requirements
4   Grease gun — A common grease gun, shown here with a detachable hose and nozzle, is needed for chassis lubrication. After use, clean it thoroughly!

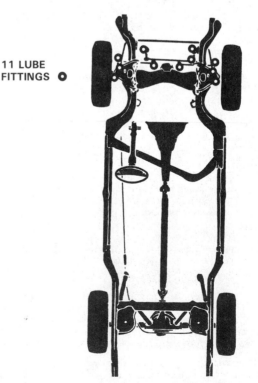

11 LUBE FITTINGS ○

13.2   This diagram shows where the lubrication points are located

fittings, which will thread into the component. A dealer or auto parts store will be able to supply the correct fittings. Straight, as well as angled, fittings are available.

3   For easier access under the vehicle, raise it with a jack and place jackstands under the frame. Make sure it's safely supported by the stands. If the wheels are to be removed at this interval for tire rotation or brake inspection, loosen the lug nuts slightly while the vehicle is still on the ground.

4   Before beginning, force a little grease out of the nozzle to remove any dirt from the end of the gun. Wipe the nozzle clean with a rag.

5   With the grease gun and plenty of clean rags, crawl under the vehicle and begin lubricating the components.

6   Wipe the balljoint grease fitting clean and push the nozzle firmly over it (see illustration). Squeeze the trigger or handle on the grease gun to force grease into the component. The balljoints should be lubricated until the rubber seal is firm to the touch. Do not pump too much grease into the fittings as it could rupture the seal. For all other suspension and steering components, continue pumping grease into the fitting until it oozes out of the joint between the two components. If it escapes around the grease gun nozzle, the nipple is clogged or the nozzle is not completely seated on the fitting. Resecure the gun nozzle to the fitting and try again. If necessary, replace the fitting with a new one.

7   Wipe the excess grease from the components and the grease fitting. Repeat the procedure for the remaining fittings.

8   If equipped with a manual transmission, lubricate the shift linkage with a little multi-purpose grease.

9   On manual transmission equipped models, lubricate the clutch linkage pivot points with clean engine oil. Lubricate the pushrod-to-fork contact points with chassis grease.

10   While you are under the vehicle, clean and lubricate the parking brake cable, along with the cable guides and levers. This can be done by smearing some of the chassis grease onto the cable and its related parts with your fingers.

11   The steering gear seldom requires the addition of lubricant, but if there is obvious leakage of grease at the seals, remove the plug or cover and check the lubricant level. If the level is low, add the specified lubricant.

12   Open the hood and smear a little chassis grease on the hood latch mechanism. Have an assistant pull the hood release lever from inside the vehicle as you lubricate the cable at the latch.

13   Lubricate all the hinges (door, hood, etc.) with engine oil to keep them in proper working order.

14   The key lock cylinders can be lubricated with spray graphite or silicone lubricant, which is available at auto parts stores.

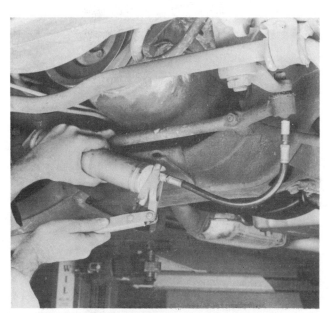

13.6   After wiping the grease fitting clean, push the nozzle firmly into place and pump the grease into the component. Usually about two pumps of the gun will be sufficient

15   Lubricate the door weatherstripping with silicone spray. This will reduce chafing and retard wear.

14   Suspension and steering check

Refer to illustration 14.4

1   Indications of a fault in these systems are excessive play in the steering wheel before the front wheels react, excessive sway around corners, body movement over rough roads or binding at some point as the steering wheel is turned.

2   Raise the front of the vehicle periodically, support it securely on jackstands and visually check the suspension and steering components for wear.

3   Check the wheel bearings. Do this by spinning the front wheels. Listen for any abnormal noises and watch to make sure the wheel spins true (doesn't wobble). Grab the top and bottom of the tire and pull in and out on it. Notice any movement which would indicate a loose wheel bearing assembly. If the bearings are suspect, refer to Section 38 and Chapter 10 for more information.

4   From under the vehicle check for loose bolts, broken or disconnected parts and deteriorated rubber bushings on all suspension and steering components. Look for grease or fluid leaking from the steering assembly. Check the power steering hoses and connections for leaks. Check the balljoints for wear (see illustration).

5   Have an assistant turn the steering wheel from side to side and check the steering components for free movement, chafing and binding. If the steering doesn't react with the movement of the steering wheel, try to determine where the slack is located.

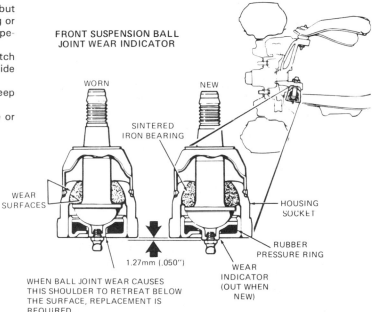

FRONT SUSPENSION BALL
JOINT WEAR INDICATOR

WORN   NEW

SINTERED
IRON BEARING

WEAR
SURFACES

HOUSING
SOCKET

RUBBER
PRESSURE RING

1.27mm (.050")

WEAR
INDICATOR
(OUT WHEN
NEW)

WHEN BALL JOINT WEAR CAUSES
THIS SHOULDER TO RETREAT BELOW
THE SURFACE, REPLACEMENT IS
REQUIRED.

14.4   Wear indicators are built into the lower balljoints to aid in their inspection

15   Exhaust system check

1   With the engine cold (at least three hours after the vehicle has been driven), check the complete exhaust system from the manifold to the end of the tailpipe. Be careful around the catalytic converter, which may be hot even after three hours. The inspection should be done with the vehicle on a hoist to permit unrestricted access. If a hoist isn't available, raise the vehicle and support it securely on jackstands.

2   Check the exhaust pipes and connections for signs of leakage and/or corrosion indicating a potential failure. Make sure that all

brackets and hangers are in good condition and tight.

3   Inspect the underside of the body for holes, corrosion, open seams, etc., which may allow exhaust gases to enter the passenger compartment. Seal all body openings with silicone or body putty.

4   Rattles and other noises can often be traced to the exhaust system, especially the hangers, mounts and heat shields. Try to move the pipes, mufflers and catalytic converter. If the components can come in contact with the body or suspension parts, secure the exhaust system with new brackets and hangers.

16   EFE (heat riser) system check

Refer to illustrations 16.2 and 16.5

1   The heat riser and the Early Fuel Evaporation (EFE) system both perform the same job, but each functions in a slightly different manner.

2   The heat riser is a valve inside the exhaust pipe, near the junction between the exhaust manifold and pipe. It can be identified by an external weight and spring **(see illustration)**.

3   With the engine and exhaust pipe cold, try moving the weight by hand. It should move freely.

4   Again with the engine cold, start the engine and watch the heat riser. Upon starting, the weight should move to the closed position. As the engine warms to normal operating temperature, the weight should move the valve to the open position, allowing a free flow of exhaust through the tailpipe. Since it could take several minutes for the system to heat up, you could mark the cold weight position, drive the vehicle, and then check the weight.

5   The EFE system also blocks off exhaust flow when the engine is cold. However, this system uses more precise temperature sensors and vacuum to open and close the exhaust pipe valve **(see illustration)**.

6   Locate the EFE actuator, which is bolted to a bracket on the right side of the engine on most vehicles. It will have an actuating rod attached to it which will lead down to the valve inside the pipe. In some cases the entire mechanism, including actuator, will be located at the exhaust pipe-to-manifold junction.

7   With the engine cold, have an assistant start the engine as you watch the actuating rod. It should immediately move to close off the valve as the engine warms. This process may take some time, so you might want to mark the position of the rod when the valve is closed, drive the vehicle to reach normal operating temperature, then open the hood and check that the rod has moved to the open position.

8   Further information on the EFE system can be found in Chapter 6.

17   Clutch pedal free play check and adjustment

Refer to illustration 17.3

Check

1   On manual transmission models, it is important to have the clutch

free play at the proper point. Free play is the distance between the clutch pedal when it is all the way up and the point at which the clutch starts to disengage.

2   Slowly depress the clutch pedal until you can feel resistance. Do this a number of times until you can pinpoint exactly where the resistance is felt.

3   Now measure the distance the pedal travels before the resistance is felt **(see illustration)**.

4   If the distance is not as specified, the clutch pedal free play should be adjusted.

Adjustment

5   Disconnect the clutch fork return spring.

6   Hold the clutch pedal against the stop and loosen the jam nut so the clutch fork pushrod can be turned out of the swivel and back against the clutch fork. The release bearing must contact the pressure plate fingers lightly.

7   Turn the clutch fork pushrod three and a half turns.

8   Tighten the jam nut, taking care not to change the pushrod length, and reconnect the return spring.

9   Recheck the free play.

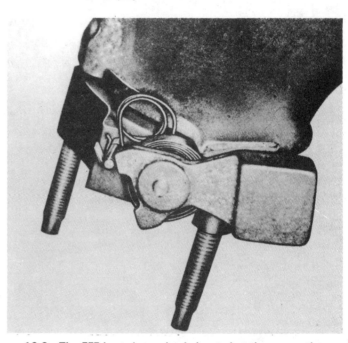

16.2   The EFE heat riser valve is located at the connection between the exhaust manifold and the exhaust pipe

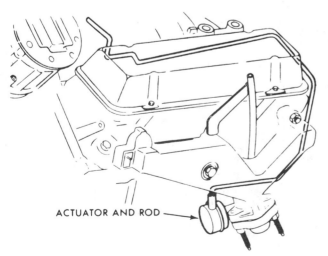

16.5   The EFE system actuator and rod system used on later models

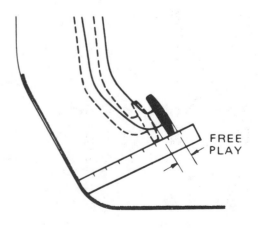

17.3   Clutch pedal free play is the distance the pedal moves before resistance is felt

18 Manual transmission lubricant level check

1   The manual transmission has an inspection and fill plug which must be removed to check the oil level. If the vehicle is raised to gain access to the plug, be sure to support it safely on jackstands — DO NOT crawl under a vehicle which is supported only by a jack!
2   Remove the plug from the transmission and use your little finger to reach inside the housing to feel the oil level. The level should be at or near the bottom of the plug hole.
3   If it isn't, add the recommended oil through the plug hole with a syringe or squeeze bottle.
4   Install and tighten the plug and check for leaks after the first few miles of driving.

19 Differential oil level check

Refer to illustrations 19.2 and 19.3
1   The differential has a check/fill plug which must be removed to check the oil level. If the vehicle is raised to gain access to the plug, be sure to support it safely on jackstands — DO NOT crawl under the vehicle when it's supported only by the jack.
2   Remove the oil check/fill plug from the side of the differential (**see illustration**).
3   The oil level should be at the bottom of the plug opening (**see illustration**). If not, use a syringe to add the recommended lubricant until it just starts to run out of the opening. On some models a tag is located in the area of the plug which gives information regarding lubricant type, particularly on models equipped with a limited slip differential.
4   Install the plug and tighten it securely.

20 Tire rotation

Refer to illustration 20.2
1   The tires should be rotated at the specified intervals and whenever uneven wear is noticed.
2   Refer to the accompanying illustration for the preferred tire rotation pattern.
3   Refer to the information in *Jacking and towing* at the front of this manual for the proper procedures to follow when raising the vehicle and changing a tire. If the brakes are to be checked, don't apply the parking brake as stated. Make sure the tires are blocked to prevent the vehicle from rolling as it's raised.

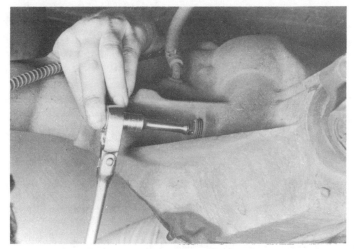

19.2   Use a ratchet and extension to remove the differential fill plug

1

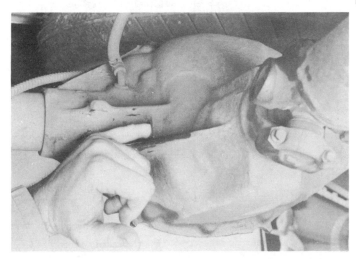

19.3   Use your little finger as a dipstick to make sure the differential oil level is even with the bottom of the opening

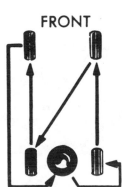

FRONT   FRONT   FRONT   FRONT

4 WHEEL ROTATION   5 WHEEL ROTATION   4 WHEEL ROTATION   5 WHEEL ROTATION

20.2   Tire rotation diagram

4   Preferably, the entire vehicle should be raised at the same time. This can be done on a hoist or by jacking up each corner and then lowering the vehicle onto jackstands placed under the frame rails. Always use four jackstands and make sure the vehicle is safely supported.
5   After rotation, check and adjust the tire pressures as necessary and be sure to check the lug nut tightness.
6   For additional information on the wheels and tires, refer to Chapter 10.

---

21   Brake check

Note: *For detailed photographs of the brake system, refer to Chapter 9.*

Warning: *Brake system dust contains asbestos, which is hazardous to your health. DO NOT blow it out with compressed air and DO NOT inhale it. DO NOT use gasoline or solvents to remove the dust. Use brake system cleaner or denatured alcohol only.*

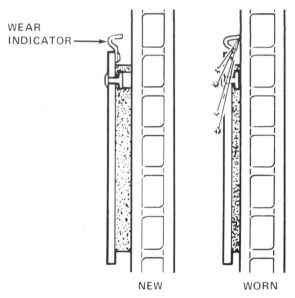

21.4   The front disc brake pad wear indicators will contact the disc and make a squealing noise when the pad is worn

21.6   The disc brake pad lining, which rubs against the disc, as well as the caliper contact points can be inspected with the wheel removed

1   In addition to the specified intervals, the brakes should be inspected every time the wheels are removed or whenever a defect is suspected.
2   To check the brakes, raise the vehicle and place it securely on jackstands. Remove the wheels (see *Jacking and towing* at the front of the manual, if necessary).

Disc brakes
Refer to illustrations 21.4 and 21.6

3   Disc brakes are used on the front wheels of later models as well as on the rear wheels of certain models. Extensive rotor damage can occur if the pads are not replaced when needed.
4   These vehicles are equipped with a wear sensor attached to the inner pad. This is a small, bent piece of metal which is visible from the inner side of the brake caliper. When the pad wears to the specified limit, the metal sensor rubs against the rotor and makes a squealing sound **(see illustration)**.
5   The disc brake calipers, which contain the pads, are visible with the wheels removed. There is an outer pad and an inner pad in each caliper. All pads should be inspected.
6   Each caliper has a ''window'' to inspect the pads. Check the thickness of the pad lining by looking into the caliper at each end and down through the inspection window at the top of the housing **(see illustration)**. If the wear sensor is very close to the rotor or the pad material has worn to about 1/8-inch or less, the pads should be replaced.
7   If you're unsure about the exact thickness of the remaining lining material, remove the pads for further inspection or replacement (refer to Chapter 9).
8   Before installing the wheels, check for leakage and/or damage (cracks, splitting, etc.) around the brake hose connections. Replace the hose or fittings as necessary, referring to Chapter 9.
9   Check the condition of the rotor. Look for score marks, deep scratches and burned spots. If these conditions exist, the hub/rotor assembly should be removed for servicing (Section 38).

Drum brakes
Refer to illustrations 21.11, 21.12 and 21.14

10   On front drum brakes, remove the hub/drum (Section 38). On rear brakes, remove the drum by pulling it off the axle and brake assembly. If this proves difficult, make sure the parking brake is released, then squirt penetrating oil around the center hub areas. Allow the oil to soak in and try to pull the drum off again.
11   If the drum still cannot be pulled off, the brake shoes will have to be adjusted. This is done by first removing the plug from the backing plate with a hammer and chisel **(see illustration)**.
12   With the plug removed, push the lever off the star wheel and then use a small screwdriver to turn the star wheel, which will move the

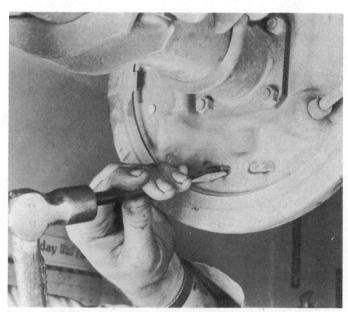

21.11   Use a hammer and chisel to remove the plug from the brake backing plate

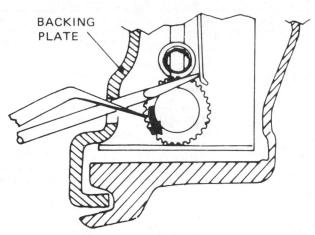

21.12 Use a screwdriver and adjusting tool to back off the rear brake shoes if necessary so the brake drum can be removed

21.14 The brake shoe lining thickness is measured from the outer surface of the lining to the metal shoe

brake shoes away from the drum **(see illustration)**.

13 With the drum removed, do not touch any brake dust (see the Warning at the beginning of this Section).

14 Note the thickness of the lining material on both the front and rear brake shoes. If the material has worn away to within 1/16-inch of the recessed rivets or metal backing, the shoes should be replaced **(see illustration and Chapter 9)**. The shoes should also be replaced if they're cracked, glazed (shiny surface) or contaminated with brake fluid.

15 Make sure that all the brake assembly springs are connected and in good condition.

16 Check the brake components for any signs of fluid leakage. With your finger, carefully pry back the rubber cups on the wheel cylinders located at the top of the brake shoes. Any leakage is an indication that the wheel cylinders should be overhauled immediately (Chapter 9). Also check brake hoses and connections for signs of leakage.

17 Wipe the inside of the drum with a clean rag and brake cleaner or denatured alcohol. Again, be careful not to breath the dangerous asbestos dust.

18 Check the inside of the drum for cracks, score marks, deep scratches and hard spots, which will appear as small discolorations. If these imperfections cannot be removed with fine emery cloth, the drum must be taken to a machine shop equipped to turn the drums.

19 If after the inspection process all parts are in good working condition, reinstall the brake drum (using a metal or rubber plug if the knockout was removed).

20 Install the wheels and lower the vehicle.

Parking brake

21 The parking brake operates from a foot pedal and locks the rear brake system. The easiest method of periodically checking the operation of the parking brake assembly is to park the vehicle on a steep hill with the parking brake set and the transmission in Neutral. If the parking brake cannot prevent the vehicle from rolling, it's in need of adjustment (see Chapter 9).

22 Fuel system check

Warning: *There are certain precautions to take when inspecting or servicing the fuel system components. Work in a well ventilated area and don't allow open flames (cigarettes, appliance pilot lights, etc.) in the work area. Mop up spills immediately and don't store fuel soaked rags where they could ignite.*

1 On most models the main fuel tank is located at the rear of the vehicle.

2 The fuel system is most easily checked with the vehicle raised on a hoist so the components underneath the vehicle are readily visible and accessible.

3 If the smell of gasoline is noticed while driving or after the vehicle has been in the sun, the system should be thoroughly inspected immediately.

4 Remove the gas tank cap and check for damage, corrosion and an unbroken sealing imprint on the gasket. Replace the cap with a new one if necessary.

5 With the vehicle raised, check the gas tank and filler neck for punctures, cracks and other damage. The connection between the filler neck and the tank is especially critical. Sometimes a rubber filler neck will leak due to loose clamps or deteriorated rubber, problems a home mechanic can usually rectify. **Warning:** *Do not, under any circumstances, try to repair a fuel tank yourself (except rubber components). A welding torch or any open flame can easily cause the fuel vapors to explode if the proper precautions are not taken!*

6 Carefully check all rubber hoses and metal lines leading away from the fuel tank. Look for loose connections, deteriorated hoses, crimped lines and other damage. Follow the lines to the front of the vehicle, carefully inspecting them all the way. Repair or replace damaged sections as necessary.

7 If a fuel odor is still evident after the inspection, refer to Section 41.

23 Carburetor choke check

Refer to illustration 23.3

1 The choke operates only when the engine is cold, so this check should be performed before the engine has been started for the day.

2 Open the hood and take off the top plate of the air cleaner assembly. It's usually held in place by a wing nut at the center. If any vacuum hoses must be disconnected, make sure you tag the hoses for reinstallation in their original positions. Place the top plate and wing nut aside, out of the way of moving engine components.

3 Look at the center of the air cleaner housing. You will notice a flat plate at the carburetor opening **(see illustration)**.

23.3 The carburetor choke plate is visible after removing the air cleaner top plate

4   Press the accelerator pedal to the floor. The plate should close completely. Start the engine while you watch the plate at the carburetor. Don't position your face near the carburetor, as the engine could backfire, causing serious burns. When the engine starts, the choke plate should open slightly.

5   Allow the engine to continue running at idle speed. As the engine warms up to operating temperature, the plate should slowly open, allowing more air to enter through the top of the carburetor.

6   After a few minutes, the choke plate should be fully open to the vertical position. Blip the throttle to make sure the fast idle cam disengages.

7   You'll notice that the engine speed corresponds with the plate opening. With the plate fully closed, the engine should run at a fast idle speed. As the plate opens and the throttle is moved to disengage the fast idle cam, the engine speed will decrease.

8   Refer to Chapter 4 for specific information on adjusting and servicing the choke components.

24   Carburetor mounting nut/bolt torque check

1   The carburetor is attached to the top of the intake manifold by several bolts or nuts. These fasteners can sometimes work loose from vibration and temperature changes during normal engine operation and cause a vacuum leak.

2   If you suspect that a vacuum leak exists at the bottom of the carburetor, obtain a length of hose. Start the engine and place one end of the hose next to your ear as you probe around the base with the other end. You will hear a hissing sound if a leak exists (be careful of hot or moving engine components).

3   Remove the air cleaner assembly, tagging each hose to be disconnected with a piece of numbered tape to make reassembly easier.

4   Locate the mounting nuts or bolts at the base of the carburetor. Decide what special tools or adapters will be necessary, if any, to tighten the fasteners.

5   Tighten the nuts or bolts to the specified torque. Don't overtighten them, as the threads could strip.

6   If, after the nuts or bolts are properly tightened, a vacuum leak still exists, the carburetor must be removed and a new gasket installed. See Chapter 4 for more information.

7   After tightening the fasteners, reinstall the air cleaner and return all hoses to their original positions.

25   Throttle linkage inspection

1   Inspect the throttle linkage for damage and missing parts and for binding and interference when the accelerator pedal is depressed.

2   Lubricate the various linkage pivot points with engine oil.

26   Thermostatic air cleaner check

Refer to illustrations 26.5 and 26.6

1   Some engines are equipped with a thermostatically controlled air cleaner which draws air to the carburetor from different locations, depending on engine temperature.

2   This is a visual check. If access is limited, a small mirror may have to be used.

3   Remove the engine cover and locate the damper door inside the air cleaner assembly. It's inside the long snorkel of the metal air cleaner housing.

4   If there is a flexible air duct attached to the end of the snorkel, leading to an area behind the grille, disconnect it at the snorkel. This will enable you to look through the end of the snorkel and see the damper inside.

5   The check should be done when the engine is cold. Start the engine and look through the snorkel at the damper, which should move to a closed position. With the damper closed, air cannot enter through the end of the snorkel, but instead enters the air cleaner through the flexible duct attached to the exhaust manifold and the heat stove passage **(see illustration)**.

6   As the engine warms up to operating temperature, the damper should open to allow air through the snorkel end **(see illustration)**. Depending on outside temperature, this may take 10- to 15 minutes. To speed up this check you can reconnect the snorkel air duct, drive the vehicle, then check to see if the damper is completely open.

7   If the thermo-controlled air cleaner isn't operating properly see Chapter 6 for more information.

27   Drivebelt check, adjustment and replacement

Refer to illustrations 27.3, 27.4 and 27.8

1   The drivebelts, or V-belts as they are often called, are located at the front of the engine and play an important role in the overall operation of the engine and accessories. Due to their function and material make-up, the belts are prone to failure after a period of time and should be inspected and adjusted periodically to prevent major engine damage.

2   The number of belts used on a particular vehicle depends on the accessories installed. Drivebelts are used to turn the alternator, power steering pump, water pump and air conditioning compressor. Depending on the pulley arrangement, more than one of these components may be driven by a single belt.

3   With the engine off, locate the drivebelts at the front of the engine. Using your fingers (and a flashlight, if necessary), move along the belts checking for cracks and separation of the belt plies. Also check for fraying and glazing, which gives the belt a shiny appearance **(see illustration)**. Both sides of each belt should be inspected, which means

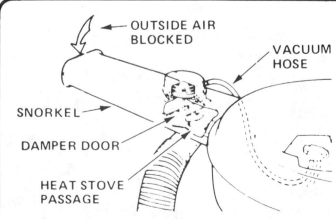

26.5   When the engine is cold, the damper door closes off the snorkel passage, allowing air warmed by the exhaust to enter the carburetor

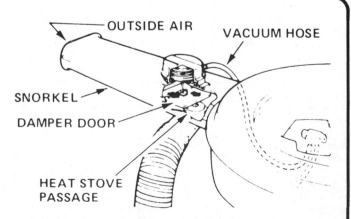

26.6   As the engine warms up, the damper door moves down to close off the heat stove passage and open the snorkel passage so outside air can enter the carburetor

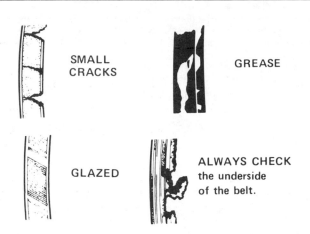

27.3 Here are some of the more common problems associated with drivebelts (check the belts very carefully to prevent untimely breakdown)

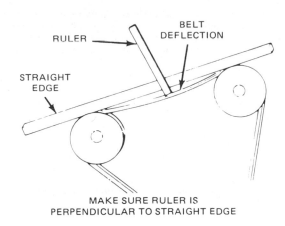

27.4 Drivebelt tension can be checked with a straightedge and a ruler

you will have to twist the belt to check the underside. Check the pulleys for nicks, cracks, distortion and corrosion.

4   The tension of each belt is checked by pushing on it at a distance halfway between the pulleys. Push firmly with your thumb and see how much the belt moves (deflects) **(see illustration)**. A rule of thumb is that if the distance from pulley center-to-pulley center is between seven and 11-inches, the belt should deflect 1/4-inch. If the belt travels between pulleys spaced 12- to 16 inches apart, the belt should deflect 1/2-inch.

5   If adjustment is needed, either to make the belt tighter or looser, it's done by moving the belt-driven accessory on the bracket.

6   For each component there will be an adjusting bolt and a pivot bolt. Both bolts must be loosened slightly to enable you to move the component.

7   After the two bolts have been loosened, move the component away from the engine to tighten the belt or toward the engine to loosen the belt. Hold the accessory in position and check the belt tension. If it's correct, tighten the two bolts until just snug, then recheck the tension. If the tension is all right, tighten the bolts.

8   To adjust the alternator drivebelt on some later models, loosen the pivot bolt and turn the adjusting bolt to tension the belt **(see illustration)**.

9   It will often be necessary to use some sort of pry bar to move the accessory while the belt is adjusted. If this must be done to gain the proper leverage, be very careful not to damage the component being moved or the part being pried against.

10 To replace a belt, follow the above procedures for drivebelt adjustment but slip the belt off the pulleys and remove it. Since belts tend to wear out more or less at the same time, it's a good idea to replace all of them at the same time. Mark each belt and the corresponding pulley grooves so the replacement belts can be installed properly.

11 Take the old belts with you when purchasing new ones in order to make a direct comparison for length, width and design.

12 Adjust the belts as described earlier in this Section.

13 When replacing a serpentine drivebelt (used on some later models), insert a 1/2-inch drive breaker bar into the tensioner and rotate it counterclockwise to release the belt tension. Make sure the new belt is routed correctly (refer to the label in the engine compartment). Also, the belt must completely engage the grooves in the pulleys.

28 Seatbelt check

1   Check the seatbelts, buckles, latch plates and guide loops for any obvious damage or signs of wear.

2   Make sure the seatbelt reminder light comes on when the key is turned on.

3   The seatbelts are designed to lock up during a sudden stop or impact, yet allow free movement during normal driving. The retractors should hold the belt against your chest while driving and rewind the belt when the buckle is unlatched.

4   If any of the above checks reveal problems with the seatbelt system, replace parts as necessary.

29 Starter/Neutral safety switch check

Warning: *During the following checks there is a chance that the vehicle could lunge forward, possibly causing damage or injuries. Allow plenty of room around the vehicle, apply the parking brake firmly and hold down the regular brake pedal during the checks.*

1   These models are equipped with a starter/Neutral safety switch which prevents the engine from starting unless the clutch pedal is depressed (manual transmission) or the shift lever is in Neutral or Park (automatic transmission).

2   On automatic transmission vehicles, try to start the vehicle in each gear. The engine should crank only in Park or Neutral.

3   If equipped with a manual transmission, place the shift lever in Neutral. The engine should crank only with the clutch pedal depressed.

27.8 On some later models, the alternator drivebelt tension is adjusted by turning the adjustment bolt (arrow)

4   Make sure the steering column lock allows the key to go into the Lock position only when the shift lever is in Park (automatic transmission) or Reverse (manual transmission).
5   The ignition key should come out only in the Lock position.

30 Ignition point replacement

Refer to illustrations 30.1, 30.2, 30.7, 30.9, 30.16, 30.17 and 30.29

1   The ignition points must be replaced at regular intervals on vehicles not equipped with electronic ignition. Occasionally the rubbing block will wear enough to require adjustment of the points. It's also possible to clean and dress them with a fine file, but replacement is recommended since they are relatively inaccessible and very inexpensive. Several special tools are required for this procedure **(see illustration)**.

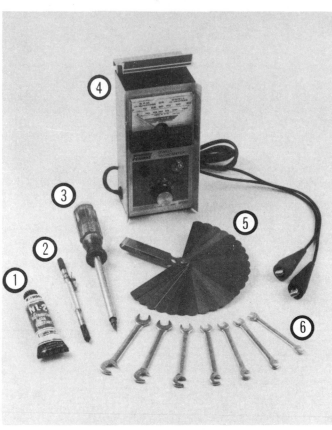

30.1 **Tools and materials needed for contact point replacement and dwell angle adjustment**

1 **Distributor cam lube** — *Sometimes this special lubricant comes with the new points; however, its a good idea to buy a tube and have it on hand*
2 **Screw starter** — *This tool has special claws which hold the screw securely as it is started, which helps prevent accidental dropping of the screw*
3 **Magnetic screwdriver** — *Serves the same purpose as 2 above. If you do not have one of these special screwdrivers, you risk dropping the point mounting screws down into the distributor body*
4 **Dwell meter** — *A dwell meter is the only accurate way to determine the point setting (gap). Connect the meter according to the instructions supplied with it*
5 **Blade-type feeler gauges** — *These are required to set the initial point gap (space between the points when they are open)*
6 **Ignition wrenches** — *These special wrenches are made to work within the tight confines of the distributor. Specifically, they are needed to loosen the nut/bolt which secures the leads to the points*

2   After removing the distributor cap and rotor (Section 45), the ignition points are plainly visible. They can be examined by gently prying them open to reveal the condition of the contact surfaces **(see illustration)**. If they're rough, pitted, covered with oil or burned, they should be replaced, along with the condenser. **Caution:** *This procedure requires the removal of small screws which can easily fall down into the distributor. To retrieve them, the distributor would have to be removed and disassembled. Use a magnetic or spring-loaded screwdriver and be extra careful.*
3   If not already done, remove the distributor cap by positioning a screwdriver in the slotted head of each latch. Press down on the latch and rotate it 1/2-turn to release the cap from the distributor body (see Section 45).
4   Position the cap (with the spark plug wires still attached) out of the way. Use a length of wire to hold it out of the way if necessary.
5   Remove the rotor (See Section 45 if necessary).
6   If equipped with a radio frequency interference shield (RFI), remove the mounting screws and the two-piece shield to gain access to the ignition points.
7   Note how they are routed, then disconnect the primary and condenser wire leads from the points **(see illustration)**. The wires may be

30.2 **Although it is possible to restore ignition points that are pitted, burned and corroded (as shown here), they should be replaced instead**

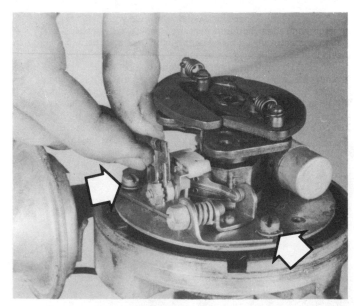

30.7 **Loosen the nut and disconnect the primary and condenser wires from the points — note the ignition point mounting screws (arrows)**

attached with a small nut (which should be loosened, but not removed) a small screw or by a spring loaded terminal. **Note:** *Some models are equipped with ignition points which include the condenser as an integral part of the point assembly. If your vehicle has this type, the condenser removal procedure below will not apply and there will be only one wire to detach from the points, rather than the two used with a separate condenser assembly.*

8   Loosen the two screws which secure the ignition points to the breaker plate, but don't completely remove the screws (most ignition point sets have slots at these locations). Slide the points out of the distributor.

9   The condenser can now be removed from the breaker plate. Loosen the mounting strap screw and slide the condenser out or completely remove the condenser and strap (**see illustration**). If you remove both the condenser and strap, be careful not to drop the mounting screw down into the distributor body.

10 Before installing the new points and condenser, clean the breaker plate and the cam on the distributor shaft to remove all dirt, dust and oil.

11 Apply a small amount of distributor cam lube (usually supplied with the new points, but also available separately) to the cam lobes.

12 Position the new condenser and tighten the mounting strap screw securely.

13 Slide the new point set under the mounting screw heads and make sure the protrusions on the breaker plate fit into the holes in the point base (to properly position the point set), then tighten the screws securely.

14 Attach the primary and condenser wires to the new points. Make sure the wires are routed so they don't interfere with breaker plate or advance weight movement.

15 Although the gap between the contact points (dwell angle) will be adjusted later, make the initial adjustment now, which will allow the engine to be started.

16 Make sure that the point rubbing block is resting on one of the high points of the cam (**see illustration**). If it isn't, turn the ignition switch to Start in short bursts to reposition the cam. You can also turn the crankshaft with a breaker bar and socket attached to the large bolt that holds the vibration damper in place.

17 With the rubbing block on a cam high point (points open), insert a 0.019-inch feeler gauge between the contact surfaces and use an Allen wrench to turn the adjustment screw until the point gap is equal to the thickness of the feeler gauge (**see illustration**). The gap is correct when a slight amount of drag is felt as the feeler gauge is withdrawn.

18 If equipped, install the RFI shield.

19 Before installing the rotor, check it as described in Section 45.

20 Install the rotor. The rotor is indexed with a square peg underneath on one side and a round peg on the other side, so it will fit on the advance mechanism only one way. If so equipped, tighten the rotor

mounting screws securely.

21 Before installing the distributor cap, inspect it as described in Section 45.

22 Install the distributor cap and lock the latches under the distributor body by depressing and turning them with a screwdriver.

23 Start the engine and check the dwell angle and ignition timing.

24 Whenever new ignition points are installed or the original points are cleaned, the dwell angle must be checked and adjusted.

25 Precise adjustment of the dwell angle requires an instrument called a dwell meter. Combination tach/dwell meters are commonly available at reasonable cost from auto parts stores. An approximate setting can be obtained if a meter isn't available.

26 *If a dwell meter is available*, hook it up following the manufacturer's instructions.

27 Start the engine and allow it to run at idle until normal operating temperature is reached (the engine must be warm to obtain an accurate reading). Turn off the engine.

28 Raise the metal door in the distributor cap. Hold it in the open position with tape if necessary.

30.9 **The condenser is attached to the breaker plate by a single screw**

30.16 **Before adjusting the point gap, the rubbing block must be resting on one of the cam lobes (which will open the points)**

30.17 **With the points open, insert a 0.019-in thick feeler gauge and turn the adjustment screw with an Allen wrench**

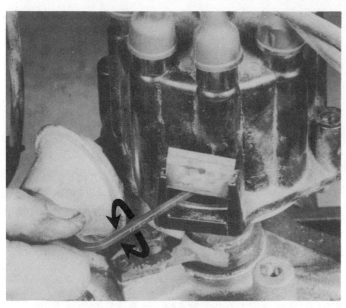

**30.29 With the door open, a 1/8-in Allen wrench can be
inserted into the adjustment screw socket and turned to
adjust the point dwell**

29 Just inside the opening is the ignition point adjustment screw. Insert a 1/8-inch Allen wrench into the adjustment screw socket **(see illustration)**.

30 Start the engine and turn the adjustment screw as required to obtain the specified dwell reading on the meter. Dwell angle specifications can be found on the tune-up decal in the engine compartment. **Note:** *When adjusting the dwell, aim for the lower end of the dwell specification range. Then, as the points wear, the dwell will remain within the specified range over a longer period of time.*

31 Remove the Allen wrench and close the door on the distributor. Turn off the engine and disconnect the dwell meter, then check the ignition timing (see Section 34).

32 *If a dwell meter isn't available*, use the following procedure to obtain an approximate dwell setting.

33 Start the engine and allow it to idle until normal operating temperature is reached.

34 Raise the metal door in the distributor cap. Hold it in the open position with tape if necessary.

35 Just inside the opening is the ignition point adjustment screw. Insert a 1/8-inch Allen wrench into the adjustment screw socket **(see illustration 30.29)**.

36 Turn the Allen wrench *clockwise* until the engine begins to misfire, then turn the screw 1/2-turn counterclockwise.

37 Remove the Allen wrench and close the door. As soon as possible have the dwell angle checked and/or adjusted with a dwell meter to ensure optimum performance.

31 Idle speed check and adjustment

Refer to illustrations 31.4a and 31.4b

1 Engine idle speed is the speed at which the engine operates when no accelerator pedal pressure is applied. On later models this speed is governed by the ECM, while on earlier models the idle speed can be adjusted. The idle speed is critical to the performance of the engine itself, as well as many engine sub-systems.

2 A hand-held tachometer must be used when adjusting idle speed to get an accurate reading. The exact hook-up for these meters varies with the manufacturer, so follow the particular directions included with the instrument.

3 Since the manufacturer used many different carburetors over the time period covered by this manual, and each varies somewhat when setting idle speed, it would be impractical to cover all types in this Section. Most later models have a label located in the engine compartment with instructions for setting idle speed.

4 For most applications, the idle speed is set by turning an adjustment screw located on the side of the carburetor. This screw changes the amount the throttle plate is held open by the throttle linkage. The screw may be on the linkage itself or may be part of a device such as an idle stop solenoid **(see illustrations)**. Refer to the tune-up label or Chapter 4.

5 Once you have found the idle screw, experiment with different length screwdrivers until the adjustment can be easily made without coming into contact with hot or moving engine components.

6 Follow the instructions on the tune-up decal or in Chapter 4, which will probably include disconnecting certain vacuum or electrical connections. To plug a vacuum hose after disconnecting, insert a suitable size metal rod into the opening, or thoroughly wrap the open end with tape to prevent any vacuum loss through the hose.

7 If the air cleaner is removed, the vacuum hose to the snorkel should be plugged.

8 Make sure the parking brake is firmly set and the wheels blocked to prevent the vehicle from rolling. This is especially true if the transmission is to be in Drive. An assistant inside the vehicle pressing on the brake pedal is the safest method.

9 For all applications, the engine must be completely warmed up to operating temperature, which will automatically render the choke fast idle inoperative.

32 Fuel filter replacement

Refer to illustrations 32.6 and 32.8

1 On these models the fuel filter is located inside the fuel inlet nut at the carburetor. It's made of either pleated paper or porous bronze and cannot be cleaned or reused.

2 The job should be done with the engine cold (after sitting at least three hours). The necessary tools include open-end wrenches to fit the fuel line nuts. Flare nut wrenches (which wrap around the nut) should be used if available. In addition, you have to obtain the replacement filter (make sure it's for your specific vehicle and engine) and some clean rags.

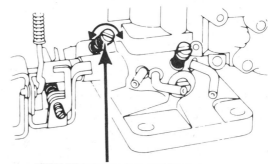

IDLE SPEED ADJUSTING SCREW

**31.4a Idle speed screws will be found in a number of
locations on a carburetor and can be easily confused with
other carburetor adjustment screws — if you are
unsure about this procedure, seek advice**

IDLE SPEED (SOLENOID) SCREW

**31.4b On some models, the idle speed screw is controlled
by an electric solenoid — the adjustment is made at the
end of the solenoid**

3 Remove the air cleaner assembly. If vacuum hoses must be disconnected, be sure to note their positions and/or tag them to ensure that they are reinstalled correctly.
4 Follow the fuel line from the fuel pump to the point where it enters the carburetor. In most cases the fuel line will be metal all the way from the fuel pump to the carburetor.
5 Place some rags under the fuel inlet fittings to catch spilled fuel as the fittings are disconnected.
6 With the proper size wrench, hold the fuel inlet nut immediately next to the carburetor body. Now loosen the fitting at the end of the metal fuel line. Make sure the fuel inlet nut next to the carburetor is held securely while the fuel line is disconnected (see illustration).

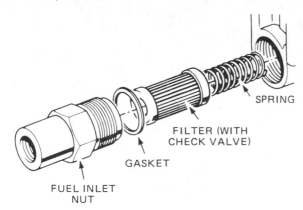

32.8 Fuel filter component layout

SPRING

FILTER (WITH CHECK VALVE)

GASKET

FUEL INLET NUT

7 After the fuel line is disconnected, move it aside for better access to the inlet nut. Don't crimp the fuel line.
8 Unscrew the fuel inlet nut, which was previously held steady. As this fitting is drawn away from the carburetor body, be careful not to lose the thin washer-type gasket on the nut or the spring, located behind the fuel filter. Also pay close attention to how the filter is installed (see illustration).
9 Compare the old filter with the new one to make sure they're the same length and design.
10 Reinstall the spring in the carburetor body.
11 Place the filter in position (a gasket is usually supplied with the new filter) and tighten the nut. Make sure it's not cross-threaded. Tighten it securely, but be careful not to overtighten it as the threads can strip easily, causing fuel leaks. Reconnect the fuel line to the fuel inlet nut, again using caution to avoid cross-threading the nut. Use a back-up wrench on the fuel inlet nut while tightening the fuel line fitting.
12 Start the engine and check carefully for leaks. If the fuel line fitting leaks, disconnect it and check for stripped or damaged threads. If the fuel line fitting has stripped threads, remove the entire line and have

a repair shop install a new fitting. If the threads look all right, purchase some thread sealing tape and wrap the threads with it. Inlet nut repair kits are available at most auto parts stores to overcome leaking at the fuel inlet nut.

33 Air filter and PCV filter replacement

Refer to illustrations 33.2, 33.4, 33.7 and 33.9

1 At the specified intervals, the air filter and (if equipped) PCV filter should be replaced with new ones. The engine air cleaner also supplies filtered air to the PCV system.
2 The filter is located on top of the carburetor and is replaced by unscrewing the wing nut from the top of the filter housing and lifting off the cover (see illustration).
3 While the top plate is off, be careful not to drop anything down into the carburetor or air cleaner assembly.
4 Lift the air filter element out of the housing (see illustration) and wipe out the inside of the air cleaner housing with a clean rag.
5 Place the new filter in the air cleaner housing. Make sure it seats properly in the bottom of the housing.
6 The PCV filter is also located inside the air cleaner housing on some models. Remove the top plate and air filter as previously described, then locate the PCV filter on the inside of the housing.

1

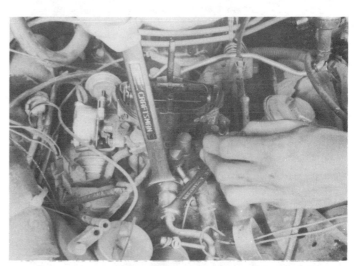

32.6 Two wrenches are required to loosen carburetor fuel filter inlet nuts

33.2 On most models, the first step in removing the air filter is unscrewing the wing nut on top of the housing

33.4 After setting the top plate aside, the filter element can be lifted out of the housing

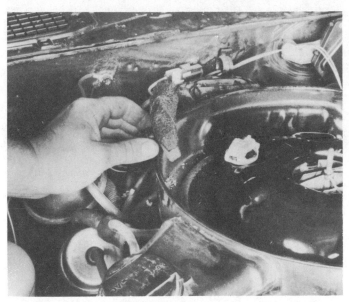

33.7 The PCV filter on most models is located in the air cleaner housing

33.9 The PCV filter used on some models is located in the rocker cover (arrow); pull the assembly out of the cover and wash it with solvent at the specified interval

7   Remove the old filter (**see illustration**).
8   Install the new PCV filter and the new air filter.
9   On some models, the PCV filter is located in the rocker cover and is connected to the air cleaner housing by a hose (**see illustration**). This type of filter doesn't require replacement; pull it out of the rocker cover and wash it with solvent at the specified intervals.
10   Install the top plate and any hoses which were disconnected.

34   Ignition timing check and adjustment

Refer to illustrations 34.2 and 34.6

Note: *It is imperative that the procedures included on the tune-up or Vehicle Emissions Control Information (VECI) label be followed when adjusting the ignition timing. The label will include all information concerning preliminary steps to be performed before adjusting the timing, as well as the timing specifications.*

1   At the specified intervals, whenever the ignition points have been replaced, the distributor removed or a change made in the fuel type, the ignition timing should be checked and adjusted.
2   Locate the Tune-up or VECI label under the hood and read through and perform all preliminary instructions concerning ignition timing. Some special tools will be needed for this procedure (**see illustration**).
3   Before attempting to check the timing, make sure the ignition point dwell angle is correct (Section 30), and the idle speed is as specified (Section 31).
4   If specified on the tune-up label, disconnect the vacuum hose from the distributor and plug the open end of the hose with a rubber plug, rod or bolt of the proper size.
5   Connect a timing light in accordance with the manufacturer's instructions. Generally, the light will be connected to power and ground sources and to the number one spark plug wire. The number one spark plug is the first spark plug on the right head (driver's side) as you are facing the engine from the front.
6   Locate the numbered timing tag on the front cover of the engine (**see illustration**). It is located just behind the lower crankshaft pulley. Clean it off with solvent if necessary to read the printing and small grooves.
7   Use chalk or paint to mark the groove in the crankshaft pulley.
8   Put a mark on the timing tab in accordance with the number of degrees called for on the VECI label or the tune-up label in the engine compartment. Each peak or notch on the timing tab represents two degrees. The word *Before* or the letter *A* indicates advance and the letter *0* indicates Top Dead Center (TDC). As an example, if your vehicle specifications call for eight degrees BTDC (Before Top Dead Center),

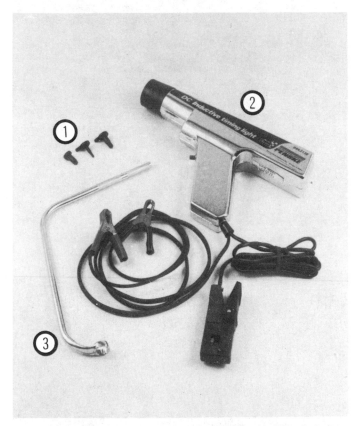

34.2 Tools needed to check and adjust the ignition timing

1   **Vacuum plugs** — *Vacuum hoses will, in most cases, have to be disconnected and plugged. Molded plugs in various shapes and sizes are available for this*
2   **Inductive pick-up timing light** — *Flashes a bright concentrated beam of light when the number one spark plug fires. Connect the leads according to the instructions supplied with the light*
3   **Distributor wrench** — *On some models, the hold-down bolt for the distributor is difficult to reach and turn with conventional wrenches or sockets. A special wrench like this must be used*

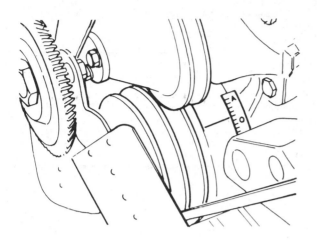
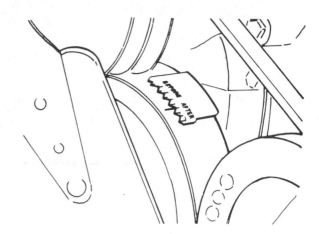

34.6 The ignition timing marks are located at the front of the engine

you will make a mark on the timing tab four notches *before* the O.
9   Check that the wiring for the timing light is clear of all moving engine components, then start the engine and warm it up to normal operating temperature.
10 Aim the flashing timing light at the timing mark by the crankshaft pulley, again being careful not to come in contact with moving parts. The marks should appear to be stationary. If the marks are in alignment, the timing is correct.
11 If the notch is not lining up with the correct mark, loosen the distributor hold-down bolt and rotate the distributor until the notch is lined up with the correct timing mark.
12 Retighten the hold-down bolt and recheck the timing.
13 Turn off the engine and disconnect the timing light. Reconnect the vacuum advance hose, if removed, and any other components which were disconnected.

35   Automatic transmission fluid and filter change

Refer to illustrations 35.7, 35.10 and 35.11
1   At the specified time intervals, the transmission fluid should be drained and replaced. Since the fluid will remain hot long after driving, perform this procedure only after the engine has cooled down completely.
2   Before beginning work, purchase the specified transmission fluid (see *Recommended lubricants and fluids* at the front of this Chapter) and a new filter.
3   Other tools necessary for this job include jackstands to support the vehicle in a raised position, a drain pan capable of holding at least eight pints, newspapers and clean rags.
4   Raise the vehicle and support it securely on jackstands.
5   With a drain pan in place, remove the front and side pan mounting bolts.
6   Loosen the rear pan bolts approximately four turns.
7   Carefully pry the transmission pan loose with a screwdriver, allowing the fluid to drain **(see illustration)**.
8   Remove the remaining bolts, pan and gasket. Carefully clean the gasket surface of the transmission to remove all traces of the old gasket and sealant.
9   Drain the fluid from the transmission pan, clean it with solvent and dry it with compressed air.
10 Remove the filter from the mount inside the transmission **(see illustration)**.

35.7   With the rear bolts in place but loose, pull the front of the pan down to let the fluid drain

35.10   After removing the bolts or screws, lower the filter from the transmission

35.11 Some models have an O-ring on the filter spout; if
it does not come out with the filter, reach up into the
opening with your finger to retrieve it

11 Install a new filter and (if equipped) O-ring **(see illustration)**.
12 Make sure the gasket surface on the transmission pan is clean,
then install a new gasket. Put the pan in place against the transmission
and, working around the pan, tighten each bolt a little at a time until
the final torque figure is reached.
13 Lower the vehicle and add the specified amount of automatic transmission fluid through the filler tube (Section 6).
14 With the transmission in Park and the parking brake set, run the
engine at a fast idle, but don't race it.
15 Move the gear selector through each range and back to Park. Check
the fluid level.
16 Check under the vehicle for leaks during the first few trips.

36 Manual transmission lubricant change

1 Raise the vehicle and support it securely on jackstands.
2 Move a drain pan, rags, newspapers and wrenches under the transmission.
3 Remove the transmission drain plug at the bottom of the case and
allow the oil to drain into the pan.
4 After the oil has drained completely, reinstall the plug and tighten
it securely.
5 Remove the fill plug from the side of the transmission case. Using
a hand pump, syringe or funnel, fill the transmission with the correct
amount of the specified lubricant. Reinstall the fill plug and tighten it
securely.

6 Lower the vehicle.
7 Drive the vehicle for a short distance then check the drain and fill
plugs for leakage.

37 Differential oil change

Refer to illustrations 37.6a, 37.6b, 37.6c and 37.8
1 Some differentials can be drained by removing the drain plug, while
on others it's necessary to remove the cover plate on the differential
housing. As an alternative, a hand suction pump can be used to remove
the differential lubricant through the filler hole. If there is no drain plug
and a suction pump isn't available, be sure to obtain a new gasket at
the same time the gear lubricant is purchased.
2 Raise the vehicle and support it securely on jackstands. Move a
drain pan, rags, newspapers and wrenches under the vehicle.
3 Remove the fill plug from the differential.
4 If equipped with a drain plug, remove the plug and allow the differential oil to drain completely. After the oil has drained, install the
plug and tighten it securely.
5 If a suction pump is being used, insert the flexible hose. Work the
hose down to the bottom of the differential housing and pump the oil
out.
6 If the differential is being drained by removing the cover plate,
remove the bolts on the lower half of the plate **(see illustration)**. Loosen
the bolts on the upper half and use them to keep the cover loosely
attached **(see illustration)**. Allow the oil to drain into the pan, then completely remove the cover **(see illustration)**.
7 Using a lint-free rag, clean the inside of the cover and the accessible
areas of the differential housing. As this is done, check for chipped
gears and metal particles in the lubricant, indicating that the differential
should be more thoroughly inspected and/or repaired.
8 Thoroughly clean the gasket mating surfaces of the differential
housing and the cover plate. Use a gasket scraper or putty knife to
remove all traces of the old gasket **(see illustration)**.
9 Apply a thin layer of RTV sealant to the cover flange and then press
a new gasket into position on the cover. Make sure the bolt holes align
properly.
10 Place the cover on the differential housing and install the bolts.
Tighten the bolts securely.
11 On all models, use a hand pump, syringe or funnel to fill the differential housing with the specified lubricant until it's level with the
bottom of the plug hole.
12 Install the filler plug and tighten it securely.

38 Front wheel bearing check, repack and adjustment

Refer to illustrations 38.1, 38.6, 38.7, 38.8, 38.11 and 38.15
1 In most cases the front wheel bearings will not need servicing until

37.6a Remove the bolts from the lower
edge of the cover . . .

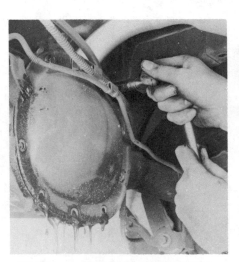

37.6b . . . then loosen the top bolts
and let the oil drain

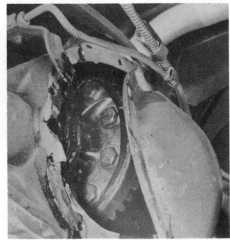

37.6c After the oil is drained, remove
the cover

37.8 Carefully scrape the old gasket material off to ensure a leak-free seal with the new gasket

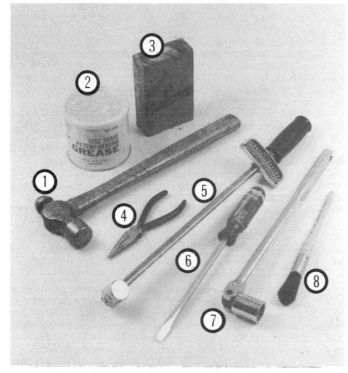

38.1 Tools and materials needed for front wheel bearing maintenance

1 **Hammer** — A common hammer will do just fine
2 **Grease** — High-temperature grease which is formulated specially for front wheel bearings should be used
3 **Wood block** — If you have a scrap piece of 2x4, it can be used to dirve the new seeal into the hub
4 **Needle-nose pliers** — Used to straighten and remove the cotter pin in the spindle
5 **Torque wrench** — This is very important in this procedure; if the bearing is too tight, the wheel won't turn freely — if it is too loose, the wheel will 'wobble' on the spindle. Either way, it could mean extensive damage
6 **Screwdriverr** — Used to remove the seal from the hub (a long screwdriver would be preferred)
7 **Socket/breaker bar** — Needed to loosen the nut on the spindle if it is extremely tight
8 **Brush** — Together with some clean solvent, this will be used to remove old grease from the hub and spindle

the brake pads are changed. However, the bearings should be checked whenever the front of the vehicle is raised for any reason. Several items, including a torque wrench and special grease, are required for this procedure **(see illustration)**.
2　With the vehicle securely supported on jackstands, spin each wheel and check for noise, rolling resistance and free play.
3　Grasp the top of each tire with one hand and the bottom with the other. Move the wheel in and out on the spindle. If there's any noticable movement, the bearings should be checked and then repacked with grease, or replaced if necessary.
4　Remove the wheel.
5　On disc brake equipped models, fabricate a wood block (1-1/16 inches by 1/2-inch by 2-inches long) which can be slid between the brake pads to keep them separated. Remove the brake caliper (Chapter 9) and hang it out of the way on a piece of wire.
6　Pry the dust cap out of the hub using a screwdriver or hammer and chisel **(see illustration)**.
7　Straighten the bent ends of the cotter pin, then pull the cotter pin out of the locking nut **(see illustration)**. Discard the cotter pin and use a new one during reassembly.

38.6 Dislodge the grease cap by working around the outer circumference with a hammer and chisel

38.7 Use needle nose pliers to straighten the cotter pin and pull it out

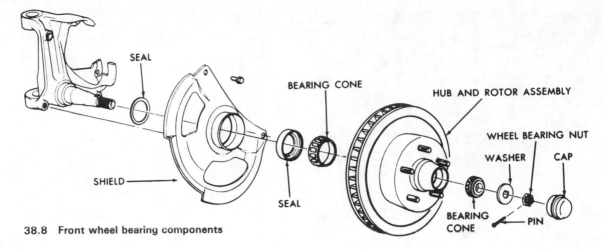

38.8   Front wheel bearing components

8   Remove the spindle nut and washer from the end of the spindle **(see illustration)**.

9   Pull the hub assembly out slightly, then push it back into its original position. This should force the outer bearing off the spindle enough so it can be removed.

10   Pull the hub off the spindle.

11   Use a screwdriver to pry the seal out of the rear of the hub **(see illustration)**. As this is done, note how the seal is installed.

12   Remove the inner wheel bearing from the hub.

13   Use solvent to remove all traces of the old grease from the bearings, hub and spindle. A small brush may prove helpful; however make sure no bristles from the brush embed themselves inside the bearing rollers. Allow the parts to air dry.

14   Carefully inspect the bearings for cracks, heat discoloration, worn rollers, etc. Check the bearing races inside the hub for wear and damage. If the bearing races are defective, the hubs should be taken to a machine shop with the facilities to remove the old races and press new ones in. Note that the bearings and races come as matched sets and old bearings should never be installed on new races.

15   Use high-temperature front wheel bearing grease to pack the bearings. Work the grease completely into the bearings, forcing it between the rollers, cone and cage from the back side **(see illustration)**.

16   Apply a thin coat of grease to the spindle at the outer bearing seat, inner bearing seat, shoulder and seal seat.

17   Put a small quantity of grease inboard of each bearing race inside the hub. Using your finger, form a dam at these points to provide extra grease availability and to keep thinned grease from flowing out of the bearing.

18   Place the grease-packed inner bearing into the rear of the hub and put a little more grease outboard of the bearing.

19   Place a new seal over the inner bearing and tap the seal evenly into place with a hammer and block of wood until it's flush with the hub.

20   Carefully place the hub assembly onto the spindle and push the grease-packed outer bearing into position.

21   Install the washer and spindle nut. Tighten the nut only slightly (no more than 12 ft-lbs of torque).

22   Spin the hub in a forward direction to seat the bearings and remove any grease or burrs which could cause excessive bearing play later.

23   Check to see that the tightness of the spindle nut is still approximately 12 ft-lbs.

24   Loosen the spindle nut until it's just loose, no more.

25   Using your hand (not a wrench of any kind), tighten the nut until it's snug. Install a new cotter pin through the hole in the spindle and spindle nut. If the nut slots don't line up, loosen the nut slightly until they do. From the hand-tight position, the nut should not be loosened more than one-half flat to install the cotter pin.

26   Bend the ends of the cotter pin until they're flat against the nut. Cut off any extra length which could interfere with the dust cap.

27   Install the dust cap, tapping it into place with a hammer.

28   Place the brake caliper near the rotor and carefully remove the wood spacer. Install the caliper (Chapter 9).

29   Install the tire/wheel assembly on the hub and tighten the lug nuts.

30   Grasp the top and bottom of the tire and check the bearings in the manner described earlier in this Section.

31   Lower the vehicle.

---

39   Cooling system servicing (draining, flushing and refilling)

Warning: *Antifreeze is a corrosive and poisonous solution, so be careful not to spill any of the coolant mixture on the vehicle's paint or your skin. If this happens, rinse immediately with plenty of clean water. Consult local authorities regarding proper disposal procedures for antifreeze before draining the cooling system. In many areas, reclamation centers have been established to collect used oil and coolant mixtures.*

1   Periodically, the cooling system should be drained, flushed and

38.11   Use a screwdriver to pry the grease seal from the back side of the hub

38.15   Work the grease completely into the rollers

CARBON DEPOSITS

Symptoms: Dry sooty deposits indicate a rich mixture or weak ignition. Causes misfiring, hard starting and hesitation.

Recommendation: Check for a clogged air cleaner, high float level, sticky choke and worn ignition points. Use a spark plug with a longer core nose for greater anti-fouling protection.

OIL DEPOSITS

Symptoms: Oily coating caused by poor oil control. Oil is leaking past worn valve guides or piston rings into the combustion chamber. Causes hard starting, misfiring and hesition.

Recommendation: Correct the mechanical condition with necessary repairs and install new plugs.

TOO HOT

Symptoms: Blistered, white insulator, eroded electrode and absence of deposits. Results in shortened plug life.

Recommendation: Check for the correct plug heat range, over-advanced ignition timing, lean fuel mixture, intake manifold vacuum leaks and sticking valves. Check the coolant level and make sure the radiator is not clogged.

PREIGNITION

Symptoms: Melted electrodes. Insulators are white, but may be dirty due to misfiring or flying debris in the combustion chamber. Can lead to engine damage.

Recommendation: Check for the correct plug heat range, over-advanced ignition timing, lean fuel mixture, clogged cooling system and lack of lubrication.

HIGH SPEED GLAZING

Symptoms: Insulator has yellowish, glazed appearance. Indicates that combustion chamber temperatures have risen suddenly during hard acceleration. Normal deposits melt to form a conductive coating. Causes misfiring at high speeds.

Recommendation: Install new plugs. Consider using a colder plug if driving habits warrant.

GAP BRIDGING

Symptoms: Combustion deposits lodge between the electrodes. Heavy deposits accumulate and bridge the electrode gap. The plug ceases to fire, resulting in a dead cylinder.

Recommendation: Locate the faulty plug and remove the deposits from between the electrodes.

NORMAL

Symptoms: Brown to grayish-tan color and slight electrode wear. Correct heat range for engine and operating conditions.

Recommendation: When new spark plugs are installed, replace with plugs of the same heat range.

ASH DEPOSITS

Symptoms: Light brown deposits encrusted on the side or center electrodes or both. Derived from oil and/or fuel additives. Excessive amounts may mask the spark, causing misfiring and hesitation during acceleration.

Recommendation: If excessive deposits accumulate over a short time or low mileage, install new valve guide seals to prevent seepage of oil into the combustion chambers. Also try changing gasoline brands.

1

WORN

Symptoms: Rounded electrodes with a small amount of deposits on the firing end. Normal color. Causes hard starting in damp or cold weather and poor fuel economy.

Recommendation: Replace with new plugs of the same heat range.

DETONATION

Symptoms: Insulators may be cracked or chipped. Improper gap setting techniques can also result in a fractured insulator tip. Can lead to piston damage.

Recommendation: Make sure the fuel anti-knock values meet engine requirements. Use care when setting the gaps on new plugs. Avoid lugging the engine.

SPLASHED DEPOSITS

Symptoms: After long periods of misfiring, deposits can loosen when normal combustion temperature is restored by an overdue tune-up. At high speeds, deposits flake off the piston and are thrown against the hot insulator, causing misfiring.

Recommendation: Replace the plugs with new ones or clean and reinstall the originals.

MECHANICAL DAMAGE

Symptoms: May be caused by a foreign object in the combustion chamber or the piston striking an incorrect reach (too long) plug. Causes a dead cylinder and could result in piston damage.

Recommendation: Remove the foreign object from the engine and/or install the correct reach plug.

refilled to replenish the antifreeze mixture and prevent formation of rust and corrosion, which can impair the performance of the cooling system and cause engine damage. When the cooling system is serviced, all hoses and the radiator cap should be checked and replaced if necessary.

2   Apply the parking brake and block the wheels. If the vehicle has just been driven, wait several hours to allow the engine to cool down before beginning this procedure.

3   Once the engine is completely cool, remove the radiator cap.

4   Move a large container under the radiator drain to catch the coolant. Attach a 3/8-inch diameter hose to the drain fitting to direct the coolant into the container, then open the drain fitting (a pair of pliers may be required to turn it).

5   After the coolant stops flowing out of the radiator, move the container under the engine block drain plug (if so equipped). Remove the plug and allow the coolant in the block to drain.

6   While the coolant is draining, check the condition of the radiator hoses, heater hoses and clamps (refer to Section 9 if necessary).

7   Replace any damaged clamps or hoses.

8   Once the system is completely drained, flush the radiator with fresh water from a garden hose until it runs clear at the drain. The flushing action of the water will remove sediments from the radiator but will not remove rust and scale from the engine and cooling tube surfaces.

9   These deposits can be removed with a chemical cleaner. Follow the procedure outlined in the manufacturer's instructions. If the radiator is severely corroded, damaged or leaking, it should be removed (Chapter 3) and taken to a radiator repair shop.

10   Remove the overflow hose from the coolant recovery reservoir. Drain the reservoir and flush it with clean water, then reconnect the hose.

11   Close and tighten the radiator drain. Install and tighten the block drain plug.

12   Place the heater temperature control in the maximum heat position.

13   Slowly add new coolant (a 50/50 mixture of water and antifreeze) to the radiator until it's full. Add coolant to the reservoir up to the lower mark.

14   Leave the radiator cap off and run the engine in a well-ventilated area until the thermostat opens (coolant will begin flowing through the radiator and the upper radiator hose will become hot).

15   Turn the engine off and let it cool. Add more coolant mixture to bring the level back up to the lip on the radiator filler neck.

16   Squeeze the upper radiator hose to expel air, then add more coolant mixture if necessary. Replace the radiator cap.

17   Start the engine, allow it to reach normal operating temperature and check for leaks.

40   Positive Crankcase Ventilation (PCV) valve check and replacement

Refer to illustration 40.2

1   The PCV valve is usually located in the rocker arm cover.

2   With the engine idling at normal operating temperature, pull the valve (with hose attached) from the rubber grommet in the cover (**see illustration**).

3   Place your finger over the valve opening. If there's no vacuum at the valve, check for a plugged hose, manifold port, or the valve itself. Replace any plugged or deteriorated hoses.

4   Turn off the engine and shake the PCV valve, listening for a rattle. If the valve doesn't rattle, replace it with a new one.

5   To replace the valve, pull it from the end of the hose, noting its installed position and direction.

6   When purchasing a replacement PCV valve, make sure it's for your particular vehicle and engine size. Compare the old valve with the new one to make sure they're the same.

7   Push the valve into the end of the hose until it's seated.

8   Inspect the rubber grommet for damage and replace it with a new one if necessary.

9   Push the PCV valve and hose securely into position.

40.2   The PCV valve simply pushes into the valve cover or manifold; place your finger under the valve and pull it out — feel for suction at the end of the valve and shake the valve, listening for a clicking sound

41   Evaporative emissions control system check

Refer to illustrations 41.2, 41.4 and 41.5

1   The function of the evaporative emissions control system is to draw fuel vapors from the gas tank and fuel system, store them in a charcoal canister and route them to the intake manifold during normal engine operation.

2   The most common symptom of a fault in the evaporative emissions

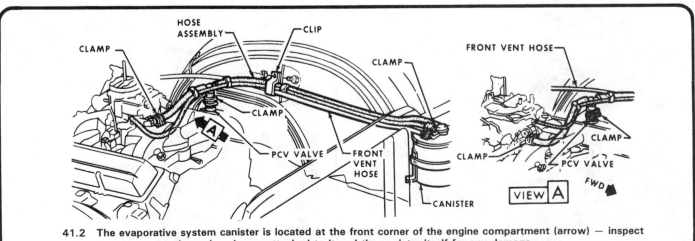

41.2   The evaporative system canister is located at the front corner of the engine compartment (arrow) — inspect the various hoses attached to it and the canister itself for any damage

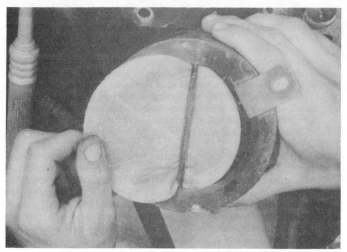

41.4 Pull the filter element out from the bottom
of the canister

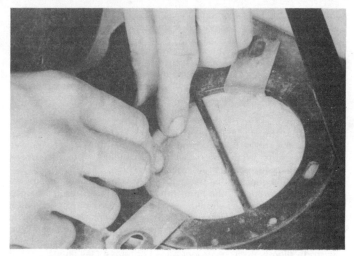

41.5 Make sure the new filter is fully seated all the way
around the bottom of the canister

1

system is a strong fuel odor in the engine compartment. If a fuel odor is detected, inspect the charcoal canister, located in the engine compartment (see illustration). Check the canister and all hoses for damage and deterioration.

3   On earlier models, the filter at the bottom of the canister should be replaced at this time.

4   Remove the retaining bolts, turn the canister upside-down and pull the old filter from the bottom of the canister (see illustration). If you cannot turn the canister enough for this due to the short length of the hoses, mark the hoses with tape and disconnect them.

5   Push the new filter into the bottom of the canister, making sure it is seated all the way around (see illustration).

6   Install the canister and connect any hoses which were disconnected.

7   The evaporative emissions control system is explained in more detail in Chapter 6.

42   Exhaust Gas Recirculation (EGR) system check

Refer to illustration 42.2

1   The EGR valve is usually located on the intake manifold, adjacent to the carburetor. Most of the time when a problem develops in this emissions system, it's due to a stuck or corroded EGR valve.

2   With the engine cold, to prevent burns, push on the EGR valve diaphragm. Using moderate pressure, you should be able to press the diaphragm in and out within the housing (see illustration).

3   If the diaphragm doesn't move or moves only with much effort, replace the EGR valve with a new one. If in doubt about the condition

of the valve, compare the free movement of your EGR valve with a new valve.

4   Refer to Chapter 6 for more information on the EGR system.

43   Spark plug replacement

Refer to illustrations 43.2, 43.5a, 43.5b, 43.6 and 43.10

1   Open the hood.

2   In most cases, the tools necessary for spark plug replacement include a spark plug socket which fits onto a ratchet (spark plug sockets are padded inside to prevent damage to the porcelain insulators on the new plugs), various extensions and a gap gauge to check and adjust the gaps on the new plugs (see illustration). A special plug wire removal

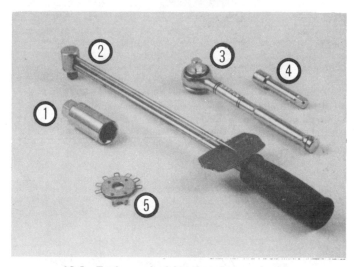

43.2   Tools required for changing spark plugs

1   **Spark plug socket** — *This will have special padding inside to protect the spark plug porcelain insulator*

2   **Torque wrench** — *Although not mandatory, use of this tool is the best way to ensure that the plugs are tightened properly*

3   **Ratchet** — *Standard hand tool to fit the plug socket*

4   **Extension** — *Depending on model and accessories, you may need special extensions and universal joints to reach one or more of the plugs*

5   **Spark plug gap gauge** — *This gauge for checking the gap comes in a variety of styles. Make sure the gap for your engine is included*

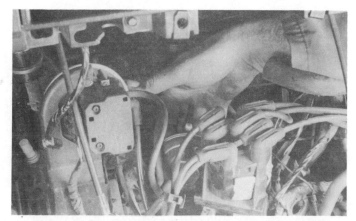

42.2   The diaphragm, located under the EGR valve, should
move easily with finger pressure

tool is available for separating the wire boots from the spark plugs, but it isn't absolutely necessary. A torque wrench should be used to tighten the new plugs.

3   The best approach when replacing the spark plugs is to purchase the new ones in advance, adjust them to the proper gap and replace them one at a time. When buying the new spark plugs, be sure to obtain the correct plug type for your particular engine. This information can be found on the *Emission Control Information label* located under the hood and in the factory owner's manual. If differences exist between the plug specified on the emissions label and in the owner's manual, assume that the emissions label is correct.

4   Allow the engine to cool completely before attempting to remove any of the plugs. While you're waiting for the engine to cool, check the new plugs for defects and adjust the gaps.

5   The gap is checked by inserting the proper thickness gauge between the electrodes at the tip of the plug (**see illustration**). The gap between the electrodes should be the same as the one specified on the *Emissions Control Information label*. The wire should just slide between the electrodes with a slight amount of drag. If the gap is incorrect, use the adjuster on the gauge body to bend the curved side electrode slightly until the proper gap is obtained (**see illustration**). If the side electrode is not exactly over the center electrode, bend it with the adjuster until it is. Check for cracks in the porcelain insulator (if any are found, the plug should not be used).

6   With the engine cool, remove the spark plug wire from one spark plug. Pull only on the boot at the end of the wire — do not pull on the wire. A plug wire removal tool should be used if available (**see illustration**).

7   If compressed air is available, use it to blow any dirt or foreign material away from the spark plug hole. A common bicycle pump will also work. The idea here is to eliminate the possibility of debris falling into the cylinder as the spark plug is removed.

8   Place the spark plug socket over the plug and remove it from the engine by turning it in a counterclockwise direction.

9   Compare the spark plug to those shown in the color photos on page 59 to get an indication of the general running condition of the engine.

10   Thread one of the new plugs into the hole until you can no longer turn it with your fingers, then tighten it with a torque wrench (if available) or the ratchet. A good idea is to slip a short length of rubber hose over the end of the plug to use as a tool to thread it into place (**see illustration**). The hose will grip the plug enough to turn it, but will start to slip if the plug begins to cross-thread in the hole — this will prevent damaged threads and the accompanying repair costs.

11   Before pushing the spark plug wire onto the end of the plug, inspect it following the procedures outlined in Section 44.

12   Attach the plug wire to the new spark plug, again using a twisting motion on the boot until it's seated on the spark plug.

13   Repeat the procedure for the remaining spark plugs, replacing them one at a time to prevent mixing up the spark plug wires.

43.5a   Spark plug manufacturers recommend using a wire-type gauge when checking the gap — if the wire does not slide between the electrodes with a slight drag, adjustment is required

43.5b   To change the gap, bend the side electrode only, as indicated by the arrows, and be very careful not to crack or chip the porcelain insulator surrounding the center electrode

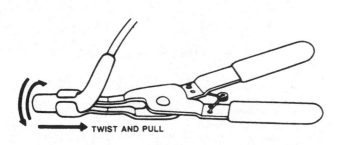

TWIST AND PULL

43.6   When removing a spark plug wire from a spark plug it is important to pull on the end of the boot and not on the wire itself. A slight twisting motion will also help

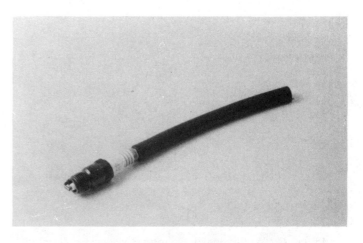

43.10   A length of 3/16-in ID rubber hose will save time and prevent damaged threads when installing the spark plugs

44 Spark plug wire check and replacement

1   The spark plug wires should be checked at the recommended intervals and whenever new spark plugs are installed in the engine.
2   The wires should be inspected one at a time to prevent mixing up the order, which is essential for proper engine operation.
3   Disconnect the plug wire from one spark plug. To do this, grab the rubber boot, twist slightly and pull the wire free. Do not pull on the wire itself, only on the rubber boot (see illustration 43.6).
4   Check inside the boot for corrosion, which will look like a white crusty powder. Push the wire and boot back onto the end of the spark plug. It should be a tight fit on the plug. If it isn't, remove the wire and use a pair of pliers to carefully crimp the metal connector inside the boot until it fits securely on the end of the spark plug.
5   Using a clean rag, wipe the entire length of the wire to remove any built-up dirt and grease. Once the wire is clean, check for holes, burned areas, cracks and other damage. Don't bend the wire excessively or the conductor inside might break.
6   Disconnect the wire from the distributor cap. A retaining ring at the top of the distributor may have to be removed to free the wires. Again, pull only on the rubber boot. Check for corrosion and a tight

fit in the same manner as the spark plug end. Reattach the wire to the distributor cap.
7   Check the remaining spark plug wires one at a time, making sure they are securely fastened at the distributor and the spark plug when the check is complete.
8   If new spark plug wires are required, purchase a new set for your specific engine model. Wire sets are available pre-cut, with the rubber boots already installed. Remove and replace the wires one at a time to avoid mix-ups in the firing order. The wire routing is extremely important, so be sure to note exactly how each wire is situated before removing it.

45 Distributor cap and rotor check and replacement

Note: *It's common practice to install a new distributor cap and rotor whenever new spark plug wires are installed. On models that have the ignition coil mounted in the cap, the coil will have to be transferred to the new cap.*

Check

Refer to illustrations 45.3a, 45.3b, 45.4, and 45.6a

1   To gain access to the distributor cap, especially on a V6 engine, it may be necessary to remove the air cleaner assembly.
2   Loosen the distributor cap mounting screws (note that the screws have a shoulder so they don't come completely out). On some models, the cap is held in place with latches that look like screws — to release them, push down with a screwdriver and turn them about 1/2-turn. Pull up on the cap, with the wires attached, to separate it from the distributor, then position it to one side.
3   The rotor is now visible on the end of the distributor shaft. Check it carefully for cracks and carbon tracks. Make sure the center terminal spring tension is adequate and look for corrosion and wear on the rotor tip **(see illustrations)**. If in doubt about its condition, replace it with a new one.
4   If replacement is required, detach the rotor from the shaft and install a new one. On some models, the rotor is press fit on the shaft and can be pried or pulled off **(see illustration)**. On other models, the rotor is attached to the distributor shaft with two screws.
5   The rotor is indexed to the shaft so it can only be installed one way. Press fit rotors have an internal key that must line up with a slot in the end of the shaft (or vice versa). Rotors held in place with screws have one square and one round peg on the underside that must fit into holes with the same shape.
6   Check the distributor cap for carbon tracks, cracks and other

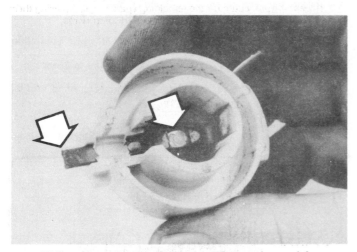

45.3a Check the distributor rotor contact (arrows) for wear and burn marks (later model remote coil-type distributor)

45.3b Carbon tracking on the rotor is caused by a leaking seal between the distributor cap and the ignition coil (always replace both the seal and rotor when this condition is present) (coil in cap-type distributor)

45.4 This type rotor can be pried off the distributor shaft with a screwdriver — other types have two screws which must be removed (be careful not to drop anything down into the distributor)

1

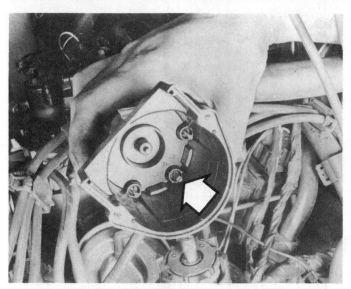

45.6a   Inspect the inside of the cap, especially the metal contacts (arrow) for corrosion and wear

between the brush and rotor will result in rotor burn-through and/or damage to the distributor cap.

Replacement

Conventional distributor

7   On models with a separately mounted ignition coil, simply separate the cap from the distributor and transfer the spark plug wires, one at a time, to the new cap. Be very careful not to mix up the wires!

8   Reattach the cap to the distributor, then tighten the screws or reposition the latches to hold it in place.

Coil-in-cap distributor

Refer to illustration 45.12

9   Use your thumbs to push the spark plug wire retainer latches away from the coil cover.

10   Lift the retainer ring away from the distributor cap with the spark plug wires attached to the ring. It may be necessary to work the wires off the distributor cap towers so they remain with the ring.

11   Disconnect the battery/tachometer/coil electrical connector from the distributor cap.

12   Remove the two coil cover screws and lift off the coil cover.

13   There are three small spade connectors on wires extending from the coil into the electrical connector hood at the side of the distributor cap. Note which terminals the wires are attached to, then use a small screwdriver to push them free.

14   Remove the four coil mounting screws and lift the coil out of the cap.

15   When installing the coil in the new cap, be sure to install a new rubber arc seal in the cap.

16   Install the coil screws, the wires in the connector hood, and the coil cover.

17   Install the cap on the distributor.

18   Plug in the coil electrical connector to the distributor cap.

19   Install the spark plug wire retaining ring on the distributor cap.

damage. Closely examine the terminals on the inside of the cap for excessive corrosion and damage **(see illustrations)**. Slight deposits are normal. Again, if in doubt about the condition of the cap, replace it with a new one. Be sure to apply a small dab of silicone lubricant to each terminal before installing the cap. Also, make sure the carbon brush (center terminal) is correctly installed in the cap — a wide gap

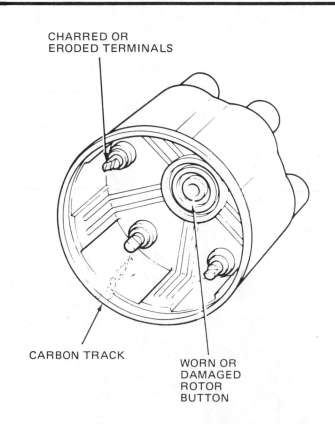

CHARRED OR ERODED TERMINALS

CARBON TRACK

WORN OR DAMAGED ROTOR BUTTON

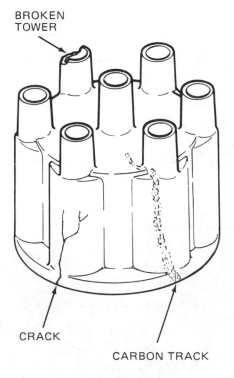

BROKEN TOWER

CRACK

CARBON TRACK

45.6b   Shown here are some of the common defects to look for when inspecting the distributor cap
(if in doubt about its condition, install a new one)

Chapter 2 Part A   Engines

Contents

2A

Specifications

Buick-built V6 engines

Firing order 1-6-5-4-3-2

Camshaft
Journal diameter (all) .... 1.785 to 1.786 in
Lobe lift — compare the readings for each intake and each exhaust valve. Replace the camshaft if readings vary more than 0.003 in.

Torque specifications   **Ft-lbs**
Intake manifold bolts 45
Exhaust manifold-to-cylinder head bolts
  thru 1985 25
  1986 20
  1987 and later 37
Cylinder head bolts
  thru 1985 80
  1986 and later
    step 1 25
    step 2* .... turn 90°
    step 3* .... turn 90°

* Do not exceed 60 ft-lbs. during steps 2 and 3

Rocker arm cover 5
Oil pan 15
Oil pump cover 10
Timing chain cover 20
Flywheel/driveplate 60
Vibration damper-to-crankshaft
  1975 .... 150 min.
  1976 and 1977 .... 175 min.
  1978 thru 1984 225
  1985 and later 200
Rocker arm shaft 30
Rocker arm cover 4

```
        RIGHT BANK
   ┌──────────────────┐
   │  2      4      6  │
   └──────────────────┘

         ◁ FWD

   ┌──────────────────┐
   │  1      3      5  │
   └──────────────────┘
   N7967
        LEFT BANK
```

Cylinder numbering—all V6's
Firing order 1-6-5-4-3-2

Buick-built V8 engines

Firing order   1-8-4-3-6-5-7-2

Camshaft

Journal diameter . . . .   1.785 to 1.786 in

Lobe lift — compare the readings for each intake and each exhaust valve. Replace the camshaft if readings vary more than 0.003 in.

Torque specifications	Ft-lbs
Intake manifold bolts	45
Exhaust manifold-to-cylinder head	25
Cylinder head bolts	
350 cu in	80
455 cu in	100
Flywheel/driveplate	60
Vibration damper-to-crankshaft	
350 cu in	
thru 1972	120
1973 thru 1975	140
1976 and 1977	175
1978 and later	225
455 cu in	
thru 1975	200
1976	225
Oil pan	14
Oil pump cover	10
Rocker arm cover	4
Timing chain cover	30
Rocker arm shaft	30

Cylinder numbering—all V8's
Firing order 1–8–4–3–5–7–2

Chevrolet-built V8 engines

Firing order   1-8-4-3-6-5-7-2

Camshaft

Lobe lift	
intake	
305 cu in	0.2485 in
350 cu in	0.2600 in
exhaust (all)	0.2733 in
Journal diameter	1.8682 to 1.8692 in
Runout — limit	0.0015 in
Endplay	0.004 to 0.014 in

Torque specifications	Ft-lbs
Intake manifold bolts	30
Exhaust manifold-to-cylinder head*	20
Camshaft sprocket bolt	20
Cylinder head bolts	65
Flywheel/driveplate	60
Vibration damper-to-crankshaft	60
Oil pan	10
Oil pump cover screws	8
Rocker arm cover	4
Timing chain cover	7
*Inner exhaust manifold bolts on 350 cu in	30

Oldsmobile-built V8 engines

Firing order   1-8-4-3-6-5-7-2

Camshaft

Journal diameter	
no. 1	2.0357 to 2.0365 in
no. 2	2.0157 to 2.0165 in
no. 3	1.9957 to 1.9965 in
no. 4	1.9757 to 1.9765 in
no. 5	1.9557 to 1.9565 in
Endplay	
thru 1984	0.011 to 0.077 in
1985 and later	0.006 to 0.022 in

Lobe lift – compare the lift readings for each intake and each exhaust valve. Replace the camshaft if readings vary more than 0.003 in. (compare intake valves to intake valves and exhaust valves to exhaust valves).

Note: For engines that lift specifications are not available for, compare the lift readings for each intake and each exhaust valve. Replace the camshaft if readings vary more than 0.003 in.

Torque specifications

	Ft-lbs
Intake manifold bolts*	40
Exhaust manifold-to-cylinder head	25
Cylinder head bolts*	
350 cu in (1977 and later) and 403 cu in	130
all others	85
Driveplate (automatic trans)	60
Flywheel (manual trans)	90
Vibration damper-to-crankshaft	200 to 310
Oil pan bolts	10
Oil pan nuts	17
Oil pump cover screws	8
Rocker arm cover	7
Rocker arm pivot bolt	25
Timing chain cover	35

* lightly oil threads

Pontiac-built V8 engines

Firing order 1-8-4-3-6-5-7-2

Camshaft

Journal diameter (all) .... 1.900 in

Lobe lift – compare the lift readings for each intake and each exhaust valve. Replace the camshaft if readings vary more than 0.003 in. (compare intake valves to intake valves and exhaust valves to exhaust valves).

Torque specifications

	Ft-lbs
Intake manifold bolts	
thru 1976	40
1977 and later	35
Exhaust manifold-to-cylinder head	
thru 1976	30
1977 and later	40
Camshaft sprocket bolt	40
Cylinder head bolts	
1977 301 cu in	85
1977 350 and 400 cu in	100
all others	95
Flywheel/driveplate	95
Vibration damper-to-crankshaft	160
Oil pan	12
Rocker arm cover	6
Rocker arm nuts	20
Timing chain cover	30

1 General information and engine identification

General information

This Part of Chapter 2 is devoted to in-vehicle repair procedures for the engine. All information concerning engine removal and installation and engine block and cylinder head overhaul can be found in Part B of this Chapter.

Since the repair procedures included in this Part are based on the assumption that the engine is still installed in the vehicle, if they are being used during a complete engine overhaul (with the engine already out of the vehicle and on a stand) many of the steps included here will not apply.

The specifications included in this Part of Chapter 2 apply only to the procedures found here. The specifications necessary for rebuilding the block and cylinder heads are included in Part B.

Engine identification
Refer to illustration 1.5

Up until 1977, most engines in GM automobiles were manufactured by the same division that marketed the body. However, since that time, GM automobiles come equipped with various engines, supplied by Oldsmobile, Chevrolet, Buick and Pontiac divisions of General Motors.

On 1972 and newer models, a check of the Vehicle Identification Number (VIN) will quickly determine from which GM plant your car's engine originated. The VIN is stamped onto a small metal plate that is affixed to the car's dashboard. The number gives information concerning the engine, the year of the car, and so on. This metal tag is located on the dashboard in the left hand corner (driver's side), up

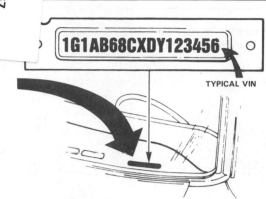

1G1AB68CXDY123456

TYPICAL VIN

1.5 The vehicle Identification Number (VIN) is on a plate attached to the left top of the instrument panel where it can be seen from the outside of the vehicle

against the windshield (see illustration). On 1972 through 1980 models, the fifth digit of the VIN is the number that tells the origin of the engine. On 1981 and newer models, the eighth digit of the VIN tells the origin of the engine. Refer to the accompanying chart to determine which engine you have. 1970 through 1976 models used engines built by the same division which marketed the body.

There are some differences between the various makes of engines but overall, repair and maintenance procedures are nearly identical. Where differences occur, they will be noted. A check of the Specifications chart at the beginning of this Chapter will alert the home mechanic to any differences in the various tolerances. Also check the Vehicle Emission Control Information label, located adjacent to the radiator, for additional engine information.

GM ENGINE IDENTIFICATION – 1977 and later

VIN CODE	ENGINE TYPE	CUBIC INCHES	LITERS	BUILT BY*
A,C,2	V6	231	3.8	B
4	V6	252	4.1	B
2	V6	260	4.3	C
F,8	V8	260	4.3	O
Y (through 1979), W	V8	301	4.9	P
U, H (1978–on)	V8	305	5.0	C
7	V8	350	5.7	C
Y (1980–on), 9	V8	307	5.0	O
X,J,H (1977 only)	V8	350	5.7	B
G,L	V8	350	5.7	C
P	V8	350	5.7	P
R	V8	350	5.7	O
E	V8	305	5.0	C
Z	V8	400	6.6	P
K	V8	403	6.6	O

*B = Buick C = Chevrolet O = Oldsmobile P = Pontiac

2 Repair operations possible with the engine in the vehicle

Many major repair operations can be accomplished without removing the engine from the vehicle.

Clean the engine compartment and the exterior of the engine with some type of pressure washer before any work is done. A clean engine will make the job easier and will help keep dirt out of the internal areas of the engine.

Depending on the components involved, it may be a good idea to remove the hood to improve access to the engine as repairs are performed (refer to Chapter 11 if necessary).

If oil or coolant leaks develop, indicating a need for gasket or seal replacement, the repairs can generally be made with the engine in the vehicle. The oil pan gasket, the cylinder head gaskets, intake and exhaust manifold gaskets, timing cover gaskets and the crankshaft oil seals are accessible with the engine in place.

Exterior engine components, such as the water pump, the starter motor, the alternator, the distributor and the fuel system components, as well as the intake and exhaust manifolds, can be removed for repair

with the engine in place.

Since the cylinder heads can be removed without pulling the engine, valve component servicing can also be accomplished with the engine in the vehicle.

Replacement of, repairs to, or inspection of the timing chain and sprockets, camshaft and the oil pump are all possible with the engine in place.

In extreme cases, caused by a lack of necessary equipment, repair or replacement of piston rings, pistons, connecting rods and rod bearings is possible with the engine in the vehicle. However, this practice is not recommended because of the cleaning and preparation work that must be performed on the components involved.

3 Top Dead Center (TDC) for number one piston — locating

Refer to illustrations 3.6 and 3.7

1 Top Dead Center (TDC) is the highest point in the cylinder that each piston reaches as it travels up and down when the crankshaft turns. Each piston reaches TDC on the compression stroke and again on the exhaust stroke, but TDC generally refers to piston position on the compression stroke. The timing marks on the vibration damper installed on the front of the crankshaft are referenced to the number one piston at TDC on the compression stroke.

2 Positioning the piston(s) at TDC is an essential part of many procedures such as rocker arm removal, valve adjustment, timing chain and sprocket replacement and distributor removal.

3 In order to bring any piston to TDC, the crankshaft must be turned using one of the methods outlined below. When looking at the front of the engine, normal crankshaft rotation is *clockwise*. **Warning:** *Before beginning this procedure, be sure to place the transmission in Neutral and unplug the wire connector at the distributor to disable the ignition system (electronic ignition) or remove the center wire from the distributor cap and ground it (conventional ignition).*

a) The preferred method is to turn the crankshaft with a large socket and breaker bar attached to the vibration damper bolt threaded into the front of the crankshaft.

b) A remote starter switch, which may save some time, can also be used. Attach the switch leads to the S (switch) and B (battery) terminals on the starter motor. Once the piston is close to TDC, use a socket and breaker bar as described in the previous paragraph.

c) If an assistant is available to turn the ignition switch to the Start position in short bursts, you can get the piston close to TDC without a remote starter switch. Use a socket and breaker bar as described in paragraph a) to complete the procedure.

4 Make a mark on the distributor housing directly below the number one spark plug wire terminal on the distributor cap. **Note:** *The terminal numbers may be be marked on the spark plug wires near the distributor.*

5 Remove the distributor cap as described in Chapter 1.

6 Turn the crankshaft (see paragraph 3 above) until the line on the vibration damper is aligned with the zero mark on the timing plate (**see illustration**). The timing plate and vibration damper are located low on

3.6 Turn the crankshaft until the line on the vibration damper is directly opposite the zero mark on the timing plate as shown here.

the front of the engine, near the pulley that turns the drivebelt.

7   The rotor should now be pointing directly at the mark on the distributor housing (**see illustration**). If it isn't, the piston may be at TDC on the exhaust stroke, so follow Step 8.

8   To get the piston to TDC on the compression stroke, turn the crankshaft one complete turn (360°) clockwise. The rotor should now be pointing at the mark. When the rotor is pointing at the number one spark plug wire terminal in the distributor cap (which is indicated by the mark on the housing) and the ignition timing marks are aligned, the number one piston is at TDC on the compression stroke.

9   After the number one piston has been positioned at TDC on the compression stroke, TDC for any of the remaining cylinders can be located by turning the crankshaft 120° at a time for V6 engines or 90° for V8 engines and following the firing order (refer to the Specifications).

4   Rocker arm covers — removal and installation

Refer to illustrations 4.7 and 4.9

1   Disconnect the negative cable from the battery.

2   Remove the air cleaner assembly.

3   Label and disconnect any emissions or vacuum lines and wires which are routed over the rocker arm cover(s).

4   Remove any braces or brackets which block access to the cover(s), noting the way they are mounted to ease reassembly.

5   Detach any remaining accessories as necessary. If removal of the air conditioning compressor is required, unbolt the unit and carefully set it aside without disconnecting the refrigerant lines. **Warning:** *The air conditioning system is under high pressure. Do not disconnect any refrigerant line or fitting without first having the system discharged by an air conditioning technician.*

6   Remove the rocker arm cover attaching bolts, along with any spark plug wire looms and hardware.

7   Remove the rocker arm cover (**see illustration**). **Caution:** *Do not pry on the sealing flange. To do so may damage the surface, causing oil leaks. Tap on the sides of the cover with a rubber hammer until it pops loose.*

8   Thoroughly clean the mating surfaces, removing all traces of old gasket material. Use acetone or lacquer thinner and a clean rag to remove any traces of oil.

9   Prepare the cover for installation by applying a continuous bead of RTV sealer (**see illustration**) or a new gasket to the sealing flange. Use the same sealing method the vehicle had, otherwise new bolts

3.7   The rotor tip should point to the mark on the distributor housing

of a different length may be required.

10   Install the cover(s) and bolts and tighten them securely. Do not overtighten them, as the covers may be deformed.

11   Reinstall the remaining parts in the reverse order of removal.

12   Run the engine and check for leaks.

5   Rocker arms and pushrods — removal, inspection and installation

Removal

Refer to illustrations 5.3a, 5.3b, 5.3c and 5.4

1   Refer to Section 4 and detach the rocker arm cover(s) from the cylinder head(s).

2   Remove each of the rocker arm nuts (Chevrolet and Pontiac engines), or bolts (Olds engines). Place them at their correct location in a carboard box or rack. Buick rocker arms and shafts can be removed as a unit once the retaining bolts are removed. **Note:** *On Chevrolet and Pontiac built engines, if the pushrods are the only items being removed, loosen each nut just enough to allow the rocker arms to be rotated to the side so the pushrods can be lifted out.*

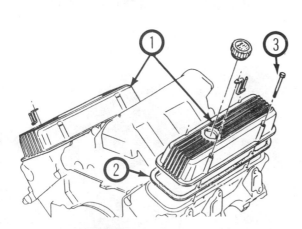

4.7   Typical rocker arm covers — exploded view

1   Rocker arm covers
2   Rocker arm cover gasket
3   Hold-down bolt

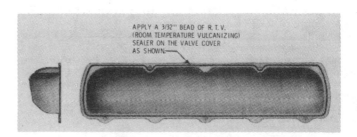

APPLY A 3/32" BEAD OF R.T.V.
(ROOM TEMPERATURE VULCANIZING)
SEALER ON THE VALVE COVER
AS SHOWN

4.9   If your engine had RTV sealer, apply a bead inside of the bolt holes as shown

3   Remove each rocker arm assembly, placing each component on the numbered box or rack. Buick rocker arms are held in place on the shaft with plastic retainers which can be pried out of place with pliers (see illustration). Small pieces of the retainer may break off inside the rocker arm shafts; be sure to remove them during the cleaning process.

4   Remove the pushrods and store them separately to make sure they don't get mixed up during installation (see illustration).

Inspection

5   Check each rocker arm for wear, cracks and other damage, especially where the pushrods and valve stems contact the rocker arm faces.

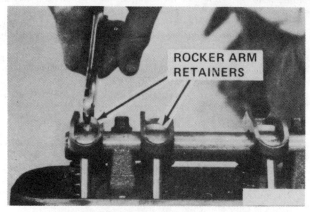

5.3a   Removing nylon retainer — Buick

5.3b   Position of service rocker arms on shaft — Buick V6

6   Make sure the hole at the pushrod end of each rocker arm is open.

7   Check each rocker arm pivot area for wear, cracks and galling. If the rocker arms are worn or damaged, replace them with new ones and use new pivot balls as well.

8   Inspect the pushrods for cracks and excessive wear at the ends. Roll each pushrod across a piece of plate glass to see if it's bent (if it wobbles, it's bent).

Installation

9   Lubricate the lower end of each pushrod with clean engine oil or moly-base grease and install them in their original locations. Make sure each pushrod seats completely in the lifter.

10 Apply moly-base grease to the ends of the valve stems and the upper ends of the pushrods before positioning the rocker arms over the studs.

11 Set the rocker arms in place, then install the pivot balls (except engines with rocker shafts) and nuts. Apply moly-base grease to the pivot balls or shafts to prevent damage to the mating surfaces before engine oil pressure builds up. Be sure to install each nut with the **flat** side against the pivot ball.

Valve adjustment

Chevrolet-built V8 engines

Refer to illustration 5.13

12 Refer to Section 3 and bring the number one piston to top dead center on the compression stroke.

13 Tighten the rocker arm nuts (number one cylinder only) until all play is removed at the pushrods. This can be determined by rotating each pushrod between your thumb and index finger as the nut is tightened (see illustration). You'll be able to feel the point at which all play is eliminated because the pushrod will no longer turn.

14 Tighten each nut an additional one full turn (360°) to center the lifters. Valve adjustment for cylinder number one is now complete.

5.3c   Position of service rocker arms on shaft — Buick V8

5.4   A perforated cardboard box can be used to store the pushrods to ensure that they are reinstalled in their original locations — note the label indicating the front of the engine

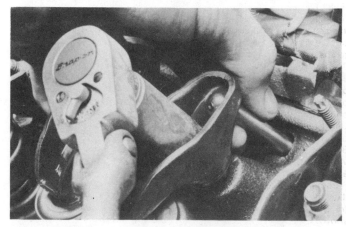

5.13   Rotate each pushrod as the rocker arm nut is tightened to determine the point at which all play is removed, then tighten each nut an additional one full turn

15 Turn the crankshaft 90° in the normal direction of rotation until the next piston in the firing order (number eight) is at TDC on the compression stroke. The distributor rotor should be pointing in the direction of terminal number eight on the cap (see Section 3 for additional information).

16 Repeat the procedure described in paragraphs 13 and 14 for the number eight cylinder valves.

17 Turn the crankshaft another 90° and adjust the number four cylinder valves. Continue turning the crankshaft 90° at a time and adjust both valves for each cylinder before proceeding. Follow the firing order sequence — a cylinder number illustration is also included — in the Specifications.

18 Refer to Section 4 and install the rocker arm covers. Start the engine, listen for unusual valvetrain noises and check for oil leaks at the rocker arm cover joints.

All other engines

19 These valves cannot be adjusted. If the clearance is excessive in the valve train, check that the pivot bolt is tightened to the proper torque Specification (or the nylon retainer is seated). Then inspect for worn components.

---

6 Valve spring, retainer and seals — replacement in vehicle

Refer to illustrations 6.8 and 6.16

Note: *Broken valve springs and defective valve stem seals can be replaced without removing the cylinder heads. Two special tools and a compressed air source are normally required to perform this operation, so read through this Section carefully and rent or buy the tools before beginning the job. If compressed air isn't available, a length of nylon rope can be used to keep the valves from falling into the cylinder during this procedure.*

1 Refer to Section 4 and remove the rocker arm cover from the affected cylinder head. If all of the valve stem seals are being replaced, remove both rocker arm covers.

2 Remove the spark plug from the cylinder which has the defective component. If all of the valve stem seals are being replaced, all of the spark plugs should be removed.

3 Turn the crankshaft until the piston in the affected cylinder is at top dead center on the compression stroke (refer to Section 3 for instructions). If you are replacing all of the valve stem seals, begin with cylinder number one and work on the valves for one cylinder at a time. Move from cylinder to cylinder following the firing order sequence (see specifications).

4 Thread an adapter into the spark plug hole and connect an air hose from a compressed air source to it. Most auto parts stores can supply the air hose adapter. **Note:** *Many cylinder compression gauges utilize a screw-in fitting that may work with your air hose quick-disconnect fitting.*

5 Remove the rocker arm(s) for the valve with the defective part and pull out the pushrod. If all of the valve stem seals are being replaced, all of the rocker arms and pushrods should be removed (refer to Section 5).

6 Apply compressed air to the cylinder. The valves should be held in place by the air pressure. If the valve faces or seats are in poor condition, leaks may prevent air pressure from retaining the valves — refer to the alternative procedure below.

7 If you don't have access to compressed air, an alternative method can be used. Position the piston at a point just before TDC on the compression stroke, then feed a long piece of nylon rope through the spark plug hole until it fills the combustion chamber. Be sure to leave the end of the rope hanging out of the engine so it can be removed easily. Use a large breaker bar and socket to rotate the crankshaft in the normal direction of rotation until **slight** resistance is felt.

8 Stuff shop rags into the cylinder head holes above and below the valves to prevent parts and tools from falling into the engine, then use a valve spring compressor to compress the spring/damper assembly. Remove the keepers with small needle-nose pliers or a magnet (**see illustration**). **Note:** *A couple of different types of tools are available for compressing the valve springs with the head in place. One type, shown here, grips the lower spring coils and presses on the retainer as the knob is turned, while the other type utilizes the rocker arm stud and nut for leverage. Both types work very well, although the lever type is usually less expensive and won't work on all cylinders of engines*

with rocker shafts.

9 Remove the spring retainer or rotator, oil shield and valve spring assembly, then remove the valve stem O-ring seal and the umbrella-type guide seal (the O-ring seal will most likely be hardened and will probably break when removed, so plan on installing a new one each time the original is removed). **Note:** *If air pressure fails to hold the valve in the closed position during this operation, the valve face and/or seat is probably damaged. If so, the cylinder head will have to be removed for additional repair operations.*

10 Wrap a rubber band or tape around the top of the valve stem so the valve won't fall into the combustion chamber, then release the air pressure. **Note:** *If a rope was used instead of air pressure, turn the crankshaft slightly in the direction opposite normal rotation.*

11 Inspect the valve stem for damage. Rotate the valve in the guide and check the end for eccentric movement, which would indicate that the valve is bent.

12 Move the valve up and down in the guide and make sure it doesn't bind. If the valve stem binds, either the valve is bent or the guide is damaged. In either case, the head will have to be removed for repair.

13 Reapply air pressure to the cylinder to retain the valve in the closed position, then remove the tape or rubber band from the valve stem. If a rope was used instead of air pressure, rotate the crankshaft in the normal direction of rotation until **slight** resistance is felt.

14 Lubricate the valve stem with engine oil and install a new umbrella-type guide seal.

15 Install the spring/damper assembly and shield in position over the valve.

16 Install the valve spring retainer or rotator. Compress the valve spring assembly and carefully install the new O-ring seal in the lower groove of the valve stem. Make sure the seal isn't twisted — it must lie perfectly flat in the groove (**see illustration**).

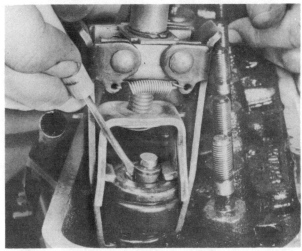

6.8 Once the spring is depressed, the keepers can be removed with a small magnet or needle-nose pliers (a magnet is preferred to prevent dropping the keepers)

6.16 Make sure the O-ring seal under the retainer is seated in the groove and not twisted before installing the keepers

2A

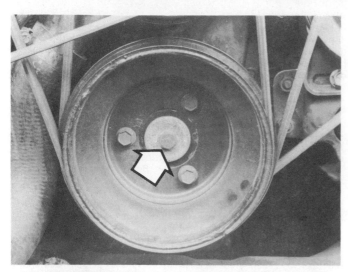

7.5a   The vibration damper bolt (arrow) is usually very tight, so use a six-point socket and a breaker bar to loosen it (the three other bolts hold the pulley to the vibration damper)

7.5b   Have an assistant hold a large screwdriver or pry bar against the ring gear

7.6   Use the recommended puller to remove the vibration damper — if a puller that applies force to the outer edge is used, the damper will be damaged!

17 Position the keepers in the upper groove. Apply a small dab of grease to the inside of each keeper to hold it in place if necessary. Remove the pressure from the spring tool and make sure the keepers are seated. Refer to Chapter 2, Part B, Section 11 and check the seals with a vacuum pump.

18 Disconnect the air hose and remove the adapter from the spark plug hole. If a rope was used in place of air pressure, pull it out of the cylinder.

19 Refer to Section 5 and install the rocker arm(s) and pushrod(s).

20 Install the spark plug(s) and hook up the wire(s).

21 Refer to Section 4 and install the rocker arm cover(s).

22 Start and run the engine, then check for oil leaks and unusual sounds coming from the rocker arm cover area.

7   Vibration damper — removal and installation

Refer to illustrations 7.5a, 7.5b, 7.6 and 7.7

1   Disconnect the negative cable from the battery.

2   Remove the fan shroud and fan assembly (Chapter 3).

3   Remove the drivebelts (Chapter 1).

4   Remove the pulley retaining bolts and detach the pulleys. **Caution:** *Before removing the pulleys, mark the location of each one in relation to the vibration damper in order to retain proper timing mark orientation during installation.*

5   Raise the vehicle and support it securely on jackstands. Remove the lower bellhousing cover. Wedge a pry bar between the flywheel/driveplate teeth to prevent the crankshaft from turning while loosening the large vibration damper bolt **(see illustrations)**.

6   Leave the damper bolt in place (with several threads still engaged), to provide the gear puller with something to push against. Use a puller to remove the damper **(see illustration)**. **Caution:** *Don't use a puller with jaws that grip the outer edge of the damper! The puller must be the type shown in the illustration that utilizes bolts to apply force to the damper hub only.*

7   To install the damper apply a dab of grease to the seal lips, position the damper on the nose of the crankshaft, align the keyway and start it onto the crankshaft with a special installation tool **(see illustration)**. Install the bolt. Tighten the bolt to the specified torque.

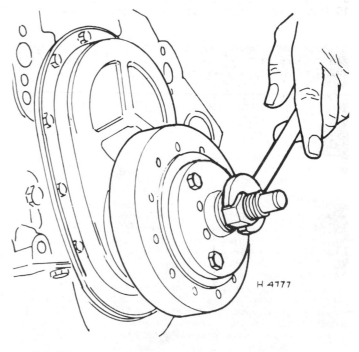

7.7   Using a special tool to push the vibration damper onto the crankshaft

8   The remaining installation steps are the reverse of the removal procedure.

8   Front crankshaft oil seal — replacement

Neoprene-type seals

Timing cover in place

1   Remove the vibration damper as described in Section 7.
2   Carefully pry the seal out of the cover with a seal removal tool or a large screwdriver. Be careful not to distort the cover or scratch the wall of the seal bore. If the engine has accumulated a lot of miles, apply penetrating oil to the seal-to-cover joint and allow it to soak in before attempting to pull the seal out.
3   Clean the bore to remove any old seal material and corrosion. Position the new seal in the bore with the open end of the seal facing IN. A small amount of oil applied to the outer edge of the new seal will make installation easier — don't overdo it!
4   Drive the seal into the bore with a large socket and hammer until it's completely seated. Select a socket that's the same outside diameter as the seal (a section of pipe can be used if a socket isn't available).
5   Reinstall the vibration damper.

Timing cover removed

Refer to illustration 8.6

6   Use a punch or screwdriver and hammer to drive the seal out of the cover from the back side. Support the cover as close to the seal bore as possible **(see illustration)**. Be careful not to distort the cover or scratch the wall of the seal bore. If the engine has accumulated a lot of miles, apply penetrating oil to the seal-to-cover joint on each side and allow it to soak in before attempting to drive the seal out.
7   Clean the bore to remove any old seal material and corrosion. Support the cover on blocks of wood and position the new seal in the bore with the open end of the seal facing IN. A small amount of oil applied to the outer edge of the new seal will make installation easier — don't overdo it!
8   Drive the seal into the bore with a large socket and hammer until it's completely seated. Select a socket that's the same outside diameter as the seal (a section of pipe can be used if a socket isn't available).

Braided-rope type seals

9   Remove the timing chain cover (see Section 12).
10 Using a punch, drive the old seal and shedder out the back of the timing chain cover.
11 Coil new seal packing around the opening so the ends of the packing are at the top. Drive the shedder in with a punch. Stake the shedder in place in at least three places.
12 Size the packing by rotating a hammer handle or similar tool around the packing until the damper hub can be inserted through the opening.
13 Lubricate the seal and install the vibration damper as described in Section 7.

9   Intake manifold — removal and installation

Refer to illustrations 9.9 and 9.14

1   Place protective covers on the fenders and disconnect the negative cable from the battery.
2   Drain the cooling system (see Chapter 1).
3   Remove the air cleaner assembly.
4   Detach all coolant hoses from the intake manifold.
5   Label and then disconnect any wiring and vacuum, emission and/or fuel lines which attach to the intake manifold.
6   Remove the EGR valve, if necessary (see Chapter 6).
7   On engines with the distributor mounted through the manifold, remove the distributor (see Chapter 5).
8   Remove the carburetor (see Chapter 4).
9   Remove the intake manifold bolts **(see illustration)** and any brackets, noting their locations, so they may be reinstalled in the same location.
10 Lift off the manifold. If it is difficult to break loose, carefully pry against a casting protrusion. **Caution:** *Do not pry against a sealing surface.* **Note:** *If your engine has a valley cover under the intake manifold, this must be removed to access the valve lifters. Unbolt the cover and lift it out.*
11 Stuff rags in the exposed ports and passages. Thoroughly clean all sealing surfaces, removing all traces of gasket material. Check the exhaust crossover passages below the carburetor for carbon blockage.
12 Position new gaskets and seals into place, using RTV sealer in the corners and to hold them in place. Use plastic gasket retainers, if provided. Follow the gasket manufacturer's instructions. On Pontiac-built engines, install a new seal ring between the intake manifold and the water pump housing.
13 Set the manifold into position. Be sure all the bolt holes are lined up and start all the bolts by hand before tightening any. On Pontiac-built engines, tighten the timing cover-to-manifold bolt first.

2A

8.6 While supporting the cover near the seal bore, drive the old seal out from the inside with a hammer and punch or screwdriver

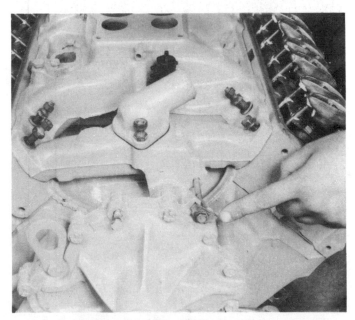

9.9 Pontiac-manufactured engines use a bolt to mate the intake manifold to the front cover

14 Tighten the bolts in three stages, following the appropriate sequence **(see illustration)** until the specified torque is reached.

15 The remainder of installation is the reverse of removal. Be sure to refill the cooling system and change the oil and filter (see Chapter 1), as coolant often gets into the oil during manifold removal.

16 Run the engine and check for fluid and vacuum leaks. Adjust the ignition timing, if the distributor was disturbed (see Chapter 1). Road test the vehicle, checking for proper operation of engine and accessories.

10 Exhaust manifolds — removal and installation

Refer to illustrations 10.7a, 10.7b, 10.11 and 10.14

1 Allow the engine to cool completely.
2 Place protective covers on the fenders.
3 Disconnect the negative cable from the battery.
4 Raise the vehicle and support it securely on jackstands.

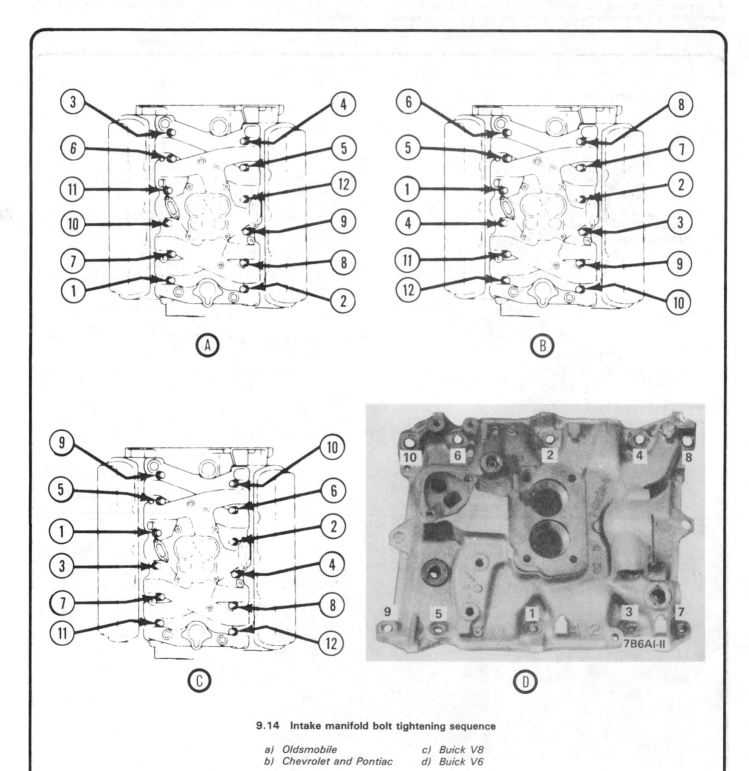

9.14 Intake manifold bolt tightening sequence

a) *Oldsmobile*   c) *Buick V8*
b) *Chevrolet and Pontiac*   d) *Buick V6*

5   Spray penetrating oil on the threads of fasteners holding the hot air shrouds and the exhaust pipe(s) to the manifold(s) you wish to remove. Go on to the next steps, allowing the penetrating oil to soak in.

6   Remove the air cleaner and hot air duct.

7   Detach the hot air shroud(s) or heat stove assembly from the manifold (see illustrations).

8   Label and then remove spark plug and oxygen sensor wires and any hoses such as EFE or AIR, as needed.

9   Unbolt any engine accessories which block access to the manifold(s) such as the alternator, air conditioning compressor or power steering pump. Refer to the appropriate Chapters (5, 3, 10) for further information. When unbolting the air conditioning compressor, leave the refrigerant lines connected and tie the compressor aside without putting a strain on the fittings. **Warning:** *Do not disconnect any air conditioning line or fitting unless the system pressure has been discharged by a qualified A/C specialist.*

10 Remove the manifold-to-exhaust pipe fasteners. **Note:** *On some models it may be necessary to remove the starter (see Chapter 5), the lower bellhousing cover, and/or a front wheel for access to the manifolds.*

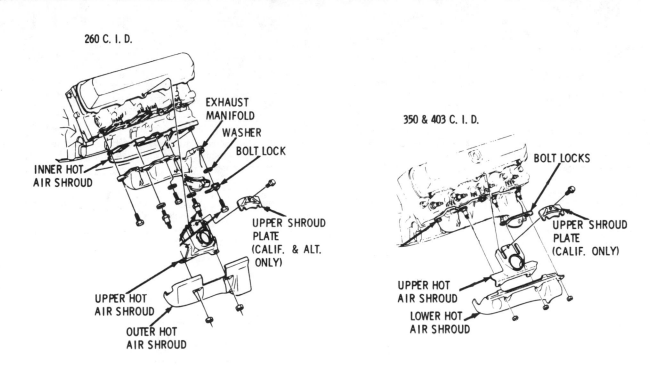

10.7a   Typical hot air shrouds (260, 350, 403 cubic inch shown)

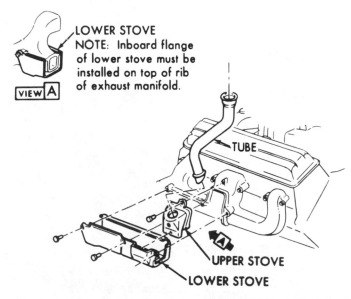

10.7b   A typical carburetor heat stove assembly (305 engine shown)

10.11   The spark plug heat shields are held in place by bolts located under the exhaust manifold (Chevrolet-built engine)

10.14   The exhaust manifold gaskets are held in place with sealant as the manifold is installed

11   Bend back any lock tabs from the manifold bolt heads and remove the bolts and any spark plug heat shields (see illustration), noting their types and locations for reassembly.

12   Remove the manifold(s) from the engine compartment.

13   Thoroughly clean and inspect the sealing surfaces, removing all traces of old gasket material. Look for cracks and damaged threads. If the gasket was leaking, take the manifold to an automotive machine shop to inspect/correct for warpage.

14   If replacing the manifold, transfer all parts to the new unit. Using new gaskets (when equipped), install the manifold (see illustration) and start the bolts by hand.

15   Working from the center outward, tighten the bolts to the specified torque. Bend the lock tabs (if equipped) against the bolt heads.

16   Reinstall the remaining components in the reverse order of removal.

17   Run the engine and check for exhaust leaks.

11   Cylinder heads — removal and installation

Refer to illustrations 11.7, 11.8 and 11.14

Caution: *The engine must be completely cool when the heads are removed. Failure to allow the engine to cool off could result in head warpage.*

Removal

1   Remove the intake manifold (see Section 9).

2   Remove the rocker arm cover(s) as described in Section 4.

3   Remove the rocker arms and pushrods (see Section 5). **Note:** *If any pushrods or head bolts cannot be removed because of interference with components such as the vacuum brake booster, lift them up as far as possible and wrap a rubber band around them to keep them from dropping during head removal. Be sure to do the same during installation.*

4   Remove the exhaust manifolds (see Section 10).

5   Unbolt the engine accessories and brackets as necessary and set them aside. See Chapter 5 for alternator removal. When removing a power steering pump (Chapter 10), leave the hoses attached and secure the unit in an upright position. Refrigerant lines should remain attached to air conditioning compressors (see Chapter 3). **Warning:** *The air conditioning system is under high pressure. Do not loosen any hose or fitting until the refrigerant gas has been discharged by an auto air conditioning technician.*

6   Recheck to be sure nothing is still connected to the head(s) you intend to remove. Remove anything which is still attached.

7   Using a new gasket, outline the cylinders and bolt pattern on a piece of cardboard (see illustration). Be sure to indicate the front of the engine for reference. Punch holes at the bolt locations.

8   Loosen the head bolts in 1/4-turn increments until they can be

removed by hand. Work from bolt to bolt in a pattern that's the reverse of the tightening sequence (see illustration). Store the bolts in the cardboard holder as they are removed; this will insure that the bolts are reinstalled in their original holes.

9   Lift the head(s) off the engine. If excessive resistance is felt, do not pry between the head and block as damage to the mating surfaces may result. To dislodge the head, place a block of wood against the end of it and strike the wood with a hammer. Store the head(s) on their sides to prevent damage to the gasket surface.

10   Cylinder head disassembly and inspection procedures are covered in detail in Chapter 2, Part B.

11   Use a gasket scraper to remove all traces of carbon and old gasket material, then clean the mating surfaces with lacquer thinner or acetone. If there's oil on the mating surfaces when the heads are installed, the gaskets may not seal properly and leaks may develop. When working on the block, cover the lifter valley with shop rags to keep out debris. Use a vacuum cleaner to remove any debris that falls into the cylinders.

12   Check the block and head mating surfaces for nicks, deep scratches and other damage. If damage is slight, it can be removed with a file. If the gasket seemed to be leaking, have the head(s) checked for cracks and warpage by an automotive machine shop. Surface damage or warpage can usually be corrected by machining. Cracks normally require replacement. Cracks normally require replacement.

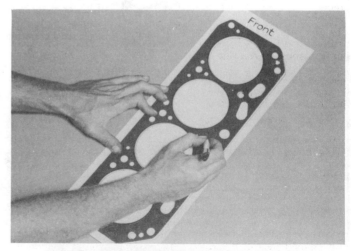

11.7   To avoid mixing up the head bolts, use a new gasket to transfer the bolt hole pattern to a piece of cardboard, then punch holes to accept the bolts

V6 prior to 1985

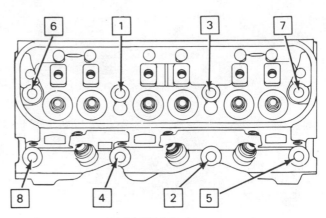

V6 1985 and newer

2A

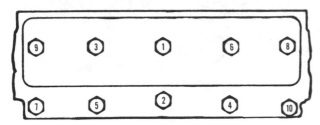

Buick V8

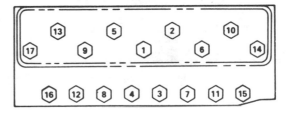

Pontiac V8

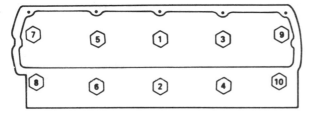

Oldsmobile V8

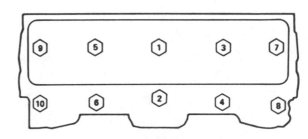

Chevrolet V8

11.8 Cylinder head bolt tightening sequence

Installation

13 Use a tap of the correct size to chase the threads in the head bolt holes. Mount each bolt in a vise and run a die down the threads to remove any corrosion and restore the threads. Dirt, corrosion, sealant and damaged threads will affect torque readings.

14 If an all-metal gasket is used, apply a thin, even coat of sealant such as K & W Copper Coat to both sides prior to installation. Metal gaskets must be installed with the raised bead UP **(see illustration)**. Most gaskets have ''This side up'' stamped into them. Composition gaskets must be installed dry — don't use sealant. Follow the gasket manufacturer's instructions, if available. Position a new gasket over the dowel pins in the block.

15 Carefully position the head on the block without denting or disturbing the gasket.

16 Be sure the head bolt holes are clean. On V6, 301 cubic inch and all Chevrolet-built engines covered by this manual, apply non-hardening sealant such as Permatex no. 2 to the head bolt threads. Apply a light coating of engine oil to the head bolts of the other engines (Buick, Olds and Pontiac V8's).

17 Install the bolts in their original locations and tighten them finger tight. Follow the recommended sequence and tighten the bolts in several steps to the specified torque.

18 The remaining installation steps are the reverse order of removal. Check the index for the appropriate Sections for installation of the various components.

19 Add coolant, change the oil and filter (see Chapter 1), then start the engine and check carefully for leaks.

11.14 Steel gaskets must be installed with the raised bead (arrow) facing UP

12.7a Timing chain cover removal and installation

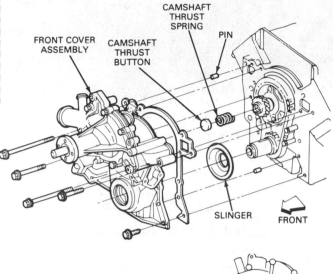

12.7b Timing chain cover components — V6

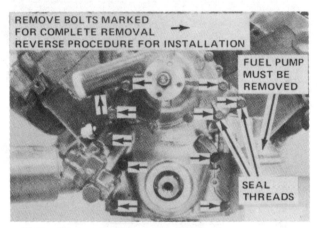

12.7c Timing chain cover bolt locations — 350 Buick-built engines

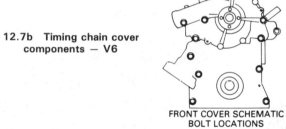

FRONT COVER SCHEMATIC BOLT LOCATIONS

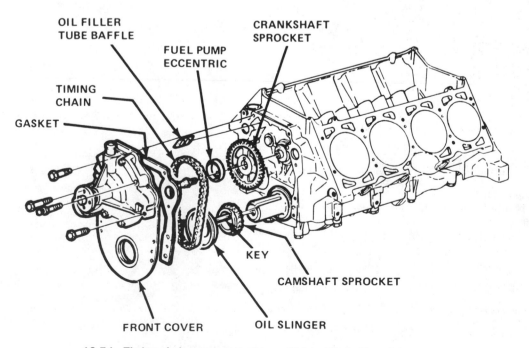

12.7d Timing chain cover assembly — Oldsmobile-built engines

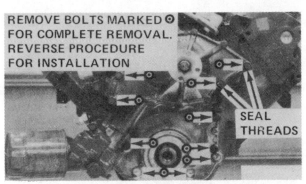

12.7e Timing chain cover bolt locations — 455 Buick-built engines

12.8 Dowel pin chamfer

12.7f A putty knife or screwdriver can be used to break the timing chain cover-to-block seal, but be careful when prying it off as damage to the cover may result

12.9 On Pontiac and Oldsmobile engines, remove the fuel pump eccentric by unscrewing the bolt in the end of the camshaft

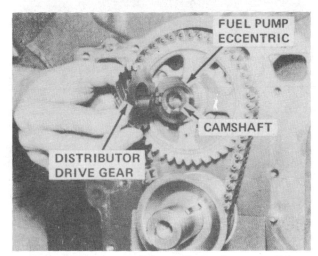

12.10 Note the way the gear fits on for reassembly (Buick engines)

12 Timing cover, chain and sprockets

Refer to illustrations 12.7a, 12.7b, 12.7c, 12.7d, 12.7e, 12.7f, 12.8, 12.9, 12.10, 12.11, 12.12a, 12.12b and 12.13

Removal

1 Disconnect the negative cable from the battery.
2 *If equipped with a Buick engine,* remove the alternator and brackets as well as the distributor (Chapter 5).
3 Drain the cooling system and disconnect the radiator hoses, heater hose (where applicable) and the small by-pass hose *(except Chevrolet engine).*
4 Remove the top radiator support, the fan shroud, the fan and pulley and the radiator (Chapter 3).
5 Remove the crankshaft drive pulley and the vibration damper (see Section 7).
6 *If equipped with a Chevrolet engine,* remove the water pump (Chapter 3). *If equipped with a Pontiac or Buick engine,* remove the

fuel pump. Unbolt and set aside any engine accessories which are in the way without disconnecting the hoses. Refer to the appropriate Chapters for further information.
7 Remove the nuts and bolts that attach the cover to the engine, then pull the cover free **(see illustrations)**. Pontiac and Buick engines have bolts attaching the oil pan to the cover (Pontiac engines also have a bolt that threads into the intake manifold). Remove the camshaft thrust spring and button, on vehicles so equipped.
8 Using vise-grip pliers, pull the dowel pins (if equipped) out of the engine block. Grind a chamfer on one end of each pin **(see illustration)**. Thoroughly clean all gasket mating surfaces (do not allow the old gasket material to fall into the oil pan), then wipe them with a cloth soaked in solvent.
9 *On Oldsmobile and Pontiac engines,* remove the fuel pump drive eccentric by unscrewing the bolt from the end of the camshaft **(see illustration)**.
10 Some Buick engines have a distributor drive gear mounted in front of the fuel pump eccentric (when removing them, note how they are aligned with each other and the camshaft) **(see illustration)**.

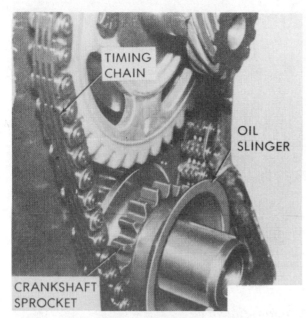

12.11   Oil slinger installation — typical

12.12a   On Buick-built V6 and V8 engines, the camshaft timing mark should be at the bottom (6 O'clock position) and the crankshaft mark at the top (12 O'clock position)

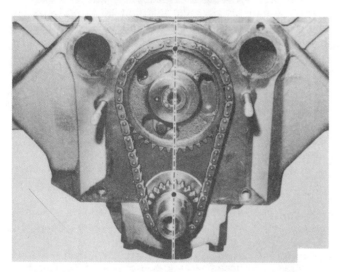

12.12b   On Chevrolet, Oldsmobile and Pontiac-built engines, both timing marks should be at the top (12 O'clock position)

12.13   Remove the three bolts from the end of the camshaft (arrows) — Chevrolet-built engine shown

11   *On Buick and Oldsmobile engines,* slide the oil slinger off of the end of the crankshaft (see illustration).

12   Turn the crankshaft until the marks on the camshaft and crankshaft sprockets are perfectly aligned (see illustrations). DO NOT attempt to remove either sprocket or the chain until this is done. Also, do not turn the camshaft or the cramkshaft after the sprockets are removed.

13   *On Chevrolet engines and 455 CID Buick engines,* remove the bolts that attach the sprocket to the end of the camshaft (see illustration). Also, on 455 CID Buick engines, the oil pan must be removed in order to slide the sprocket off of the crankshaft (see Section 14).

14   Generally speaking, the camshaft sprocket, the crankshaft sprocket and the timing chain can be slipped off the shafts together. If resistance is encountered, it may be necessary to use two screwdrivers to carefully pry the sprockets off of the shafts. If extreme resistance is encountered (which may happen with the crankshaft sprocket), a gear puller will be required. It should be noted that on Oldsmobile engines, the key that indexes the sprocket to the crankshaft must be removed before sliding or pulling the sprocket off of the shaft. On models with spring loaded timing chain dampers, hold the damper back as you slip the chain off.

15   If the crankshaft and the camshaft are not disturbed while the tim-ing chain and sprockets are out of place, then installation can begin with Step 18. If the engine is completely dismantled, or if the crankshaft or camshaft are disturbed while the timing chain is off, then the No. 1 piston must be positioned at TDC before the timing chain and sprockets are installed.

16   Align the hole in the camshaft sprocket with the dowel pin in the end of the camshaft, then slip the sprocket onto the end of the camshaft. *On Buick engines,* turn the camshaft until the timing mark on the sprocket is pointed straight down. **Note:** *On Chevrolet, Pontiac and Oldsmobile engines, with the No. 1 piston at TDC, the timing mark on the camshaft sprocket must be pointed straight up* (see illustrations 12.12a and 12.12b).

17   Slip the crankshaft sprocket onto the end of the crankshaft (make sure the key and keyway are properly aligned), then turn the crankshaft until the timing mark on the sprocket is pointed straight up (all engines).

18   Next, remove the camshaft sprocket from the camshaft and lay the chain over it. Slip the other end of the chain over the crankshaft sprocket (keep the timing marks aligned as this is done) and reinstall the camshaft sprocket. When the sprockets are properly installed, the timing marks on the sprockets will be perfectly aligned opposite each other (except on Chevrolet, Pontiac and Oldsmobile engines; refer to

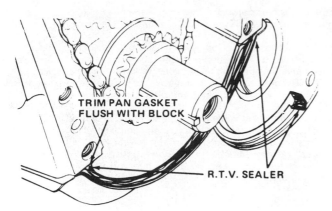

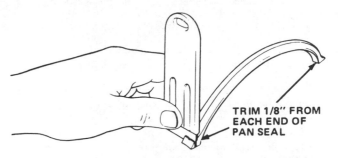

12.22   On Oldsmobile engines, trim the oil pan gasket as shown before installing the front cover

12.23   Trimming the oil pan seal — Oldsmobile engines

26 Apply engine oil to the bolt threads and loosely install two of the bolts to hold the cover in place.
27 Install the dowel pins, chamfered end first, into the engine block.
28 Install the water pump with a new gasket (if removed from cover).
29 Tighten all bolts to the proper torque specifications and install all components in the reverse order of removal. Apply lubricant to the front hub seal before installing the crankshaft hub.

Installation (Chevrolet built engines)

2A

30 Ensure that all gasket surfaces are clean and free of excess gasket material.
31 Use a sharp knife to trim any protruding gasket material at the front of the oil pan.
32 Apply a 1/8-inch bead of RTV gaket sealer to the joint formed at the oil pan and engine block, as well as the front lip of the oil pan.
33 Coat the cover gasket with a non-setting sealant, position it on the cover, then loosely install the cover. First install the top four bolts loosely, then install two 1/4 — 20 x 1/2 inch long screws at the lower cover holes. Apply a bead of sealer on the bottom of the cover, then install the cover, tightening the screws alternately and evenly and at the same time aligning the dowel pins.
34 Remove the two 1/4 – 20 x 1/2 inch long screws and install the remaining cover bolts. Torque all cover bolts to the proper specifications.
35 Install the water pump using new gaskets (see Chapter 3).
36 Follow the removal steps in the reverse order for the remaining components.

Installation (Pontiac built engines)

37 Remove the O-ring seal from the recess in the intake manifold water recirculation passage.
38 Transfer the water pump to the new cover, if used.
39 Position a new gasket over the studs against the engine block. If the oil pan gasket was damaged during removal, new front portions should be cemented in place on the oil pan flanges.
40 Install a new O-ring into the intake manifold passage.
41 Place the cover in position over the indexing studs and secure with the bolts and nuts. Install the oil pan-to-timing cover screws after the other fasteners are installed.
42 Install the remaining components in the reverse order of disassembly, referring to the appropriate Sections in this Chapter or other Chapters.

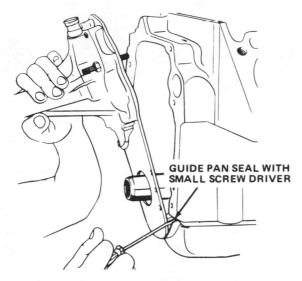

12.25   Guide the oil pan seal into place with a small screwdriver — Oldsmobile engines

illustrations 12.12a and 12.12b and Step 16).
19 On Chevrolet engines and 455 CID Buick engines, install the bolts that attach the sprocket to the camshaft, then recheck the alignment of the timing marks. On Oldsmobile engines, install the crankshaft key after the sprocket is in place (use a brass hammer to seat the key in the keyway).
20 The rest of the installation procedure is basically the reverse of removal. On Pontiac engines, the camshaft should extend through the sprocket so that the hole in the fuel pump drive eccentric will locate on the end of the shaft. Install the eccentric and index the tangs on the eccentric with the small hole in the sprocket hub. On 350 CID Buick engines, make sure the oil groove in the eccentric faces out.
21 Be sure to tighten the crankshaft and camshaft sprocket retaining bolts to the specified torque (if applicable).

Installation (Oldsmobile built engines)
Refer to illustrations 12.22, 12.23 and 12.25

22 Cut off the excess gasket material at the front of the oil pan until it is flush with the engine block (see illustration).
23 Using a razor knife, trim about 1/8-inch from each end of the new front pan seal (see illustration).
24 Install a new gasket to the engine block and a new front seal on the cover (see Section 8). Use RTV gasket sealant on these gaskets and also at the junction of the cover, block and oil pan.
25 Tilt the cover into place and press downward to compress the lower pan seal. Rotate the cover back and forth and guide the pan seal into the cavity using a small screwdriver (see illustration).

Installation (Buick built engines)

43 Before re-installing the timing chain cover, remove the oil pump cover and pack petroleum jelly around the oil pump gears so that there is no air space left inside the pump. If this is not done, the pump may "lose its prime" and not begin pumping oil immediately when the engine is started.
44 Re-install the pump cover, using a new gasket, and torque the bolts to specifications.
45 Make sure that the gasket surface of the block and timing chain cover are smooth and clean and install a new gasket on the cover.
46 Lubricate the vibration damper shaft where it will go through the timing chain cover seal so that the seal will not be damaged when the engine is first started.
47 Using the dowel pins on the block, engage the dowel holes in the cover and position the cover against the block.

48 Apply sealer to the bolt threads and tighten the bolts to the Specifications.
49 Install the vibration damper, bolt and washer (see Section 7).

13   Camshaft, bearings and lifters — removal, inspection and installation

Refer to illustrations 13.3, 13.12a, 13.12b, and 13.18

Camshaft lobe lift check

1   In order to determine the extent of cam lobe wear, the lobe lift should be checked prior to camshaft removal. Refer to Section 4 and remove the rocker arm covers.
2   Position the number one piston at TDC on the compression stroke (see Section 3).
3   Beginning with the number one cylinder valves, mount a dial indicator on the engine and position the plunger against the top surface of the first rocker arm. The plunger should be directly above and in line with the pushrod **(see illustration)**.
4   Zero the dial indicator, then very slowly turn the crankshaft in the normal direction of rotation (clockwise) until the indicator needle stops and begins to move in the opposite direction. The point at which it

13.3   When checking the camshaft lobe lift, the dial indicator plunger must be positioned directly above the pushrod

stops indicates maximum cam lobe lift.
5   Record this figure for future reference, then reposition the piston at TDC on the compression stroke.
6   Move the dial indicator to the remaining number one cylinder rocker arm and repeat the check. Be sure to record the results for each valve.
7   Repeat the check for the remaining valves. Since each piston must be at TDC on the compression stroke for this procedure, work from cylinder to cylinder following the firing order sequence (refer to the Specifications).
8   After the check is complete, compare the results to the Specifications. If camshaft lobe lift is less than specified, cam lobe wear has occurred and a new camshaft should be installed.
Note: *On air conditioning equipped models, have the refrigerant discharged and remove the condenser prior to commencing the following procedure (see Chapter 3).*

Removal

9   Refer to the appropriate Sections and remove the intake manifold, the rocker arms, the pushrods and the timing chain and camshaft sprocket. The radiator, fuel pump and distributor should be removed as well (see Chapters 3, 4 and 5).
10 There are several ways to extract the lifters from the bores. A special tool designed to grip and remove lifters is manufactured by many tool companies and is widely available, but it may not be required in every case. On newer engines without a lot of varnish buildup, the lifters can often be removed with a small magnet or even with your fingers. A machinist's scribe with a bent end can be used to pull the lifters out by positioning the point under the retainer ring in the top of each lifter. **Caution:** *Do not use pliers to remove the lifters unless you intend to replace them with new ones (along with the camshaft). The pliers may damage the precision machined and hardened lifters, rendering them useless.*
11 Before removing the lifters, arrange to store them in a clearly labelled box to ensure that they are reinstalled in their original locations. Remove the lifters and store them where they will not get dirty. Do not attempt to withdraw the camshaft with the lifters in place.
12 Unbolt and remove the thrust plate, if equipped **(see illustration)**. Thread a long bolt of the proper thread into one of the camshaft sprocket bolt holes to use as a handle when removing the camshaft from the block **(see illustration)**.
13 Carefully pull the camshaft out. Support the cam near the block so the lobes do not nick or gouge the bearings as it is withdrawn.

Inspection

Camshaft and bearings
14 After the camshaft has been removed from the engine, cleaned with solvent and dried, inspect the bearing journals for uneven wear, pitting and evidence of seizure. If the journals are damaged, the bearing inserts in the block are probably damaged as well. Both the camshaft

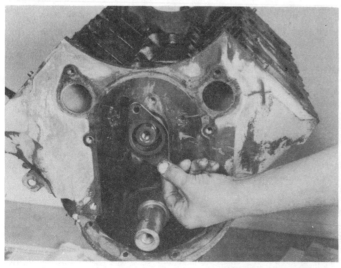

13.12a   Removing the camshaft thrust plate (Pontiac engine)

13.12b   A long bolt can be threaded into one of the camshaft bolt holes to provide a handle for removal and installation of the camshaft

and bearings will have to be replaced.

15 Measure the bearing journals with a micrometer to determine if they are excessively worn or out-of-round.

16 Check the camshaft lobes for heat discoloration, score marks, chipped areas, pitting and uneven wear. If the lobes are in good condition and if the lobe lift measurements are as specified, the camshaft can be reused.

Conventional lifters

17 Clean the lifters with solvent and dry them thoroughly without mixing them up.

18 Check each lifter wall, pushrod seat and foot for scuffing, score marks and uneven wear. Each lifter foot (the surface that rides on the cam lobe) must be slightly convex, although this can be difficult to determine by eye **(see illustration)**. If the base of the lifter is concave, the lifters and camshaft must be replaced. If the lifter walls are damaged or worn (which is not very likely), inspect the lifter bores in the engine block as well. If the pushrod seats are worn, check the pushrod ends.

19 If new lifters are being installed, a new camshaft must also be installed. If a new camshaft is installed, use new lifters as well. Never install used lifters unless the original camshaft is used and the lifters can be installed in their original locations.

Roller lifters

20 Check the rollers carefully for wear and damage and make sure they turn freely without excessive play. The inspection procedure for conventional lifters also applies to roller lifters.

21 Unlike conventional lifters, used roller lifters can be reinstalled with a new camshaft, and the original camshaft can be used if new lifters are installed.

Bearing replacement

22 Camshaft bearing replacement requires special tools and expertise that place it outside the scope of the home mechanic. Take the block to an automotive machine shop to ensure that the job is done correctly.

Installation

23 Lubricate the camshaft bearing journals and cam lobes with moly-base grease or engine assembly lube.

24 Slide the camshaft into the engine. Support the cam near the block and be careful not to scrape or nick the bearings.

25 Lubricate and then install the thrust plate, if equipped.

26 Refer to Section 12 and install the timing chain and sprockets.

27 Lubricate the lifters with clean engine oil and install them in the block. If the original lifters are being reinstalled, be sure to return them to their original locations. If a new camshaft is being installed, be sure to install new lifters as well (except for engines with roller lifters).

28 The remaining installation steps are the reverse of removal.

29 Before starting and running the engine, change the oil and install a new oil filter (see Chapter 1).

14 Oil pan — removal and installation

Refer to illustrations 14.18, 14.20, 14.21a and 14.21b

Warning: *Do not place any part of your body below the engine when it is supported solely by a jack or hoist.*

1 Disconnect the negative battery cable.

2 Remove the air cleaner assembly and set aside.

3 Remove the distributor cap to prevent breakage as the engine is raised (models with distributor at rear of engine only).

4 Unbolt the radiator shroud from the radiator support and hang the shroud over the cooling fan.

5 If necessary, remove the oil dipstick and dipstick tube.

6 Raise the car and support firmly on jack stands.

7 Drain the engine oil into a suitable container.

8 Disconnect the exhaust crossover pipe at the exhaust manifold flanges. Lower the exhaust pipes and suspend them from the frame with wire.

9 If equipped with an automatic transmission, remove the converter underpan.

10 If equipped with a manual transmission, remove the starter (Chapter 5) and the flywheel cover.

11 Use the bolt at the center of the vibration damper to rotate the engine until the timing mark is straight down, at the 6 o'clock position. This will move the forward crankshaft throw upward, providing clearance at the front of the oil pan.

12 Remove the through bolt at each engine mount.

13 At this time the engine must be raised slightly to enable the oil pan to slide clear of the crossmember. The preferred method is to use an engine hoist or ''cherry picker''. Hook up the lifting chains as described in Part B, Section 5.

14 An alternative method can be used if extreme care is exercised. Use a floor jack and a block of wood placed under the oil pan. The wood block should spread the load across the oil pan, preventing damage or collapse of the oil pan metal. The oil pump pickup and screen is very close to the oil pan bottom, so any collapsing of the pan may damage the pickup or prevent the oil pump from drawing oil properly.

15 With either method, raise the engine slowly until wood blocks can be placed between the frame front crossmember and the engine block. The blocks should be approximately three inches thick. Check clearances all around the engine as it is raised. Pay particular attention to the distributor and the cooling fan.

16 Lower the engine onto the wood blocks. Make sure it is firmly supported. If a hoist is being used, keep the lifting chains secured to the engine.

17 Remove the oil pan bolts. Note the different sizes used and their locations.

18 Remove the oil pan by tilting it downwards at the rear and then working the front clear of the crossmember **(see illustration)**. It may

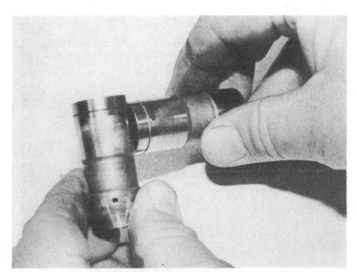

13.18 The foot of each lifter should be slightly convex — the side of another lifter can be used as a straightedge to check it; if it appears flat, it is worn and must not be reused

14.18 Tilt the oil pan down (as shown) at the rear to clear the front crossmember

be necessary to use a rubber mallet to break the seal.
19 Before installing, thoroughly clean the gasket sealing surfaces on the engine block and on the oil pan. All sealer and gasket material must be removed.
20 Apply a thin film of sealer to the new side gaskets and fit them to the engine block. All bolt holes should line up properly. Use the retainers, if equipped **(see illustration)**.
21 Again using sealer, install the front and rear seals to the engine. Make sure the ends butt with the ends of the side gaskets **(see illustrations)**.
22 Lift the pan into position and install all bolts finger-tight. There is no specific order for tightening the bolts; however, it is a good policy to tighten the end bolts first.

23 Lower the engine onto its mounts and install the through bolts. Tighten the nuts/bolts securely.
24 Follow the removal steps in a reverse order. Fill the engine with the correct grade and quantity of oil, start the engine and check for leaks.

15 Oil pump — removal, inspection and installation

Buick engines
Refer to illustration 15.4
Removal
1 Unscrew and remove the oil filter (see Chapter 1).
2 Remove the screws attaching the oil pump cover assembly to the timing chain cover. Remove the cover assembly and slide out the oil pump gear.

Inspection
3 Wash off the gears with a proper solution and inspect for wear, scoring, etc. Replace any unserviceable gears with new ones.
4 Unscrew the oil pressure relief valve cap, spring and valve **(see illustration)**. Do not remove the oil filter by-pass valve and spring, as they are staked in place.
5 Wash the parts thoroughly in the proper solvent and inspect the relief valve for wear and scoring. Check to make sure that the relief valve spring is not collapsed or worn on its side. Any relief valve spring which is questionable should be replaced with a new one.

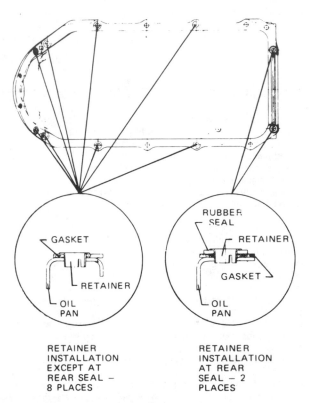

14.20 Oil pan gasket retaining clips are used on some engines

14.21a Sealant is applied at the area where the front gasket meets the side gasket (Chevrolet engine shown)

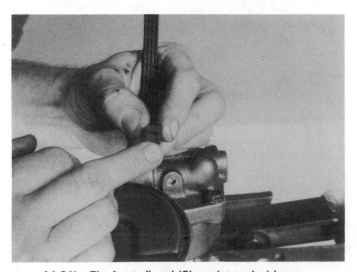

14.21b The front oil seal (Chevrolet engine) has an indentation which fits into the side gasket

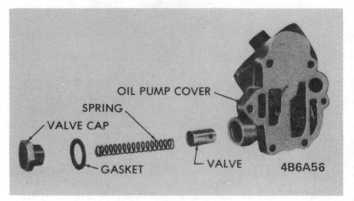

15.4 Oil pump cover and pressure relief components — typical Buick engine

6   Check the relief valve in its bore in the cover. It should be an easy slip-fit only, and any side shake that can be felt is too much. The valve and/or cover should be replaced with a new one in this case.

7   The filter by-pass valve should be flat and free of nicks, cracks or warping and scratches.

8   Lubricate the pressure relief valve and spring, and install it in the bore of the oil pump case. Install the cap and gasket, and tighten the cap securely.

9   If the above inspections reveal wear or if high mileage/low oil pressure indicate a faulty pump, replace it with a new one.

10 If the condition of the pump is satisfactory at this point, remove the gears and pack the pocket full of petroleum jelly. Do not use chassis lube.

Installation

11 Re-install the gears, making sure that petroleum jelly is forced into every cavity of the gear pocket and between the teeth of the gears. The pump may not prime itself when the engine is started if the pump is not packed with the petroleum jelly.

12 Install the pump cover assembly screws and tighten them alternately and evenly. Torque-tighten to Specifications.

13 Install oil filter and check oil level with the dipstick. Pay close at-tention to the oil pressure gauge or warning light during the initial start-up and driving period. Shut off the engine and inspect all work if a lack of pressure is indicated.

Chevrolet, Oldsmobile and Pontiac engines — all
Refer to illustration 15.17

Removal

14 Remove the oil pan as described in Section 14.

15 Remove the bolts securing the oil pump assembly to the main bearing cap. Remove the oil pump with its pickup tube and screen as an assembly from the engine block. Once the pump is removed, the oil pump driveshaft can be withdrawn from the block. **Note:** *On Oldsmobile engines, do not attempt to remove the washers from the driveshaft. Note that the end with the washers fits into the pump.*

Inspection

16 In most cases it will be more practical and economical to replace a faulty oil pump with a new or rebuilt unit. If it is decided to overhaul the oil pump, check on internal parts availability before beginning.

17 Remove the pump cover retaining screws (**see illustration**) and the

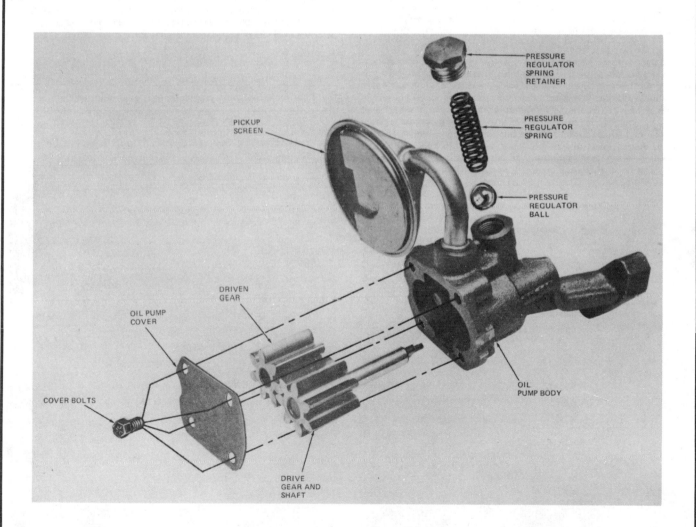

**15.17 Typical oil pump assembly — exploded view
(except V6 and Buick-built engines)**

PRESSURE REGULATOR SPRING RETAINER

PRESSURE REGULATOR SPRING

PRESSURE REGULATOR BALL

PICKUP SCREEN

DRIVEN GEAR

OIL PUMP COVER

COVER BOLTS

DRIVE GEAR AND SHAFT

OIL PUMP BODY

2A

pump cover (Oldsmobile engines also have a gasket installed). Index mark the gear teeth to permit reassembly in the same position.

18   Remove the idler gear, drive gear and shaft from the body.

19   Remove the pressure regulator valve retaining pin (Pontiac engines utilize a threaded cap), the regulator valve and the related parts.

20   If necessary, the pick-up screen and pipe assembly can be extracted from the pump body. **Note:** *On Pontiac engines, the oil pickup tube/screen assembly should not be disturbed.*

21   Wash all the parts in solvent and thoroughly dry them. Inspect the body for cracks, wear or other damage. Similarly inspect the gears.

22   Check the drive gear shaft for looseness in the pump body, and the inside of the pump cover for wear that would permit oil leakage past the end of the gears.

23   Inspect the pick-up screen and pipe assembly for damage to the screen, pipe or relief grommet.

24   Apply a gasket sealant to the end of the pipe (pick-up screen and pipe assembly) and tap it into the pump body, taking care that no damage occurs. If the original press-fit cannot be obtained, a new assembly must be used to prevent air leaks and loss of pressure.

25   Install the pressure regulator valve and related parts.

26   Install the drive gear and shaft in the pump body, followed by the idler gear, with the smooth side towards the pump cover opening. **Note:** *On Oldsmobile engines, check the gear end clearance by resting a straightedge on the pump body. Try to slip a feeler gauge between the ends of the gears and the straightedge. The clearance should be between 0.0015- and 0.0085-inch. If it is not, the pump should be replaced with a new one. Lubricate the parts with engine oil.*

27   Install the cover and torque-tighten the screws to Specifications.

28   Turn the driveshaft to ensure that the pump operates freely.

Installation

29   To install, move the pump assembly into position and align the slot on the top end of the driveshaft with the drive tang on the lower end of the distributor. The distributor drives the oil pump, so it is essential that these two components mate properly. On Pontiac and Oldsmobile engines, the driveshaft fits into the distributor drive gear.

30   Install the bolts and tighten them securely. Pontiac engines require a new gasket between the pump body and the block.

31   Make sure the oil pump screen is parallel with the oil rails. The screen must be in this position to fit into the oil pan properly.

16   Flywheel/driveplate — removal and installation

Refer to illustrations 16.3 and 16.4

1   Raise the vehicle and support it securely on jackstands, then refer to Chapter 7 and remove the transmission.

2   Remove the pressure plate assembly and clutch disc (Chapter 8) (manual transmission equipped vehicles).

3   Use paint to draw a line from the flywheel to the end of the crankshaft for correct alignment during reinstallation **(see illustration)**.

4   Remove the bolts that secure the flywheel to the crankshaft rear flange. If difficulty is experienced in removing the bolts due to movement of the crankshaft, wedge a screwdriver to keep the flywheel from turning **(see illustration)**.

5   Remove the flywheel/driveplate from the crankshaft flange.

6   Clean any grease or oil from the flywheel. Inspect the surface of the flywheel for rivet grooves, burned areas and score marks. Light scoring can be removed with emery cloth. Check for cracked or broken teeth. Lay the flywheel on a flat surface and use a straightedge to check for warpage.

7   Clean the mating surfaces of the flywheel/driveplate and the crankshaft.

8   Position the flywheel/driveplate against the crankshaft, matching the alignment marks made during removal. Before installing the bolts, apply Loc-Tite to the threads.

9   Wedge a screwdriver through the driveplate or into the ring gear teeth to keep the crankshaft from turning. Tighten the bolts to the specified torque in two or three steps, working in a criss-cross pattern.

10   The remainder of installation is the reverse of the removal procedure.

17   Rear main oil seal — replacement (engine in car)

Two-piece neoprene type seal
Refer to illustrations 17.5, 17.9, 17.13 and 17.14

1   Always replace both halves of the rear main oil seal as a unit. While the replacement of this seal is much easier with the engine removed

16.3   To insure proper balance, mark the flywheel's relation to the crankshaft

16.4   A large screwdriver wedged in the starter ring gear teeth or one of the holes in the driveplate can be used to keep the flywheel/driveplate from turning as the mounting bolts are removed

from the car, the job can be done with engine in place.

2   Remove the oil pan and oil pump as described previously in this Chapter.

3   Remove the rear main bearing cap from the engine.

4   Using a screwdriver, pry the lower half of the oil seal from the bearing cap.

5   To remove the upper half of the seal, use a small hammer and a brass pin punch to roll the seal around the crankshaft journal. Tap one end of the seal with the hammer and punch (be careful not to strike the crankshaft) until the other end of the seal protrudes enough to pull the seal out with a pair of pliers (see illustration).

6   Clean all seal and and foreign material from the bearing cap and block. Do not use an abrasive cleaner for this.

7   Inspect components for nicks, scratches or burrs at all sealing surfaces.

8   Coat the seal lips of the new seal with light engine oil. Do not get oil on the seal mating ends.

9   Included in the purchase of the rear main oil seal should be a small plastic installation tool. If not included, make your own by cutting an old feeler gauge blade or shim stock (see illustration).

10   Position the narrow end of this installation tool between the crankshaft and the seal seat. The idea is to protect the new seal from being damaged by the sharp edge of the seal seat.

11   Raise the new upper half of the seal into position with the seal lips facing towards the front of the engine. Push the seal onto its seat, using the installation tool as a protector against the seal contacting the sharp edge.

12   Roll the seal around the crankshaft, all the time using the tool as a "shoehorn" for protection. When both ends of the seal are flush with the engine block, remove the installation tool, being careful not to withdraw the seal as well.

13   Install the lower half of the oil seal in the bearing cap, again using the installation tool to protect the seal against the sharp edge (see illustration). Make sure the seal is firmly seated, then withdraw the installation tools.

14   Smear a bit of sealant on the bearing cap areas immediately adjacent to the seal ends (see illustration).

15   Install the bearing cap (with seal) and torque the attaching bolts to about 10-12 ft-lbs only. Now tap the end of the crankshaft first rearward, then forward to line up the thrust surfaces. Retorque the bearing cap bolts to the proper Specification (see Chapter 2B).

2A

17.5   A hammer and brass drift should be used to push the upper seal half around the crankshaft

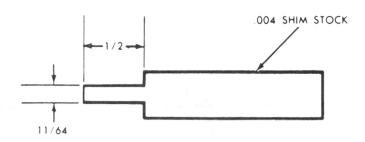

17.9   Neoprene type crankshaft rear oil seal installation tool

17.13   Use a protector tool (arrow) when pushing the main seal into place

17.14   Sealant should be used where the rear main cap touches the engine block

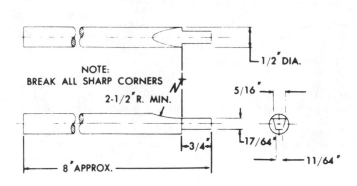

17.16a Packing tool fabrication details

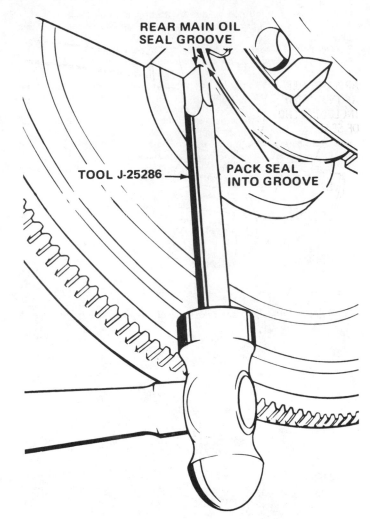

17.16b Packing upper half of braided fabric type crankshaft rear oil seal into block

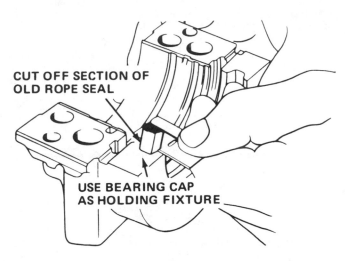

17.17 Use the bearing cap as a holding fixture when cutting short sections of the old seal

Braided fabric type seal

Refer to illustrations 17.16a, 17.16b, 17.17, 17.20a and 17.20b

16 With the oil pan, oil pump and main bearing cap removed (see previous Sections), insert the special GM seal packing tool or equivalent (see illustration) against the seal. Drive the old seal into its groove until it is packed tight at each end (see illustration).

17 Measure the amount which the seal was driven upwards, then add 1/16-inch. Cut two pieces that length from the old seal taken from the bearing cap. Use the bearing cap as a guide when cutting (see illustration).

18 Place a drop of sealant on each end of these seal pieces and then pack them into the upper groove to fill the gap made previously.

19 Trim the remaining material perfectly flush with the block. Be careful not to harm the bearing surface.

20 Install a new rope seal into the main bearing cap groove and push firmly all around using a hammer handle or special GM tool (see illustration). Make sure the seal is firmly seated, then trim the ends flush with the bearing cap mating surface (see illustration).

21 Install cap and remaining components in reverse order, tightening all parts to Specifications (See Chapter 2B for main bearing cap torque specifications).

One-piece neoprene type seal

22 Later models equipped with a one-piece seal require an entirely different installation procedure. The flywheel/driveplate must be removed first and then the housing unbolted from the block (see illustration).

23 Check the seal contact surface very carefully for scratches and nicks that could damage the new seal lip and cause oil leaks. If the crankshaft is damaged, the only alternative is a new or different crankshaft.

24 The old seal can be removed from the housing by inserting a large screwdriver into the notches provided and prying it out (see illustration). Be sure to note how far it is recessed into the housing bore before removing it; the new seal will have to be recessed an equal amount. Be very careful not to scratch or otherwise damage the bore in the housing or oil leaks could develop.

25 Make sure the housing is clean, then apply a thin coat of engine oil to the outer edge of the new seal. The seal must be pressed squarely into the housing bore, so hammering it into place is not recommended. If you do not have access to a press, sandwich the housing and seal between two smooth pieces of wood and press the seal into place with the jaws of a large vise. The pieces of wood must be thick enough to distribute the force evenly around the entire circumference of the seal. Work slowly and make sure the seal enters the bore squarely.

26 The seal lips must be lubricated with clean engine oil or moly-based grease before the seal/housing is slipped over the crankshaft and bolted to the block. Use a new gasket — no sealant is required — and make sure the dowel pins are in place before installing the housing.

27 Tighten the nuts/screws a little at a time until they are all snug.

28 Reinstall the remaining parts in the reverse order of removal.

29 Be sure to add oil, then run the engine and check for oil leaks.

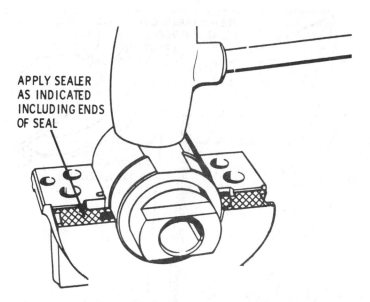

17.20a Installing the rear main oil seal in bearing cap

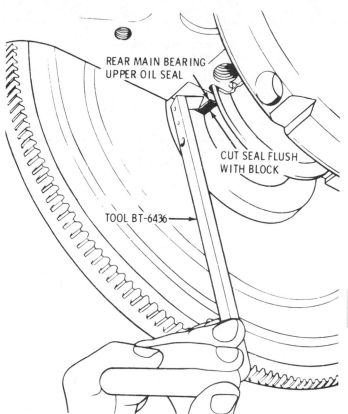

17.20b Using a special tool to trim the upper seal ends

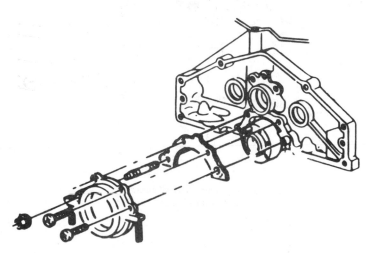

17.22 One-piece rear main oil seal fits into a housing bolted to the block

18 Engine mounts — check and replacement

Refer to illustration 18.7

1 Engine mounts seldom require attention, but broken or deteriorated mounts should be replaced immediately or the added strain placed on the driveline components may cause damage.

Check

2 During the check, the engine must be raised slightly to remove the weight from the mounts. Disconnect the negative battery cable from the battery.

3 Raise the vehicle and support it securely on jackstands, then position the jack under the engine oil pan. Place a large block of wood between the jack head and the oil pan, then carefully raise the engine just enough to take the weight off the mounts.

4 Check the mounts to see if the rubber is cracked, hardened or separated from the metal plates. Sometimes the rubber will split right down the center. Rubber preservative may be applied to the mounts to slow deterioration.

5 Check for relative movement between the mount plates and the

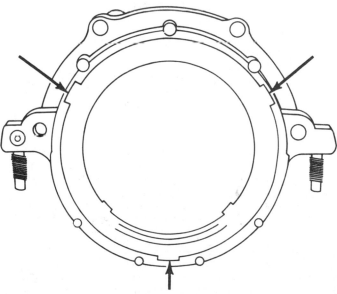

17.24 To remove the seal from the housing, insert the tip of the screwdriver into each notch (arrows) and lever the seal out

engine or frame (use a large screwdriver or pry bar to attempt to move the mounts). If movement is noted, lower the engine and tighten the mount fasteners.

Replacement

6 Remove the fan shroud mounting screws and place the shroud over the fan.

7   Remove the engine mount through-bolts **(see illustration)**.
8   Disconnect the shift linkage where it connects the transmission to the body (Chapter 7).
9   Raise the engine high enough to clear the clevis brackets. Do not force the engine up too high. If it touches anything before the mounts are free, remove the part for clearance. Place a block of wood between the oil pan and crossmember as a safety precaution.
10   Unbolt the mount from the engine block and remove it from the vehicle. **Note:** *On vehicles equipped with self-locking nuts and bolts,*

replace them with new ones whenever they are disassembled. Prior to assembly, remove hardened residual adhesive from the engine block holes with a proper-size bottoming tap.
11   Attach the new mount to the engine block and install the fasteners in the appropriate locations. Tighten the fasteners securely.
12   Remove the wooden block and lower the engine into place. Install the through-bolts and tighten the nuts securely.
13   Complete the installation by reinstalling all parts removed to gain access to the mounts.

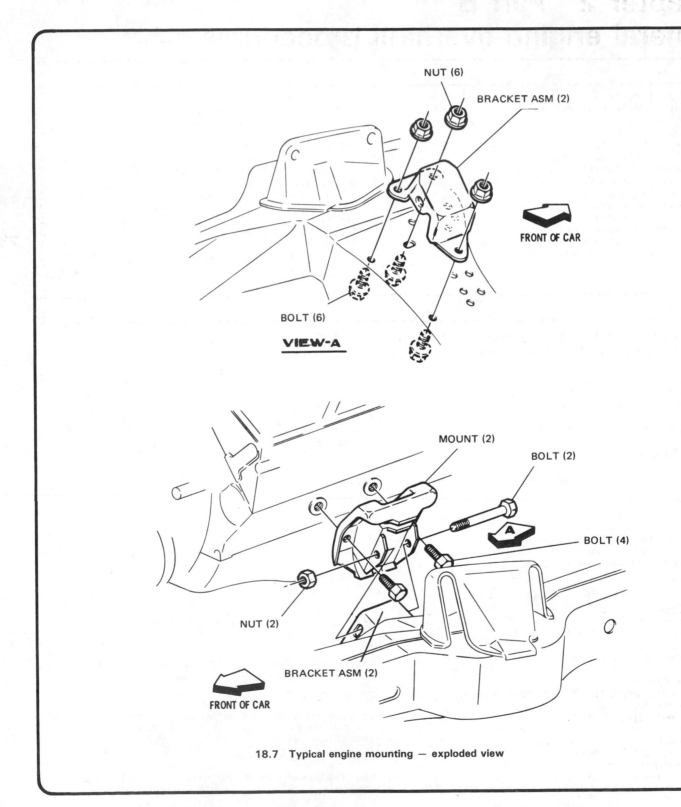

18.7 Typical engine mounting — exploded view

Chapter 2   Part B
General engine overhaul procedures

Contents

2B

Specifications

231 and 252 cu in Buick-built V6 engines, 1977 and later — VIN codes A, C, 2 and 4
See Chapter 2A Section 1 for additional information

General
Oil pressure	
at 2600 rpm	37 psi
Compression pressure	
minimum	100 psi
allowable variation between cylinders	20%

Cylinder head
Warpage limit	0.006 in

Valves
Valve stem diameter	
intake	0.3401 to 0.3412 in
exhaust	0.3405 to 0.3412 in
Valve margin width (limit)	1/32 in
Valve spring installed height	1.727 in
Valve stem-to-guide clearance	
intake	0.0015 to 0.0035 in
exhaust	0.0015 to 0.0032 in

Engine block
Cylinder bore diameter	
231 cu in	3.800 in
252 cu in	3.965 in
Cylinder bore taper/out-of-round	Less than 0.0005 in

Pistons and rings
Piston-to-bore clearance (measured at top of skirt)	0.0008 to 0.0020 in
Piston ring end gap	
compression rings	0.010 to 0.0020 in
oil rings	
thru 1980	0.015 to 0.035 in
1981 and later	0.015 to 0.055 in
Piston ring side clearance	
compression rings	0.003 to 0.005 in
oil control rings	0.0035 max

Crankshaft, connecting rods and main bearings

Connecting rod side clearance (total — both rods)
1975 thru 1980	0.006 to 0.027 in
1981 thru 1984	0.006 to 0.023 in
1985 and later	0.003 to 0.015 in

Connecting rod journal diameter
1975 thru 1977	1.9910 to 2.0000 in
1978 and later	2.2487 to 2.2495 in
Connecting rod bearing oil clearance	0.0005 to 0.0026 in
Rod and main journal taper/out-of-round limit	0.0015 in

Crankshaft endplay
1975 thru 1978	0.004 to 0.008 in
1979 and later	0.003 to 0.011 in
Main bearing journal diameter	2.4995 in

Main bearing oil clearance
1975 thru 1977	0.0004 to 0.0015 in
1978 and later	0.0003 to 0.0018 in

Torque specifications*

Ft-lbs

Main bearing cap bolts
1975 and 1976	115
1977 and later	100
Connecting rod cap nut	40

* **Note:** *Refer to Part A for additional torque specifications.*

350 and 455 cu in Buick-built engines, 1977 and later — VIN codes J, X and H (up to 1978)
See Chapter 2A Section 1 for additional information

General

Oil pressure
350 cu in	37 psi @ 2600 rpm
455 cu in	40 psi @ 2400 rpm

Compression pressure
allowable variation between cylinders	20%
minimum	100 psi

Cylinder head
Warpage limit	0.006 in

Valves

Valve stem diameter
intake	0.3720 to 0.3730 in
exhaust	0.3723 to 0.3730 in
Valve margin width minimum	1/32 in

Valve spring installed height
350 cu in	1 23/32 in
455 cu in	1 29/32 in

Valve stem-to-guide clearance
intake (350 and 455 cu in)	0.0015 to 0.0035 in
exhaust (350 and 455 cu in)	0.0015 to 0.0032 in

Engine block

Cylinder bore diameter
350 cu in	3.800 in
455 cu in	4.3125 in

Piston-to-bore clearance (measured at top of skirt)
350 cu in	0.0008 to 0.0020 in
455 cu in	0.0010 to 0.0016 in

Pistons and rings

Piston ring end gap — 350 and 455 cu in
top and second compression ring	0.013 to 0.023 in

oil ring
350 cu in	0.015 to 0.035 in
455 cu in	0.015 to 0.055 in

Piston ring side clearance
top and second compression ring	0.0030 to 0.0050 in
oil control ring	0.0035 in max

Crankshaft, connecting rods and main bearings

Rod end play — total for two (side clearance)

350 cu in
thru 1972	0.006 to 0.014 in
1973 and 1974	0.006 to 0.020 in

1975 thru 1979	0.006 to 0.026 in
1980 and later	0.006 to 0.023 in
455 cu in	
thru 1974	0.005 to 0.019 in
1975 and later	0.005 to 0.026 in
Crankshaft endplay (all)	0.003 to 0.009 in
Main bearing journal diameter	
350 cu in	
thru 1973	2.9995 in
1974 and later	3.0000 in
455 cu in	3.2500 in
Connecting rod journal diameter	
350 cu in	1.991 to 2.000 in
455 cu in	2.2487 to 2.2495 in
Main bearing oil clearance	
350 cu in	0.0004 to 0.0015 in
455 cu in	0.0007 to 0.0018 in
Connecting rod bearing oil clearance	
thru 1974	0.0002 to 0.0023 in
1975 and later	0.0005 to 0.0026 in

Torque specifications*   Ft-lbs

Connecting rod cap	
350 cu in thru 1973 with nut	35
350 cu in with cap screw	40
455 cu in (all)	45
Main bearing cap bolts	
350 cu in thru 1972	95
1973 thru 1976 (all)	115
1977 and later	100

* **Note:** *Refer to Part A for additional torque specifications.*

2B

305 and 350 cu in Chevrolet-built engines, 1977 and later — VIN codes G, L, U and H (1978 and later)
See Chapter 2A Section 1 for additional information

General

Oil pressure	
at 2400 rpm	30 to 45 psi
Compression pressure	
allowable variation between cylinders	20%
minimum	100 psi

Cylinder head

Warpage limit	0.006 in

Valves

Valve stem diameter (all)	0.3410 to 0.3417 in
Valve margin width (minimum)	1/32 in
Valve spring free length outer spring (all)	2.03 in
Valve spring installed height (all)	1 23/32 in
Valve stem-to-guide clearance (all)	0.0010 to 0.0027 in

Engine block

Cylinder bore diameter	
305 cu in	3.7350 to 3.7385 in
350 cu in	3.9995 to 4.0025 in
Cylinder bore taper limit	0.005 in
Cylinder bore out-of-round limit	0.002 in
Piston-to-bore clearance — service limit	0.0027 in

Piston rings

Piston ring side clearance	
compression rings	0.0012 to 0.0032 in
oil control rings	0.005 in max

Crankshaft, connecting rods and main bearings

Connecting rod end play (total — both rods)	0.008 to 0.014 in
Crankshaft end play	0.002 to 0.008 in
Main bearing journal diameter	2.448 to 2.449 in
Connecting rod journal diameter	2.0986 to 2.0998 in
Journal taper/out-of-round limit	0.001 in
Main bearing oil clearance wear limits	
no. 1 journal	0.0020 in
all others	0.0035 in

Connecting rod bearing oil clearance wear limit . . . .   0.0035 in

Note: *Bearing oil clearances vary considerably between model years and applications. Refer to the bearing manufacturer's specifications when assembling an engine.*

Torque specifications*	Ft-lbs
Main bearing cap bolts **	70
Connecting rod cap nut	45
Rear oil seal housing bolts (when equipped)	135 in-lbs

* **Note:** *Refer to Part A for additional torque specifications.*

** *Tighten outer bolts on four-bolt caps to 65 ft-lbs.*

260, 307, 350, 403 and 455 cu in Oldsmobile built engines, 1977 and later — VIN codes F, K, 8, 9, Y (1980 and later), R

See Chapter 2A Section 1 for additional information

General
Oil pressure
260, 350 and 403 cu in	40 psi @ 2000 rpm
307 cu in	30 to 40 psi @ 1500 rpm
455 cu in	30 to 50 psi @ 1500 rpm

Compression pressure
allowable variation between cylinders	20%
minimum	100 psi

Cylinder head
Warpage limit . . . .   0.006 in

Valves
Valve stem diameter
intake	0.3425 to 0.3432 in
exhaust	0.3420 to 0.3427 in
Valve margin width (minimum)	1/32 in

Valve spring installed height
455 cu in	1.62 in
all others	1.67 in

Valve stem-to-guide clearance
intake	0.0010 to 0.0027 in
exhaust	0.0015 to 0.0032 in

Engine block
Cylinder bore diameter
260 cu in	3.500 in
307 cu in	3.800 in
350 cu in	4.057 in
403 cu in	4.351 in
455 cu in	4.126 in
Cylinder bore taper/out-of-round	Less than 0.001 in

Piston-to-bore clearance
thru 1978	0.0010 to 0.0020 in
1979 and 1980	
260 and 350 cu in	0.0007 to 0.0018 in
307 and 403 cu in	0.0005 to 0.0015 in
1981 and later	0.0007 to 0.0018 in

Pistons and rings
Piston ring end gap*
compression rings	
307 cu in	0.009 to 0.019 in
all others	0.010 to 0.023 in
oil ring	0.015 to 0.055 in

* *Varies by ring manufacturer — use ring maker's specifications, if different.*

Piston compression ring side clearance
thru 1985	0.0020 to 0.0040 in
1986 and later	0.0018 to 0.0038 in

Crankshaft, connecting rods and main bearings
Connecting rod end play (side clearance)	0.006 to 0.020 in

Crankshaft end play
thru 1976	0.004 to 0.008 in
1977 and later	0.0035 to 0.0135 in

Connecting rod journal diameter
260, 307, 350 and 403 cu in	2.1238 to 2.1248 in
455 cu in	2.4988 to 2.4998 in

Main bearing journal diameter
  260, 307, 350 and 403 cu in
    front (no.1) journal .... 2.4988 to 2.4998 in
    all other journals .... 2.4985 to 2.4995 in
  455 cu in (all) .... 2.9993 to 3.0003 in
Main bearing oil clearance
  bearings no. 1 through no. 4 (all engines) .... 0.0005 to 0.0021 in
  rear (no. 5)
    455 cu in .... 0.0020 to 0.0034 in
    all other engines .... 0.0015 to 0.0031 in
Connecting rod bearing oil clearance (all)................ 0.0004 to 0.0033 in

Torque specifications* Ft-lbs
Main bearing cap bolts rear (no. 5) cap — all 120
caps no. 1 through no. 4
  455 cu in only 120
  all other engines 80
Connecting rod cap nut
  thru 1986...................................... 42
  1987 48
  1988
    step one 18
    step two .... turn additional 70°

* Note: *Refer to Part A for additional torque specifications.*

301, 350, 400 and 455 cu in Pontiac-built engines, 1977 and later — VIN codes Y (through 1979), P, W and Z

See Chapter 2A Section 1 for additional information

2B

General
Oil pressure
  minimum .... 30 psi @ 2600 rpm
Compression pressure
  allowable variation between cylinders 20%
  minimum .... 100 psi

Cylinder head
Warpage limit..................................... 0.006 in

Valves
Valve stem diameter
  intake
    thru 1977 (except 301 cu in).................... 0.3416 in
    1978 and later, and all 301 cu in .... 0.3425 in
  exhaust
    thru 1977 (except 301 cu in).................... 0.3411 in
    1978 and later, and all 301 cu in .... 0.3425 in
Valve margin width (minimum) .... 1/32 in
Valve spring installed height
  two-barrel carb engines through 1977 (except 301 cu in)1 19/32 in
  four-barrel carb engines through 1977 .... 1 9/16 in
  1978 and later 350 and 400 cu in.................... 1 27/50 in
  301 cu in engines .... 1 21/32 in
Valve stem-to-guide clearance
  intake
    301 cu in .... 0.0010 to 0.0027 in
    all others .... 0.0016 to 0.0033 in
  exhaust
    301 cu in .... 0.0010 to 0.0027 in
    all others .... 0.0021 to 0.0038 in

Engine block
Cylinder bore diameter (nominal)
  301 cu in .... 4.00 in
  350 cu in .... 3.88 in
  400 cu in .... 4.12 in
  455 cu in .... 4.15 in
Piston-to-bore clearance*
  thru 1972 (all) .... 0.0025 to 0.0033 in
  1973 and 1974 (350 and 400 cu in only) .... 0.0029 to 0.0037 in
  1974 and later (455 cu in only) .... 0.0021 to 0.0029 in
  1980 and 1981 (301 cu in only) .... 0.0017 to 0.0025 in
  all others .... 0.0025 to 0.0033 in

* Measure pistons at top of skirt, perpendicular to pin

Pistons and rings

Piston ring end gap
  compression rings
    thru 1976 . . . . 0.0010 to 0.0020 in
    1977 and later . . . . 0.0010 to 0.0025 in
  oil rings . . . . 0.0015 to 0.0035 in
Piston ring side clearance (compression rings only)
  thru 1976 . . . . 0.0015 to 0.0050 in
  1977 and later 301 and 400 cu in . . . . 0.0015 to 0.0035 in

Crankshaft, connecting rods and main bearings

Connecting rod end play (side clearance)
  thru 1977 (except 301 cu in) . . . . 0.012 to 0.017 in
  1978 and later, and all 301 cu in . . . . 0.006 to 0.022 in
Crankshaft end play . . . . 0.003 to 0.009 in
Main bearing journal diameter
  455 cu in . . . . 3.2500 in
  all others . . . . 3.0000 in
Connecting rod journal diameter
  thru 1977 . . . . 2.250 in
  1978 and 1979 models . . . . 2.240 or 2.250 in
  1980 and later . . . . 2.000 in
Connecting rod bearing oil clearance
  455 cu in thru 1975 . . . . 0.0010 to 0.0031 in
  all others . . . . 0.0005 to 0.0026 in
Main bearing oil clearance
  455 cu in . . . . 0.0005 to 0.0021 in
  all others thru 1976 . . . . 0.0002 to 0.0017 in
  1977 and later . . . . 0.0004 to 0.0020 in

Torque specifications*   Ft-lbs

Main bearing cap bolts
  rear (no. 5) main
    301 cu in 100
    all other engines 120
  caps no. 1 through no. 4
    301 cu in
      with 7/16 in bolt 70
      with 1/2 in bolt 100
    all other engines 100
Connecting rod cap nut
  thru 1976 43
  301 cu in only 30
  all others 40

* Note: *Refer to Part A for additional torque specifications.*

1 General information

Included in this portion of Chapter 2 are the general overhaul procedures for the cylinder heads and internal engine components.

The information ranges from advice concerning preparation for an overhaul and the purchase of replacement parts to detailed, step-by-step procedures covering removal and installation of internal engine components and the inspection of parts.

The following Sections have been written based on the assumption that the engine has been removed from the vehicle. For information concerning in-vehicle engine repair, as well as removal and installation of the external components necessary for the overhaul, see Part A of this Chapter and Section 7 of this Part.

The Specifications included in this Part are only those necessary for the inspection and overhaul procedures which follow. Refer to Part A for additional Specifications.

2 Engine overhaul — general information

Refer to illustration 2.4

It's not always easy to determine when, or if, an engine should be completely overhauled, as a number of factors must be considered.

High mileage is not necessarily an indication that an overhaul is needed, while low mileage doesn't preclude the need for an overhaul. Frequency of servicing is probably the most important consideration. An engine that's had regular and frequent oil and filter changes, as well as other required maintenance, will most likely give many thousands of miles of reliable service. Conversely, a neglected engine may require an overhaul very early in its life.

Excessive oil consumption is an indication that piston rings, valve seals and/or valve guides are in need of attention. Make sure that oil leaks aren't responsible before deciding that the rings and/or guides are bad. Perform a cylinder compression check to determine the extent of the work required (see Section 3).

Check the oil pressure with a gauge installed in place of the oil pressure sending unit **(see illustration)** and compare it to the Specifications. If it's extremely low, the bearings and/or oil pump are probably worn out.

Loss of power, rough running, knocking or metallic engine noises, excessive valve train noise and high fuel consumption rates may also point to the need for an overhaul, especially if they're all present at the same time. If a complete tune-up doesn't remedy the situation, major mechanical work is the only solution.

An engine overhaul involves restoring the internal parts to the specifications of a new engine. During an overhaul, the piston rings are replaced and the cylinder walls are reconditioned (rebored and/or honed).

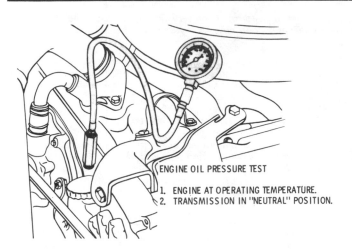

**2.4 On Oldsmobile-built engines (shown) the sending unit
is located at the top-front. On Buick, Pontiac and V6
engines, the sender is adjacent to the oil filter.
Chevrolet-built engines have the sender near
the base of the distributor**

**3.5 If your engine has a coil-in-cap distributor, disconnect
the wire from the BAT terminal on the distributor cap when
checking the compression**

If a rebore is done by an automotive machine shop, new oversize
pistons will also be installed. The main bearings, connecting rod bearings and camshaft bearings are generally replaced with new ones and,
if necessary, the crankshaft may be reground to restore the journals.
Generally, the valves are serviced as well, since they're usually in less-
than-perfect condition at this point. While the engine is being overhauled, other components, such as the distributor, starter and alternator, can be rebuilt as well. The end result should be a like-new engine
that will give many trouble-free miles. **Note:** *Critical cooling system
components such as the hoses, drivebelts, thermostat and water pump
MUST be replaced with new parts when an engine is overhauled. The
radiator should be checked carefully to ensure that it isn't clogged or
leaking (see Chapter 3). Also, we don't recommend overhauling the
oil pump — always install a new one when an engine is rebuilt.*

Before beginning the engine overhaul, read through the entire procedure to familiarize yourself with the scope and requirements of the
job. Overhauling an engine isn't difficult, but it is time consuming. Plan
on the vehicle being tied up for a minimum of two weeks, especially
if parts must be taken to an automotive machine shop for repair or
reconditioning. Check on availability of parts and make sure that any
necessary special tools and equipment are obtained in advance. Most
work can be done with typical hand tools, although a number of precision measuring tools are required for inspecting parts to determine if
they must be replaced. Often an automotive machine shop will handle
the inspection of parts and offer advice concerning reconditioning and
replacement. **Note:** *Always wait until the engine has been completely
disassembled and all components, especially the engine block, have
been inspected before deciding what service and repair operations must
be performed by an automotive machine shop.* Since the block's condition will be the major factor to consider when determining whether
to overhaul the original engine or buy a rebuilt one, never purchase
parts or have machine work done on other components until the block
has been thoroughly inspected. As a general rule, time is the primary
cost of an overhaul, so it doesn't pay to install worn or substandard
parts.

As a final note, to ensure maximum life and minimum trouble from
a rebuilt engine, everything must be assembled with care in a spotlessly
clean environment.

3 Cylinder compression check

Refer to illustrations 3.5 and 3.6

1   A compression check will tell you what mechanical condition the
upper end (pistons, rings, valves, head gaskets) of your engine is in.
Specifically, it can tell you if the compression is down due to leakage
caused by worn piston rings, defective valves and seats or a blown
head gasket. **Note:** *The engine must be at normal operating temperature*
*and the battery must be fully charged for this check. Also, the choke
valve must be all the way open to get an accurate compression reading
(if the engine's warm, the choke should be open).*

2   Begin by cleaning the area around the spark plugs before you
remove them (compressed air should be used, if available, otherwise
a small brush or even a bicycle tire pump will work). The idea is to
prevent dirt from getting into the cylinders as the compression check
is being done.

3   Remove all of the spark plugs from the engine (Chapter 1).

4   Block the throttle wide open.

5   On vehicles with "point-type" ignition, detach the coil wire from
the center of the distributor cap and ground it on the engine block.
Use a jumper wire with alligator clips on each end to ensure a good
ground. On electronic ignition equipped vehicles, the ignition circuit
should be disabled by unplugging the "BAT" wire going to the
distributor. **(see illustration).**

6   Install the compression gauge in the number one spark plug hole
(see illustration).

7   Crank the engine over at least seven compression strokes and
watch the gauge. The compression should build up quickly in a healthy
engine. Low compression on the first stroke, followed by gradually in-
creasing pressure on successive strokes, indicates worn piston rings.
A low compression reading on the first stroke, which doesn't build up

**3.6 A compression gauge with a threaded fitting for the
plug hole is preferred over the type that requires hand
pressure to maintain the seal**

during successive strokes, indicates leaking valves or a blown head gasket (a cracked head could also be the cause). Deposits on the undersides of the valve heads can also cause low compression. Record the highest gauge reading obtained.

8   Repeat the procedure for the remaining cylinders and compare the results to the Specifications.

9   Add some engine oil (about three squirts from a plunger-type oil can) to each cylinder, through the spark plug hole, and repeat the test.

10 If the compression increases after the oil is added, the piston rings are definitely worn. If the compression doesn't increase significantly, the leakage is occurring at the valves or head gasket. Leakage past the valves may be caused by burned valve seats and/or faces or warped, cracked or bent valves.

11 If two adjacent cylinders have equally low compression, there's a strong possibility that the head gasket between them is blown. The appearance of coolant in the combustion chambers or the crankcase would verify this condition.

12 If one cylinder is 20 percent lower than the others, and the engine has a slightly rough idle, a worn exhaust lobe on the camshaft could be the cause.

13 If the compression is unusually high, the combustion chambers are probably coated with carbon deposits. If that's the case, the cylinder heads should be removed and decarbonized.

14 If compression is way down or varies greatly between cylinders, it would be a good idea to have a leak-down test performed by an automotive repair shop. This test will pinpoint exactly where the leakage is occurring and how severe it is.

---

4   Engine removal — methods and precautions

If you've decided that an engine must be removed for overhaul or major repair work, several preliminary steps should be taken.

Locating a suitable place to work is extremely important. Adequate work space, along with storage space for the vehicle, will be needed. If a shop or garage isn't available, at the very least a flat, level, clean work surface made of concrete or asphalt is required.

Cleaning the engine compartment and engine before beginning the removal procedure will help keep tools clean and organized.

An engine hoist or A-frame will also be necessary. Make sure the equipment is rated in excess of the combined weight of the engine and accessories. Safety is of primary importance, considering the potential hazards involved in lifting the engine out of the vehicle.

If the engine is being removed by a novice, a helper should be available. Advice and aid from someone more experienced would also be helpful. There are many instances when one person cannot simultaneously perform all of the operations required when lifting the engine out of the vehicle.

Plan the operation ahead of time. Arrange for or obtain all of the tools and equipment you'll need prior to beginning the job. Some of the equipment necessary to perform engine removal and installation safely and with relative ease are (in addition to an engine hoist) a heavy duty floor jack, complete sets of wrenches and sockets as described in the front of this manual, wooden blocks and plenty of rags and cleaning solvent for mopping up spilled oil, coolant and gasoline. If the hoist must be rented, make sure that you arrange for it in advance and perform all of the operations possible without it beforehand. This will save you money and time.

Plan for the vehicle to be out of use for quite a while. A machine shop will be required to perform some of the work which the do-it-yourselfer can't accomplish without special equipment. These shops often have a busy schedule, so it would be a good idea to consult them before removing the engine in order to accurately estimate the amount of time required to rebuild or repair components that may need work.

Always be extremely careful when removing and installing the engine. Serious injury can result from careless actions. Plan ahead, take your time and a job of this nature, although major, can be accomplished successfully.

---

5   Engine — removal and installation

Refer to illustrations 5.5 and 5.20
Warning: *The air conditioning system is under high pressure! Have a*

dealer service department or service station discharge the system before disconnecting any A/C system hoses or fittings.

Removal

1   Disconnect the negative cable from the battery.

2   Cover the fenders and cowl and remove the hood (see Chapter 11). Special pads are available to protect the fenders, but an old bedspread or blanket will also work.

3   Remove the air cleaner assembly.

4   Drain the cooling system (see Chapter 1).

5   Label the vacuum lines, emissions system hoses, wiring connectors, ground straps and fuel lines, to ensure correct reinstallation, then detach them. Pieces of masking tape with numbers or letters written on them work well **(see illustration)**. If there's any possibility of confusion, make a sketch of the engine compartment and clearly label the lines, hoses and wires.

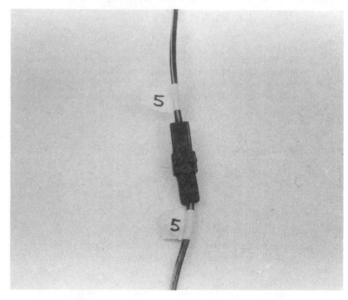

5.5   Flag each wire and hose to ease reassembly

6   Label and detach all coolant hoses from the engine.

7   Remove the cooling fan, shroud and radiator (see Chapter 3).

8   Remove the drivebelts (see Chapter 1).

9   **Warning:** *Gasoline is extremely flammable, so extra precautions must be taken when working on any part of the fuel system. DO NOT smoke or allow open flames or bare light bulbs near the vehicle. Also, don't work in a garage if a natural gas appliance with a pilot light is present.* Disconnect the fuel lines running from the engine to the chassis (see Chapter 4). Plug or cap all open fittings/lines.

10 Disconnect the throttle linkage (and TV linkage/speed control cable, if equipped) from the engine (see Chapter 4).

11 On power steering equipped vehicles, unbolt the power steering pump (see Chapter 10). Leave the lines/hoses attached and make sure the pump is kept in an upright position in the engine compartment (use wire or rope to restrain it out of the way).

12 On A/C equipped vehicles, unbolt the compressor (see Chapter 3) and set it aside. Do not disconnect the hoses.

13 Drain the engine oil (Chapter 1) and remove the filter.

14 Remove the starter motor (see Chapter 5).

15 Remove the alternator (see Chapter 5).

16 Unbolt the exhaust system from the engine (see Chapter 4).

17 If you're working on a vehicle with an automatic transmission, refer to Chapter 7 and remove the torque converter-to-driveplate fasteners.

18 Support the transmission with a jack. Position a block of wood between them to prevent damage to the transmission. Special transmission jacks with safety chains are available — use one if possible.

19 Attach an engine sling or a length of chain to the lifting brackets on the engine.

20 Roll the hoist into position and connect the sling to it **(see illustration)**. Take up the slack in the sling or chain, but don't lift the engine. **Warning:** *DO NOT place any part of your body under the engine when it's supported only by a hoist or other lifting device.*

5.20 Properly attached engine chain

21 Remove the transmission-to-engine block bolts.
22 Remove the engine mount-to-frame bolts.
23 Recheck to be sure nothing is still connecting the engine to the transmission or vehicle. Disconnect anything still remaining.
24 Raise the engine slightly. Carefully work it forward to separate it from the transmission. If you're working on a vehicle with an automatic transmission, be sure the torque converter stays in the transmission (clamp a pair of vise-grips to the housing to keep the converter from sliding out). If you're working on a vehicle with a manual transmission, the input shaft must be completely disengaged from the clutch. Slowly raise the engine out of the engine compartment. Check carefully to make sure nothing is hanging up.
25 Remove the flywheel/driveplate and mount the engine on an engine stand.

Installation

26 Check the engine and transmission mounts. If they're worn or damaged, replace them.
27 If you're working on a manual transmission equipped vehicle, install the clutch and pressure plate (Chapter 7). Now is a good time to install a new clutch.
28 Carefully lower the engine into the engine compartment — make sure the engine mounts line up.
29 If you're working on an automatic transmission equipped vehicle, guide the torque converter into the crankshaft following the procedure outlined in Chapter 7.
30 If you're working on a manual transmission equipped vehicle, apply a dab of high-temperature grease to the input shaft and guide it into the crankshaft pilot bearing until the bellhousing is flush with the engine block.
31 Install the transmission-to-engine bolts and tighten them securely.
Caution: *DO NOT use the bolts to force the transmission and engine together!*
32 Reinstall the remaining components in the reverse order of removal.
33 Add coolant, oil, power steering and transmission fluid as needed.
34 Run the engine and check for leaks and proper operation of all accessories, then install the hood and test drive the vehicle.
35 Have the A/C system recharged and leak tested.

---

6   Engine rebuilding alternatives

The do-it-yourselfer is faced with a number of options when performing an engine overhaul. The decision to replace the engine block, piston/connecting rod assemblies and crankshaft depends on a number of factors, with the number one consideration being the condition of the block. Other considerations are cost, access to machine shop facilities, parts availability, time required to complete the project and the extent of prior mechanical experience on the part of the do-it-yourselfer.

Some of the rebuilding alternatives include:

Individual parts — If the inspection procedures reveal that the engine block and most engine components are in reusable condition, purchasing individual parts may be the most economical alternative. The block, crankshaft and piston/connecting rod assemblies should all be inspected carefully. Even if the block shows little wear, the cylinder bores should be surface honed.

Short block — A short block consists of an engine block with a crankshaft and piston/connecting rod assemblies already installed. All new bearings are incorporated and all clearances will be correct. The existing camshaft, valve train components, cylinder heads and external parts can be bolted to the short block with little or no machine shop work necessary.

Long block — A long block consists of a short block plus an oil pump, oil pan, cylinder heads, rocker arm covers, camshaft and valve train components, timing sprockets and chain or gears and timing cover. All components are installed with new bearings, seals and gaskets incorporated throughout. The installation of manifolds and external parts is all that's necessary.

Give careful thought to which alternative is best for you and discuss the situation with local automotive machine shops, auto parts dealers and experienced rebuilders before ordering or purchasing replacement parts.

---

7   Engine overhaul — disassembly sequence

Refer to illustrations 7.3a and 7.3b

1   It's much easier to disassemble and work on the engine if it's mounted on a portable engine stand. A stand can often be rented quite cheaply from an equipment rental yard. Before the engine is mounted on a stand, the flywheel/driveplate should be removed from the engine.
2   If a stand isn't available, it's possible to disassemble the engine with it blocked up on the floor. Be extra careful not to tip or drop the engine when working without a stand.
3   If you're going to obtain a rebuilt engine, all external components must come off first, to be transferred to the replacement engine, just as they will if you're doing a complete engine overhaul yourself. These include:

Alternator and brackets
Emissions control components
Distributor, spark plug wires and spark plugs
Thermostat and housing cover
Water pump
Carburetor
Intake/exhaust manifolds
Oil filter
Engine mounts
Clutch and flywheel/driveplate
Engine rear plate

Note: *When removing the external components from the engine, pay close attention to details that may be helpful or important during installation. Note the installed position of gaskets, seals, spacers, pins, brackets, washers, bolts and other small items* (**see illustrations**).

4   If you're obtaining a short block, which consists of the engine block, crankshaft, pistons and connecting rods all assembled, then the cylinder heads, oil pan and oil pump will have to be removed as well. See *Engine rebuilding alternatives* for additional information regarding the different possibilities to be considered.
5   If you're planning a complete overhaul, the engine must be disassembled and the internal components removed in the following order:

Rocker arm covers
Intake and exhaust manifolds
Rocker arms and pushrods
Valve lifters
Cylinder heads
Timing cover
Timing chain and sprockets
Camshaft
Oil pan
Oil pump
Piston/connecting rod assemblies
Crankshaft and main bearings

2B

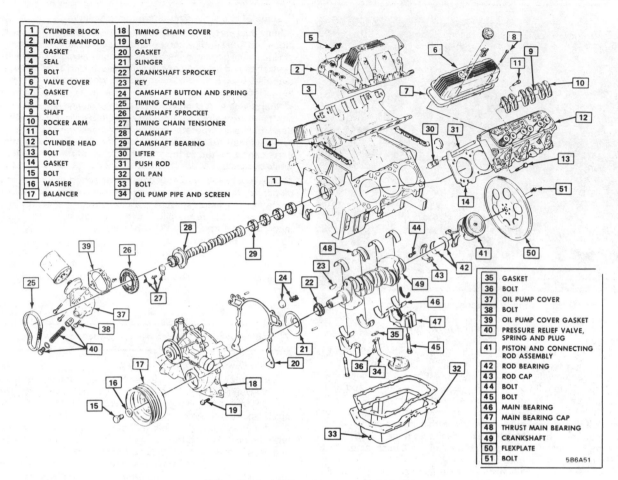

1	CYLINDER BLOCK	18	TIMING CHAIN COVER
2	INTAKE MANIFOLD	19	BOLT
3	GASKET	20	GASKET
4	SEAL	21	SLINGER
5	BOLT	22	CRANKSHAFT SPROCKET
6	VALVE COVER	23	KEY
7	GASKET	24	CAMSHAFT BUTTON AND SPRING
8	BOLT	25	TIMING CHAIN
9	SHAFT	26	CAMSHAFT SPROCKET
10	ROCKER ARM	27	TIMING CHAIN TENSIONER
11	BOLT	28	CAMSHAFT
12	CYLINDER HEAD	29	CAMSHAFT BEARING
13	BOLT	30	LIFTER
14	GASKET	31	PUSH ROD
15	BOLT	32	OIL PAN
16	WASHER	33	BOLT
17	BALANCER	34	OIL PUMP PIPE AND SCREEN

35	GASKET
36	BOLT
37	OIL PUMP COVER
38	BOLT
39	OIL PUMP COVER GASKET
40	PRESSURE RELIEF VALVE, SPRING AND PLUG
41	PISTON AND CONNECTING ROD ASSEMBLY
42	ROD BEARING
43	ROD CAP
44	BOLT
45	BOLT
46	MAIN BEARING
47	MAIN BEARING CAP
48	THRUST MAIN BEARING
49	CRANKSHAFT
50	FLEXPLATE
51	BOLT

5B6A51

7.3a Typical V6 engine — exploded view

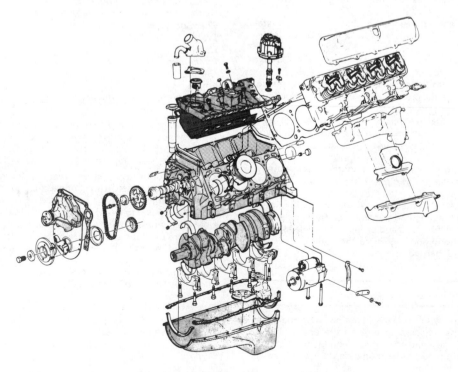

7.3b Typical V8 engine — exploded view

6   Before beginning the disassembly and overhaul procedures, make sure the following items are available. Also, refer to *Engine overhaul — reassembly sequence* for a list of tools and materials needed for engine reassembly.

Common hand tools
Small cardboard boxes or plastic bags for storing parts
Gasket scraper
Ridge reamer
Vibration damper puller
Micrometers
Telescoping gauges
Dial indicator set
Valve spring compressor
Cylinder surfacing hone
Piston ring groove cleaning tool
Electric drill motor
Tap and die set
Wire brushes
Oil gallery brushes
Cleaning solvent

8 Cylinder head — disassembly

Refer to illustrations 8.2, 8.3 and 8.4

Note: *New and rebuilt cylinder heads are commonly available for most engines at dealerships and auto parts stores. Due to the fact that some specialized tools are necessary for the disassembly and inspection procedures, and replacement parts may not be readily available, it may be more practical and economical for the home mechanic to purchase replacement heads rather than taking the time to disassemble, inspect and recondition the originals.*

1   Cylinder head disassembly involves removal of the intake and exhaust valves and related components. If they're still in place, remove the rocker arm nuts, pivot balls and rocker arms from the cylinder head studs. Label the parts or store them separately so they can be reinstalled in their original locations.
2   Before the valves are removed, arrange to label and store them, along with their related components, so they can be kept separate and reinstalled in the same valve guides they are removed from **(see illustration).**
3   Compress the springs on the first valve with a spring compressor and remove the keepers **(see Illustration).** Carefully release the valve spring compressor and remove the retainer, the spring and the spring seat (if used).
4   Pull the valve out of the head, then remove the oil seal from the

guide. If the valve binds in the guide (won't pull through), push it back into the head and deburr the area around the keeper groove with a fine file or whetstone **(see illustration).**
5   Repeat the procedure for the remaining valves. Remember to keep all the parts for each valve together so they can be reinstalled in the same locations.
6   Once the valves and related components have been removed and stored in an organized manner, the heads should be thoroughly cleaned and inspected. If a complete engine overhaul is being done, finish the engine disassembly procedures before beginning the cylinder head cleaning and inspection process.

9 Cylinder head — cleaning and inspection

1   Thorough cleaning of the cylinder heads and related valve train components, followed by a detailed inspection, will enable you to decide how much valve service work must be done during the engine overhaul. **Note:** *If the engine was severely overheated, the cylinder head is probably warped (see Step 12).*

8.2 A small plastic bag, with an appropriate label, can be used to store the valve train components so they can be kept together and reinstalled in the correct guide

8.3 Use a valve spring compressor to compress the spring, then remove the keepers from the valve stem

8.4 If the valve won't pull through the guide, deburr the edge of the stem end and the area around the top of the keeper groove with a file

2B

Cleaning

2   Scrape all traces of old gasket material and sealing compound off the head gasket, intake manifold and exhaust manifold sealing surfaces. Be very careful not to gouge the cylinder head. Special gasket removal solvents that soften gaskets and make removal much easier are available at auto parts stores.

3   Remove all built up scale from the coolant passages.

4   Run a stiff wire brush through the various holes to remove deposits that may have formed in them.

5   Run an appropriate size tap into each of the threaded holes to remove corrosion and thread sealant that may be present. If compressed air is available, use it to clear the holes of debris produced by this operation. **Warning:** *Wear eye protection when using compressed air!*

6   Clean the rocker arm pivot stud threads, when equipped, with a wire brush.

7   Clean the cylinder head with solvent and dry it thoroughly. Compressed air will speed the drying process and ensure that all holes and recessed areas are clean. **Note:** *Decarbonizing chemicals are available and may prove very useful when cleaning cylinder heads and valve train components. They are very caustic and should be used with caution. Be sure to follow the instructions on the container.*

8   Clean the rocker arm components and pushrods with solvent and dry them thoroughly (don't mix them up during the cleaning process). Compressed air will speed the drying process and can be used to clean out the oil passages.

9   Clean all the valve springs, spring seats, keepers and retainers (or rotators) with solvent and dry them thoroughly. Do the components from one valve at a time to avoid mixing up the parts.

10   Scrape off any heavy deposits that may have formed on the valves, then use a motorized wire brush to remove deposits from the valve heads and stems. Again, make sure the valves don't get mixed up.

Inspection

Note: *Be sure to perform all of the following inspection procedures before concluding that machine shop work is required. Make a list of the items that need attention.*

Cylinder head

Refer to illustrations 9.12, 9.14a and 9.14b

11   Inspect the head very carefully for cracks, evidence of coolant leakage and other damage. If cracks are found, check with an automotive machine shop concerning repair. If repair isn't possible, a new cylinder head should be obtained.

12   Using a straightedge and feeler gauge, check the head gasket mating surface for warpage **(see illustration)**. If the warpage exceeds the specified limit, it can be resurfaced at an automotive machine shop. **Note:** *If the heads are resurfaced, the intake manifold flanges will also require machining.*

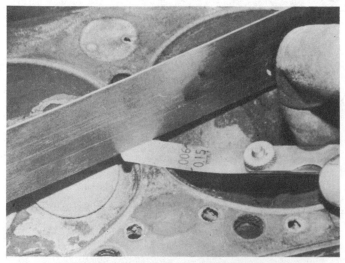

9.12   Check the cylinder head gasket surface for warpage by trying to slip a feeler gauge under the straightedge (see the Specifications for the maximum warpage allowed and use a feeler gauge of that thickness)

13   Examine the valve seats in each of the combustion chambers. If they're pitted, cracked or burned, the head will require valve service that's beyond the scope of the home mechanic.

14   Check the valve stem-to-guide clearance by measuring the lateral movement of the valve stem with a dial indicator attached securely to the head **(see illustration)**. The valve must be in the guide and approximately 1/16-inch off the seat. The total valve stem movement indicated by the gauge needle must be divided by two to obtain the actual clearance. After this is done, if there's still some doubt regarding the condition of the valve guides they should be checked by an automotive machine shop (the cost should be minimal). Oversize valves may be used to compensate for guide wear **(see illustration)**.

Valves

Refer to illustrations 9.15a, 9.15b and 9.16

15   Carefully inspect each valve face for uneven wear, deformation, cracks, pits and burned areas **(see illustration)**. Check the valve stem

9.14a   A dial indicator can be used to determine the valve stem-to-guide clearance (move the valve stem as indicated by the arrows)

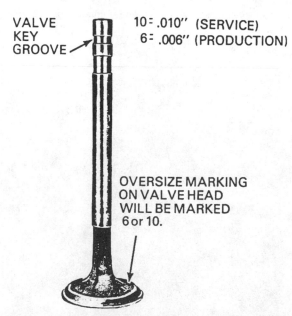

9.14b   Some engines are equipped with slightly oversized valves from the factory. Valves with larger diameter stems are available to compensate for guide wear; however, a machine shop must resize the guides

for scuffing and galling and the neck for cracks. Rotate the valve and check for any obvious indication that it's bent. Look for pits and excessive wear on the end of the stem. The presence of any of these conditions indicates the need for valve service by an automotive machine shop.

16 Measure the margin width on each valve (see illustration). Any valve with a margin narrower than specified will have to be replaced with a new one.

Valve components

Refer to illustrations 9.18 and 9.19

17 Check each valve spring for wear (on the ends) and pits. Any springs that are shorter than specified have sagged and should not be reused. The tension of all springs should be checked with a special fixture before deciding that they're suitable for use in a rebuilt engine (take the springs to an automotive machine shop for this check).

18 Stand each spring on a flat surface and check it for squareness (see illustration). If any of the springs are distorted or sagged, replace

all of them with new parts.

19 Check the spring retainers (or rotators) and keepers for obvious wear and cracks. Any questionable parts should be replaced with new ones, as extensive damage will occur if they fail during engine operation. Make sure the rotators operate smoothly with no binding or excessive play (see illustration).

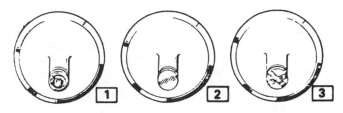

9.15b Valve stem wear patterns

1 Proper tip pattern (rotator functioning properly)
2 No rotation pattern (replace rotator and check rotation)

3 Partial rotation pattern (replace rotator and check rotation)

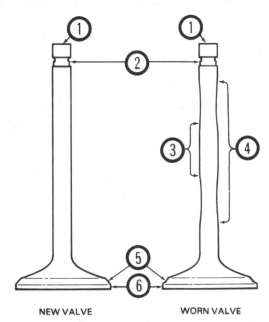

9.15a Check for valve wear at the points shown here

1 Valve tip
2 Keeper groove
3 Stem (least worn area)
4 Stem (most worn area)
5 Valve face
6 Margin

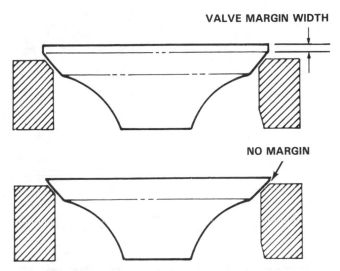

9.16 The margin width on each valve must be as specified (if no margin exists, the valve cannot be reused)

9.18 Check each valve spring for squareness

9.19 The exhaust valve rotators can be checked by turning the inner and outer sections in opposite directions — feel for smooth movement and excessive play

2B

Rocker arm components

20 Check the rocker arm faces (the areas that contact the pushrod ends and valve stems) for pits, wear, galling, score marks and rough spots. Check the rocker arm pivot contact areas and pivot as well. Look for cracks in each rocker arm and nut or bolt.

21 Inspect the pushrod ends for scuffing and excessive wear. Roll each pushrod on a flat surface, like a piece of plate glass, to determine if it's bent.

22 Check the rocker arm studs in the cylinder heads for damaged threads and secure installation.

23 Any damaged or excessively worn parts must be replaced with new ones.

24 If the inspection process indicates that the valve components are in generally poor condition and worn beyond the limits specified, which is usually the case in an engine that's being overhauled, reassemble the valves in the cylinder head and refer to Section 10 for valve servicing recommendations.

10 Valves — servicing

1 Because of the complex nature of the job and the special tools and equipment needed, servicing of the valves, the valve seats and the valve guides, commonly known as a valve job, should be done by a professional.

2 The home mechanic can remove and disassemble the heads, do the initial cleaning and inspection, then reassemble and deliver them to a dealer service department or an automotive machine shop for the actual service work. Doing the inspection will enable you to see what condition the heads and valvetrain components are in and will ensure that you know what work and new parts are required when dealing with an automotive machine shop.

3 The dealer service department, or automotive machine shop, will remove the valves and springs, recondition or replace the valves and valve seats, recondition the valve guides, check and replace the valve springs, spring retainers or rotators and keepers (as necessary), replace the valve seals with new ones, reassemble the valve components and make sure the installed spring height is correct. The cylinder head gasket surfaces will also be resurfaced if they're warped.

4 After the valve job has been performed by a professional, the heads will be in like-new condition. When the heads are returned, be sure to clean them again before installation on the engine to remove any metal particles and abrasive grit that may still be present from the valve service or head resurfacing operations. Use compressed air, if available, to blow out all the oil holes and passages.

11 Cylinder head — reassembly

Refer to illustrations 11.3, 11.5a, 11.5b, 11.6, 11.8 and 11.9

1 Regardless of whether or not the heads were sent to an automotive repair shop for valve servicing, make sure they are clean before beginning reassembly.

2 If the heads were sent out for valve servicing, the valves and related components will already be in place. Begin the reassembly procedure with Step 8.

3 Install new seals on each of the intake valve guides. Using a hammer and a deep socket, gently tap each seal into place until it is completely seated on the guide **(see illustration)**. Do not twist or cock the seals during installation or they will not seal properly on the valve stems. The umbrella-type seals are installed over the exhaust valves after the valves are in place.

4 Beginning at one end of the head, lubricate and install the first valve. Apply moly-base grease or clean engine oil to the valve stem.

5 Drop the spring seat or shim(s) over the valve guide and set the valve springs, shield and retainer (or rotator) in place **(see illustrations)**.

6 Compress the springs with a valve spring compressor and carefully install the O-ring oil seal in the lower groove of the valve stem. Make sure the seal is not twisted — it must lie perfectly flat in the groove. Position the keepers in the upper groove, then slowly release the com-

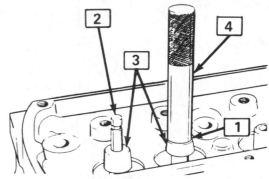

11.3   Make sure the new valve stem seals are seated against the tops of the valve guides

1 Valve seal seated in tool
2 Deburr the end of the valve stem before installing the seal
3 Seal
4 Valve seal installation tool

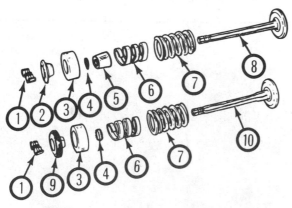

11.5a   Typical engine valves and related components — exploded view

1 Keeper
2 Retainer
3 Oil shield
4 O-ring oil seal
5 Umbrella seal
6 Damper
7 Spring
8 Intake valve
9 Rotator
10 Exhaust valve

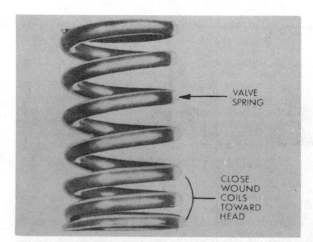

11.5b   If the valve springs are wound closer at one end, install them as shown

pressor and make sure the keepers seat properly. Apply a small dab of grease to each keeper to hold it in place if necessary (**see illustration**).

7   Repeat the procedure for the remaining valves. Be sure to return the components to their original locations — do not mix them up!

8   Once all the valves are in place in both heads, the valve stem O-ring seals must be checked to make sure they do not leak. This procedure requires a vacuum pump and special adapter (GM tool no. J-23994), so it may be a good idea to have it done by a dealer service department, repair shop or automotive machine shop. The adapter is positioned on each valve retainer or rotator and vacuum is applied with the hand pump (**see illustration**). If the vacuum cannot be maintained, the seal is leaking and must be checked/replaced before the head is installed on the engine.

9   Check the installed valve spring height with a ruler graduated in 1/32-inch increments or a dial caliper. If the heads were sent out for service work, the installed height should be correct (but don't automatically assume that it is). The measurement is taken from the top of each spring seat or shim(s) to the top of the oil shield (or the bottom of the retainer/rotator, the two points are the same) (**see illustration**). If the height is greater than specified, shims can be added under the springs to correct it. **Caution:** *Do not, under any circumstances, shim the springs to the point where the installed height is less than specified.*

10   Apply moly-base grease to the rocker arm faces and the pivot balls, then install the rocker arms and pivots on the cylinder head studs. Thread the nuts on three or four turns only at this time (when the heads are installed, the nuts will be tightened following a specific procedure).

12   Pistons/connecting rod assembly — removal

Refer to illustrations 12.1, 12.3 and 12.6

Note: *Prior to removing the piston/connecting rod assemblies, remove the cylinder heads, the oil pan and the oil pump (except externally mounted pumps) by referring to the appropriate Sections in Chapter 2.*

1   Use your fingernail to feel if a ridge has formed at the upper limit of ring travel (about 1/4-inch down from the top of each cylinder). If carbon deposits or cylinder wear have produced ridges, they must be completely removed with a special tool (**see illustration**). Follow the manufacturer's instructions provided with the tool. Failure to remove the ridges before attempting to remove the piston/connecting rod assemblies may result in piston breakage.

2   After the cylinder ridges have been removed, turn the engine upside-down so the crankshaft is facing up.

3   Before the connecting rods are removed, check the end play with feeler gauges. Slide them between the first connecting rod and the crankshaft throw until the play is removed (**see illustration**). The end play is equal to the thickness of the feeler gauge(s). If the end play

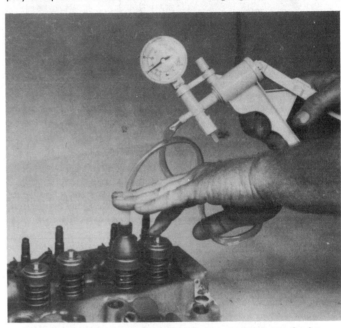

11.6   Apply a small dab of grease to each keeper as shown here before installation — it will hold them in place on the valve stem as the spring is released

11.8   A special adapter and a vacuum pump are required to check the O-ring valve stem seals for leaks

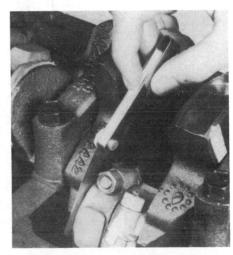

11.9   Be sure to check the valve spring installed height (the distance from the top of the seat/shims to the top of the shield)

12.1   A ridge reamer is required to remove the ridge from the top of the cylinder — do this before removing the pistons!

12.3   Check the connecting rod side clearance with a feeler gauge as shown

2B

exceeds the service limit, new connecting rods will be required. If new rods (or a new crankshaft) are installed, the end play may fall under the specified minimum (if it does, the rods will have to be machined to restore it — consult an automotive machine shop for advice if necessary). Repeat the procedure for the remaining connecting rods.

4   Check the connecting rods and caps for identification marks. If they aren't plainly marked, use a small center punch to make the appropriate number of indentations on each rod and cap (1, 2, 3, etc., depending on the engine type and cylinder they're associated with).

5   Loosen each of the connecting rod cap nuts 1/2-turn at a time until they can be removed by hand. Remove the number one connecting rod cap and bearing insert. Don't drop the bearing insert out of the cap.

6   Slip a short length of plastic or rubber hose over each connecting rod cap bolt to protect the crankshaft journal and cylinder wall as the piston is removed (**see illustration**).

7   Remove the bearing insert and push the connecting rod/piston

assembly out through the top of the engine. Use a wooden hammer handle to push on the upper bearing surface in the connecting rod. If resistance is felt, double-check to make sure that all of the ridge was removed from the cylinder.

8   Repeat the procedure for the remaining cylinders.

9   After removal, reassemble the connecting rod caps and bearing inserts in their respective connecting rods and install the cap nuts finger tight. Leaving the old bearing inserts in place until reassembly will help prevent the connecting rod bearing surfaces from being accidentally nicked or gouged.

10 Don't separate the pistons from the connecting rods (see Section 17 for additional information).

12.6   To prevent damage to the crankshaft journals and cylinder walls, slip sections of hose over the rod bolts before removing the pistons

---

13   Crankshaft — removal

Refer to illustrations 13.1, 13.3, 13.4a and 13.4b

Note: *The crankshaft can be removed only after the engine has been removed from the vehicle. It's assumed that the flywheel or driveplate, vibration damper, timing chain, oil pan, oil pump and piston/connecting rod assemblies have already been removed. If your engine is equipped with a one-piece rear main oil seal, the seal housing must be unbolted and separated from the block before proceeding with crankshaft removal.*

1   Before the crankshaft is removed, check the end play. Mount a dial indicator with the stem in line with the crankshaft and just touching one of the crank throws (**see illustration**).

2   Push the crankshaft all the way to the rear and zero the dial indicator. Next, pry the crankshaft to the front as far as possible and check the reading on the dial indicator. The distance that it moves is the end play. If it's greater than specified, check the crankshaft thrust surfaces for wear. If no wear is evident, new main bearings should correct the end play.

3   If a dial indicator isn't available, feeler gauges can be used. Gently pry or push the crankshaft all the way to the front of the engine. Slip feeler gauges between the crankshaft and the front face of the thrust main bearing to determine the clearance (**see illustration**).

4   Check the main bearing caps to see if they're marked to indicate their locations. They should be numbered consecutively from the front of the engine to the rear. If they aren't, mark them with number stamping dies or a center punch (**see illustration**). Main bearing caps generally have a cast-in arrow, which points to the front of the engine (**see**

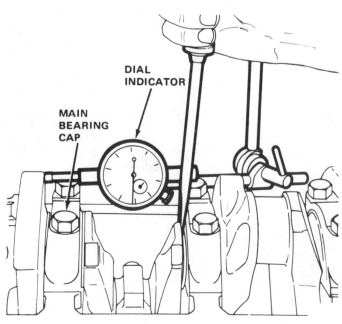

13.1   Checking crankshaft end play with a dial indicator

13.3   Checking crankshaft end play with a feeler gauge

illustration). Loosen the main bearing cap bolts 1/4-turn at a time each, until they can be removed by hand. Note if any stud bolts are used and make sure they're returned to their original locations when the crankshaft is reinstalled.

5   Gently tap the caps with a soft-face hammer, then separate them from the engine block. If necessary, use the bolts as levers to remove the caps. Try not to drop the bearing inserts if they come out with the caps.

6   Carefully lift the crankshaft out of the engine. It may be a good idea to have an assistant available, since the crankshaft is quite heavy. With the bearing inserts in place in the engine block and main bearing caps, return the caps to their respective locations on the engine block and tighten the bolts finger tight.

oil holes and galleries. **Warning:** *Wear eye protection when using compressed air!*

7   If the block isn't extremely dirty or sludged up, you can do an adequate cleaning job with hot soapy water and a stiff brush. Take plenty of time and do a thorough job. Regardless of the cleaning method used, be sure to clean all oil holes and galleries very thoroughly, dry the block completely and coat all machined surfaces with light oil.

8   The threaded holes in the block must be clean to ensure accurate torque readings during reassembly. Run the proper size tap into each of the holes to remove rust, corrosion, thread sealant or sludge and restore damaged threads. If possible, use compressed air to clear the holes of debris produced by this operation. Now is a good time to clean the threads on the head bolts and the main bearing cap bolts as well.

9   Reinstall the main bearing caps and tighten the bolts finger tight.

14 Engine block — cleaning

Refer to illustrations 14.1 and 14.10

Caution: *The core plugs (also known as freeze or soft plugs) may be difficult or impossible to retrieve if they're driven into the block coolant passages.*

1   Drill a small hole in the center of each core plug and pull them out with an auto body type dent puller **(see illustration).**

2   Using a gasket scraper, remove all traces of gasket material from the engine block. Be very careful not to nick or gouge the gasket sealing surfaces.

3   Remove the main bearing caps and separate the bearing inserts from the caps and the engine block. Tag the bearings, indicating which cylinder they were removed from and whether they were in the cap or the block, then set them aside.

4   Remove all of the threaded oil gallery plugs from the block. The plugs are usually very tight — they may have to be drilled out and the holes retapped. Use new plugs when the engine is reassembled.

5   If the engine is extremely dirty it should be taken to an automotive machine shop to be steam cleaned or hot tanked.

6   After the block is returned, clean all oil holes and oil galleries one more time. Brushes specifically designed for this purpose are available at most auto parts stores. Flush the passages with warm water until the water runs clear, dry the block thoroughly and wipe all machined surfaces with a light, rust preventive oil. If you have access to compressed air, use it to speed the drying process and to blow out all the

13.4a Use a center punch or number stamping dies to mark the main bearing caps to ensure that they are reinstalled in their original locations on the block (make the punch marks near one of the bolt heads)

13.4b The arrow on the main bearing cap indicates the front of the engine

14.1 Using an auto body dent puller to remove the engine core plugs

2B

10 After coating the sealing surfaces of the new core plugs with Permatex no. 2 sealant, install them in the engine block **(see illustration)**. Make sure they're driven in straight and seated properly or leakage could result. Special tools are available for this purpose, but a large socket, with an outside diameter that will just slip into the core plug, a 1/2-inch drive extension and a hammer will work just as well.

11 Apply non-hardening sealant (such as Permatex no. 2 or Teflon pipe sealant) to the new oil gallery plugs and thread them into the holes in the block. Make sure they're tightened securely.

12 If the engine isn't going to be reassembled right away, cover it with a large plastic trash bag to keep it clean.

15 Engine block — inspection

Refer to illustrations 15.4a, 15.4b and 15.4c

1 Before the block is inspected, it should be cleaned as described in Section 14.

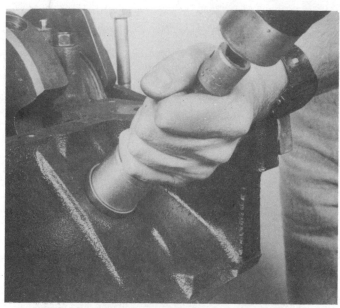

14.10   A large socket on an extension can be used to drive the new soft plugs into the bores

2 Visually check the block for cracks, rust and corrosion. Look for stripped threads in the threaded holes. It's also a good idea to have the block checked for hidden cracks by an automotive machine shop that has the special equipment to do this type of work. If defects are found, have the block repaired, if possible, or replaced.

3 Check the cylinder bores for scuffing and scoring.

4 Measure the diameter of each cylinder at the top (just under the ridge area), center and bottom of the cylinder bore, parallel to the crankshaft axis (**see illustrations**).

5 Next, measure each cylinder's diameter at the same three locations *across* the crankshaft axis. Compare the results to the Specifications.

6 If the required precision measuring tools aren't available, the piston-to-cylinder clearances can be obtained, though not quite as accurately, using feeler gauge stock. Feeler gauge stock comes in 12-inch lengths and various thicknesses and is generally available at auto parts stores.

7 To check the clearance, select a feeler gauge and slip it into the cylinder along with the matching piston. The piston must be positioned exactly as it normally would be. The feeler gauge must be between the piston and cylinder on one of the thrust faces (90° to the piston pin bore).

8 The piston should slip through the cylinder (with the feeler gauge in place) with moderate pressure.

9 If it falls through or slides through easily, the clearance is excessive and a new piston will be required. If the piston binds at the lower end of the cylinder and is loose toward the top, the cylinder is tapered. If tight spots are encountered as the piston/feeler gauge is rotated in the cylinder, the cylinder is out-of-round.

10 Repeat the procedure for the remaining pistons and cylinders.

11 If the cylinder walls are badly scuffed or scored, or if they're out-

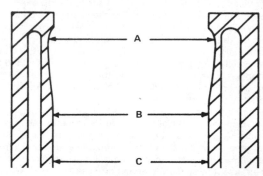

15.4a   Measure the diameter of each cylinder just under the wear ridge (A), at the center (B) and at the bottom (C)

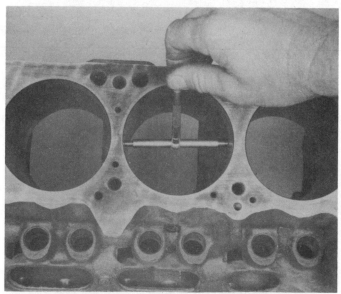

15.4b   The ability to "feel" when the telescoping gauge is at the correct point will be developed over time, so work slowly and repeat the check until you are satisfied that the bore measurement is accurate

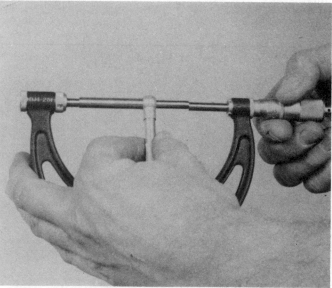

15.4c   The gauge is then measured with a micrometer to determine the bore size

of-round or tapered beyond the limits given in the Specifications, have the engine block rebored and honed at an automotive machine shop. If a rebore is done, oversize pistons and rings will be required.

12 If the cylinders are in reasonably good condition and not worn to the outside of the limits, and if the piston-to-cylinder clearances can be maintained properly, then they don't have to be rebored. Honing is all that's necessary (Section 16).

16 Cylinder honing

Refer to illustrations 16.3a and 16.3b

1 Prior to engine reassembly, the cylinder bores must be honed so the new piston rings will seat correctly and provide the best possible combustion chamber seal. **Note:** *If you don't have the tools or don't want to tackle the honing operation, most automotive machine shops will do it for a reasonable fee.*

2 Before honing the cylinders, install the main bearing caps and tighten the bolts to the specified torque.

3 Two types of cylinder hones are commonly available — the flex hone, or "bottle brush," type and the more traditional surfacing hone with spring-loaded stones. Both will do the job, but for the less experienced mechanic the "bottle brush" hone will probably be easier to use. You'll also need some kerosene or honing oil, rags and an electric drill motor. Proceed as follows:

  a) Mount the hone in the drill motor, compress the stones and slip it into the first cylinder **(see illustration)**. Be sure to wear safety goggles or a face shield!

  b) Lubricate the cylinder with plenty of honing oil, turn on the drill and move the hone up and down in the cylinder at a pace that will produce a fine crosshatch pattern on the cylinder walls. Ideally, the crosshatch lines should intersect at approximately a 60° angle **(see illustration)**. Be sure to use plenty of lubricant and don't take off any more material than is absolutely necessary to produce the desired finish. **Note:** *Piston ring manufacturers may specify a smaller crosshatch angle than the traditional 60° — read and follow any instructions included with the new rings.*

  c) Don't withdraw the hone from the cylinder while it's running. Instead, shut off the drill and continue moving the hone up-and-down in the cylinder until it comes to a complete stop, then compress the stones and withdraw the hone. If you're using a "bottle brush" type hone, stop the drill motor, then turn the chuck in the normal direction of rotation while withdrawing the hone from the cylinder.

  d) Wipe the oil out of the cylinder and repeat the procedure for the remaining cylinders.

4 After the honing job is complete, chamfer the top edges of the cylinder bores with a small file so the rings won't catch when the pistons are installed. **Be very careful not to nick the cylinder walls with the end of the file.**

5 The entire engine block must be washed again very thoroughly with warm, soapy water to remove all traces of the abrasive grit produced during the honing operation. **Note:** *The bores can be considered clean when a lint-free white cloth — dampened with clean engine oil — used to wipe them out doesn't pick up any more honing residue, which will show up as gray areas on the cloth.* Be sure to run a brush through all oil holes and galleries and flush them with running water.

6 After rinsing, dry the block and apply a coat of light rust preventive oil to all machined surfaces. Wrap the block in a plastic trash bag to keep it clean and set it aside until reassembly.

16.3a A "bottle brush" hone will produce better results if you have never done cylinder honing before

17 Piston/connecting rod assembly — inspection

Refer to illustrations 17.4a, 17.4b, 17.10 and 17.11

1 Before the inspection process can be carried out, the piston/connecting rod assemblies must be cleaned and the original piston rings removed from the pistons. **Note:** *Always use new piston rings when the engine is reassembled.*

2 Using a piston ring installation tool, carefully remove the rings from the pistons. Be careful not to nick or gouge the pistons in the process.

3 Scrape all traces of carbon from the top of the piston. A handheld wire brush or a piece of fine emery cloth can be used once the majority of the deposits have been scraped away. Do not, under any circumstances, use a wire brush mounted in a drill motor to remove deposits from the pistons. The piston material is soft and may be eroded away by the wire brush.

4 Use a piston ring groove cleaning tool to remove carbon deposits

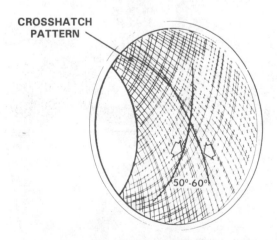

16.3b The cylinder hone should leave a smooth, crosshatch pattern with the lines intersecting at approximately a 60-degree angle

CROSSHATCH PATTERN

50°-60°

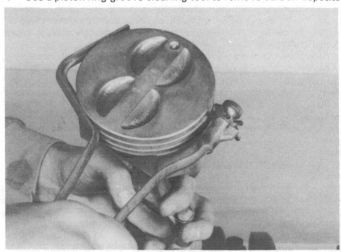

17.4a The piston ring grooves can be cleaned with a special tool, as shown here, . . .

2B

17.4b   . . . or a section of a broken ring

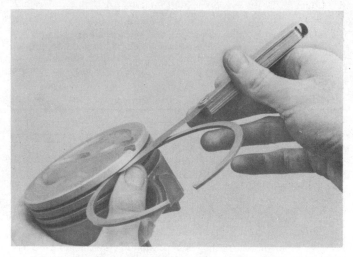

17.10   Check the ring side clearance with a feeler gauge at several points around the groove

from the ring grooves. If a tool isn't available, a piece broken off the old ring will do the job. Be very careful to remove only the carbon deposits — don't remove any metal and do not nick or scratch the sides of the ring grooves (**see illustrations**).

5   Once the deposits have been removed, clean the piston/rod assemblies with solvent and dry them with compressed air (if available). Make sure the oil return holes in the back sides of the ring grooves are clear.

6   If the pistons and cylinder walls aren't damaged or worn excessively, and if the engine block is not rebored, new pistons won't be necessary. Normal piston wear appears as even vertical wear on the piston thrust surfaces and slight looseness of the top ring in its groove. New piston rings, however, should always be used when an engine is rebuilt.

7   Carefully inspect each piston for cracks around the skirt, at the pin bosses and at the ring lands.

8   Look for scoring and scuffing on the thrust faces of the skirt, holes in the piston crown and burned areas at the edge of the crown. If the skirt is scored or scuffed, the engine may have been suffering from overheating and/or abnormal combustion, which caused excessively high operating temperatures. The cooling and lubrication systems should be checked thoroughly. A hole in the piston crown is an indication that abnormal combustion (preignition) was occurring. Burned areas at the edge of the piston crown are usually evidence of spark knock (detonation). If any of the above problems exist, the causes must be corrected or the damage will occur again. The causes may include intake air leaks, incorrect fuel/air mixture, incorrect ignition timing and EGR system malfunctions.

9   Corrosion of the piston, in the form of small pits, indicates that coolant is leaking into the combustion chamber and/or the crankcase. Again, the cause must be corrected or the problem may persist in the rebuilt engine.

10   Measure the piston ring side clearance by laying a new piston ring in each ring groove and slipping a feeler gauge in beside it (**see illustration**). Check the clearance at three or four locations around each groove. Be sure to use the correct ring for each groove — they are different. If the side clearance is greater than specified, new pistons will have to be used.

11   Check the piston-to-bore clearance by measuring the bore (see Section 15) and the piston diameter. Make sure the pistons and bores are correctly matched. Measure the piston across the skirt, at a 90° angle to and in line with the piston pin (**see illustration**). Subtract the piston diameter from the bore diameter to obtain the clearance. If it's greater than specified, the block will have to be rebored and new pistons and rings installed.

12   Check the piston-to-rod clearance by twisting the piston and rod in opposite directions. Any noticeable play indicates excessive wear, which must be corrected. The piston/connecting rod assemblies should be taken to an automotive machine shop to have the pistons and rods resized and new pins installed.

13   If the pistons must be removed from the connecting rods for any reason, they should be taken to an automotive machine shop. While

they are there have the connecting rods checked for bend and twist, since automotive machine shops have special equipment for this purpose. **Note:** *Unless new pistons and/or connecting rods must be installed, do not disassemble the pistons and connecting rods.*

14   Check the connecting rods for cracks and other damage. Temporarily remove the rod caps, lift out the old bearing inserts, wipe the rod and cap bearing surfaces clean and inspect them for nicks, gouges and scratches. After checking the rods, replace the old bearings, slip the caps into place and tighten the nuts finger tight. **Note:** *If the engine is being rebuilt because of a connecting rod knock, be sure to install new rods.*

---

18   Crankshaft — inspection

1   Clean the crankshaft with solvent and dry it with compressed air (if available). Be sure to clean the oil holes with a stiff brush and flush them with solvent.

2   Check the main and connecting rod bearing journals for uneven wear, scoring, pits and cracks.

3   Rub a penny across each journal several times. If a journal picks up copper from the penny, it's too rough and must be reground.

4   Remove all burrs from the crankshaft oil holes with a stone, file or scraper.

17.11   Measure the piston diameter at a 90° angle to the piston pin and in line with it

5   Check the rest of the crankshaft for cracks and other damage. It should be magnafluxed to reveal hidden cracks — an automotive machine shop will handle the procedure.

6   Using a micrometer, measure the diameter of the main and connecting rod journals and compare the results to the Specifications. By measuring the diameter at a number of points around each journal's circumference, you'll be able to determine whether or not the journal is out-of-round. Take the measurement at each end of the journal, near the crank throws, to determine if the journal is tapered.

7   If the crankshaft journals are damaged, tapered, out-of-round or worn beyond the limits given in the Specifications, have the crankshaft reground by an automotive machine shop. Be sure to use the correct size bearing inserts if the crankshaft is reconditioned.

8   Check the oil seal journals at each end of the crankshaft for wear and damage. If the seal has worn a groove in the journal, or if it's nicked or scratched, the new seal may leak when the engine is reassembled. In some cases, an automotive machine shop may be able to repair the journal by pressing on a thin sleeve. If repair isn't feasible, a new or different crankshaft should be installed.

9   Refer to Section 19 and examine the main and rod bearing inserts.

19   Main and connecting rod bearings — inspection

Refer to illustration 19.1

1   Even though the main and connecting rod bearings should be replaced with new ones during the engine overhaul, the old bearings should be retained for close examination, as they may reveal valuable information about the condition of the engine (**see illustration**).

2   Bearing failure occurs because of lack of lubrication, the presence of dirt or other foreign particles, overloading the engine and corrosion. Regardless of the cause of bearing failure, it must be corrected before the engine is reassembled to prevent it from happening again.

3   When examining the bearings, remove them from the engine block, the main bearing caps, the connecting rods and the rod caps and lay them out on a clean surface in the same general position as their location in the engine. This will enable you to match any bearing problems with the corresponding crankshaft journal.

4   Dirt and other foreign particles get into the engine in a variety of ways. It may be left in the engine during assembly, or it may pass through filters or the PCV system. It may get into the oil, and from

there into the bearings. Metal chips from machining operations and normal engine wear are often present. Abrasives are sometimes left in engine components after reconditioning, especially when parts are not thoroughly cleaned using the proper cleaning methods. Whatever the source, these foreign objects often end up embedded in the soft bearing material and are easily recognized. Large particles will not embed in the bearing and will score or gouge the bearing and journal. The best prevention for this cause of bearing failure is to clean all parts thoroughly and keep everything spotlessly clean during engine assembly. Frequent and regular engine oil and filter changes are also recommended.

5   Lack of lubrication (or lubrication breakdown) has a number of interrelated causes. Excessive heat (which thins the oil), overloading (which squeezes the oil from the bearing face) and oil leakage or throw off (from excessive bearing clearances, worn oil pump or high engine speeds) all contribute to lubrication breakdown. Blocked oil passages, which usually are the result of misaligned oil holes in a bearing shell, will also oil starve a bearing and destroy it. When lack of lubrication is the cause of bearing failure, the bearing material is wiped or extruded from the steel backing of the bearing. Temperatures may increase to the point where the steel backing turns blue from overheating.

6   Driving habits can have a definite effect on bearing life. Full throttle, low speed operation (lugging the engine) puts very high loads on bearings, which tends to squeeze out the oil film. These loads cause the bearings to flex, which produces fine cracks in the bearing face (fatigue failure). Eventually the bearing material will loosen in pieces and tear away from the steel backing. Short trip driving leads to corrosion of bearings because insufficient engine heat is produced to drive off the condensed water and corrosive gases. These products collect in the engine oil, forming acid and sludge. As the oil is carried to the engine bearings, the acid attacks and corrodes the bearing material.

7   Incorrect bearing installation during engine assembly will lead to bearing failure as well. Tight fitting bearings leave insufficient bearing oil clearance and will result in oil starvation. Dirt or foreign particles trapped behind a bearing insert result in high spots on the bearing which lead to failure.

2B

20   Engine overhaul — reassembly sequence

1   Before beginning engine reassembly, make sure you have all the necessary new parts, gaskets and seals as well as the following items on hand:

Common hand tools
A 1/2-inch drive torque wrench
Piston ring installation tool
Piston ring compressor
Vibration damper installation tool
Short lengths of rubber or plastic hose
*   to fit over connecting rod bolts*
Plastigage
Feeler gauges
A fine-tooth file
New engine oil
Engine assembly lube or moly-base grease
Gasket sealant
Thread locking compound

2   In order to save time and avoid problems, engine reassembly must be done in the following general order:

New camshaft bearings (must be installed by an auto machine shop)
Piston rings
Crankshaft and main bearings
Piston/connecting rod assemblies
Oil pump — except external-mount type
Camshaft and lifters
Oil pan
Timing chain and sprockets
Cylinder heads, pushrods and rocker arms
Timing cover (and oil pump — external-mount type)
Intake and exhaust manifolds
Rocker arm covers
Engine rear plate
Flywheel/driveplate

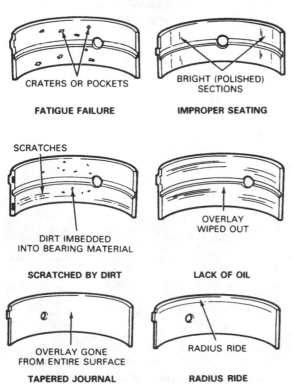

CRATERS OR POCKETS

FATIGUE FAILURE

BRIGHT (POLISHED) SECTIONS

IMPROPER SEATING

SCRATCHES

DIRT IMBEDDED INTO BEARING MATERIAL

SCRATCHED BY DIRT

OVERLAY WIPED OUT

LACK OF OIL

OVERLAY GONE FROM ENTIRE SURFACE

TAPERED JOURNAL

RADIUS RIDE

RADIUS RIDE

19.1   Typical indications of bearing failure

21 Piston rings — installation

Refer to illustrations 21.3, 21.4, 21.5, 21.9a, 21.9b, 21.12a and 21.12b

1   Before installing the new piston rings, the ring end gaps must be checked. It's assumed that the piston ring side clearance has been checked and verified correct (Section 17).

2   Lay out the piston/connecting rod assemblies and the new ring sets so the ring sets will be matched with the same piston and cylinder during the end gap measurement and engine assembly.

3   Insert the top (number one) ring into the first cylinder and square it up with the cylinder walls by pushing it in with the top of the piston (**see illustration**). The ring should be near the bottom of the cylinder, at the lower limit of ring travel.

4   To measure the end gap, slip feeler gauges between the ends of the ring until a gauge equal to the gap width is found (**see illustration**). The feeler gauge should slide between the ring ends with a slight amount of drag. Compare the measurement to the Specifications. If the gap is larger or smaller than specified, double-check to make sure you have the correct rings before proceeding.

5   If the gap is too small, it must be enlarged or the ring ends may come in contact with each other during engine operation, which can cause serious damage to the engine. The end gap can be increased by filing the ring ends very carefully with a fine file. Mount the file in a vise equipped with soft jaws, slip the ring over the file with the ends contacting the file face and slowly move the ring to remove material from the ends. When performing this operation, file only from the outside in (**see illustration**).

6   Excess end gap isn't critical unless it's greater than 0.040-inch. Again, double-check to make sure you have the correct rings for your engine.

7   Repeat the procedure for each ring that will be installed in the first cylinder and for each ring in the remaining cylinders. Remember to keep rings, pistons and cylinders matched up.

8   Once the ring end gaps have been checked/corrected, the rings can be installed on the pistons.

9   The oil control ring (lowest one on the piston) is usually installed first. It's composed of three separate components. Slip the spacer/ex-

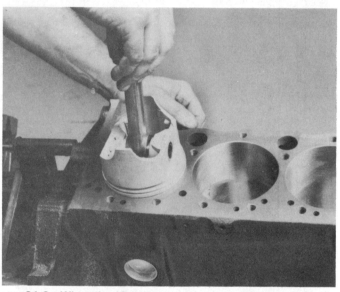

21.3   When checking piston ring end gap, the ring must be square in the cylinder bore (this is done by pushing the ring down with the top of a piston as shown)

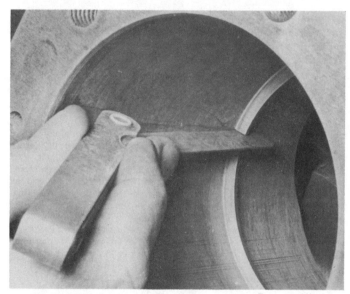

21.4   With the ring square in the cylinder, measure the end gap with a feeler gauge

21.5   If the end gap is too small, clamp a file in a vise and file the ring ends (from the outside in only) to enlarge the gap slightly

21.9a   Installing the spacer/expander in the oil control ring groove

pander into the groove (**see illustration**). If an anti-rotation tang is used, make sure it's inserted into the drilled hole in the ring groove. Next, install the lower side rail. Don't use a piston ring installation tool on the oil ring side rails, as they may be damaged. Instead, place one end of the side rail into the groove between the spacer/expander and the ring land, hold it firmly in place and slide a finger around the piston while pushing the rail into the groove (**see illustration**). Next, install the upper side rail in the same manner.

10 After the three oil ring components have been installed, check to make sure that both the upper and lower side rails can be turned smoothly in the ring groove.

11 The number two (middle) ring is installed next. It's usually stamped with a mark which must face up, toward the top of the piston. **Note:** *Always follow the instructions printed on the ring package or box — different manufacturers may require different approaches. Do not mix up the top and middle rings, as they have different cross sections.*

12 Use a piston ring installation tool and make sure the identification mark is facing the top of the piston (**see illustration**), then slip the ring into the middle groove on the piston (**see illustration**). Don't expand

the ring any more than necessary to slide it over the piston.

13 Install the number one (top) ring in the same manner. Make sure the mark is facing up. Be careful not to confuse the number one and number two rings.

14 Repeat the procedure for the remaining pistons and rings.

22 Crankshaft — installation and main bearing oil clearance check

Refer to illustrations 22.11, 22.15 and 22.16

1 Crankshaft installation is the first step in engine reassembly. It's assumed at this point that the engine block and crankshaft have been cleaned, inspected and repaired or reconditioned.

2 Position the engine with the bottom facing up.

3 Remove the main bearing cap bolts and lift out the caps. Lay them out in the proper order to ensure correct installation.

4 If they're still in place, remove the original bearing inserts from the block and the main bearing caps. Wipe the bearing surfaces of the block and caps with a clean, lint-free cloth. They must be kept spotlessly clean.

Main bearing oil clearance check

5 Clean the back sides of the new main bearing inserts and lay one in each main bearing saddle in the block. If one of the bearing inserts from each set has a large groove in it, make sure the grooved insert is installed in the block. Lay the other bearing from each set in the corresponding main bearing cap. Make sure the tab on the bearing insert fits into the recess in the block or cap. **Caution:** *The oil holes in the block must line up with the oil holes in the bearing insert. Do not hammer the bearing into place and don't nick or gouge the bearing faces. No lubrication should be used at this time.*

6 The flanged thrust bearing must be installed in the proper cap and saddle.

7 Clean the faces of the bearings in the block and the crankshaft main bearing journals with a clean, lint-free cloth.

8 Check or clean the oil holes in the crankshaft, as any dirt here can go only one way — straight through the new bearings.

9 Once you're certain the crankshaft is clean, carefully lay it in position in the main bearings.

10 Before the crankshaft can be permanently installed, the main bearing oil clearance must be checked.

11 Cut several pieces of the appropriate size Plastigage (they must be slightly shorter than the width of the main bearings) and place one

2B

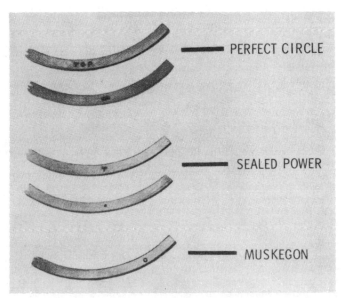
21.9b DO NOT use a piston ring installation tool when installing the oil ring side rails

21.12a Piston ring TOP marks — typical

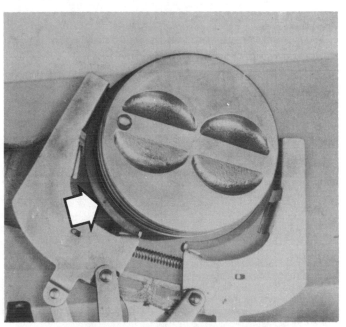
21.12b Installing the compression rings with a ring expander — the mark (arrow) must face up

22.11 Lay the Plastigage strips (arrow) on the main bearing journals, parallel to the crankshaft centerline

22.15 Compare the width of the crushed Plastigage to the scale on the container to determine the main bearing oil clearance (always take the measurement at the widest point of the Plastigage); be sure to use the correct scale — standard and metric scales are included

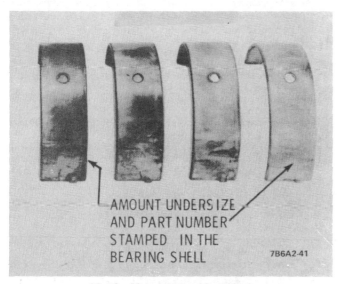

AMOUNT UNDERSIZE
AND PART NUMBER
STAMPED IN THE
BEARING SHELL

7B6A2-41

22.16 Main bearing identification

piece on each crankshaft main bearing journal, parallel with the journal axis (**see illustration**).

12 Clean the faces of the bearings in the caps and install the caps in their respective positions (don't mix them up) with the arrows pointing toward the front of the engine. Don't disturb the Plastigage.

13 Starting with the center main and working out toward the ends, tighten the main bearing cap bolts, in three steps, to the specified torque. Don't rotate the crankshaft at any time during this operation.

14 Remove the bolts and carefully lift off the main bearing caps. Keep them in order. Don't disturb the Plastigage or rotate the crankshaft. If any of the main bearing caps are difficult to remove, tap them gently from side to side with a soft-face hammer to loosen them.

15 Compare the width of the crushed Plastigage on each journal to the scale printed on the Plastigage envelope to obtain the main bearing oil clearance (**see illustration**). Check the Specifications to make sure it's correct.

16 If the clearance is not as specified, the bearing inserts (**see illustration**) may be the wrong size (which means different ones will be re-

quired). Before deciding that different inserts are needed, make sure that no dirt or oil was between the bearing inserts and the caps or block when the clearance was measured. If the Plastigage was wider at one end than the other, the journal may be tapered (refer to Section 18).

17 Carefully scrape all traces of the Plastigage material off the main bearing journals and/or the bearing faces. Use your fingernail or the edge of a credit card — don't nick or scratch the bearing faces.

Final crankshaft installation

18 Carefully lift the crankshaft out of the engine.

19 Clean the bearing faces in the block, then apply a thin, uniform layer of moly-base grease or engine assembly lube to each of the bearing surfaces. Be sure to coat the thrust faces as well as the journal face of the thrust bearing.

20 Make sure the crankshaft journals are clean, then lay the crankshaft back in place in the block.

21 Clean the faces of the bearings in the caps, then apply lubricant to them.

22 Install the caps in their respective positions with the arrows pointing toward the front of the engine.

23 Install the bolts.

24 Tighten all except the thrust bearing cap bolts to the specified torque (work from the center out and approach the final torque in three steps).

25 Tighten the thrust bearing cap bolts to 10-to-12 ft-lbs.

26 Tap the ends of the crankshaft forward and backward with a lead or brass hammer to line up the main bearing and crankshaft thrust surfaces.

27 Retighten all main bearing cap bolts to the specified torque, starting with the center main and working out toward the ends.

28 On manual transmission equipped models, install a new pilot bearing in the end of the crankshaft (see Chapter 8).

29 Rotate the crankshaft a number of times by hand to check for any obvious binding.

30 The final step is to check the crankshaft end play with a feeler gauge or a dial indicator as described in Section 13. The end play should be correct if the crankshaft thrust faces aren't worn or damaged and new bearings have been installed.

31 If you are working on an engine with a one-piece rear main oil seal, refer to Section 23 and install the new seal, then bolt the housing to the block.

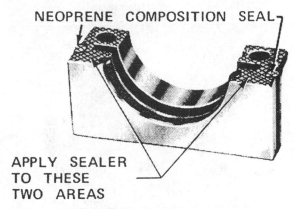

NEOPRENE COMPOSITION SEAL

APPLY SEALER TO THESE TWO AREAS

23.6 Areas for applying sealer to main bearing cap

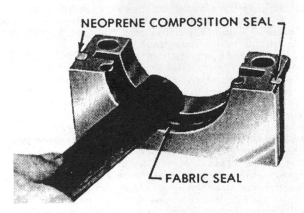

NEOPRENE COMPOSITION SEAL

FABRIC SEAL

23.3 Using a wood hammer handle for installing the rear main bearing seal

2B

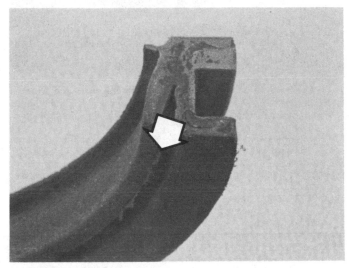

23.9 The rear main oil seal may have two lips — the oil seal (arrow) must point toward the front of the engine, which means that the dust seal will face out, toward the rear of the engine

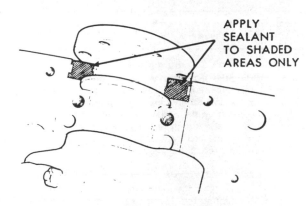

APPLY SEALANT TO SHADED AREAS ONLY

23.11 Before installing the rear main bearing cap, apply the specified sealant to the shaded areas of the block (or the equivalent areas on the cap)

23 Rear main oil seal installation

Split-type (two-piece) fabric seal

Refer to illustrations 23.3 and 23.6

1 Braided fabric seals pressed into grooves formed in the crankcase and rear bearing cap are used to seal against oil leakage around the crankshaft. The crankshaft must be removed for this operation.

2 With the bearing caps and the crankshaft removed, remove the old oil seal and place a new seal in the groove with both ends projecting above the parting surface of the cap.

3 Use a handle of a hammer or similar tool to force the seal into the groove by rubbing down until the seal projects above the groove not more then 1/16-inch **(see illustration)**. Cut the ends of the seal flush with the surface of the cap with a single-edged razor blade.

4 Soak the neoprene seals (if equipped), which go into the grooves in the sides of the bearing cap in kerosene for one to two minutes.

5 Install the neoprene seals (if equipped) in the groove between the bearing cap and the crankcase. The seals are slightly undersized and swell in the presence of heat and oil. They are slightly longer than the groove in the bearing cap and must not be cut to fit.

6 Apply a small amount of RTV sealer at the joint where the bearing cap meets the crankcase to help eliminate oil leakage **(see illustration)**. A very thin coat is all that is necessary.

7 Install the bearing cap in the crankcase. Force the seals up into the bearing cap with a blunt instrument to be sure of a good seal at the upper parting line between the cap and case.

Split-type (two-piece) neoprene seal

Refer to illustrations 23.9 and 23.11

8 Inspect the rear main bearing cap and engine block mating surfaces, as well as the seal grooves, for nicks, burrs and scratches. Remove any defects with a fine file or deburring tool.

9 Install one seal section in the block with the lip facing the front of the engine (if the seal has two lips, the one with the helix must face the front) **(see illustration)**. Leave one end protruding from the block approximately 1/4- to 3/8-inch and make sure it's completely seated.

10 Repeat the procedure to install the remaining seal half in the rear main bearing cap. In this case, leave the opposite end of the seal protruding from the cap the same distance the block seal is protruding from the block.

11 During final installation of the crankshaft (after the main bearing oil clearances have been checked with Plastigage) as described in Section 22, apply a thin, even coat of anaerobic-type gasket sealant to the shaded areas of the cap or block **(see illustration)**. Don't get any sealant on the bearing face, crankshaft journal, seal ends or seal lips. Also, lubricate the seal lips with moly-base grease or engine assembly lube.

Housing that bolts to block

12 Some models are equipped with a one-piece seal that fits into a housing attached to the block. The crankshaft must be installed first and the main bearing caps bolted in place, then the new seal should be installed in the housing and the housing bolted to the block **(see illustration in Chapter 2A)**.

13   Before installing the crankshaft, check the seal contact surface very carefully for scratches and nicks that could damage the new seal lip and cause oil leaks. If the crankshaft is damaged, the only alternative is a new or different crankshaft.

14   The old seal can be removed from the housing with a screwdriver by prying it out from the front (see illustration in Chapter 2A). Be sure to note how far it's recessed into the housing bore before removing it; the new seal will have to be recessed an equal amount. Be very careful not to scratch or otherwise damage the bore in the housing or oil leaks could develop.

15   Make sure the housing is clean, then apply a thin coat of engine oil to the outer edge of the new seal. The seal must be pressed squarely into the housing bore, so hammering it into place is not recommended. If you don't have access to a press, sandwich the housing and seal between two smooth pieces of wood and press the seal into place with the jaws of a large vise. The pieces of wood must be thick enough to distribute the force evenly around the entire circumference of the seal. Work slowly and make sure the seal enters the bore squarely.

16   The seal lips must be lubricated with moly-base grease or engine assembly lube before the seal/housing is slipped over the crankshaft and bolted to the block. Use a new gasket — no sealant is required — and make sure the dowel pins are in place before installing the housing.

17   Tighten the screws a little at a time until they're all at the specified torque.

---

24   Piston/connecting rod assembly — installation and rod bearing oil clearance check

Refer to illustrations 24.5, 24.9 and 24.11

1   Before installing the piston/connecting rod assemblies, the cylinder walls must be perfectly clean, the top edge of each cylinder must be chamfered, and the crankshaft must be in place.

2   Remove the cap from the end of the number one connecting rod (refer to the marks made during removal). Remove the original bearing inserts and wipe the bearing surfaces of the connecting rod and cap with a clean, lint-free cloth. They must be kept spotlessly clean.

Connecting rod bearing oil clearance check

3   Clean the back side of the new upper bearing insert, then lay it in place in the connecting rod. Make sure the tab on the bearing fits into the recess in the rod. Don't hammer the bearing insert into place and be very careful not to nick or gouge the bearing face. Don't lubricate the bearing at this time.

4   Clean the back side of the other bearing insert and install it in the rod cap. Again, make sure the tab on the bearing fits into the recess in the cap, and don't apply any lubricant. It's critically important that the mating surfaces of the bearing and connecting rod are perfectly clean and oil-free when they're assembled.

5   Position the piston ring gaps at 120° intervals around the piston (see illustration).

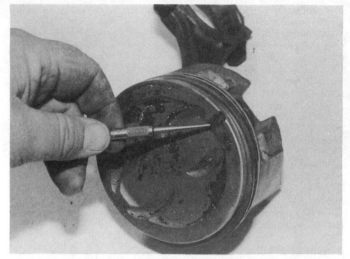

24.9   The notch in each piston must face the FRONT of the engine as the pistons are installed

6   Slip a section of plastic or rubber hose over each connecting rod cap bolt.

7   Lubricate the piston and rings with clean engine oil and attach a piston ring compressor to the piston. Leave the skirt protruding about 1/4-inch to guide the piston into the cylinder. The rings must be compressed until they're flush with the piston.

8   Rotate the crankshaft until the number one connecting rod journal is at BDC (bottom dead center) and apply a coat of engine oil to the cylinder walls.

9   With the mark or notch on top of the piston (see illustration) facing the front of the engine, gently insert the piston/connecting rod assembly into the number one cylinder bore and rest the bottom edge of the ring compressor on the engine block.

10   Tap the top edge of the ring compressor to make sure it's contacting the block around its entire circumference.

11   Gently tap on the top of the piston with the end of a wooden hammer handle (see illustration) while guiding the end of the connecting rod into place on the crankshaft journal. The piston rings may try to pop out of the ring compressor just before entering the cylinder bore, so keep some downward pressure on the ring compressor. Work slowly, and if any resistance is felt as the piston enters the cylinder, stop immediately. Find out what's hanging up and fix it before proceeding. Do not, for any reason, force the piston into the cylinder — you might break a ring and/or the piston.

12   Once the piston/connecting rod assembly is installed, the connecting rod bearing oil clearance must be checked before the rod cap is permanently bolted in place.

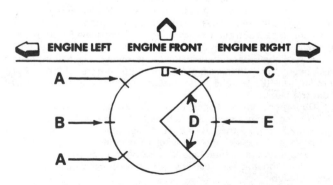

← ENGINE LEFT   ↑ ENGINE FRONT   ENGINE RIGHT →

24.5   Position the piston ring gaps as shown here before installing the piston/connecting rod assemblies in the engine

A   Oil ring rail gaps
B   2nd compression ring gap
C   Notch in position
D   Oil ring spacer gap (tang in hole or slot with arc)
E   Top compression ring gap

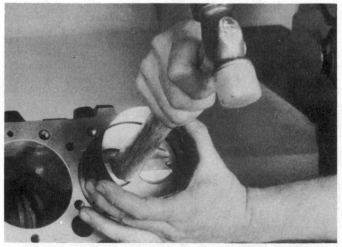

24.11   The piston can be driven (gently) into the cylinder bore with the end of a wooden hammer handle

13 Cut a piece of the appropriate size Plastigage slightly shorter than the width of the connecting rod bearing and lay it in place on the number one connecting rod journal, parallel with the journal axis.
14 Clean the connecting rod cap bearing face, remove the protective hoses from the connecting rod bolts and install the rod cap. Make sure the mating mark on the cap is on the same side as the mark on the connecting rod.
15 Install the nuts and tighten them to the specified torque, working up to it in three steps. **Note:** *Use a thin-wall socket to avoid erroneous torque readings that can result if the socket is wedged between the rod cap and nut. If the socket tends to wedge itself between the nut and the cap, lift up on it slightly until it no longer contacts the cap.* Do not rotate the crankshaft at any time during this operation.
16 Remove the nuts and detach the rod cap, being very careful not to disturb the Plastigage.
17 Compare the width of the crushed Plastigage to the scale printed on the Plastigage envelope to obtain the oil clearance. Compare it to the Specifications to make sure the clearance is correct.
18 If the clearance is not as specified, the bearing inserts may be the wrong size (which means different ones will be required). Before deciding that different inserts are needed, make sure that no dirt or oil was between the bearing inserts and the connecting rod or cap when the clearance was measured. Also, recheck the journal diameter. If the Plastigage was wider at one end than the other, the journal may be tapered (refer to Section 18).

Final connecting rod installation

19 Carefully scrape all traces of the Plastigage material off the rod journal and/or bearing face. Be very careful not to scratch the bearing — use your fingernail or the edge of a credit card.
20 Make sure the bearing faces are perfectly clean, then apply a uniform layer of clean moly-base grease or engine assembly lube to both of them. You'll have to push the piston into the cylinder to expose the face of the bearing insert in the connecting rod — be sure to slip the protective hoses over the rod bolts first.
21 Slide the connecting rod back into place on the journal, remove the protective hoses from the rod cap bolts, install the rod cap and tighten the nuts to the specified torque. Again, work up to the torque in three steps.
22 Repeat the entire procedure for the remaining pistons/connecting rods.
23 The important points to remember are:
   a) Keep the back sides of the bearing inserts and the insides of the connecting rods and caps perfectly clean when assembling them.
   b) Make sure you have the correct piston/rod assembly for each cylinder.
   c) The notch or mark on the piston must face the front of the engine.
   d) Lubricate the cylinder walls with clean oil.
   e) Lubricate the bearing faces when installing the rod caps after the oil clearance has been checked.
24 After all the piston/connecting rod assemblies have been properly installed, rotate the crankshaft a number of times by hand to check for any obvious binding.
25 As a final step, the connecting rod end play must be checked. Refer to Section 12 for this procedure.
26 Compare the measured end play to the Specifications to make sure it's correct. If it was correct before disassembly and the original crankshaft and rods were reinstalled, it should still be right. If new rods or a new crankshaft were installed, the end play may be inadequate. If so, the rods will have to be removed and taken to an automotive machine shop for resizing.

25 Pre-oiling engine after overhaul

Note: *This procedure does not apply to V6 or Buick-built V8 engines. For those engines, go on the Section 26.*
Refer to illustrations 25.3 and 25.5

1 After an overhaul it is a good idea to pre-oil the engine before it is installed in the vehicle and started for the first time. Pre-oiling will reveal any problems with the lubrication system at a time when corrections can be made easily and will prevent major engine damage. It will also allow the internal engine parts to be lubricated thoroughly in the normal fashion without the heavy loads associated with combustion placed on them.

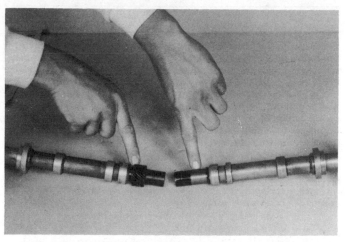
25.3 The pre-oil distributor (right) has the gear ground off and the advance weights (if equipped) removed

2 The engine should be completely assembled with the exception of the distributor and rocker arm covers. The oil filter and oil pressure sending unit must be in place and the specified amount of oil must be in the crankcase (see Chapter 1).
3 An old distributor will be needed for this procedure — a salvage yard should be able to supply one for a reasonable price. In order to function as a pre-oil tool, the distributor must have the gear on the lower end of the shaft ground off (**see illustration**) and, if equipped, the advance weights on the upper end of the shaft removed.
4 Install the pre-oil distributor in place of the original distributor and make sure the lower end of the shaft mates with the upper end of the oil pump driveshaft. Turn the distributor shaft until they are aligned and the distributor body seats on the block. Install the distributor hold-down clamp and bolt.
5 Mount the upper end of the shaft in the chuck of an electric drill and use the drill to turn the pre-oil distributor shaft, which will drive the oil pump and circulate the oil throughout the engine (**see illustration**). **Note:** *The drill must turn in a clockwise direction on Chevrolet-built engines. On Pontiac and Oldsmobile-built engines, the shaft must be turned counterclockwise as viewed from above.*
6 It may take two or three minutes, but oil should soon start to flow out of all of the rocker arm holes, indicating that the oil pump is working properly. Let the oil circulate for several seconds, then shut off the drill motor.
7 Remove the pre-oil distributor, then install the rocker arm covers. The distributor should be installed after the engine is installed in the vehicle, so plug the hole with a clean cloth.

25.5 A drill motor connected to the modified distributor shaft drives the oil pump

2B

26   Initial start-up and break-in after overhaul

Warning: *Have a fire extinguisher handy when starting the engine for the first time.*

1   Once the engine has been installed in the vehicle, double-check the engine oil and coolant levels.

2   With the spark plugs out of the engine and the ignition system disabled (see Section 3), crank the engine until oil pressure registers on the gauge or the indicator light goes out.

3   Install the spark plugs, hook up the plug wires and restore the ignition system functions (Section 3).

4   Start the engine. It may take a few moments for the fuel system to build up pressure, but the engine should start without a great deal of effort. **Note:** *If backfiring occurs through the carburetor, recheck the carburetor and ignition timing. If that fails to correct it, check for improper timing chain installation.*

5   After the engine starts, it should be allowed to warm up to normal operating temperature. While the engine is warming up, make a thorough check for fuel, oil and coolant leaks.

6   Shut the engine off and recheck the engine oil and coolant levels.

7   Drive the vehicle to an area with minimum traffic, accelerate at full throttle from 30 to 50 mph, then allow the vehicle to slow to 30 mph with the throttle closed. Repeat the procedure 10 or 12 times. This will load the piston rings and cause them to seat properly against the cylinder walls. Check again for oil and coolant leaks.

8   Drive the vehicle gently for the first 500 miles (no sustained high speeds) and keep a constant check on the oil level. It is not unusual for an engine to use oil during the break-in period.

9   At approxmately 500 to 600 miles, change the oil and filter.

10 For the next few hundred miles, drive the vehicle normally. Do not pamper it or abuse it.

11 After 2000 miles, change the oil and filter again and consider the engine broken in.

HEATER HOSES.

64" × 3/4" FROM WATER PUMP TO HEATER GOES PAST CHOKE ON CARBURATOR.

24" × 5/8" FROM REAR OF MOTOR TO HEATER.

Chapter 3   Cooling, heating and air conditioning systems

Contents

3

Specifications

General
Radiator cap pressure rating .... 14 to 17 psi
Thermostat rating
  high altitude .... 180 to 185° F
  standard .... 192 to 198° F

Torque specifications   Ft-lbs
Water pump mounting bolts
  V6 7
  V8 engines
    Buick-built 7
    Chevrolet-built 30
    Oldsmobile-built 13
    Pontiac-built
      1/4 in 12
      1/2 in 20
      3/8 in 30
Thermostat housing cover
  V6 20
  V8 engines
    Buick-built 20
    Chevrolet-built 30
    Oldsmobile-built V8 20
    Pontiac-built V8 30

1   General information

Engine cooling system

All vehicles covered by this manual employ a pressurized engine cooling system with thermostatically controlled coolant circulation. An impeller type water pump mounted on the front of the block pumps coolant through the engine. The coolant flows around each cylinder and toward the rear of the engine. Cast-in coolant passages direct coolant around the intake and exhaust ports, near the spark plug areas and in close proximity to the exhaust valve guides.

A wax pellet type thermostat is located in the thermostat housing near the front of the engine. During warm up, the closed thermostat prevents coolant from circulating through the radiator. When the engine reaches normal operating temperature, the thermostat opens and allows hot coolant to travel through the radiator, where it is cooled before returning to the engine.

The cooling system is sealed by a pressure type radiator cap. This raises the boiling point of the coolant, and the higher boiling point of the coolant increases the cooling efficiency of the radiator. If the system pressure exceeds the cap pressure relief value, the excess pressure in the system forces the spring-loaded valve inside the cap off its seat and allows the coolant to escape through the overflow tube into a coolant reservoir. When the system cools, the excess coolant is automatically drawn from the reservoir back into the radiator.

The coolant reservoir does double duty as both the point at which fresh coolant is added to the cooling system to maintain the proper fluid level and as a holding tank for overheated coolant.

This type of cooling system is known as a closed design because coolant that escapes past the pressure cap is saved and reused.

Heating system

The heating system consists of a blower fan and heater core located within the heater box, the inlet and outlet hoses connecting the heater core to the engine cooling system and the heater/air conditioning control head on the dashboard. Hot engine coolant is circulated through the heater core. When the heater mode is activated, a flap door opens to expose the heater box to the passenger compartment. A fan switch on the control head activates the blower motor, which forces air through the core, heating the air.

Air conditioning system

The air conditioning system consists of a condenser mounted in front of the radiator, an evaporator mounted adjacent to the heater core, a compressor mounted on the engine, a filter-drier (accumulator) which contains a high pressure relief valve and the plumbing connecting all of the above.

A blower fan forces the warmer air of the passenger compartment through the evaporator core (sort of a radiator-in-reverse), transferring the heat from the air to the refrigerant. The liquid refrigerant boils off into low pressure vapor, taking the heat with it when it leaves the evaporator.

2   Antifreeze — general information

Warning: *Do not allow antifreeze to come in contact with your skin or painted surfaces of the vehicle. Flush contacted areas immediately with plenty of water. Antifreeze can be fatal to children and pets. They like it because it is sweet. Ingestion of even very small amounts may be fatal. Wipe up garage floor and drip pan coolant spills immediately. Keep antifreeze containers covered and repair leaks in your cooling system immediately.*

The cooling system should be filled with a water/ethylene glycol based antifreeze solution, which will prevent freezing down to at least −20°F, or lower if local climate requires it. It also provides protection against corrosion and increases the coolant boiling point.

The cooling system should be drained, flushed and refilled at least every other year (see Chapter 1). The use of antifreeze solutions for periods of longer than two years is likely to cause damage and encourage the formation of rust and scale in the system. If your tap water is "hard", use distilled water with the antifreeze.

Before adding antifreeze to the system, check all hose connections, because antifreeze tends to search out and leak through every minute openings. Engines do not normally consume coolant. Therefore, if the level goes down find the cause and correct it.

The exact mixture of antifreeze-to-water which you should use depends on the relative weather conditions. The mixture should contain at least 50 percent antifreeze, but should never contain more than 70 percent antifreeze. Consult the mixture ratio chart on the antifreeze container before adding coolant. Hydrometers are available at most auto parts stores to test the ratio of antifreeze to water. Use antifreeze which meets GM Specification 1825-M (Part No. 1052753) or equivalent.

3   Thermostat — check and replacement

Warning: *Do not attempt to remove the radiator cap, coolant or thermostat until the engine has cooled completely.*

Caution: *Do not drive the vehicle without a thermostat. The computer (when equipped) may stay in open loop and emissions and fuel economy will suffer.*

Check

1   Before assuming the thermostat is to blame for a cooling system problem, check coolant level (Chapter 1), drivebelt tension (Chapter 1) and temperature gauge (or light) operation.
2   If the engine takes a long time to warm up, the thermostat is probably stuck open. Replace the thermostat.
3   If the engine runs hot, use your hand to check the temperature of the upper radiator hose. If the hose is not hot, but the engine is, the thermostat is probably stuck in the closed position, preventing the coolant inside the engine from escaping to the radiator. Replace the thermostat.
4   If the upper radiator hose is hot, it means that the coolant is flowing and the thermostat is open. Consult the Troubleshooting Section at the front of this manual for further diagnosis.

Replacement

Refer to illustration 3.9
5   Disconnect the negative battery cable.
6   Drain the cooling system (Chapter 1).
7   Remove the upper radiator hose from the thermostat housing.
8   On Oldsmobile-built engines, remove the smaller coolant hose from the thermosat housing.
9   Remove the bolts from the thermostat housing and detach the housing **(see illustration)**. Be prepared for some coolant to spill as the gasket seal is broken.
10   Remove the thermostat, noting the way it was installed.
11   Remove all traces of gasket material from the sealing surfaces.
12   Apply gasket sealer to both sides of a new gasket and position it on the engine.

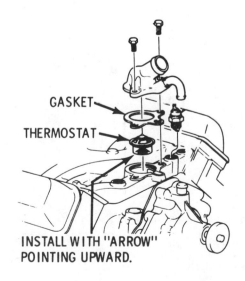

GASKET
THERMOSTAT
INSTALL WITH "ARROW" POINTING UPWARD.

3.9   Thermostat installation (typical)

13 Install the thermostat, housing and bolts. Tighten the bolts to the specified torque.
14 Refill the cooling system (Chapter 1).

4 Radiator — removal and installation

Refer to illustrations 4.4a, 4.4b, 4.4c and 4.5
Warning: *The engine must be completely cool before beginning this procedure!*

1 Disconnect the negative battery cable.
2 Drain the radiator, referring to Chapter 1.
3 Disconnect the radiator upper and lower hoses and the automatic transmission cooling lines if applicable.
4 Disconnect the radiator shroud and hang it over the fan. The shroud is attached with screws going into the radiator with clips or staples across the bottom **(see illustrations)**.
5 Remove the upper metal panel at the top of the radiator **(see illustration)**.
6 Lift the radiator straight up and out of the engine compartment. Be careful not to scratch the paint on the front nosepiece. If coolant drips on any body paint, immediately wash it off with clear water as the antifreeze solution can damage the finish.
7 With the radiator removed, it can be inspected for leaks or damage.

If in need of repairs, have a professional radiator shop or dealer perform the work, as special equipment and techniques are required.
8 Bugs and dirt can be cleaned from the radiator by using compressed air and a soft brush. Do not bend the cooling fins as this is done.
9 Inspect the rubber mounting pads which the radiator sits on and replace as necessary.
10 Lift the radiator into position making sure it is seated in the mounting pads.
11 Install the upper panel, shroud and hoses in the reverse order of removal.
12 Connect the negative battery cable and fill the radiator as described in Chapter 1.
13 Start the engine and check for leaks. Allow the engine to reach normal operating temperature (upper radiator hose hot) and add coolant until the level reaches the bottom of the filler neck.
14 Install cap with arrows aligned with the overflow tube.

5 Engine cooling fan and clutch — check and replacement

Check

1 Most vehicles covered by this manual are equipped with thermostatically controlled fan clutches. Some non-air conditioned models are equipped with solid-hub type fans.

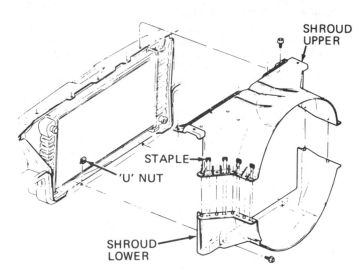

4.4a Typical V6 radiator mount and shroud

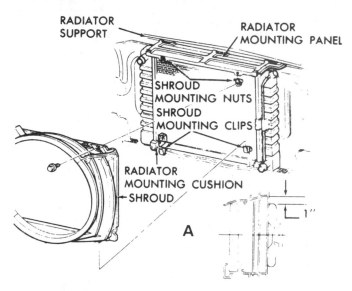

4.4b Typical radiator mount and shroud (early)

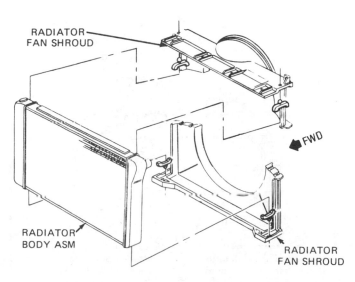

4.4c Typical radiator mount and shroud (late)

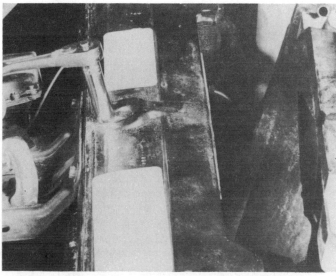

4.5 Removing radiator upper panel bolts

5.10a   On models with a clutch assembly, the fan is attached to the assembly or water pump hub with four nuts or bolts (arrow)

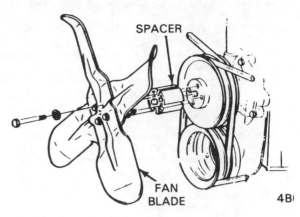

5.10b   Installation details of fan on models without automatic fan clutch

2   Begin the clutch check with a lukewarm engine (start it when cold and let it run for two minutes only).
3   Remove the key from the ignition switch for safety purposes.
4   Turn the fan blades and note the resistance. There should be moderate resistance, depending on temperature.
5   Drive the vehicle until the engine is warmed up. Shut it off and remove the key.
6   Turn the fan blades and again note the resistance. There should be a noticeable increase in resistance.
7   If the fan clutch fails this check or is locked up, replacement is indicated. If excessive fluid is leaking from the hub or lateral play over 1/4-inch is noted, replace the fan clutch.
8   If any fan blades are bent, don't straighten them! The metal will be weakened and blades could fly off during engine operation. Replace the fan with a new one.

Replacement

Refer to illustrations 5.10a and 5.10b

9   Remove the upper fan shroud.
10 Remove the fasteners holding the fan assembly to the water pump hub (see illustrations).
11 Detach the fan and clutch assembly.
12 Unbolt the fan from the clutch (if equipped).
13 Installation is the reverse of removal.
14 Tighten all fasteners securely.

6   Coolant temperature sending unit — check and replacement

Refer to illustrations 6.1a, 6.1b and 6.1c

Temperature warning light system check

1   If the light doesn't come on when the ignition switch is turned on, check the bulb. If the light stays on even with the engine cold, unplug the wire at the sending unit (see illustrations). If the light goes off, replace the sending unit. If the light stays on, the wire is grounded somewhere in the harness.

Temperature gauge system check

2   If the gauge is inoperative, check the fuse (Chapter 12).
3   If the fuse is OK, unplug the wire connected to the sending unit and ground it with a jumper wire. Turn on the ignition switch momentarily. The gauge should register at maximum. If it does, replace the sending unit. If it's still inoperative, the gauge or wiring may be faulty.

Sending unit replacement

4   Allow the engine to cool completely.
5   Unplug the wire connected to the sending unit.
6   Unscrew the sending unit and quickly install the new unit to prevent loss of coolant.
7   Connect the wire and check indicator operation.

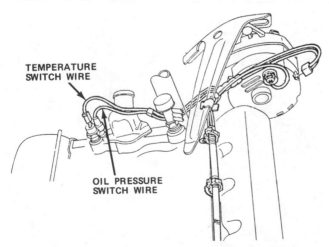

6.1a   Coolant temperature sending unit location — typical V8 except Chevrolet-built engines

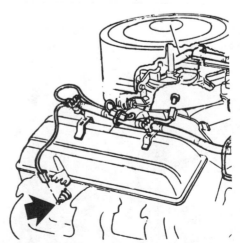

6.1b   Most Chevrolet-built engines have the coolant temperature sending unit on the left side between the number one and number three spark plugs (arrow)

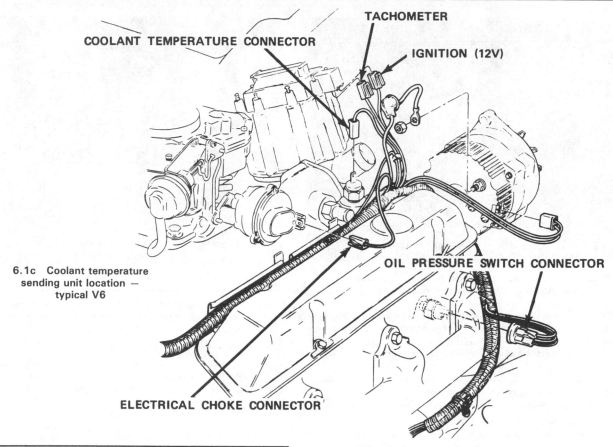

6.1c Coolant temperature sending unit location — typical V6

3

7 Coolant reservoir — removal and installation

Refer to illustration 7.1

1   Disconnect the coolant overflow hose at the radiator neck **(see illustration)**.
2   Remove the screws attaching the reservoir to the inner fender.
3   Lift the reservoir straight up off the mounting bracket.
4   Installation is the reverse of removal.

8 Water pump — check

Refer to illustration 8.3

1   Water pump failure can cause overheating of and serious damage to the engine. There are three ways to check the operation of the water pump while it's installed on the engine. If any one of the three following quick checks indicates water pump failure, it should be replaced immediately.
2   Start the engine and warm it up to normal operating temperature. Squeeze the upper radiator hose. If the water pump is working properly, a pressure surge should be felt as the hose is released.
3   A seal protects the water pump impeller shaft bearing from contamination by engine coolant. If the seal fails, weep holes in the top and bottom of the water pump snout **(see illustration)** will leak coolant under the vehicle. If the weep hole is leaking, shaft bearing failure will follow. Replace the water pump immediately.
4   Besides contamination by coolant after a seal failure, the water pump impeller shaft bearing can also be prematurely worn out by an improperly tensioned drivebelt. When the bearing wears out, it emits a high pitched squealing sound. If noise is coming from the water pump during engine operation, the shaft bearing has failed. Replace the water pump immediately.

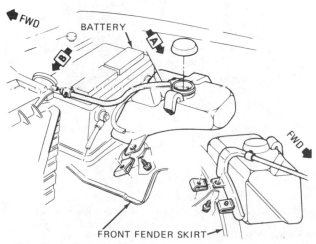

7.1 Typical coolant recovery system (late model shown)

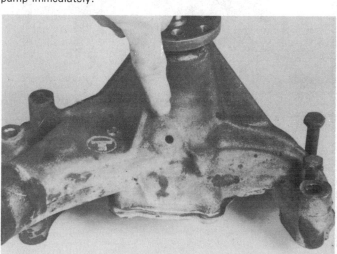

8.3 Water pump weep hole location

9.6a Note the location and position of all related mounting brackets for ease of reassembly

9.6b The long pivot bolt for the power steering pump also mounts to the water pump

5   To identify excessive bearing wear before the bearing actually fails, grasp the water pump pulley and try to force it up and down or from side to side. If the pulley can be moved either horizontally or vertically, the bearing is nearing the end of its service life. Replace the water pump.

9 Water pump — removal and installation

Refer to illustrations 9.6a, 9.6b and 9.8

Note: *It is not economical or practical to overhaul a water pump. If failure occurs, a new or rebuilt unit should be purchased to replace the faulty water pump.*

1   Disconnect the negative battery cable.
2   Drain the radiator, referring to Chapter 1 if necessary.
3   Reaching inside the radiator shroud, remove the bolts which secure the fan to the water pump hub (see Section 5). Remove the fan and

spacer (if equipped). A thermostatic fan clutch must remain in the ''in car'' position.
4   Remove the radiator shroud for better access to the water pump.
5   It is now necessary to loosen and remove all drivebelts from the water pump pulley. The number of belts will depend upon model, year, and equipment. Loosen the adjusting and pivot bolts of each affected component (air pump, alternator, air conditioning compressor, power steering pump) and push the component inward to loosen the belt enough to be removed from the water pump pulley (see Chapter 1).
6   Disconnect and remove all mounting brackets which are attached to the water pump. These may include on late model vehicles the alternator, air conditioning compressor, and power steering brackets **(see illustrations)**.
7   Disconnect the lower radiator hose, heater hose, and bypass hose at the water pump.
8   Remove the remaining bolts which secure the water pump to the front cover of the engine **(see illustration)**. Lift the water pump hous-

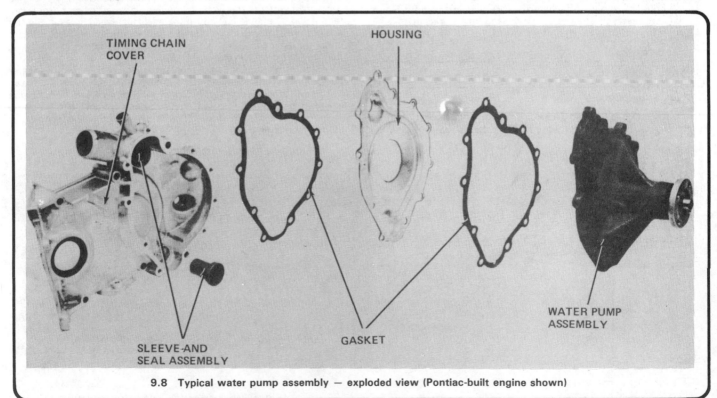

9.8 Typical water pump assembly — exploded view (Pontiac-built engine shown)

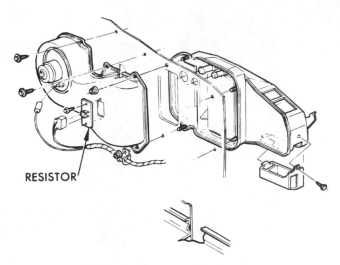

10.1a   Typical blower and case

10.1b   Later model blowers are mounted vertically near the right hood hinge

ing away from the engine.

9   If installing a new or rebuilt water pump, transfer all fittings and studs to the new water pump.

10   Clean the gasket surfaces of the front cover completely using a gasket scraper or putty knife.

11   Use a thin coat of gasket sealant on the new gaskets and install the new water pump. Place the pump into position on the front cover and secure loosely with the bolts. Do not torque tighten these bolts until all brackets have been installed to their original position on the water pump.

12   Tighten all water pump bolts to torque specifications.

13   Install the engine components in the reverse order of removal, tightening the appropriate fasteners securely.

14   Adjust all drivebelts to the proper tension (see Chapter 1).

15   Connect the negative battery cable and fill the radiator with a mixture of ethylene glycol antifreeze and water in a 50/50 mixture. Start the engine and allow it to idle until the upper radiator hose gets hot. Check for leaks. With the engine hot, fill it with more coolant mixture until the level is at the bottom of the filler neck. Install the radiator cap and check coolant level periodically over the next few miles of driving.

10   Blower unit — removal and installation

Refer to illustrations 10.1a and 10.1b

1   Disconnect the battery ground cable, then remove all wiring, hoses, etc., to the right-hand fender skirt. On 1977 and later models, the assembly is accessible from under the hood **(see illustrations)**. Simply disconnect the blower lead wire at the motor and remove the blower-to-case attaching screws.

2   Raise the front of the vehicle and support it securely on jackstands.

3   Remove all fender skirt attaching bolts except those fastened to the radiator support.

4   Pull outwards then down on the fender skirt and place a 2 x 4-inch wooden block between the skirt and fender.

5   Remove the blower wheel retaining nut and separate the wheel from the blower.

6   Pass the blower throught the fender skirt opening (paragraph 4).

7   Installation is the reverse of the removal procedure, but be sure the blower wheel is installed with the open end away from the motor.

11   Air conditioning system — check and maintenance

Refer to illustrations 11.4a, 11.4b and 11.5

1   The following maintenance steps should be performed on a regular basis to ensure that the air conditioner continues to operate at peak efficiency.

a)   Check the tension of the A/C compressor drivebelt and adjust it if necessary (refer to Chapter I).

b)   Visually inspect the condition of the hoses, looking for any cracks, hardening and other deterioration. **Note:** *Don't remove any hoses until the system has been discharged.*

c)   Make sure the fins of the condenser aren't covered with foreign material, such as leaves or bugs. A soft brush and compressed air can be used to remove them.

d)   Be sure the evaporator drain is open by slipping a wire into the drain tube occasionally.

2   The A/C compressor should be run about 10 minutes at least once every month. This is especially important to remember during the winter months because long-term non-use can cause hardening of the seals.

3   Due to the complexity of the air conditioning system and the special equipment required to effectively work on it, accurate troubleshooting and repair of the system usually cannot be done by a home mechanic and should be left to a professional. In any case, due to the toxic nature of the refrigerant, prior to disconnecting any part of the system, the vehicle should be taken to your dealer or a repair shop to have the system discharged. If the system should lose its cooling action, some causes can be diagnosed by the home mechanic. Look for other symptoms of trouble such as those that follow. In all cases, it's a good idea to have the system serviced by a professional.

4   Most of the earlier (non-accumulator) systems **(see illustration)** used a thermal limiter circuit to protect the compressor. When the thermal limiter fuse burns out, the compressor clutch won't engage. Simply

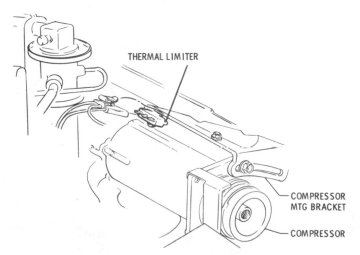

11.4a   Thermal limiters are usually mounted on the compressor bracket (models without accumulators)

11.4b   Vehicles with accumulators (arrow) do not use a thermal limiter fuse

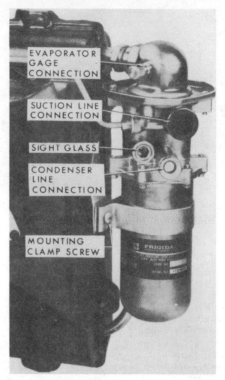

11.5   Sight glass location — typical

plug in a new one. Later models, with an accumulator, do not use a thermal limiter fuse **(see illustration).**

5   If bubbles appear in the sight glass (located near the top of the receiver-drier or accumulator) **(see illustration)**, this is an indication of either a small refrigerant leak or air in the refrigerant. If air is in the refrigerant, the receiver-dryer or accumulator is probably contaminated with moisture and should be replaced.

6   If the view glass takes on a mist-like appearance or shows many bubbles, this indicates a large refrigerant leak. In such a case, do not operate the compressor at all until the fault has been corrected.

7   Sweating or frosting of the expansion valve inlet indicates that the expansion valve is clogged or defective. It should be cleaned or replaced as necessary.

8   Sweating or frosting of the suction line (which runs between the suction throttle valve and the compressor) indicates that the expansion valve is stuck open or defective. It should be corrected or replaced as necessary.

9   Frosting on the evaporator indicates a defective suction throttle valve, requiring replacement of the valve.

10   Frosting of the high pressure liquid line (which runs between the condenser, accumulator and expansion valve) indicates that either the drier or the high pressure line is restricted. The line will have to be cleared or the accumulator replaced.

11   The combination of bubbles in the sight glass, a very hot suction line and, possibly, overheating of the engine is an indication that either the condenser is not operating properly or the refrigerant is overcharged. Check the tension of the drivebelt and adjust if necessary (Chapter 1). Check for foreign matter covering the fins of the condenser and clean

if necessary. Also check for proper operation of the cooling system. If no fault can be found in these checks, the condenser may have to be replaced.

12   Air conditioning system accumulator/receiver-drier — removal and installation

Refer to illustrations 12.1 and 12.2

Warning: *Before removing the accumulator/receiver-drier, the system must be discharged by an air conditioning technician. Do not attempt to do this yourself. The refrigerant in the system can cause serious injury and respiratory irritation.*

1   The accumulator/receiver-drier, which acts as a reservoir and filter for the refrigerant, is the canister-shaped object mounted near the right

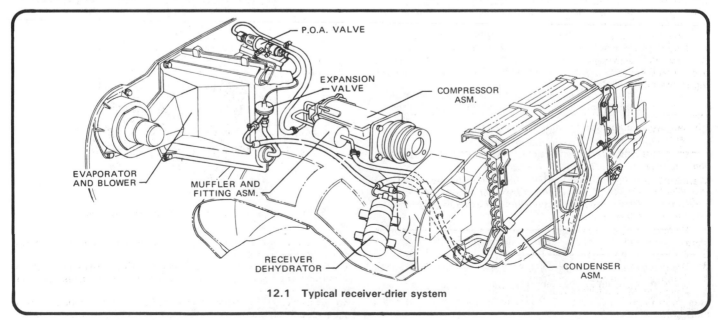

12.1   Typical receiver-drier system

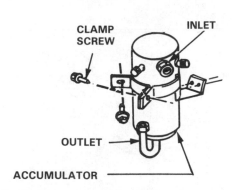

CLAMP SCREW   INLET

OUTLET

ACCUMULATOR

12.2   Liquid line inlet and outlets, and mounting details — typical accumulator system

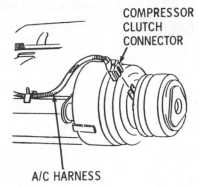

COMPRESSOR CLUTCH CONNECTOR

A/C HARNESS

13.3   All compressors have wiring going to the clutch connector — some have wiring to the rear of the compressor as well

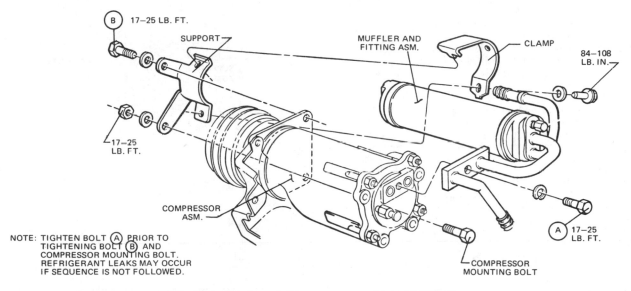

B 17—25 LB. FT.

SUPPORT

MUFFLER AND FITTING ASM.

CLAMP

84—108 LB. IN.

17—25 LB. FT.

COMPRESSOR ASM.

A 17—25 LB. FT.

COMPRESSOR MOUNTING BOLT

NOTE: TIGHTEN BOLT (A) PRIOR TO TIGHTENING BOLT (B) AND COMPRESSOR MOUNTING BOLT. REFRIGERANT LEAKS MAY OCCUR IF SEQUENCE IS NOT FOLLOWED.

13.5   Exploded view of A6 compressor refrigerant fittings

front fender well or adjacent to the condenser **(see illustration)** in the engine compartment.

2   Disconnect the two liquid lines from the accumulator or receiver-drier. Cap the open fittings immediately to prevent moisture from entering the system **(see illustration)**.

3   Remove the accumulator or receiver-drier from its bracket.

4   Installation procedures are the reverse of those for removal.

5   Have the system evacuated, charged and leak tested. If a new accumulator or receiver-drier was installed, add refrigerant oil according to the part manufacturer's instructions.

13   Air conditioning system compressor — removal and installation

Refer to illustrations 13.3, 13.5, and 13.6

Warning: *The air conditioning system is under high pressure. DO NOT disassemble any part of the system (hoses, compressor, line fittings, etc.) until after the system has been depressurized by a dealer service department or service station.*

1   Have the A/C system discharged by a dealer or air conditioning shop.

2   Disconnect the negative battery cable.

3   Disconnect the compressor clutch wiring harness **(see illustration)**.

4   Remove the drivebelt (see Chapter 1).

5   Disconnect the refrigerant lines from the rear of the compressor **(see illustration)**. Plug the open fittings to prevent entry of dirt and moisture.

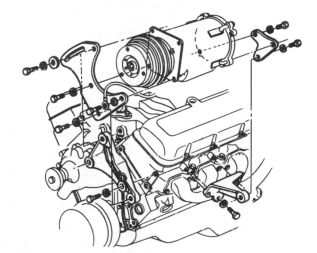

13.6   Typical air conditioner compressor mounting

6   Unbolt the compressor from the mounting brackets and lift it out of the vehicle **(see illustration)**.

7   If a new compressor is being installed, follow the directions which come with the compressor regarding the draining of excess oil prior to installation.

8   Installation is the reverse of removal. Replace any O-rings with new ones specifically made for the purpose and lubricate them with re-

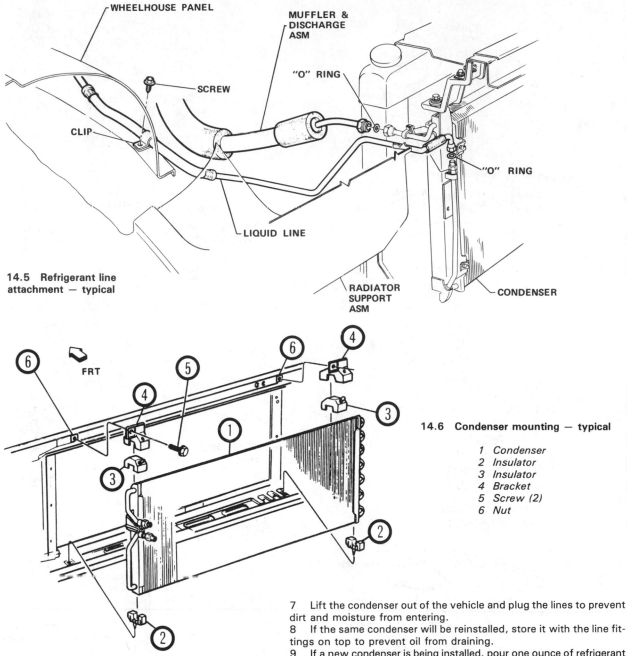

14.5   Refrigerant line attachment — typical

14.6   Condenser mounting — typical

1 *Condenser*
2 *Insulator*
3 *Insulator*
4 *Bracket*
5 *Screw (2)*
6 *Nut*

7   Lift the condenser out of the vehicle and plug the lines to prevent dirt and moisture from entering.
8   If the same condenser will be reinstalled, store it with the line fittings on top to prevent oil from draining.
9   If a new condenser is being installed, pour one ounce of refrigerant oil into the new condenser prior to installation.
10 Reinstall the components in the reverse order of removal. Be sure the rubber pads are in place under the condenser.
11 Have the system evacuated, recharged and leak tested by the shop that discharged it.

frigerant oil.
9   Have the system evacuated, recharged and leak tested by the shop that discharged it.

14   Air conditioning system condenser — removal and installation

Refer to illustrations 14.5 and 14.6

Warning: *The air conditioning system is under high pressure. DO NOT disassemble any part of the system (hoses, compressor, line fittings, etc.) until after the system has been depressurized by a dealer service department or service station.*

1   Have the A/C system discharged by a dealer or air conditioning shop.
2   Disconnect the negative cable from battery.
3   Drain the cooling system (Chapter 1).
4   Remove the radiator (Section 4).
5   Disconnect the refrigerant lines from the condenser **(see illustration)**.
6   Remove the mounting bolts from the condenser brackets **(see illustration)**.

15   Air conditioner and heater control assembly — removal and installation

Refer to illustrations 15.3, 15.4, 15.5 and 15.6

1   Disconnect the negative battery cable from the battery.
2   Remove the trim ring around the instrument cluster (see Chapter 11).
3   Remove the screws and pull the control assembly out of the dashboard **(see illustration)**.
4   Label and then disconnect the control cables **(see illustration)**.
5   Disconnect the vacuum hoses (where equipped) **(see illustration)**.
6   Disconnect the wire harnesses **(see illustration)**.
7   Installation is the reverse of removal.

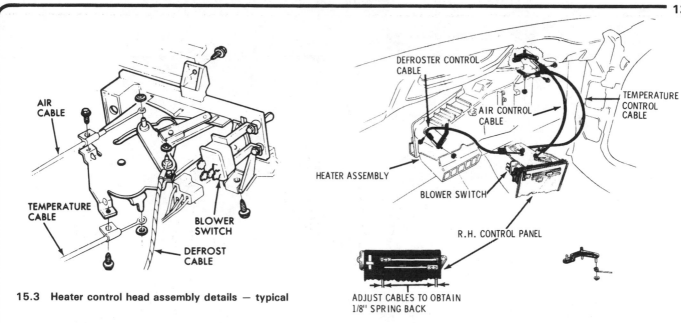

AIR CABLE

TEMPERATURE CABLE

BLOWER SWITCH

DEFROST CABLE

15.3   Heater control head assembly details — typical

DEFROSTER CONTROL CABLE

AIR CONTROL CABLE

TEMPERATURE CONTROL CABLE

HEATER ASSEMBLY

BLOWER SWITCH

R.H. CONTROL PANEL

ADJUST CABLES TO OBTAIN 1/8" SPRING BACK

15.4   Heater control cables — mounting details (typical)

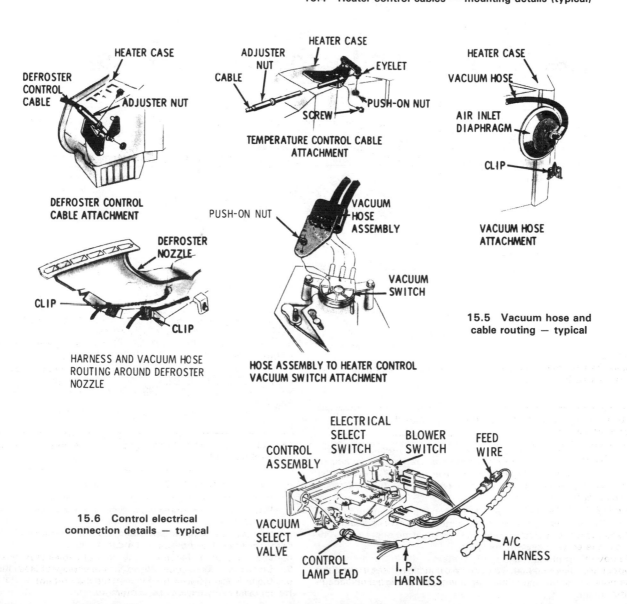

HEATER CASE

DEFROSTER CONTROL CABLE

ADJUSTER NUT

DEFROSTER CONTROL CABLE ATTACHMENT

ADJUSTER NUT

HEATER CASE

CABLE

EYELET

PUSH-ON NUT

SCREW

TEMPERATURE CONTROL CABLE ATTACHMENT

HEATER CASE

VACUUM HOSE

AIR INLET DIAPHRAGM

CLIP

VACUUM HOSE ATTACHMENT

3

DEFROSTER NOZZLE

CLIP

CLIP

HARNESS AND VACUUM HOSE ROUTING AROUND DEFROSTER NOZZLE

PUSH-ON NUT

VACUUM HOSE ASSEMBLY

VACUUM SWITCH

HOSE ASSEMBLY TO HEATER CONTROL VACUUM SWITCH ATTACHMENT

15.5   Vacuum hose and cable routing — typical

ELECTRICAL SELECT SWITCH

BLOWER SWITCH

FEED WIRE

CONTROL ASSEMBLY

VACUUM SELECT VALVE

CONTROL LAMP LEAD

I. P. HARNESS

A/C HARNESS

15.6   Control electrical connection details — typical

Chapter 4 Fuel and exhaust systems

Contents

1 General information

The fuel system consists of a rear-mounted fuel tank, a fuel pump, an air cleaner and a carburetor.

Employment of a carburetor, either a two- or a four-barrel type, depends on the engine displacement and the date of production of the vehicle.

The exhaust system consists of a pair of exhaust manifolds, a catalytic converter, a muffler and the pipes connecting them.

2 Fuel lines and fittings — general information

Warning: *Gasoline is extremely flammable, so extra precautions must be taken when working on any part of the fuel system. Do not smoke or allow open flames or bare light bulbs near the work area. Finally, do not work in an enclosed space where a natural gas-type appliance with a pilot light is present.*

1 The fuel feed and return lines extend from the fuel tank to the carburetor. The lines are secured to the underbody with clip and screw assemblies. Both fuel feed and return lines must be occasionally inspected for leaks, kinks or dents.

2 If evidence of dirt is found in the system or fuel filter during disassembly, the line should be disconnected and blown out. Check the fuel strainer on the fuel gauge sending unit (see Section 5) for damage or deterioration.

Steel tubing

3 If a fuel line must be replaced, use welded steel tubing meeting GM specifications. (Your GM dealer parts department will be able to supply you with tubing of the proper specification for your vehicle.)

4 Do not use copper or aluminum tubing to replace steel tubing. These materials do not have the durability to withstand normal vehicle vibration.

5 Most feed and return pipes use screw couplings with O-rings. Any time these fittings are loosened to service or replace components, ensure that:
   a) A backup wrench is used while loosening and tightening the fittings.
   b) Check all O-rings for cuts, cracking or deterioration. Replace any that appear worn or damaged.
   c) If the lines are replaced, always use original equipment parts, or parts that meet GM standards.

Rubber hose

6 When rubber hose is used to replace a metal line, you must use reinforced, fuel resistant hose meeting GM specifications. Hose(s) not meeting proper specifications could cause premature failure or could fail to meet Federal emission standards. Hose inside diameter must match pipe outside diameter.

7 Do not use rubber hose within four inches of any part of the exhaust system or within 10 inches of the catalytic converter. Metal lines and rubber hoses must never be allowed to chafe against the frame. A

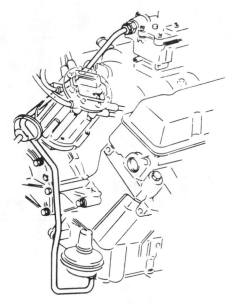

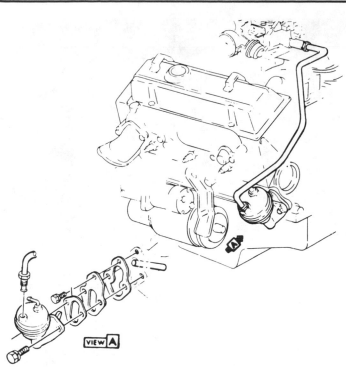

3.1b   Fuel pump location on a 231 V6

3.1a   Exploded view of typical fuel pump assembly on a 229 V6

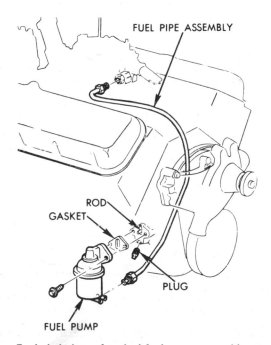

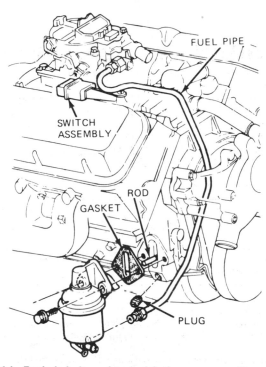

3.1d   Exploded view of typical fuel pump assembly on a big-block V8

3.1c   Exploded view of typical fuel pump assembly on a small-block V8

If the line is too corroded to withstand bead operation without damage, the line should be replaced.

10   Use a screw-type hose clamp. Slide the clamp onto the line and push the hose on. Tighten the clamps on each side of the repair.

11   Secure the lines properly to the frame to prevent chafing.

minimum 1/4-inch clearance must be maintained around a line or hose to prevent contact with the frame.

Repair

8   In repairable areas, cut a piece of fuel hose four inches longer than the portion of the line removed. If more than a six-inch length of line is removed, use a combination of steel line and hose so that hose lengths will not be more than 10 inches. Always follow the same routing as the original line.

9   Cut the ends of the line with a tube cutter. Using the first step of a double flaring tool, form a bead on the end of both line sections.

3   Fuel pump — check

Refer to illustrations 3.1a, 3.1b, 3.1c and 3.1d

1   The mechanical fuel pump (**see illustrations**) is actuated by the engine camshaft. A pushrod is used between the camshaft and the pump rocker. Fuel pumps on 231 V6 engines are driven directly from the camshaft eccentric without a pushrod.

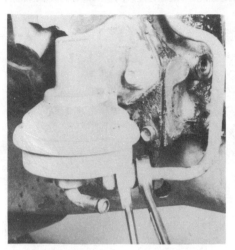

4.1 When detaching the fuel lines from a mechanical pump, use two wrenches so you don't bend or kink the metal fuel lines or the pipes protruding from the pump (small-block V8 shown)

4.2a To remove a mechanical pump from the engine, remove the two mounting bolts . . .

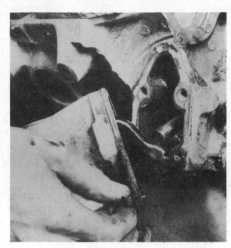

4.2b . . . then separate the pump and gasket from the block (be sure to remove all old gasket material from the pump and block mating surfaces)

2   If the pump is suspected of being faulty, carry out the following test.
3   Verify that gas is in the fuel tank. Tighten any loose fuel line connections and look for kinks or bends.
4   Disconnect the wiring harness from the distributor to prevent the engine from firing when the starter motor is actuated.
5   Disconnect the fuel line from the carburetor and place its open end in a container.
6   Operate the starter motor and verify that well-defined spurts of fuel are being ejected from the open end of the line. If so, the pump is operating correctly; if not, replace the pump as described in the following Section.

4 Fuel pump — removal and installation

Refer to illustrations 4.1, 4.2a, 4.2b and 4.3

1   To remove the pump, remove the fuel inlet and outlet lines. Use two wrenches to prevent damage to the pump and connections **(see illustration)**.
2   Remove the fuel pump mounting bolts, the pump and the gasket **(see illustrations)**.

3   If the pushrod is to be removed, first remove the pipe plug or the pump adapter and gasket, as appropriate **(see illustration)**.
4   When installing, first install the pushrod using the gasket sealant on the pipe lug or gasket (where applicable). Retain the pushrod in position using heavy grease. This is not necessary with the V6 engine.
5   Install the pump using a new gasket. On the 231 V6 engine, insert the fuel pump into position. Ensure that its rocker arm contacts the camshaft. Use gasket sealant on the screw threads.
6   Connect the fuel lines, start the engine and check for leaks.

5 Fuel tank — removal and installation

Refer to illustrations 5.8a, 5.8b and 5.8c
Warning: *Gasoline is extremely flammable, so extra precautions must be taken when working on any part of the fuel system. Do not smoke or allow open flames or bare light bulbs near the work area. Also, do not work in a garage if a natural gas-type appliance with a pilot light is present. While performing any work on the fuel tank it is advisable to wear safety glasses and to have a dry chemical (Class B) fire extinguisher on hand. If you spill any fuel on your skin, rinse it off immediately with soap and water.*

4.3 The pushrod (on a pushrod-type mechanical pump) is easy to pull out once the pump and gasket are removed

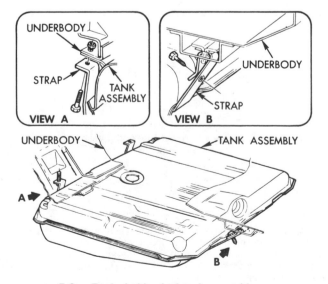

5.8a Typical older fuel tank assembly

1   Remove the fuel filler neck cap to relieve fuel tank pressure.
2   Detach the cable from the negative terminal of the battery.
3   If the tank is full or nearly full, use a hand-operated pump to remove as much fuel through the filler tube as possible (if no such pump is available, you can drain the tank at the fuel feed line after raising the vehicle).
4   Raise the vehicle and place it securely on jackstands.
5   Disconnect the fuel lines, the vapor return line and the fuel filler neck. **Note:** *The fuel feed and return lines and the vapor return line are three different diameters, so reattachment is simplified. If you have* any doubts, however, clearly label the three lines and their respective inlet or outlet pipes. Be sure to plug the hoses to prevent leakage and contamination of the fuel system.
6   If you didn't have a hand pump, siphon the fuel from the tank at the fuel feed — not the return — line.
7   Support the fuel tank with a floor jack or other suitable means. Place a sturdy plank between the jack head and the fuel tank to protect the tank.
8   Disconnect both fuel tank retaining straps and pivot them down until they are hanging out of the way **(see illustrations)**.

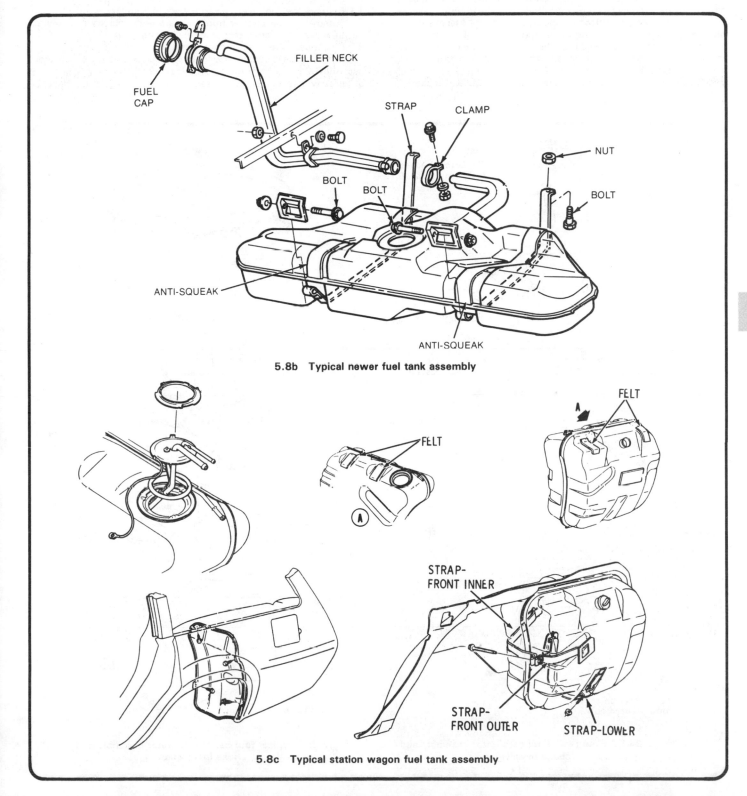

5.8b   Typical newer fuel tank assembly

5.8c   Typical station wagon fuel tank assembly

9   Lower the tank far enough to disconnect the electrical wires and ground strap from the fuel pump/fuel gauge sending unit, if you have not already done so.
10   Remove the tank from the vehicle.
11   Installation is the reverse of removal.

---

6 Fuel tank cleaning and repair — general information

1   Any repairs to the fuel tank or filler neck should be carried out by a professional who has experience in this critical and potentially dangerous work. Even after cleaning and flushing of the fuel system, explosive fumes can remain and ignite during repair of the tank.
2   If the fuel tank is removed from the vehicle, it should not be placed in an area where sparks or open flames could ignite the fumes coming out of the tank. Be especially careful inside garages where a natural gas type appliance is located, because the pilot light could cause an explosion.

---

7 Carburetor — removal and installation

Refer to illustrations 7.8a and 7.8b

Warning: *Gasoline is extremely flammable so extra precautions must be taken when working on any part of the fuel system. DO NOT smoke or allow open flames or bare light bulbs in or near the work area. Also, don't work in a garage if a natural gas appliance such as a water heater or clothes dryer is present.*

Removal

1   Remove the fuel filler cap to relieve fuel tank pressure.
2   Remove the air cleaner from the carburetor. Be sure to label all vacuum hoses attached to the air cleaner housing.
3   Disconnect the throttle cable from the throttle lever.
4   If the vehicle is equipped with an automatic transmission, disconnect the TV cable from the throttle lever.
5   Clearly label all vacuum hoses and fittings, then disconnect the hoses.

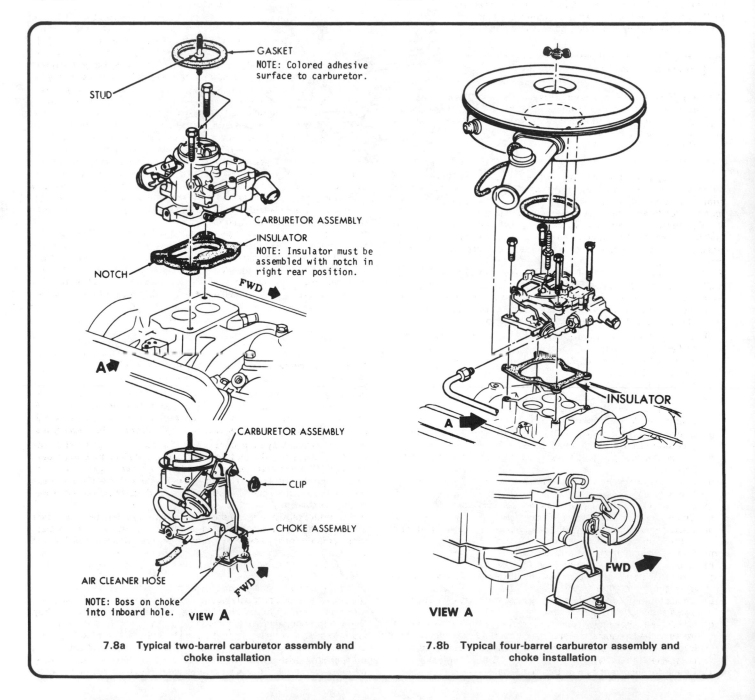

7.8a Typical two-barrel carburetor assembly and choke installation

7.8b Typical four-barrel carburetor assembly and choke installation

6   Disconnect the fuel line from the carburetor.

7   Label the wires and terminals, then unplug all wire harness connectors.

8   Remove the mounting fasteners **(see illustrations)** and detach the carburetor from the intake manifold. Remove the carburetor mounting gasket. Stuff a shop rag into the intake manifold openings.

Installation

9   Use a gasket scraper to remove all traces of gasket material and sealant from the intake manifold (and the carburetor, if it's being re-installed), then remove the shop rag from the manifold openings. Clean the mating surfaces with lacquer thinner or acetone.

10   Place a new gasket on the manifold.

11   Position the carburetor on the gasket and install the mounting fasteners.

12   To prevent carburetor distortion or damage, tighten the fasteners securely in a criss-cross pattern, 1/2-turn at a time.

13   The remaining installation steps are the reverse of removal.

14   Check and, if necessary, adjust the idle speed.

15   If the vehicle is equipped with an automatic taransmission, refer to Chapter 7B for the TV cable adjustment procedure.

16   Start the engine and check carefully for fuel leaks.

8   Carburetor — diagnosis and overhaul

Warning: *Gasoline is extremely flammable, so extra precautions must be taken when working on any part of the fuel system. DO NOT smoke or allow open flames or bare light bulbs in or near the work area. Also, don't work in a garage if a natural gas appliance such as a water heater or clothes dryer is present.*

Diagnosis

1   A thorough road test and check of carburetor adjustments should be done before any major carburetor service work. Specifications for some adjustments are listed on the *Vehicle Emissions Control Information (VECI) label* found in the engine compartment.

2   Carburetor problems usually show up as flooding, hard starting, stalling, severe backfiring and poor acceleration. A carburetor that's leaking fuel and/or covered with wet looking deposits definitely needs attention.

3   Some performance complaints directed at the carburetor are actually a result of loose, out-of-adjustment or malfunctioning engine or electrical components. Others develop when vacuum hoses leak, are disconnected or are incorrectly routed. The proper approach to analyzing carburetor problems should include the following items:

a)   Inspect all vacuum hoses and actuators for leaks and correct installation (see Chapters 1 and 6).

b)   Tighten the intake manifold and carburetor mounting nuts/bolts evenly and securely.

c)   Perform a cylinder compression test (see Chapter 2).

d)   Clean or replace the spark plugs as necessary (see Chapter 1).

e)   Check the spark plug wires (see Chapter 1).

f)   Inspect the ignition primary wires.

g)   Check the ignition timing (follow the instructions printed on the *Emissions Control Information label*).

h)   Check the fuel pump pressure/volume (see Section 3 of this Chapter).

i)   Check the heat control valve in the air cleaner for proper operation (see Chapter 1).

j)   Check/replace the air filter element (see Chapter 1).

k)   Check the PCV system (see Chapter 6).

l)   Check/replace the fuel filter (see Chapter 1). Also, the strainer in the tank could be restricted.

m)   Check for a plugged exhaust system.

n)   Check EGR valve operation (see Chapter 6).

o)   Check the choke — it should be completely open at normal engine operating temperature (see Chapter 1).

p)   Check for fuel leaks and kinked or dented fuel lines (see Chapter 1 and Section 2 of this Chapter).

q)   Check the accelerator pump operation with the engine off (remove the air cleaner cover and operate the throttle as you look into the carburetor throat — you should see a stream of gasoline enter the carburetor).

r)   Check for incorrect fuel or bad gasoline.

s)   Check the valve clearances (if applicable) and camshaft lobe lift (see Chapters 1 and 2).

t)   Have a dealer service department or repair shop check the electronic and carburetor controls.

4   Diagnosing carburetor problems may require that the engine be started and run with the air cleaner off. While running the engine without the air cleaner, backfires are possible. This situation is likely to occur if the carburetor is malfunctioning, but just the removal of the air cleaner can lean the fuel/air mixture enough to produce an engine backfire. **Warning:** *Do not position any part of your body, especially your face, directly over the carburetor during inspection and servicing procedures. Wear eye protection!*

Overhaul

5   Once it's determined that the carburetor needs an overhaul, several options are available. If you're going to attempt to overhaul the carburetor yourself, first obtain a good quality carburetor rebuild kit (which will include all necessary gaskets, internal parts, instructions and a parts list). You'll also need some special solvent and a means of blowing out the internal passages of the carburetor with air.

6   An alternative is to obtain a new or rebuilt carburetor. They are readily available from dealers and auto parts stores. Make absolutely sure the exchange carburetor is identical to the original. A tag is usually attached to the top of the carburetor or a number is stamped on the float bowl. It will help determine the exact type of carburetor you have. When obtaining a rebuilt carburetor or a rebuild kit, make sure the kit or carburetor matches your application exactly. Seemingly insignificant differences can make a large difference in the engine performance.

7   If you choose to overhaul your own carburetor, allow enough time to disassemble it carefully, soak the necessary parts in the cleaning solvent (usually for at least one-half day or according to the instructions listed on the carburetor cleaner) and reassemble it, which will usually take much longer than disassembly. When disassembling the carburetor, match each part with the illustration in the carburetor kit and lay the parts out in order on a clean work surface. Overhauls by inexperienced mechanics can result in an engine which runs poorly or not at all. To avoid this, use care and patience when disassembling the carburetor so you can reassemble it correctly.

8   Because carburetor designs are constantly modified by the manufacturer in order to meet increasingly more stringent emissions regulations, it isn't feasible to include a step-by-step overhaul of each type. You'll receive a detailed, well illustrated set of instructions with any carburetor overhaul kit; they will apply in a more specific manner to the carburetor on your vehicle. An exploded view of a typical carburetor is included here.

9   Exhaust system servicing — general information

Warning: *Inspection and repair of exhaust system components should be done only after enough time has elapsed after driving the vehicle to allow the system components to cool completely. Also, when working under the vehicle, make sure it is securely supported on jackstands.*

1   The exhaust system consists of the exhaust manifold(s), the catalytic converter, the muffler, the tailpipe and all connecting pipes, brackets, hangers and clamps. The exhaust system is attached to the body with mounting brackets and rubber hangers. If any of these parts are improperly installed, excessive noise and vibration will be transmitted to the body.

2   Conduct regular inspections of the exhaust system to keep it safe and quiet. Look for any damaged or bent parts, open seams, holes, loose connections, excessive corrosion or other defects which could allow exhaust fumes to enter the vehicle. Deteriorated exhaust system components should not be repaired; they should be replaced with new parts.

3   If the exhaust system components are extremely corroded or rusted together, they will probably have to be cut from the exhaust system. The convenient way to accomplish this is to have a muffler repair shop remove the corroded sections with a cutting torch. If, however, you want to save money by doing it yourself (and you don't have an oxy/acetylene welding outfit with a cutting torch), simply cut off the old components with a hacksaw. If you have compressed air, special pneumatic cutting chisels can also be used. If you do decide to tackle

the job at home, be sure to wear OSHA-approved safey goggles to protect your eyes from metal chips and work gloves to protect your hands.

4   Here are some simple guidelines to apply when repairing the exhaust system:

a) Work from the back to the front when removing exhaust system components.

b) Apply penetrating oil to the exhaust system component fasteners to make them easier to remove.

c) Use new gaskets, hangers and clamps when installing exhaust system components.

d) Apply anti-seize compound to the threads of all exhaust system fasteners during reassembly.

e) Be sure to allow sufficient clearance between newly installed parts and all points on the underbody to avoid overheating the floor pan and possibly damaging the interior carpet and insulation. Pay particularly close attention to the catalytic converter and its heat shield.

Chapter 5   Engine electrical systems

Contents

5

---

1   General information and precautions

The engine electrical systems include all ignition, charging and starting components. Because of their engine-related functions, these components are discussed separately from chassis electrical devices such as the lights, the instruments, etc. (which are included in Chapter 12).

Always observe the following precautions when working on the electrical systems:

  a) Be extremely careful when servicing engine electrical components. They are easily damaged if checked, connected or handled improperly.
  b) The alternator is driven by an engine drivebelt which could cause serious injury if your hands, hair or clothes become entangled in it with the engine running.
  c) Both the alternator and the starter are connected directly to the battery and could arc or even cause a fire if mishandled, overloaded or shorted out.
  d) Never leave the ignition switch on for long periods of time with the engine off.

  e) Don't disconnect the battery cables while the engine is running.
  f) Maintain correct polarity when connecting a battery cable from another source, such as a vehicle, during jump starting.
  g) Always disconnect the negative cable first and hook it up last or the battery may be shorted by the tool being used to loosen the cable clamps.

It's also a good idea to review the safety-related information regarding the engine electrical systems located in the *Safety First* section near the front of this manual before beginning any operation included in this Chapter.

---

2   Battery — removal and installation

Refer to illustration 2.2

1   **Caution:** *Always disconnect the negative cable first and hook it up last or the battery may be shorted by the tool being used to loosen the cable clamps.* Disconnect both cables from the battery terminals.

2.2   Typical battery hold-down clamp illustration

2   Remove the battery hold-down clamp (see illustration).
3   Lift out the battery. Use the proper lifting technique — the battery is heavy.
4   While the battery is out, inspect the battery carrier (tray) for corrosion (See Chapter 1).
5   If you are replacing the battery, make sure that you get an identical battery, with the same dimensions, amperage rating, "cold cranking" rating, etc.
6   Installation is the reverse of removal.

3   Battery — emergency jump starting

Refer to the *Booster battery (jump) starting* procedure at the front of this manual.

4   Battery cables — check and replacement

1   Periodically inspect the entire length of each battery cable for damage, cracked or burned insulation and corrosion. Poor battery cable connections can cause starting problems and decreased engine performance.
2   Check the cable-to-terminal connections at the ends of the cables for cracks, loose wire strands and corrosion. The presence of white, fluffy deposits under the insulation at the cable terminal connection is a sign that the cable is corroded and should be replaced. Check the terminals for distortion, missing mounting bolts and corrosion.
3   When removing the cables, **always disconnect the negative cable first and hook it up last** or the battery may be shorted by the tool used to loosen the cable clamps. Even if only the positive cable is being replaced, be sure to disconnect the negative cable from the battery first (see Chapter 1 for further information regarding battery cable removal).
4   Disconnect the old cables from the battery, then trace each of them to their opposite ends and detach them from the starter solenoid and ground. Note the routing of each cable to insure correct installation.
5   If you are replacing either or both of the old cables; take them with you when buying new cables. It is vitally important that you replace the cables with identical parts. Cables have characteristics that make them easy to identify: positive cables are usually red, larger in cross-section and have a larger diameter battery post clamp; ground cables are usually black, smaller in cross-section and have a slightly smaller diameter clamp for the negative post.
6   Clean the threads of the solenoid or ground connection with a wire brush to remove rust and corrosion. Apply a light coat of battery terminal corrosion inhibitor, or petroleum jelly, to the threads to prevent future corrosion.
7   Attach the cable to the solenoid or ground connection and tighten the mounting nut/bolt securely.
8   Before connecting a new cable to the battery, make sure that it reaches the battery post without having to be stretched.
9   Connect the positive cable first, followed by the negative cable.

5   Ignition system — general information

1   In order for the engine to run correctly, it is necessary for an electrical spark to ignite the fuel/air mixture in the combustion chamber at exactly the right moment in relation to engine speed and load. The ignition coil converts low tension (LT) voltage from the battery into high tension (HT) voltage, powerful enough to jump the spark plug gap in the cylinder, providing that the system is in good condition and that all adjustments are correct.
2   The ignition system fitted to all pre-1975 cars as standard equipment is a conventional distributor with mechaical contact breaker points. On 1975 and later models, a breakerless high energy ignition (HEI) system is used.

Pre-1975 ignition systems

3   The ignition system is divided into the primary (low tension) circuit and the secondary (high tension) circuit.
4   The primary circuit consists of the battery lead to the starter motor, the lead to the ignition switch, the calibrated resistance wire from the ignition switch to the primary coil winding and the lead from the low tension coil windings to the contact breaker points and condenser in the distributor.
5   The secondary circuit consists of the secondary coil winding, the high tension lead from the coil to the distributor cap, the rotor and the spark plug leads and spark plugs.
6   The system functions in the following manner. Low tension voltage in the coil is converted into high tension voltage by the opening and closing of the contact breaker points in the distributor. This high tension voltage is carried via the brush in the center of the distributor cap contacts to the rotor arm of the distribututor cap. Every time the rotor contacts one of the spark plug terminals on the cap, it jumps the gap from the rotor arm to the terminal and is carried by the spark plug lead to the spark plug, where it jumps the spark plug gap to ground.
7   Ignition advance is controlled by both mechanical and vacuum-operated systems. The mechanical governor mechanism consists of two weights, which due to centrifugal force move out from the distributor shaft as the engine speed rises. As they move outwards they rotate the cam relative to the distributor shaft, advancing spark timing. The weights are held in position by two light springs. It is the tension of these springs which determines correct spark advancement.
8   The vacuum control system consists of a diaphragm, one side of which is connected via a vacuum line to the carburetor, the other side to the contact breaker plate. Vacuum in the intake manifold and carburetor varies with engine speed and throttle opening. As the vacuum changes, it moves the diaphragm, which rotates the contact breaker plate slightly in relation to the rotor, thus advancing or retarding the spark. Control is fine-tuned by a spring in the vacuum assembly.
9   On some models, a Transmission Controlled Spark (TCS) system eliminates vacuum advance (see Chapter 6).

HEI ignition systems (1975 through 1980)

10   The high energy ignition (HEI) system is a pulse triggered, transistor controlled, inductive discharge system.
11   A magnetic pick-up inside the distributor contains a permanent magnet, pole-piece and pick-up coil. A time core, rotating inside the pole piece, induces a voltage in the pick-up coil. When the teeth on the timer and pole piece line up, a signal passes to the electronic module to open the coil primary circuit. The primary circuit current collapses and a high voltage is induced in the coil secondary winding. This high voltage is directed to the spark plugs by the distributor rotor in a manner similar to a conventional system. A capacitor suppresses radio interference.
12   The HEI system features a longer spark duration than a conventional breaker point ignition system, and the dwell period increases automatically with engine speed. These characteristics are desirable for lean firing and EGR-diluted mixtures (see Chapter 6).
13   The ignition coil and the electronic module are both housed in the distributor cap on the HEI system. The distributor does not require routine servicing.
14   Spark timing is advanced by mechanical and vacuum devices similar to those used on conventional breaker point distributors (described above). The TCS system is eliminated.

7.5   After turning the rotor until it is pointing at the terminal for the number 1 spark plug, paint or scribe a mark on the edge of the distributor base directly beneath it

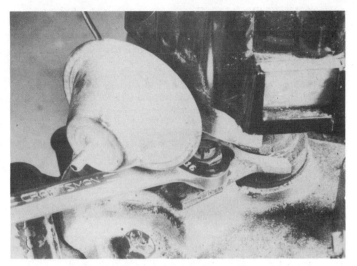

7.6a   Some distributor hold-down bolts can be removed with a combination wrench . . .

HEI systems (1981 and later)

15   Since 1981, HEI systems have been equipped with electronic spark timing (EST). All spark timing changes are carried out by the Electronic Control Module (ECM), which monitors data from various engine sensors, computes the desired spark timing and signals the distributor to alter spark timing accordingly. Vacuum and mechanical advance is eliminated.

16   An Electronic Spark Control (ESC) system utilizes a knock sensor, and the ECM, to allow maximum spark advance without spark knock. The ESC system improves driveability and fuel economy.

6   Ignition system — check

1   Attach an inductive timing light to each plug wire, one at a time, and crank the engine.
    a) If the light flashes, voltage is reaching the plug.
    b) If the light does not flash, proceed to the next Step.
2   Inspect the spark plug wire(s), distributor cap, rotor and spark plug(s) (see Chapter 1).
3   If the engine still won't start, check the ignition coil (see Section 11).

7   Distributor — removal and installation

Refer to illustrations 7.5, 7.6a and 7.6b

Removal

1   After disconnecting the negative battery terminal cable, unplug the primary lead from the coil.
2   Unplug or detach all electrical leads from the distributor. To find the connectors, trace the wires from the distributor.
3   Look for a raised ''1'' on the distributor cap This marks the location for the number one cylinder spark plug wire terminal. If the cap does not have a mark for the mumber one spark plug, locate the number one spark plug and trace the wire back to its corresponding terminal on the cap.
4   Remove the distributor cap (see Chapter 1) and turn the engine over until the rotor is pointing toward the number one spark plug terminal (see locating TDC procedure in Chapter 2).
5   Make a mark on the edge of the distributor base directly below the rotor tip and in line with it (see illustration). Also, mark the distributor base and the engine block to ensure that the distributor is installed correctly.
6   Remove the distributor hold-down bolt and clamp (see illustrations), then pull the distributor straight up to remove it. Be careful not to disturb the intermediate driveshaft. Caution: DO NOT turn the engine while the distributor is removed, or the alignment marks will be useless.

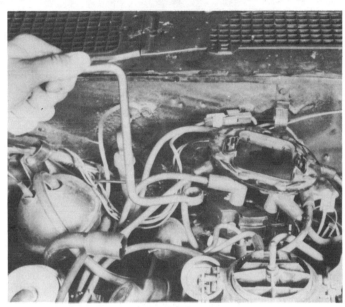

7.6b   . . . others may require a special distributor wrench

Installation

Note: If the crankshaft has been moved while the distributor is out, locate Top Dead Center (TDC) for the number one piston (see Chapter 2) and position the distributor and rotor accordingly.

7   Insert the distributor into the engine in exactly the same relationship to the block that it was in when removed.
8   To mesh the helical gears on the camshaft and the distributor, it may be necessary to turn the rotor slightly. If the distributor doesn't seat completely, the hex shaped recess in the lower end of the distributor shaft is not mating properly with the oil pump shaft. Recheck the alignment marks between the distributor base and the block to verify that the distributor is in the same position it was in before removal. Also check the rotor to see if it's aligned with the mark you made on the edge of the distributor base.
9   Place the hold-down clamp in position and loosely install the bolt.
10   Install the distributor cap and tighten the cap screws securely.
11   Plug in the module electrical connector.
12   Reattach the spark plug wires to the plugs (if removed).
13   Connect the cable to the negative terminal of the battery.
14   Check the ignition timing (see Chapter 1) and tighten the distributor hold-down bolt securely.

5

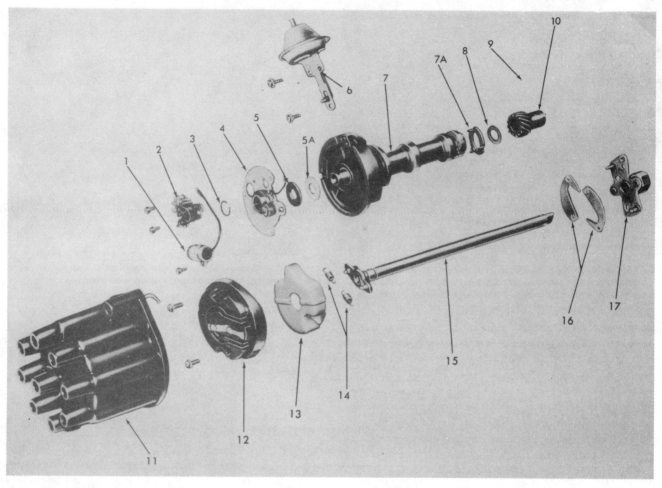

8.2 Exploded view of a typical contact breaker type distributor

1	Condenser	9	Drive gear pin
2	Contact point assembly	10	Drive gear
3	Retaining ring	11	Cap
4	Breaker plate	12	Rotor
5	Felt washer	13	Radio frequency
5a	Plastic seal		interference shield
6	Vacuum advance unit	14	Weight springs
7	Housing	15	Mainshaft
7a	Tanged washer	16	Advance weights
8	Shim washer	17	Cam weight base assembly

8   HEI distributor (1970 through 1974) — overhaul

Refer to illustration 8.2

1   Remove the distributor (See Section 7).
2   Remove the rotor (two screws), the advance weight springs and the weights. Where applicable, also remove the radio frequency interference (RFI) shield **(see illustration)**.
3   Drive out the roll pin retaining the gear to the shaft then pull off the gear and spacers.
4   Ensure that the shaft is not burred, then slide it from the housing.
5   Remove the cam weight base assembly.
6   Remove the screws retaining the vacuum unit and lift off the unit itself.
7   Remove the spring retainer (snap-ring) then remove the breaker plate assembly.
8   Remove the contact points and condenser, followed by the felt washer and plastic seal located beneath the breaker plate.
9   Wipe all components clean with a solvent-moistened cloth and examine them for wear, distortion and scoring. Replace parts as necessary. Pay particular attention to the rotor and distributor cap to ensure that they are not cracked.
10 Fill the lubricating cavity in the housing with general purpose grease, then fit a new plastic seal and felt washer.
11 Install the vacuum unit and the breaker plate in the housing, and the spring retainer on the upper bushing.
12 Lubricate the cam weight base and slide it on the mainshaft; install the weights and springs.
13 Insert the mainshaft in the housing then fit the shims and drivegear. Install a new roll pin.
14 Install the contact point set (see Chapter 1).
15 Install the rotor, aligning the round and square pilot holes.
16 Install the distributor (see Section 7).

9   HEI distributor (1975 through 1981) — overhaul

Refer to illustrations 9.2, 9.3, 9.5 and 9.9

1   Remove the distributor (see Section 7).
2   Remove the rotor (two screws) **(see illustration)**.
3   Remove the two screws retaining the module. Move the module aside and remove the connector from the 'B' and 'C' terminals **(see illustration)**.
4   Remove the connections from the 'W' and 'G' terminals.
5   Carefully drive out the roll pin from the drive gear **(see illustration)**.
6   Remove the gear, shim and tanged washer from the distributor shaft.
7   Ensure that the shaft is not burred, then remove it from the housing.
8   Remove the washer from the upper end of the distributor housing.
9   Remove the three screws and take out the pole-piece, magnet and pick-up coil **(see illustration)**.
10 Remove the lock ring, then take out the pick-up coil retainer, shim and felt washer.
11 Remove the vacuum unit (two screws).
12 Disconnect the capacitor lead and remove the capacitor (one screw).
13 Disconnect the wiring harness from the distributor housing.

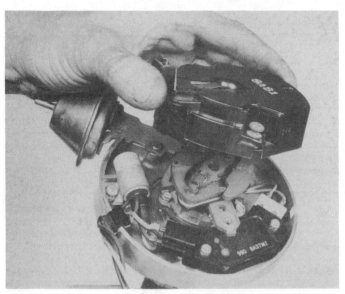

9.2 To detach the rotor from the HEI distributor, remove the two screws on top that attach it to the centrifugal advance mechanism

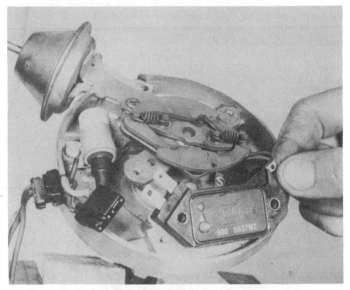

9.3 To detach the ignition module from the HEI distributor, remove the two mounting screws and unplug the connector from the B and C terminals

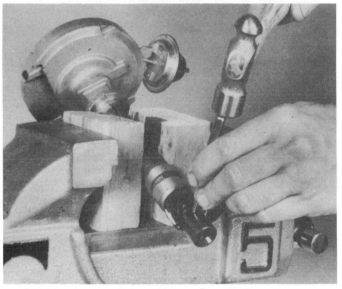

9.5 To remove the distributor shaft, drive the roll pin out of the shaft with a hammer and punch, remove the gear, shim and tanged washer from the shaft, inspect the shaft for any burrs that might prevent its removal, then pull it out (be careful not to lose the washer at the upper end of the shaft)

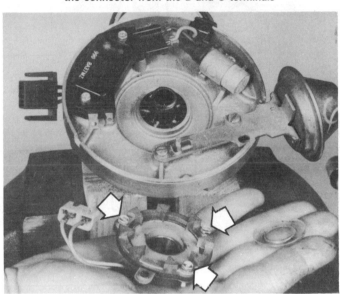

9.9 Remove the three screws (arrows) and detach the pole piece, magnet and pick-up coil

14 Wipe all components clean with a solvent-moistened cloth and examine them for wear, distortion and other damage. Replace parts as necessary.

15 To assemble, position the vacuum unit to the housing and secure with the two screws.

16 Position the felt washer over the lubricant reservoir at the top of the housing, then position the shim on top of the felt washer.

17 Position the pick-up coil retainer to the housing. The vacuum advance arm goes over the actuating pin of the advance mechanism. Secure it with the lock-ring.

18 Install the pick-up coil magnet and pole-piece. Loosely install the three screws to retain the pole-piece.

19 Install the washer to the top of the housing. Install the distributor shaft, then rotate it and check for equal clearance all round between the shaft projections and pole-piece. Secure the pole-piece when correctly positioned.

20 Install the tanged washer, shim and drivegear. Align the gear and

install a new roll pin.

21 Loosely install the capacitor with one screw.

22 Install the connector to the 'B' and 'C' terminals on the module, with the tab at the top.

23 Apply silicone grease to the base of the module and secure it with two screws. The grease is essential to ensure good heat conduction.

24 Position the wiring harness, with the grommet in the housing notch, then connect the pink wire to the capacitor stud and the black wire to the capacitor mounting screw. Tighten the screw.

25 Connect the white wire from the pick-up coil to the module "W" terminal and the green to the 'G' terminal.

26 Install the advance weights, weight retainer (dimple downwards), and springs.

27 Install the rotor and secure with the two screws. Ensure that the notch on the side of the rotor engages with the tab on the cam weight base.

28 Install the distributor (see Section 7).

10   HEI distributor (1981 and later) — overhaul

Refer to illustrations 10.1, 10.3, 10.8 and 10.9

1   Later model HEI distributors (see illustration) vary somewhat from those described in Section 9. Most later distributors are not equipped with vacuum advance units, as advance is controlled by electronic control module (ECM).

2   Unplug the electrical connector(s), disengage the latches and remove the distributor cap.

3   To test the pick-up coil, remove the rotor and pick-up leads and connect an ohmmeter as shown (see illustration).

4   The distributor is equipped with a vacuum advance unit, connect a vacuum source or pump to it.

5   Apply vacuum to the advance unit and verify that the indicated resistance remains steady as vacuum is applied. Replace the advance unit if it is inoperative or the ohmmeter reading changes. Make sure the application of vacuum does not cause the teeth to align (indicated by a jump in the ohmmeter reading).

6   With the ohmmeter attached as shown in Step 1 in the illustrations, the indicated resistance should be infinite. With the ohmmeter attached as shown in Step 2, the reading should be between 500 and 1500 ohms. Replace the coil if it fails either test.

7   Place the distributor in a vice, using blocks of wood to protect it.

8   Mark the relative positions of the gear and shaft. Drive the roll pin out (see illustration). Remove the gear and pull the shaft from the distributor housing.

9   Remove the aluminum shield for access to the pick-up coil and

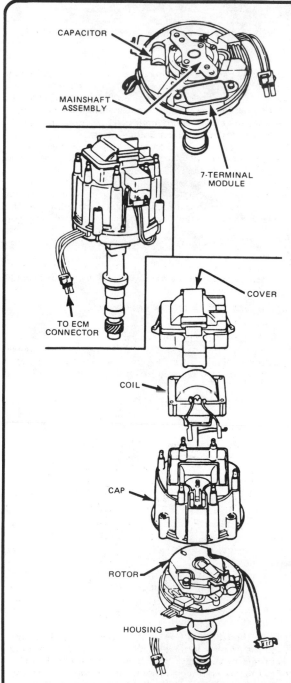

10.1   Exploded view of a typical late-model HEI distributor

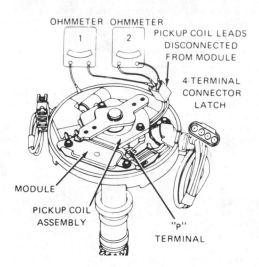

10.3   To test the pickup coil on a later model HEI distributor, remove the rotor and pickup leads and connect an ohmmeter as shown

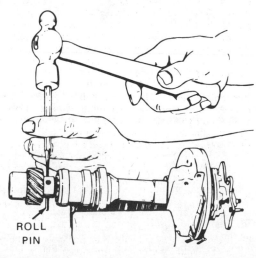

10.8   To remove the distributor shaft, mark the relative positions of the gear and shaft, drive out the pin retaining the distributor gear to the shaft, remove the gear and pull out the shaft

module **(see illustration)**.The pick-up coil can be lifted out after removal of the C washer. Remove the two screws and lift the module, capacitor and harness assembly from the distributor base.

10   Wipe the distributor base and module with a clean cloth and inspect it for cracks and damage.

11   Reassembly is the reverse of the disassembly procedure. Be sure to apply a coat of silicone lubricant to the distributor base under the module. After reassembly, spin the distributor shaft to make sure there is no contact by the pick-up coil and/or the Hall effect pick-up teeth. Loosen and retighten the teeth to eliminate the contact.

---

11   Ignition coil — check and replacement

Check

1   If the engine is hard to start (particularly when it's already hot), misses at high speed or cuts out during acceleration, the coil may be faulty. First, make sure that the battery and the distributor are in good condition, the points (pre-1975 vehicles) are properly adjusted and the plugs and plug wires are in good shape. If the problem persists, perform the following test:

Separately mounted coils (pre-1975)

2   Before performing any of the following coil electrical checks, make sure that the coil is clean, free of any carbon tracks and that all connections are tight and free of corrosion. Also make sure that both battery terminals are clean and that the cables are securely attached (especially the ground strap at the negative terminal).

3   Detach the coil high tension cable from the distributor cap. Hold the end of the cable about 3/16-inch away from some grounded part of the engine and operate the starter with the ignition turned on. A bright blue spark should jump the gap.

  a) If the spark is weak, yellowish or red, spark voltage is insufficient. If the points, condenser and battery are in good condition, the coil is probably weak. Take it to a dealer and have the output checked. If it tests weak when compared to a new coil of the same specifications, replace it.

  b) If there is no spark at all, try to locate the trouble before replacing the coil. Remove the distributor cap. Turn the engine until the points are open, or separate the points with a small piece of cardboard. Turn on the ignition switch. Using a 12-volt bulb with two test leads, attach one lead to ground somewhere on the engine and the other lead to first one of the coil's primary terminals and then the other.

  1) If the bulb lights when touched to the primary terminal that leads to the distributor, the coil is getting current and the primary windings are okay.

  2) If the bulb lights when touched to the other primary terminal but not when attached to the one leading to the distributor, the primary windings are faulty and the coil is no good.

  3) If the light does not go on when connected to either primary connection, the coil is not the problem. Check the ignition switch and starter solenoid.

  4) If the bulb lights when touched to both primary terminals (the coil is receiving current at both primary terminals), remove the high-tension cable from the center distributor cap tower and try shorting across the open distributor points with the tip of a clean (no oil) screwdriver.

  a) If a spark jumps from the coil's high tension secondary wire to a grounded point on the engine as the screwdriver is removed, the points are either contaminated by oil, dirt or water, or they're burned.

  b) If the screwdriver fails to produce a spark at the high tension wire, disconnect the primary wire that passes between the coil and the distributor and attach a test wire to the coil in its place. Ground the other end of the wire against the engine block, then pull it away (the test wire is simulating the points: grounding the wire is just like closing the points; pulling it away creates the same effect — producing a spark from the coil's high tension wire — as opening the points).

  1) If a spark jumps from the high-tension cable when the test wire is removed from the ground, the coil is okay. Either the points are grounded or the condenser is shorted.

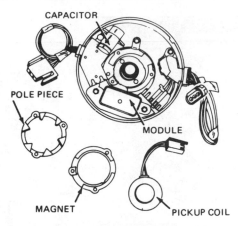

10.9   Exploded view of pickup coil assembly, capacitor and module

  2) If a spark does not jump during this test, the secondary windings of the coil are faulty. Replace the coil.

4   Sometimes, a coil checks out perfectly but the engine is still hard to start and misses at higher speeds. The problem may be inadequate spark voltage caused by reversed coil polarity. If you have recently tuned up the engine or performed any service work involving the coil, it's possible that the primary leads to the coil were accidentally reversed. To check for reversed polarity, remove one of the spark plug leads and hold it about 1/4-inch from the spark plug terminal or any ground point. Then insert the point of a pencil between the ignition lead and the plug while the engine is running (if the plug connector terminals are deeply recessed in a boot or insulating shield, straighten all but one bend in a paper clip and insert the looped end into the plug connector).

  a) If the spark flares on the ground or spark plug side of the pencil, the polarity is correct.

  b) If the spark flares between the ignition lead and the pencil, however, the polarity is wrong and the primary wires should be switched at the coil.

HEI-type coil-in-cap (1975 and later vehicles)
Refer to illustration 11.6

5   Remove the distributor cap (see Chapter 1).

6   Attach the two leads of an ohmmeter to the two primary terminals as shown **(see illustration)**. The indicated resistance should be zero or very near zero. If it isn't, replace the coil.

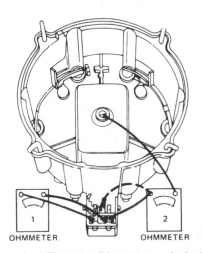

11.6   To test the HEI type coil-in-cap, attach the leads of an ohmmeter to the primary terminals and verify that the indicated resistance is zero or very near zero, then, using the high scale, attach one lead to the high tension terminal and the other to each of the primary terminals and verify that both of the readings are not infinite — if the indicated resistance is not as specified, replace the coil

11.10   To remove a conventional coil, simply detach the
high tension cable and the two primary leads and remove
the mounting bracket screws

11.14   To get at the coil, remove the coil cover screws
and the cover

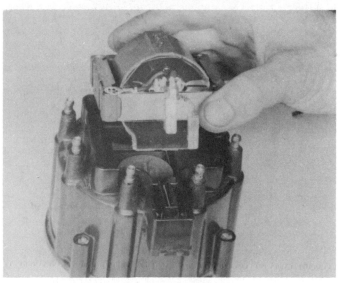

11.16   To separate the coil from the distributor cap,
clearly mark the wires, detach the coil ground wire and
push the leads from the underside of the connectors

11.17   Before installing a new coil, make sure that the
center electrode is in good condition

7   Using the high scale, attach one lead of the ohmmeter to the high
tension terminal in the middle of the distributor and the other lead to
each of the primary terminals. If *both* of the readings indicate infinite
resistance, replace the coil.

Replacement

Separately mounted coils (pre-1975)

Refer to Illustration 11.10

8   Detach the cable from the negative terminal of the battery.
9   Disconnect the high tension cable from the coil.
10   Detach the electrical connections from the coil primary and secondary terminals. Be sure to mark the connections before removal to
ensure that they are re-installed correctly. Remove the coil (see
illustration).
11   Installation is the reverse of removal

HEI-type coil-in-cap (1975 and later)

Refer to Illustrations 11.14, 11.16 and 11.17

12   Detach the cable from the negative terminal of the battery.
13   Disconnect the battery wire and harness connector from the

distributor cap.
14   Remove the coil cover screws and the cover (see illustration).
15   Remove the coil assembly screws.
16   Note the position of each wire, duly marking them if necessary.
Remove the coil ground wire, then push the leads from the underside
of the connectors. Remove the coil from the distributor cap (see
illustration).
17   Installation is the reverse of the removal procedure. Be sure that
the center electrode is in good shape (see illustration) and that the leads
are connected to their original positions.

12   Charging system — general information and precautions

Refer to illustrations 12.1, 12.2a and 12.2b

   The charging system (see illustration) includes the alternator, either
an internal or an external voltage regulator, a charge indicator, the battery, a fusible link and the wiring between all the components. The
charging system supplies electrical power for the ignition system, the
lights, the radio, etc. The alternator is driven by a drivebelt at the front

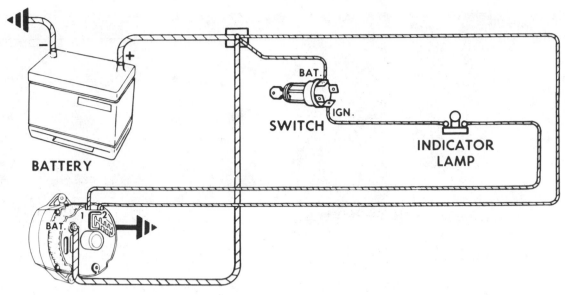

12.1 Wiring schematic for a typical charging system

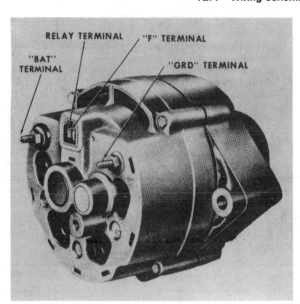

12.2a A Series 1D Delcotron alternator, which uses an external voltage regulator (Series 10DN and 100B types are similar)

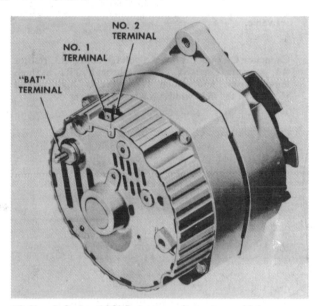

12.2b A Series 10SI Delcotron alternator, which uses an internal voltage regulator (Series CS-121, 130 and 144 types are similar, but are not rebuildable)

(right end) of the engine.

The alternator fitted to all models is a Delco-Remy Delcotron. Several units have been used. Early units (see illustration), such as the Series 1D, 10DN and 100B, are fitted with an external voltage regulator. Later units (see illustration), such as the Series 10SI and the CS-121, CS-130 and CS-144, are fitted with an internal voltage regualtor. Finally, it should be noted that the CS series alternators cannot be rebuilt. If one becomes inoperative, it must be replaced.

The purpose of the voltage regulator is to limit the alternator's voltage to a preset value. This prevents power surges, circuit overloads, etc., during peak voltage output.

The fusible link is a short length of insulated wire integral with the engine compartment wiring harness. The link is four wire gauges smaller in diameter than the circuit it protects. Production fusible links and their identification flags are identified by the flag color. See Chapter 12 for additional information regarding fusible links.

The charging system doesn't ordinarily require periodic maintenance. However, the drivebelt, battery and wires and connections should be inspected at the intervals outlined in Chapter 1.

The dashboard warning light should come on when the ignition key is turned to Start, then should go off immediately. If it remains on,

there is a malfunction in the charging system (see Section 13). Some vehicles are also equipped with a voltage gauge. If the voltage gauge indicates abnormally high or low voltage, check the charging system (see Section 13).

Be very careful when making electrical circuit connections to a vehicle equipped with an alternator and note the following:

a) When reconnecting wires to the alternator from the battery, be sure to note the polarity.

b) Before using arc welding equipment to repair any part of the vehicle, disconnect the wires from the alternator and the battery terminals.

c) Never start the engine with a battery charger connected.

d) Always disconnect both battery leads before using a battery charger.

e) The alternator is driven by an engine drivebelt which could cause serious injury if your hands, hair or clothes become entangled in it with the engine running.

f) Because the alternator is connected directly to the battery, it could arc or cause a fire if overloaded or shorted out.

g) Wrap a plastic bag over the alternator and secure it with rubber bands before steam cleaning the engine.

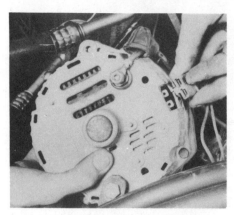

14.2   The first step in alternator removal is disconnecting all electrical leads (which will vary somewhat with alternator type and year of manufacture)

14.3a   To remove the drivebelt, loosen the alternator mounting bolt . . .

14.3b   . . . then loosen the adjustment bolt and slip off the belt — finally, remove the mounting and adjusting bolts and remove the alternator

13   Charging system — check

1   If a malfunction occurs in the charging circuit, don't automatically assume that the alternator is causing the problem. First check the following items:
  a)   Check the drivebelt tension and its condition. Replace it if worn or deteriorated.
  b)   Make sure that the alternator mounting and adjustment bolts are tight.
  c)   Inspect the alternator wiring harness and the connectors at the alternator and voltage regulator. They must be in good condition and tight.
  d)   Check the fusible link (if equipped) located between the starter solenoid and the alternator. If it's burned, determine the cause, repair the circuit and replace the link (the vehicle won't start and/or the accessories won't work if the fusible link blows).
  e)   Start the engine and check the alternator for abnormal noises (a shrieking or squealing sound indicates a bad bushing).
  f)   Check the specific gravity of the battery electrolyte. If it's low, charge the battery (doesn't apply to maintenance free batteries).
  g)   Make sure that the battery is fully charged (one bad cell in a battery can cause overcharging by the alternator).
  h)   Disconnect the battery cables (negative first, then positive). Inspect the battery posts and the cable clamps for corrosion. Clean them thoroughly if necessary (see Chapter 1).
  i)   With the key off, insert a test light between the negative battery post and the disconnected negative cable clamp.
    1)   If the test light does not come on, reattach the clamp and proceed to the next Step.
    2)   If the test light comes on, there is a short in the electrical system of the vehicle. The short must be repaired before the charging system can be checked.
    3)   Disconnect the alternator wiring harness.
      a)   If the light goes out, the alternator is bad.
      b)   If the light stays on, pull each fuse until the light goes out (this will tell you which component is shorted).
2   Using a voltmeter, check the battery voltage with the engine off. It should be approximately 12 volts.
3   Start the engine and check the battery voltage again. It should now be approximately 14 to 15 volts.
4   Turn on the headlights. The voltage should drop, and then come back up, if the charging system is working properly.
5   If the voltage reading is less or more than the specified charging voltage, replace the voltage regulator (refer to Section 16).

14   Alternator — removal and installation

Refer to illustrations 14.2, 14.3a, 14.3b and 14.3c
1   Detach the cable from the negative terminal of the battery.
2   Detach the electrical connectors from the alternator and the voltage regulator (**see illustration**).
3   Loosen the alternator adjustment and pivot bolts and detach the drivebelt (**see illustrations**).
4   Remove the adjustment and pivot bolts and separate the alternator from the engine.
5   If you are replacing the alternator, take the old alternator with you when purchasing a replacement unit. Make *sure* that the new/rebuilt unit is identical to the old alternator. Look at the terminals — they should be the same in number, size and location as the terminals on the old alternator. Finally, look at the identification markings — they will be stamped in the housing or printed on a tag or plaque affixed to the housing. Make sure that these numbers are the same on both alternators.
6   Many new/rebuilt alternators do not have a pulley installed, so you may have to switch the pulley from the old unit to the new/rebuilt one. When buying an alternator, find out the shop's policy regarding pulleys — some shops will perform this service free of charge.
7   Installation is the reverse of removal.
8   After the alternator is installed, adjust the drivebelt tension (see Chapter 1).
9   Check the charging voltage to verify proper operation of the alternator (see Section 13).

15   Alternator — brush replacement and overhaul

Refer to Illustration 15.7
Note: *Due to the critical nature of the disassembly and testing of the various alternator components it may be advisable for the home mechanic to simply replace a faulty unit with a new or factory rebuilt model. If you decide to perform the overhaul procedure yourself, make sure that replacement parts are available before proceeding.*
1   Remove the alternator and pulley (see Section 14).
2   Secure the alternator in the jaws of a vice, applying the pressure to the mounting flange.
3   Remove the four through-bolts, and separate the slip-ring, end frame and stator assembly from the drive-end and rotor assembly. Use a screwdriver to lever them apart and mark the relative position of the end frames to facilitate reassembly.
4   Remove the stator lead securing nuts and separate the stator from the end frame.

1D, 10DN and 100B series

5   Extract the screws and remove the brush holder assembly.
6   Remove the heat sink from the end frame after extracting the BAT and GRD terminals and single securing screws.

10 S1 series

7   Continue dismantling, by removing the rectifier bridge, securing screw and the BAT terminal screw. Disconnect the capacitor lead and remove the rectifier bridge from the end-frame (**see illustration**).

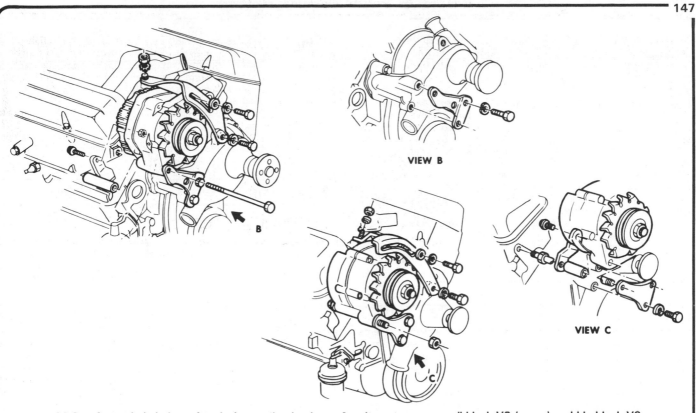

14.3c An exploded view of typical mounting hardware for alternator on a small-block V8 (upper) and big-block V8 (lower) — mounting hardware on V6 installations is similar

VIEW B

VIEW C

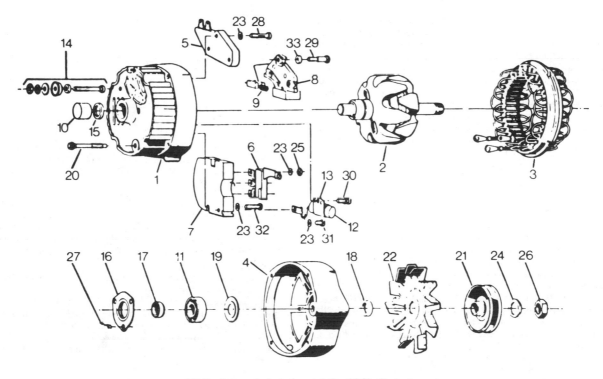

15.7 An exploded view of the 10SI alternator

1	Slip-ring end frame	8	Brush assembly	15	Seal	22 Fan
2	Rotor	9	Brush holder	16	Plate	23 Washer
3	Stator	10	Bearing	17	Collar	24 Washer
4	Drive end frame	11	Bearing	18	Collar	25 Nut
5	Regulator	12	Capacitor	19	Washer	26 Nut
6	Diode	13	Bracket	20	Through-bolt	27 to 32 Screws
7	Rectifier bridge	14	Terminal components	21	Pulley	33 Washer

5

8   Unscrew the two securing screws and remove the brush holder and regulator. Carefully retain the insulating sleeves and washers.
9   Remove the capacitor (one screw) from the end-frame.

All models

10 If the slip ring end-frame bearing is dry or noisy when rotated, it must be replaced (not greased). Greasing will not extend its service life. Press out the old bearing and discard the oil seal. Press in the new bearing, squarely, until the bearing is flush with the outside of the end-frame. Install a new oil seal. During these operations, support the end-frame adequately to prevent cracking or distorting the frame.
11 Now insert a 5/16-inch Allen wrench into the socket in the center of the shaft at the drive pulley end. Using this to prevent the shaft from rotating, unscrew the pulley retaining nut and remove the washer, pulley, fan and the spacer.
12 Remove the rotor and spacers from the drive end-frame.
13 If the bearing in the drive end-frame is dry or noisy it must be replaced. Do not grease it in the hope that this will extend its life. Access to the bearing is obtained after removing the retainer place bolts and separating the plate/seal assembly. Press the bearing out by using a piece of tube applied to the inner race and press the new one in by applying the tube to the outer race. Make sure that the slinger is correctly located and recommended grease is applied to the bearing before installation.
14 With the alternator completely dismantled, wipe all components clean (do not use solvent on the stator or rotor windings), and examine for wear or damage. Purchase new components as necessary.
15 If the slip rings are dirty they should be cleaned by spinning the rotor and holding a piece of 400-grain abrasive paper against them. This method will avoid the creation of flat spots on the rings. If the rings are badly scored, out-of-round or otherwise damaged, the complete rotor assembly must be replaced.
16 Check the brushes for wear. If they are worn halfway or more in length, do not re-use them. Purchase new springs only if they appear weak or are distorted.
17 Reassembly is a reversal of dismantling. Observe the following points:
   a) Tighten the pulley nut securely. Take great care to position the insulating washers and sleeves correctly on the brush clip screws.
   b) Clean the brush contact surfaces before installing the slip ring end-frame and hold the brushes up in their holders by passing a thin rod through the opening in the slip ring end-frame to permit the brushes to pass over the slip rings.
   c) Finally, make sure that the marks on the slip ring and drive end-frame (which were made before dismantling) are in alignment.

16 External voltage regulator — check and replacement

Refer to Illustration 16.4

1   A discharged battery will normally be due to a fault in the voltage regulator, but before testing the unit, do the following:
   a) Check the drivebelt tension.
   b) Test the condition of the battery.
   c) Check the charging circuit for loose connections and broken wires.
   d) Made sure that lights or other electrical accessories have not been switched on inadvertently.
   e) Check the generator indicator lamp for normal illumination with the ignition switched on and off, and with the engine idling and stationary.
2   Disconnect the battery ground cable. Disconnect the harness connector from the regulator.
3   Under no circumstances should the voltage regulator or field relay contacts be cleaned since any abrasive materials will destroy the contact material.
4   Voltage regulator point (0.014-inch) and air-gap (0.067-inch) adjustments can be checked with a feeler gauge of the specified thickness. Check the voltage regulator point opening of the upper contacts with the lower contacts just touching. Adjustments are made by carefully bending the upper contact arm. Check the voltage regulator air gap with the lower contacts touching and adjust it, if necessary, by turning the nylon nut (**see illustration**).

5   The field relay point opening may be adjusted by bending the armature stop. The air gap is checked with the points just touching and is adjusted by bending the flat contact support spring. **Note:** *The field relay will normally operate satisfactorily even if the air-gap is outside the specified limits, and should not be adjusted when the system is functioning satisfactorily.*
6   If the regulator must be replaced, simply remove the mounting screws.
7   Installation is the reverse of the removal procedure. Ensure that the rubber gasket is in place on the reulator base.

17 Starting system — general information and precautions

The sole function of the starting system is to turn over the engine quickly enough to allow it to start.
The starting system consists of the battery, the starter motor, the starter solenoid and the wires connecting them. The solenoid is mounted directly on the starter motor or is a separate component located in the engine compartment.
The solenoid/starter motor assembly is installed on the lower part of the engine, next to the transmission bellhousing.
When the ignition key is turned to the Start position, the starter solenoid is actuated through the starter control circuit. The starter solenoid then connects the battery to the starter. The battery supplies the electrical energy to the starter motor, which does the actual work of cranking the engine.
The starter motor on a vehicle equipped with a manual transmission can only be operated when the clutch pedal is depressed; the starter on a vehicle equipped with an automatic transmission can only be operated when the transmission selector lever is in Park or Neutral.
Always observe the following precautions when working on the starting system:
   a) Excessive cranking of the starter motor can overheat it and cause serious damage. Never operate the starter motor for more than 30 seconds at a time without pausing to allow it to cool for at least two minutes.
   b) The starter is connected directly to the battery and could arc or cause a fire if mishandled, overloaded or shorted out.
   c) Always detach the cable from the negative terminal of the battery before working on the starting system.

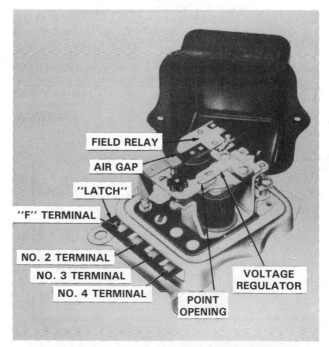

16.4 The voltage regulator point and air gap adjustments can be checked with a feeler gauge of the specified thickness (point opening, 0.014-inch; air gap, 0.067-inch)

18 Starter motor — testing in vehicle

Note: *Before diagnosing starter problems, make sure that the battery is fully charged.*

1 If the starter motor does not turn at all when the ignition switch is operated, make sure that the shift lever is in Neutral or Park (automatic transaxle) or that the clutch pedal is depressed (manual transaxle).

2 Make sure that the battery is charged and that all cables, both at the battery and starter solenoid terminals, are clean and secure.

3 If the starter motor spins but the engine is not cranking, the over-running clutch in the starter motor is slipping and the starter motor must be replaced.

4 If, when the switch is actuated, the starter motor does not operate at all but the solenoid clicks, then the problem lies with either the battery, the main solenoid contacts or the starter motor itself, or the engine is seized.

5 If the solenoid plunger cannot be heard when the switch is actuated, the battery is bad, the fusible link is burned (the circuit is open) or the solenoid itself is defective.

6 To check the solenoid, connect a jumper lead between the battery (positive terminal) and the ignition switch terminal (the small terminal) on the solenoid. If the starter motor now operates, the solenoid is OK and the problem is in the ignition switch, neutral start switch or in the wiring.

7 If the starter motor still does not operate, remove the starter/solenoid assembly for disassembly, testing and repair.

8 If the starter motor cranks the engine at an abnormally slow speed, first make sure that the battery is charged and that all terminal connections are tight. If the engine is partially seized, or has the wrong viscosity oil in it, it will crank slowly.

9 Run the engine until normal operating temperature is reached, then disconnect the coil wire from the distributor cap and ground it on the engine.

10 Connect a voltmeter positive lead to the battery positive post and then connect the negative lead to the negative post.

11 Crank the engine and take the voltmeter readings as soon as a steady figure is indicated. Do not allow the starter motor to turn for more than 30 seconds at a time. A reading of nine volts or more, with the starter motor turning at normal cranking speed, is normal. If the reading is nine volts or more but the cranking speed is slow, the motor is faulty. If the reading is less than nine volts and the cranking speed is slow, the solenoid contacts are probably burned, the starter motor is bad, the battery is discharged or there is a bad connection.

19 Starter motor — removal and installation

Refer to illustrations 19.4a, 19.4b and 19.4c

1 Detach the cable from the negative terminal of the battery.

2 Raise the vehicle and support it securely on jackstands.

3 Clearly label, then disconnect the wires from the terminals on the starter motor and solenoid.

4 Remove the starter motor mounting bolts **(see illustrations)**. Remove the starter.

5 Installation is the reverse of removal.

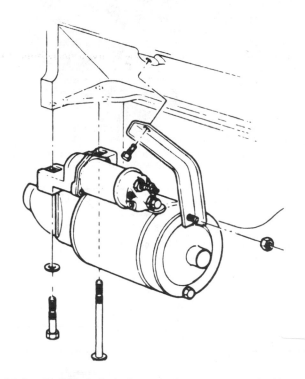

19.4a Exploded view of a typical starter motor installation

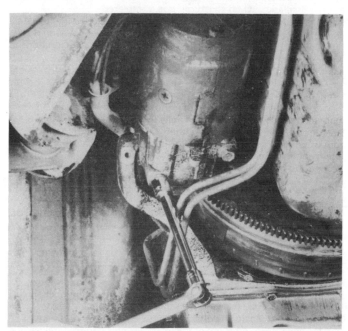

19.4b Working from underneath the vehicle (placed securely on jackstands), remove the starter motor mounting bolts ...

19.4c ... and remove the starter and solenoid (arrow) as an assembly

20.3   To disengage the solenoid from the starter, turn it in a clockwise direction

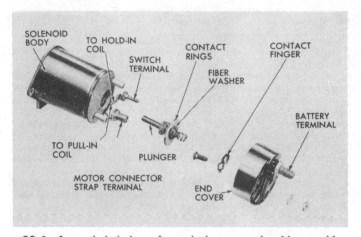

20.4   An exploded view of a typical starter solenoid assembly

20   Starter motor solenoid — removal, repair and installation

Refer to Illustrations 20.3 and 20.4

1   After removing the starter/solenoid unit (see Section 19), disconnect the connector strap from the solenoid MOTOR terminal.
2   Remove the two screws which secure the solenoid housing to the end-frame assembly.
3   Twist the solenoid in a clockwise direction to disengage the flange key and then withdraw the solenoid **(see illustration)**.
4   Remove the nuts and washers from the solenoid terminals and then unscrew the two solenoid end-cover retaining screws and washers and pull off the end-cover **(see illustration)**.
5   Unscrew the nut washer from the battery terminal on the end-cover and remove the terminal.
6   Remove the resistor bypass terminal and contactor.
7   Remove the motor connector strap terminal and solder a new terminal in position.
8   Use a new battery terminal and install it to the end-cover. Install the bypass terminal and contactor.
9   Install the end-cover and the remaining terminal nuts.
10   Install the solenoid to the starter motor by first checking that the return spring is in position on the plunger and then insert the solenoid body into the drive housing and turn the body counter clockwise to engage the flange key.
11   Install the two solenoid securing screws and connect the MOTOR connector strap.

21   Starter motor — overhaul

Refer to Illustration 21.2

Note: *Due to the critical nature of the disassembly and testing of the starter motor it may be advisable for the home mechanic to simply purchase a new or factory-rebuilt unit. If it is decided to overhaul the starter, check on the availability of singular replacement components before proceeding.*

1   Disconnect the starter motor field coil connectors from the solenoid terminals.
2   Unscrew and remove the through-bolts **(see illustration)**.
3   Remove the commutator end-frame, field frame assembly and the armature from the drive housing.
4   Slide the two-section thrust collar off the end of the armature shaft and then, using a piece of suitable tube, drive the stop/retainer up the armature shaft to expose the snap-ring.
5   Extract the snap-ring from its shaft groove and then slide the

stop/retainer and overrunning clutch assembly from the armature shaft.
6   Dismantle the brush components from the field frame.
7   Release the V-shaped springs from the brushholder supports.
8   Remove the brushholder support pin and then lift the complete brush assembly upwards.
9   Disconnect the leads from the brushes if they are worn down to half their original length and they are to be replaced.
10   The starter motor is now completely dismantled except for the field coils. If these are found to be defective during the tests described later in this Section, removal of the pole shoe screws is best left to a service facility which has the necessary pressure driver.
11   Clean all components and replace any obviously worn components.
12   Never attempt to undercut the insulation between the commutator segments on starter motors having the molded type commutators. On commutators of conventional type, the insulation should be undercut (below the level of the segments) by 1/32-inch. Use an old hacksaw blade to do this, and make sure that the undercut is the full width of the insulation and the groove is quite square at the bottom. When the undercutting is completed, brush away all dirt and dust.
13   Clean the commutator by spinning it while a piece of '00' sandpaper is wrapped round it. Never use any other type of abrasive material for this work.
14   If necessary, because the commutator is in such bad shape, it may be turned down in a lathe to provide a new surface. Make sure to undercut the insulation when the turning is completed.
15   *To test the armature for ground:* use a lamp-type circuit tester. Place one lead on the armature core or shaft and the other on a segment of the commutator. If the lamp lights, then the armature is grounded and must be replaced.
16   *To test the field coils for open circuit:* place one test probe on the insulated brush and the other on the field connector bar. If the lamp does not light, the coils are open and must be replaced.
17   *To test the field coils for ground:* place one test probe on the connector bar and the other on the grounded brush. If the lamp lights, then the field coils are grounded.
18   The overrunning clutch cannot be repaired, and if faulty, it must be replaced as a complete assembly.
19   Install the brush assembly to the field frame as follows:
20   Install the brushes to their holders.
21   Assemble the insulated and grounded brushholders together with the V-spring and then locate the unit on its support pin.
22   Push the holders and spring to the bottom of the support and then rotate the spring to engage the V in the support slot.
23   Connect the ground wire to the grounded brush and the field lead wire to the insulated brush.
24   Repeat the operations for the second set of brushes.
25   Smear silicone oil onto the drive end of the armature shaft and then slide the clutch assembly (pinion to the front) onto the shaft.
26   Slide the pinion stop/retainer onto the shaft so that its open end is facing away from the pinion.
27   Stand the armature vertically on a piece of wood and then position the snap-ring on the end of the shaft. Using a hammer and a piece of hardwood, drive the snap-ring onto the shaft.
28   Slide the snap-ring down the shaft until it drops into its groove.

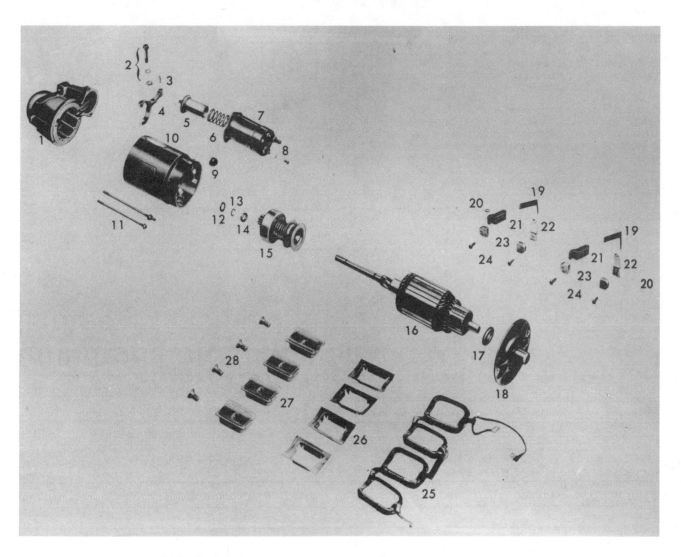

21.2 Exploded view of a typical starter motor and solenoid assembly

1 Drive housing	7 Solenoid case	15 Overrunning clutch	22 Grounded brush
2 Shift lever bolt, nut	8 Screw and lock washer	assembly	holders
and lockwasher	9 Grommet	16 Armature	23 Brushes
3 Pin	10 Field frame	17 Braking washer	24 Screws
4 Shift lever	11 Through-bolts	18 Commutator end frame	25 Field coils
5 Solenoid plunger	12 Thrust collar	19 Brush springs	26 Insulators
6 Solenoid return	13 Snap-ring	20 Washer	27 Pole shoes
spring	14 Retainer	21 Insulated brush holders	28 Screws

29 Install the thrust collar on the shaft so that the shoulder is next to the snap-ring. Using two pairs of pliers, squeeze the thrust collar and stop/retainer together until the snap-ring fully enters the retainer.

30 Lubricate the drive housing bushing with silicone oil and after ensuring that the thrust collar is in position against the snap-ring, slide the armature and clutch assembly into the drive housing so that, at the same time, the shift lever engages with the clutch.

31 Postion the field frame over the armature and apply sealing compound between the frame and the solenoid case.

32 Position the field frame against the drive housing, taking care not to damage the brushes.

33 Lubricate the bushing in the commutator end-frame using silicone oil; place the leather brake washer on the armature shaft and then slide the commutator end-frame onto the shaft.

34 Reconnect the field coil connectors to the MOTOR terminal of the solenoid.

35 Now check the pinion clearance. To do this, connect a 12-volt battery between the solenoid S terminal and ground and at the same time fix a heavy connecting cable between the MOTOR terminal and ground (to prevent any possibility of the starter motor rotating). As the solenoid is energized it will push the pinion forward into its normal cranking position and retain it there. With the fingers, push the pinion away from the stop/retainer in order to eliminate any slack, then check the clearance between the face of the pinion and the face of stop/retainer using a feeler gauge. The clearance should be between 0.010 and 0.140-inch to ensure correct engagement of the pinion with the flywheel (or driveplate — automatic transmission) ring-gear. If the clearance is incorrect, the starter will have to be dismantled again and any worn or distorted components replaced, no adjustment being provided for.

5

Chapter 6   Emission control systems

Contents

1   General information

Refer to illustrations 1.6a, 1.6b, 1.6c, 1.6d, 1.6e and 1.6f

To prevent pollution of the atmosphere from incompletely burned or evaporating gases, and to maintain good driveability and fuel economy, a number of emission control systems, such as the following, are used on your vehicle:

Air Injection Reactor (AIR) system
Exhaust Gas Recirculation (EGR) system
Evaporation Control System (ECS)
Positive Crankcase Ventilation (PCV) system
Inlet air temperature control system
Catalytic converter
Electronic Spark Timing (EST)
Transmission Controlled Spark (TCS) system
Computer Controlled Catalytic Converter (C4) system
Computer Command Control (C3) system

The Sections in this Chapter include general descriptions, checking procedures within the scope of the home mechanic and component replacement procedures (when possible) for each of the systems listed above.

Before assuming that an emissions control system is malfunctioning, check the fuel and ignition systems carefully. The diagnosis of some emission control devices requires specialized tools, equipment and training. If checking and servicing become too difficult or if a procedure is beyond your ability, consult a dealer service department.

This doesn't mean, however, that emission control systems are particularly difficult to maintain and repair. You can quickly and easily perform many checks and do most of the regular maintenance at home with common tune-up and hand tools. **Note:** *Because of a Federally mandated extended warranty which covers the emission control system components, check with your dealer about warranty coverage before working on any emissions-related systems. Once the warranty has expired, you may wish to perform some of the component checks and/or replacement procedures in this Chapter to save money.*

Pay close attention to any special precautions outlined in this Chapter. It should be noted that the illustrations of the various systems may not exactly match the system installed on your vehicle because of changes made by the manufacturer during production or from year to year. Remember — the most frequent cause of emissions problems is simply a loose or broken vacuum hose or wire, so always check the hose and wiring connections first.

The accompanying emission component location schematics **(see illustrations)** will give you a good idea where various emission devices are located on your vehicle. (Unfortunately, these charts are not available for '70's-era vehicles.) If there is a discrepancy between the included chart and the Vehicle Control Information (VECI) label on your vehicle, always refer to the VECI sticker. The VECI label is located in the engine compartment. This label contains important emissions specifications and adjustment information, and a vacuum hose routing and emission component location schematic. When servicing the engine or emissions systems, the VECI label in your particular vehicle should always be checked for up-to-date information.

1.6a Emission control component location, 1984 V8-equipped vehicles (Oldsmobile shown, others similar)

COMPUTER SYSTEM

C1	Electronic Control Module (ECM)
C2	ALCL Connector
C3	"CHECK ENGINE" Light
C4	Remote Lamp Driver
C5	System Ground
C6	Fuse Panel
C8	Computer Control Harness
C9	Cold Start Module

AIR/FUEL SYSTEM

1	Mixture Control
2	Idle Load Compensator
3	EFE Valve
4	Rear Vacuum Brake
4A	ILC/RVB Solenoid

TRANSMISSION CONVERTER CLUTCH CONTROL SYSTEM

5	Trans. Conv. Clutch Connector

IGNITION SYSTEM

6	Electronic Spark Timing Connector

AIR INJECTION SYSTEM

8	Air Injection Pump
9	Air Control Solenoid Valve
10	Air Switching Solenoid Valve

EXHAUST GAS RECIRCULATION CONTROL SYSTEM

11	Exhaust Gas Recirculation Valve
12	Exhaust Gas Recirculation Solenoid Valve

SENSORS/SWITCHES

A	Differential Pressure Sensor	D	Coolant Sensor
B	Exhaust Oxygen Sensor	E	Barometric Pressure Sensor
C	Throttle Position Sensor	F	Vehicle Speed Sensor

FUEL VAPOR CONTROL SYSTEM

15	Vapor Canister

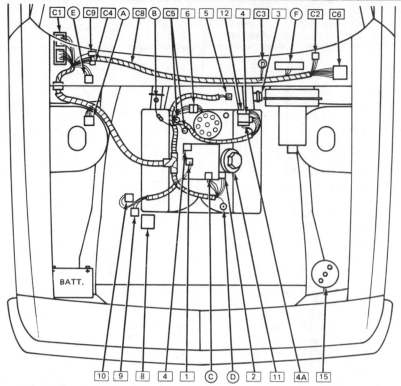

1.6b Emission control component location, 1984 V6-equipped vehicles (Oldsmobile shown, others similar)

COMPUTER SYSTEM

C1	Electronic Control Module (ECM)
C2	ALCL Connector
C3	"CHECK ENGINE" Light
C4	System Power
C5	System Ground
C6	Fuse Panel
C8	Computer Control Harness

AIR/FUEL SYSTEM

1	Mixture Control
2	Idle Speed Control
4	Heated Grid EFE
4A	EFE Relay

TRANSMISSION CONVERTER CLUTCH CONTROL SYSTEM

5	Trans. Conv. Clutch Connector

IGNITION SYSTEM

6	Electronic Spark Timing Connector
7	Electronic Spark Control (ESC)

AIR INJECTION SYSTEM

8	Air Injection Pump
9	Air Control Solenoid Valve (Divert)
10	Air Switching Solenoid Valve

EXHAUST GAS RECIRCULATION CONTROL SYSTEM

11	Exhaust Gas Recirculation Valve
12	Exhaust Gas Recirculation Solenoid Valve

FUEL VAPOR CONTROL SYSTEM

15	Vapor Canister

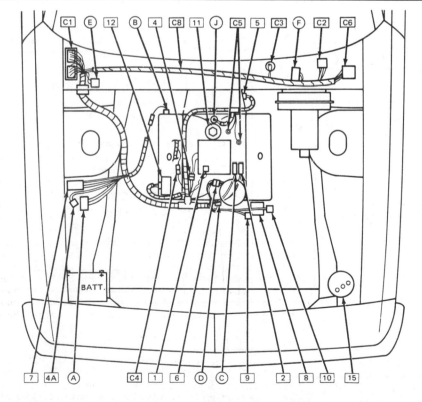

SENSORS/SWITCHES

A	Differential Pressure Sensor	C	Throttle Position Sensor	F	Vehicle Speed Sensor
B	Exhaust Oxygen Sensor	D	Coolant Sensor	J	ESC Sensor (Knock)
		E	Barometric Pressure Sensor		

6

1.6c Emission control component location, 1985 V8-equipped vehicles (Pontiac shown, others similar)

COMPUTER HARNESS

C1 Electronic Control Module
C2 ALCL connector (Data Access)
C3 "CHECK ENG/SERV ENG SOON" light
C4 ECM power
C5 ECM harness ground
C6 Fuse panel
C7 "C.E./S.E.S." lamp driver
C10 M/C dwell connector

NOT ECM CONNECTED

N1 Crankcase vent (PCV)
N2 Intake manifold warming (EFE)
N16 Fuel vapor canister valve(TVS)
N17 Fuel vapor canister

CONTROLLED DEVICES

1 Mixture control solenoid
2 Electric throttle kicker (idle solenoid)
5 Trans. Conv. Clutch connector
6 Electronic Spark Timing connector
7 Electronic Spark Control
9 Air divert solenoid
10 Air switching solenoid
12 Exh. Gas Recirc. vac. solenoid (PWM)

⬡ Exhaust Gas Recirculation valve

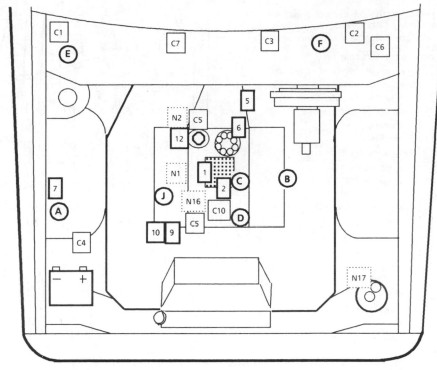

INFORMATION SENSORS

A Pressure differential (vacuum)
B Exhaust oxygen
C Throttle position
D Coolant temperature
E Barometric pressure
F Vehicle speed
J Detonation (ESC)

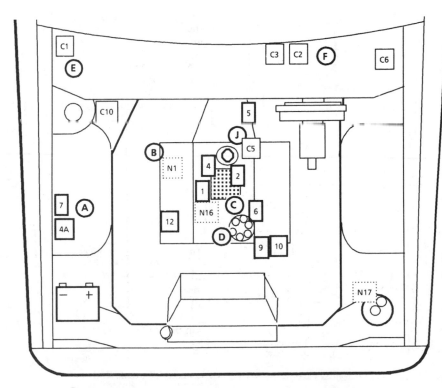

1.6d Emission control component location, 1985 V6-equipped vehicles (Pontiac shown, others similar)

COMPUTER HARNESS

C1 Electronic Control Module
C2 ALCL connector (Data Access)
C3 "CHECK ENG/SERV ENG SOON" light
C5 ECM harness ground
C6 Fuse panel
C10 M/C dwell connector

NOT ECM CONNECTED

N1 Crankcase vent (PCV)
N16 Fuel vapor canister valve(TVS)
N17 Fuel vapor canister

CONTROLLED DEVICES

1 Mixture control solenoid
2 Idle speed control motor
4 Heated EFE grid
4A Heated EFE grid relay
5 Trans. Conv. Clutch connector
6 Electronic Spark Timing connector
7 Electronic Spark Control (ESC)
9 Air control solenoid
10 Air switching solenoid
12 Exh. Gas Recirc. vac. solenoid (PWM)

⬡ Exhaust Gas Recirculation valve

INFORMATION SENSORS

A Manifold Absolute Pressure
B Exhaust oxygen
C Throttle position
D Coolant temperature
E Barometric pressure
F Vehicle speed
J Detonation (ESC)

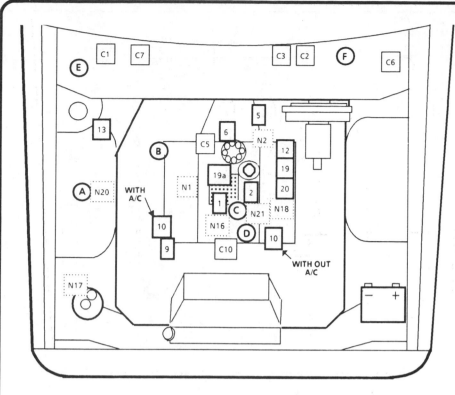

1.6e Emission control component location, 1987-on V8-equipped vehicles (Buick shown, others similar)

COMPUTER HARNESS
C1 Electronic Control Module (ECM)
C2 ALDL diagnostic connector
C3 "SERVICE ENGINE SOON" light
C5 ECM harness ground
C6 Fuse panel
C7 "C.E./S.E.S." lamp driver
C10 M/C dwell connector

NOT ECM CONNECTED
N1 Crankcase vent valve (PCV)
N2 EFE valve
N16 Fuel vapor canister valve
N17 Fuel vapor canister
N18 Anti-dieseling solenoid (VIN Y only)
N20 Anti-dieseling vac. tank (VIN Y only)
N21 Idle Speed Solenoid (VIN 9 only)

CONTROLLED DEVICES
1   Mixture control solenoid
2   Idle load Compensator (VIN Y only)
5   Trans. Conv. Clutch connector
6   Electronic Spark Timing (EST)connector
9   Air injection divert valve
10 Air injection switching valve
12 Exh. Gas Recirc. vacuum solenoid
13 A/C compressor relay
19 Rear vacuum break solenoid
19a Rear vacuum break
20 ILC Solenoid

Exhaust Gas Recirculation valve

INFORMATION SENSORS
A Differential Pressure (Vac)   D Coolant temperature
B Exhaust oxygen   E Barometric pressure
C Throttle position   F Vehicle speed

1.6f Emission control component location, 1987 and 1988 V6-equipped vehicles (Buick shown, others similar)

COMPUTER HARNESS
C1 Electronic Control Module (ECM)
C2 ALDL connector
C3 "SERVICE ENGINE SOON" light
C5 ECM harness ground
C6 Fuse panel
C10 M/C dwell connector

NOT ECM CONNECTED
N1 Crankcase vent (PCV)
N16 Fuel vapor canister valve(TVS)
N17 Fuel vapor canister

CONTROLLED DEVICES
1   Mixture control solenoid
2   Idle speed control motor
4   Heated EFE grid
4A Heated EFE grid relay
5   Trans. Conv. Clutch connector
6   Electronic Spark Timing connector
7   Electronic Spark Control (ESC)
9   Air control solenoid
10 Air switching solenoid
12 Exh. Gas Recirc. vac. solenoid (PWM)

Exhaust Gas Recirculation valve

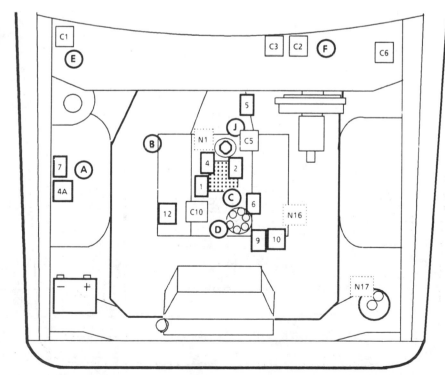

INFORMATION SENSORS
A Manifold Absolute Pressure   D Coolant temperature
B Exhaust oxygen   E Barometric pressure
C Throttle position   F Vehicle speed
                                    J Detonation (ESC)

6

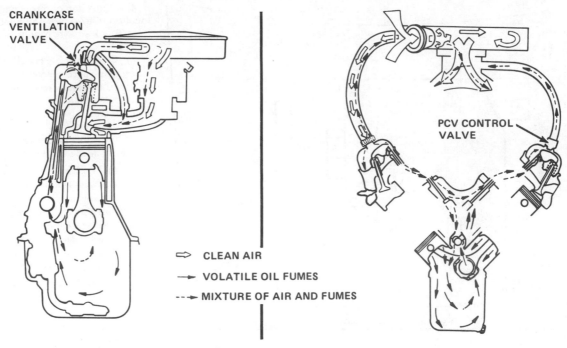

2.1   Operation of a typical Positive Crankcase Ventilation (PCV) system

2   Positive Crankcase Ventilation system

General description

Refer to illustrations 2.1 and 2.2

1   The positive crankcase ventilation, or PCV as it is more commonly called, reduces hydrocarbon emissions by circulating fresh air through the crankcase to pick up blow-by gases, which are then re-routed through the carburetor or intake manifold to be reburned by the engine (**see illustration**).

2   The main components of this simple system are vacuum hoses and a PCV valve which regulates the flow of gases according to engine speed and manifold vacuum (**see illustration**).

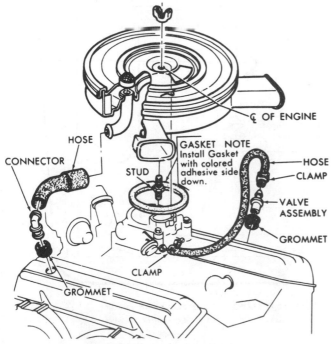

2.2   Exploded view of a typical PCV system

Checking

Refer to illustrations 2.6 and 2.9

3   The PCV system can be checked for proper operation quickly and easily. This system should be checked regularly, as carbon and gunk deposited by the blow-by gases will eventually clog the PCV valve and/or system hoses. When the flow of the PCV system is reduced or stopped, common symptoms are rough idling or a reduced engine speed at idle.

4   To check for proper vacuum in the system, remove the top plate of the air cleaner and locate the small PCV filter on the inside of the air cleaner housing.

5   Disconnect the hose leading to this filter. Be careful not to break the molded fitting on the filter.

6   With the engine idling, place your thumb lightly over the end of the hose (**see illustration**). Leave it there for about 30 seconds. You should feel a slight pull, or vacuum. The suction may be heard as your

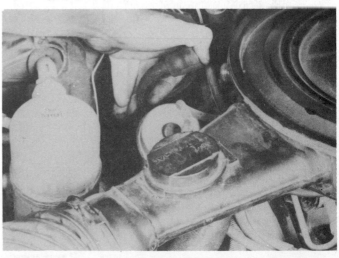

2.6   To check for proper vacuum, remove the top plate of the air cleaner housing, locate the small PCV filter on the inside of the air cleaner housing, detach the hose leading to the this filter and, with the engine idling, place your thumb lightly over the end of the hose and leave it there for about 30 seconds — you should feel a slight suction

thumb is released. This will indicate that air is being drawn all the way through the system. If a vacuum is felt, the system is functioning properly. Check that the filter inside the air cleaner housing is not clogged or dirty. If in doubt, replace the filter with a new one, which is an inexpensive safeguard.

7   If there is very little vacuum, or none at all, at the end of the hose, the system is clogged and must be inspected further.

8   Shut off the engine and locate the PCV valve. Carefully pull it from its rubber grommet. Shake it and listen for a clicking sound. If the valve does not click freely, replace the valve with a new one.

9   Now start the engine and run it at idle speed with the PCV valve removed. Place your thumb over the end of the valve and feel for suction (see illustration). This should be relatively strong vacuum which will be felt immediately.

10   If little or no vacuum is felt at the PCV valve, turn off the engine and disconnect the vacuum hose from the other end of the valve. Run the engine at idle speed and check for vacuum at the end of the hose just disconnected. No vacuum at this point indicates that the vacuum hose or inlet fitting at the engine is plugged. If it is the hose which is blocked, replace it with a new one or remove it from the engine and blow it out sufficiently with compressed air. A clogged passage at the carburetor or manifold requires that the component be removed and thoroughly cleaned of carbon build-up. A strong vacuum felt going into the PCV valve, but little or no vacuum coming out of the valve, indicates a failure of the PCV valve, requiring replacement with a new one.

11   When purchasing a new PCV valve make sure it is the proper one. Each PCV valve is metered for specific engine sizes and model years. An incorrect PCV valve may pull too much or too little vacuum, possibly causing damage to the engine.

12   Information on removing and installing the PCV valve can be found in Chapter 1.

3   Air Injection Reactor (AIR) system

General description

Refer to illustrations 3.1, 3.3a, 3.3b, 3.3c 3.4a and 3.4b

1   The Air Injection Reactor (AIR) system reduces hydrocarbons in the exhaust by pumping additional oxygen into the exhaust port of the cylinder head, exhaust manifold (see illustration), or the catalytic converter. The oxygen-rich air helps combust the unburned hydrocarbons before they are expelled as exhaust.

2   The AIR system operates at all engine speeds, but it bypasses air for a short time during deceleration and at high speeds, because air added to the over-rich fuel/air mixture present in the exhaust during these conditions can cause backfiring or popping through the exhaust.

3   The AIR system consists of an engine-driven injection pump at the front of the engine, air diverter valve attached to the pump housing (see illustration), the manifold and injection tubes running into each port at the exhaust manifolds, and a check valve for each hose between

2.9   To check for a clogged PCV valve, remove the valve from the rocker arm cover and, with the engine running, place your finger over the end of the valve and feel for suction — it should be fairly strong

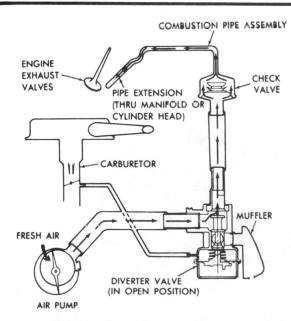

3.1   The Air Injection Reactor (AIR) system reduces hydrocarbons in the exhaust by pumping fresh air directly into the exhaust manifold ports of each cylinder — the fresh oxygen-rich air helps combust the unburned hydrocarbons before they are expelled as exhaust

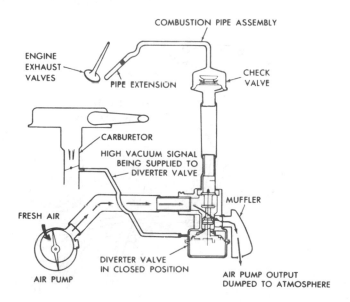

3.3a   During deceleration and at high speeds, the air diverter valve bypasses air from the air pump and dumps it into the atmosphere to prevent backfiring or popping through the exhaust

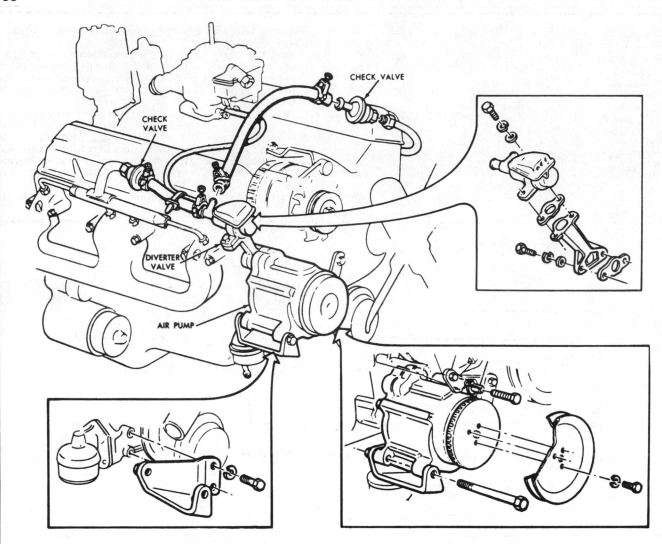

CHECK VALVE

CHECK VALVE

AIR PUMP

DIVERTER VALVE

3.3b   A typical AIR system installation on a small block V8

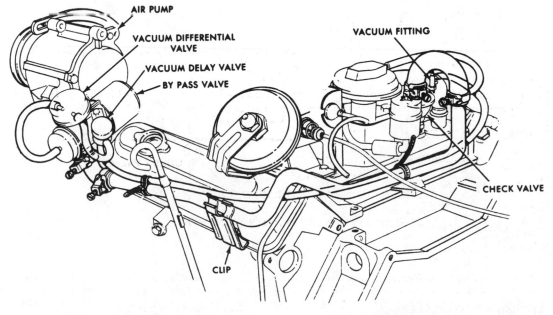

AIR PUMP

VACUUM DIFFERENTIAL VALVE

VACUUM DELAY VALVE

BY PASS VALVE

VACUUM FITTING

CHECK VALVE

CLIP

3.3c   A typical AIR system installation on a 231 V6

the pump and the injection tubes on either side of the engine **(see illustration)**. Instead of a diverter valve, some 231 V6 models use a bypass valve in conjunction with a vacuum differential valve. On these models, fresh air is pumped into the rear of the manifold and then to the exhaust ports **(see illustration)**.

4   Later versions of the AIR system **(see illustrations)** are under ECM control:

  a) When the engine is cold, the ECM energizes an AIR control solenoid. This allows air to flow to an AIR switching valve. The AIR switching valve is energized to direct air to the exhaust ports.

  b) On a warm engine, or in "closed loop" mode, the ECM de-energizes the AIR switching valve, directing air between the beds of the catalytic converter. This provides extra oxygen for the oxidizing catalyst to decrease HC and CO levels, while keeping oxygen levels low in the first bed of the converter. This enables the

reducing catalyst to effectively decrease the levels of oxides of nitrogen (NOX).

  c) If the AIR control valve detects a rapid increase in manifold vacuum (deceleration) certain operating modes (wide open throttle, for example), or the ECM self-diagnostic system detects a problem in the CCC system, air is diverted (divert mode) to the air cleaner or directly to the atmosphere.

  d) The divert mode prevents backfiring through the exhaust system. Throttle closure at deceleration creates a fuel-air mixture which is temporarily too rich to burn completely. This mixture, when it reaches the exhaust, becomes burnable when combined with injected air. The next spark would ignite this mixture, causing an exhaust backfire, but momentary diverting of injected air prevents it.

  e) The air flow and control hoses transmit pressurized air to the cat-

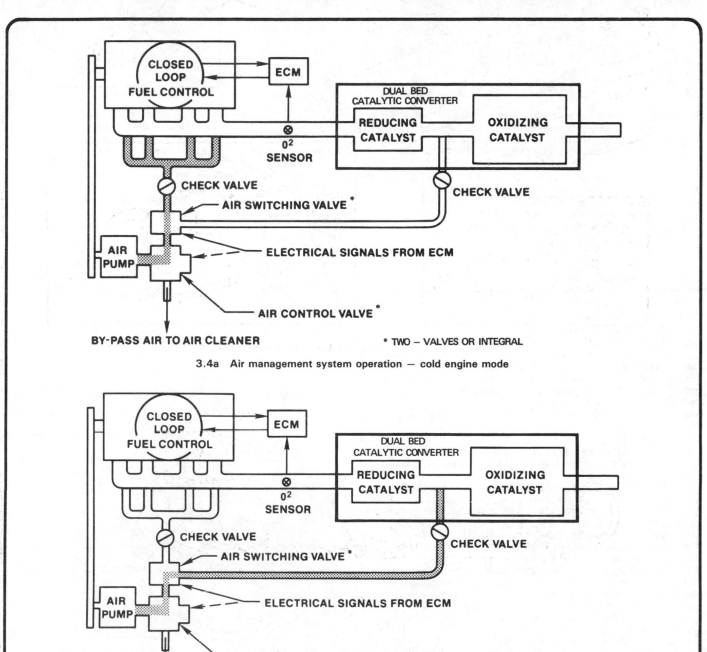

3.4a   Air management system operation — cold engine mode

3.4b   Air management system operation — warm engine mode

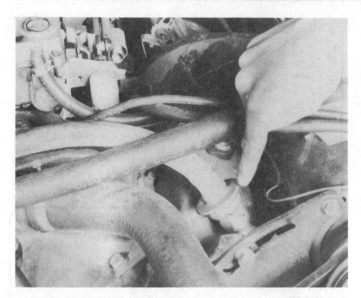

3.6   To check for proper air delivery from the pump, follow the hoses from the pump to where they meet the injection tube/manifold assembly on each side of the engine, loosen the clamps, disconnect the hoses . . .

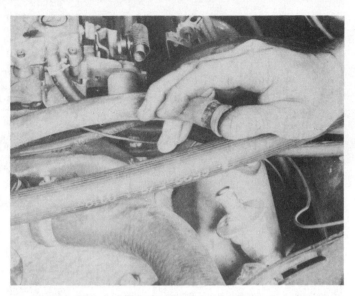

3.7   . . . start the engine and, with your fingers or a piece of paper, verify that air is flowing out of these hoses, then accelerate the engine and note the air flow, which should increase in relation to engine speed — if it does, the pump is working satisfactorily; if it doesn't, check for crimps in the hoses, a loose drivebelt or a leaky diverter valve

alytic converter or to the exhaust ports via internal passages in the intake manifold, or through external firing.

f) The check valve prevents backflow of exhaust gas into the AIR distribution system. The valve prevents backflow when the air pump bypasses at high speeds and loads, or when the air pump malfunctions.

Checking

Note: *The following checks generally apply to all AIR systems. However, where ECM controlled systems differ in design from older types, diagnosis is beyond the scope of the home mechanic.*

Refer to illustrations 3.6, 3.7 and 3.8

5   Properly installed and adjusted air injection systems are fairly reliable and seldom cause problems. However, a malfunctioning system can cause engine surge, backfiring and over-heated spark plugs. The air pump is the most critical component of this system and the belt at the front of the engine which drives the pump should be your first check. If the belt is cracked or frayed, replace it with a new one. Check the tension of the drive belt by pressing it with your finger. There should be about 1/2-inch of play in the belt when pushed halfway between the pulleys. If the belt is too loose, adjust it (see Chapter 1).

6   To check for proper air delivery from the pump, follow the hoses from the pump to where they meet the injection tube/manifold assembly on each side of the engine **(see illustration)**. Loosen the clamps and disconnect the hoses.

7   Start the engine and, with your fingers or a piece of paper, verify that air is flowing out of these hoses **(see illustration)**. Accelerate the engine and observe the air flow, which should increase in relation to engine speed. If this is the case, the pump is working satisfactorily. If air flow was not present, or did not increase, check for crimps in the hoses, proper drivebelt tension and for a leaking diverter valve, which can be heard with the pump operating.

8   To check the diverter valve, sometimes called the 'gulp' valve or anti-backfire valve, make sure all hoses are connected and start the engine. Locate the muffler on the valve, which is a canister unit with holes in it **(see illustration)**. The 231 V6 bypass valve closely resembles a diverter valve. The vacuum differential valve is located on top of the bypass valve.

9   Being careful not to touch any of the moving engine components, place your hand near the muffler outlet holes and check that no air is escaping with the engine at idle speed. Now have an assistant depress the accelerator pedal to accelerate the engine and then quickly let off the pedal. A momentary blast of air should be felt discharging through the diverter valve muffler. The vacuum differential valve on the 231 V6 (located on top of the bypass valve) is checked the same way as a diverter valve. The bypass valve is checked by disconnecting

and blocking the vacuum source, which should produce a continuous blast of air until the line is reconnected.

10   If no air discharge was felt, disconnect the smaller vacuum hose at the diveter valve. Place your finger over the end of the hose and again have your assistant depress the accelerator and let it off. As the engine is decelerating, a vacuum should be felt. If vacuum was felt, replace the diverter valve with a new one. If no vacuum was felt, the vacuum hose or engine vacuum source is plugged, requiring a thorough cleaning to eliminate the problem.

11   Two check valves are located on the air manifold assembly. Their function is to prevent exhaust gases from flowing back into the air pump. To find out if they are functioning properly, disconnect the two air supply hoses where they attach to the check valves. Start the engine and, being careful not to touch any moving engine components, place

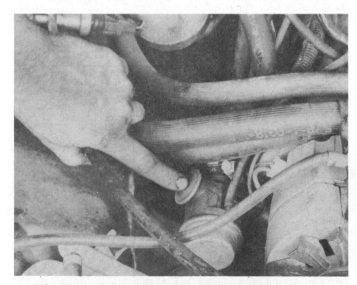

3.8   To check the diverter valve, make sure all hoses are connected, start the engine, locate the muffler (the small perforated canister) on the valve, place your hand near the muffler outlet holes and verify that no air is escaping while the engine is idling, then accelerate the engine and quickly let off the pedal — a momentary blast of air should be felt discharging through the diverter valve muffler

your hand over the outlet of the check valve. No exhaust should flow out of the check valve. The valve can be further checked by turning off the engine, allowing it to cool, and orally blowing through the check valve (toward the air manifold). Then attempt to suck back through it. If the valve is allowing you to suck back towards the air pump, it is faulty and should be replaced.

12 Another check for this system is for leaks in the hose connection and/or hoses themselves. Leaks can often be detected by sound or feel with the pump in operation. If a leak is suspected, use a soapy water solution to verify this. Pour or sponge the solution of detergent and water on the hoses and connections. With the pump running, bubbles will form if a leak exists. The air delivery hoses are of a special design to withstand engine temperatures, so if they are replaced make sure the new hoses are of the proper standards.

Component replacement

Air pump

13 As mentioned earlier, some air pumps share a common drivebelt with the alternator while others use their own belt. The particular layout on the vehicle being serviced will affect the removal and installation procedure somewhat.

14 Disconnect the air delivery hoses at the air pump. Note the position of each hose for assembly.

15 Disconnect the vacuum source hose at the diverter valve.

16 Compress the drivebelt to keep the air pump pulley from turning, and remove the bolts and washers securing the pulley to the pump.

17 To get some slack in the belt, loosen the alternator adjusting bolt and the pivot bolt. Push the alternator inward until the belt and air pump pulley can be removed from the pump.

18 Remove the bolts which secure the air pump to its brackets and then lift the pump and diverter valve assembly from the engine compartment.

19 If the diverter valve is to be installed onto the new air pump, remove the bolts securing it to the pump and separate the two components.

20 Check the pump for evidence that exhaust gas has entered it, indicating a failure of one or both check valves.

21 Install the diverter valve to the new air pump using a new gasket. Tighten the attaching bolts securely.

22 Install the air pump to its engine mounting brackets with the attaching bolts loose. The exception to this is on models where the mounting bolts are inaccessible with the pulley installed. In this case, the pump mounting bolts should be tightened securely at this point.

23 Install the pump pulley with the bolts, only hand tight at this time.

24 Place the drive belt into position on the air pump pulley and adjust the belt by gently prying on the alternator until about 1/2-inch of play is felt in the belt when pushed with your fingers half-way between the pulleys. Tighten the alternator bolts, keeping the belt tension at this point.

25 Keep the pump pulley from turning by compressing the drive belt and tighten the pulley bolts securely.

26 Connect the hoses to the air pump and diverter valve. Make sure the connections are tight.

27 Tighten the mounting bolts for the pump securely.

28 Check the operation of the air pump as outlined previously.

Diverter valve

29 Disconnect the vacuum signal line and air delivery hoses at the diverter valve. Note the position of each for assembly.

30 Remove the bolts which secure the valve to the air pump and remove the diverter valve from the engine compartment.

31 When purchasing a new diverter or bypass valve, keep in mind that although many of the valves are similar in appearance, each is designed to meet particular requirements of various engines. Therefore, be sure to install the correct valve.

32 Install the new diverter valve to the air pump or pump extension with a new gasket. Tighten the securing bolts.

33 Connect the air delivery and vacuum source hoses and check the operation of the valve as outlined previously.

Air manifold and injection tubes

Refer to illustrations 3.36 and 3.38

34 Due to the high temperatures at this area, the connections at the exhaust manifold may be difficult to loosen. Commercial penetrating oil applied to the thread of the injection tubes may help in the removal procedure.

3.36 To remove the injector tubes, detach the air delivery hoses at the manifold check valves, loosen the threaded connectors on the exhaust manifold at each exhaust port, slide the connectors upward on the injection tubes so the threads are out of the exhaust manifold and pull the injection tube/air manifold assembly from the engine exhaust manifold (on some model years, the injection tube extensions leading inside the engine may come out with the assembly)

35 Disconnect the air delivery hoses at the manifold check valves.

36 Loosen the threaded connectors on the exhaust manifold at each exhaust port (see illustration). Slide the connectors upwards on the injection tubes so the threads are out of the exhaust manifold.

37 Pull the injection tube/air manifold assembly from the engine exhaust manifold and out of the engine compartment. Depending on the model year, injection tube extensions leading inside the engine may come out with the assembly.

38 On models where the extension tubes remain inside the exhaust manifold, they must be pressed out after the exhaust manifold is removed from the engine (see illustration).

39 If the exhaust manifold was removed from the engine to clean or replace the extensions, reinstall the manifold with extensions to the

6

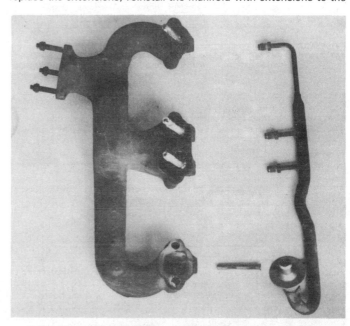

3.38 External extension tubes must be pressed out after the exhaust manifold is removed from the engine

3.44 To remove the check valve from the air manifold assembly, use two wrenches (one as a backup) on the threaded fittings — be sure that you don't bend or twist the delicate manifold or injection tubes while loosening the check valve

engine, using a new gasket. Torque to the proper specifications (see Chapter 2).

40 Thread each of the injection tube connectors loosely into the exhaust manifold, using an anti-seize compound on the threads. After each of the connectors is sufficiently started, tighten each securely.

41 Connect the air supply hoses to the check valves.

42 Start the engine and check for leaks as previously described.

Check valve

Refer to illustration 3.44

43 Disconnect the air supply hose at the check valve.

44 Using two wrenches on the flats provided, remove the check valve from the air manifold assembly **(see illustration)**. Be careful not to bend or twist the delicate manifold or injection tubes as this is done.

45 Installation is a reversal of the removal procedure.

4   Transmission Controlled Spark (TCS) system

General description

Refer to illustrations 4.2a, 4.2b, 4.2c and 4.2d

1 This system is designed to eliminate the vacuum advance at the distributor under certain driving conditions. The system is incorporated on all vehicles with manual transmissions. The Transmission Controlled Spark (TCS) system used for 1971 models is also known as the Combination Emission Control (CEC) system.

2 Vacuum for the advancing mechanism in the distributor is shut off until the transmission is in High gear or 3rd and 4th gears with the 4-speed transmission **(see illustrations)**. Vacuum is allowed in

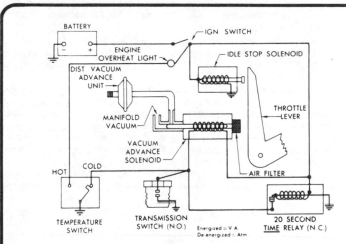

4.2a Transmission Controlled Spark (TCS) system — engine off

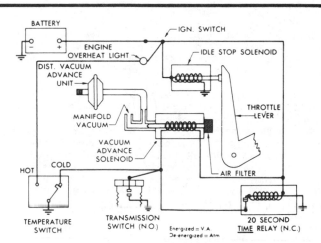

4.2b TCS system — cold override energized

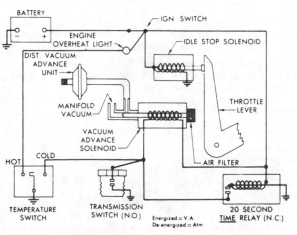

4.2c TCS system — low gear operation

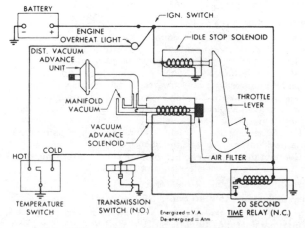

4.2d TCS system — high gear operation

Reverse for the Turbo Hydra-Matic automatic transmissions.

3   This system is made up of: a transmission switch; engine coolant temperature switch; time delay relay; vacuum advance solenoid; and an idle stop solenoid. Although this system is somewhat more difficult to service, check and maintain than the other emissions systems, when each component is examined individually the operation of the TCS system can be easily understood.

Transmission switch

Refer to illustration 4.4

4   On manual transmissions, the electrical switch is actuated by the internal shifter shaft. The switch (see illustration) is located on the outside of the transmission case, adjacent to the shifter shaft.

5   Automatic transmissions use a pressure-sensitive switch which is actuated by the fluid pressure as the transmission reaches High gear (and Reverse in the case of the Turbo Hydra-Matics). This switch is located on the outside of the transmission on Powerglide and Turbo Hydra-Matic 350 transmissions. Turbo Hydra-Matic 400 transmissions have the switch mounted internally in the transmission.

6   When activated in the proper transmission gears, the switch sends an electrical input to the vacuum advance solenoid. This TCS component remained basically unchanged through the four years in which it was used.

Temperature switch

Refer to illustration 4.7

7   The function of this switch is to sense the engine temperature and send a signal to the vacuum advance solenoid. It is the same switch which operates the dashboard-mounted warning light or water temperature gauge. The switch (see illustration) is located in the left cylinder head, between the number one and number three exhaust ports

4.4   TCS system — manual transmission switch location (arrow)

on small-block V8 engines, and between the number three and number five exhaust ports on Mark IV big-block engines.

8   The temperature switch monitors engine coolant temperatures and sends electrical current to the vacuum advance solenoid. On 1969 through 1972 vehicles, the temperature switch reacts with the vacuum advance solenoid to allow full vacuum advance whenever the engine temperature is below 82 degrees. For 1973 and 1974 this temperature was raised to 93 degrees. This means that regardless of the transmission gear or any other engine condition, the TCS system is not functional and should have no effect on engine operation until the engine has warmed up to these operating temperatures.

Time delay relay

Refer to illustration 4.13

9   This electrically-operated relay has undergone some changes in the various TCS systems. In each model year, however, its main fuction is to delay the operation of the vacuum advance solenoid.

10   In all years except 1972, the time delay relay will allow full distributor vacuum advance during the first 20 seconds of engine operation. This means that every time the ignition switch is turned on, no matter if the engine is warm or cold, the delay relay will render the TCS system inoperative for the first 20 seconds.

11   On 1972 models the delay relay performs a different function. The relay does not come into play until the transmission reaches High gear as signalled by the transmission switch. When this happens, the time relay delays the operation of the vacuum advance solenoid for about 23 seconds. In other words, the engine distributor does not receive full vacuum until about 20 seconds after the transmission reaches High gear.

12   It should also be noted that the 1972 delay relay automatically recycles whenever the transmission is taken out of High gear, as in a downshift or when put into passing gear. Once the transmission is back into High, it will again take about 20 seconds to achieve full vacuum advance at the distributor.

13   The 1972 relay is located under the dashboard, on the center reinforcement brace. For the other years, the relay is mounted inside the engine compartment, on the firewall (see illustration).

Vacuum advance solenoid

14   This is the heart of the TCS system, with its function being to supply or deny vacuum to the distributor.

15   This canister-shaped unit is located on the right side of the engine, attached to the intake manifold. It can be readily located by simply following the vacuum hose out of the distributor vacuum advance unit.

16   In the energized position, the plunger inside the solenoid opens the vacuum port from the carburetor to the vacuum advance unit, and at the same time blocks off the clean air port at the other end. In the de-energized mode, the clean air port is uncovered, which allows the distributor to vent to the atmosphere and shuts off vacuum to the distributor.

Idle stop solenoid

Refer to illustrations 4.17 and 4.18

17   This solenoid is attached to the right side of the carburetor with brackets. It can be identified by a wiring connector at one end and a

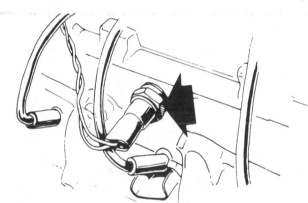

4.7   TCS system — typical coolant temperature switch location

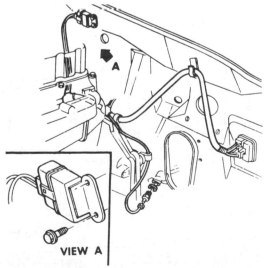

4.13   The TCS system time delay relay is located on the firewall (except on 1972 models, on which it is located under the dash, on the center reinforcement brace)

6

4.17   The idle stop solenoid, which is attached to the right side of the carburetor, can be identified by this wiring connector at one end and the bolt-head plunger at the other

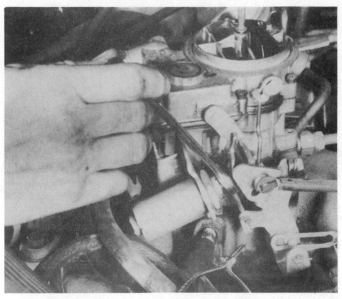

4.18   The idle stop solenoid is an electrically operated, two-position control device that can be used to provide a predetermined throttle setting

bolt-head plunger on the other **(see illustration)**.

18   The idle stop solenoid is an electrically operated, two-position control. It is used to provide a predetermined throttle setting **(see illustration)**.

19   In the energized position, the plunger extends from the solenoid body and contacts the carburetor throttle lever. This prevents the carburetor throttle plates from closing fully. When de-energized (key off), the solenoid plunger retracts into the solenoid body to allow the throttle plates to fully close, which 'starves' the engine and prevents run-on, or 'dieseling'.

20   The 1971 system also incorporates a solid state timing device which allows the air conditioning compressor (if equipped) to come on when the ignition is turned off. The added load of the air conditioning compressor helps to shut off the engine to further prevent dieseling.

Checking

21   This system is difficult to check due to the fact that the vehicle must be in full operation. This means that the checks must be made with the car travelling at speed.

22   If a problem in this system is suspected, first check that all electrical wires and connections are in good condition and intact. Also inspect the vacuum hoses at the vacuum advance solenoid and the distributor vacuum advance unit. A blown fuse in the fuse box can also cause problems in this system.

23   To ascertain if the TCS system is in fact malfunctioning, connect a vacuum gauge in the hose between the solenoid and the distributor. A length of vacuum hose must be used to enable you to route the gauge inside the passenger's compartment. Make sure the hose is not crimped and will not be damaged by moving or hot engine parts.

24   Drive the car and have an assistant watch the vacuum gauge. Make a log of vacuum gauge readings and transmission gears. If the system is functioning properly, the following conditions will be met:

   a)   When the engine is cold, vacuum will show on the gauge until the engine has warmed to operating temperature.

   b)   Vacuum should be present on the gauge during the first 20 seconds after the engine is started, regardless of temperature.

   c)   At normal operating temperature there should be vacuum showing on the gauge in High gear only.

25   The system should be tested with the engine cold, and also after it has reached normal operating temperature. Don't forget about the time delay function and how it relates to your particular vehicle.

26   The above test will tell you if the system as a whole is functioning properly. The following are test procedures for the individual TCS components if a fault is detected in the driving test.

Idle stop solenoid

27   Have an assistant turn the ignition switch on as you watch the idle stop solenoid plunger. With the key on, the plunger should extend against the throttle linkage. With the key off, the plunger should retract into the solenoid.

Transmission switch

28   With the engine warm and running, have an assistant put the transmission in a low forward gear (make sure the front wheels are blocked, parking brake is on and the assistant has the brake pedal depressed). There should be no vacuum going to the distributor. If there is vacuum going to the distributor, remove the transmission switch connection. Replace the transmission switch if the vacuum stops when the transmission switch connection was removed.

Temperature switch

29   When the engine is cold, there should be vacuum going to the distributor. If this is not the case, ground the wire from the cold terminal of the temperature switch. If the vacuum advance solenoid energizes, replace the temperature switch with a new one.

30   A failure of the temperature switch may also show up on the driving test with the engine at different operating temperatures, and/or as a malfunction of the temperature gauge or dash warning light.

Vacuum advance solenoid

31   Check the vacuum running into the solenoid from the intake manifold or carburetor. You should be able to feel this vacuum with the engine running.

32   Now reconnect the vacuum inlet hose and disconnect the vacuum hose leading to the distributor. Disconnect the electrical connectors at the solenoid and run a 12-volt jumper wire to the solenoid. The solenoid should be energized, allowing vacuum to reach the distributor.

Time delay relay (1972)

33   With the ignition on, check for 12 volts at the tan colored lead to the relay. Use a test light for this.

34   Install a 12-volt jumper wire to the terminal with the tan lead, and ground the terminal with the black lead. If, after 26 seconds, the advance solenoid does not energize (meaning vacuum to the distributor), replace the delay relay.

Time delay relay (except 1972)

35   Remove the temperature switch connector at the time delay relay.

36   Check to make sure the relay is cool, then turn the ignition to the On position.

37   The vacuum advance solenoid should energize for about 20 seconds and then de-energize. If it does not de-energize, remove the blue lead from the time relay. If this causes the solenoid to de-energize, the relay is faulty and should be replaced.

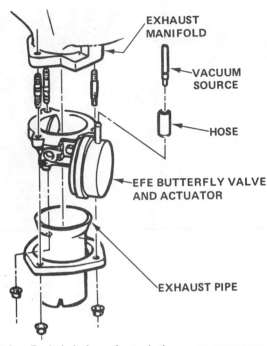

5.2a Exploded view of a typical vacuum servo type
EFE assembly

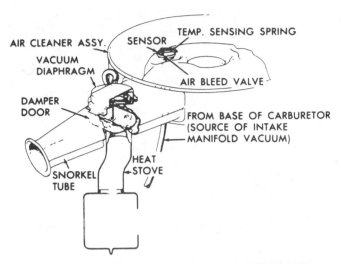

5.2b A typical Thermostatic Air Cleaner (THERMAC)
system — this design draws warm air from the exhaust
manifold directly into the carburetor

5 Inlet air temperature control system

General description
Refer to illustrations 5.2a, 5.2b, and 5.5

1 Various versions of this system go by different names, but their purpose is always the same — to improve engine efficiency and reduce hydrocarbon emissions during the initial warm-up period of the vehicle.
2 Two basic methods are used to achieve this goal:
  a) Forced air pre-heat system: Some form of exhaust valve is incorporated inside the exhaust pipe **(see illustration)** to recirculate warm exhaust gases which are then used to pre-heat the carburetor and choke.
  b) Warm air from the exhaust manifold is routed into the air cleaner, then through the carburetor **(see illustration)**.
3 This system has its greatest effect on engine performance and emissions output during the first few miles of driving (depending on the outside temperature). Once the engine reaches its normal operating temperature, the flapper valves in the exhaust pipe and air cleaner open, allowing for normal engine operation.
4 Because of this cold-engine-only function, it is important to periodically check this system to prevent poor cold engine performance and overheating of the fuel mixture once the engine has reached operating temperatures. If either the exhaust heat valve or air cleaner valve sticks in the 'no heat' position, the engine will run poorly, stall and waste gas until it has warmed up on its own. A valve sticking in the 'heat' position causes the engine to run as if it is out of tune, because of the constant flow of hot air to the carburetor.
5 The main component of the initial system is a heat valve **(see illustration)** inside the exhaust pipe on the right side of the engine (called a heat riser on 1969 through 1974 models). In 1975, General Motors introduced a new inlet air temperature control system known as the Early Fuel Evaporation (EFE) system. It also has a valve in the exhaust pipe, but uses manifold vacuum to actuate the valve. Instead of a spring and weight, an actuator and Thermal Vacuum Switch TVS control the heat valve. A Thermostatic Air Cleaner (TAC or THERMAC) consisting of a temperature sensor, vacuum diaphragm and heat stove completes the system. Initial checking procedures can be found in Chapter 1.

Check

Forced air pre-heat system
6 The conventional heat riser, installed on cars built through 1974, should be checked often for free operation. Because of the high exhaust temperatures and its location, which is open to the elements, corrosion frequently keeps the valve from operating freely, or even freezes it in position.
7 To check the heat riser operation, locate it on the exhaust manifold (it can be identified by an external weight and spring), and with the engine cold, try moving the counterweight. The valve should move freely with no binding. Now have an assistant start the engine (still cold) while the counterweight is observed. The valve should move to the closed position and then slowly open as the engine warms.
8 A stuck or binding heat riser valve can usually be loosened by soaking the valve shaft with solvent as the counterweight is moved back and forth. Light taps with a hammer may be necessary to free a tightly stuck valve. If this proves unsuccessful, the heat riser must be replaced with a new one after disconnecting it from the exhaust pipe.

Early Fuel Evaporation (EFE) System
Refer to illustrations 5.10 and 5.11

9 In 1975, General Motors introduced a replacement for the heat riser known as the Early Fuel Evaporation (EFE) system. The EFE system performs the same function as the heat riser but uses manifold vacuum to open and close the heat valve. Some vehicles are equipped with an electrical type EFE, which uses a ceramic heater grid located underneath the primary base of the carburetor.

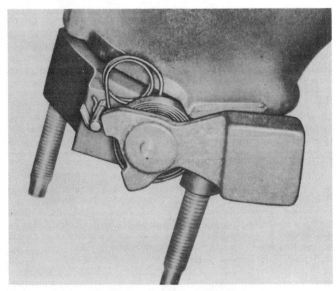

5.5 Typical manifold heat control valve (or heat riser, as
it's known on 1970 through 1974 models)

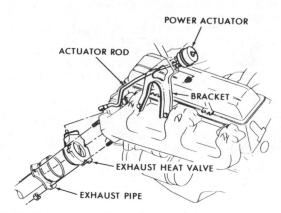

5.10 Typical Early Fuel Evaporation (EFE) system uses manifold vacuum to open and close the heat valve

10 To check the EFE system, locate the actuator and rod assembly **(see illustration)** which is located on a bracket attached to the right (left on some 231 V6 models) exhaust manifold. Have an assistant start the engine (it must be cold). Observe the movement of the actuator rod which leads to the heat valve inside the exhaust pipe. It should immediately operate the valve to the closed position. If it does, the system is operating correctly.

11 If the actuator rod doesn't move, disconnect the vacuum hose at the actuator and place your thumb over the open end **(see illustration)**. With the engine cold and at idle, you should feel a suction, indicating proper vacuum. If there is vacuum at this point, replace the actuator with a new one.

12 If there is no vacuum in the line, this is an indication that either the hose is crimped or plugged, or the thermal vacuum switch threaded into the water outlet is not functioning properly. Replace the hose or switch as necessary.

13 To make sure the Early Fuel Evaporation System is disengaging once the engine has warmed, continue to observe the actuating rod as the engine reaches normal operating temperature (approximately 180 degrees depending on engine size). The rod should again move, indicating the valve is in the open position.

14 If after the engine has warmed, the valve does not open, disconnect the vacuum hose at the actuator and check for vacuum with your thumb. If there is no vacuum, replace the actuator. If there is vacuum, replace the TVS switch on the water outlet housing.

Thermostatic Air Cleaner (TAC/THERMAC)

15 THERMAC components can be quickly and easily checked for proper operation, (see Chapter 1 for routine checking procedures and illustrations).

16 With the engine off, observe the damper door inside the air cleaner snorkel. If this is difficult because of the direction in which the snorkel is pointing, use a small mirror. The valve should be open (all air flows through the snorkel and none through the exhaust manifold hot-air duct at the underside of the air cleaner housing). **Note:** *Thermal sensors on some V6's have a check valve which keeps the damper door closed when the air cleaner is cold and the engine if off.*

17 Have an assistant start the engine while you observe the flapper door inside the snorkel. With the engine cold and at idle, the damper door should close off all air from the snorkel, allowing heated air from the exhaust manifold to enter the air cleaner intake. As the engine warms to operating temperature, the damper door should move, allowing outside air through the snorkel to be included in the mixture. Eventually, the door should recede to the point where most of the incoming air is through the snorkel and not the exhaust manifold passage.

18 If the damper door does not close off the snorkel to outside air when the cold engine is first started, disconnect the vacuum hose at the snorkel vacuum motor, place your thumb over the hose end and check for vacuum. If there is vacuum to the motor, verify that the damper door and link are not frozen or binding within the air cleaner snorkel. Replace the vacuum motor if the hose routing is correct and the damper door moves freely.

19 If there is no vacuum to the motor in the above test, check the hoses for cracks, crimps or disconnections. If the hoses are clear and in good condition, replace the temperature sensor inside the air cleaner housing.

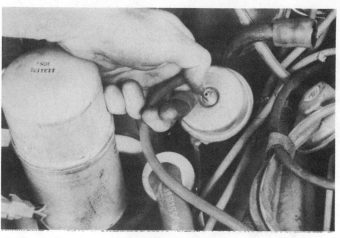

5.11 If the actuator rod is not working properly, you can check the EFE system by disconnecting the vacuum hose at the actuator and placing your thumb over the open end — with the engine cold and at idle, you should feel a suction indicating proper vacuum — if you do, replace the actuator

Replacement

Actuator and rod assembly

20 Disconnect the vacuum hose from the actuator.

21 Remove the two nuts which attach the actuator to the bracket.

22 Disconnect the rod from the heat valve and remove the actuator and rod from the engine compartment.

23 Installation is the reverse of removal.

Exhaust heat valve

24 Remove the crossover exhaust pipe.

25 Disconnect the actuating rod from the heat valve.

26 Remove the valve from inside the exhaust pipe.

27 Installation is the reverse of removal.

Thermal vacuum switch (TVS)

28 Drain the engine coolant until the fluid level is below the engine water outlet (thermostat) housing. (On some of the V6's, the TVS is located on the engine manifold).

29 Disconnect the hoses from the TVS switch. Note their positions for reassembly.

30 Using a suitable wrench, remove the TVS switch.

31 Apply a soft setting sealant uniformly to the threads of the new TVS switch. Make sure that none of the sealant gets on the sensor end of the switch.

32 Install the switch and tighten it securely.

33 Connect the vacuum hoses to the switch in their original positions and add coolant as necessary.

Air cleaner vacuum motor

Refer to illustration 5.35

34 Remove the air cleaner assembly from the engine and disconnect the vacuum hose from the motor.

35 Drill out the two spot welds **(see illustration)** which secure the vacuum motor retaining strap to the snorkel tube.

36 Remove the motor attaching strap.

37 Lift up the motor, cocking it to one side to unhook the motor linkage at the control damper assembly.

38 To install, drill a 7/64-inch hole in the snorkel tube at the center of the retaining strap.

39 Insert the vacuum motor linkage into the control damper assembly.

40 Using the sheet metal screw supplied with the motor service kit, attach the motor and retaining strap to the snorkel. Make sure the sheet metal screw does not interfere with the operation of the damper door.

41 Connect the vacuum hose to the motor and install the air cleaner assembly.

Air cleaner temperature sensor

42 Remove the air cleaner from the engine and disconnect the vacuum hoses at the sensor.

43 Carefully note the position of the sensor. The new sensor must be installed in exactly the same position.

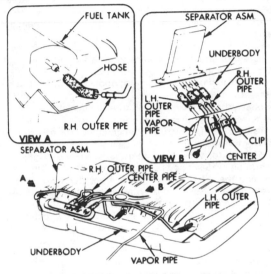

DRILL 7/64" HOLE IN CENTER POSITION OF STRAP

SPOTWELDS

VACUUM DIAPHRAGM

RETAINING STRAP

INSTALL REPLACEMENT SENSOR ASSM. IN SAME POSITION AS ORIGINAL ASSM.

5.35 To replace the air cleaner vacuum motor, drill out the two spot welds which secure the motor retaining strap, remove the attaching strap, lift up the motor, then cock it to one side to unhook the linkage at the control damper assembly

44 Pry up the tabs on the sensor retaining clip and remove the sensor and clip from the air cleaner.
45 Install the new sensor with a new gasket in the same position as the old one.
46 Press the retaining clip on the sensor, taking care not to damage the control mechanism in the center of the sensor.
47 Connect the vacuum hoses and install the air cleaner on the engine.

6 Evaporation Control System (ECS)/Evaporative Emission Control System (EECS)

Refer to illustrations 6.4a and 6.4b

General description

1 The Evaporation Control System is one of the most trouble-free systems in the emissions network. Its function is to reduce hydrocarbon emissions. Basically, this is a closed fuel system which reroutes wasted fuel back to the gas tank and stores fuel vapors instead of venting them to the atmosphere.
2 Because it has few moving parts, the ECS/EECS system requires no periodic maintenance other than replacement of the filter in the bottom the the charcoal canister at the recommended intervals.
3 The strong smell of fuel vapors is a tip-off that the system is not operating properly. So is engine starvation induced by lack of fuel during acceleration.
4 A pressure/vacuum gasoline filler cap must be used on vehicles equipped with ECS/EECS. A standard cap can render the system ineffective and possibly even collapse the fuel tank. The ECS/EECS system consists of a special gas tank with fill limiters and vent connections, a charcoal canister with an integral purge valve and a filter which stores vapor from the fuel tank to be burned by the carburetor, a carburetor bowl vent valve and the system of hoses connecting these components (see illustrations).

6.4a Typical fuel tank hose routing for the Evaporation Control System (ECS)

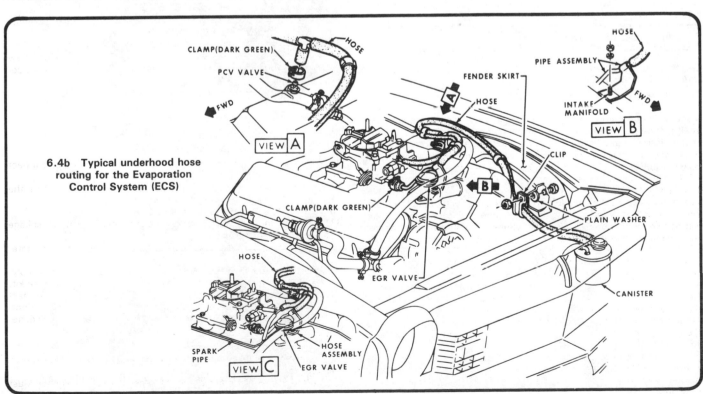

6.4b Typical underhood hose routing for the Evaporation Control System (ECS)

5   Earlier versions of the purge valve are regulated by coolant temperature: at coolant temperatures below the switching point, canister purge is controlled by an internal orifice in the switch. At coolant temperatures above the switching point, the switch opens, allowing canister purge to be controlled by manifold vacuum from the carburetor port. 1983 and later versions of the EECS are equipped with a canister purge valve under ECM control.

6   With the engine cold and at room temperature, disconnect the fuel tank line at the charcoal canister (on all models, the canister is located inside the engine compartment). Each of the hose connections should be duly labeled. Make sure you label them yourself if they're not already marked, to prevent improper assembly.

7   As this hose is disconnected, check for the presence of liquid fuel in the line. Fuel in this vapor hose is an indication that the vent controls or pressure-vacuum relief valve in the gas cap are not functioning properly.

8   Hook up a pressure suction device on the end of the fuel vapor line. Apply 15 psi pressure to the line and check for excessive loss of pressure.

9   Check for a fuel vapor smell in the engine compartment and around the gas tank.

10   Remove the fuel filler cap and check for pressure in the gas tank.

11   If there is a large loss of pressure or a fuel odor, inspect all lines for leaks or deterioration.

12   With the fuel filler cap removed, apply pressure again and check for obstructions in the vent line.

13   To check the purge valve built into the canister, start the engine, allow it to reach normal operating temperatures, and disconnect the vacuum signal line running from the engine to the canister. With your thumb over the end of the hose, raise the engine speed to about 1500 rpm and check for vaccum. If there is no vacuum signal, check the EGR operation as described in this Chapter. The vacuum signal for the canister and the EGR valve originate from the same source.

14   The purge line to the charcoal canister functions with the PCV vacuum source, so if there is no vacuum when this hose is disconnected from the canister, check the PCV valve vacuum.

15   Checking an ECM-controlled purge valve is beyond the scope of the home mechanic.

Charcoal canister and filter — replacement

16   Chapter 1 contains all information concerning the servicing of the Evaporation Control System, in particular the replacement of the canister filter.

---

7   Exhaust Gas Recirculation (EGR) system

General description
Refer to illustrations 7.1, 7.2, 7.3a and 7.3b

1   The EGR system (**see illustration**) is used to reduce oxides of nitrogen (NOX) from the exhaust. Formation of these pollutants takes place at very high temperatures; consequently, it occurs during the peak temperature period of the combustion process. To reduce peak temperatures, and thus the formation of NOX, a small amount of exhaust gas is taken from the exhaust system and recirculated in the combustion cycle.

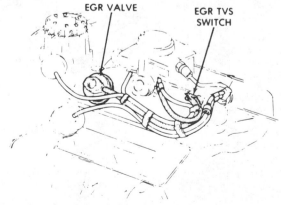

7.1   A typical Exhaust Gas Recirculation (EGR) system

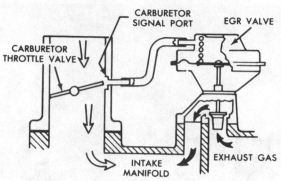

7.2   You can't see much of the EGR exhaust passages, because they are cast into the intake manifold

2   To tap this exhaust supply without an extensive array of pipes and connections in the exhaust system, additional exhaust passages are cast into the intricate runner system of the intake manifold (**see illustration**). Because of this arrangement, most of the EGR routing components are hidden from view under the manifold.

3   Two basic types of EGR valves are used — Vacuum Modulated EGR and Exhaust Back Pressure EGR. When Vacuum Modulated EGR is used, the amount of exhaust gas admitted to the intake manifold depends on a vacuum signal (ported vacuum) which is controlled by throttle position. When the throttle is closed (idle or deceleration), there is no vacuum signal to the EGR valve because the vacuum port is above the closed throttle valve. As the throttle valve is opened, a ported vacuum signal is supplied to the EGR valve, admitting exhaust gas to the intake manifold. The Exhaust Backpressure Modulated EGR uses a transducer located inside the EGR valve to control the operating vacuum signal. The vacuum signal is generated in the same manner as for the Vacuum Modulated EGR system. The integral transducer uses exhaust gas pressure to control an air bleed within the valve to modify the vacuum signal from the carburetor. Two types of back pressure EGR valves are used; negative transducer (**see illustration**) and positive transducer (**see illustration**).The latest versions of the EGR

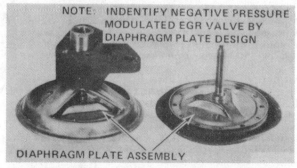

7.3a   Typical positive backpressure EGR valve diaphragm plate design

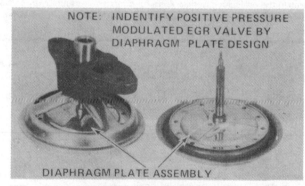

7.3b   Typical negative backpressure EGR valve diaphragm plate design

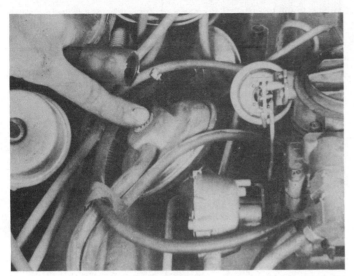

7.6 On most models, the EGR valve is located on the intake manifold, adjacent to the carburetor

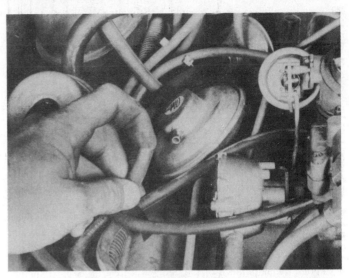

7.13 If a check of the EGR valve reveals that it's not working, verify that vacuum is reaching the EGR valve: detach the vacuum hose from the valve and, with the engine running slightly above idle, place your thumb over the end of the hose — if there is vacuum, replace the EGR valve; if there isn't, trace the vacuum hose to its source and look for cracks, breaks or blockage

valve are ECM-controlled. EGR flow is regulated by an ECM-controlled solenoid in the vacuum line. The ECM uses data from various combinations of sensors — such as the coolant temperature sensor, throttle positon sensor, MAP sensor and distributor signal — to regulate the solenoid. The negative transducer EGR valve is used on V6 engines; the positive transducer valve is used on V8 engines.

4   The EGR system does not recirculate gases when the engine is idling or decelerating. The system is also regulated by the thermal vacuum switch, which does not allow the system to operate until the engine has reached normal operating temperature.

5   Common engine problems associated with the EGR system are: rough idling or stalling when at idle, rough engine performance upon light throttle application and stalling on deceleration.

Check

Refer to illustrations 7.6 and 7.13

6   Locate the EGR valve. The location varies from year to year, but on most models it is located on the intake manifold, adjacent to the right side of the carburetor **(see illustration)**. Initial checking, with illustrations, can be found in Chapter 1.

7   Place your finger under the EGR valve and push upwards on the diaphragm plate. The diaphragm should move freely from the open to the closed position. If it doesn't, replace the EGR valve.

8   Now start the engine and run it at idle speed. With your finger, manually depress the EGR diaphragm. If the valve or adjacent accessories are hot, wear gloves to prevent burning your fingers. When the diaphragm is pressed (valve closed to recirculate exhaust), the engine should lose speed, stumble or even stall. If the engine does not change speed, the EGR passages should be checked for blockage. This will require that the intake manifold be removed (see Chapter 2). Any further checking of the positive backpressure type EGR valve will require special tools, so a questionable valve is best replaced with a new one at this point. Negative backpressure type EGR valves can be further tested as follows:

9   Allow the engine to reach its normal operating temperature. Have an assistant depress the accelerator slightly and hold the engine at a constant speed above idle.

10   Detach the vacuum signal line at the EGR valve and verify that the diaphragm plate moves downward and engine speed increases.

11   Reattach the vacuum line to the valve. The diaphragm plate should move upward with a decrease in engine speed.

12   If the diaphragm doesn't move, make sure the engine is at its normal operating temperature. Repeat the test if in doubt.

13   To verify that vacuum is reaching the EGR valve, detach the vacuum hose at the valve and, with the engine running and the accelerator slightly pressed, verify that there's vacuum at the end of the hose with your thumb **(see illustration)**. If there is vacuum, replace the EGR valve with a new one. If there is no vacuum signal, follow the vacuum hose to its source, inspecting for disconnections, cracks, breaks or blockage in the lines.

14   On all model years except 1973, the EGR system uses some kind of vacuum valve to regulate the amount of exhaust gas admitted to the intake air-fuel mixture. Some of the more common valves are the Vacuum Controlled Valve (VCV), which regulates the EGR in accordance with engine intake vacuum; the Thermal Vacuum Switch (TVS) which regulates EGR valve operation in relation to engine temperature; and the electronically operated, ECM-controlled solenoid, which also acts in accordance with engine coolant temperature. 1973 vehicles have the vacuum source routed directly to the caburetor.

15   This vacuum switch opens as the coolant temperature increases, allowing vacuum to reach the EGR valve. The exact temperature varies from year to year, but is indicative of the normal operating temperature of the particular engine.

16   To test a vacuum-actuated switch, check the vacuum signal with a vacuum gauge (if the switch on your vehicle is a solenoid under ECM control, diagnosis should be left to a dealer).

17   Disconnect the vacuum hose at the EGR valve, connect the vacuum gauge to the disconnected end of the hose and start the idle, then have an assistant depress the accelerator slightly and note this reading. As the accelerator is depressed, the vacuum reading should increase.

18   If the gauge does not respond to the throttle opening, disconnect the hose which leads from the carburetor to the vacuum switch. Repeat the test with the vacuum gauge attached to the vacuum hose end of the switch. If the vacuum gauge responds to accelerator opening, the vacuum switch is defective and should be replaced with a new one.

19   If the gauge still does not respond to an increase in throttle opening, check for a plugged hose or a problem with the carburetor.

Replacement

EGR valve

20   Disconnect the vacuum hose at the EGR valve.

21   Remove the nuts or bolts which secure the valve to the intake manifold.

22   Lift the EGR valve from the engine.

23   Clean the mounting surfaces of the EGR valve. Remove all traces of gasket material.

24   Place the new EGR valve, with a new gasket, on the intake manifold. Install the spacer, if used. Tighten the attaching bolts or nuts.

25   Connect the vacuum signal hose.

Thermal vacuum switch

26   Drain the engine coolant until the coolant level is beneath the switch.

27   Disconnect the vacuum hose at the EGR valve, connect the vacuum gauge to the disconnected end of the hose and start the engine, noting their positions for reassembly.

6

28 Using a suitable wrench, remove the switch.
29 When installing the switch, apply thread sealer to the threads, being careful not to allow the sealant to touch the bottom sensor.
30 Install the switch and tighten it securely.

ECM-controlled EGRs

31 Diagnosis of ECM-controlled EGRs is beyond the scope of the home mechanic.

8   Catalytic converter

General description

1   The catalytic converter is an emission control device added to the exhaust system to reduce hydrocarbon and carbon monoxide pollutants. This converter contains beads which are coated with a catalytic substance containing platinum and palladium.
2   It is imperative that only unleaded gasoline be used in a vehicle equipped with a catalytic converter. Unleaded fuel reduces combustion chamber deposits, corrosion and prevents lead contamination of the catalyst.
3   Periodic maintenance of the catalytic converter is not required; however, if the car is raised for other service it is advisable to inspect the overall condition of the catalytic converter and related exhaust components.
4   If the catalytic converter has been ruled by an official inspection station to be ineffective, the converter can be replaced with a new one, or the coated beads drained and replaced. Physical damage and the use of leaded fuels are the main causes of a malfunctioning catalytic converter.
5   It should be noted that the catalytic converter can reach very high temperatures in operation. Because of this, any work performed to the converter or in the general area where it is located should be done only after the system has sufficiently cooled. Also, caution should be exercised when lifting the vehicle with a hoist, as the converter can be damaged if the lifting pads are not properly positioned.
6   There are no functional tests which the home mechanic can make to determine if the catalytic converter is performing its task.

Component replacement

Catalytic converter

Refer to illustration 8.8

7   Raise the car and support it firmly with jackstands. The converter and exhaust system should be cool before proceeding.
8   Disconnect the converter at the front and rear (see illustration).

On most models a flange is used with four bolts and nuts to secure the converter to its mating exhaust pipes. If the fasteners are frozen in place due to high temperatures and corrosion, apply a penetrating oil liberally and allow it to soak in. As a last resort, the fasteners will have to be carefully cut off with a hacksaw.
9   Gently separate the inlet and outlet converter flanges from the exhaust pipes and remove the converter from under the vehicle.
10 Installation is a reversal of the removal process; however, always use new nuts and bolts.

Catalyst

Refer to illustration 8.17

11 Two types of catalytic converters are used on the vehicles covered in this manual. The monolith converter has coated rods which cannot be serviced. If failure occurs, the entire converter must be replaced with a new one. The catalyst in bead type converters can be changed by draining and filling the beads through a plug at the bottom of the converter.
12 With specialized equipment, the beads can be replaced with the converter still positioned under the car. This is definitely a job for a dealer who has the equipment and training necessary to perform this operation.
13 Bead replacement is more easily done with the converter removed from the car (see above).
14 With the converter on a suitable work bench, remove the pressed fill plug. This is done by driving a small chisel between the converter shell and the fill plug lip. Deform the lip until pliers can be used to remove the plug. Be careful not to damage the converter shell surface where the plug seals.
15 Once the plug is removed, drain the beads into a suitable container for disposal. Shake the converter vigorously to remove all beads.
16 To fill the catalytic converter with new beads, raise the front of the converter to approximately 45 degrees and pour the beads through the fill hole. Tapping lightly on the converter belt with a hammer as the beads are poured in will help to settle them. Continue tapping and pouring until the converter is full.
17 A special service fill plug will be required to replace the stock one which was removed. This consists of a bridge, bolt and fill plug (see illustration) and is installed as follows:

a) Install the bolt into the bridge and put the bridge into the converter opening. Move it back and forth to loosen the beads across the opening (bolt centered).
b) Remove the bolt from the bridge and put the washer and fill plug, dished side out, over the bolt.
c) While holding the fill plug and washer against the bolt head, thread the bolt four or five turns into the bridge.

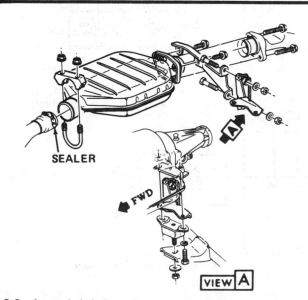

8.8   An exploded view of a typical catalytic converter assembly

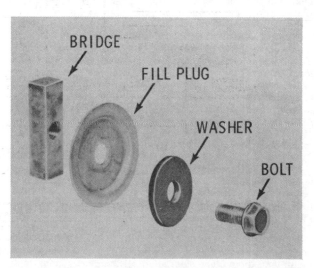

8.17   A typical catalytic converter service fill plug assembly

d) After fill plug has seated against the converter housing, tighten the bolt to 28 ft-lbs.

18 Install the converter, start the engine and check for leaks.

9 Computer Controlled Catalytic Converter (C4) Computer Command Control (C3 or CCC) system and information sensors

General description

Refer to illustrations 9.1a and 9.1b

1 The C4 system first became available on 1979-1/2 models. In 1981, the C4 system was replaced by the Computer Command Control

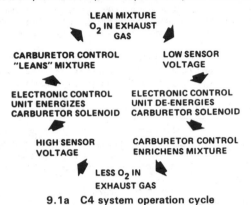

9.1a C4 system operation cycle

(CCC or C3) System. Both systems control exhaust emissions while retaining drivability by maintaining a continuous interaction between all of the emissions systems on your vehicle **(see illustrations)**. A malfunction in the system is signaled by a Check Engine or Service Engine Soon light on the dash. On the C4 system, the Check Engine light will remain on as long as the engine is running. With the CCM diagnostic system activated, this same lamp will flash the trouble code related to the cause of the malfunction. On the C3 system, the Check Engine or Service Engine Soon light will remain on until the problem is identified and repaired and the code is erased from memory. In other words, the C3 system stores trouble codes in its memory, but the C4 system doesn't.

2 The C4/C3 System requires special tools for maintenance and repair, so most service work on it should be left to your dealer or a qualified technician. Although it seems complex, the system is easily understood in terms of its various components and their functions.

Electronic control module (ECM)

3 The electronic control module (ECM) is essentially a small on-board computer (located under the dash on most vehicles) which monitors numerous (up to 14) engine functions and controls as many as nine engine-related systems. The ECM contains a Programmable Read Only Memory (PROM) calibration unit which tailors each ECM's performance to conform to the vehicle. The PROM is programmed with the vehicle's particular design, weight, axle ratio, etc., and cannot be used in another ECM in a car which differs in any way.

4 The ECM receives continuous data from the various information sensors, processes it in accordance with PROM instructions, then sends electronic signals to system components, modifying their performance (see next Section).

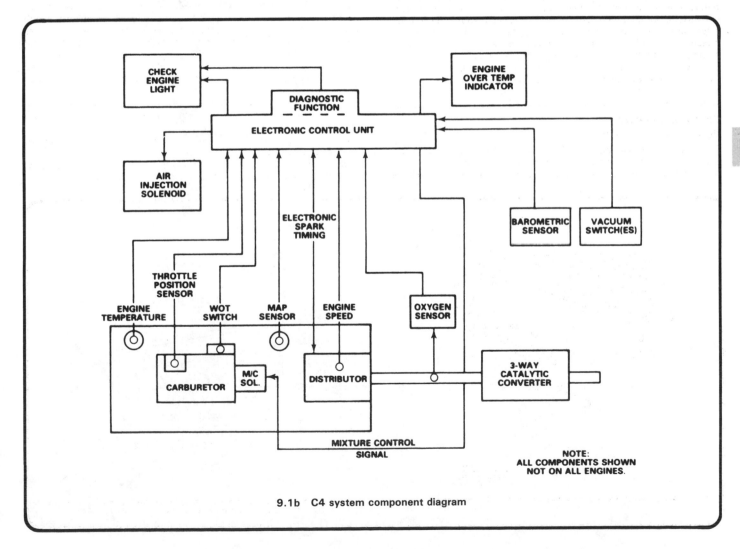

9.1b C4 system component diagram

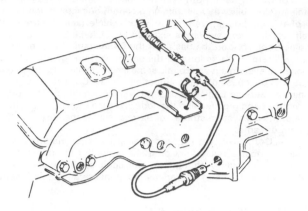

9.5   An exploded view of a typical oxygen sensor installation on a 5.0-liter V8 — on V6 engines, the sensor is located just behind the junction of the two exhaust manifold pipes

Oxygen (O₂) sensor

Refer to illustration 9.5

5   The oxygen sensor **(see illustration)** is mounted in the exhaust pipe, upstream of the catalytic converter. It monitors the exhaust stream and sends information to the ECM on how much oxygen is present. The oxygen level is determined by how rich or lean the fuel mixture is.

Mixture Control (M/C) solenoid

6   The M/C solenoid controls the fuel flow through the carburetor idle and main metering circuits. The solenoid cycles ten times per second, constantly adjusting the fuel/air mixture. The ECM energizes the solenoid to keep emissions within limits based on information it receives from the oxygen sensor.

Coolant temperature sensor

7   This sensor monitors coolant temperature and sends this information to the ECM. The ECM alters the air fuel ratio accordingly for conditions such as cold starting. The ECM also performs various switching functions on the EGR, EFE and AIR management systems, depending on engine temperature. This feedback from the coolant sensor can also activate the hot temperature light.

Pressure sensors

Refer to illustrations 9.9a and 9.9b

8   The ECM uses information from the Barometric Pressure Sensor (BARO) and Manifold Absolute Pressure (MAP) sensor, or the Differential Pressure Sensor (DPS or VAC) to adjust engine performance. The BARO sensor senses ambient pressure changes that occur as a result of changes in the weather and the altitude of the vehicle. It then sends an electronic signal to the ECM that is used to adjust the air fuel ratio and spark timing.

9   The MAP or DPS/VAC sensor **(see illustrations)** measures changes in manifold pressure and provides this information to the ECM. The pressure changes reflect the need for adjustments in air-fuel mixture, spark timing (EST), etc., that are needed to maintain good vehicle performance under various driving conditions.

10   The DPS also measures engine load. It produces a low voltage when manifold vacuum is low and a high voltage when manifold vacuum is high. It's called a differential pressure sensor because it measures the difference between atmospheric pressure and manifold pressure.

Throttle position sensor (TPS)

11   Mounted on the carburetor body, the TPS is actuated by the throttle plate and sends a variable voltage signal to the ECM: when the throttle plate is closed, the voltage signal is low, but as the throttle plate is opened, the voltage increases. The ECM uses this voltage signal to recognize throttle position.

Idle speed control (ISC)

12   The idle speed control maintains a low idle speed without stalling under changing conditions. The ECM controls the idle speed control motor on the carburetor to adjust the idle.

Electronic spark timing (EST)

13   The High Energy Ignition (HEI) distributor used with the C4 system does not use centrifugal or vacuum advance. Spark timing is controlled electronically by the ECM, except under certain conditions, such as cranking the engine.

Transmission Converter Clutch/Torque Converter Clutch (TCC)

14   The ECM controls an electrical solenoid mounted in the automatic transmission. When the vehicle reaches a specified speed, the ECM energizes the solenoid and allows the torque converter to mechanically couple the engine to the transmission. When operating conditions indicate the transmission should operate as a normal, fluid-coupled transmission (deceleration, passing, etc.), the solenoid is de-energized. The transmission also returns to normal (fluid-coupled) automatic operation when the brake pedal is depressed.

Air injection reactor (AIR)

15   When the engine is cold, the ECM energizes an air switching valve which allows air to flow to the exhaust ports to lower carbon monoxide (CO) and hydrocarbon (HC) levels in the exhaust.

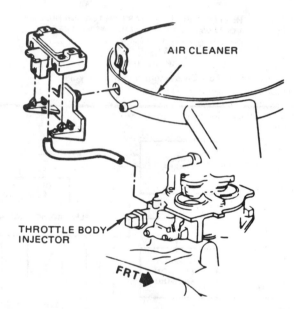

9.9a   An exploded view of a typical MAP sensor assembly (on some vehicles, the MAP sensor is located on the firewall instead — check the VECI label for the location of the MAP sensor on your vehicle)

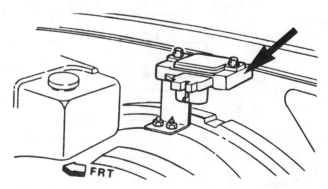

9.9b   A typical firewall installation of a pressure differential (DPS or VAC) sensor assembly — check the VECI label for the location of the DPS/VAC sensor on your vehicle

Exhaust gas recirculation (EGR)

16 The ECM controls ported vacuum to the EGR with a solenoid valve. When the engine is cold, the solenoid is energized to block vacuum to the EGR valve until the engine is warm.

Evaporative emission system (ECS/EECS)

17 When the engine is cold or idling, the ECM solenoid blocks vacuum to the valve at the top of the charcoal canister. When the engine is warm and at a specified rpm, the ECM de-energizes the valve, releasing the collected vapors into the intake manifold.

Early fuel evaporation (EFE)

18 The ECM controls a valve which shuts off the system until the engine is warm.

---

10 C4/C3 system and trouble codes

Refer to illustration 10.4

The C4 system is analogous to the central nervous system in the human body. The sensors (nerve endings) constantly relay information to the ECM (brain), which processes the data and, if necessary, sends out a command to change the operating parameters of the engine (body).

Here's a specific example of how one portion of this system operates: An oxygen sensor, located in the exhaust manifold, constantly monitors the oxygen content of the exhaust gas. If the percentage of oxygen in the exhaust gas is incorrect, an electrical signal is sent to the ECM. The ECM takes this information, processes it and then sends a command to the fuel injection system, telling it to change the air/fuel mixture. This happens in a fraction of a second and it goes on continuously when the engine is running. The end result is an air/fuel mixture ratio which is constantly maintained at a predetermined ratio, regardless of driving conditions.

One might think that a system which uses an on-board computer and electrical sensors whould be difficult to diagnose. This is not necessarily the case. The C4 system has a built-in diagnostic feature which indicates a problem by flashing a Check Engine or Service Engine Soon light on the instrument panel. When this light comes on during normal vehicle operation, a fault in one of the information sensor circuits or the ECM itself has been detected. More importantly, the source of the malfunction is stored in the ECM's memory.

To retrieve this information from the ECM memory, you must use a short jumper wire to ground a diagnostic terminal. This terminal is part of a wiring connector known as the Assembly Line Communica-

10.4 Typical Assembly Line Data Link (ALDL) terminal — (Assembly Line Communications Link, or ALCL, terminals similar)

A Ground	E Serial data (special tool
B Diagnostic terminal	required — do not use)
C AIR (if used)	F TCC (if used)
D Check Engine (or Service	G Fuel pump (if used)
Engine Soon) light	H Brake sensor speed input

tions Link (ALCL) or Assembly Line Data Link (ALDL) (see illustration). The ALCL/ALDL is located underneath the dashboard, just below the instrument panel and to the left of the center console.

To use the link, remove the plastic cover by sliding it toward you. With the connector exposed to view, push one end of the jumper wire into the diagnostic terminal and the other end into the ground terminal.

When the diagnostic terminal is grounded with the ignition On and the engine stopped, the system will enter the Diagnostic Mode. In this mode the ECM will display a Code 12 by flashing the light, indicating that the system is operating. A Code 12 is simply one flash, followed by a brief pause, then two flashes in quick succession. This code will be flashed three times. If no other codes are stored, Code 12 will continue to flash until the diagnostic terminal ground is removed.

After flashing Code 12 three times, the ECM will display any stored trouble codes. Each code will be flashed three times, then Code 12 will be flashed again, indicating that the display of any stored trouble codes has been completed.

When the ECM sets a trouble code, the light will come on and a trouble code will be stored in memory. If the problem is intermittent, the light will go out after ten seconds, when the fault goes away. However, the trouble code will stay in the ECM memory until the battery voltage to the ECM is interrupted. Removing battery voltage for ten seconds will clear all stored trouble codes. Trouble codes should always be cleared after repairs have been completed. **Caution:** *To prevent damage to the ECM, the ignition switch must be Off when disconnecting power to the ECM.*

Following is a list of the typical trouble codes which may be encountered while diagnosing the C4 System. Also included are simplified troubleshooting procedures. If the problem persists after these checks have been made, more detailed service procedures will have to be done by a dealer service department.

6

Trouble codes	Circuit or system	Probable cause
Code 12 (1 flash, pause, 2 flashes)	Distributor-to-ECM	This is the normal code when the engine isn't running. It is not stored in memory. It will flash only when a fault is present, the diagnostic terminal is grounded with the ignition turned on and the engine is not running. If additional codes are stored in the ECM, they will appear after this code has flashed 3 times. If the code appears while the engine is running, no reference pulses from the distributor are reaching the ECM.
Code 13 (1 flash, pause, 3 flashes)	Oxygen sensor	The engine must run up to 5 minutes at part throttle under road load before this code will set. Check for a sticking or misadjusted throttle position sensor. Check the oxygen sensor wires and connectors. Replace the oxygen sensor if necessary.
Code 14 (1 flash, pause, 4 flashes)	Coolant sensor	This code indicates a shorted coolant sensor circuit. The engine must run up to 2 minutes before this code will set. If the engine is experiencing overheating problems, the problem must be rectified before continuing. Check all wiring and connectors associated with the coolant temperature sensor. Replace the sensor if necessary.
Code 13 and 14 at same time	Coolant sensor	See Code 43.
Code 13 and 43 at same time	Coolant sensor	See Code 43.
Code 15 (1 flash, pause, 5 flashes)	Coolant sensor	The temperature sensor circuit is open. The engine must run for 5 minutes under 800 rpm to set this code. See Code 14 probable cause, then check the wiring connections at the ECM.

Trouble codes (cont.)	Circuit or system	Probable cause
Code 21 (2 flashes, pause, 1 flash)	WOT switch	The Wide Open Throttle (WOT) switch is shorted or the closed throttle switch (if equipped) is open. On some year models, Code 21 may refer to the TPS switch (see below) or to both WOT and TSP switches.
Code 21 (2 flashes, pause, 1 flash)	TPS switch	Check for a sticking or misadjusted Throttle Position Sensor (TPS) plunger. The engine must run for at least 10 seconds at 800 rpm, or at the specified curb idle, to set the code. Check all wiring and connectors between the TPS and the ECM. Adjust or replace the TPS if necessary.
Code 22 (1979 only) (2 flashes, pause, 2 flashes)	WOT switch	The Wide Open Throttle (WOT) switch circuit is grounded.
Code 22 (2 flashes, pause, 2 flashes)	TPS switch	The engine must run 20 seconds at the specified curb idle to set this code. Check the Throttle Position Sensor (TPS) adjustment. Check the ECM connector. Replace the TPS.
Code 21 and 22 at same time	WOT switch	Grounded Wide Open Throttle (WOT) switch.
Code 23 (2 flashes, pause, 3 flashes)	M/C solenoid	The Mixture Control (MC) solenoid is open or grounded.
Code 24 (2 flashes, pause, 4 flashes)	VSS	A fault in the Vehicle Speed Sensor (VSS) circuit should appear only when the vehicle is in motion and the engine has run at least 5 minutes. Disregard this code if it is set when the drive wheels are not turning. Check the connectors at the ECM. Check the TPS adjustment.
Code 32 (3 flashes, pause, 2 flashes)	BARO sensor	The Barometric Pressure (BARO) sensor circuit output voltage is low.
Code 32 and 55 at the same time	ECM	The BV reference terminal at the ECM is grounded, or the ECM is faulty.
Code 34 (3 flashes, pause, 4 flashes)	Vacuum sensor or MAP sensor	This code will set when the signal voltage from the Manifold Absolute Pressure (MAP) sensor circuit signal is too high. The engine must idle for up to 5 minutes to set this code. The ECM will substitute a fixed MAP value and use the TPS to control fuel delivery. Replace the MAP sensor.
Code 35 (3 flashes, pause, 5 flashes)	ISC switch	The Idle Speed Control (ISC) switch is shorted. It takes at least 2 seconds at half throttle to set this code. Replace the ISC switch.
Code 41 (4 flashes, pause, 1 flash)	EST circuit	No distributor reference pulses to the ECM at specified engine vacuum (about 8 inches Hg). This code will store in memory. *Also, see below*
Code 41 (4 flashes, pause, 1 flash)	EST circuit	The Electronic Spark Timing (EST) bypass circuit or the EST circuit is grounded or open. A malfunctioning HEI module can set this code.
Code 42 (4 flashes, pause, 2 flashes)	EST circuit	Electronic Spark Timing bypass circuit or EST circuit is grounded or open. A malfunctioning HEI module can cause this code.
Code 43 (4 flashes, pause, 3 flashes)	TPS switch	Throttle Position Sensor (TPS) out of adjustment. Engine must run for at least 10 seconds to set this code. *Also, see below.*
Code 43 (4 flashes, pause, 3 flashes)	ESC unit	The Electronic Spark Control (ESC) retard signal has been on for too long or the voltage is too low.
Code 44 (4 flashes, pause, 4 flashes)	Oxygen sensor	The exhaust is lean. Indicated by the oxygen sensor after the engine has run in closed loop, part throttle at road load up to 5 minutes. Check the ECM wiring connectors. Check for vacuum leakage at the base gasket, vacuum hoses or the intake manifold gasket. Replace the oxygen sensor. **Note:** *A Code 33 or 34 may also cause a Code 44 — so check them first.*
Code 45 (4 flashes, pause, 5 flashes)	Oxygen sensor	The exhaust is rich. Indicated by the oxygen sensor after the vehicle has run in closed loop, part throttle at road load up to 5 minutes. Check the evaporative charcoal canister and its components for the presence of fuel. Replace the oxygen sensor. **Note:** *A Code 33 or 34 may also cause a Code 45 — so check them first.*
Code 44 and 45 at same time	Oxygen sensor	Indicates a faulty oxygen sensor circuit.
Code 51 (1979 only) (5 flashes, pause, 1 flash)	ECM unit	Faulty Electronic Control Module (ECM).
Code 51 (5 flashes, pause, 1 flash)	PROM unit	Faulty Programmed Read Only Memory (PROM) or improper PROM installation. Make sure that the PROM or MEM-CAL is properly in the ECM. Replace the PROM or MEM-CAL.
Code 52 (5 flashes, pause, 2 flashes)	ECM unit	Faulty ECM. Replace the ECM.
Code 53 (5 flashes, pause, 3 flashes)	EGR valve	Exhaust Gas Recirculation (EGR) valve vacuum sensor is receiving improper vacuum signal. The EGR valve is faulty. Replace the EGR.
Code 52 and 53 at same time	ECM unit	If the Check Engine light is off, there is an intermittent ECM problem. If the Check Engine light is on, the ECM is faulty. Replace it.

Trouble codes (cont.)	**Circuit or system**	**Probable cause**

Code 54 . . . . M/C solenoid . . . . The Mixture Control (M/C) solenoid voltage is high at the ECM because of
(5 flashes, pause, 4 flashes) | | a shorted M/C solenoid circuit and/or faulty ECM.

Code 55 (1979 only) . . . . TPS or ECM . . . . Faulty Throttle Position Sensor (TPS) or Electronic Control Module.
(5 flashes, pause, 5 flashes)

Code 55 . . . . ECM or oxygen sensor . . . . Make sure that the ECM ground connectors are tight. If they are, either the
(5 flashes, pause, 5 flashes) | | ECM or the oxygen sensor is faulty. Replace the ECM and/or the oxygen
| | sensor.

Note: *Where replacement of one of the above systems, units or devices is recommended, it should be recognized that simply replacing some of the above components will not always solve the problem. For this reason, you may want to seek professional advice before purchasing any replacement parts.*

---

11   Electronic Control Module (ECM)/Programmable Read Only Memory (PROM)/CALPAK

---

1   The Electronic Control Module (ECM) is located inside the body in front of the right front door.
2   To remove it, disconnect the negative battery cable from the battery.
3   Remove the screws from the trim panel under the right end of the dash.
4   Remove the right hush panel retaining screw and detach the panel.
5   Remove the retaining bolts and carefully slide the ECM out far enough to unplug the electrical connector.
6   Unplug both electrical connectors from the ECM. **Caution:** *The ignition switch must be Off when pulling out or plugging in the connectors, to prevent damage to the ECM.*

PROM

Refer to illustration 11.7
7   To allow one model of ECM to be used for many different vehicles, a device called a PROM (Programmable Read Only Memory) is used. To access the PROM, remove the cover. The PROM **(see illustration)** is located inside the ECM and contains information on the vehicle's weight, engine, transmission, axle ratio, etc. One ECM part number can be used by many GM vehicles but the PROM is very specific and must be used only in the vehicle for which it was designed.
8   For this reason, it is essential to check the latest parts book and Service Bulletin information for the correct part number when replacing a PROM. An ECM purchased at the dealer is purchased without a PROM. The PROM from the old ECM must be carefully removed and installed in the new ECM.

CALPAK

9   A device known as a CALPAK **(see illustration 11.7)** is used to allow fuel delivery if other parts of the ECM are damaged. The CALPAK

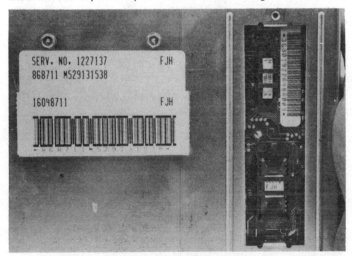

11.7   The CALPAK (top right) and PROM (bottom right) inside an ECM for a V6 (ECM for V8 is similar)

has an access door in the ECM, and replacement is the same as that described for the PROM.

ECM/PROM/CALPAK replacement

Refer to illustrations 11.12, 11.14 and 11.17
10   Turn the ECM so that the bottom cover is facing up and place it on a clean work surface.
11   Remove the PROM/PAK access cover.
12   Using a PROM removal tool (available at your dealer), grasp the PROM carrier at the narrow ends **(see illustration)**. Gently rock the carrier from end to end while applying firm upward force.

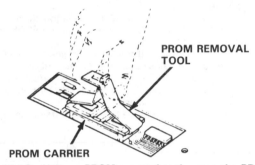

PROM REMOVAL TOOL

PROM CARRIER

11.12   Using a PROM removal tool, grasp the PROM carrier at the narrow ends and gently rock the removal tool until the PROM is unplugged from the socket

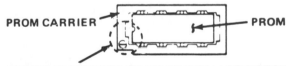

PROM CARRIER — **PROM**

NOTCH IN PROM MATCHES TO SMALLER NOTCH IN CARRIER AND ⊖

11.14   Note how the notch in the PROM is matched up with the smaller notch in the carrier

13   The PROM carrier and PROM should lift off the PROM socket easily. **Caution:** *The PROM carrier should only be removed with the special rocker-type PROM removal tool. Removal without this tool or with any other type of tool may damage the PROM or the PROM socket* **(see illustration).**
14   Note the reference end of the PROM carrier **(see illustration)** before setting it aside.
15   If you are replacing the ECM, remove the new ECM from its container and check the service number to make sure that it is the same as the number on the old ECM.
16   If you are replacing the PROM, remove the new PROM from its container and check the service number to make sure that it is the same as the number of the old PROM.
17   Position the PROM/PROM carrier assembly squarely over the PROM socket with the small notched end of the carrier aligned with the small notch in the socket at the pin one end. Press on the PROM carrier until

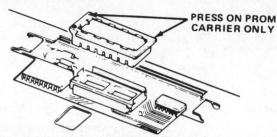

PRESS ON PROM
CARRIER ONLY

**11.17   Press only on the ends of the PROM carrier — pressure
on the area in between could result in bent or broken pins
or damage to the PROM itself**

it seats firmly in the socket (see illustration)

18 If the PROM is new, make sure that the notch in the PROM is
matched to the small notch in the carrier. **Caution:** *If the PROM is installed backwards and the ignition switch is turned on, the PROM will
be destroyed.*

19 Using the tool, install the new PROM carrier in the PROM socket
of the ECM. The small notch of the carrier should be aligned with the
small notch in the socket. Press on the PROM carrier until it is firmly
seated in the socket. **Caution:** *Do not press on the PROM — press only
on the carrier.*

20 Attach the access cover to the ECM and tighten the two screws.

21 Install the ECM in the support bracket, plug in the electrical connectors to the ECM and install the hush panel.

22 Start the engine.

23 Enter the diagnostic mode by grounding the diagnostic lead of the
ALCL (see Section 10). If no trouble codes occur, the PROM is correctly installed.

24 If Trouble Code 51 occurs, or if the Check Engine/Service Engine
Soon light comes on and remains constantly lit, the PROM is not fully
seated, is installed backwards, has bent pins or is defective.

25 If the PROM is not fully seated, pressing firmly on both ends of
the carrier should correct the problem.

26 If the pins have been bent, remove the PROM, straighten the pins

and reinstall the PROM. If the bent pins break or crack when you attempt to straighten them, discard the PROM and replace it with a new
one.

27 If careful inspection indicates that the PROM is fully seated, has
not been installed backwards and has no bent pins, but the Check
Engine/Service Engine Soon light remains lit, the PROM is probably
faulty and must be replaced.

12   Electronic Spark Timing (EST)

General description

1   To provide improved engine performance, fuel economy and control
of exhaust emissions, the Electronic Control Module (ECM) controls
distributor spark advance (ignition timing) with the Electronic Spark
Timing (EST) system.

2   The ECM receives a reference pulse from the distributor, which
indicates both engine rpm and crankshaft position. The ECM then determines the proper spark advance for the engine operating conditions
and sends an EST pulse to the distributor.

Checking

3   The ECM will set spark timing at a specified value when the
diagnostic test terminal in the ALCL connector is grounded. To check
for EST operation, the timing should be checked at 2000 rpm with
the terminal ungrounded. Then ground the test terminal. If the timing
changes at 2000 rpm, the EST is operating. A fault in the EST system
will usually set Trouble Code 42.

Setting base timing

4   To set the initial base timing, locate, then disconnect the timing
connector (the location and wire color of the timing connector is on
the VECI label).

5   Set the timing as specified on the VECI label. This will cause a
Code 42 to be stored in the ECM memory. Be sure to clear the memory
after setting the timing (see Section 10).

6   For further information regarding the testing and component
replacement procedures for the distributor, refer to Chapter 5.

Chapter 7 Part A Manual transmission

Contents

Specifications

Torque specifications

	Ft-lb
Cover-to-case bolt	17
Drain and fill plugs	14
Transmission-to-clutch housing bolt	55
Transmission-to-engine bolt	40
Extension housing-to-case bolt	46
Transmission mount bolt	30
Input shaft retainer bolt	22
Trunnion jam nut	30
Shift fork-to-shifter rail set screw	14
Shift linkage clamp screw	20
Crossmember bolt	25

1 General information

All vehicles covered in this manual come equipped with either a 3-speed manual transmission or an automatic transmission. All information on the manual transmission is included in this Part of Chapter 7. Information on the automatic transmission can be found in Part B of this Chapter.

The manual transmission used in these models is a 3-speed all-synchromesh unit.

Due to the complexity, unavailability of replacement parts and the special tools necessary, internal repair by the home mechanic is not recommended. The information in this Chapter is limited to general information and removal and installation of the transmission.

Depending on the expense involved in having a faulty transmission overhauled, it may be a good idea to replace the unit with either a new or rebuilt one. Your local dealer or transmission shop should be able to supply you with information concerning cost, availability and exchange policy. Regardless of how you decide to remedy a transmission problem, you can still save a lot of money by removing and installing the unit yourself.

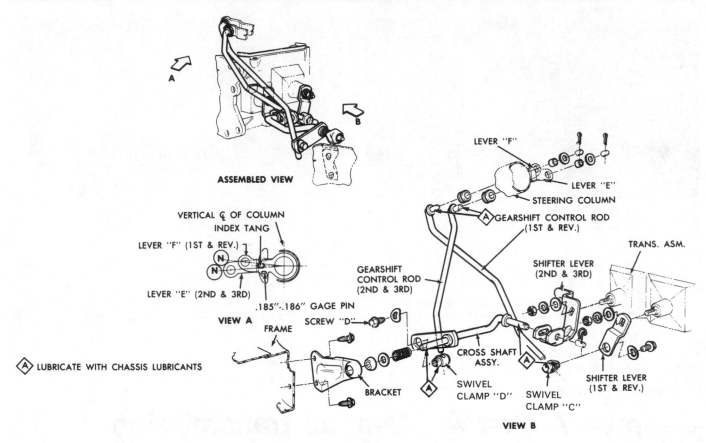

2.3 Column shift and backdrive adjustment details

2 Column shift and backdrive linkage — adjustment

Refer to illustrations 2.3 and 2.8

1   Shift the transmission into Reverse and turn the ignition key to
the Lock position.
2   Raise the vehicle and support it securely on jackstands.
3   Loosen the swivel clamp screws "C" at the transmission lever
(Reverse and 1st gear) and "D" at the cross shaft (see View B in accompanying illustration 2.3).
4   Place the front (2nd and 3rd gear) transmission shift lever in Neutral
and the rear shift lever (Reverse and 1st gear) in Reverse.
5   Tighten swivel clamp screw "C" securely, unlock the steering
column and place the shift lever in Neutral.
6   Line up the lower shift levers ("E" and "F") and insert a 0.185
to 0.186-inch gage pin through the hole in the levers shown in **View A**.
7   Tighten swivel clamp screw "D" and remove the gage pin. Check
the operation of the linkage by moving it through the complete shift
pattern.
8   Shift the transmission into 3rd gear and adjust the Transmission
Controlled Spark (TCS) switch so that the plunger is fully depressed
against the lever in 3rd and 4th gear (see illustration).

3 Transmission mount — check and replacement

1   Insert a large screwdriver or pry bar into the space between the
transmission extension housing and the crossmember and pry up.
2   The transmission should not spread excessively away from the
insulator.
3   To replace, remove the nuts attaching the insulator to the crossmember and the bolts attaching the insulator to the transmission.

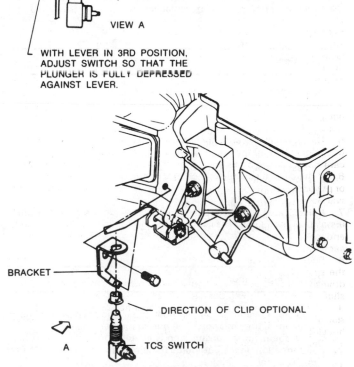

VIEW A

WITH LEVER IN 3RD POSITION,
ADJUST SWITCH SO THAT THE
PLUNGER IS FULLY DEPRESSED
AGAINST LEVER.

2.8 Transmission Controlled Spark (TCS) switch
adjustment details

4.5 Use a seal removal tool or a long screwdriver to carefully pry the seal out of the end of the transmission

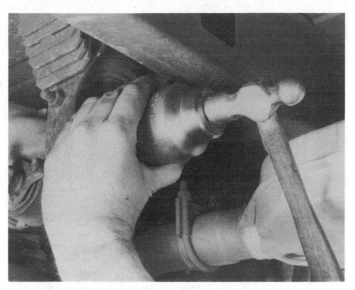

4.7 A large socket works well for installing the seal — the socket should come in contact with the outer edge of the seal

4 Raise the transmission slightly with a jack and remove the insulator, noting which holes are used in the crossmember for proper alignment during installation.
5 Installation is the reverse of the removal procedure.

4 Transmission oil seal — replacement

Refer to illustrations 4.5 and 4.7

1 Oil leaks frequently occur due to wear of the extension housing oil seal and bushing (if equipped), and/or the speedometer drive gear oil seal and O-ring. Replacement of these seals is relatively easy, since the repairs can usually be performed without removing the transmission from the vehicle.
2 The extension housing oil seal is located at the extreme rear of the transmission, where the driveshaft is attached. If leakage at the seal is suspected, raise the vehicle and support it securely on jackstands. If the seal is leaking, transmission lubricant will be built up on the front of the driveshaft and may be dripping from the rear of the transmission.
3 Refer to Chapter 8 and remove the driveshaft.
4 Using a soft faced hammer, carefully tap the dust shield (if equipped) to the rear and remove it from the transmission. Be careful not to distort it.
5 Using a screwdriver or pry bar, carefully pry the oil seal and bushing (if equipped) out of the rear of the transmission **(see illustration)**. Take care not to damage the splines on the transmission output shaft.
6 If the oil seal and bushing cannot be removed with a screwdriver or pry bar, a special oil seal removal tool (available at auto parts stores) will be required.
7 Using a large section of pipe or a very large deep socket as a drift, install the new oil seal **(see illustration)**. Drive it into the bore squarely and make sure it's completely seated. Install a new bushing using the same method.
8 Reinstall the dust shield by carefully tapping it into place. Lubricate the splines of the transmission output shaft and the outside of the driveshaft sleeve yoke with lightweight grease, then install the driveshaft. Be careful not to damage the lip of the new seal.
9 The speedometer cable and driven gear housing is located on the side of the extension housing. Look for transmission oil around the cable housing to determine if the seal and O-ring are leaking.
10 Disconnect the speedometer cable.
11 Using a hook, remove the seal.
12 Using a small socket as a drift, install the new seal.
13 Install a new O-ring in the driven gear housing and reinstall the driven gear housing and cable assembly on the extension housing.

5 Manual transmission — removal and installation

Removal

1 Disconnect the negative cable at the battery. Place the cable out of the way so it cannot accidentally come in contact with the negative terminal of the battery, as this would once again allow power into the electrical system of the vehicle.
2 Disconnect the shift linkage.
3 Raise the vehicle and support it securely on jackstands.
4 Disconnect the speedometer cable and wire harness connectors from the transmission.
5 Remove the driveshaft (Chapter 8). Use a plastic bag to cover the end of the transmission to prevent fluid loss and contamination.
6 Remove the exhaust system components as necessary for clearance (Chapter 4).
7 Support the engine. This can be done from above with an engine hoist, or by placing a jack (with a block of wood as an insulator) under the engine oil pan. The engine should remain supported at all times while the transmission is out of the vehicle.
8 Support the transmission with a jack — preferably a special jack made for this purpose. Safety chains will help steady the transmission on the jack.
9 Remove the rear transmission support-to-crossmember nuts/bolts.
10 Remove the nuts from the crossmember bolts. Raise the transmission slightly and remove the crossmember.
11 Remove the bolts securing the transmission to the clutch housing.
12 Make a final check that all wires and hoses have been disconnected from the transmission and then move the transmission and jack toward the rear of the vehicle until the transmission input shaft is clear of the clutch housing. Keep the transmission level as this is done.
13 Once the input shaft is clear, lower the transmission and remove it from under the vehicle. **Caution:** *Do not depress the clutch pedal while the transmission is out of the vehicle.*
14 The clutch components can be inspected by removing the clutch housing from the engine (Chapter 8). In most cases, new clutch components should be routinely installed if the transmission is removed.

Installation

15 If removed, install the clutch components (Chapter 8).
16 If removed, attach the clutch housing to the engine and tighten the bolts securely (Chapter 8).
17 With the transmission secured to the jack, as on removal, raise the transmission into position behind the clutch housing and then carefully slide it forward, engaging the input shaft with the clutch plate hub. Do not use excessive force to install the transmission — if the input shaft does not slide into place, readjust the angle of the trans-

7A

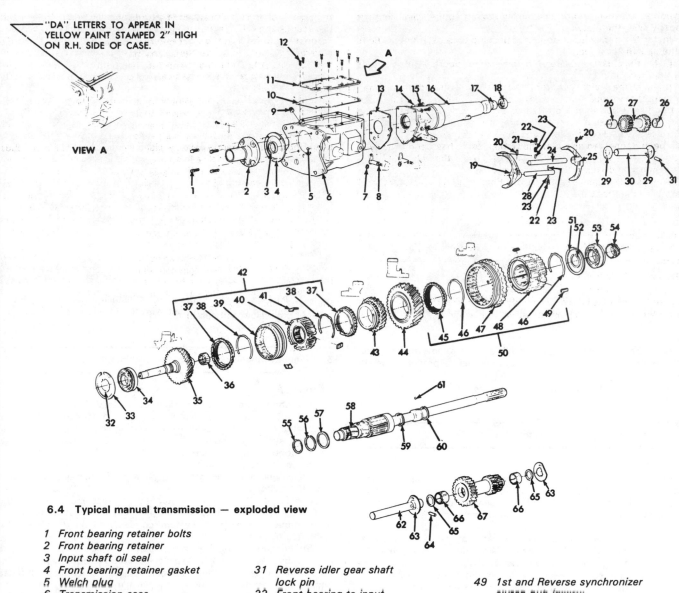

"DA" LETTERS TO APPEAR IN YELLOW PAINT STAMPED 2" HIGH ON R.H. SIDE OF CASE.

VIEW A

6.4 Typical manual transmission — exploded view

1 Front bearing retainer bolts
2 Front bearing retainer
3 Input shaft oil seal
4 Front bearing retainer gasket
5 Welch plug
6 Transmission case
7 Shifter shaft oil seals
8 Shifter shafts
9 Filler plug
10 Case cover gasket
11 Transmission case cover
12 Cover-to-case screws and washers
13 Extension-to-case gasket
14 Lockwashers
15 Extension-to-case bolts
16 Extension
17 Extension bushing
18 Extension oil seal
19 2nd and 3rd shift fork
20 Shift fork-to-rail set screws
21 Interlock spring retainer screw
22 Shifter interlock springs
23 Shifter interlock rod pins
24 1st and Reverse shifter rod
25 1st and Reverse shift fork
26 Reverse idler gear bushings
27 Reverse idler gear
28 2nd and 3rd shifter rail
29 Reverse idler gear thrust washers
30 Reverse idler gear shaft

31 Reverse idler gear shaft lock pin
32 Front bearing-to-input shaft snap-ring
33 Front bearing retainer ring
34 Front bearing
35 Input shaft (main drive gear)
36 Mainshaft roller bearings
37 2nd and 3rd synchronizer blocking rings
38 2nd and 3rd synchronizer retainer springs
39 2nd and 3rd synchronizer clutch hub sleeve
40 2nd and 3rd synchronizer clutch hub
41 2nd and 3rd synchronizer clutch hub inserts
42 2nd and 3rd gear synchronizer assembly
43 2nd speed gear
44 1st speed gear
45 1st and Reverse synchronizer blocking ring
46 1st and Reverse synchronizer retainer springs
47 1st and Reverse sliding gear
48 1st and Reverse synchronizer clutch hub

49 1st and Reverse synchronizer clutch hub inserts
50 1st and Reverse gear synchronizer assembly
51 Rear bearing retainer ring
52 1st and Reverse gear sychronizer assembly
53 Rear bearing
54 Speedometer drive gear
55 2nd and 3rd synchronizer hub-to-shaft snap-ring
56 1st speed gear thrust washer-to-shaft snap-ring
57 1st speed gear thrust washer
58 Main shaft
59 Rear bearing-to-shaft snap-ring
60 Speedometer gear-to-shaft snap-ring
61 Speedometer gear retaining ball
62 Countershaft
63 Countershaft gear thrust washers
64 Countershaft retaining pin
65 Countershaft washers
66 Countershaft roller bearings
67 Countershaft gear

mission so it is level and/or turn the input shaft so the splines engage properly with the clutch.

18 Install the transmission-to-clutch housing bolts. Tighten the bolts to the specified torque.

19 Install the crossmember and transmission support. Tighten all nuts and bolts securely.

20 Remove the jacks supporting the transmission and the engine.

21 Install the various items removed previously, referring to Chapter 8 for the installation of the driveshaft and Chapter 4 for information regarding the exhaust system components.

22 Make a final check that all wires, hoses and the speedometer cable have been connected and that the transmission has been filled with lubricant to the proper level (Chapter 1). Lower the vehicle.

23 Connect and adjust the shift linkage.

24 Connect the negative battery cable. Road test the vehicle for proper operation and check for leakage.

6 Manual transmission overhaul — general information

Refer to illustration 6.4

Overhauling a manual transmission is a difficult job for the do-it-yourselfer. It involves the disassembly and reassembly of many small parts. Numerous clearances must be precisely measured and, if necessary, changed with select fit spacers and snap-rings. As a result, if transmission problems arise, it can be removed and installed by a competent do-it-yourselfer, but overhaul should be left to a transmission repair shop. Rebuilt transmissions may be available — check with your dealer parts department and auto parts stores. At any rate, the time and money involved in an overhaul is almost sure to exceed the cost of a rebuilt unit.

Nevertheless, it's not impossible for an inexperienced mechanic to rebuild a transmission if the special tools are available and the job is done in a deliberate step-by-step manner so nothing is overlooked.

The tools necessary for an overhaul include internal and external snap-ring pliers, a bearing puller, a slide hammer, a set of pin punches, a dial indicator and possibly a hydraulic press. In addition, a large, sturdy workbench and a vise or transmission stand will be required.

During disassembly of the transmission, make careful notes of how each piece comes off, where it fits in relation to other pieces and what holds it in place. An exploded view is included **(see illustration)** to show where the parts go — but actually noting how they are installed when you remove the parts will make it much easier to get the transmission back together.

Before taking the transmission apart for repair, it will help if you have some idea what area of the transmission is malfunctioning. Certain problems can be closely tied to specific areas in the transmission, which can make component examination and replacement easier. Refer to the *Troubleshooting* section at the front of this manual for information regarding possible sources of trouble.

7A

Chapter 7 Part B Automatic transmission

Contents

Specifications

Torque specifications

	Ft-lb
Transmission-to-engine bolt	40
Floor shift lever-to-shift cable pin retaining nut	11 to 15
Torque converter-to-driveplate bolt	
1970 through 1985 models	25 to 35
1986 through 1988 models	46

1 General information

All vehicles covered in this manual come equipped with either a 3-speed manual transmission or an automatic transmission. All information on the automatic transmission is included in this Part of Chapter 7. Information on the manual transmission can be found in Part A of this Chapter.

Due to the complexity of the automatic transmissions covered in this manual and the need for specialized equipment to perform most service operations, this Chapter contains only general diagnosis, routine maintenance, adjustment and removal and installation procedures.

If the transmission requires major repair work, it should be left to a dealer service department or an automotive or transmission repair shop. You can, however, remove and install the transmission yourself and save the expense, even if the repair work is done by a transmission shop.

2 Diagnosis — general

Note: *Automatic transmission malfunctions may be caused by five general conditions: poor engine performance, improper adjustments, hydraulic malfunctions, mechanical malfunctions or malfunctions in the computer or its signal network. Diagnosis of these problems should always begin with a check of the easily repaired items: fluid level and condition (Chapter 1), shift linkage adjustment and throttle linkage adjustment. Next, perform a road test to determine if the problem has been corrected or if more diagnosis is necessary. If the problem persists after the preliminary tests and corrections are completed, additional diagnosis should be done by a dealer service department or transmission repair shop. Refer to the* Troubleshooting Section *at the front of this manual for information on symptoms of transmission problems.*

Preliminary checks

1 Drive the vehicle to warm the transmission to normal operating temperature.
2 Check the fluid level as described in Chapter 1:
   a) If the fluid level is unusually low, add enough fluid to bring the level within the designated area of the dipstick, then check for external leaks (see below).
   b) If the fluid level is abnormally high, drain off the excess, then check the drained fluid for contamination by coolant. The presence of engine coolant in the automatic transmission fluid indicates that a failure has occurred in the internal radiator walls that separate the coolant from the transmission fluid (see Chapter 3).
   c) If the fluid is foaming, drain it and refill the transmission, then check for coolant in the fluid or a high fluid level.
3 Check the engine idle speed. **Note:** *If the engine is malfunctioning, do not proceed with the preliminary checks until it has been repaired and runs normally.*
4 Check the throttle valve cable for freedom of movement. Adjust it if necessary (Section 9). **Note:** *The throttle cable may function properly when the engine is shut off and cold, but it may malfunction once the engine is hot. Check it cold and at normal engine operating temperature.*
5 Inspect the shift control linkage (Sections 4/5). Make sure that it's properly adjusted and that the linkage operates smoothly.

Fluid leak diagnosis

6 Most fluid leaks are easy to locate visually. Repair usually consists of replacing a seal or gasket. If a leak is difficult to find, the following procedure may help.
7 Identify the fluid. Make sure it's transmission fluid and not engine oil or brake fluid (automatic transmission fluid is a deep red color).
8 Try to pinpoint the source of the leak. Drive the vehicle several miles, then park it over a large sheet of cardboard. After a minute or two, you should be able to locate the leak by determining the source of the fluid dripping onto the cardboard.
9 Make a careful visual inspection of the suspected component and the area immediately around it. Pay particular attention to gasket mating surfaces. A mirror is often helpful for finding leaks in areas that are hard to see.
10 If the leak still cannot be found, clean the suspected area thoroughly with a degreaser or solvent, then dry it.
11 Drive the vehicle for several miles at normal operating temperature and varying speeds. After driving the vehicle, visually inspect the suspected component again.
12 Once the leak has been located, the cause must be determined before it can be properly repaired. If a gasket is replaced but the sealing flange is bent, the new gasket will not stop the leak. The bent flange must be straightened.
13 Before attempting to repair a leak, check to make sure that the following conditions are corrected or they may cause another leak. **Note:** *Some of the following conditions cannot be fixed without highly specialized tools and expertise. Such problems must be referred to a transmission repair shop or a dealer service department.*

Gasket leaks

14 Check the pan periodically. Make sure the bolts are tight, no bolts are missing, the gasket is in good condition and the pan is flat (dents in the pan may indicate damage to the valve body inside).
15 If the pan gasket is leaking, the fluid level or the fluid pressure may be too high, the vent may be plugged, the pan bolts may be too tight, the pan sealing flange may be warped, the sealing surface of the transmission housing may be damaged, the gasket may be damaged or the transmission casting may be cracked or porous. If sealant instead of gasket material has been used to form a seal between the pan and the transmission housing, it may be the wrong sealant.

Seal leaks

16 If a transmission seal is leaking, the fluid level or pressure may be too high, the vent may be plugged, the seal bore may be damaged, the seal itself may be damaged or improperly installed, the surface of the shaft protruding through the seal may be damaged or a loose bearing may be causing excessive shaft movement.
17 Make sure the dipstick tube seal is in good condition and the tube is properly seated. Periodically check the area around the speedometer gear or sensor for leakage. If transmission fluid is evident, check the O-ring for damage.

Case leaks

18 If the case itself appears to be leaking, the casting is porous and will have to be repaired or replaced.
19 Make sure the oil cooler hose fittings are tight and in good condition.

Fluid comes out vent pipe or fill tube

20 If this condition occurs, the transmission is overfilled, there is coolant in the fluid, the case is porous, the dipstick is incorrect, the vent is plugged or the drain back holes are plugged.

3 Transmission identification

Refer to illustration 3.1

1 Besides checking the transmission serial number, there is a quick way to determine which of the four automatic transmissions a particular vehicle is equipped with. Read the following transmission oil pan descriptions and refer to accompanying illustration 3.1 to identify the various models.

Powerglide

2 This transmission case is made of either cast iron or aluminum. The word 'powerglide' is plainly stamped on the case. The shift quadrant indicator is set up in one of two ways: P-N-D-L-R or P-R-N-D-L.

7B

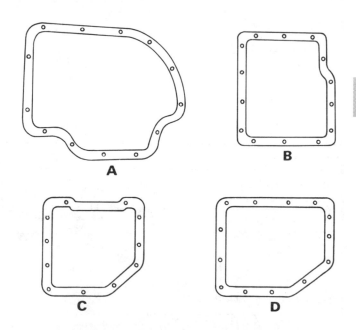

3.1 The oil pan gasket shape can help you determine which transmission your vehicle is equipped with

A Turbo Hydra-Matic 400   C Turbo Hydra-Matic 200
B Powerglide   D Turbo Hydra-Matic 250/350

Turbo Hydra-Matic 200/200C/2004R

3   This transmission is a two-piece design with a downshift cable running from the accelerator to the right side of the transmission case. The oil pan has 11 bolts and is square-shaped with one corner angled.

Turbo Hydra-Matic 250/350

4   This closely resembles the THM 200 but the oil pan has 13 bolts.

Turbo Hydra-Matic 375/400

5   The case of the 400 is also two-piece, but the downshifting is electrically controlled from a switch at the carburetor to the left side of the transmission. The oil pan also has 13 bolts. The shape of the pan is elongated and irregular.

---

4   Column shift linkage — checking and adjustment

1   The selector linkage will be in need of adjustment if at any time 'Low' or 'Reverse' can be obtained without first having to lift the shift control lever to enable it to pass over the mechanical stop.

1970 through 1973 models
Refer to illustration 4.2

2   If adjustment is required, release the control rod swivel or clamp and set the lever on the side of the transmission in the 'Drive' or L2 detent **(see illustration)**. This can be clearly defined by placing the lever in L or L1 and moving the lever back one detent (click).
3   Position the shift control lever up against the 'Drive' stop and then tighten the swivel or clamp on the control rod.
4   Check all selector positions, especially 'Park'. In some cases, especially with worn linkage, it may be necessary to readjust slightly in order to ensure that the 'Park' detent is fully engaged.

1974 through 1988 models
Refer to illustration 4.7

5   Place the shift lever in the Neutral position of the shift indicator.
6   Position the transmission shift lever in the Neutral detent.
7   Install the clamp spring and screw assembly on the equalizer lever control rod **(see illustration)**.
8   Hold the clamp flush against the equalizer lever and tighten the clamp screw finger tight. Make sure that no force is exerted in either direction on the rod or equalizer lever while the screw is tightened.
9   Tighten the screw securely.
10   Check that the ignition key can be moved freely to the 'Lock' position when the shift lever is in 'Park' and not in any other position.

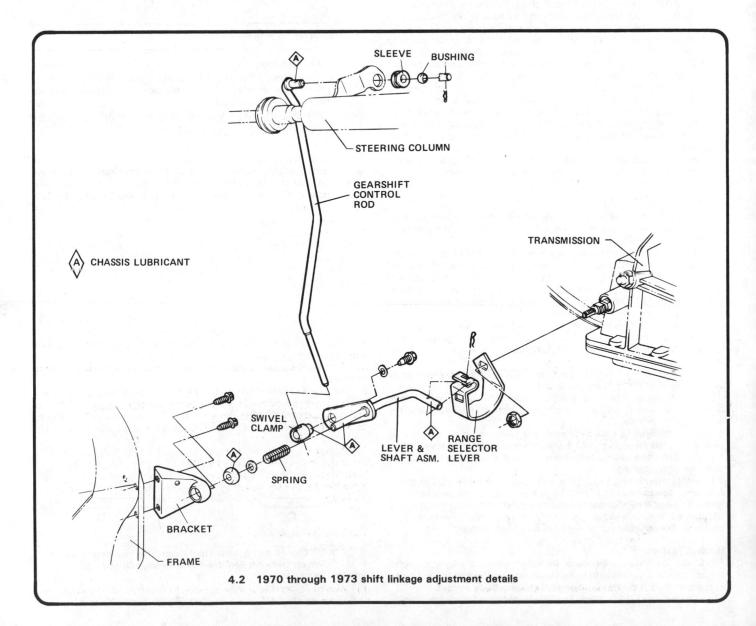

4.2   1970 through 1973 shift linkage adjustment details

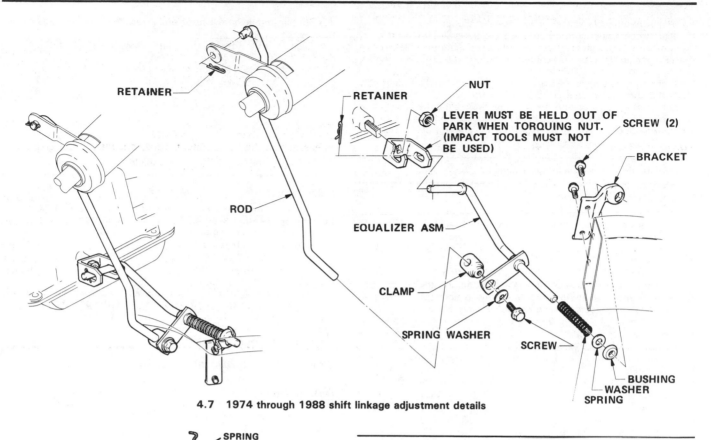

4.7 1974 through 1988 shift linkage adjustment details

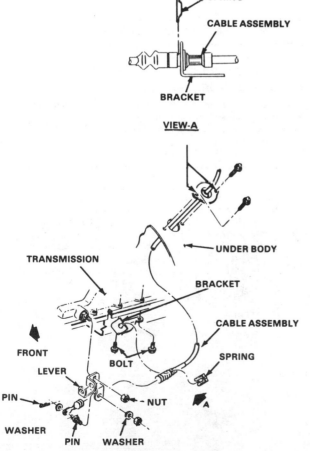

5.11 Components involved in floor shift linkage adjustment

5 Floor shift linkage — check and adjustment

1   If the engine can be started in any of the Drive positions and the Neutral start switch is properly adjusted (Section 11), the shift linkage must be adjusted.

Powerglide

2   Set the shift lever in 'Drive'.
3   Working under the vehicle, disconnect the selector cable from the lever on the side of the transmission.
4   Move the lever on the side of the transmission to the 'Drive' detent.
5   Measure the distance from the rear face of the cable mounting bracket to the center of the cable pivot stud. This should be 5-1/2 inches. Adjust the position of the stud if necessary to achieve this measurement.
6   Adjust the cable in its mounting bracket so that the cable end fits freely onto the pivot stud. Install the cable retaining clip.
7   Working inside the vehicle, remove the shift quadrant cover, plate and illumination bulbs.
8   Remove the selector cable clip and disconnect the cable from the shift lever.
9   Insert a gauge (0.07-inch thick) between the pawl and the detent plate, then measure the distance between the front face of the shifter assembly bracket and the center of the cable pivot pin. This should be 6-1/4 inches. If it is not, loosen bolt A and move the lever as necessary.
10   Adjust the cable mounting to the shifter bracket until the cable eye freely enters over the pivot pin. If at any time depressing the handle button does not clear the cut-outs in the detent plate, or conversely if the handle can be moved to P and R positions without depressing the buttom, raise or lower the detent plate after loosening the retaining bolt.

Turbo Hydra-Matic
Refer to illustration 5.11

Note: Apply the parking brake and block the wheels to prevent the vehicle from rolling.

11   Working under the vehicle, loosen the nut attaching the shift lever to the pin on the shift cable assembly (see illustration).

7B

12 Place the console shifter (inside the vehicle) in Park.
13 Place the manual shifting shaft on the transmission in Park.
14 Move the pin to give a 'free pin' fit, making sure that the console shifter is still in the Neutral position, and tighten the pin-to-lever retaining nut to the specified torque.
15 Make sure the engine will start in the Park and Neutral positions only.
16 If the engine can be started in any of the drive positions (as indicated by the shifter inside the vehicle), repeat the steps above or have the vehicle examined by a dealer, because improper linkage adjustment can lead to band or clutch failure and possible personal injury.

6 Powerglide — on-vehicle adjustments

Low band adjustment

1   This adjustment should normally be carried out at the time of the first oil change and thereafter only when unsatisfactory performance indicates it to be necessary (see *Troubleshooting*).
2   Raise the vehicle to provide access to the transmission, making sure to secure the vehicle on jackstands.
3   Place the selector lever in the Neutral position.
4   Remove the protective cap from the transmission adjusting screw.
5   Release and unscrew the adjusting screw locknut one-quarter turn and hold it in this position with a wrench.
6   Using the special tool J-21848 or a torque wrench and adaptor, tighten the adjusting screw to 70 in-lbs., then back off the screw the exact number of turns as follows:
  a) For a band which has been in operation for less than 6000 miles — three complete turns.
  b) For a band which has been in operation for more than 6000 miles — four complete turns.
7   Tighten the adjusting screw locknut.

Throttle valve/linkage adjustment

8   Remove the air cleaner. Disconnect the accelerator linkage at the carburetor, and the accelerator and throttle valve return springs.
9   Pull the throttle valve upper rod forward with the right hand then open the carburetor throttle side with the left hand.
10 Adjust the swivel on the end of the upper throttle valve rod so that the ball stud contacts the end of the slot in the upper throttle valve rod as the carburetor reaches the wide open throttle (WOT) position.
11 Connect and adjust the accelerator linkage.

Neutral start switch alignment

12 This operation will only be required if a new switch is being installed.

13 Set the shift lever in Neutral and locate the lever tang against the transmission selector plate.
14 Align the slot in the contact support with the hole in the switch by inserting a 3/32-inch diameter pin.
15 Place the contact support drive slot over the shifter tube drive tang and tighten the screws. Withdraw the pin.
16 Connect the switch wires and check that the operation of the switch is correct when the ignition is switched on.

7 Turbo Hydra-Matic 250 — on-vehicle adjustments

Intermediate band adjustment

1   This adjustment should be carried out every 24,000 miles or if the performance of the transmission indicates the need for it.
2   Raise the vehicle to gain access to the transmission, making sure to secure the vehicle on jackstands.
3   Place the speed selector lever in Neutral.
4   The adjusting screw and locknut for the intermediate band is located on the right-hand side of the transmission case.
5   Loosen the locknut 1/4-turn using a wrench or special tool J-24367. Hold the locknut in this position and tighten the adjusting screw to a torque of 30 in-lbs. Now back off the screw three complete turns exactly.
6   Without moving the adjusting screw, tighten the locknut to 15 ft-lbs.

Downshift (detent) cable adjustment

7   The cable will normally only require adjustment if a new one has been installed.
8   Depress the accelerator pedal fully. The ball will slide into the cable sleeve and automatically pre-set the cable tension.

8 Turbo Hydra-Matic 350 downshift (detent) cable — adjustment

Refer to illustration 8.1

1970 through 1980 models

1   Insert a screwdriver on each side of the snap-lock and pry out to release (see illustration).
2   Compress the locking tabs and disconnect the snap-lock assembly from its bracket.

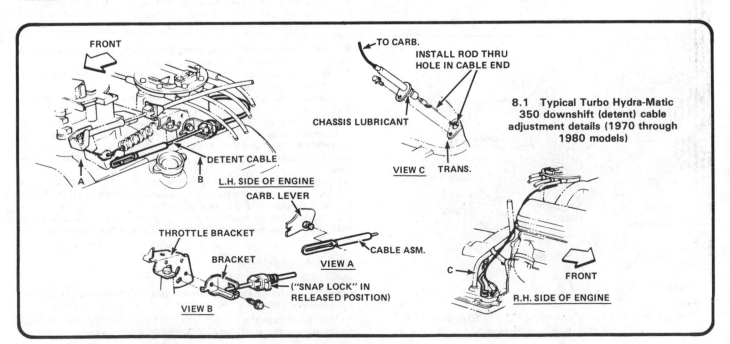

8.1 Typical Turbo Hydra-Matic 350 downshift (detent) cable adjustment details (1970 through 1980 models)

3   Manually set the carburetor in the fully open position with the throttle lever fully against its stop.
4   With the carburetor in the fully open position, push the snap-lock on the detent cable into the locked position and release the throttle lever.

1981 through 1988 models

5   This will normally be required only after installation of a new cable.
6   Depress the accelerator pedal to the fully open position. The cable ball will slide into the sleeve of the cable and automatically adjust the setting of the detent cable.

---

9   Throttle valve (TV) cable — description, inspection and adjustment

Description

1   The throttle valve cable used on these transmissions should not be thought of as merely a "downshift" cable, as in earlier transmissions. The TV cable controls line pressure, shift points, shift feel, part throttle downshifts and detent downshifts.
2   If the TV cable is broken, sticky, misadjusted or is the incorrect part, the vehicle will experience a number of problems.

Inspection

Refer to illustration 9.4

3   Inspection should be made with the engine running at idle speed with the selector lever in Neutral. Set the parking brake firmly and block the wheels to prevent any vehicle movement. As an added precaution, have an assistant in the driver's seat applying the brake pedal.
4   Grab the inner cable a few inches behind where it attaches to the throttle linkage and pull the cable forward. It should easily slide through the cable housing with no binding or jerky operation **(see illustration)**.
5   Release the cable and it should return to its original location with the cable stop against the cable terminal.
6   If the TV cable does not operate as above, the cause is a defective or misadjusted cable or damaged components at either end of the cable.

Adjustment

7   The engine should not be running during this adjustment.

1976 through 1980 models

Refer to illustration 9.8

8   Disengage the snap-lock and check that the cable is free to slide through the lock **(see illustration)**.
9   Move the carburetor throttle lever to the fully open position.
10 Push the snap-lock down until it is flush and then gently release the throttle lever.

1981 through 1988 models

Refer to illustration 9.11

11 Depress the re-adjust tab and move the slider back through the fitting away from the throttle linkage until the slider stops against the fitting **(see illustration)**.
12 Release the re-adjust tab.
13 Turn the throttle lever to the wide open throttle (WOT) position, which will automatically adjust the cable. Release the throttle lever.
Caution: *Don't use excessive force at the throttle lever to adjust the TV cable. If great effort is required to adjust the cable, disconnect the cable at the transmission end and check for free operation. If it's still difficult, replace the cable. If it's now free, suspect a bent TV link in the transmission or a problem with a throttle lever.*
14 After adjustment check for proper operation as described in Steps 3 through 6 above.

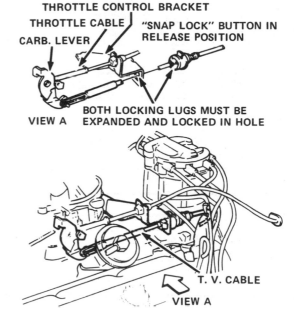

9.8   1976 through 1980 model TV cable adjustment details

7B

9.4   To check for free operation, pull forward on the throttle valve (TV) inner cable, feeling for smooth operation through the full range of travel — the cable should retract evenly and rapidly when released

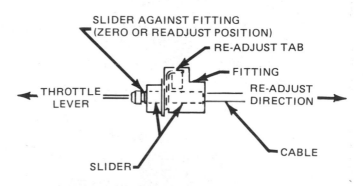

9.11   On 1981 through 1988 models, depress the throttle valve (TV) cable re-adjust tab and pull the slider back (arrow) until it rests on its stop — release the tab and open the throttle completely

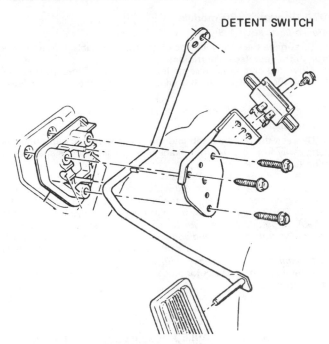

DETENT SWITCH

10.1   Turbo Hydra-Matic downshift (detent) switch details

10   Turbo Hydra-Matic 400 downshift (detent) switch — adjustment

Refer to illustration 10.1

1   The switch is mounted on the pedal bracket **(see illustration)**.
2   The switch is set by pushing the plunger as far forward as possible. At the first full depression of the accelerator pedal, the switch is automatically adjusted.

11   Turbo Hydra-Matic switch — check and adjustment

Refer to illustrations 11.6a and 11.6b

1   When the switch is operating properly, the engine should crank over with the selector lever in Park or Neutral only. Also, the backup lights should come on when the lever is in Reverse.
2   If a new switch is being installed, set the shift lever against the 'Neutral' gate by rotating the lower lever on the shift tube in a counterclockwise direction as viewed from the driver's seat.
3   Locate the switch actuating tang in the shifter tube slot and then tighten the securing screws.
4   Connect the wiring harness and switch on the ignition and check that the starter motor will actuate.
5   If the switch operates correctly, move the shift lever out of Neutral, which will cause the alignment pin (installed during production of the switch) to shear.
6   If an old switch is being installed or readjusted, use a pin (0.093 to 0.097-inch diameter) to align the hole in the switch with the actuating tang. Insert the pin to a depth of 1/4-in. Remove the pin before moving the shift lever out of Neutral **(see illustration)**. On later models the switch automatically ratchets to the proper adjustment when the shift lever is moved to Park. To readjust a later model switch, move the switch assembly housing to the Low gear position and then shift into Park **(see illustration)**.

12   Automatic transmission — removal and installation

Refer to illustrations 12.5 and 12.6

Removal

1   Disconnect the negative cable at the battery. Place the cable out of the way so it cannot accidentally come in contact with the negative terminal of the battery, as this would once again allow power into the electrical system of the vehicle.
2   Raise the vehicle and support it securely.
3   Drain the transmission fluid (Chapter 1).
4   Remove the torque converter cover.

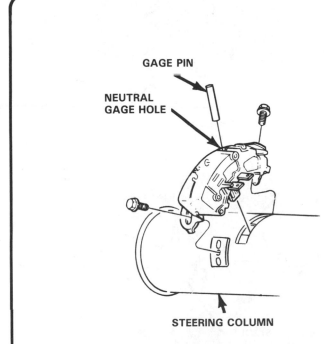

GAGE PIN

NEUTRAL GAGE HOLE

STEERING COLUMN

11.6a   On earlier models, insert a pin into the gage hole to adjust the neutral start switch

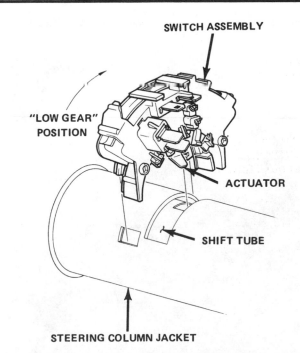

SWITCH ASSEMBLY

"LOW GEAR" POSITION

ACTUATOR

SHIFT TUBE

STEERING COLUMN JACKET

11.6b   Later model neutral start switches are adjusted by moving the assembly housing to the Low gear position and then shifting into Park

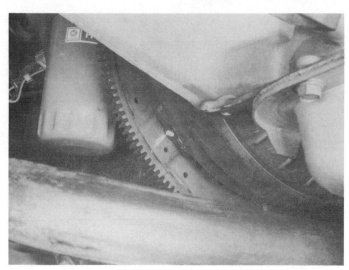

12.5 Mark the relationship of the torque converter to the flywheel with white paint

12.6 Remove the torque converter-to-flywheel retaining bolts (here, a flywheel wrench is being used to prevent the flywheel from turning, but a wrench on the crankshaft vibration damper will also work)

5 Mark the relation of the flywheel and the torque converter with white paint so they can be reinstalled in the same position **(see illustration)**.
6 Remove the torque converter-to-flywheel nuts/bolts **(see illustration)**. Turn the crankshaft bolt for access to each nut in turn.
7 Remove the starter motor (Chapter 5).
8 Remove the driveshaft (Chapter 8).
9 Disconnect the speedometer cable.
10 Disconnect the electrical connectors from the transmission.
11 On models so equipped, disconnect the vacuum hoses.
12 Remove any exhaust component which will interfere with transmission removal (Chapter 4).
13 Disconnect the TV linkage rod or cable.
14 Disconnect the shift linkage.
15 Support the engine using a jack and a block of wood under the oil pan to spread the load.
16 Support the transmission with a jack — preferably a jack made for this purpose. Safety chains will help steady the transmission on the jack.
17 Remove the rear mount-to-crossmember attaching bolts and the crossmember-to-frame attaching bolts.
18 Remove the two engine rear support-to-transmission extension housing attaching bolts.
19 Raise the transmission sufficiently to allow removal of the crossmember.
20 Remove the bolts securing the transmission to the engine.
21 Lower the transmission slightly and disconnect and plug the transmission cooler lines.
22 Remove the transmission fluid filler tube.
23 Move the transmission to the rear to disengage it from the engine block dowel pins and make sure the torque converter is detached from the flywheel. Secure the torque converter to the transmission so that it will not fall out during removal. Lower the transmission from the vehicle.

Installation

24 Make sure prior to installation that the torque converter hub is securely engaged in the pump.
25 With the transmission secured to the jack, raise the transmission into position, making sure to keep it level so the torque converter does not slide forward. Connect the transmission cooler lines.
26 Turn the torque converter to line up the torque converter and flywheel bolt holes. The white paint mark on the torque converter and the stud made during Step 5 must line up.
27 Move the transmission carefully forward until the dowel pins are engaged and the torque converter is engaged.
28 Install the transmission housing-to-engine bolts and nuts. Tighten the bolts and nuts to the specified torque.
29 Install the torque converter-to-flywheel nuts. Tighten the nuts to the specified torque.
30 Install the transmission mount crossmember and through-bolts. Tighten the bolts and nuts securely.
31 Remove the jacks supporting the transmission and the engine.
32 Install the fluid filler tube.
33 Install the starter.
34 Connect the vacuum hose(s) (if equipped).
35 Connect the shift and TV linkage.
36 Plug in the transmission electrical connectors.
37 Install the torque converter cover.
38 Connect the driveshaft.
39 Connect the speedometer.
40 Adjust the shift linkage.
41 Install any exhaust system components which were removed.
42 Lower the vehicle.
43 Fill the transmission with the specified fluid (Chapter 1), run the vehicle and check for fluid leaks.

7B

Chapter 8   Clutch and drivetrain

Contents

Specifications

Clutch

Type . . . .   Single dry plate, diaphragm spring
Pedal free play check and adjustment . . . .   See Chapter 1

Torque specifications   **Ft-lbs**
Pressure plate-to-flywheel bolts   25
Bellhousing to engine bolts   40
Transmission case-to-clutch bellhousing bolts   55

Driveshaft

Torque specifications   **Ft-lbs**
Universal joint strap bolts   15
Universal U-bolt nuts   15
Universal flange bolts   70

Rear axle

Torque specifications   **Ft-lbs**
Differential cover bolts   20
Pinion shaft lock bolt   25

B and O type axle

Axleshaft end play . . . .   0.001 to 0.022 in

1 General information

The information in this Chapter deals with the components from the rear of the engine to the rear wheels, except for the transmission, which is dealt with in the previous Chapter. For the purposes of this Chapter, these components are grouped into three categories; clutch, driveshaft and rear axle. Separate Sections within this Chapter offer general descriptions and checking procedures for components in each of the three groups.

Since nearly all the procedures covered in this Chapter involve working under the vehicle, make sure it's securely supported on sturdy jackstands or on a hoist where the vehicle can be easily raised and lowered.

2 Clutch — description and check

Refer to illustration 2.1

1   All vehicles with a manual transmission use a single dry plate, diaphragm spring type clutch **(see illustration)**. The clutch disc has a splined hub which allows it to slide along the splines of the transmission input shaft. The clutch and pressure plate are held in contact by spring pressure exerted by the diaphragm in the pressure plate.

2   The mechanical release system includes the clutch pedal, the clutch linkage which actuates the clutch release lever and the release bearing.

3   When pressure is applied to the clutch pedal to release the clutch, mechanical pressure is exerted against the outer end of the clutch release lever. As the lever pivots, the shaft fingers push against the release bearing. The bearing pushes against the fingers of the diaphragm spring of the pressure plate assembly, which in turn releases the clutch plate.

4   Terminology can be a problem when discussing the clutch components because common names are in some cases different from those used by the manufacturer. For example, the driven plate is also called the clutch plate or disc, and the clutch release bearing is sometimes called a throwout bearing.

5   Other than to replace components with obvious damage, some preliminary checks should be performed to diagnose clutch problems.

   a) To check ''clutch spin down time,'' run the engine at normal idle speed with the transmission in Neutral (clutch pedal up — engaged). Disengage the clutch (pedal down), wait several seconds and shift the transmission into Reverse. No grinding noise should be heard. A grinding noise would most likely indicate a problem in the pressure plate or the clutch disc.

   b) To check for complete clutch release, run the engine (with the parking brake applied to prevent movement) and hold the clutch pedal approximately 1/2-inch from the floor. Shift the transmission between 1st gear and Reverse several times. If the shift is rough, component failure is indicated.

   c) Visually inspect the pivot bushing at the top of the clutch pedal to make sure there is no binding or excessive play.

   d) On vehicles with mechanical release systems, a clutch pedal that is difficult to operate is most likely caused by faulty linkage. Check it for worn bushings and bent or distorted parts.

   e) Crawl under the vehicle and make sure the clutch release lever is solidly mounted on the ball stud.

3 Clutch components — removal, inspection and installation

Warning: *Dust produced by clutch wear and deposited on clutch components contains asbestos, which is hazardous to your health. DO NOT blow it out with compressed air and DO NOT inhale it. DO NOT use gasoline or petroleum-based solvents to remove the dust. Brake system cleaner should be used to flush the dust into a drain pan. After the clutch components are wiped clean with a rag, dispose of the contaminated rags and cleaner in a covered, marked container.*

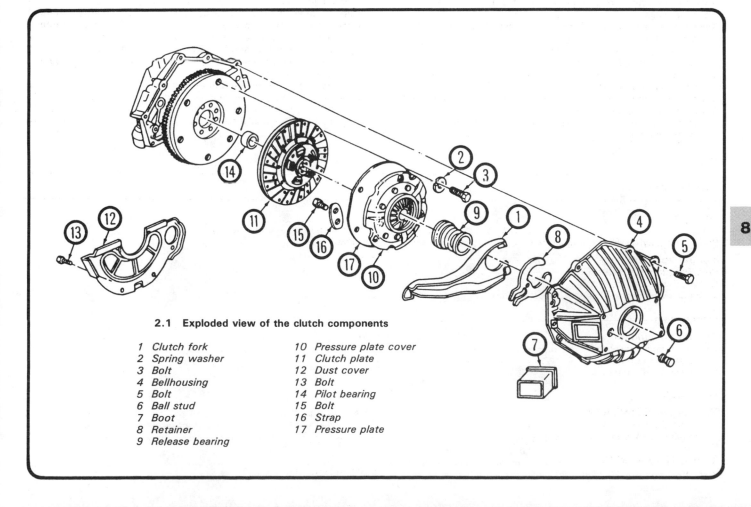

2.1 Exploded view of the clutch components

1 Clutch fork	10 Pressure plate cover
2 Spring washer	11 Clutch plate
3 Bolt	12 Dust cover
4 Bellhousing	13 Bolt
5 Bolt	14 Pilot bearing
6 Ball stud	15 Bolt
7 Boot	16 Strap
8 Retainer	17 Pressure plate
9 Release bearing	

8

Removal

Refer to illustration 3.7

1   Access to the clutch components is normally accomplished by removing the transmission, leaving the engine in the vehicle. If, of course, the engine is being removed for major overhaul, then check the clutch for wear and replace worn components as necessary. However, the relatively low cost of the clutch components compared to the time and trouble spent gaining access to them warrants their replacement anytime the engine or transmission is removed, unless they are new or in near perfect condition. The following procedures are based on the assumption the engine will stay in place.

2   Referring to Chapter 7 Part A, remove the transmission from the vehicle. Support the engine while the transmission is out. Preferably, an engine hoist should be used to support it from above. However, if a jack is used underneath the engine, make sure a piece of wood is positioned between the jack and oil pan to spread the load. **Caution:** *The pickup for the oil pump is very close to the bottom of the oil pan. If the pan is bent or distorted in any way, engine oil starvation could occur.*

3   Remove the return spring and the clutch release lever pushrod.

4   Remove the bellhousing-to-engine bolts and then detach the housing. It may have to be gently pried off the alignment dowels with a screwdriver or pry bar.

5   The clutch fork and release bearing can remain attached to the housing for the time being.

6   To support the clutch disc during removal, install a clutch alignment tool through the clutch disc hub.

7   Carefully inspect the flywheel and pressure plate for indexing marks. The marks are usually an X, an O or a white letter. If they cannot be found, scribe marks yourself so the pressure plate and the flywheel will be in the same alignment during installation **(see illustration)**.

8   Turning each bolt only 1/4-turn at a time, loosen the pressure plate-to-flywheel bolts. Work in a criss-cross pattern until all spring pressure is relieved. Then hold the pressure plate securely and completely remove the bolts, followed by the pressure plate and clutch disc.

Inspection

Refer to illustrations 3.12 and 3.14

9   Ordinarily, when a problem occurs in the clutch, it can be attributed to wear of the clutch driven plate assembly (clutch disc). However, all components should be inspected at this time.

10   Inspect the flywheel for cracks, heat checking, grooves and other obvious defects. If the imperfections are slight, a machine shop can machine the surface flat and smooth, which is highly recommended regardless of the surface appearance. Refer to Chapter 2 for the flywheel removal and installation procedure.

11   Inspect the pilot bearing (Section 5).

12   Inspect the lining on the clutch disc. There should be at least 1/16 inch of lining above the rivet heads. Check for loose rivets, distortion, cracks, broken springs and other obvious damage **(see illustration)**. As mentioned above, ordinarily the clutch disc is routinely replaced, so if in doubt about the condition, replace it with a new one.

13   The release bearing should also be replaced along with the clutch disc (see Section 4).

14   Check the machined surfaces and the diaphragm spring fingers

3.7   After removal of the transmission, this will be the view of the clutch components

1 *Pressure plate*   2 *Flywheel*

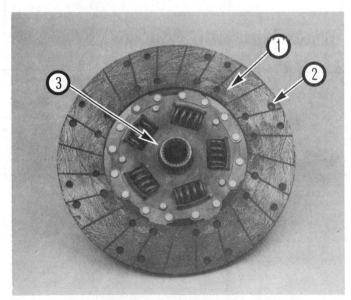

3.12   The clutch plate

1 *Lining — this will wear down in use*
2 *Rivets — these secure the lining and will damage the flywheel or pressure plate if allowed to contact the surfaces*
3 *Markings — "Flywheel side" or something similar*

3.14   The machined face of the pressure plate must be inspected for score marks and other damage — if damage is slight, a machine shop can make the surface smooth again

of the pressure plate (see illustration). If the surface is grooved or otherwise damaged, replace the pressure plate. Also check for obvious damage, distortion, cracking, etc. Light glazing can be removed with medium grit emery cloth. If a new pressure plate is required, new and factory-rebuilt units are available.

Installation
Refer to illustration 3.16

15   Before installation, clean the flywheel and pressure plate machined surfaces with lacquer thinner or acetone. It's important that no oil or grease is on these surfaces or the lining of the clutch disc. Handle the parts only with clean hands.

16   Position the clutch disc and pressure plate against the flywheel with the clutch held in place with an alignment tool (see illustration). Make sure it's installed properly (most replacement clutch plates will be marked ''flywheel side'' or something similar — if not marked, install the clutch disc with the damper springs toward the transmission).

17   Tighten the pressure plate-to-flywheel bolts only finger tight, working around the pressure plate.

18   Center the clutch disc by ensuring the alignment tool extends through the splined hub and into the pilot bearing in the crankshaft. Wiggle the tool up, down or side-to-side as needed to bottom the tool

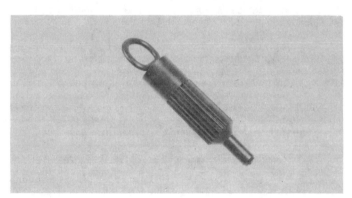

3.16   A clutch alignment tool can be purchased at most auto parts stores and eliminates all guesswork when centering the clutch plate in the pressure plate

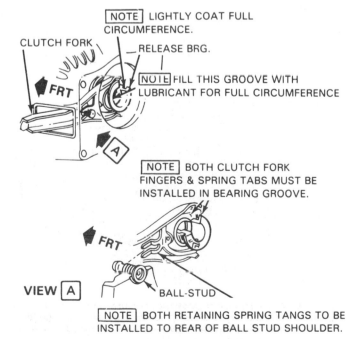

4.6   Release bearing and fork installation and lubrication details

in the pilot bearing. Tighten the pressure plate-to-flywheel bolts a little at a time, working in a criss-cross pattern to prevent distorting the cover. After all of the bolts are snug, tighten them to the specified torque. Remove the alignment tool.

19   Using high temperature grease, lubricate the inner groove of the release bearing (refer to Section 4). Also place grease on the release lever contact areas and the transmission input shaft bearing retainer.

20   Install the clutch release bearing as described in Section 4.

21   Install the bellhousing and tighten the bolts to the specified torque.

22   Install the transmission, slave cylinder and all components removed previously. Tighten all fasteners to the proper torque specifications.

23   Refer to Chapter 1 for clutch pedal free play check and adjustment information.

4   Clutch release bearing and lever — removal, inspection and installation

Refer to illustrations 4.6 and 4.7

Warning: *Dust produced by clutch wear and deposited on clutch components may contain asbestos, which is hazardous to your health. DO NOT blow it out with compressed air and DO NOT inhale it. DO NOT use gasoline or petroleum-based solvents to remove the dust. Brake system cleaner should be used to flush the dust into a drain pan. After the clutch components are wiped clean with a rag, dispose of the contaminated rags and cleaner in a covered, marked container.*

Removal

1   Disconnect the negative cable from the battery.

2   Remove the transmission (Chapter 7).

3   Remove the bellhousing (Section 3).

4   Remove the clutch release lever from the ball stud, then remove the bearing from the lever.

Inspection

5   Hold the center of the bearing and rotate the outer portion while applying pressure. If the bearing doesn't turn smoothly or if it's noisy, replace it with a new one. Wipe the bearing with a clean rag and inspect it for damage, wear and cracks. Don't immerse the bearing in solvent — it's sealed for life and to do so would ruin it.

Installation

6   Lightly lubricate the clutch lever crown and spring retention crown where they contact the bearing with high-temperature grease. Fill the inner groove of the bearing with the same grease (see illustration).

7   Attach the release bearing to the clutch lever so that both fork tabs fit into the bearing recess (see illustration).

4.7   When installing the release bearing, make sure the fingers and the tabs fit into the bearing recess

8

8   Lubricate the clutch release lever ball socket with high-temperature grease and push the lever onto the ball stud until it's firmly seated.
9   Apply a light coat of high-temperature grease to the face of the release bearing, where it contacts the pressure plate diaphragm fingers.
10 Install the bellhousing and tighten the bolts to the specified torque.
11 Prior to installing the transmission, apply a light coat of grease to the transmission front bearing retainer.
12 The remainder of installation is the reverse of the removal procedure. Tighten all bolts to the specified torque.

5   Pilot bearing — inspection and replacement

Refer to illustration 5.9

1   The clutch pilot bearing is a needle roller type bearing which is pressed into the rear of the crankshaft. It is greased at the factory and does not require additional lubrication. Its primary purpose is to support the front of the transmission input shaft. The pilot bearing should be inspected whenever the clutch components are removed from the engine. Due to its inaccessibility, if you are in doubt as to its condition, replace it with a new one. **Note:** *If the engine has been removed from the vehicle, disregard the following steps which do not apply.*
2   Remove the transmission (refer to Chapter 7 Part A).
3   Remove the clutch components (Section 3).
4   Inspect for any excessive wear, scoring, lack of grease, dryness or obvious damage. If any of these conditions are noted, the bearing should be replaced. A flashlight will be helpful to direct light into the recess.
5   Removal can be accomplished with a special puller and slide hammer, but an alternative method also works very well.
6   Find a solid steel bar which is slightly smaller in diameter than the bearing. Alternatives to a solid bar would be a wood dowel or a socket with a bolt fixed in place to make it solid.
7   Check the bar for fit — it should just slip into the bearing with very little clearance.
8   Pack the bearing and the area behind it (in the crankshaft recess) with heavy grease. Pack it tightly to eliminate as much air as possible.
9   Insert the bar into the bearing bore and strike the bar sharply with a hammer, which will force the grease to the back side of the bearing and push it out **(see illustration)**. Remove the bearing and clean all grease from the crankshaft recess.
10 To install the new bearing, lightly lubricate the outside surface with lithium-based grease, then drive it into the recess with a soft-face hammer.

5.9   Pack the recess behind the pilot bearing with heavy grease and force it out hydraulically with a steel rod slightly smaller than the bore in the bearing — when the hammer strikes the rod, the bearing will pop out of the crankshaft

11 Install the clutch components, transmission and all other components removed previously, tightening all fasteners properly.

6   Clutch pedal — removal and installation

Refer to illustration 6.4

1   Disconnect the negative cable from the battery.
2   Disconnect and remove the starter safety switch (see Section 7).
3   Disconnect the clutch and brake pedal pushrods and pedal return springs.
4   Remove the pedal pivot nut and slide the pedal to the left to remove it.
5   Wipe clean all parts; however, don't use cleaning solvent on the bushings. Replace all worn parts with new ones.
6   Installation is the reverse of removal. Check that the starter safety switch allows the vehicle to be started only with the clutch pedal fully depressed.

7   Clutch safety switch — removal, installation and adjustment

1   Disconnect the cable from the negative terminal of the battery.
2   Unplug the electrical connector from the switch **(see illustration 6.4)**.
3   Remove the mounting screws and compress the switch actuating shaft retainer, then detach the switch from the mounting bracket and clutch pedal.
4   To install the switch, reverse the removal procedure.
5   Check for proper operation.

8   Driveshaft and universal joints — description and check

1   The driveshaft is a tube running between the transmission and the rear end. Universal joints are located at either end of the driveshaft and permit power to be transmitted to the rear wheels at varying angles.
2   The driveshaft features a splined yoke at the front, which slips into the extension housing of the transmission. This arrangement allows the driveshaft to slide back and forth within the transmission as the vehicle is in operation.
3   An oil seal is used to prevent leakage of fluid at this point and to keep dirt and contaminants from entering the transmission. If leakage is evident at the front of the driveshaft, replace the oil seal, referring to the procedures in Chapter 7.
4   The driveshaft assembly requires very little service. The universal joints are lubricated for life and must be replaced if problems develop. The driveshaft must be removed from the vehicle for this procedure.
5   Since the driveshaft is a balanced unit, it's important that no undercoating, mud, etc., be allowed to stay on it. When the vehicle is raised for service it's a good idea to clean the driveshaft and inspect it for any obvious damage. Also check that the small weights used to originally balance the driveshaft are in place and securely attached. Whenever the driveshaft is removed it's important that it be reinstalled in the same relative position to preserve this balance.
6   Problems with the driveshaft are usually indicated by a noise or vibration while driving the vehicle. A road test should verify if the problem is the driveshaft or another vehicle component:
   a) On an open road, free of traffic, drive the vehicle and note the engine speed (rpm) at which the problem is most evident.
   b) With this noted, drive the vehicle again, this time manually keeping the transmission in 1st, then 2nd, then 3rd gear ranges and running the engine up to the engine speed noted.
   c) If the noise or vibration occurs at the same engine speed regardless of which gear the transmission is in, the driveshaft is not at fault because the speed of the driveshaft varies in each gear.
   d) If the noise or vibration decreased or was eliminated, visually inspect the driveshaft for damage, material on the shaft which would effect balance, missing weights and damaged universal joints. Another possibility for this condition would be tires which are out of balance.
7   To check for worn universal joints:
   a) On an open road, free of traffic, drive the vehicle slowly until

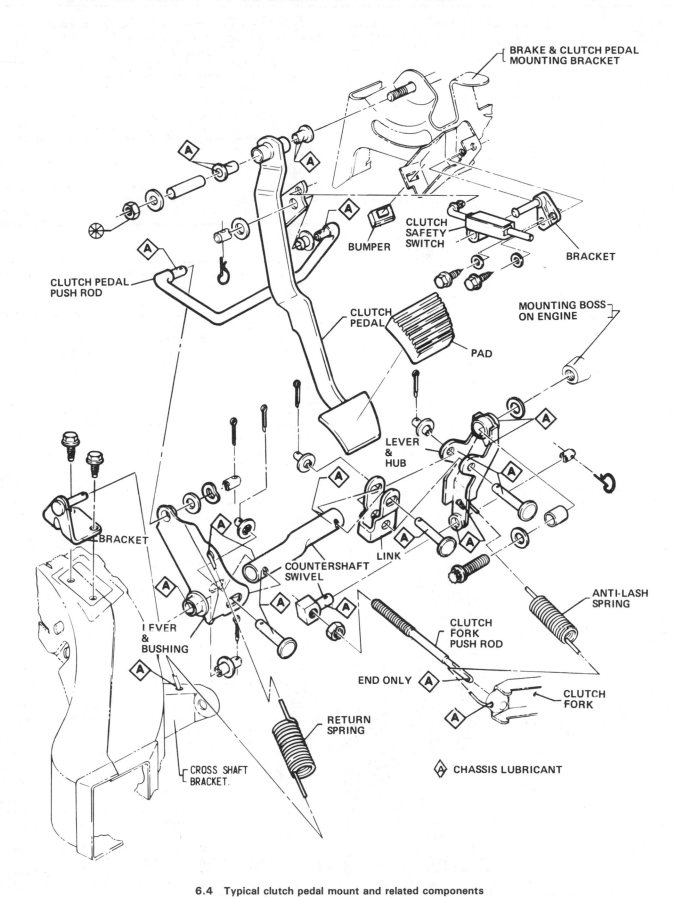

BRAKE & CLUTCH PEDAL MOUNTING BRACKET

CLUTCH SAFETY SWITCH

BUMPER

BRACKET

CLUTCH PEDAL PUSH ROD

MOUNTING BOSS ON ENGINE

CLUTCH PEDAL

PAD

LEVER & HUB

LINK

COUNTERSHAFT SWIVEL

ANTI-LASH SPRING

CLUTCH FORK PUSH ROD

BRACKET

LEVER & BUSHING

END ONLY

CLUTCH FORK

RETURN SPRING

CROSS SHAFT BRACKET.

⬦ CHASSIS LUBRICANT

8

6.4 Typical clutch pedal mount and related components

the transmission is in High gear. Let off on the accelerator, allowing the vehicle to coast, then accelerate. A clunking or knocking noise will indicate worn universal joints.
b) Drive the vehicle at a speed of about 10 to 15 mph and then place the transmission in Neutral, allowing the vehicle to coast. Listen for abnormal driveline noises.
c) Raise the vehicle and support it securely on jackstands. With the transmission in Neutral, manually turn the driveshaft, watching the universal joints for excessive play.

9   Driveshaft — removal and installation

Refer to illustration 9.3 and 9.4

Removal

1   Disconnect the negative cable from the battery.
2   Raise the vehicle and support it securely on jackstands. Place the transmission in Neutral with the parking brake off.
3   Using a sharp scribe, white paint or a hammer and punch, place marks on the driveshaft and the differential flange in line with each other **(see illustration)**. This is to make sure the driveshaft is reinstalled

9.3   Before removing the driveshaft, mark the relationship of the driveshaft yoke to the differential flange — to prevent the driveshaft from turning when loosening the strap bolts, insert a screwdriver through the yoke

in the same position to preserve the balance.
4   Disconnect the rear universal joint by unscrewing and removing the nuts from the U-bolts or strap retaining bolts, or by removing the flange bolts. Turn the driveshaft (or tires) as necessary to bring the bolts into the most accessible position **(see illustration)**.
5   Tape the bearing caps to the spider to prevent the caps from coming off during removal.
6   Lower the rear of the driveshaft and then slide the front out of the transmission.
7   To prevent loss of fluid and protect against contamination while the driveshaft is out, wrap a plastic bag over the transmission housing and hold it in place with a rubber band.

Installation

8   Remove the plastic bag on the transmission and wipe the area clean. Inspect the oil seal carefully. Procedures for replacement of this seal can be found in Chapter 7.
9   Slide the front of the driveshaft into the transmission.
10   Raise the rear of the driveshaft into position, checking to be sure that the marks are in alignment. If not, turn the rear wheels to match the pinion flange and the driveshaft.
11   Remove the tape securing the bearing caps and install the straps and bolts. Tighten the bolts to the specified torque.

10   Universal joints — replacement

Note: *A press or large vise will be required for this procedure. It may be advisable to take the driveshaft to a local dealer or machine shop where the universal joints can be replaced for you, normally at a reasonable charge.*

Cleveland type joint

Refer to illustrations 10.1 and 10.2

1   Clean away all dirt from the ends of the bearings on the yokes so that the snap-rings can be removed using a pair of snap-ring pliers. If the snap-rings are very tight, tap the end of the bearing cup (inside the snap-ring) to relieve the pressure **(see illustration)**.
2   Support the trunnion yoke on a short piece of tube or the open end of a socket, then use a suitably sized socket to press out the cross (trunnion) by means of a vise **(see illustration)**.
3   Press the trunnion through as far as possible, then grip the bearing cup in the jaws of a vise to fully remove it. Repeat the procedure for the remaining cups.
4   On some models, the slip yoke at the transmission end has a vent hole. When dismantling, ensure that this vent hole is not blocked.
5   A universal joint repair kit will contain a new trunnion, seals, bearings, cups and snap-rings. Some replacement universal joints are equipped with a grease fitting. Be sure it is offset in the proper direction (toward the driveshaft).

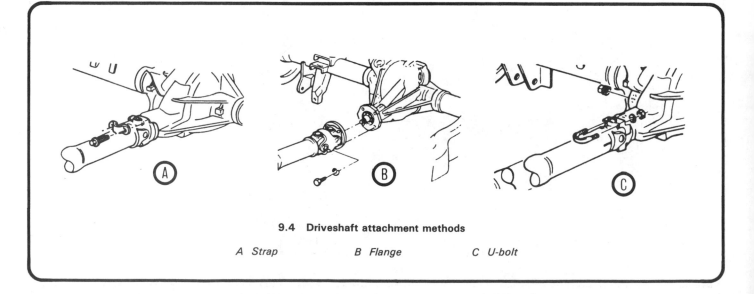

9.4   Driveshaft attachment methods

A Strap   B Flange   C U-bolt

6   Commence reassembly by packing each of the reservoirs at the trunnion ends with lubricant.

7   Make sure that the dust seals are correctly located on the trunnion, so that the cavities in the seals are nearer the trunnion.

8   Using a vise, press one bearing cup into the yoke so that it enters not more than 1/4-inch.

9   Using a thick grease, stick each of the needle rollers inside the cup.

10   Insert the trunnion into the partially fitted bearing cup, taking care not to displace the needle rollers.

11   Stick the needle bearings into the opposite cup and then, holding the trunnion in correct alignment, press both cups fully home in the jaws of the vise.

12   Install the new snap-rings.

13   Repeat the operations on the other two bearing cups.

14   In extreme cases of wear or neglect, it is possible that the bearing cup housings in the yoke will have worn so much that the cups are a loose fit in the yokes. In such cases, replace the complete driveshaft assembly.

15   Always check the wear in the sliding sleeve splines and replace the sleeve if worn.

Saginaw type joint
Refer to illustrations 10.16 and 10.18

16   Where a Saginaw joint is to be disassembled, the procedure given in the previous Section for pressing out the bearing cup is applicable. If the joint has been previously repaired it will be necessary to remove the snap-rings inboard of the yokes; if this is to be the first time that servicing has been carried out, there are no snap-rings to remove, but the pressing operation in the vise will shear the plastic molding material **(see illustration)**.

17   Having removed the cross (trunnion), remove the remains of the plastic material from the yoke. Use a small punch to remove the material from the injection holes.

18   Reassembly is similar to that given for the Cleveland type joint except that the snap-rings are installed inside the yoke. If difficulty is encountered, strike the yoke firmly with a hammer to assist in seating **(see illustration)**.

Double cardan type constant velocity joint
Refer to illustrations 10.19 and 10.21

19   An inspection kit containing two bearing cups and two retainers is available to permit the joint to be dismantled to the stage where the

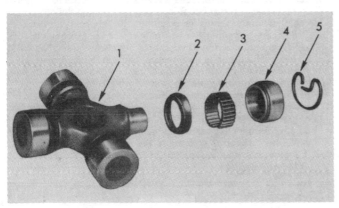

10.1   Cleveland type universal joint repair kit

1 Trunnion	4 Cap
2 Seal	5 Snap-ring
3 Bearings	

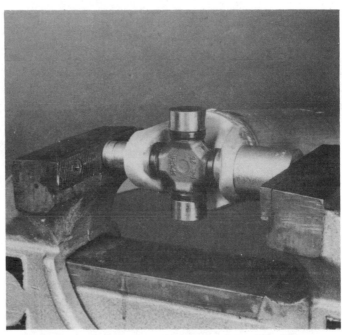

10.2   To press the universal joint out of the driveshaft, set it up in a vise with the small socket (on the left) pushing the joint and bearing cap into the large socket

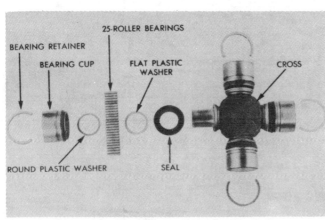

10.16   Saginaw type universal joint repair kit

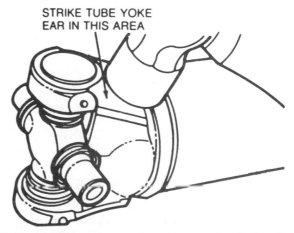

STRIKE TUBE YOKE EAR IN THIS AREA

10.18   To relieve stress produced by pressing the bearing caps into the yokes, strike the yoke in the area shown

8

joint can be inspected. Before any dismantling is started, mark the flange yoke and coupling yoke so that they can be reassembled in the same relative position **(see illustration)**.

20   Dismantle the joint by removing the bearing cups in a similar way to that described in the preceding Section, according to type.

21   Disengage the flange yoike and trunnion from the centering ball. Pry the seal from the ball socket and remove the washers, spings and three ball seats **(see illustration)**.

22   Clean the ball seat insert bushing and inspect for wear. If evident, the flange yoke and trunnion assembly must be replaced.

23   Clean the seal, ball seats, spring and washers and inspect for wear. If excessive wear is evident or parts are broken, a replacement service kit must be used.

24   Remove all plastic material from the groove of the coupling yoke (if this type of joint is used).

25   Inspect the centering ball; if damaged, it must be replaced.

26   Withdraw the centering ball from the stud using a suitable extractor. Provided that the ball is not to be re-used, it will not matter if it is damaged.

27   Press a new ball onto the stud until it seats firmly on the stud shoulder. It is extremely important that no damage to the ball occurs during this stage, and suitable protection must be given to it.

28   Using the grease provided in the repair kit, lubricate all the parts and insert them into the ball seat cavity in the following order: spring, washer (small OD), three ball seats (largest opening outwards to receive the ball), washer (large OD) and the seal.

29   Lubricate the seal lips and press it (lip inwards) into the cavity. Fill the cavity with the grease provided.

30   Install the flange yoke to the centering ball, ensuring that the alignment marks are correctly positioned.

31   Install the trunnion caps as described previously for the Cleveland or Saginaw types.

***

11   Rear axle — description and check

***

Refer to illustration 11.3

Description

1   The rear axle assembly is a hypoid, semi-floating type (the center-line of the pinion gear is below the centerline of the ring gear). The differential carrier is a casting with a pressed steel cover, and the axle tubes are made of steel, pressed and welded into the carrier.

2   An optional locking rear axle is also available. This differential allows for normal differential operation until one wheel loses traction. The unit utilizes multi-disc clutch packs and a speed sensitive engagement mechanism which locks both axleshafts together, applying equal rotational power to both wheels.

3   In order to undertake certain operations, particularly replacement of the axleshafts, it's important to know the axle identification number. It's located on the front face of the right side axle tube. The third letter of the code identifies the manufacturer of the axle. This is important, as axle design varies slightly among manufacturers. Manufacturer's code letter B or O indicates that the wheel bearings are pressed onto the axleshafts, whereas all other lettered axles have bearings pressed into the axle tubes, and the axleshafts are retained with C-locks **(see illustration)**.

Check

4   Many times a fault is suspected in the rear axle area when, in fact, the problem lies elsewhere. For this reason, a thorough check should be performed before assuming a rear axle problem.

5   The following noises are those commonly associated with rear axle diagnosis procedures:

a)   Road noise is often mistaken for mechanical faults. Driving the vehicle on different surfaces will show whether the road surface is the cause of the noise. Road noise will remain the same if the vehicle is under power or coasting.

b)   Tire noise is sometimes mistaken for mechanical problems. Tires which are worn or low on pressure are particularly susceptible to emitting vibrations and noises. Tire noise will remain about the same during varying driving situations, where rear axle noise will change during coasting, acceleration, etc.

c)   Engine and transmission noise can be deceiving because it will travel along the driveline. To isolate engine and transmission noises, make a note of the engine speed at which the noise is most pronounced. Stop the vehicle and place the transmission in Neutral and run the engine to the same speed. If the noise is the same, the rear axle is not at fault.

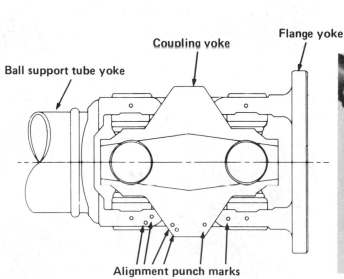

10.19   CV joint alignment marks made before disassembly

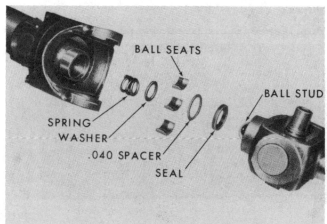

10.21   CV joint centering ball mechanism

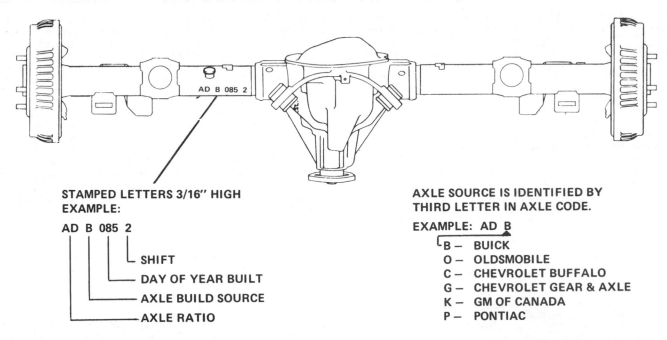

STAMPED LETTERS 3/16'' HIGH
EXAMPLE:

AD B 085 2
|_ SHIFT
|_ DAY OF YEAR BUILT
|_ AXLE BUILD SOURCE
|_ AXLE RATIO

AXLE SOURCE IS IDENTIFIED BY
THIRD LETTER IN AXLE CODE.
EXAMPLE: AD B
▲
B – BUICK
O – OLDSMOBILE
C – CHEVROLET BUFFALO
G – CHEVROLET GEAR & AXLE
K – GM OF CANADA
P – PONTIAC

11.3 Location of the rear axle identification number — early models have only a three-letter code

6   Overhaul and general repair of the rear axle is beyond the scope of the home mechanic due to the many special tools and critical measurements required. Thus, the procedures listed here will involve axleshaft removal and installation, axleshaft oil seal replacement, axleshaft bearing replacement and removal of the entire unit for repair or replacement.

12   Axleshaft — removal and installation (except B and O type axles)

Refer to illustrations 12.3a, 12.3b, 12.4 and 12.5

1   Raise the rear of the vehicle, support it securely and remove the wheel and brake drum (refer to Chapter 9).
2   Remove the cover from the differential carrier and allow the oil to drain into a container.
3   Remove the lock bolt from the differential pinion shaft. Remove the pinion shaft (**see illustrations**).
4   Push the outer (flanged) end of the axleshaft in and remove the C-lock from the inner end of the shaft (**see illustration**).

12.3a   Remove the pinion shaft lock bolt . . .

12.3b   . . . then carefully remove the pinion shaft from the differential carrier (don't turn the wheels or the carrier after the shaft has been removed, or the spider gears may fall out)

12.4   Push the axle flange in, then remove the C-lock from the inner end of the axleshaft

8

5   Withdraw the axleshaft, taking care not to damage the oil seal in the end of the axle housing as the splined end of the axleshaft passes through it **(see illustration)**.
6   Installation is the reverse of removal. Tighten the lock bolt to the specified torque.
7   Always use a new cover gasket and tighten the cover bolts to the specified torque.
8   Refill the axle with the correct quantity and grade of lubricant (Chapter 1).

13   Axleshaft oil seal — replacement (except B and O type axles)

Refer to illustrations 13.2 and 13.3

1   Remove the axleshaft as described in the preceding Section.
2   Pry the old oil seal out of the end of the axle housing, using a large screwdriver or the inner end of the axleshaft itself as a lever **(see illustration)**.
3   Using a large socket as a seal driver, tap the seal into position so that the lips are facing in and the metal face is visible from the end of the axle housing **(see illustration)**. When correctly installed, the face of the oil seal should be flush with the end of the axle housing. Lubricate

the lips of the seal with gear oil.
4   Installation of the axleshaft is described in the preceding Section.

14   Axleshaft bearing — replacement (except B and O type axles)

Refer to illustrations 14.3 and 14.4

1   Remove the axleshaft (refer to Section 12) and the oil seal (refer to Section 13).
2   A bearing puller will be required, or a tool which will engage behind the bearing will have to be fabricated.
3   Attach a slide hammer and pull the bearing from the axle housing **(see illustration)**.
4   Clean out the bearing recess and drive in the new bearing using GM tool no. J8902 and J23765 or equivalent **(see illustration)**. **Caution:** *Failure to use this tool could result in bearing damage.* Lubricate the new bearing with gear lubricant. Make sure that the bearing is tapped into the full depth of its recess and that the numbers on the bearing are visible from the outer end of the housing.
5   Discard the old oil seal and install a new one, then install the axleshaft.

12.5   Carefully pull the axleshaft from the housing to avoid damaging the seal

13.2   The axleshaft oil seal can sometimes be pried out with the end of the axle

13.3   A large socket can be used to install the new seal squarely

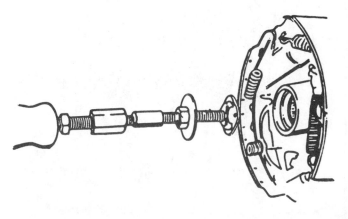

14.3   A slide hammer with a special bearing puller attachment is required to pull the axleshaft bearing from the axle housing

15   Axleshaft — removal, overhaul and installation (B and O type)

Refer to illustrations 15.3a, 15.3b, 15.4, and 15.6

1   The usual reason for axleshaft removal on this type of axle is that the shaft end play has become excessive. To check this, remove the wheel and brake drum (see Chapter 9) and attach a dial gauge with its stylus against the axleshaft end flange. If the shaft is then moved in and out by hand, the end play should not exceed 0.022-inch. If the end play is excessive, carry out the following operations, as the shaft bearing is probably worn.

2   Unscrew and remove the bolts which attach the axleshaft retainer plate to the brake backing plate.

3   Attach a slide hammer to the wheel mounting studs and withdraw the axleshaft. Do not attempt to pull the axleshaft by hand from the housing, as you will only succeed in pulling the vehicle off the support stands **(see illustrations)**.

4   As the axleshaft is removed, it is possible that the bearing will become separated into three parts. This does not indicate that the bearing is unserviceable. If this happens, remove the two sections left behind from the axle tube **(see illustration)**.

5   With the axleshaft removed, hold it in the jaws of a vise so that the bearing retainer ring rests on the edges of the jaws.

6   Using a hammer and a sharp chisel, nick the retainer in two places. This will have the effect of spreading the retainer so that it will slide

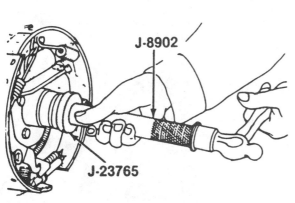

14.4   A special bearing driver is needed to install the axleshaft bearing without damaging it

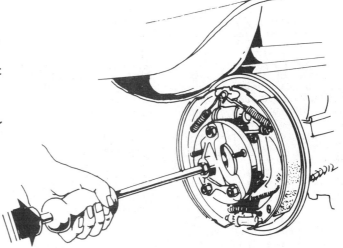

15.3a   Using a slide hammer to remove a B and O type axleshaft

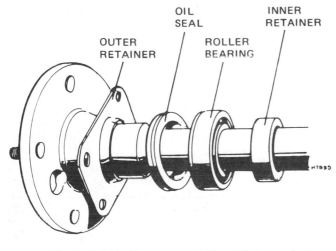

15.3b   Axleshaft components (B and O type axles)

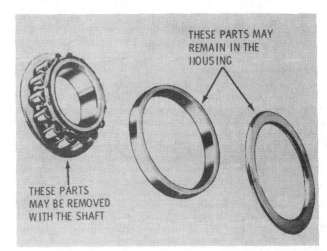

15.4   B and O type axle bearing components

8

off the shaft. Do not damage the shaft in the process and never attempt to cut the retainer away with a torch, as the temper of the shaft will be ruined **(see illustration)**.

7   Using a suitable press or extractor, withdraw the bearing from the axleshaft.

8   Remove and discard the oil seal.

9   When installing the new bearing, make sure that the retainer plate and the seal are installed to the shaft first. Press on the bearing and the retaining ring tight up against it.

10 Before installing the axleshaft assembly, smear wheel bearing grease onto the bearing end and in the bearing recess in the axle housing tube.

11 Apply rear axle oil to the axleshaft splines.

12 Hold the axleshaft horizontal and insert it into the axle housing. Feel when the shaft splines have picked up those in the differential side gears and then push the shaft fully into position, using a soft faced hammer on the end flange as necessary.

13 Bolt the retainer plate to the brake backplate, install the brake drum and wheel and lower the vehicle to the ground.

16 Rear axle assembly — removal and installation

1   Raise the rear of the vehicle and support it securely on stands placed under the body frame rails.

2   Position an adjustable floor jack under the differential housing and just take up the weight. Do not raise the jack sufficiently to take the weight of the vehicle from the frame stands.

3   Disconnect the lower shock absorber mountings (Chapter 10).

4   Remove the driveshaft.

5   Remove the rear wheels and brake drums. See Chapter 9 for information if difficulty is experienced in removing the brake drums.

6   Disconnect the hydraulic brake lines from their clips on the axle housing.

7   Unbolt and remove the differential cover, allowing the fluid to drain into a container.

8   Remove the axleshafts as described in Section 12 or Section 15 of this Chapter, depending on type.

9   Depending on axle type, unbolt the brake backing plates, carefully withdraw the brake assemblies and wire them up to the frame without bending the hydraulic lines or disconnecting them.

10 Remove the leaf springs or coil springs as described in Chapter 10.

11 Withdraw the axle assembly from under the vehicle.

12 Installation is a reversal of removal, but tighten all suspension bolts and nuts to the specified torque (refer to Chapters 9 and 10). Fill the axle assembly with the proper grade and amount of lubricant (see Specifications, Chapter 1).

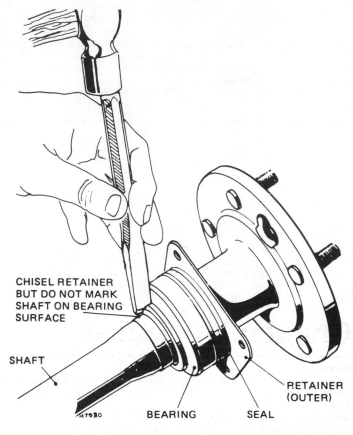

CHISEL RETAINER BUT DO NOT MARK SHAFT ON BEARING SURFACE

SHAFT

RETAINER (OUTER)

H7980   BEARING   SEAL

15.6 Spreading the bearing retaining ring (B and O type)

Chapter 9 Brakes

Contents

Specifications

Brake fluid type .... See Chapter 1

Disc brakes
Minimum brake pad thickness .... See Chapter 1
Rotor discard thickness .... Refer to minimum thickness casting on rotor
Lateral runout.............................. 0.004 in maximum
Rotor thickness variation (parallelism) .... 0.0005 in
Caliper-to-knuckle clearance .... 0.005 to 0.012 in

Drum brakes
Minimum brake lining thickness .... See Chapter 1
Drum discard thickness .... Refer to minimum thickness casting on drum
Out-of-round .... 0.006 in maximum
Taper................................ 0.003 in maximum

Torque specifications   Ft-lbs
Master cylinder mounting nuts 24
Power booster mounting nuts 24
Caliper mounting bolts 37
Wheel cylinder mounting bolts 13
Brake hose-to-caliper inlet fitting bolt 32
Wheel lug nuts............................ 90 to 100

9

1   General information

The vehicles covered by this manual are equipped with hydraulically operated front and rear brake systems. The front brakes are disc or drum type and the rear brakes are drum type. Both the front and rear brakes are self adjusting. The front disc brakes automatically compensate for pad wear, while the drum brakes incorporate an adjustment mechanism which is activated as the brakes are applied when the vehicle is driven in Reverse.

Hydraulic system

The hydraulic system consists of two separate circuits. The master cylinder has separate reservoirs for the two circuits and in the event of a leak or failure in one hydraulic circuit, the other circuit will remain operative. A visual warning of circuit failure or air in the system is given by a warning light activated by displacement of the piston in the pressure differential switch portion of the combination valve from its normal ''in balance'' position.

Combination valve

A combination valve, located in the engine compartment below the master cylinder, consists of three sections providing the following functions. The metering section limits pressure to the front brakes until a predetermined front input pressure is reached and until the rear brakes are activated. There is no restriction at inlet pressures below three psi, allowing pressure equalization during non-braking periods. The proportioning section proportions outlet pressure to the rear brakes after a predetermined rear input pressure has been reached, preventing early rear wheel lock-up under heavy brake loads. The valve is also designed to assure full pressure to one brake system should the other system fail. The pressure differential warning switch incorporated into the combination valve is designed to continuously compare the front and rear brake pressure from the master cylinder and energize the dash warning light in the event of either a front or rear brake system failure. The design of the switch and valve are such that the switch will stay in the ''warning'' position once a failure has occurred. The only way to turn the light off is to repair the cause of the failure and apply a brake pedal force of 450 psi.

Power brake booster

The power brake booster, utilizing engine manifold vacuum and atmospheric pressure to provide assistance to the hydraulically operated brakes, is mounted on the firewall in the engine compartment.

Parking brake

The parking brake operates the rear brakes only, through cable actuation. It's activated by a pedal mounted on the left side kick panel.

Service

After completing any operation involving disassembly of any part of the brake system, always test drive the vehicle to check for proper braking performance before resuming normal driving. When testing the brakes, perform the tests on a clean, dry flat surface. Conditions other than these can lead to inaccurate test results.

Test the brakes at various speeds with both light and heavy pedal pressure. The vehicle should stop evenly without pulling to one side or the other. Avoid locking the brakes, because this slides the tires and diminishes braking efficiency and control of the vehicle.

Tires, vehicle load and front-end alignment are factors which also affect braking performance.

2   Disc brake pads — replacement

Refer to illustrations 2.5 and 2.6a through 2.6g

Warning: *Disc brake pads must be replaced on both front wheels at the same time — never replace the pads on only one wheel. Also, the dust created by the brake system may contain asbestos, which is harmful to your health. Never blow it out with compressed air and don't inhale any of it. An approved filtering mask should be worn when working on the brakes. Do not, under any circumstances, use petroleum-based solvents to clean brake parts. Use brake cleaner or denatured alcohol only!*

Note: *When servicing the disc brakes, use only high quality, nationally recognized name-brand pads.*

1   Remove the cover from the brake fluid reservoir.
2   Loosen the wheel lug nuts, raise the front of the vehicle and support it securely on jackstands.
3   Remove the front wheels. Work on one brake assembly at a time, using the assembled brake for reference if necessary.
4   Inspect the brake disc carefully as outlined in Section 4. If machining is necessary, follow the information in that Section to remove the disc, at which time the pads can be removed from the calipers as well.
5   Push the piston back into the bore to provide room for the new brake pads. A C-clamp can be used to accomplish this **(see illustration)**. As the piston is depressed to the bottom of the caliper bore, the fluid in the master cylinder will rise. Make sure it doesn't overflow. If necessary, siphon off some of the fluid.
6   Follow the accompanying illustrations, beginning with 2.6a, for the actual pad replacement procedure. Be sure to stay in order and read the caption under each illustration.
7   When reinstalling the caliper, be sure to tighten the mounting bolts to the specified torque. After the job has been completed, firmly depress the brake pedal a few times to bring the pads into contact with the disc.

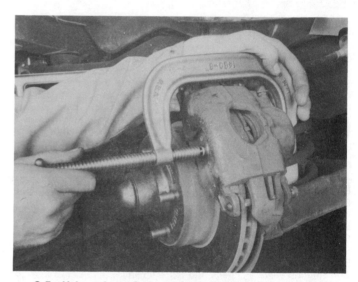

2.5   Using a large C-clamp, push the piston back into the caliper bore — note that one end of the clamp is on the flat area near the brake hose fitting and the other end (screw end) is pressing against the outer brake pad

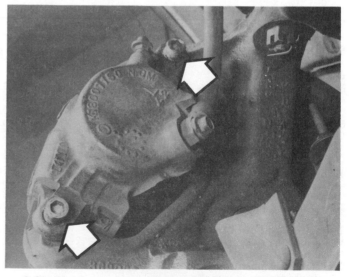

2.6a   Remove the two caliper-to-steering knuckle mounting bolts (arrows) (this will require the use of an Allen head or Torx head socket wrench)

2.6b   Slide the caliper up and off the rotor

2.6c   Pull the inner pad straight out, disengaging the retainer spring from the caliper piston

2.6d   Transfer the retainer spring from the old inner pad to the new one — hook the end of the spring in the hole at the top of the pad, then insert the two prongs of the spring into the slot on the pad backing plate

2.6e   Lubricate the caliper mounting ears with multi-purpose grease

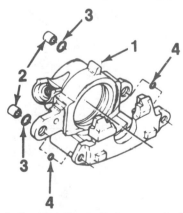

2.6f   Push the mounting bolt sleeves out of the bores, remove the old bushings and install the new ones supplied with the brake pads

1 Caliper   3 Bushings
2 Sleeves   4 Bushings

2.6g   Slide the caliper assembly over the rotor, install the mounting bolts, then insert a screwdriver between the rotor and outer brake pad, pry up, then strike the pad ears with a hammer to eliminate all play between the pad and caliper

9

3   Disc brake caliper — removal, overhaul and installation

Warning: *Dust created by the brake system may contain asbestos, which is harmful to your health. Never blow it out with compressed air and don't inhale any of it. An approved filtering mask should be worn when working on the brakes. Do not, under any circumstances, use petroleum-based solvents to clean brake parts. Use brake cleaner or denatured alcohol only!*

Note: *If an overhaul is indicated (usually because of fluid leakage) explore all options before beginning the job. New and factory rebuilt calipers are available on an exchange basis, which makes this job quite easy. If it's decided to rebuild the calipers, make sure a rebuild kit is available before proceeding. Always rebuild the calipers in pairs — never rebuild just one of them.*

Removal

Refer to illustration 3.4

1   Remove the cover from the brake fluid reservoir, siphon off two-thirds of the fluid into a container and discard it.
2   Loosen the wheel lug nuts, raise the front of the vehicle and support it securely on jackstands. Remove the front wheels.
3   Bottom the piston in the caliper bore **(see illustration 2.5)**.
4   **Note:** *Do not remove the brake hose from the caliper if you are*

only removing the caliper. Remove the brake hose inlet fitting bolt and detach the hose **(see illustration)**. On models with a hydraulic fitting (tube nut), use a flare nut wrench. Have a rag handy to catch spilled fluid and wrap a plastic bag tightly around the end of the hose to prevent fluid loss and contamination.
5   Remove the two mounting bolts and detach the caliper from the vehicle (refer to Section 2 if necessary).

Overhaul

Refer to illustrations 3.8, 3.9, 3.10, 3.11, 3.15, 3.16, 3.17 and 3.18

6   Refer to Section 2 and remove the brake pads from the caliper.
7   Clean the exterior of the caliper with brake cleaner or denatured alcohol. **Never use gasoline, kerosene or petroleum-based cleaning solvents.** Place the caliper on a clean workbench.
8   Position a wooden block or several shop rags in the caliper as a cushion, then use compressed air to remove the piston from the caliper **(see illustration)**. Use only enough air pressure to ease the piston out of the bore. If the piston is blown out, even with the cushion in place, it may be damaged. **Warning:** *Never place your fingers in front of the piston in an attempt to catch or protect it when applying compressed air, as serious injury could occur.*
9   Carefully pry the dust boot out of the caliper bore **(see illustration)**.
10   Using a wood or plastic tool, remove the piston seal from the groove in the caliper bore **(see illustration)**. Metal tools may cause bore damage.

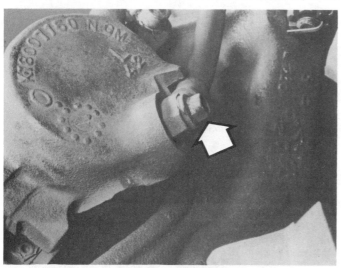

3.4   It's easier to remove the barke hose inlet fitting bolt (arrow) before removing the caliper mounting bolts

3.8   With the caliper padded to catch the piston, use compressed air to force the piston out of the bore — make sure your hands or fingers are not between the piston and caliper!

3.9   When prying the dust boot out of the caliper, be very careful not to scratch the bore surface

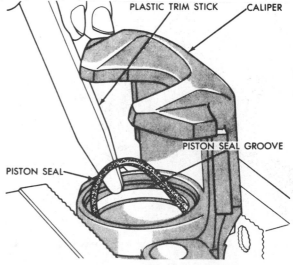

3.10   Remove the piston seal with a wooden or plastic tool to avoid scratching the bore and seal groove

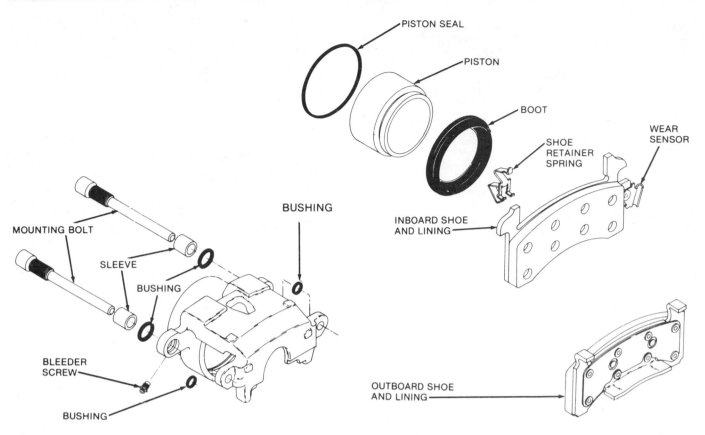

3.11 Exploded view of the disc brake caliper components

11 Remove the caliper bleeder screw, then remove and discard the sleeves and bushings from the caliper ears. Discard all rubber parts **(see illustration)**.

12 Clean the remaining parts with brake system cleaner or denatured alcohol, then blow them dry with compressed air.

13 Carefully examine the piston for nicks and burrs and loss of plating. If surface defects are present, the parts must be replaced.

14 Check the caliper bore in a similar way. Light polishing with crocus cloth is permissible to remove light corrosion and stains. Discard the mounting bolts if they're corroded or damaged.

15 When assembling, lubricate the piston bores and seal with clean brake fluid. Position the seal in the caliper bore groove **(see illustration)**.

16 Lubricate the piston with clean brake fluid, then install a new boot in the piston groove with the fold toward the open end of the piston **(see illustration)**.

17 Insert the piston squarely into the caliper bore, then apply force

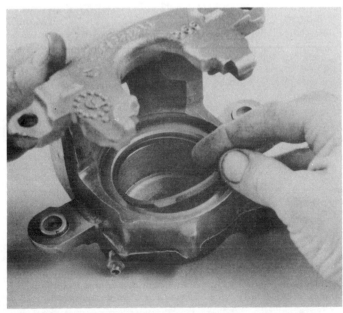

3.15 Position the seal in the caliper bore groove, making sure it isn't twisted

3.16 Install the new dust boot in the piston groove (note that the folds are at the open end of the piston)

9

3.17　Install the piston squarely in the caliper bore then bottom it by pushing down evenly

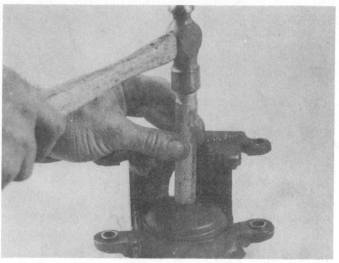

3.18　Seat the boot in the counterbore (a seal driver is being used in this photo, but a drift punch will work if care is exercised)

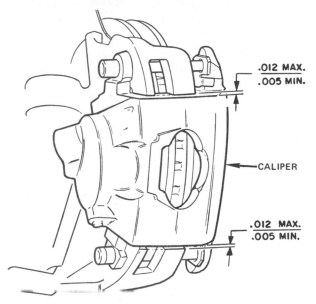

.012 MAX.
.005 MIN.

CALIPER

.012 MAX.
.005 MIN.

3.23　The dimension between each caliper stop and the caliper should be 0.005- to 0.012-inch

4.3　Check the rotor for deep grooves and score marks (be sure to inspect both sides of the rotor)

to bottom it (see illustration).

18　Position the dust boot in the caliper counterbore, then use a drift to drive it into position (see illustration). Make sure the boot is recessed evenly below the caliper face.

19　Install the bleeder screw.

20　Install new bushings in the mounting bolt holes and fill the area between the bushings with the silicone grease supplied in the rebuild kit. Push the sleeves into the mounting bolt holes.

Installation

Refer to illustration 3.23

21　Inspect the mounting bolts for excessive corrosion.

22　Place the caliper in position over the rotor and mounting bracket, install the bolts and tighten them to the specified torque.

23　Check to make sure the total clearance between the caliper and the bracket stops is between 0.005- and 0.012-inch (see illustration).

24　Install the brake hose and inlet fitting bolt, using new copper washers, then tighten the bolt to the specified torque.

25　If the line was disconnected, be sure to bleed the brakes (Section 10).

26　Install the wheels and lower the vehicle.

27　After the job has been completed, firmly depress the brake pedal a few times to bring the pads into contact with the disc.

28　Check brake operation before driving the vehicle in traffic.

4　Brake disc — inspection, removal and installation

Inspection

Refer to illustrations 4.3, 4.4a, 4.4b and 4.5

1　Loosen the wheel lug nuts, raise the vehicle and support it securely on jackstands. Remove the wheel.

2　Remove the brake caliper as outlined in Section 3. Remove caliper mounting bracket on models so equipped. It's not necessary to disconnect the brake hose. After removing the caliper bolts, suspend the caliper out of the way with a piece of wire. Don't let the caliper hang by the hose and don't stretch or twist the hose.

3　Visually check the disc surface for score marks and other damage. Light scratches and shallow grooves are normal after use and may not always be detrimental to brake operation, but deep score marks — over 0.015-inch (0.38 mm) — require disc removal and refinishing by an automotive machine shop. Be sure to check both sides of the disc (see illustration). If pulsating has been noticed during application of the brakes, suspect disc runout. Be sure to check the wheel bearings to make sure they're properly adjusted.

4　To check disc runout, place a dial indicator at a point about 1/2-inch from the outer edge of the disc (see illustration). Set the indicator to

**4.4a Check rotor runout with a dial indicator — if the
reading exceeds the maximum allowable runout, the rotor
will have to be resurfaced or replaced**

**4.4b Using a swirling motion, remove the glaze from the
rotor with medium-grit emery cloth**

zero and turn the disc. The indicator reading should not exceed the specified allowable runout limit. If it does, the disc should be refinished by an automotive machine shop. **Note:** *Professionals recommend resurfacing of brake discs regardless of the dial indicator reading (to produce a smooth, flat surface that will eliminate brake pedal pulsations and other undesirable symptoms related to questionable discs). At the very least, if you elect not to have the discs resurfaced, deglaze them with medium-grit emery cloth (use a swirling motion to ensure a non-directional finish)* **(see illustration).**

5   The disc must not be machined to a thickness less than the specified minimum refinish thickness. The minimum wear (or discard) thickness is cast into the inside of the disc. The disc thickness can be checked with a micrometer **(see illustration).**

Removal

6   Refer to Chapter 1, *Front wheel bearing check, repack and adjustment* for the hub/disc removal procedure. Remove the two lug nuts

that were installed to hold the disc in place and pull the disc from the hub.

Installation

7   Install the disc and hub assembly and adjust the wheel bearing (Chapter 1).
8   Install the caliper and brake pad assembly over the disc and position it on the steering knuckle (refer to Section 3 for the caliper installation procedure, if necessary). Tighten the caliper bolts to the specified torque.
9   Install the wheel, then lower the vehicle to the ground. Depress the brake pedal a few times to bring the brake pads into contact with the disc. Bleeding of the system will not be necessary unless the brake hose was disconnected from the caliper. Check the operation of the brakes carefully before placing the vehicle into normal service.

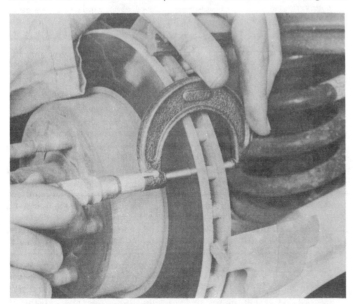

**4.5 A micrometer is used to measure rotor thickness —
this can be done on the vehicle (as shown) or on the bench
(the minimum thickness is cast into the inside of the rotor)**

---

5   Drum brake shoes (front and rear) — replacement

Refer to illustrations 5.4a through 5.4v

Warning: *Drum brake shoes must be replaced on both wheels at the same time — never replace the shoes on only one wheel. Also, the dust created by the brake system may contain asbestos, which is harmful to your health. Never blow it out with compressed air and don't inhale any of it. An approved filtering mask should be worn when working on the brakes. Do not, under any circumstances, use petroleum-based solvents to clean brake parts. Use brake cleaner or denatured alcohol only!*

Caution: *Whenever the brake shoes are replaced, the retractor and hold-down springs should also be replaced. Due to the continuous heating/cooling cycle that the springs are subjected to, they lose their tension over a period of time and may allow the shoes to drag on the drum and wear at a much faster rate than normal. When replacing the brake shoes, use only high quality nationally recognized brand-name parts.*

1   Loosen the wheel lug nuts, raise the rear of the vehicle and support it securely on jackstands. Block the front wheels to keep the vehicle from rolling.
2   Release the parking brake.
3   Remove the wheel. **Note:** *All four rear brake shoes must be replaced at the same time, but to avoid mixing up parts, work on only one brake assembly at a time.*

9

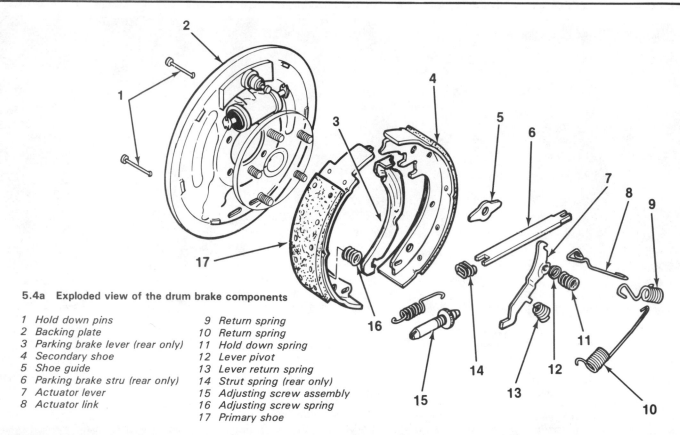

5.4a Exploded view of the drum brake components

1 Hold down pins	9 Return spring
2 Backing plate	10 Return spring
3 Parking brake lever (rear only)	11 Hold down spring
4 Secondary shoe	12 Lever pivot
5 Shoe guide	13 Lever return spring
6 Parking brake stru (rear only)	14 Strut spring (rear only)
7 Actuator lever	15 Adjusting screw assembly
8 Actuator link	16 Adjusting screw spring
	17 Primary shoe

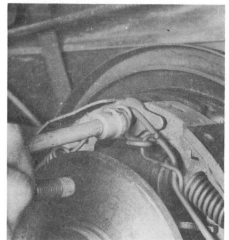

5.4b Remove the shoe return springs — the spring tool shown here is available at most auto parts stores and makes this job much easier and safer

5.4c Pull the bottom of the actuator lever toward the secondary brake shoe, compressing the lever return spring — the actuator link can now be removed

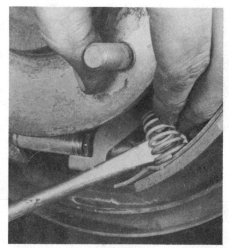

5.4d Pry the actuator lever spring out with a large screwdriver

4   Follow the accompanying photos (**illustrations 5.4a through 5.4v**) for the inspection and replacement of the brake shoes. Be sure to stay in order and read the caption under each illustration. **Note:** *If the brake drum cannot be easily pulled off the axle and shoe assembly, make sure that the parking brake is completely released, then apply some penetrating oil at the hub-to-drum joint. Allow the oil to soak in and try to pull the drum off. If the drum still cannot be pulled off, the brake shoes will have to be retracted. This is accomplished by first removing the plug from the backing plate. With the plug removed, pull the lever off the adjusting star wheel with one small screwdriver while turning the adjusting wheel with another small screwdriver, moving the shoes away from the drum. The drum should now come off.*

5   Before reinstalling the drum it should be checked for cracks, score marks, deep scratches and hard spots, which will appear as small dis-colored areas. If the hard spots cannot be removed with fine emery cloth or if any of the other conditions listed above exist, the drum must be taken to an automotive machine shop to have it turned. **Note:** *Pro-fessionals recommend resurfacing the drums whenever a brake job is done. Resurfacing will eliminate the possibility of out-of-round drums. If the drums are worn so much that they can't be resurfaced without exceeding the maximum allowable diameter (stamped into the drum), then new ones will be required. At the very least, if you elect not to have the drums resurfaced, remove the glazing from the surface with medium-grit emery cloth using a swirling motion.*

6   Install the brake drum on the axle flange.

7   Mount the wheel, install the lug nuts, then lower the vehicle.

8   Make a number of forward and reverse stops to adjust the brakes until satisfactory pedal action is obtained.

9   Check brake operation before driving the vehicle in traffic.

5.4e Slide the parking brake strut out from between the axle flange and primary shoe (rear drum brakes only)

5.4f Remove the hold-down springs and pins — the hold-down spring tool shown here is available at most auto parts stores

5.4g Remove the actuator lever and pivot — be careful not to let the pivot fall out of the lever

5.4h Spread the top of the shoes apart and slide the assembly around the axle

5.4i Unhook the parking brake lever from the secondary shoe (rear drum brake only)

5.4j Spread the bottom of the shoes apart and remove the adjusting screw assembly

5.4k Clean the adjusting screw with solvent, dry it off and lubricate the threads and end with multi-purpose grease, then reinstall the adjusting screw assembly between the new brake shoes

5.4l Lubricate the shoe contact points on the backing plate with high-temperature brake grease

5.4m Insert the parking brake lever into the opening in the secondary brake shoe (rear drum brake only)

9

5.4n Spread the shoes apart and slide them into position on the backing plate

5.4o Install the hold-down pin and spring through the backing plate and primary shoe

5.4p Insert the lever pivot into the actuator lever, place the lever over the secondary shoe hold-down pin and install the hold-down spring

5.4q Guide the parking brake strut behind the axle flange and engage the rear end of it in the slot on the parking brake lever — spread the shoes enough to allow the other end to seat against the primary shoe (rear drum brake only)

5.4r Place the shoe guide over the anchor pin

5.4s Hook the lower end of the actuator link to the actuator lever, then loop the top end over the anchor pin

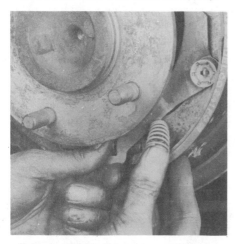

5.4t Install the lever return spring over the tab on the actuator lever, then push the spring up onto the brake shoe

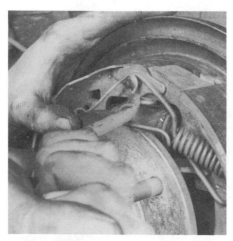

5.4u Install the primary and secondary shoe return springs

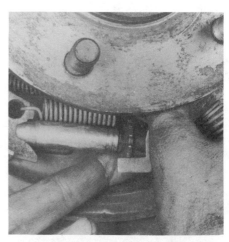

5.4v Pull out on the actuator lever to disengage it from the adjusting screw wheel, turn the wheel to adjust the shoes in or out as necessary — the brake drum should slide over the shoes and turn with a very slight amount of drag

6   Wheel cylinder — removal, overhaul and installation

Note: *If an overhaul is indicated (usually because of fluid leakage or sticky operation) explore all options before beginning the job. New wheel cylinders are available, which makes this job quite easy. If it's decided to rebuild the wheel cylinder, make sure that a rebuild kit is available before proceeding. Never overhaul only one wheel cylinder — always rebuild both of them at the same time.*

Removal

Refer to illustration 6.4

1   Raise the rear of the vehicle and support it securely on jackstands. Block the front wheels to keep the vehicle from rolling.
2   Remove the brake shoe assembly (Section 5).
3   Remove all dirt and foreign material from around the wheel cylinder.
4   Unscrew the brake line fitting **(see illustration)**. Don't pull the brake line away from the wheel cylinder.
5   Remove the wheel cylinder mounting bolts.
6   Detach the wheel cylinder from the brake backing plate and place it on a clean workbench. Immediately plug the brake line to prevent

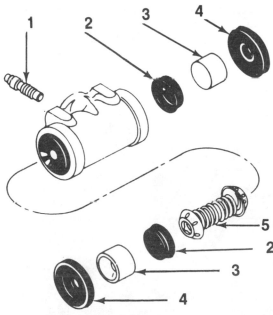

6.4   Completely loosen the brake line fitting (A) then remove the two wheel cylinder mounting bolts (B)

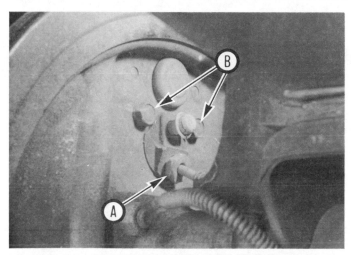

6.7   Exploded view of the wheel cylinder components

1 Bleeder valve	4 Boot
2 Seal	5 Spring assembly
3 Piston	

fluid loss and contamination. **Note:** *If the brake shoe linings are contaminated with brake fluid, install new brake shoes.*

Overhaul

Refer to illustration 6.7

7   Remove the bleeder screw, cups, pistons, boots and spring assembly from the wheel cylinder body **(see illustration)**.
8   Clean the wheel cylinder with brake fluid, denatured alcohol or brake system cleaner. **Warning:** *Do not, under any circumstances, use petroleum based solvents to clean brake parts!*
9   Use compressed air to remove excess fluid from the wheel cylinder and to blow out the passages.
10   Check the cylinder bore for corrosion and score marks. Crocus cloth can be used to remove light corrosion and stains, but the cylinder must be replaced with a new one if the defects cannot be removed easily, or if the bore is scored.
11   Lubricate the new cups with brake fluid.
12   Assemble the wheel cylinder components. Make sure the cup lips face in **(see illustration)**.

Installation

13   Place the wheel cylinder in position and install the bolts.
14   Connect the brake line and tighten the fitting. Install the brake shoe assembly.
15   Bleed the brakes (Section 10).
16   Check brake operation before driving the vehicle in traffic.

7   Master cylinder — removal, overhaul and installation

Removal

Refer to illustrations 7.2, 7.5 and 7.6

Warning: *Failure to fully depressurize the powermaster unit before performing service operations could result in personal injury and damage to painted surfaces. The use of rubber hoses other than those furnished specifically for the powermaster may lead to functional problems requiring major overhaul. To depressurize the powermaster unit, make sure the ignition switch is Off, and apply and release the brake pedal a minimum of ten times, using approximately 50 pounds of force on the pedal.*

Note: *Before deciding to overhaul the master cylinder, investigate the availability and cost of a new or factory rebuilt unit and also the availability of a rebuild kit.*

1   Place rags under the brake line fittings and prepare caps or plastic bags to cover the ends of the lines once they are disconnected. **Caution:** *Brake fluid will damage paint. Cover all body parts and be careful not to spill fluid during this procedure.*
2   Loosen the tube nuts at the ends of the brake lines where they enter the master cylinder. To prevent rounding off the flats on these nuts, a flare-nut wrench, which wraps around the nut, should be used **(see illustration)**.

7.2   Disconnect the brake lines from the master cylinder — a flare-nut wrench should be used

9

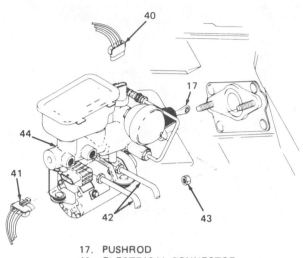

17. PUSHROD
40. ELECTRICAL CONNECTOR
41. ELECTRICAL CONNECTOR
42. BRAKE PIPE
43. NUT
44. POWERMASTER UNIT

7.5   Powermaster unit

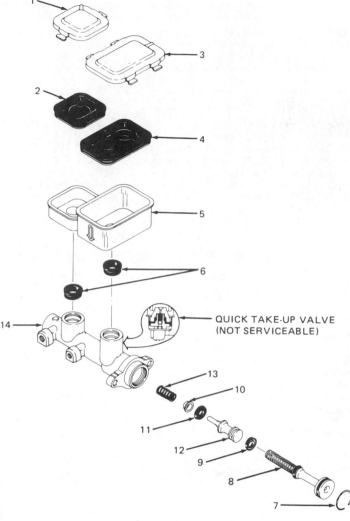

7.9a   Exploded view of a plastic master cylinder assembly

1 *Reservoir cover*	8 *Primary piston assembly*
2 *Reservoir diaphragm*	9 *Secondary seal*
3 *Reservoir cover*	10 *Spring retainer*
4 *Reservoir diaphragm*	11 *Primary seal*
5 *Reservoir*	12 *Secondary piston*
6 *Reservoir grommet*	13 *Spring*
7 *Lock ring*	14 *Cylinder body*

**7.6   Pull the combination valve forward, being careful not
to bend or kink the lines, then slide the master cylinder
off the mounting studs**

3   Pull the brake lines away from the master cylinder slightly and plug
the ends to prevent contamination.
4   On manual and powermaster brakes, disconnect the pushrod at
the brake pedal inside the car.
5   On the powermaster unit, two electrical connectors must be
removed **(see illustration)**.
6   Remove the two master cylinder mounting nuts. If there is a bracket
retaining the combination valve, move it forward slightly, taking care
not to bend the hydraulic lines running to the combination valve, and
remove the master cylinder from the vehicle **(see illustration)**.
7   Remove the reservoir covers and reservoir diaphragms, then discard
any fluid remaining in the reservoir.

Overhaul

Plastic reservoir master cylinder
*Refer to illustrations 7.9a, 7.9b, 7.10, 7.11, 7.16, 7.17a, 7.17b,
7.17c, 7.17d and 7.18*

8   Mount the master cylinder in a vise. Be sure to line the vise jaws
with blocks of wood to prevent damage to the cylinder body.
9   Remove the primary piston lock ring by depressing the piston and
prying the ring out with a screwdriver **(see illustrations)**.

7.9b   Push the primary piston in and remove the lock ring

7.10   Pull the primary piston and spring assembly out of the bore

7.11   To remove the secondary piston, tap the cylinder against a block of wood

10 Remove the primary piston assembly from the cylinder bore (**see illustration**).

11 Remove the secondary piston assembly from the cylinder bore. It may be necessary to remove the master cylinder from the vise and invert it, carefully tapping it against a block of wood to expel the piston (**see illustration**).

12 Pry the reservoir from the cylinder body with a screwdriver. Remove the grommets.

13 Do not attempt to remove the quick take-up valve from the master cylinder body — it's not serviceable.

14 Inspect the cylinder bore for corrosion and damage. If any corrosion or damage is found, replace the master cylinder body with a new one, as abrasives cannot be used on the bore.

15 Lubricate the new reservoir grommets with silicone lubricant and press them into the master cylinder body. Make sure they're properly seated.

16 Lay the reservoir on a hard surface and press the master cylinder body onto the reservoir, using a rocking motion (**see illustration**).

17 Remove the old seals from the secondary piston assembly and install the new secondary seals with the lips facing *away* from each other (**see illustrations**). The lip on the primary seal must face in (**see illustration**).

7.16   Lay the reservoir face down on the bench, with the secondary reservoir propped up on a block of wood — push the master cylinder straight down over the reservoir tubes using a rocking motion

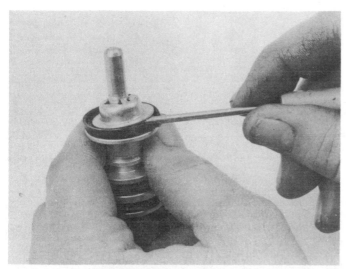

7.17a   Pry the secondary piston spring retainer off with a small screwdriver, then remove the seal

7.17b   Remove the secondary seals from the piston (some only have one seal)

9

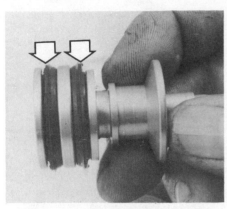

7.17c Install the secondary seals with the lips facing away from each other (on the single seal design, the seal lip should face away from the center of the piston)

7.17d Install a new primary seal on the secondary piston with the seal lip facing in the direction shown

7.18 Install a new spring retainer over the end of the secondary piston and push it into place with a socket

18 Attach the spring retainer to the secondary piston assembly (see illustration).

19 Lubricate the cylinder bore with clean brake fluid and install the spring and secondary piston assembly.

20 Install the primary piston assembly in the cylinder bore, depress it and install the lock ring.

21 Inspect the reservoir cover and diaphragm for cracks and deformation. Replace any damaged parts with new ones and attach the diaphragm to the cover.

22 Note: Whenever the master cylinder is removed, the complete hydraulic system must be bled. The time required to bleed the system can be reduced if the master cylinder is filled with fluid and bench bled (refer to Steps 40 through 44) before the master cylinder is installed on the vehicle.

Cast iron master cylinder

Refer to illustrations 7.25a, 7.25b, 7.26a, 7.26b, 7.29a, 7.29b, 7.30, 7.32a, 7.32b and 7.33

23 Drain all fluid from the master cylinder and place the unit in a vise. Use wood blocks to cushion the jaws of the vise.

24 On manual brakes remove the pushrod retaining ring.

25 Remove the secondary stop bolt from the bottom of the front fluid reservoir (Delco Moraine) or from the base of the master cylinder body

(Bendix) (see illustration).

26 Remove the retaining ring from the groove and take out the primary piston assembly (see illustration). Following the primary piston out of the bore will be the secondary piston, spring and retainer. A piece of bent stiff wire can be used to draw these assemblies out of the cylinder bore (see illustration).

27 Examine the inside surface of the master cylinder and the secondary piston. If there is evidence of scoring or 'bright' wear areas, the entire master cylinder should be replaced with a new one.

28 If the components are in good condition, wash in clean hydraulic fluid. Discard all the rubber components and the primary piston. Purchase a rebuild kit which will contain all the necessary parts for the overhaul.

29 Inspect the line seats which are located in the master cylinder body where the lines connect. If they appear damaged they should be replaced with new ones, which come in the overhaul kit. They are forced out of the body by threading a screw into the tube and then prying outwards (see illustration). The new ones are forced into place using a spare brake line nut (see illustration). All parts necessary for this should be included in the rebuild kit.

30 Place the new secondary seals in the grooves of the secondary piston (see illustration).

31 Assemble the primary seals and seal protector over the end of the secondary piston.

32 Lubricate the cylinder bore and secondary piston with clean brake

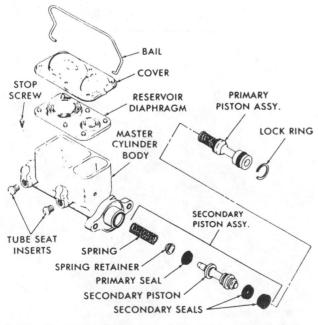

7.25a Typical exploded view of a cast iron master cylinder

BAIL
COVER
STOP SCREW
RESERVOIR DIAPHRAGM
PRIMARY PISTON ASSY.
LOCK RING
MASTER CYLINDER BODY
SECONDARY PISTON ASSY.
TUBE SEAT INSERTS
SPRING
SPRING RETAINER
PRIMARY SEAL
SECONDARY PISTON
SECONDARY SEALS

7.25b Removing secondary stop bolt

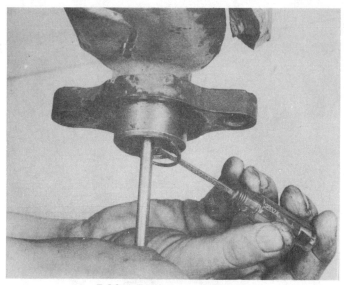

7.26a Removing retaining ring

7.26b Drawing out piston assembly with wire

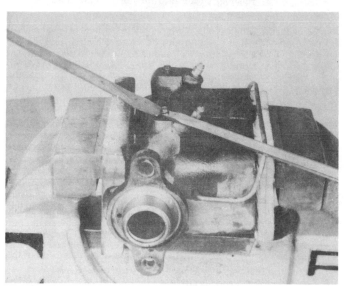

7.29a Removing line seats

7.29b Installing new line seat (note the cone-shaped end is installed facing up)

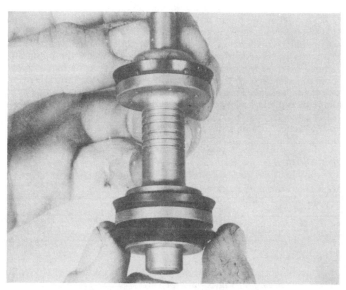

7.30 Seals correctly installed on piston

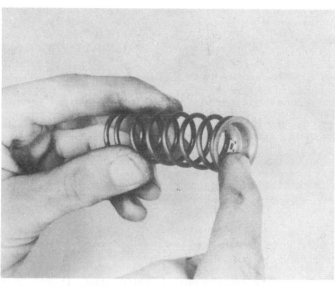

7.32a Assembling retainer and spring

9

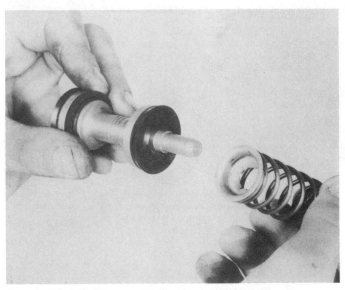

7.32b   Assembling spring and piston

7.33   Pushing piston into master cylinder bore

fluid. Insert the spring retainer into the spring then place the retainer and spring over the end of the secondary piston **(see illustrations)**. The retainer should locate inside the primary seal lips.

33 With the master cylinder vertical, push the secondary piston into the bore to seat its spring **(see illustration)**.

34 Coat the seals of the primary piston with brake fluid and fit it into the cylinder bore. Hold it down while the retaining ring is installed in the cylinder groove.

35 Continue to hold the piston down while the stop screw is installed.

36 Install the reservoir diaphragm into the reservoir cover plate, making sure it is fully collapsed inside the recess lid.

37 **Note:** *Whenever the master cylinder is removed, the complete hydraulic system must be bled. The time required to bleed the system can be reduced if the master cylinder is filled with fluid and bench bled (refer to Step 40 through 44) before the master cylinder is installed on the vehicle.*

Powermaster brakes

38 Because of the special tools, equipment and expertise required to disassemble, overhaul and reassemble this assembly, it is recommended that it be left to a dealer service department or a repair shop. This unit can be removed and installed by a competent do-it-yourselfer

39 **Note:** *Whenever the master cylinder is removed, the complete hydraulic system must be bled. The time required to bleed the system can be reduced if the master cylinder is filled with fluid and bench bled (refer to Steps 40 through 44) before the master cylinder is installed on the vehicle.*

Bench bleeding master cylinder

Note: *On powermaster systems, only the master cylinder portion can be bench bled. See Steps 45 through 50 for powermaster bleed and fill.*

40 Insert threaded plugs of the correct size into the cylinder outlet holes and fill the reservoirs with brake fluid. The master cylinder should be supported in such a manner that brake fluid will not spill during the bench bleeding procedure.

41 Loosen one plug at a time and push the piston assembly into the bore to force air from the master cylinder. To prevent air from being drawn back into the cylinder, the appropriate plug must be replaced before allowing the piston to return to its original position.

42 Stroke the piston three or four times for each outlet to ensure that all air has been expelled.

43 Since high pressure is not involved in the bench bleeding procedure, an alternative to the removal and replacement of the plugs with each stroke of the piston assembly is available. Before pushing in on the piston assembly, remove one of the plugs completely. Before releasing the piston, however, instead of replacing the plug, simply put your finger tightly over the hole to keep air from being drawn back into the master cylinder. Wait several seconds for the brake fluid to be drawn from the reservoir to the piston bore, then repeat the procedure. When you push down on the piston it will force your finger off the hole, allow-

ing the air inside to be expelled. When only brake fluid is being ejected from the hole, replace the plug and go on to the other port.

44 Refill the master cylinder reservoirs and install the diaphragm and cover assembly. **Note:** *The reservoirs should only be filled to the top of the reservoir divider to prevent overflowing when the cover is installed.*

Powermaster bleed and fill

Note: *Bench bleed the master cylinder portion of powermaster before installing the unit on the vehicle.*

45 Fill both sides of the reservoir to the Full marks on the inside of the reservoir. Use only clean, new brake fluid meeting DOT specifications shown on the reservoir cover.

46 Turn the ignition On. With the pump running, the brake fluid level in the booster side of the reservoir should decrease as brake fluid is moved to the accumulator. If the booster side of the reservoir begins to run dry, add brake fluid to just cover the reservoir pump or until the pump stops. **Note:** *The pump must shut off within 20 seconds. Turn ignition Off after 20 seconds have elapsed. Check for leaks or flow back into the reservoir from the booster return port.*

47 Install the reservoir cover assembly to the reservoir.

48 Check that the ignition is Off and apply and release the brake pedal 10 times. Remove the reservoir cover and adjust the booster fluid level to the Full mark.

49 Turn the ignition On. The pump will run and refill the accumulator. Make sure that the pump does not run longer than 20 seconds and that the fluid level remains above the pump sump port in the reservoir.

50 Install the reservoir cover. With the ignition On, apply and release the brake pedal on and off 10 to 15 times, to cycle the pump and remove air from the booster section. Do not allow the pump to run more than 20 seconds for each cycle. Recheck the high and low reservoir fluid levels per Steps 45 and 46. If fluid levels do not stabilize at the high and low levels, if the pump runs more than 20 seconds, or if the pump cycles without brake applications, have your car towed to the nearest dealer or repair shop. Do not drive with powermaster brakes not working properly.

Installation

51 Carefully install the master cylinder by reversing the removal steps, then bleed the brakes (refer to Section 10).

---

8   Combination valve — check and replacement

Check

1   Disconnect the wire from the pressure differential switch. **Note:** *When unplugginging the connector, squeeze the side lock releases, moving the inside tabs away from the switch, then pull up.* Pliers may

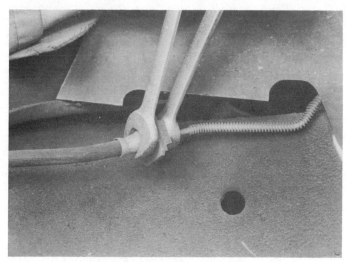

9.2 Place a wrench on the hose fitting to prevent it from turning and disconnect the line with a flare-nut wrench

be used as an aid if necessary.
2   Using a jumper wire, connect the switch wire to a good ground, such as the engine block.
3   Turn the ignition key to the On position. The warning light in the instrument panel should light.
4   If the warning light does not light, either the bulb is burned out or the electrical circuit is defective. Replace the bulb (refer to Chapter 12) or repair the electrical circuit as necessary.
5   When the warning light functions correctly, turn the ignition switch off, disconnect the jumper wire and reconnect the wire to the switch terminal.
6   Make sure the master cylinder reservoirs are full, then attach a bleeder hose to one of the rear wheel bleeder valves and immerse the other end of the hose in a container partially filled with clean brake fluid.
7   Turn the ignition switch On.
8   Open the bleeder valve while a helper applies moderate pressure to the brake pedal. The brake warning light on the instrument panel should light.
9   Close the bleeder valve before the helper releases the brake pedal.
10   Reapply the brake pedal with moderate to heavy pressure. The brake warning light should go out.
11   Attach the bleeder hose to one of the front brake bleeder valves and repeat Steps 8 through 10. The warning light should react in the same manner as in Steps 8 and 10.
12   Turn the ignition switch Off.
13   If the warning light did not come on in Steps 8 and 11, but does light when a jumper is connected to ground, the warning light switch portion of the combination valve is defective and the combination valve must be replaced with a new one since the components of the combination valve are not individually serviceable.

Replacement

14   Place a container under the combination valve and protect all painted surfaces with newspapers or rags.
15   Disconnect the hydraulic lines at the combination valve, then plug the lines to prevent further loss of fluid and to protect the lines from contamination.
16   Disconnect the electrical connector from the pressure differential switch.
17   Remove the bolt holding the valve to the mounting bracket and remove the valve from the vehicle.
18   Installation is the reverse of the removal procedure.
19   Bleed the entire brake system.

---

9   Brake hoses and lines — inspection and replacement

Inspection

1   About every six months, with the vehicle raised and supported securely on jackstands, the rubber hoses which connect the steel brake

lines with the front and rear brake assemblies should be inspected for cracks, chafing of the outer cover, leaks, blisters and other damage. These are important and vulnerable parts of the brake system and inspection should be complete. A light and mirror will be helpful for a thorough check. If a hose exhibits any of the above conditions, replace it with a new one.

Replacement
Front brake hose
Refer to illustration 9.2

2   Using a back-up wrench, disconnect the brake line from the hose fitting, being careful not to bend the frame bracket or brake line **(see illustration)**.
3   Use a pair of pliers to remove the U-clip from the female fitting at the bracket, then detach the hose from the bracket.
4   Unscrew the brake hose from the caliper. At the caliper end of the hose, remove the bolt from the fitting block, then remove the hose and the copper washers on either side of the fitting block.
5   To install the hose, first thread it into the caliper, tightening it securely. When installing the hose, always use new copper washers on either side of the fitting block and lubricate all bolt trreads with clean brake fluid before installation.
6   With the fitting engaged with the caliper locating ledge, attach the hose to the caliper, tightening the fitting bolt to the specified torque.
7   Without twisting the hose, install the female fitting in the hose bracket. It will fit the bracket in only one position.
8   Install the U-clip retaining the female fitting to the frame bracket.
9   Using a back-up wrench, attach the brake line to the hose fitting.
10   When the brake hose installation is complete, there should be no kinks in the hose. Make sure the hose doesn't contact any part of the suspension. Check this by turning the wheels to the extreme left and right positions. If the hose makes contact, remove it and correct the installation as necessary. Bleed the system (Section 10).

Rear brake hose
11   Using a back-up wrench, disconnect the hose at the frame bracket, being careful not to bend the bracket or steel lines.
12   Remove the U-clip with a pair of pliers and separate the female fitting from the bracket.
13   Disconnect the two hydraulic lines at the junction block, then unbolt and remove the hose.
14   Bolt the junction block to the axle housing and connect the lines, tightening them securely. Without twisting the hose, install the female end of the hose in the frame bracket.
15   Install the U-clips retaining the female end to the bracket.
16   Using a back-up wrench, attach the steel line fittings to the female fittings. Again, be careful not to bend the bracket or steel line.
17   Make sure the hose installation did not loosen the frame bracket. Tighten the bracket if necessary.
18   Fill the master cylinder reservoir and bleed the system (refer to Section 10).

Metal brake lines
19   When replacing brake lines be sure to use the correct parts. Don't use copper tubing for any brake system components. Purchase steel brake lines from a dealer or auto parts store.
20   Prefabricated brake line, with the tube ends already flared and fittings installed, is available at auto parts stores and dealers. These lines are also bent to the proper shapes.
21   If prefabricated lines are not available, obtain the recommended steel tubing and fittings to match the line to be replaced. Determine the correct length by measuring the old brake line (a piece of string can usually be used for this) and cut the new tubing to length, allowing about ½-inch extra for flaring the ends.
22   Install the fitting over the cut tubing and flare the ends of the line with a flaring tool. A double-flare is the only acceptable type for automotive brake system applications.
23   If necessary, carefully bend the line to the proper shape. A tube bender is recommended for this **Warning:** *Do not crimp or damage the line.*
24   When installing the new line make sure it's securely supported in the brackets and has plenty of clearance between moving or hot components.
25   After installation, check the master cylinder fluid level and add fluid as necessary. Bleed the brake system as outlined in the next Section and test the brakes carefully before driving the vehicle in traffic.

9

10   Brake system bleeding

Refer to illustration 10.8

Warning: *Wear eye protection when bleeding the brake system. If the fluid comes in contact with your eyes, immediately rinse them with water and seek medical attention.*

Note: *Bleeding the hydraulic system is necessary to remove any air that manages to find its way into the system when it's been opened during removal and installation of a hose, line, caliper or master cylinder.*

1   It will probably be necessary to bleed the system at all four brakes if air has entered the system due to low fluid level, or if the brake lines have been disconnected at the master cylinder.

2   If a brake line was disconnected only at a wheel, then only that caliper or wheel cylinder must be bled.

3   If a brake line is disconnected at a fitting located between the master cylinder and any of the brakes, that part of the system served by the disconnected line must be bled.

4   Remove any residual vacuum from the brake power booster by applying the brake several times with the engine off.

5   Remove the master cylinder reservoir cover and fill the reservoir with brake fluid. Reinstall the cover. **Note:** *Check the fluid level often during the bleeding operation and add fluid as necessary to prevent the fluid level from falling low enough to allow air bubbles into the master cylinder.*

6   Have an assistant on hand, as well as a supply of new brake fluid, a clear container partially filled with clean brake fluid, a length of 3/16-inch plastic, rubber or vinyl tubing to fit over the bleeder valve and a wrench to open and close the bleeder valve.

7   Beginning at the right rear wheel, loosen the bleeder valve slightly, then tighten it to a point where it is snug but can still be loosened quickly and easily.

8   Place one end of the tubing over the bleeder valve and submerge the other end in brake fluid in the container **(see illustration)**.

9   Have the assistant pump the brakes slowly a few times to get pressure in the system, then hold the pedal firmly depressed.

10 While the pedal is held depressed, open the bleeder valve just enough to allow a flow of fluid to leave the valve. Watch for air bubbles to exit the submerged end of the tube. When the fluid flow slows after a couple of seconds, close the valve and have your assistant release the pedal.

11 Repeat Steps 9 and 10 until no more air is seen leaving the tube, then tighten the bleeder valve and proceed to the left rear wheel, the right front wheel and the left front wheel, in that order, and perform the same procedure. Be sure to check the fluid in the master cylinder reservoir frequently.

12 Never use old brake fluid. It contains moisture which will deteriorate the brake system components.

13 Refill the master cylinder with fluid at the end of the operation.

14 Check the operation of the brakes. The pedal should feel solid when depressed, with no sponginess. If necessary, repeat the entire process. **Warning:** *Do not operate the vehicle if you are in doubt about the effectiveness of the brake system.*

11   Parking brake — adjustment

Refer to illustration 11.3

1   The adjustment of the parking brake cable may be necessary whenever the rear brake cables have been disconnected or the parking brake cables have stretched due to age and stress.

2   Depress the parking brake pedal exactly three ratchet clicks and then raise the car for access underneath, supporting it securely on jackstands.

3   Tighten the adjusting nut until the left rear tire can just barely be turned in a rearward motion **(see illustration)**. The tire should be completely locked from moving in a forward rotation.

4   Carefully release the parking brake pedal and check that the tire is able to rotate freely in either direction. It is important that there is no drag on the rear brakes with the pedal released.

11.3   To adjust the parking brake cable, turn the adjusting nut on the equalizer while preventing the cable from turning with a pair of locking pliers clamped to the end of the adjuster rod (later model cable)

12   Parking brake cables — replacement

Rear cables

Refer to illustrations 12.4 and 12.5

1   Loosen the wheel lug nuts, raise the rear of the vehicle and support it securely on jackstands. Remove the wheel(s).

2   Loosen the equalizer nut to slacken the cables, then disconnect the cable to be replaced from the equalizer.

3   Remove the brake drum from the axle flange. Refer to Section 5 if any difficulty is encountered.

4   Remove the brake shoe assembly far enough to disconnect the cable end from the parking brake lever **(see illustration)**.

5   Depress the tangs on the cable housing retainer and push the housing and cable through the backing plate **(see illustration)**.

6   To install the cable, reverse the removal procedure and adjust the cable as described in the preceding Section.

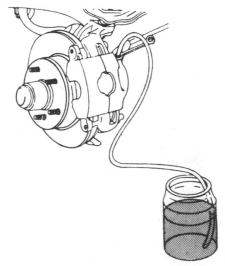

10.8   When bleeding the brakes, a hose is connected to the bleeder valve and then submerged in brake fluid — air will be seen as bubbles in the container and the hose

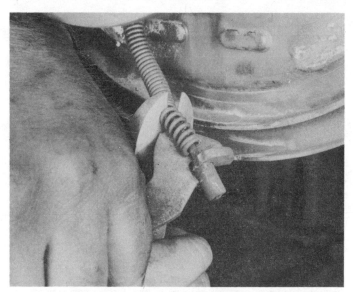

12.4 To disconnect the cable end from the parking brake lever, pull back on the return spring and maneuver the cable out of the slot in the lever

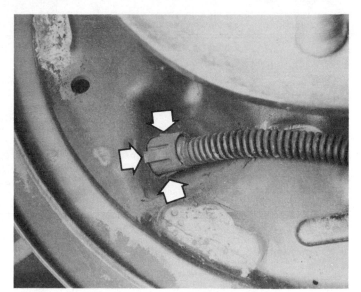

12.5 Depress the retention tangs (arrows) to free the cable and housing from the backing plate

Front cable

Refer to illustration 12.9

7   Raise the vehicle and support it securely on jackstands.
8   Loosen the equalizer assembly to provide slack in the cable.
9   Disconnect the front cable from the cable joiner near the equalizer **(see illustration)**.
10   Disconnect the cable from the pedal assembly.
11   Free the cable from the routing clips and push the cable and grommet through the firewall.
12   To install the cable, reverse the removal procedure and adjust the cable as described in the preceding Section.

13   Parking brake pedal — removal and installation

1   Disconnect the battery ground cable and the parking brake warning switch wire.
2   Remove the clip and ball from the clevis (if necessary, the equalizer nut can be loosened) **(see illustration 12.9)**.
3   Remove the pedal rear mounting bolt and the nuts from the mounting studs at the front of the dash panel (under the hood).
4   Remove the pedal assembly.
5   Installation is the reverse of the removal procedure.

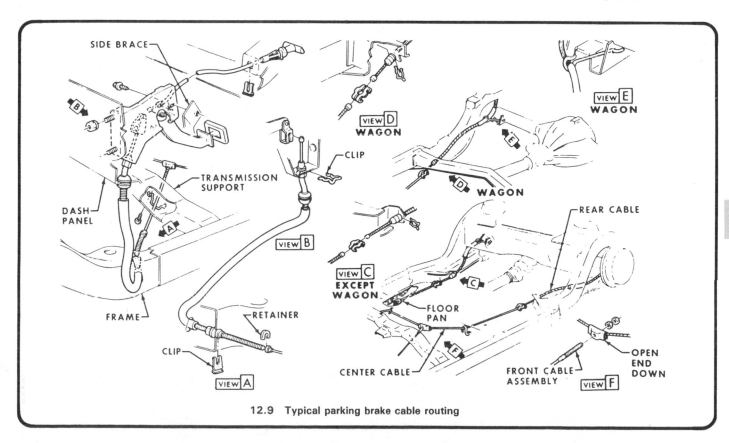

12.9 Typical parking brake cable routing

14   Brake pedal — removal and installation

Refer to illustration 14.2

1970 through 1973

1   On manual transmission models, disconnect the clutch pedal return spring and disconnect the clutch pushrod from the pedal arm.

2   If a power booster is not fitted, disconnect the brake pedal return spring and then disconnect the master cylinder pushrod from the pedal arm. Remove the retainer from the right-hand side of the pedal pivot shaft. Slide the clutch pedal to the left and remove it from the supprt braces. Remove the brake pedal and nylon bushings **(see illustration)**.

3   If a power booster is fitted, loosen the booster mounting nuts enough to allow the pushrod to slide off the pedal pin. Remove the clip retainer from the pedal pin and remove the pushrod. Remove the pedal pivot shaft nut and slide the pivot bolt out of the mounting bracket. The brake pedal and bushings can now be removed. Replace any worn bushings and lubricate upon reassembly, which is the reversal of the removal and dismantling sequence.

4   On vehicles without a power booster, adjust the brake pedal by releasing the pushrod locknut and turning the pushrod in or out to give between 1/16- and 1/4-inch of free movement. Tighten the locknut securely.

5   Adjust the brake light switch as described in Section 16.

6   Check the clutch pedal free play as described in Chapter 1.

1974 and later

7   Disconnect the clutch pedal return spring (if equipped).

8   Remove the clip retainer from the pushrod pin.

9   Unscrew the nut from the end of the pedal pivot shaft and withdraw the shaft far enough to be able to remove the pedal spacer and bushings.

10   Replace and/or lubricate the bushings as necessary.

11   Installation is the reverse of removal.

15   Power brake booster — inspection, removal and installation

1   The power brake booster unit requires no special maintenance apart from periodic inspection of the vacuum hose and the case.

2   Dismantling of the power unit requires special tools and is not ordinarily done by the home mechanic. If a problem develops, install a new or factory rebuilt unit.

3   Remove the nuts attaching the master cylinder to the booster and carefully pull the master cylinder forward until it clears the mounting studs. Don't bend or kink the brake lines.

4   Disconnect the vacuum hose where it attaches to the power brake booster.

5   From the passenger compartment, disconnect the power brake pushrod from the top of the brake pedal.

6   Also from this location, remove the nuts attaching the booster to the firewall.

7   Carefully lift the booster unit away from the firewall and out of the engine compartment.

8   To install, place the booster in position and tighten the nuts to the Specifications. Connect the brake pedal.

9   Install the master cylinder and vacuum hose.

10   Carefully test the operation of the brakes before placing the vehicle in normal service.

16   Brake light switch — removal, installation and adjustment

Refer to illustration 16.1

1   This switch is located on a flange or bracket protruding from the brake pedal support **(see illustration)**.

2   With the brake pedal in the fully released position, the plunger on the body of the switch should be fully pressed in. When the pedal is pushed in, the plunger releases and sends electrical current to the stop lights at the rear of the car.

3   Electrical contact should be made when the pedal is depressed 0.38- to 0.64-inch. If this is not the case, the switch can be adjusted by turning it in or out as required.

4   To replace the switch if it is faulty, disconnect the electrical coupler (two couplers if car is equipped with cruise control) and loosen the switch locknut until the switch can be unscrewed from the bracket. Installation is a reversal of this procedure.

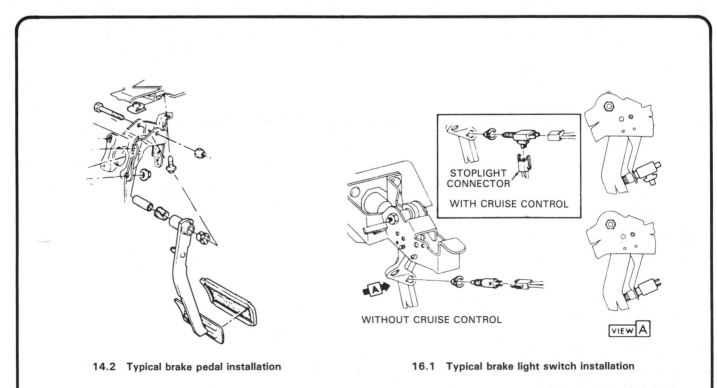

14.2   Typical brake pedal installation   16.1   Typical brake light switch installation

Chapter 10 Steering and suspension systems

Contents

Specifications

Torque specifications

	Ft-lbs
Upper control arm nuts................................	80
Upper balljoint stud-to-steering knuckle nut	40
Lower balljoint stud-to-steering knuckle nut	80
Lower control arm-to-frame pivot bolt nut	90
Front shock absorber upper stud nut	10
Front shock absorber-to-lower control arm bolts	20
Front stabilizer bar link-to-shaft nut....................	15
Front stabilizer bar bracket-to-frame bolts	25
Rear control arm bolt nuts	
all except rear upper	110
rear upper..	80
Rear shock absorber-to-lower mount	65
Rear shock absorber-to-upper mount	15
Rear stabilizer bar-to-lower control arm nut	50
Rear stabilizer bar insulator bracket nuts	30
Rear stabilizer bar clamp bolts	20

(Continued on page 225)

10

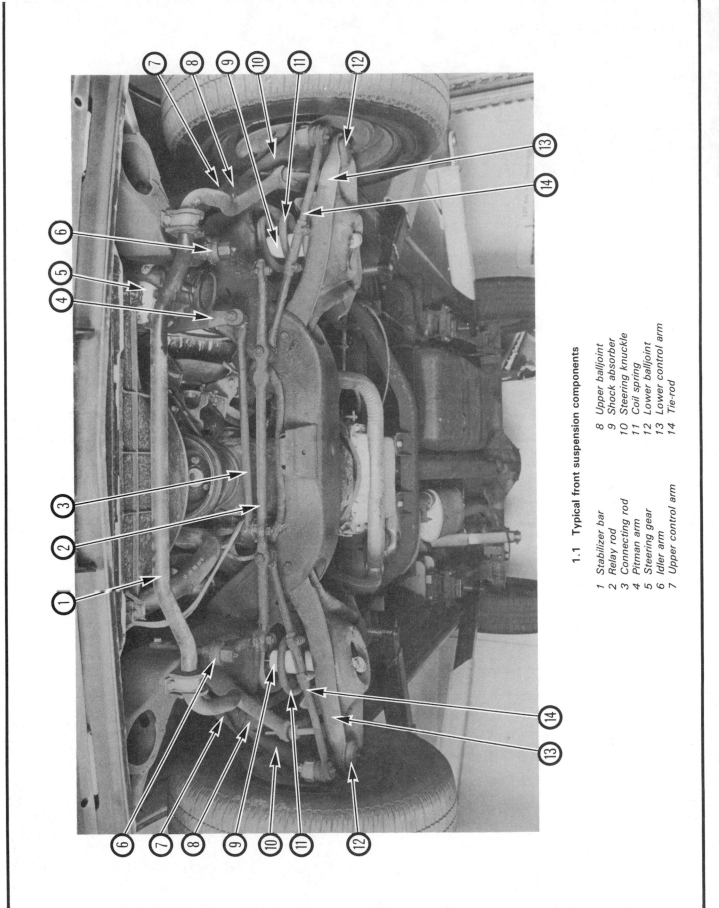

1.1 Typical front suspension components

1 Stabilizer bar	8 Upper balljoint
2 Relay rod	9 Shock absorber
3 Connecting rod	10 Steering knuckle
4 Pitman arm	11 Coil spring
5 Steering gear	12 Lower balljoint
6 Idler arm	13 Lower control arm
7 Upper control arm	14 Tie-rod

Torque specifications (continued)

	Ft-lbs
Leaf spring anchor plate nuts	40
Leaf spring front eye nuts	75
Leaf spring rear shackle pin nuts	95
Wheel lug nuts	70
Steering wheel-to-steering shaft nut	30
Tie-rod end-to-steering knuckle nut	30
Tie-rod adjuster sleeve clamp nut	20
Steering gear-to-frame bolts	70
Pitman shaft nut	185
Pitman arm-to-intermediate rod nut	40
Tie-rod end-to-intermediate rod nut	50
Idler arm-to-intermediate rod nut	35
Idler arm-to-frame nuts	40
Intermediate shaft pinch bolts	50

1 General information

Refer to illustration 1.1

Caution: *Whenever any suspension or steering fasteners are loosened or removed they must be inspected and, if necessary, replaced with new ones of the same part number or of original equipment quality and design. Cotter keys, used extensively on steering components, should never be reused — always replace them with new ones. Torque specifications must be followed for proper reassembly and component retention. Never attempt to heat, straighten or weld any steering or suspension component. Always replace bent or damaged parts with new ones.*

Each front wheel is connected to the frame by upper and lower control arms (A-frames), through a steering knuckle and upper and lower balljoints. A coil spring is installed between the lower control arm and the frame, and a telescopic shock absorber is positioned inside the coil spring. A stabilizer bar connected to the frame rails and to the lower control arms on each side aids in controlling body roll **(see illustration)**.

The rear suspension on coupe, sedan and convertible models consists of a solid axle located by upper and lower control arms, with coil springs supplying the suspension. On station wagon models the control arms and coil springs are replaced with multi-leaf springs. All models utilize telescopic shock absorbers installed between the spring mounts or seats and the frame rails.

The steering system consists of the steering wheel and column, an articulated intermediate shaft, a recirculating ball steering gear and steering linkage. Power steering is standard on all models.

2 Front stabilizer bar — removal and installation

Refer to illustrations 2.2 and 2.3

Removal

1   Raise the vehicle and support it securely on jackstands. Apply the parking brake.
2   Remove the stabilizer bar link nuts, noting how the washers and bushings are positioned **(see illustration)**. Clamp a pair of locking pliers to the stabilizer bar link to prevent it from turning.
3   Remove the stabilizer bar bracket bolts and detach the bar from the vehicle **(see illustration)**.
4   Pull the brackets off the stabilizer bar and inspect the bushings for cracks, hardening and other signs of deterioration. If the bushings are damaged, cut them from the bar.

Installation

5   Position the stabilizer bar bushings on the bar with the slits facing the front of the vehicle. **Note:** *The offset in the bar must face down.*
6   Push the brackets over the bushings and raise the bar up to the frame. Install the bracket bolts but don't tighten them completely at this time.
7   Install the stabilizer bar link nuts, washers and rubber bushings and tighten the nuts securely.
8   Tighten the bracket bolts.

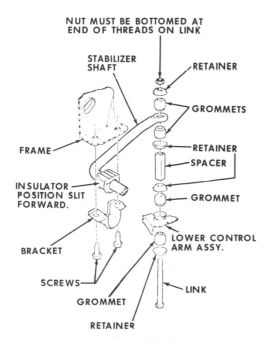

2.2   Typical front stabilizer bar to lower control arm linkage

2.3   Remove the brackets and rubber bushings on each side which attach the stabilizer bar to the frame

10

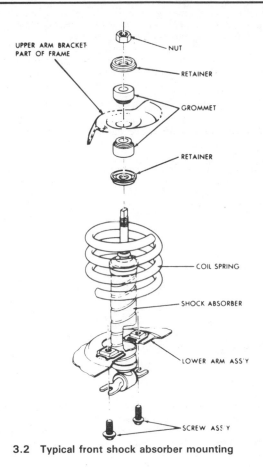

UPPER ARM BRACKET-
PART OF FRAME

NUT

RETAINER

GROMMET

RETAINER

COIL SPRING

SHOCK ABSORBER

LOWER ARM ASS'Y

SCREW ASS'Y

3.2   Typical front shock absorber mounting

3   Front shock absorbers — removal and installation

Refer to illustration 3.2

Removal

1   Loosen the wheel lug nuts, raise the vehicle and support it securely on jackstands. Apply the parking brake. Remove the wheel.
2   Remove the upper shock absorber stem nut **(see illustration)**. Use an open end wrench to keep the stem from turning. If the nut won't loosen because of rust, squirt some penetrating oil on the stem threads and allow it to soak in for awhile. It may be necessary to keep the stem from turning with a pair of locking pliers, since the flats provided for a wrench are quite small.
3   Remove the two lower shock mount bolts and pull the shock absorber out through the bottom of the lower control arm. Remove the washers and the rubber grommets from the top of the shock absorber.

4.4   A special GM tool (J-23742) is used to push the balljoint out of the steering knuckle, but an alternative tool can be fabricated from a large bolt, nut, washer and socket

Installation

4   Extend the new shock absorber as far as possible. Position a new washer and rubber grommet on the stem and guide the shock up through the coil spring and into the upper mount.
5   Install the upper rubber grommet and washer and wiggle the stem back-and-forth to ensure that the grommets are centered in the mount. Tighten the stem nut securely.
6   Install the lower mounting bolts and tighten them securely.

4   Balljoints — replacement

Refer to illustrations 4.4, 4.5 and 4.8

Upper balljoint

1   Loosen the wheel lug nuts, raise the vehicle and support it securely on jackstands. Apply the parking brake. Remove the wheel.
2   Place a jack or a jackstand under the lower control arm. **Note:** *The jack or jackstand must remain under the control arm during removal and installation of the balljoint to hold the spring and control arm in position.*
3   Remove the cotter pin from the balljoint stud and back off the nut two turns.
4   Separate the balljoint from the steering knuckle (use GM tool no. J-23742 or equivalent to press the balljoint out of the steering knuckle) **(see illustration)**. An equivalent tool can be fabricated from a large bolt, nut, washer and socket. Countersink the center of the bolt head with a large drill bit to prevent the tool from slipping off the balljoint stud. Install the tool as shown in the illustration, hold the bolt head with a wrench and tighten the nut against the washer until the balljoint pops out. Notice that the balljoint nut hasn't been completely removed.
5   Using a 1/8-inch drill bit, drill a 1/4-inch deep hole in the center of each rivet head **(see illustration)**.
6   Using a 1/2-inch diameter drill bit, drill off the rivet heads.
7   Use a punch to knock the rivet shanks out, then remove the balljoint from the control arm.
8   Position the new balljoint on the control arm and install the bolts and nuts supplied in the kit **(see illustration)**. Be sure to tighten the nuts to the torque specified on the balljoint kit instruction sheet.
9   Insert the balljoint stud into the steering knuckle and install the nut, tightening it to the specified torque.
10   Install a new cotter pin, tightening the nut slightly if necessary to align a slot in the nut with the hole in the balljoint stud.
11   Install the balljoint grease fitting and fill the joint with grease.
12   Install the wheel, tightening the lug nuts to the specified torque.
13   Drive the vehicle to an alignment shop to have the front end alignment checked and, if necessary, adjusted.

Lower balljoint

14   The lower balljoint is a press fit in the lower control arm and requires special tools to remove and replace it. Refer to Section 6, remove

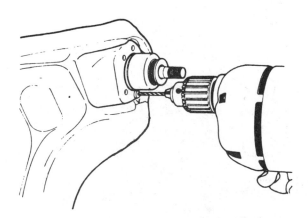

4.5   Drill pilot holes into the heads of the balljoint rivets with a 1/8-inch bit, then use a 1/2-inch bit to cut the rivet heads off — be careful not to enlarge the holes in the control arm

4.8 Install the replacement balljoint in the upper control arm with the nuts on top

the lower control arm and take it to an automotive machine shop to have the old balljoint pressed out and the new balljoint pressed in.

5 Upper control arm — removal and installation

Refer to illustration 5.4

Removal

1 Loosen the wheel lug nuts, raise the front of the vehicle and support it securely on jackstands. Apply the parking brake. Remove the wheel.
2 Support the lower control arm with a jack or jackstand. The support point must be as close to the balljoint as possible to give maximum leverage on the lower control arm.

3 Disconnect the upper balljoint from the steering knuckle (refer to Section 4). **Note:** *DO NOT use a "pickle fork" type balljoint separator — it may damage the balljoint seals.*
4 Remove the control arm-to-frame nuts and bolts, recording the position of any alignment shims. They must be reinstalled in the same location to maintain wheel alignment **(see illustration)**.
5 Detach the control arm from the vehicle. **Note:** *The control arm bushings are pressed into place and require special tools for removal and installation. If the bushings must be replaced, take the control arm to a dealer service department or an automotive machine shop to have the old bushings pressed out and the new ones pressed in.*

Installation

6 Position the control arm on the frame and install the bolts and nuts. Install any alignment shims that were removed. Tighten the nuts to the specified torque.
7 Insert the balljoint stud into the steering knuckle and tighten the nut to the specified torque. Install a new cotter pin, tightening the nut slightly, if necessary, to align a slot in the nut with the hole in the balljoint stud.
8 Install the wheel and lug nuts and lower the vehicle. Tighten the lug nuts to the specified torque.
9 Drive the vehicle to an alignment shop to have the front end alignment checked and, if necessary, adjusted.

6 Lower control arm — removal and installation

Refer to illustration 6.6

Removal

1 Loosen the wheel lug nuts, raise the vehicle and support it securely on jackstands. Apply the parking brake. Remove the wheel.
2 Unbolt the shock absorber from the lower control arm and push it up into the coil spring.
3 Disconnect the stabilizer bar from the lower control arm (Section 2).
4 Remove the coil spring as described in Section 8.
5 Remove the cotter pin and back off the lower control arm balljoint stud nut two turns. Separate the balljoint from the steering knuckle (Section 4).
6 Remove the control arm from the vehicle **(see illustration). Note:**

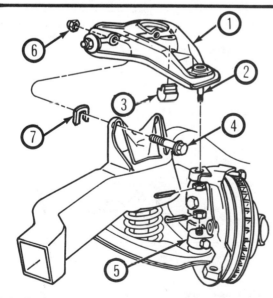

5.4 Typical upper control arm mounting details. Note the position of the alignment shims and return them to their original positions

1 Upper control arm	5 Steering knuckle
2 Upper balljoint	6 Nut
3 Bumper	7 Alignment shim
4 Bolt	

6.6 Typical lower control arm mounting details

1 Pivot bolt	4 Bumper
2 Lower control arm	5 Pivot bolt
3 Nut	

10

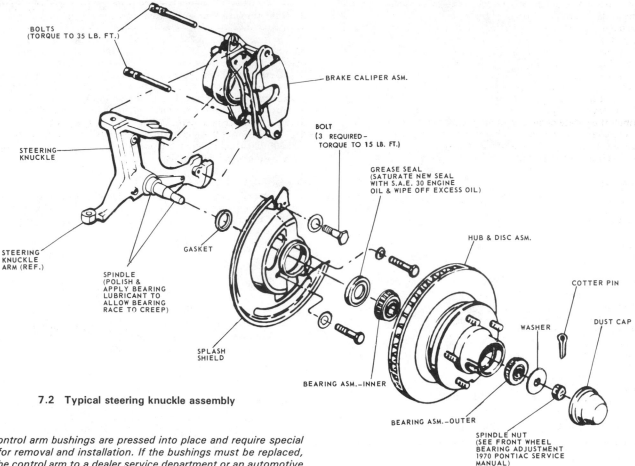

BOLTS
(TORQUE TO 35 LB. FT.)

BRAKE CALIPER ASM.

BOLT
(3 REQUIRED –
TORQUE TO 15 LB. FT.)

STEERING
KNUCKLE

GREASE SEAL
(SATURATE NEW SEAL
WITH S.A.E. 30 ENGINE
OIL & WIPE OFF EXCESS OIL)

HUB & DISC ASM.

STEERING
KNUCKLE
ARM (REF.)

GASKET

SPINDLE
(POLISH &
APPLY BEARING
LUBRICANT TO
ALLOW BEARING
RACE TO CREEP)

COTTER PIN

WASHER

DUST CAP

SPLASH
SHIELD

BEARING ASM.–INNER

BEARING ASM.–OUTER

SPINDLE NUT
(SEE FRONT WHEEL
BEARING ADJUSTMENT
1970 PONTIAC SERVICE
MANUAL)

7.2 Typical steering knuckle assembly

The control arm bushings are pressed into place and require special tools for removal and installation. If the bushings must be replaced, take the control arm to a dealer service department or an automotive machine shop to have the old bushings pressed out and the new ones pressed in.

Installation

7   Insert the balljoint stud into the steering knuckle, tighten the nut to the specified torque and install a new cotter pin. If necessary, tighten the nut slightly to align a slot in the nut with the hole in the balljoint stud.
8   Install the coil spring (Section 8) and the lower control arm pivot bolts and nuts, but don't completely tighten them at this time.
9   Connect the stabilizer bar to the lower control arm.
10   Install the wheel and lug nuts, lower the vehicle and tighten the lug nuts to the specified torque.
11   With the vehicle at normal ride height, tighten the lower control arm pivot bolt nuts to the specified torque.
12   Drive the vehicle to an alignment shop to have the front end alignment checked and, if necessary, adjusted.

7   Steering knuckle — removal and installation

Refer to illustration 7.2

Removal

1   Loosen the wheel lug nuts, raise the vehicle and support it securely on jackstands placed under the frame. Apply the parking brake. Remove the wheel.
2   Remove the brake caliper (**see illustration**) and suspend it with a piece of wire (Chapter 9). Do not let it hang by the brake hose!
3   Remove the brake rotor and hub assembly (see Chapter 1).
4   Remove the splash shield from the steering knuckle.
5   Separate the tie-rod end from the steering arm (see Section 17).
6   If the steering knuckle must be replaced, remove the dust seal from the spindle by prying it off with a screwdriver. If it's damaged, replace it with a new one.
7   Position a floor jack under the lower control arm and raise it slightly

to take the spring pressure off the suspension stop. The jack must remain in this position throughout the entire procedure.
8   Remove the cotter pins from the upper and lower balljoint studs and back off the nuts two turns each.
9   Break the balljoints loose from the steering knuckle with a ball-joint separator (Section 4). **Note:** *A pickle fork type balljoint separator may damage the balljoint seals.*
10   Remove the nuts from the balljoint studs, separate the control arms from the steering knuckle and remove the knuckle from the vehicle.

Installation

11   Place the knuckle between the upper and lower control arms and insert the balljoint studs into the knuckle, beginning with the lower balljoint. Install the nuts and tighten them to the specified torque. Install new cotter pins, tightening the nuts slightly to align the slots in the nuts with the holes in the balljoint studs, if necessary.
12   Install the splash shield.
13   Connect the tie-rod end to the steering arm and tighten the nut to the specified torque. Be sure to use a new cotter pin.
14   Install the brake rotor and adjust the wheel bearings following the procedure outlined in Chapter 1.
15   Install the brake caliper.
16   Install the wheel and lug nuts. Lower the vehicle to the ground and tighten the nuts to the specified torque.

8   Front coil springs — removal and installation

Removal

1   Loosen the wheel lug nuts, raise the vehicle and support it securely on jackstands placed under the frame. Apply the parking brake. Remove the wheel.
2   Remove the shock absorber (Section 3).
3   Disconnect the stabilizer bar from the lower control arm (Section 2).

4   Position a jack under the inner edge of the lower control arm. Make sure the jack is centered from front to rear.

5   Loop a length of safety chain up through the control arm and coil spring and bolt the ends of the chain together. Make sure there's enough slack in the chain so it won't inhibit spring extension when the control arm is lowered.

6   Raise the jack slightly to relieve spring pressure from the control arm pivot bolts and remove the nuts and bolts. If the bolts are hard to remove, drive them out with a long, narrow drift.

7   Slowly lower the jack until the coil spring is fully extended.

8   Unbolt the safety chain and maneuver the coil spring out. Do not apply downward pressure on the lower control arm as it may damage the balljoint. If the upper coil spring insulator is not on the top of the spring, reach up in the spring pocket and retrieve it.

Installation

9   Place the insulators on the top and bottom of the coil spring (the top of the spring is flat on the end, with a gripper notch near the end of the spring coil).

10   Install the top of the spring into the spring pocket and the bottom in the lower control arm. The end of the lower spring coil must be seated in the lowest recessed portion of the spring seat.

11   Place the jack under the lower control arm, install the safety chain and slowly raise the control arm into place. When the bolt holes are aligned, install the bolts with the bolt heads towards the center of the control arm. It may be necessary to insert a punch through the mounting bracket and into the control arm bushing to align the holes. Do not completely tighten the nuts at this time.

12   Install the shock absorber (Section 3).

13   Attach the stabilizer bar to the lower control arm (Section 2).

14   Install the wheel and lug nuts. Lower the vehicle and tighten the lug nuts to the specified torque.

15   Reach under the vehicle and tighten the lower control arm pivot bolt nuts to the specified torque.

16   Drive the vehicle to an alignment shop to have the front end alignment checked and, if necessary, adjusted.

9   Rear stabilizer bar — removal and installation

Refer to illustrations 9.2 and 9.6

Coil spring models

1   Raise the rear of the vehicle and support it securely on jackstands.

2   Remove the two nuts and bolts on each side securing the stabilizer bar to the lower control arms (see illustration).

3   Remove the stabilizer bar and, if present, the shims installed between the bar and lower control arm on each side.

4   Installation is the reverse of the removal procedure, being sure to replace the shims (if any were removed) and tightening the nuts and bolts to the specified torque.

Leaf spring models

5   Raise the rear of the vehicle and support it securely on jackstands.

6   Disconnect the lower end of each support assembly from the stabilizer bar by removing the clamp bolts (see illustration).

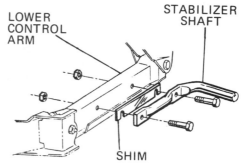

9.2   On coil spring models, the rear stabilizer bar bolts to the lower control arm on each side
(right side shown — left side opposite)

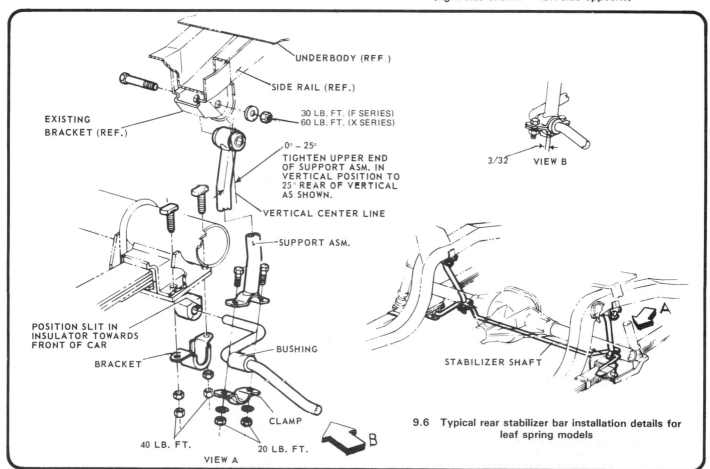

9.6   Typical rear stabilizer bar installation details for leaf spring models

10

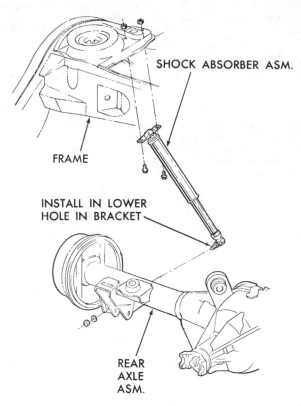

10.3a Typical shock absorber mounting on coil spring models

7   Remove the insulator and bracket from each spring anchor plate and lower the stabilizer bar from the vehicle.
8   Installation is the reverse of the removal procedure, being sure to tighten the insulator bracket nuts and the support assembly clamp bolts to the specified torque. **Note:** *When installing the insulators on the stabilizer bar, the slit in the insulator should face the front of the vehicle.*

---

10   Rear shock absorbers — removal and installation

Refer to illustrations 10.3a and 10.3b
1   Raise the rear of the vehicle and support it securely on jackstands.
2   On leaf spring models, remove the wheel and tire.
3   On models where the lower end of the shock absorber is retained to the axle by a stud, remove the nut and washer **(see illustrations)**.
4   On models where the lower end of the shock absorber is retained to the axle by a through-bolt, remove the nut, lockwasher and bolt.
5   Remove the two upper bolts securing the shock absorber to the frame and remove the shock absorber from the vehicle.
6   Installation is the reverse of the removal procedure.

---

11   Rear coil springs — removal and installation

Refer to illustration 11.6
1   Raise the rear of the vehicle and support it securely on jackstands under the frame rails.
2   Remove the rear wheels.
3   Place a floor jack under the center of the differential housing and raise the axle until the coil springs just start to compress. **Warning:** *When the springs are removed, the floor jack will be the sole support for the rear axle assembly, so be sure it is positioned correctly.*
4   Disconnect the lower ends of both shock absorbers from the rear axle.
5   Remove the clip attaching the brake line to the frame crossmember.
6   Carefully lower the jack just enough to remove the spring and rubber insulator (on top of the spring) **(see illustration)**. **Note:** *When remov-*

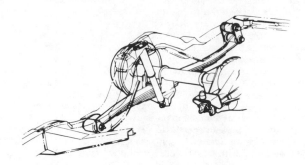

10.3b   Typical shock absorber mounting on leaf spring models

ing the spring make note of the position of the coil ends, top and bottom. The spring must be reinstalled with the coil ends in the same position.
7   Installation is the reverse of the removal procedure.

---

12   Rear control arms — removal and installation

Refer to illustration 12.3
1   Raise the vehicle and support it securely with jackstands placed under the axle housing.

Upper arm
2   Support the nose of the differential with a floor jack to keep the axle housing from pivoting when the control arms are removed.
3   Remove the pivot bolt holding the rear of the control arm to the ear on the axle housing **(see illustration)** and pry the control arm upwards until it clears the ear.
4   On early models, unbolt the upper control arm bracket from the frame crossmember.
5   On later models, remove the control arm pivot bolt at the frame crossmember.

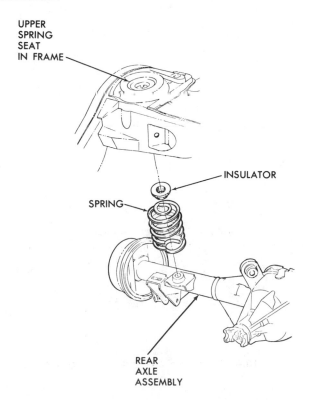

11.6   Typical rear coil spring and insulator details

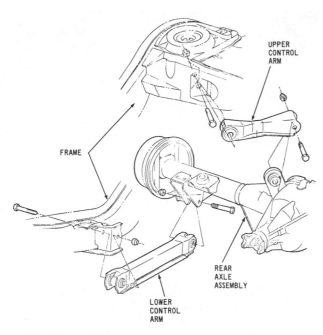

12.3   **Typical rear upper and lower control arms used on coil spring models**

6   Remove the control arm.
7   Installation is the reverse of the removal procedure.
8   Lower the vehicle to the ground and tighten all control arm bolts to the specified torque.

Lower control arm

9   Support the nose of the differential with a floor jack to keep the axle housing from pivoting when the control arms are removed.
10   Remove the pivot bolt holding the rear of the control arm to the lower spring seat and pry the control arm downwards until it clears the spring seat flanges.
11   Remove the control arm pivot bolt at the frame rail.
12   Remove the control arm.
13   Installation is the reverse of the removal procedure.
14   Lower the vehicle to the ground and tighten all control arm bolts to the specified torque.

13   Leaf springs — removal and installation

Refer to illustration 13.4

1   Raise the vehicle and support it securely on jackstands placed beneath the frame rails, just in front of the front spring mounts.
2   Remove the lower shock absorber mounting nut or bolt and compress the shock absorber upwards to move it out of the way.
3   Place a floor jack under the axle housing and lift the axle housing slightly.
4   Remove the anchor plate nuts and withdraw the anchor plate and lower spring cushion pad **(see illustration)**.

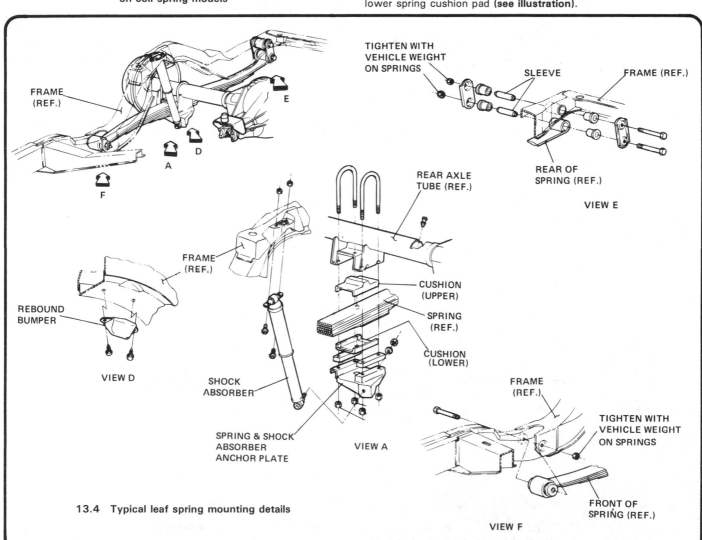

13.4   **Typical leaf spring mounting details**

10

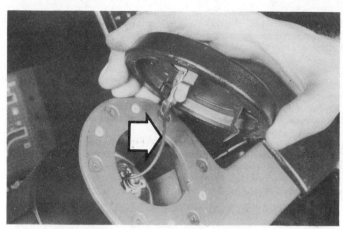

14.2   Although the shapes may vary on different models, the horn pad is removed by gripping it firmly and pulling it from the steering wheel — be sure to detach the horn wire (arrow)

14.3   Snap-ring pliers are used to remove the safety clip from the steering shaft

14.4   Check to be sure that there are alignment marks on the steering shaft and steering wheel (arrow) — if they aren't there or don't line up, scribe or paint new marks

14.5   Remove the steering wheel from the shaft with a puller — do not hammer on the shaft!

5   Use the floor jack to lift the axle off the spring and remove the upper spring cushion pad.
6   Loosen the upper and lower shackle pin nuts at the rear of the spring.
7   Support the front of the spring, remove the front eye bolt and let the spring swing downward.
8   Remove the lower shackle pin from the rear of the spring and withdraw the spring from the vehicle.
9   Installation is the reverse of the removal procedure. With the vehicle lowered to the ground and the full weight on the springs, tighten all fasteners to the specified torque.

15.2   Mark the relationship of the intermediate shaft to the steering shaft (arrow) and the steering gear input shaft

14   Steering wheel — removal and installation

Refer to illustrations 14.2, 14.3, 14.4 and 14.5

1   Disconnect the cable from the negative terminal of the battery.
2   Pull the horn pad from the steering wheel and disconnect the wire to the horn switch (see illustration).
3   Remove the safety clip from the steering shaft (see illustration).
4   Remove the steering wheel retaining nut then mark the relationship of the steering shaft to the hub (if marks don't already exist or don't line up) to simplify installation and ensure steering wheel alignment (see illustration).
5   Use a puller to disconnect the steering wheel from the shaft (see illustration).
6   To install the wheel, align the mark on the steering wheel hub with the mark on the shaft and slip the wheel onto the shaft. Install the hub nut and tighten it to the specified torque. Install the safety clip.
7   Connect the horn wire and install the horn pad.
8   Connect the negative battery cable.

15   Intermediate shaft — removal and installation

Refer to illustrations 15.2 and 15.3

1   Turn the front wheels to the straight ahead position.
2   Using white paint, place alignment marks on the upper universal joint, the steering shaft, the lower universal joint and the steering gear input shaft (see illustration).

INTERMEDIATE SHAFT INSTALLATION

1. COUPLING MUST BE FULLY ENGAGED WITH SPLINES OF STEERING GEAR BEFORE INSTALLING PINCH BOLT.

2. COUPLING SHIELD LATCH MUST BE SEATED AROUND THE RETURN PIPE NUT.

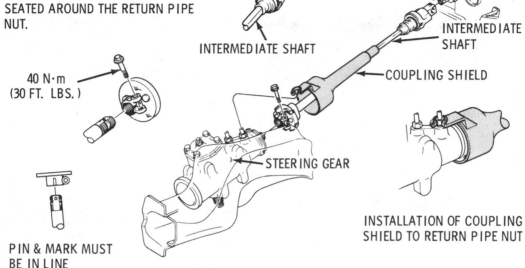

70 N·m (50 FT. LBS.)

40 N·m (30 FT. LBS.)

INTERMEDIATE SHAFT

INTERMEDIATE SHAFT

COUPLING SHIELD

STEERING GEAR

INSTALLATION OF COUPLING SHIELD TO RETURN PIPE NUT

PIN & MARK MUST BE IN LINE

15.3 Typical intermediate shaft installation details

3 Remove the upper and lower universal joint pinch bolts (see illustration). Some models require the steering gear to be lowered for shaft removal.
4 Pry the intermediate shaft out of the steering shaft universal joint with a large screwdriver, then pull the shaft from the steering gearbox.
5 Installation is the reverse of the removal procedure. Be sure to align the marks and tighten the pinch bolts to the specified torque.

16 Steering gear — removal and installation

Refer to illustrations 16.4 and 16.5

Removal

1 Raise the front of the vehicle and support it securely on jackstands. Apply the parking brake.
2 Place a drain pan under the steering gear (power steering only). Remove the power steering pressure and return lines and cap the ends to prevent excessive fluid loss and contamination.

3 Mark the relationship of the lower intermediate shaft universal joint to the steering gear input shaft. Remove the lower intermediate shaft pinch bolt.
4 Mark the relationship of the Pitman arm to the Pitman shaft so it can be installed in the same position (see illustration). Remove the nut and washer.
5 Remove the Pitman arm from the shaft with a two-jaw puller (see illustration).
6 Support the steering gear and remove the steering gear-to-frame mounting bolts. Lower the unit, separate the intermediate shaft from the steering gear input shaft and remove the steering gear from the vehicle.

Installation

7 Raise the steering gear into position and connect the intermediate shaft, aligning the marks.
8 Install the mounting bolts and washers and tighten them to the specified torque.
9 Slide the Pitman arm onto the Pitman shaft, ensuring that the marks

16.4 Paint alignment marks on the Pitman arm and the steering gear output shaft, then remove the nut and washer

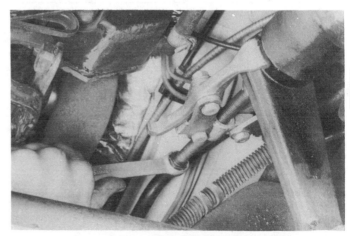

16.5 Use a puller to remove the Pitman arm from the steering gear output shaft

10

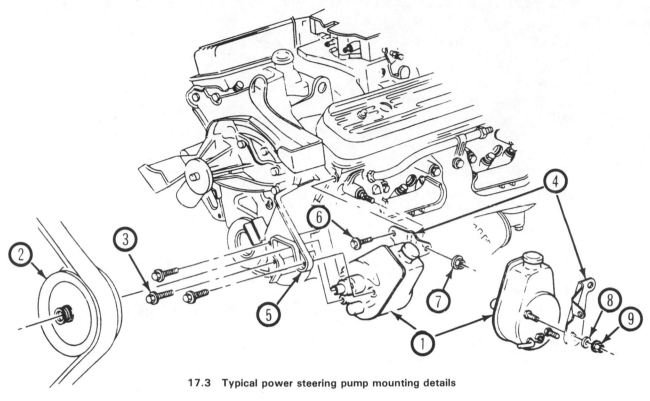

17.3 Typical power steering pump mounting details

1 Pump	6 Brace bolt
2 Pulley	7 Brace to stud nut
3 Mounting bolt	8 Washer
4 Rear brace	9 Brace to pump nut
5 Bracket	

are aligned. Install the washer and nut and tighten the nut to the specified torque.

10 Install the lower intermediate shaft pinch bolt and tighten it to the specified torque.

11 Connect the power steering pressure and return hoses to the steering gear and fill the power steering pump reservoir with the recommended fluid (Chapter 1).

12 Lower the vehicle and bleed the steering system as outlined in Section 18.

17 Power steering pump — removal and installation

Refer to illustration 17.3

1 Disconnect the hydraulic lines from either the pump or the steering gear and support them in a raised position to keep the fluid from draining.

2 Loosen the pump mounting bolts and pivot the pump inwards (towards the engine) until the drivebelt can be removed.

3 Remove the pump mounting bolts and braces and remove the pump **(see illustration)**.

4 Reinstall the pump by reversing the removal procedure. Before installing the drivebelt, prime the pump by filling the reservoir with fluid, then turn the pulley in the opposite direction to normal rotation until no more air bubbles are observed in the reservoir.

5 Install the drivebelt (Chapter 1) and bleed the system as described in Section 18.

18 Power steering system — bleeding

1 Following any operation in which the power steering fluid lines have been disconnected, the power steering system must be bled to remove all air and obtain proper steering performance.

2 With the front wheels in the straight ahead position, check the power steering fluid level and, if low, add fluid until it reaches the Cold mark on the dipstick.

3 Start the engine and allow it to run at fast idle. Recheck the fluid level and add more if necessary to reach the Cold mark on the dipstick.

4 Bleed the system by turning the wheels from side-to-side, without hitting the stops. This will work the air out of the system. Keep the reservoir full of fluid as this is done.

5 When the air is worked out of the system, return the wheels to the straight ahead position and leave the vehicle running for several more minutes before shutting it off.

6 Road test the vehicle to be sure the steering system is functioning normally and noise free.

7 Recheck the fluid level to be sure it is up to the Hot mark on the dipstick while the engine is at normal operating temperature. Add fluid if necessary (see Chapter 1).

19 Steering linkage — inspection, removal and installation

Warning: *Whenever any of the suspension or steering fasteners are loosened or removed they must be inspected and if necessary, replaced with new ones of the same part number or of original equipment quality and design. Torque specifications must be followed for proper reassembly and component retention. Never attempt to heat, straighten or weld any suspension or steering component. Instead, replace any bent or damaged part with a new one.*

Caution: *DO NOT use a "pickle fork" type balljoint separator — it may damage the balljoint seals.*

Inspection
Refer to illustrations 19.1 and 19.5

1 The steering linkage connects the steering gear to the front wheels

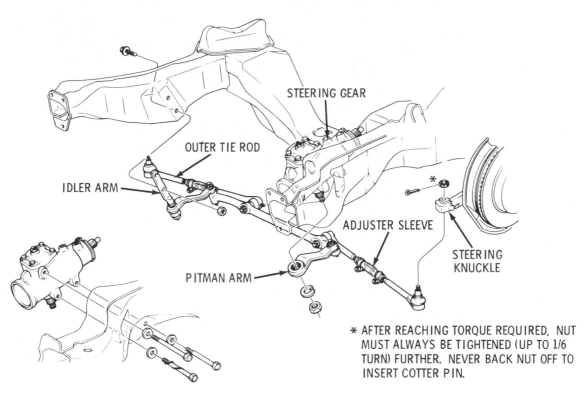

19.1 Typical steering linkage arrangement

* AFTER REACHING TORQUE REQUIRED, NUT
  MUST ALWAYS BE TIGHTENED (UP TO 1/6
  TURN) FURTHER. NEVER BACK NUT OFF TO
  INSERT COTTER PIN.

and keeps the wheels in proper relation to each other **(see illustration)**. The linkage consists of the Pitman arm, fastened to the steering gear shaft, which moves the relay rod back-and-forth through the connecting rod. The relay rod is supported on each end by frame-mounted idler arms. The back-and-forth motion of the relay rod is transmitted to the steering knuckles through a pair of tie-rod assemblies. Each tie-rod is made up of an inner and outer tie-rod end, a threaded adjuster tube and two clamps.

2   Set the wheels in the straight ahead position and lock the steering wheel.

3   Raise one side of the vehicle until the tire is approximately 1-inch off the ground.

4   Mount a dial indicator with the needle resting on the outside edge of the wheel. Grasp the front and rear of the tire and using light pressure, wiggle the wheel back-and-forth and note the dial indicator reading. The gauge reading should be less than 0.108-inch. If the play in the steering system is more than specified, inspect each steering linkage pivot point and ball stud for looseness and replace parts if necessary.

5   Raise the vehicle and support it on jackstands. Push up, then pull down on the relay rod end of the idler arm, exerting a force of approximately 25 pounds each way. Measure the total distance the end of the arm travels **(see illustration)**. If the play is greater than 1/4-inch, replace the idler arm.

6   Check for torn ball stud boots, frozen joints and bent or damaged linkage components.

Removal and installation
Refer to illustrations 19.9, 19.11, 19.13, 19.15a and 19.15b
Tie-rod

7   Loosen the wheel lug nuts, raise the vehicle and support it securely on jackstands. Apply the parking brake. Remove the wheel.

8   Remove the cotter pin and loosen, but do not remove, the castellated nut from the ball stud.

9   Using a two jaw puller, separate the tie-rod end from the steering knuckle **(see illustration)**. Remove the castellated nut and pull the tie-rod end from the knuckle.

10 Remove the nut securing the inner tie-rod end to the relay rod. Separate the inner tie-rod end from the relay rod in the same manner as in Step 9.

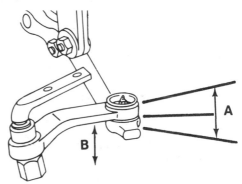

19.5 To check for excessive idler arm play, apply approximately 25 lbs. of force up and down (B) on the idler arm — if the total movement (A) is greater than 1/4-inch, replace the idler arm

19.9 Use a puller to press the tie-rod end out of the steering knuckle

10

19.11   Measure the distance from the adjuster tube to the ball stud centerline so the new tie-rod end can be set to the same length

19.13   It may be necessary to force the ball stud into the tapered hole to keep it from turning while the nut is tightened

11 If the inner or outer tie-rod end must be replaced, measure the distance from the end of the adjuster tube to the center of the ball stud and record it **(see illustration)**. Loosen the adjuster tube clamp and unscrew the tie-rod end.

12 Lubricate the threaded portion of the tie-rod end with chassis grease. Screw the new tie-rod end into the adjuster tube and adjust the distance from the tube to the ball stud to the previously measured dimension. The number of threads showing on the inner and outer tie-rod ends should be equal within three threads. Don't tighten the clamp yet.

13 To install the tie-rod, insert the inner tie-rod end ball stud into the relay rod until it's seated. Install the nut and tighten it to the specified torque. If the ball stud spins when attempting to tighten the nut, force it into the tapered hole with a large pair of pliers **(see illustration)**.

14 Connect the outer tie-rod end to the steering knuckle and install the castellated nut. Tighten the nut to the specified torque and install a new cotter pin. If necessary, tighten the nut slightly to align a slot in the nut with the hole in the ball stud.

15 Tighten the clamp nuts. The center of the bolt should be nearly horizontal and the adjuster tube slot must not line up with the gap in the clamps **(see illustrations)**.

16 Install the wheel and lug nuts, lower the vehicle and tighten the lug nuts to the specified torque. Drive the vehicle to an alignment shop to have the front end alignment checked and, if necessary, adjusted.

Idler arm

17 Raise the vehicle and support it securely on jackstands. Apply the parking brake.

18 Loosen but do not remove the idler arm-to-relay rod nut.

19 Separate the idler arm from the relay rod with a two jaw puller **(see illustration 19.9)**. Remove the nut.

20 Remove the idler arm-to-frame bolts.

21 To install the idler arm, position it on the frame and install the bolts, tightening them to the specified torque.

22 Insert the idler arm ball stud into the relay rod and install the nut. Tighten the nut to the specified torque. If the ball stud spins when attempting to tighten the nut, force it into the tapered hole with a large pair of pliers.

Relay rod

23 Raise the vehicle and support it securely on jackstands. Apply the parking brake.

24 Separate the two inner tie-rod ends from the relay rod.

25 Separate the connecting rod from the relay rod.

26 Separate both idler arms from the relay rod.

27 Installation is the reverse of the removal procedure. If the ball studs spin when attempting to tighten the nuts, force them into the tapered holes with a large pair of pliers. Be sure to tighten all of the nuts to the specified torque.

Connecting rod

28 Raise the front of the vehicle and support it securely on jackstands. Apply the parking brake.

29 Loosen, but do not remove, the nut securing the connecting rod ball stud to the relay rod. Separate the joint with a two jaw puller then remove the nut.

30 Separate the connecting rod from the Pitman arm.

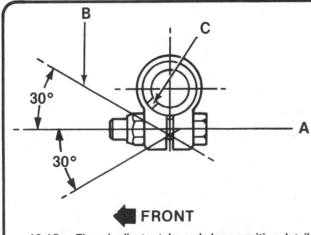

19.15a   Tie-rod adjuster tube and clamp position details

A *Horizontal*
B *The clamp bolts must be within 30° of horizontal*
C *The adjuster tube slot MUST NOT line up with the gap in the clamps*

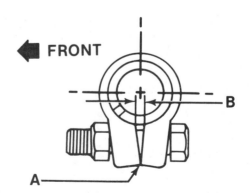

19.15b   The clamp ends (A) may touch when tightened, but there must be a gap between the inner portions of the clamp next to the adjuster tube (B)

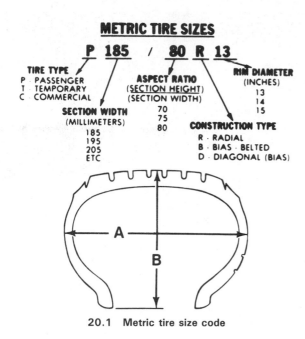

20.1 Metric tire size code

A Section width   *B Section height*

31 Installation is the reverse of the removal procedure. If the ball studs spin when attempting to tighten the nuts, force them into the tapered holes with a large pair of pliers. Be sure to tighten all of the nuts to the specified torque.

Pitman arm
32 Refer to Section 16 of this Chapter for the Pitman arm removal procedure.

---

20 Wheels and tires — general information

Refer to illustration 20.1

All vehicles covered by this manual are equipped with metric-sized fiberglass or steel belted radial tires **(see illustration)**. Use of other size or type of tires may affect the ride and handling of the vehicle. Don't mix different types of tires, such as radials and bias belted, on the same vehicle as handling may be seriously affected. It's recommended that tires be replaced in pairs on the same axle, but if only one tire is being replaced, be sure it's the same size, structure and tread design as the other.

Because tire pressure has a substantial effect on handling and wear, the pressure on all tires should be checked at least once a month or before any extended trips (see Chapter 1).

Wheels must be replaced if they are bent, dented, leak air, have elongated bolt holes, are heavily rusted, out of vertical symmetry or if the lug nuts won't stay tight. Wheel repairs that use welding or peening are not recommended.

Tire and wheel balance is important in the overall handling, braking and performance of the vehicle. Unbalanced wheels can adversely affect handling and ride characteristics as well as tire life. Whenever a tire is installed on a wheel, the tire and wheel should be balanced by a shop with the proper equipment.

---

21 Front end alignment — general information

Refer to illustration 21.1

A front end alignment refers to the adjustments made to the front wheels so they are in proper angular relationship to the suspension and the ground. Front wheels that are out of proper alignment not only affect steering control, but also increase tire wear. The front end adjustments normally required are camber, caster and toe-in **(see illustration)**.

Getting the proper front wheel alignment is a very exacting process, one in which complicated and expensive machines are necessary to

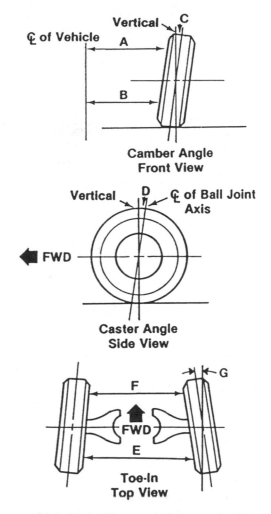

21.1 Typical front end alignment details

A minus B	= C (degrees camber)
D	= caster (measured in degrees
E minus F	= toe-in (measured in inches)
G	= toe-in (expressed in degrees)

perform the job properly. Because of this, you should have a technician with the proper equipment perform these tasks. We will, however, use this space to give you a basic idea of what is involved with front end alignment so you can better understand the process and deal intelligently with the shop that does the work.

Toe-in is the turning in of the front wheels. The purpose of a toe specification is to ensure parallel rolling of the front wheels. In a vehicle with zero toe-in, the distance between the front edges of the wheels will be the same as the distance between the rear edges of the wheels. The actual amount of toe-in is normally only a fraction of an inch. Toe-in adjustment is controlled by the tie-rod end position on the inner tie-rod. Incorrect toe-in will cause the tires to wear improperly by making them scrub against the road surface.

Camber is the tilting of the front wheels from the vertical when viewed from the front of the vehicle. When the wheels tilt out at the top, the camber is said to be positive (+). When the wheels tilt in at the top the camber is negative (−). The amount of tilt is measured in degrees from the vertical and this measurement is called the camber angle. This angle affects the amount of tire tread which contacts the road and compensates for changes in the suspension geometry when the vehicle is cornering or travelling over an undulating surface.

Caster is the tilting of the top of the front steering axis from the vertical. A tilt toward the rear is positive caster and a tilt toward the front is negative caster.

Caster is adjusted by moving shims from one end of the upper control arm mount to the other.

10

Chapter 11 Body

Contents

1 General information

These models have a separate frame and body. Certain components are particularly vulnerable to accident damage and can be unbolted and repaired or replaced. Among these parts are the body moldings, bumpers, the hood and trunk lids and all glass.

Only general body maintenance practices and body panel repair procedures within the scope of the do-it-yourselfer are included in this Chapter.

2 Body — maintenance

1   The condition of your vehicle's body is very important, because the resale value depends a great deal on it. It's much more difficult to repair a neglected or damaged body than it is to repair mechanical components. The hidden areas of the body, such as the wheel wells, the frame and the engine compartment, are equally important, although they don't require as frequent attention as the rest of the body.
2   Once a year, or every 12,000 miles, it's a good idea to have the underside of the body steam cleaned. All traces of dirt and oil will be removed and the area can then be inspected carefully for rust, damaged brake lines, frayed electrical wires, damaged cables and other problems. The front suspension components should be greased after completion of this job.
3   At the same time, clean the engine and the engine compartment with a steam cleaner or water soluble degreaser.
4   The wheel wells should be given close attention, since undercoating can peel away and stones and dirt thrown up by the tires can cause the paint to chip and flake, allowing rust to set in. If rust is found, clean down to the bare metal and apply an anti-rust paint.
5   The body should be washed about once a week. Wet the vehicle thoroughly to soften the dirt, then wash it down with a soft sponge and plenty of clean soapy water. If the surplus dirt is not washed off very carefully, it can wear down the paint.
6   Spots of tar or asphalt thrown up from the road should be removed with a cloth soaked in solvent.
7   Once every six months, wax the body and chrome trim. If a chrome cleaner is used to remove rust from any of the vehicle's plated parts, remember that the cleaner also removes part of the chrome, so use it sparingly.

3 Vinyl trim — maintenance

Don't clean vinyl trim with detergents, caustic soap or petroleum-based cleaners. Plain soap and water works just fine, with a soft brush to clean dirt that may be ingrained. Wash the vinyl as frequently as the rest of the vehicle.

After cleaning, application of a high quality rubber and vinyl protectant will help prevent oxidation and cracks. The protectant can also be applied to weatherstripping, vacuum lines and rubber hoses, which often fail as a result of chemical degradation, and to the tires.

4 Upholstery and carpets — maintenance

1 Every three months remove the carpets or mats and clean the interior of the vehicle (more frequently if necessary). Vacuum the upholstery and carpets to remove loose dirt and dust.
2 Leather upholstery requires special care. Stains should be removed with warm water and a very mild soap solution. Use a clean, damp cloth to remove the soap, then wipe again with a dry cloth. Never use alcohol, gasoline, nail polish remover or thinner to clean leather upholstery.
3 After cleaning, regularly treat leather upholstery with a leather wax. Never use car wax on leather upholstery.
4 In areas where the interior of the vehicle is subject to bright sunlight, cover leather seats with a sheet if the vehicle is to be left out for any length of time.
5 Use of an interior-type windshield sun deflector is also recommended.

5 Body repair — minor damage

See color photo sequence ''Repair of minor scratches''

1 If the scratch is superficial and does not penetrate to the metal of the body, repair is very simple. Lightly rub the scratched area with a fine rubbing compound to remove loose paint and built up wax. Rinse the area with clean water.
2 Apply touch-up paint to the scratch, using a small brush. Continue to apply thin layers of paint until the surface of the paint in the scratch is level with the surrounding paint. Allow the new paint at least two weeks to harden, then blend it into the surrounding paint by rubbing with a very fine rubbing compound. Finally, apply a coat of wax to the scratch area.
3 If the scratch has penetrated the paint and exposed the metal of the body, causing the metal to rust, a different repair technique is required. Remove all loose rust from the bottom of the scratch with a pocket knife, then apply rust-inhibiting paint to prevent the formation of rust in the future. Using a rubber or nylon applicator, coat the scratched area with glaze-type filler. If required, the filler can be mixed with thinner to provide a very thin paste, which is ideal for filling narrow scratches. Before the glaze filler in the scratch hardens, wrap a piece of smooth cotton cloth around the tip of a finger. Dip the cloth in thinner and then quickly wipe it along the surface of the scratch. This will ensure that the surface of the filler is slightly hollow. The scratch can now be painted over as described earlier in this Section.

Repair of dents

4 When repairing dents, the first job is to pull the dent out until the affected area is as close as possible to its original shape. There is no point in trying to restore the original shape completely as the metal in the damaged area will have stretched on impact and cannot be restored to its original contours. It is better to bring the level of the dent up to a point which is about 1/8-inch below the level of the surrounding metal. In cases where the dent is very shallow, it is not worth trying to pull it out at all.
5 If the back side of the dent is accessible, it can be hammered out gently from behind using a soft-face hammer. While doing this, hold a block of wood firmly against the opposite side of the metal to absorb the hammer blows and prevent the metal from being stretched.
6 If the dent is in a section of the body which has double layers, or some other factor makes it inaccessible from behind, a different technique is required. Drill several small holes through the metal inside the damaged area, particularly in the deeper sections. Screw long, self-tapping screws into the holes just enough for them to get a good grip in the metal. Now the dent can be pulled out by pulling on the protruding heads of the screws with locking pliers.
7 The next stage of repair is the removal of paint from the damaged area and from an inch or so of the surrounding metal. This is easily done with a wire brush or sanding disk in a drill motor, although it can be done just as effectively by hand with sandpaper. To complete the preparation for filling, score the surface of the bare metal with a screwdriver or the tang of a file, or drill small holes in the affected area. This will provide a good grip for the filler material. To complete the repair, see the Section on filling and painting.

Repair of rust holes or gashes

8 Remove all paint from the affected area and from an inch or so of the surrounding metal using a sanding disk or wire brush mounted in a drill motor. If these are not available, a few sheets of sandpaper will do the job just as effectively.
9 With the paint removed, you will be able to determine the severity of the corrosion and decide whether to replace the whole panel, if possible, or repair the affected area. New body panels are not as expensive as most people think, and it is often quicker to install a new panel than to repair large areas of rust.
10 Remove all trim pieces from the affected area except those which will act as a guide to the original shape of the damaged body, such as headlight shells, etc. Using metal snips or a hacksaw blade, remove all loose metal and any other metal that is badly affected by rust. Hammer the edges of the hole inward to create a slight depression for the filler material.
11 Wire brush the affected area to remove the powdery rust from the surface of the metal. If the back of the rusted area is accessible, treat it with rust-inhibiting paint.
12 Before filling is done, block the hole in some way. This can be done with sheet metal riveted or screwed into place, or by stuffing the hole with wire mesh.
13 Once the hole is blocked off, the affected area can be filled and painted. See the following subsection on filling and painting.

Filling and painting

14 Many types of body fillers are available, but generally speaking, body repair kits which contain filler paste and a tube of resin hardener are best for this type of repair work. A wide, flexible plastic or nylon applicator will be necessary for imparting a smooth and contoured finish to the surface of the filler material. Mix up a small amount of filler on a clean piece of wood or cardboard (use the hardener sparingly). Follow the manufacturer's instructions on the package, otherwise the filler will set incorrectly.
15 Using the applicator, apply the filler paste to the prepared area. Draw the applicator across the surface of the filler to achieve the desired contour and to level the filler surface. As soon as a contour that approximates the original one is achieved, stop working the paste. If you continue, the paste will begin to stick to the applicator. Continue to add thin layers of paste at 20-minute intervals until the level of the filler is just above the surrounding metal.
16 Once the filler has hardened, the excess can be removed with a body file. From then on, progressively finer grades of sandpaper should be used, starting with a 180-grit paper and finishing with 600-grit wet-or-dry paper. Always wrap the sandpaper around a flat rubber or wooden block, otherwise the surface of the filler will not be completely flat. During the sanding of the filler surface, the wet-or-dry paper should be periodically rinsed in water. This will ensure that a very smooth finish is produced in the final stage.
17 At this point, the repair area should be surrounded by a ring of bare metal, which in turn should be encircled by the finely feathered edge of good paint. Rinse the repair area with clean water until all of the dust produced by the sanding operation is gone.
18 Spray the entire area with a light coat of primer. This will reveal any imperfections in the surface of the filler. Repair the imperfections with fresh filler paste or glaze filler and once more smooth the surface with sandpaper. Repeat this spray-and-repair procedure until you are satisfied that the surface of the filler and the feathered edge of the paint are perfect. Rinse the area with clean water and allow it to dry completely.
19 The repair area is now ready for painting. Spray painting must be carried out in a warm, dry, windless and dust-free atmosphere. These conditions can be created if you have access to a large indoor work area, but if you are forced to work in the open, you will have to pick the day very carefully. If you are working indoors, dousing the floor in the work area with water will help settle the dust which would otherwise be in the air. If the repair area is confined to one body panel, mask off the surrounding panels. This will help minimize the effects of a slight mismatch in paint color. Trim pieces such as chrome strips, door handles, etc., will also need to be masked off or removed. Use masking tape and several thicknesses of newspaper for the masking operations.
20 Before spraying, shake the paint can thoroughly, then spray a test area until the spray painting technique is mastered. Cover the repair area with a thick coat of primer. The thickness should be built up using several thin layers of primer rather than one thick one. Using 600-grit

wet-or-dry sandpaper, rub down the surface of the primer until it is very smooth. While doing this, the work area should be thoroughly rinsed with water and the wet-or-dry sandpaper periodically rinsed as well. Allow the primer to dry before spraying additional coats.

21   Spray on the top coat, again building up the thickness by using several thin layers of paint. Begin spraying in the center of the repair area and then, using a circular motion, work out until the whole repair area and about two inches of the surrounding original paint is covered. Remove all masking material 10 to 15 minutes after spraying on the final coat of paint. Allow the new paint at least two weeks to harden, then use a very fine rubbing compound to blend the edges of the new paint into the existing paint. Finally, apply a coat of wax.

6 Body repair — major damage

1   Major damage must be repaired by an auto body shop specifically equipped to perform unibody repairs. These shops have the specialized equipment required to do the job properly.

2   If the damage is extensive, the body must be checked for proper alignment or the vehicle's handling characteristics may be adversely affected and other components may wear at an accelerated rate.

3   Due to the fact that all of the major body components (hood, fenders, etc.) are separate and replaceable units, any seriously damaged components should be replaced rather than repaired. Sometimes the components can be found in a wrecking yard that specializes in used vehicle components, often at considerable savings over the cost of new parts.

7 Hinges and locks — maintenance

Once every 3000 miles, or every three months, the hinges and latch assemblies on the doors, hood and trunk should be given a few drops of light oil or lock lubricant. The door latch strikers should also be lubricated with a thin coat of grease to reduce wear and ensure free movement. Lubricate the door and trunk locks with spray-on graphite lubricant.

8 Hood — removal, installation and adjustment

Refer to illustrations 8.1, 8.2 and 8.4

Note: *The hood is heavy and somewhat awkward to remove and install — at least two people should perform this procedure.*

Removal and installation

1   Use blankets or pads to cover the cowl area of the body and the fenders **(see illustration)**. This will protect the body and paint as the hood is lifted off.

2   Scribe or paint alignment marks around the bolt heads to insure proper alignment during installation **(see illustration)**.

3   Disconnect any cables or wire harnesses which will interfere with removal.

4   Have an assistant support the weight of the hood. Remove the hinge-to-hood nuts or bolts **(see illustration)**.

5   Lift off the hood.

6   Installation is the reverse of removal.

Adjustment

7   Fore-and-aft and side-to-side adjustment of the hood is done by moving the hood in relation to the hinge plate after loosening the bolts or nuts.

8   Scribe a line around the entire hinge plate so you can judge the amount of movement **(see illustration 8.2)**.

9   Loosen the bolts or nuts and move the hood into correct alignment. Move it only a little at a time. Tighten the hinge bolts or nuts and carefully lower the hood to check the alignment.

10 If necessary after installation, the entire hood lock assembly can be adjusted up and down as well as from side to side on the radiator support so the hood closes securely and is flush with the fenders. To do this, scribe a line around the hood lock mounting bolts to provide a reference point (Section 12). Then loosen the bolts and reposition the latch assembly as necessary. Following adjustment, retighten the mounting bolts.

11 Finally, adjust the hood bumpers on the radiator support so the hood, when closed, is flush with the fenders.

12 The hood latch assembly, as well as the hinges, should be periodically lubricated with white lithium-base grease to prevent sticking and wear.

9 Bumpers (front) — removal and installation

1970 through 1972 models

Refer to illustration 9.5

1   Raise the hood and disconnect the battery.

2   Remove the radiator grille.

3   Remove the parking lights from their mounts and place to one side; also remove the side marker lights.

4   Remove the valance panel.

5   Unbolt the bumper bracket from the frame and remove the bumper **(see illustration)**.

1973 through 1988 models

Refer to illustrations 9.6 and 9.9

Note: *Vehicles manufactured from 1973 on are fitted with energy absorbing devices between the bumpers and vehicle frame to meet Federal Safety Standards under impact load. These are filled with hydraulic*

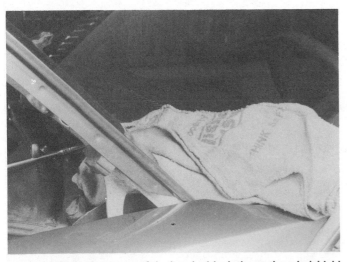

8.1   Pad the back corners of the hood with cloths so the windshield won't be damaged if the hood accidentally swings rearward

8.2   Use white paint or a scribe to mark the hood bolt locations

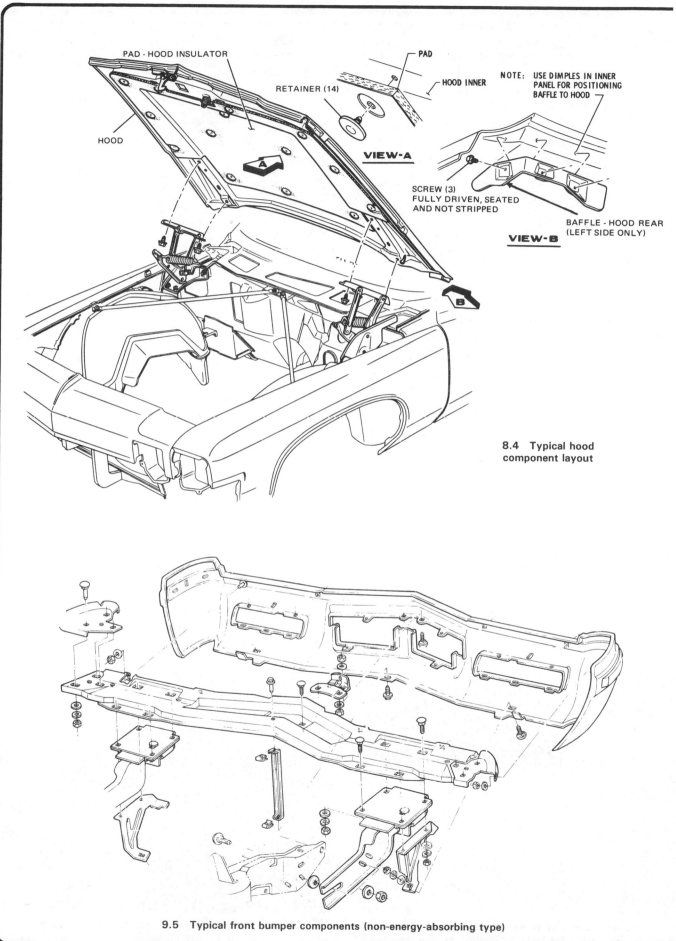

PAD - HOOD INSULATOR

PAD

HOOD INNER

RETAINER (14)

NOTE: USE DIMPLES IN INNER PANEL FOR POSITIONING BAFFLE TO HOOD

VIEW-A

HOOD

A

B

SCREW (3) FULLY DRIVEN, SEATED AND NOT STRIPPED

BAFFLE - HOOD REAR (LEFT SIDE ONLY)

VIEW-B

8.4 Typical hood component layout

9.5 Typical front bumper components (non-energy-absorbing type)

11

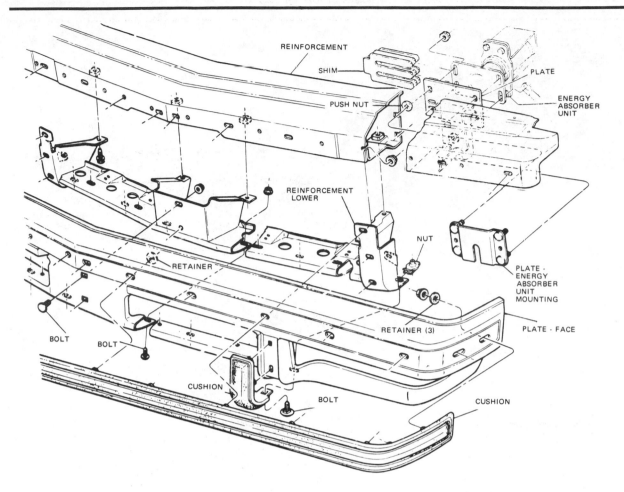

9.6 Typical energy-absorbing type front bumper installation details

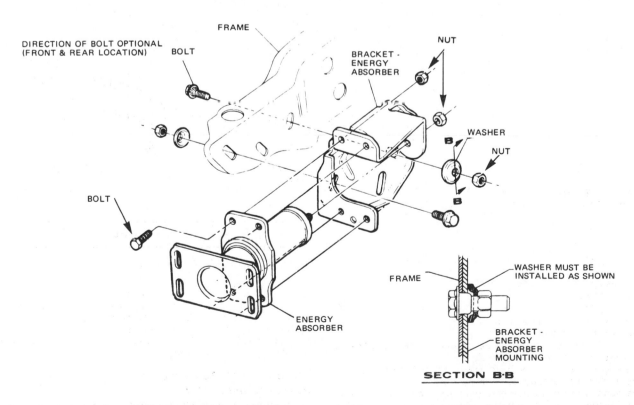

9.9 Bumper energy absorber used on 1973 and later models (front shown)

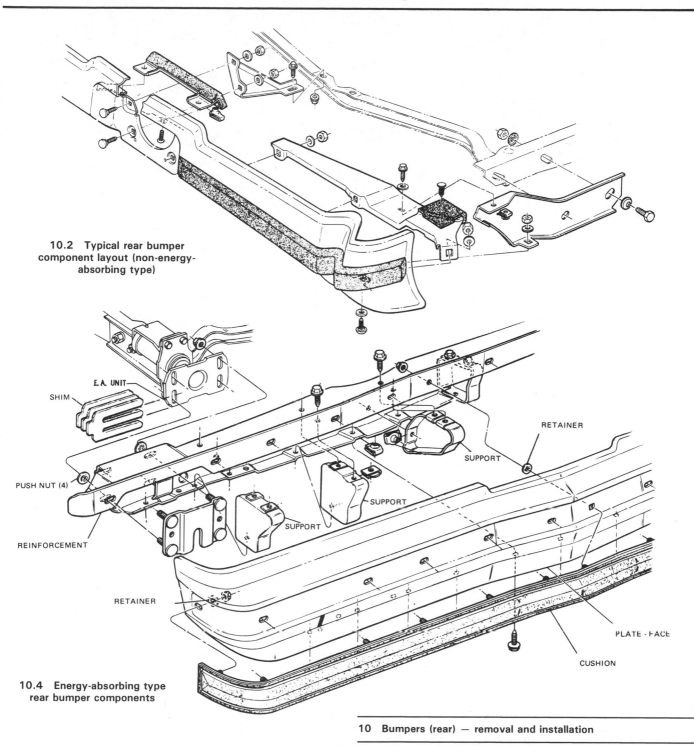

10.2 Typical rear bumper component layout (non-energy-absorbing type)

10.4 Energy-absorbing type rear bumper components

fluid and gas under high pressure and should not be interfered with or subjected to heat.

6   Unscrew and remove the nuts which hold the reinforcement plate to the energy absorber (see illustration).
7   Withdraw the bumper.
8   If the reinforcement plate must be removed, detach the license plate bracket and other reinforcement plate brackets.
9   If the energy absorber must be removed, unbolt it from the frame and slide it from the vehicle (see illustration).
10 Installation of all types is a reversal of removal, but move the position of the bumper up and down or from side to side in order to equalize the bumper-to-body clearance before tightening the mounting bolts and nuts.

10 Bumpers (rear) — removal and installation

1970 through 1972 models
Refer to illustration 10.2

1   Disconnect the license plate light.
2   Unscrew and remove all bumper mounting bolts and lower the bumper to the floor. Some of these bolts are accessible from within the trunk on sedans (see illustration).
3   The operations are similar on wagons except that various step pads and clips must be removed.

1973 through 1988 models
Refer to illustration 10.4

4   On these bumpers with energy absorbers, the removal operations are similar to those described in Paragraphs 6 to 9 of the preceding Section (see illustration).

11

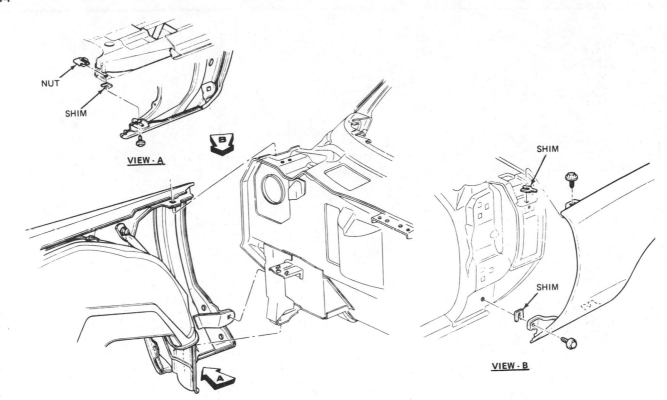

11.8a Typical front fender installation details

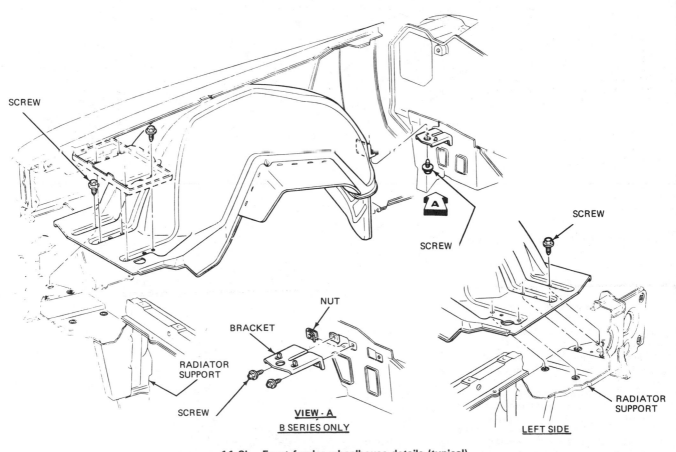

11.8b Front fender wheelhouse details (typical)

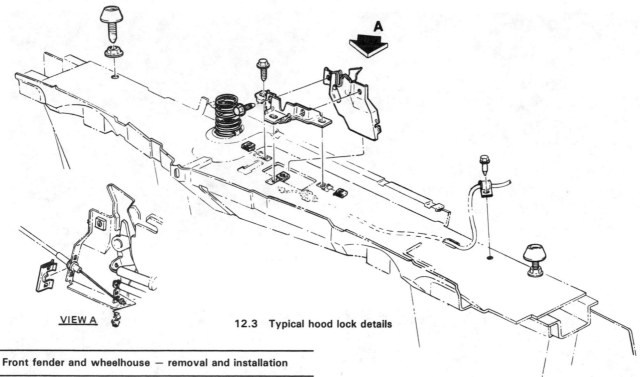

12.3 Typical hood lock details

VIEW A

11 Front fender and wheelhouse — removal and installation

Refer to illustrations 11.8a and 11.8b

1   Disconnect the battery ground lead. If the right-hand fender and wheelhouse are to be removed, remove the battery also.
2   Raise the vehicle using a hoist, then remove the wheel. Remove the front bumper.
3   Remove the hood and hinges.
4   Disconnect all electrical wiring, clips and other items attached to the assembly.
5   Disconnect the filler panel, header panel, valance panel and brace.
6   Remove the headlight and bezel.
7   Remove the headlight retainer support screws where applicable.
8   Remove the fender and wheelhouse assembly attachment screws. Note the number of shims fitted to assist in installation **(see illustrations)**.
9   Remove the side-marker light connections as the assembly is being carefully lifted away from the vehicle.
10   Installation is a reversal of the removal procedure, but the fender and wheelhouse should be guided in at the bottom adjacent to the door first of all. Adjust the assembly before finally tightening the screws using the original shims, then add or remove shims as necessary.

12 Hood lock mechanism — removal and installation

Refer to illustration 12.3

1   Remove the catch plate assembly by removing the screws retaining the catch to the radiator support, center support and tie-bar or grille upper bar.
2   Disconnect the hood release cable.
3   Scribe a line around the lockplate to aid alignment when installing, then remove the screws retaining it to the hood **(see illustration)**. Remove the lockplate.
4   Installation is the reverse of the removal procedure. Adjust the hood lock bolts so that the hood engages securely when closed and the hood bumpers are slightly compressed.

13 Trunk lid — removal, installation and adjustment

Refer to illustrations 13.3

1   Open the trunk lid and cover the edges of the trunk compartment with pads or cloths to protect the painted surfaces when the lid is removed.

2   Disconnect any cables or wire harness connectors attached to the trunk lid that would interfere with removal.
3   Scribe or paint alignment marks around the hinge bolt mounting flanges **(see illustration)**.
4   While an assistant supports the lid, remove the hinge bolts from both sides and lift it off.
5   Installation is the reverse of removal. **Note:** *When reinstalling the trunk lid, align the hinge bolt flanges with the marks made during removal.*
6   After installation, close the lid and see if it's in proper alignment with the surrounding panels. Fore-and-aft and side-to-side adjustments of the lid are controlled by the position of the hinge bolts in the slots. To adjust it, loosen the hinge bolts, reposition the lid and retighten the bolts.
7   The height of the lid in relation to the surrounding body panels when closed can be adjusted by loosening the lock striker bolts, repositioning the striker and retightening the bolts.

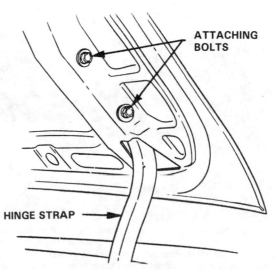

ATTACHING BOLTS

HINGE STRAP

13.3 Scribe or paint around the trunk lid attaching bolts before loosening them

11

This photo sequence illustrates the repair of a dent and damaged paintwork. The procedure for the repair of a hole is similar. Refer to the text for more complete instructions

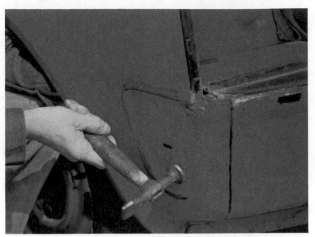

After removing any adjacent body trim, hammer the dent out. The damaged area should then be made slightly concave

Use coarse sandpaper or a sanding disc on a drill motor to remove all paint from the damaged area. Feather the sanded area into the edges of the surrounding paint, using progressively finer grades of sandpaper

The damaged area should be treated with rust remover prior to application of the body filler. In the case of a rust hole, all rusted sheet metal should be cut away

Carefully follow manufacturer's instructions when mixing the body filler so as to have the longest possible working time during application. Rust holes should be covered with fiberglass screen held in place with dabs of body filler prior to repair

Apply the filler with a flexible applicator in thin layers at 20 minute intervals. Use an applicator such as a wood spatula for confined areas. The filler should protrude slightly above the surrounding area

Shape the filler with a surform-type plane. Then, use water and progressively finer grades of sandpaper and a sanding block to wet-sand the area until it is smooth. Feather the edges of the repair area into the surrounding paint.

Use spray or brush applied primer to cover the entire repair area so that slight imperfections in the surface will be filled in. Prime at least one inch into the area surrounding the repair. Be careful of over-spray when using spray-type primer

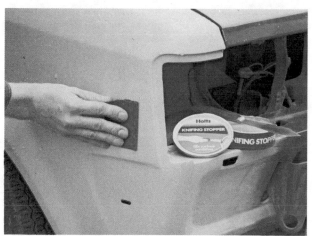

Wet-sand the primer with fine (approximately 400 grade) sandpaper until the area is smooth to the touch and blended into the surrounding paint. Use filler paste on minor imperfections

After the filler paste has dried, use rubbing compound to ensure that the surface of the primer is smooth. Prior to painting, the surface should be wiped down with a tack rag or lint-free cloth soaked in lacquer thinner

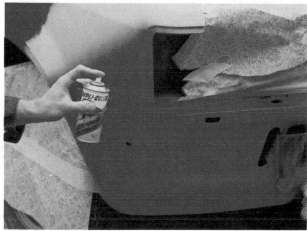

Choose a dry, warm, breeze-free area in which to paint and make sure that adjacent areas are protected from over-spray. Shake the spray paint can thoroughly and apply the top coat to the repair area, building it up by applying several coats, working from the center

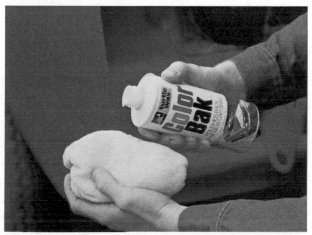

After allowing at least two weeks for the paint to harden, use fine rubbing compound to blend the area into the original paint. Wax can now be applied

11

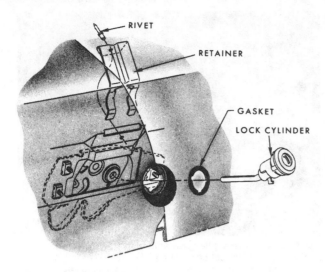

14.4   The rivet must be removed before the lock cylinder retainer can be pulled off

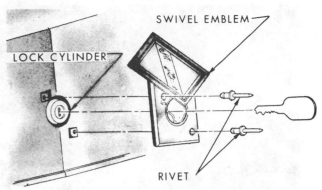

14.5   On models so equipped, the swivel-type emblem must be removed before the lock cylinder can be withdrawn

3   When installing, ensure that the lid lock is correctly aligned before finally tightening the bolts.
4   The striker is retained with bolts or screws. Before removing a striker, scribe around the adjacent panel to facilitate installation in the original position. If necessary, adjustment can be made by repositioning.

14   Trunk lid lock cylinder — removal and installation

Early models

1   Open the trunk and remove the lock cylinder retainer screw(s).
2   Pull the retainer down or away from the lock cylinder and remove the cylinder from the body.
3   Installation is the reverse of the removal procedure.

Later models

Refer to illustrations 14.4 and 14.5

4   The procedure for later models is basically as described above, but in some instances the retainer is secured with stud nuts or rivets **(see illustration)**.
5   On models with swivel-type emblems, it will be necessary to drill out the rivets and remove the emblem so the lock cylinder can be withdrawn **(see illustration)**.
6   When drilling out rivets, use a 1/8-inch drill, taking care not to enlarge the rivet hole. A 1/8 x 5/16-inch pop rivet is suitable for a replacement when installing.

15   Trunk lid lock and striker — removal and installation

1   Remove the lid lock cylinder (Section 14).
2   The lid lock is retained by bolts which can readily be removed with a wrench.

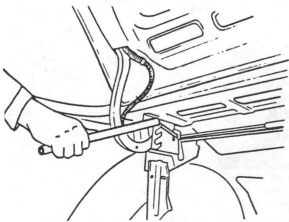

16.2   Use a piece of pipe to move the torque rod end to a different notch

16   Trunk lid torque rods — adjustment and removal

Refer to illustration 16.2

1   Torque rods are used to control the amount of effort needed to operate the trunk lid. These can be adjusted, if necessary, by moving the rods to different notches.
2   To move the rod, push a length of 1/2-inch internal diameter pipe over its end and use the pipe as a lever **(see illustration)**.
3   Removal is carried out in a similar way, but relieve the torque rod tension gently.

17   Wagon tailgate (hinged type) — removal and installation

Refer to illustrations 17.1 and 17.9

1   Remove the screws and the upper finishing molding from the interior at the top of the tailgate opening **(see illustration)**.
2   Disconnect the battery ground cable.
3   The wiring loom must now be cut to enable the tailgate to be removed. To do this, peel away the outer insulating tape and examine the color coding of the inner wires. Depending on the electrical equipment installed on the particular vehicle, there will be one or more wires. Cut these wires, making the cuts by staggering their length so that when the wires are eventually rejoined, a bulge will not be formed due to tape being all in one place.
4   Remove the screw from the grommet/tube clip at the roof reinforcement.
5   Disengage the grommet, pull the harness through the hole and tape it to the tailgate inner panel.
6   To prevent damage to paint, place a piece of thick cloth between the upper edge of the tailgate and the roof panel.
7   Have one or two assistants support the tailgate in the fully open position and then carry out the following operations.
8   Remove both of the side counterbalance assembly nuts connecting the assemblies to the tailgate, disengage from the tailgate and allow the counterbalance assembly to rest against the base of the body aperture.
9   Drive out the hinge pins using a 3/16-inch diameter rod. Strike the rod hard enough to shear the retaining clip tabs **(see illustration)**.
10 Lift the tailgate from the vehicle.
11 The tailgate counterbalance support mounting nuts must never be unscrewed unless the tailgate is in the fully open position, otherwise personal injury could result.
12 Installation is the reverse of removal, but observe the following points.
13 Install new retaining rings into the hinge pin notches so that the tabs are toward the head of the pin. Make sure the pointed end of the hinge pins faces out. Lubricate the pins.

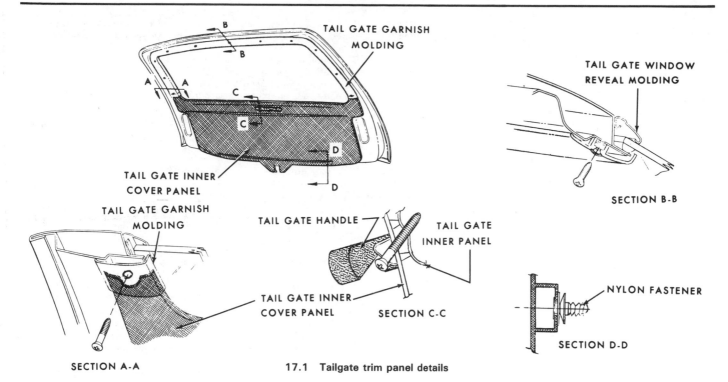

17.1 Tailgate trim panel details

14 If possible, use new nuts for the counterbalance support, otherwise apply thread locking compound to the old nuts. Tighten the nuts to 18 ft-lbs. torque.
15 The rest of the installation operations are the reverse of removal.
16 The tailgate trim panel can be removed by withdrawing any control handles and removing the panel clips and screws.

---

18 Wagon tailgate (hinged type) counterbalance assemblies — removal and installation

---

Refer to illustration 18.4

Warning: *Personal injury may result if the tailgate is not in the fully open position any time the counterbalance support assembly attaching nuts are loosened or removed.*

1 These assemblies contain heavy coil springs that are always under tension, even when removed. Do not deviate from the following procedure during removal or personal injury could result.
2 Remove the filler from the rear body pillar upper finishing molding, then remove the molding.

3 Remove the pillar anchor plate cover.
4 Have one or two assistants support the tailgate in the fully open position, remove the counterbalance nuts from one assembly and remove it from the vehicle **(see illustration)**.
5 Install the new counterbalance assembly, making sure that the black painted end is attached to the body pillar anchor plate. Use new nuts or apply thread locking compound to the old nuts. Tighten the nuts to a torque of 18 ft-lbs.
6 Do not attempt to dismantle the old assemblies, but to make them safe before disposal, the outer casing can be crimped using two pieces of steel rod and a vise.

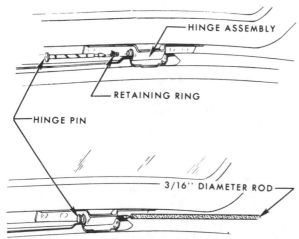

17.9 Use a 3/16-inch rod and a hammer to drive out the hinge pins

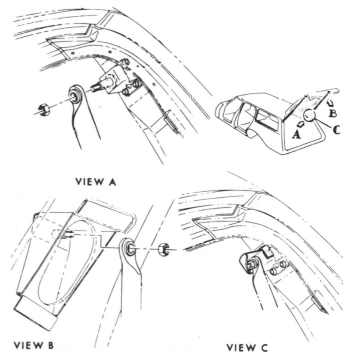

18.4 Hinged type tailgate counterbalance installation details — the tailgate must be fully open whenever the nuts are loosened or removed

11

19 Wagon tailgate (retractable type) — removal and installation

Refer to illustrations 19.2 and 19.4

1   The tailgate retracts into a storage area beneath the load compartment floor.
2   Cover the upper surface of the rear bumper to protect the tailgate. Obtain a bolt (1/4-inch 20 x 1) to serve as a roller stop during subsequent operations **(see illustration)**.
3   Raise the tailgete to its latched position and remove the left-hand access hole cover.
4   Remove the screws which attach the regulator hinge arm to the tailgate **(see illustration)**. On manually-operated tailgates, unlock the gate and lower it sufficiently to clear the lock assembly. Pivot the gate to the rear 45 degrees.

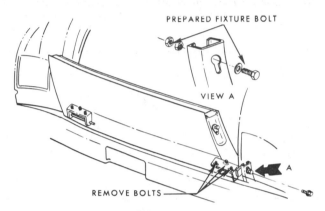

19.2   Use a 1/4-inch bolt as a roller stop during the removal procedure

5   Insert the temporary bolt and nut into the keyhole slot at the top end of the right-hand channel guide below the roller to hold the synchronizing tube in position.
6   Scribe the position of the right-hand lower roller support on the tailgate and remove the mounting bolts.
7   Move the right-hand side of the tailgate to the rear so that it clears the body opening, then slide it to the right and out of engagement with the left-hand torque roller shaft. Remove the tailgate.
8   Installation is the reverse of removal, but remove the temporary bolt before raising the tailgate.

20 Door trim panel — removal and installation

Refer to illustrations 20.2a, 20.2b and 20.3

1   Disconnect the negative cable from the battery.
2   Remove all door trim panel retaining screws, door handles and door pull/armrest assemblies **(see illustrations)**.
3   On manual window regulator equipped models, remove the window crank **(see illustration)**. On power regulator models, pry out the control switch assembly and unplug it.
4   Insert a putty knife between the trim panel and the door and disengage the retaining clips. Work around the outer edge until the panel is free.
5   Once all of the clips are disengaged, detach the trim panel, unplug any wire harness connectors and remove the trim panel from the vehicle.
6   For access to the inner door, carefully peel back the plastic watershield.
7   Prior to installation of the door panel, be sure to reinstall any clips in the panel which may have come out during the removal procedure and remain in the door itself.
8   Plug in the wire harness connectors and place the panel in position in the door. Press the door panel into place until the clips are seated and install the armrest/door pulls. Install the manual regulator window crank or power window switch assembly.

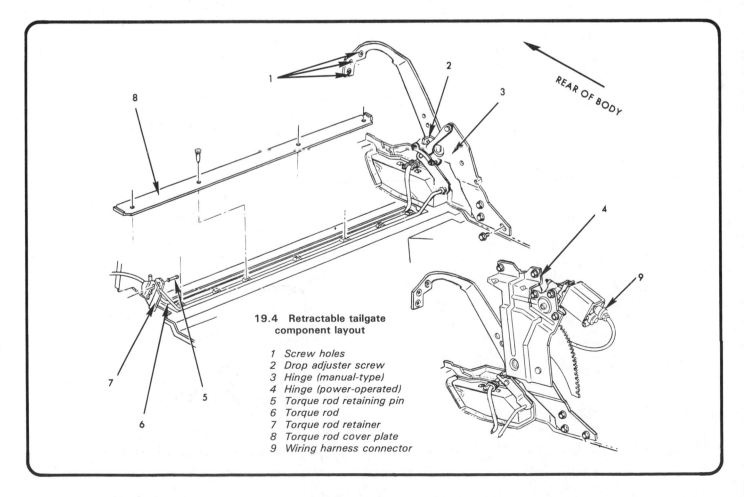

19.4   Retractable tailgate component layout

1 Screw holes
2 Drop adjuster screw
3 Hinge (manual-type)
4 Hinge (power-operated)
5 Torque rod retaining pin
6 Torque rod
7 Torque rod retainer
8 Torque rod cover plate
9 Wiring harness connector

21 Door lock assembly — removal and installation

Front door

Refer to illustration 21.1

1   To remove the lock cylinder, remove the trim panel and the water defelector. Raise the window, then use a screwdriver to slide the lock cylinder retaining clip out of engagement **(see illustration)**. Installation is the reverse of the removal procedure.

2   To remove the lock assembly, raise the window, remove the trim panel and water deflector.

3   Working through the large access hole, disengage the remote control-to-lock connecting rod (spring clip). On coupe models it may be necessary to disengage the inside locking rod from the lock, which can be achieved by sliding the plastic retaining sleeves toward each other.

4   Remove the screws securing the lock to the door lock pillar; remove the assembly from the door. On some four-door models, the inside lock-ing rod must be removed from the lock after removal of the lock assembly.

5   Installation is the reverse of removal.

Rear door

6   Raise the door glass fully and remove the upper trim panel.

7   Working through the access hole, disengage the lock connecting rods and then extract the lock securing screws. Withdraw the lock.

8   Installation is the reverse of removal.

22 Door exterior handle — removal and installation

Refer to illustrations 22.3a, 22.3b and 22.3c

1   Different designs of outside door handles are used according to vehicle model and date of production, but removal is similar for all types.

2   Raise the window completely, remove the door trim and peel away the upper corner of the water deflector in order to gain access to the

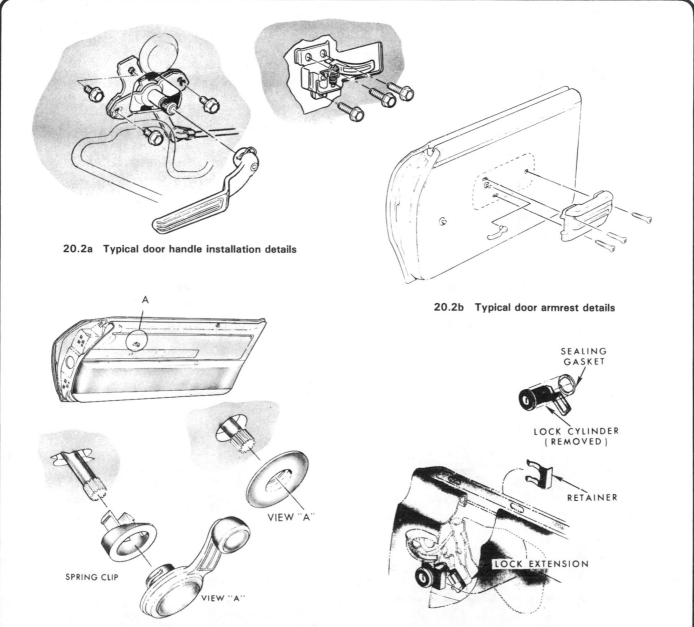

20.2a Typical door handle installation details

20.2b Typical door armrest details

20.3 Typical manual window crank installation details

21.1 Typical door lock cylinder details

11

outside handle mounting nuts or bolts.
3   Unscrew the nuts or bolts and remove the handle and gaskets **(see illustrations)**.
4   Installation is the reverse of removal.

23   Front door glass — removal and installation

Refer to illustration 23.3

1   Remove the door trim panel and water deflector.
2   Remove the weatherstrip clips, the travel stops and the stabilizer guide assembly.
3   Set the window to the half-raised position and remove the lower sash channel nuts **(see illustration)**. Now raise the window glass completely and remove the nut.

4   Mark the position of the bolts and remove them, disengage the guide from the roller and rest the guide in the bottom of the door.
5   Tilt the top of the glass until the rear roller is clear of the inner panel and then lift the glass from the door.
6   Installation is the reverse of removal, but adjust the channels, guides and stops as necessary to give smooth operation before finally tightening their mounting nuts.

24   Front door window regulator — removal and installation

Refer to illustration 24.2

1   Remove the door trim panel and water deflector.
2   Raise the window completely and prop it in this position by inserting

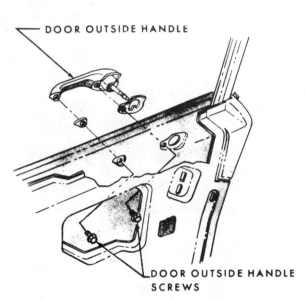

22.3a   Pushbutton-type outside handle details

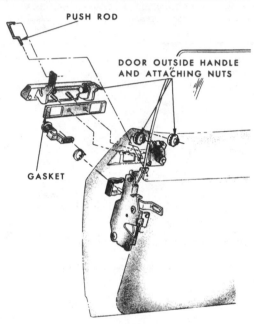

22.3b   Liftbar-type outside handle details

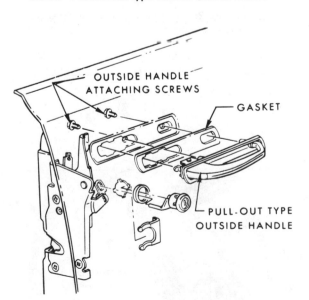

22.3c   Pullout-type exterior handle component layout

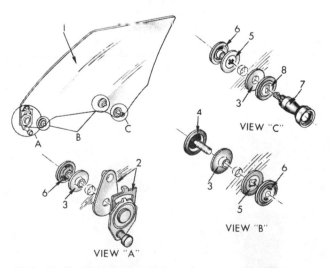

23.3   Typical front door window glass component layout

1 Window assembly	5 Plastic washer
2 Bellcrank assembly	6 Nut
3 Bushing	7 Window roller
4 Inner panel cam bolt	8 Metal washer

two rubber wedges between the glass and the door panel (see illustration).

3   Mark the position of the cam attaching bolts and remove the regulator bolts.

4   With electrically-operated regulators, disconnect the wiring harness. **Warning:** *It is imperative that the regulator sector gear on electrically-operated regulators be locked into position before removing the motor from the regulator. The control arms are under pressure and can cause serious injury if the motor is removed without performing the operation described in Chapter 12, Section 27, Steps 12 through 18.*

5   Slide the front regulator upper arm from the sash, then slide the rear lift arm forward from the sash cam.

6   Slide the regulator to the rear and withdraw it through the lower rear access hole.

7   Installation is the reverse of removal.

25   Rear door glass — removal and installation

1   Remove the upper section of the trim panel.

2   Remove the front and rear travel stop and the weatherstrip retainers.

3   Raise the window almost to the fully up position and then remove the lower sash guide plate-to-glass mounting nuts.

4   Tilt the upper edge of the glass to disengage the glass from the sash plate and then withdraw the window by lifting it straight up.

5   Installation is the reverse of removal.

26   Rear door window regulator — removal and installation

Manually-operated regulator

1   Remove the door trim panel and water deflector.

2   Raise the window completely and secure in this position with two rubber wedges inserted between the glass and the door panel (see illustration 24.2).

3   Unscrew and remove the regulator mounting bolts.

4   Disengage the regulator lift arm from the lower sash guide plate cam and withdraw the regulator through the access hole.

Electrically-operated regulator

Warning: *It is imperative that the regulator sector gear on electrically-operated regulators be locked into position before removing the motor from the regulator. The control arms are under pressure and can cause serious injury if the motor is removed without performing the operation described in Chapter 12, Section 27, Steps 12 through 18.*

5   Remove the window glass as previously described.

6   Unscrew and remove the regulator mounting bolts. Disengage the regulator lift arm from the sash plate guide cam assembly.

7   Unscrew and remove the upper and lower guide tube mounting screws, and then withdraw the guide tube and lower sash guide plate from the door.

24.2   Use rubber doorstops to hold the glass in the raised position

8   Disconnect the wiring harness and withdraw the regulator assembly.

9   Installation of both manual and electric regulators is the reverse of removal.

27   Door — removal and installation

1   Remove the door trim panel. Disconnect any wire harness connectors and push them through the door opening so they won't interfere with door removal.

2   Place a jack or jackstand under the door or have an assistant on hand to support it when the hinge bolts are removed. **Note:** *If a jack or jackstand is used, place a rag between it and the door to protect the door's painted surfaces.*

3   Scribe around the door hinges.

4   Remove the hinge-to-door bolts or drive out the pins and carefully lift off the door.

5   Installation is the reverse of removal.

6   Following installation of the door, check the alignment and adjust it if necessary as follows:

  a) Up-and-down and forward-and-backward adjustments are made by loosening the hinge-to-body bolts and moving the door as necessary.

  b) The door lock striker can also be adjusted both up and down and sideways to provide positive engagement with the lock mechanism. This is done by loosening the mounting bolts and moving the striker as necessary.

11

Chapter 12   Chassis electrical system

Contents

1   General information

The electrical system is a 12-volt, negative ground type. Power for the lights and all electrical accessories is supplied by a lead/acid-type battery which is charged by the alternator.

This Chapter covers repair and service procedures for the various electrical components not associated with the engine. Information on the battery, alternator, distributor and starter motor can be found in Chapter 5.

It should be noted that when portions of the electrical system are serviced, the negative battery cable should be disconnected from the battery to prevent electrical shorts and/or fires.

2   Electrical troubleshooting — general information

A typical electrical circuit consists of an electrical component, any switches, relays, motors, fuses, fusible links or circuit breakers related to that component and the wiring and connectors that link the component to both the battery and the chassis. To help you pinpoint an electrical circuit problem, wiring diagrams are included at the end of this book.

Before tackling any troublesome electrical circuit, first study the appropriate wiring diagrams to get a complete understanding of what makes up that individual circuit. Trouble spots, for instance, can often be narrowed down by noting if other components related to the circuit are operating properly. If several components or circuits fail at one time, chances are the problem is in a fuse or ground connection, because several circuits are often routed through the same fuse and ground connections.

Electrical problems usually stem from simple causes, such as loose or corroded connections, a blown fuse, a melted fusible link or a bad relay. Visually inspect the condition of all fuses, wires and connections in a problem circuit before troubleshooting it.

If testing instruments are going to be utilized, use the diagrams to plan ahead of time where you will make the necessary connections in order to accurately pinpoint the trouble spot.

The basic tools needed for electrical troubleshooting include a circuit tester or voltmeter (a 12-volt bulb with a set of test leads can also be used), a continuity tester, which includes a bulb, battery and set of test leads, and a jumper wire, preferably with a circuit breaker incorporated, which can be used to bypass electrical components. Before attempting to locate a problem with test instruments, use the wiring diagram(s) to decide where to make the connections.

Voltage checks

Voltage checks should be performed if a circuit is not functioning properly. Connect one lead of a circuit tester to either the negative battery terminal or a known good ground. Connect the other lead to a connector in the circuit being tested, preferably nearest to the battery or fuse. If the bulb of the tester lights, voltage is present, which means that the part of the circuit between the connector and the battery is problem free. Continue checking the rest of the circuit in the same fashion. When you reach a point at which no voltage is present, the problem lies between that point and the last test point with voltage. Most of the time the problem can be traced to a loose connection. **Note:** *Keep in mind that some circuits receive voltage only when the ignition key is in the Accessory or Run position.*

Finding a short

One method of finding shorts in a circuit is to remove the fuse and connect a test light or voltmeter in its place to the fuse terminals. There should be no voltage present in the circuit. Move the wiring harness from side to side while watching the test light. If the bulb goes on, there is a short to ground somewhere in that area, probably where the insulation has rubbed through. The same test can be performed on each component in the circuit, even a switch.

Ground check

Perform a ground test to check whether a component is properly grounded. Disconnect the battery and connect one lead of a self-powered test light, known as a continuity tester, to a known good ground. Connect the other lead to the wire or ground connection being tested. If the bulb goes on, the ground is good. If the bulb does not go on, the ground is not good.

Continuity check

A continuity check is done to determine if there are any breaks in a circuit — if it is passing electricity properly. With the circuit off (no power in the circuit), a self-powered continuity tester can be used to check the circuit. Connect the test leads to both ends of the circuit (or to the "power" end and a good ground), and if the test light comes on, the circuit is passing current properly. If the light doesn't come on, there is a break somewhere in the circuit. The same procedure can be used to test a switch, by connecting the continuity tester to the switch terminals. With the switch turned On, the test light should come on.

Finding an open circuit

When diagnosing for possible open circuits, it is often difficult to locate them by sight because oxidation or terminal misalignment are hidden by the connectors. Merely wiggling a connector on a sensor or in the wiring harness may correct the open circuit condition. Remember this when an open circuit is indicated when troubleshooting a circuit. Intermittent problems may also be caused by oxidized or loose connections.

Electrical troubleshooting is simple if you keep in mind that all electrical circuits are basically electricity running from the battery, through the wires, switches, relays, fuses and fusible links to each electrical component (light bulb, motor, etc.) and to ground, from which it is passed back to the battery. Any electrical problem is an interruption in the flow of electricity to and from the battery.

3   Fuses — general information

Refer to illustrations 3.1 and 3.4

The electrical circuits of the vehicle are protected by a combination of fuses, circuit breakers and fusible links. The fuse block is located under the instrument panel on the left side of the dashboard **(see illustration)**. On some later models, the fuse block is incorporated into the wiring harness adjacent to the steering column.

Each of the fuses is designed to protect a specific circuit, and the various circuits are identified on the fuse panel itself.

A blown fuse on earlier models can be readily identified by inspecting the element inside the glass tube. If this metal element is broken, the fuse is inoperable and must be replaced with a new one.

On later models, miniaturized fuses are employed in the fuse block. These compact fuses, with blade terminal design, allow fingertip removal and replacement. If an electrical component fails, always check the fuse first. A blown fuse is easily identified through the clear plastic body. Visually inspect the element for evidence of damage **(see illustration)**. If a continuity check is called for, the blade terminal tips are exposed in the fuse body.

Be sure to replace blown fuses with the correct type. Fuses of different ratings are physically interchangeable, but only fuses of the proper rating should be used. Replacing a fuse with one of a higher or lower value than specified is not recommended. Each electrical circuit needs a specific amount of protection. The amperage value of each fuse is molded into the fuse body.

If the replacement fuse immediately fails, don't replace it again until the cause of the problem is isolated and corrected. In most cases, the cause will be a short circuit in the wiring caused by a broken or deteriorated wire.

4   Fusible links — general information

Some circuits are protected by fusible links. The links are used in circuits which are not ordinarily fused, such as the ignition circuit.

Although the fusible links appear to be of a heavier gauge than the wire they are protecting, the appearance is due to the thick insulation.

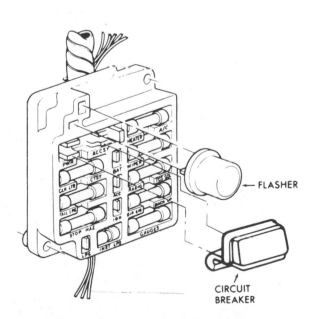

3.1   On most models the fuse block is located under the dash to the left of the driver (on later models it may be in the wiring harness adjacent to the steering column)

3.4   To test for a blown fuse on later models, pull it out and inspect it for an open circuit (1), then, with the circuit activated, use a test light across the terminals (2)

12

All fusible links are four wire gauges smaller than the wire they are designed to protect.

Fusible links cannot be repaired, but a new link of the same size wire can be put in its place. The procedure is as follows:

a) Disconnect the negative cable from the battery.
b) Disconnect the fusible link from the wiring harness.
c) Cut the damaged fusible link out of the wiring just behind the connector.
d) Strip the insulation back approximately 1/2-inch.
e) Position the connector on the new fusible link and crimp it into place.
f) Use rosin core solder at each end of the new link to obtain a good solder joint.
g) Use plenty of electrical tape around the soldered joint. No wires should be exposed.
h) Connect the battery ground cable. Test the circuit for proper operation.

5   Circuit breakers — general information

Circuit breakers protect components such as power windows, power door locks and headlights. Some circuit breakers are located in the fuse box.

On some models the circuit breaker resets itself automatically, so an electrical overload in a circuit breaker protected system will cause the circuit to fail momentarily, then come back on. If the circuit does not come back on, check it immediately. Once the condition is corrected, the circuit breaker will resume its normal function. Some circuit breakers must be reset manually.

6   Relays — general information

Several electrical accessories in the vehicle use relays to transmit the electrical signal to the component. If the relay is defective, that component will not operate properly.

The various relays are grouped together in several locations. If a faulty relay is suspected, it can be removed and tested by a dealer service department or a repair shop. Defective relays must be replaced as a unit.

7   Turn signal and hazard flashers — check and replacement

Turn signal flasher

1   The turn signal flasher, a small canister-shaped unit located in the fuse block or in the wiring harness under the dash, flashes the turn signals.
2   When the flasher unit is functioning properly, an audible click can be heard during its operation. If the turn signals fail on one side or the other and the flasher unit does not make its characteristic clicking sound, a faulty turn signal bulb is indicated.
3   If both turn signals fail to blink, the problem may be due to a blown fuse, a faulty flasher unit, a broken switch or a loose or open connection. If a quick check of the fuse box indicates that the turn signal fuse has blown, check the wiring for a short before installing a new fuse.
4   To replace the flasher, simply pull it out of the fuse block or wiring harness.
5   Make sure that the replacement unit is identical to the original. Compare the old one to the new one before installing it.
6   Installation is the reverse of removal.

Hazard flasher

7   The hazard flasher, a small canister-shaped unit located in the fuse block or the wiring harness, flashes all four turn signals simultaneously when activated.
8   The hazard flasher is checked in a fashion similar to the turn signal flasher (see Steps 2 and 3).
9   To replace the hazard flasher, pull it from the back of fuse block.
10   Make sure the replacement unit is identical to the one it replaces. Compare the old one to the new one before installing it.
11   Installation is the reverse of removal.

8   Headlight — removal and installation

Refer to illustration 8.2

1   Whenever replacing a headlight, be careful not to turn the spring-loaded adjusting screws of the headlight, as this will alter the aim.
2   Remove the headlight bezel screws and remove the decorative bezel **(see illustration)**.
3   Use a cotter pin removal tool or similar device to unhook the spring from the retaining ring.
4   Remove the two screws which secure the retaining ring and withdraw the ring. Support the light as this is done.
5   Pull the sealed beam unit outward slightly and disconnect the electrical connector from the rear of the light. Remove the light from the vehicle.
6   Position the new unit close enough to connect the electrical connector. Make sure that the numbers molded into the lens are at the top.
7   Install the retaining ring with its mounting screws and spring.
8   Install the decorative bezel and check for proper operation. If the adjusting screws were not altered, the new headlight will not need to have its aim adjusted.

9   Headlights — adjustment

Refer to illustration 9.1

Note: *The headlights must be aimed correctly. If adjusted incorrectly*

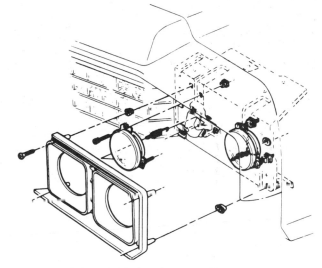

8.2   Typical headlight installation details

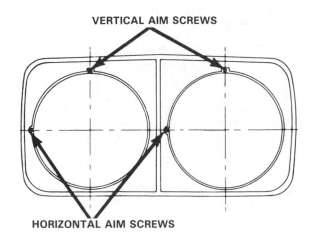

9.1   Typical headlight adjusting screw locations

they could blind the driver of an oncoming vehicle and cause a serious accident or seriously reduce your ability to see the road. The headlights should be checked for proper aim every 12 months and any time a new headlight is installed or front end body work is performed. It should be emphasized that the following procedure is only an interim step which will provide temporary adjustment until the headlights can be adjusted by a properly equipped shop.

1 Headlights have two spring loaded adjusting screws, one on the top controlling up-and-down movement and one on the side controlling left-and-right movement **(see illustration)**.

2 There are several methods of adjusting the headlights. The simplest method requires a blank wall 25 feet in front of the vehicle and a level floor.

3 Position masking tape vertically on the wall in reference to the vehicle centerline and the centerlines of both headlights.

4 Position a horizontal tape line in reference to the centerline of all the headlights. **Note:** *It may be easier to position the tape on the wall with the vehicle parked only a few inches away.*

5 Adjustment should be made with the vehicle sitting level, the gas tank half-full and no unusually heavy load in the vehicle.

6 Starting with the low beam adjustment, position the high intensity zone so it is two inches below the horizontal line and two inches to the right of the headlight vertical line. Adjustment is made by turning the top adjusting screw *clockwise* to raise the beam and *counterclockwise* to lower the beam. The adjusting screw on the side should be used in the same manner to move the beam left or right.

7 With the high beams on, the high intensity zone should be vertically centered with the exact center just below the horizontal line. **Note:** *It may not be possible to position the headlight aim exactly for both high and low beams. If a compromise must be made, keep in mind that the low beams are the most used and have the greatest effect on driver safety.*

8 Have the headlights adjusted by a dealer service department or service station at the earliest opportunity.

10 Bulb replacement — front end

Parking light
1970 models
1 Remove the lens screws, take the lens off and withdraw the bulb from its holder.

1971 through 1973 models
2 Twist the socket out of the rear of the housing.

1974 through 1988 models
3 The bulb holder is twisted out of the rear of the light body, depending on year and model.

Front side marker light
1970 and 1971 models
4 Twist the bulb holder at the rear of the light 1/4-turn to release it. The bulb can then be withdrawn from its socket.

1972 through 1988 models
5 The side marker light lens can be taken off after removing two screws.

11 Bulb replacement — rear end

Refer to illustration 11.1

Stop, tail, turn signal and back-up lights
1970 models
1 Access to all bulbs is obtained by removing the lens screws and the lens **(see illustration)**.

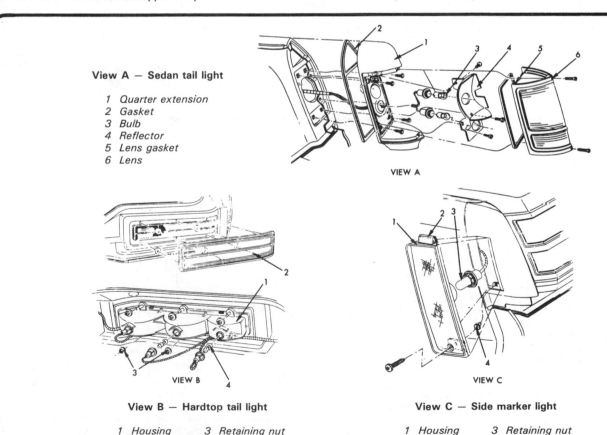

View A — Sedan tail light

1 Quarter extension
2 Gasket
3 Bulb
4 Reflector
5 Lens gasket
6 Lens

VIEW A

VIEW B

View B — Hardtop tail light

1 Housing   3 Retaining nut
2 Bezel   4 Bulb

VIEW C

View C — Side marker light

1 Housing   3 Retaining nut
2 Retainer   4 Bulb

11.1 Typical earlier model rear bulb replacement details

12

1971 and 1972 models

2   The bulb holders can be twisted from the backs of the housings by working within the trunk.

1973 through 1988 models

3   The bulbs are accessible from within the trunk on sedan models and from under the bumper on wagon models, depending on year and model.

License plate light

1970 through 1973 models

4   Access to the bulb is obtained after removing the lens securing screws and taking off the lens.

1974 through 1988 models

5   Remove the light mounting screws and lower the light until the bulb holder can be twisted from its socket in the light body.

Rear marker light

6   Twist the bulb holder from its socket after reaching into the trunk or up under the rear fender, according to design.

12   Bulb replacement — interior

Center console lights

1   Pry up the switch assembly from the console and remove the bulb from its socket.
2   The courtesy light bulb is accessible after removing the lens screws and taking off the lens.

Automatic floor shift quadrant lights

3   Remove the quadrant trim plate from the console and withdraw the light socket.

Interior (roof) light

4   Pinch the sides of the plastic lens together and remove it.
5   The festoon-type bulb can now be carefully pried from between the spring contacts.

13   Bulb replacement — instrument cluster

1   Most instrument panel bulbs are accessible after first removing the lens and trim plate in the following way.
2   Disconnect the battery ground cable.
3   If the vehicle is equipped with automatic transmission, remove the shift indicator (earlier models) or disconnect the shift indicator cable from the steering column.
4   On some models, it may be necessary to remove the steering column upper support screws and lower the column.
5   Remove the screws and snap fasteners from the outer edge of the instrument cluster and the screws from the upper surface of the trim plate.
6   On later models some bulbs are accessible from the rear of the instrument cluster after removing the cluster (Section 19).

14   Headlight switch — removal and installation

Early models
Refer to illustration 14.3

1   Disconnect the battery ground cable.
2   Pull the headlight control knob to the On position.
3   Reach up under the instrument panel and depress the switch shaft retainer **(see illustration)**. Remove the knob and shaft assembly.
4   Remove the bezel nut and switch from the instrument panel and then disconnect the wiring plug.

Later models
Refer to illustration 14.5

5   Removal is the same as for earlier models except that the instrument panel pad is fixed, and access to the switch is gained by removing the instrument bezel. The switch is then removed by reaching up under the instrument panel **(see illustration)**.

15   Windshield wiper/washer switch — removal and installation

1   Disconnect the battery ground cable.

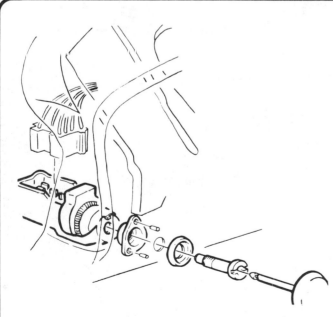
14.3   Early model headlight switch installation details

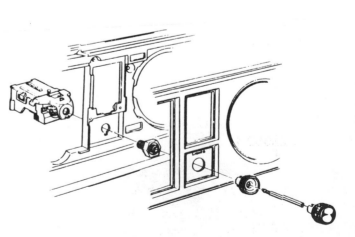
14.5   On later models the bezel may have to be removed for access to the headlight switch nut

Earlier models

2   Extract the screws holding the control shroud to the instrument panel. On some models, one of these screws is hidden above the head-light switch shaft and one above the cigar lighter knob.

3   Lift off the shroud and remove the remaining screws so that the switch can be withdrawn and unplugged.

Later models

Refer to illustration 15.10

4   The wiper/washer switch is located on the left-hand side of the steering column, under the turn signal switch.

5   To remove the wiper/washer switch, first remove the steering wheel (Chapter 10) and the turn signal switch (Section 16).

6   Remove the upper mounting screw on the ignition and dimmer switch. This releases the dimmer switch and actuator rod assembly. Be careful not to move the ignition switch. If this does happen, it will require adjustment before reassembly.

7   The wiper/washer switch and pivot assembly can now be removed from the column housing after disconnecting the wire harness.

8   During installation, place the wiper/washer switch and pivot assembly into the housing and feed the connector down through the bowl and shroud assembly.

9   Install the switch as outlined in Section 16.

10   Install the pinched end of the dimmer switch actuator rod into the dimmer switch . Feed the other end of the rod through the hose in the shroud and into the wiper/washer switch and pivot assembly drive. Do not tighten the mounting screw yet. Depress the dimmer switch slightly and use a 3/32-inch drill bit to locate the switch correctly **(see illustration)**. Push the switch up to remove the play between the ignition and dimmer switches and the actuator rod. Tighten the switch screw securely. Remove the drill bit and check the dimmer switch function by operating the lever.

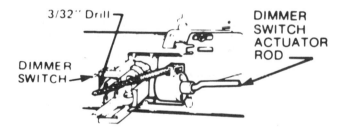

15.10   A 3/32-inch drill bit oan be used to align the dimmer switch prior to tightening the screw

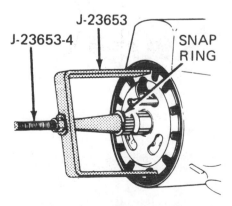

16.4   A special tool is required to depress the steering lockplate so the retaining ring can be removed

16   Turn signal switch — removal and installation

Refer to illustrations 16.3, 16.4, 16.5 and 16.8

1   Disconnect the negative battery cable and remove the steering wheel (Chapter 10).

2   Remove the steering column trim cover located at the base of the dashboard.

3   At the end of the steering column, late models have a plastic cover plate which should be pried out of the column, using a screwdriver in the slots provided **(see illustration)**.

4   The lock plate will now have to be removed from the steering col-umn. This is held in place with a snap-ring which fits into a groove in the steering shaft. The lock plate must be depressed to relieve pressure on the snap-ring. A special U-shaped tool which fits on the shaft should be used to depress the lock plate as the snap-ring is re-moved from its groove **(see illustration)**.

5   Slide the canceling cam, upper bearing preload spring and thrust washer off the end of the shaft **(see illustration)**.

16.3   Use a screwdriver to pry up the cover plate

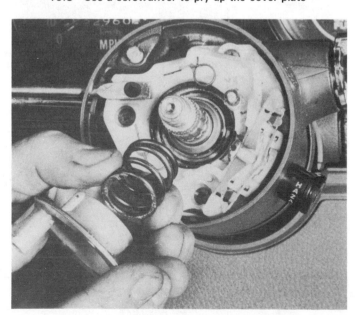

16.5   Lift off the cancelling plate and spring

6   Remove the turn signal lever attaching screw and withdraw the turn signal lever from the side of the column.
7   Push in the hazard warning knob and unscrew the knob from the threaded shaft.
8   Remove the three turn signal assembly mounting screws (see illustration).
9   Pull the switch wiring connector out of the bracket on the steering column jacket. Tape the connector terminals to prevent damage. Feed the wiring connector up through the column support bracket and pull the switch, wiring harness and connectors out the top of the steering column.
10   Installation is the reverse of removal; however, make sure the wiring harness is in the protector as it is pulled into position. Before installing the thrust washer, upper bearing preload spring and canceling cam, make sure the switch is in the neutral position and the warning knob is pulled out. Always use a new snap-ring on the shaft for the lock plate.

17   Ignition lock cylinder — removal and installation

1970 through 1978 models

Refer to illustration 17.3

1   The lock cylinder is located on the upper right-hand side of the steering column. On these models, the lock cylinder should be removed only in the Run position, otherwise damage to the warning buzzer switch may occur.

2   Remove the steering wheel (Chapter 10) and turn signal switch (Section 16). **Note:** *The turn signal switch need not be fully removed provided that it is pushed to the rear far enough for it to be slipped over the end of the shaft. Do not pull the harness out of the column.*
3   Insert a thin blade screwdriver into the slot in the turn signal switch housing. Break the housing flash loose and at the same time depress the spring latch at the lower end of the lock cylinder. Holding the latch depressed, withdraw the lock cylinder from the housing (see illustration).
4   To install the new lock cylinder/sleeve assembly, hold the sleeve and rotate the lock clockwise against the stop.
5   Insert the cylinder/sleeve assembly into the housing so the key on the cylinder sleeve is aligned with the housing keyway.
6   Insert a 0.070-inch diameter drill between the lock bezel and the housing and then rotate the cylinder counterclockwise, maintaining pressure on the cylinder until the drive section mates with the sector.
7   Press in the lock cylinder until the snap-ring engages in the grooves and secures the cylinder in the housing. Remove the drill and check the lock action.
8   Install the turn signal switch and the steering wheel.

1979 through 1988 models

Refer to illustration 17.12

9   The lock cylinder should be removed in the Run position only.
10   Remove the steering wheel (Chapter 10) and turn signal switch (Section 16). It is not necessary to completely remove the switch. Pull it up and over the end of the steering shaft. Do not pull the wiring harness out of the column.
11   Remove the ignition key warning switch.

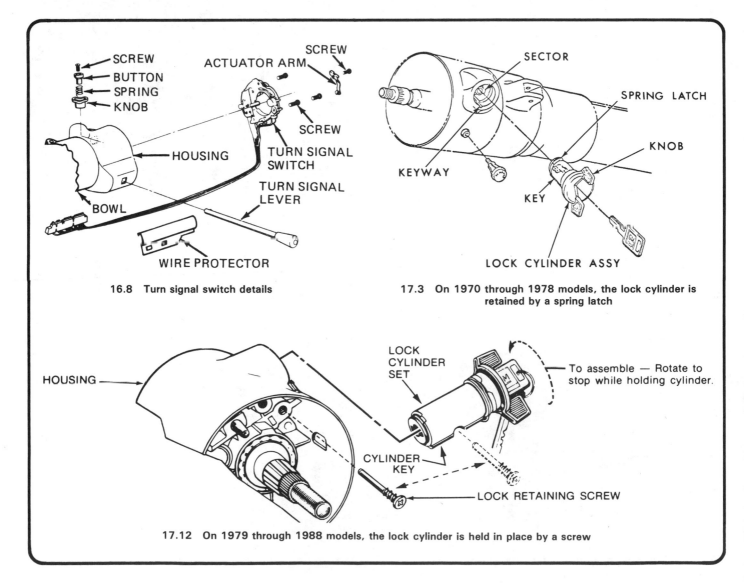

16.8   Turn signal switch details

17.3   On 1970 through 1978 models, the lock cylinder is retained by a spring latch

17.12   On 1979 through 1988 models, the lock cylinder is held in place by a screw

12 Using a magnetized screwdriver, remove the lock retaining screw. Do not allow this screw to drop down into the column, as this will require a complete disassembly of the steering column to retrieve the screw **(see illustration)**.
13 Pull the lock cylinder out of the side of the steering column.
14 To install, rotate the lock cylinder set and align the cylinder key with the keyway in the steering column housing.
15 Push the lock all the way in and install the retaining screw.
16 Install the remaining components referring to the appropriate Sections.

18 Speedometer cable — replacement

Refer to illustrations 18.1 and 18.2

1 The instrument cluster must first be removed as described in Section 19 **(see illustration)**.
2 Once the end of the speedometer drive cable is exposed, grip the inner cable with pliers and draw it out of the housing **(see illustration)**.
3 Installation is the reverse of removal, but on 1970 through 1974 models, lubricate the lower three-quarters of the inner cable before

inserting it. On later models, lubricate the entire cable. Use special speedometer cable lubricant, not oil, for this purpose.
4 Insert the cable into the housing using a twisting movement until the lower end is felt to engage with the pinion gear at the transmission.

19 Instrument cluster — removal and installation

Refer to illustration 19.5

1 Disconnect the negative cable at the battery. Place the cable out of the way so it cannot accidentally come in contact with the negative terminal of the battery, as this would once again allow power into the electrical system of the vehicle.
2 Remove the instrument cluster trim plate and steering column cover.
3 Remove the shift indicator (early models) or detach the indicator cable (later models).
4 On some models it may be necessary to remove the headlight switch (Section 14) and/or wiper/washer switch (Section 15).
5 Remove the cluster retaining screws or nuts, pull the cluster out and disconnect the speedometer cable **(see illustration)**. On some later

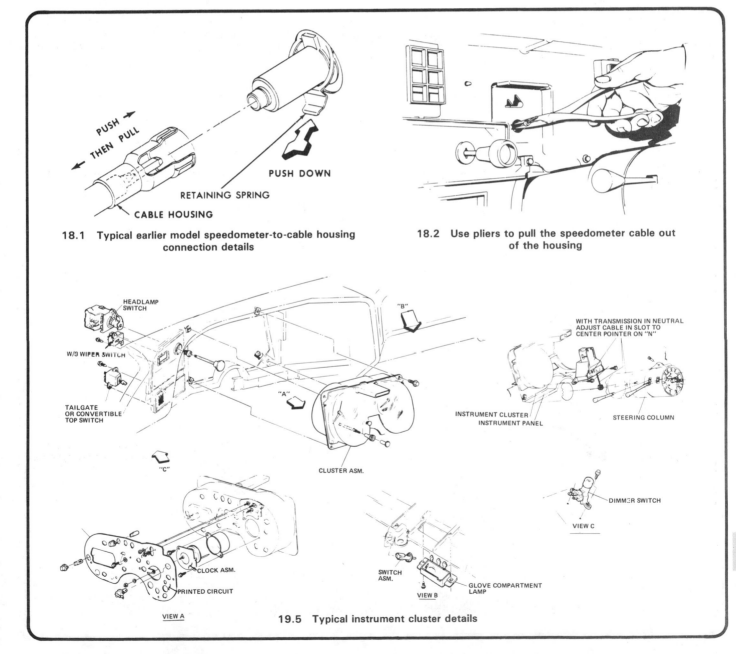

18.1 Typical earlier model speedometer-to-cable housing connection details

18.2 Use pliers to pull the speedometer cable out of the housing

19.5 Typical instrument cluster details

models it may be necessary to disconnect the cable at the transmission to provide sufficient slack for the cluster to be pulled out for access to the connectors.

6   Unplug any electrical connectors which would interfere with removal.

7   Detach the cluster from the instrument panel.

8   Installation is the reverse of removal.

20 Windshield wiper arm — removal and installation

1   Make sure the wiper arms are in the self-parked position, the motor having been switched off in the low speed mode.

2   Note carefully the position of the wiper arm in relation to the windshield lower reveal molding. Use tape on the windshield to mark the exact location of the wiper arm on the glass.

3   Using a hooked tool or a small screwdriver, pull aside the small spring tang which holds the wiper arm to the splined transmission shaft and at the same time pull the arm from the shaft.

4   Installation is the reverse of removal, but do not push the arm fully home on the shaft until the alignment of the arm has been checked. If necessary, the arm can be pulled off again and turned through one or two serrations of the shaft to correct the alignment without the necessity of pulling aside the spring tang.

5   Finally, press the arm fully home on its shaft and then wet the windshield glass and operate the motor on low speed to ensure the arc of travel is correct.

21 Windshield wiper motor — removal and installation

Refer to illustration 21.5

1   Raise the hood and remove the cowl screen.

2   Reaching through the opening, loosen the drive link-to-crank arm nuts.

3   Remove the transmission drive link from the motor crank arm.

4   Disconnect the wiring and the washer hoses from the wiper motor.

5   Remove the three motor mounting screws and withdraw the motor, guiding the crank arm through the hole in the rear firewall **(see illustration)**.

6   Installation is the reverse of removal, but before connecting the drive link, check that the motor is in Park.

22 Radio — removal and installation

Refer to illustrations 22.2 and 22.3

1   Disconnect the negative cable at the battery. Place the cable out of the way so it cannot accidentally come in contact with the negative terminal of the battery, as this would once again allow power into the electrical system of the vehicle.

2   On earlier models, remove the control knobs and bezel. Use a socket to remove the control shaft nuts and washers **(see illustration)**.

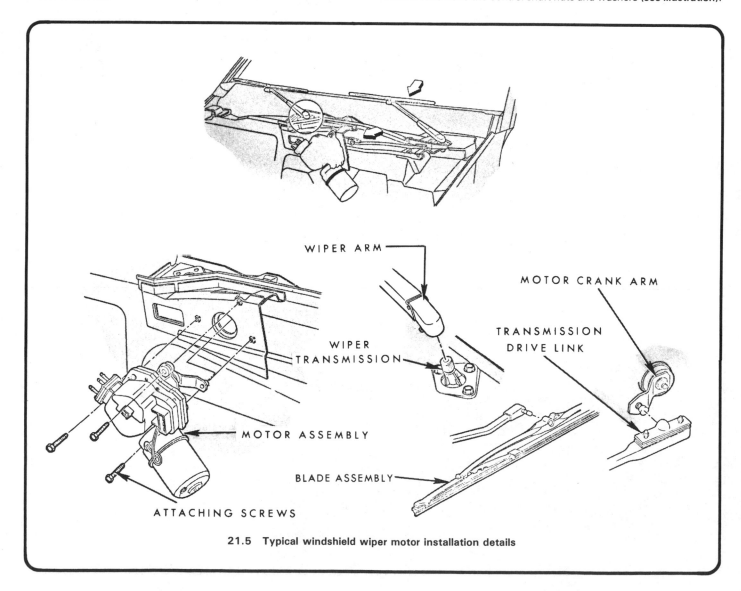

21.5 **Typical windshield wiper motor installation details**

3   On later models, remove the radio trim cover. Remove the retaining screws (see illustration).
4   On all models, pull the radio from the instrument panel until the wiring can be reached and disconnected. Remove the radio.
5   Installation is the reverse of removal. Make sure all speaker leads, the antenna lead and any other connectors are plugged in before turning on the power to the radio.

23   Electric grid-type rear defogger — testing and repair

Refer to illustrations 23.5a, 23.5b and 23.11

1   This option consists of a rear window with a number of horizontal elements that are baked into the glass surface during the glass forming operation.

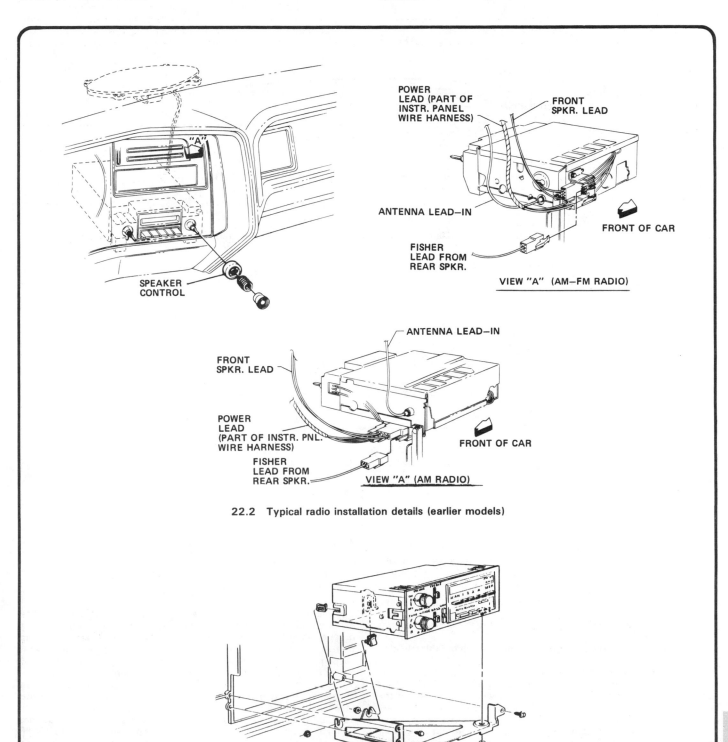

22.2   Typical radio installation details (earlier models)

22.3   Later model radio installation details

12

ZONES OF BULB BRILLIANCE

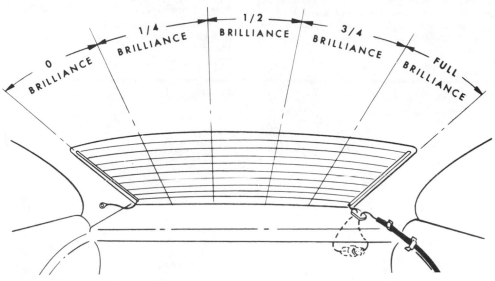

23.5a   The test light should increase in brilliance as the probe is moved from left to right across the defogger element

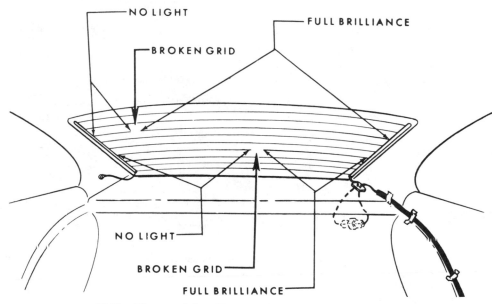

23.5b   The test light will respond as shown here if there
are broken grid lines

2   Small breaks in the element system can be successfully repaired without removing the rear window.
3   To test the grids for proper operation, start the engine and turn on the system.
4   Ground one lead of a test light and lightly touch the other lead to each grid line.
5   The brilliance of the test light should increase as the probe is moved across the element from left to right **(see illustration)**. If the test light doesn't change exactly as described above, check for breaks in the element or a loose ground wire for the system **(see illustration)**. All of the grid lines should be checked in at least two places.
6   To repair a break in a grid line it is recommended that a repair kit specifically for this purpose be purchased from a GM dealer. Included in the repair kit will be a decal, a container of silver plastic and hardener, a mixing stick and instructions.
7   To repair a break, first turn off the system and allow it to de-energize for a few minutes.
8   Lightly buff the grid line area with fine steel wool and then clean the area thoroughly with alcohol.

9   Use the decal supplied in the repair kit, or use electrician's tape above and below the area to be repaired. The space between the pieces of tape should be the same as existing grid lines. This can be checked from outside the car. Press the tape tightly against the glass to prevent seepage.
10   Mix the hardener and silver plastic thoroughly.
11   Using the wood spatula, apply the silver plastic mixture between the pieces of tape, overlapping the damaged area slightly on either end **(see illustration)**.
12   Carefully remove the decal or tape and apply a constant stream of hot air directly to the repaired area. A heat gun set at 500° to 700°F is recommended. Hold the gun about one inch from the glass for one to two minutes.
13   If the new grid line appears off color, tincture of iodine can be used to clean the repair and bring it back to the proper color. This mixture should not remain on the repair for more than 30 seconds.
14   Although the defogger is now fully operational, the repaired area should not be disturbed for at least 24 hours.

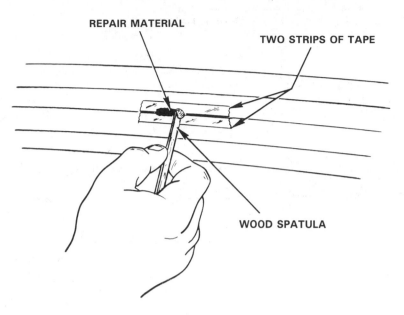

23.11   Use a wood spatula to apply the repair material to the grid lines

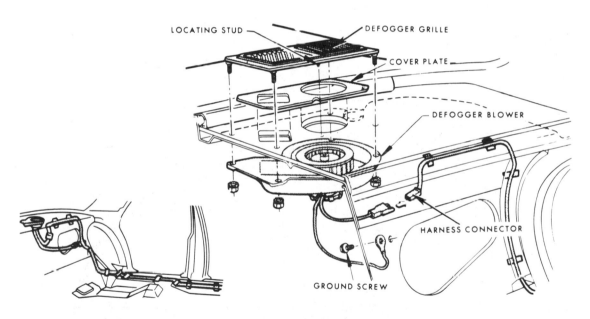

24.1   Typical blower-type defogger details

24 Electric blower type defogger — description

Refer to illustration 24.1

1   This type of rear window defogger consists of a motor and fan assembly **(see illustration)**
2   Access to the motor can usually be obtained from within the trunk on sedan models.
3   On wagon models the defogger motor is mounted on the tailgate inner panel. Air is drawn into the blower from the passenger compartment through a grille.

25 Cruise control system — description and check

The cruise control system maintains vehicle speed with a vacuum

actuated servo motor, located in the engine compartment, which is connected to the throttle linkage by a cable. The system consists of the servo motor, clutch switch, brake switch, control switches, a relay and associated vacuum hoses.

Because of the complexity of the cruise control system and the special tools and techniques required for diagnosis, repair should be left to a dealer service department or a repair shop. However, it is possible for the home mechanic to make simple checks of the wiring and vacuum connections for minor faults which can be easily repaired. These include:

a) Inspecting the cruise control actuating switches for broken wires and loose connections.
b) Checking the cruise control fuse.
c) Checking the hoses in the engine compartment for tight connections, cracks and obvious vacuum leaks. The cruise control system is operated by vacuum, so it's critical that all vacuum switches, hoses and connections are secure.

12

26   Power door lock system — description and solenoid replacement

Refer to illustration 26.4

1   This optional system incorporates a solenoid actuator inside each door. The solenoid is electrically operated from a control switch on the instrument panel and operates the lock through a linkage. Each actuator has an internal circuit breaker which may require one to three minutes to reset.
2   To remove the solenoid, raise the door window and remove the door panel trim pad as described in Chapter 11.
3   After prying away the water deflector, the solenoid can be seen through the large access hole. The solenoid can be mounted to either the rear door lock pillar or the inner metal door panel.
4   Early models use attaching screws through the door panel and into the solenoid bracket (**see illustration**). Later models use rivets to secure the solenoid to the pillar. These must be drilled out using a 1/4-inch drill bit.

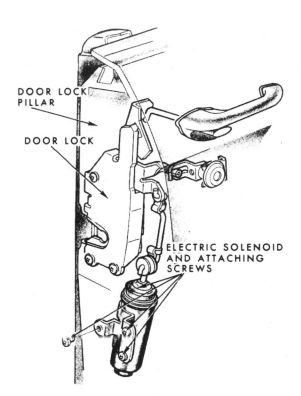

DOOR LOCK PILLAR

DOOR LOCK

ELECTRIC SOLENOID AND ATTACHING SCREWS

26.4   Typical power door lock solenoid installation details

5   Once the securing devices are removed, disconnect the wiring harness at the solenoid and the actuating link, held in place with a metal clip. Remove the solenoid from the door cavity.
6   To install, place the solenoid in position and connect the electrical connector and actuating link. If rivets were drilled out, new aluminum rivets (1/4 x 0.500-inch size) can be used upon reassembly. Optionally, 1/4 – 20 screws and U-nuts can be used.
7   Check the operation of the door locks before installing the water deflector and trim panel.

27   Power window system — description and motor replacement

1   This system incorporates an electric motor and an independent control switch for each of the door windows. The driver's door has a master control switch permitting operation of all windows.
2   The electric motor which powers the window regulator is a reversible-direction motor and operates on 12 volts. It features an internal

circuit breaker for protection. The motor is secured to the regulator with bolts.
3   The electrical motor can be removed from the regulator with the remainder of the window system intact only if the door glass is intact and attached to the regulator. If the door glass is broken or removed from the door, the motor must be separated after the regulator is removed from inside the door.

Glass intact and attached

Refer to illustration 27.7

4   Raise the window and remove the door trim panel and water deflector as described in Chapter 11.
5   Reach inside the door access cavity and disconnect the wiring harness at the motor.
6   It is imperative at this point that the window glass be taped or blocked in the up position. This will prevent the glass from falling into the door and possibly causing injury or damage.
7   Since the bolts used to secure the motor to the regulator are inaccessible, it is necessary to drill three large access holes in the metal door panel. The position of these holes is critical. Use the full-size templates as shown in the accompanying illustration. 1978 and later models have locating dimples stamped into the inner door skin to eliminate the need for templates. The template should be positioned on the door with tape after properly aligning it with the regulator attaching rivets (late models) or bolts (early models).
8   Use a centerpunch to dimple the panel at the center of the template access holes and then cut the 3/4-inch holes with a hole saw.

ALIGN TEMPLATE USING REFERENCE POINTS ''I, II, OR III'' WITH REGULATOR LOWER ATTACHING BOLTS ON DOOR

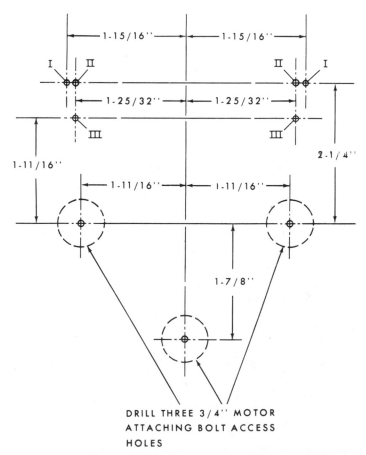

DRILL THREE 3/4'' MOTOR ATTACHING BOLT ACCESS HOLES

27.7   On 1970 through 1978 models, use this template for locating the power window motor bolts

9 Reach in through the access hole and support the motor as the attaching bolts are removed. Remove the motor through the access hole, being careful that the window glass is firmly supported in the up position.

10 Before installation, the motor drive gear and regulator sector teeth should be lubricated.

11 Upon positioning the motor, make sure the drive gear properly engages with the regulator sector teeth. Install remaining components in the reverse order of removal. Waterproof tape can be used to seal the three access holes drilled in the metal inner panel.

Glass broken or not attached

12 Remove the window regulator as described in Chapter 11. Make sure the wiring harness to the motor is disconnected first.

13 It is imperative that the regulator sector gear be locked into position before removing the motor from the regulator. The control arms are under pressure and can cause serious injury if the motor is removed without performing the following operation.

14 Drill a hole through the regulator sector gear and backplate. Install a bolt and nut to lock the gear in position. Do not drill closer than 1/2-inch to the edge of the sector gear or backplate.

15 Remove the three motor attaching bolts and remove the motor assembly from lthe regulator.

16 Prior to installation, the motor drive gear and regulator sector teeth should be lubricated. The lubricant should be cold weather approved to at least –20°F. Lubriplate Spray Lube 'A' is recommended by GM.

17 When installing the motor to the regulator, make sure the sector gear teeth and drive gear teeth properly mesh.

18 Once the motor attaching bolts are tightened, the locking nut and bolt can be removed. Install the regulator as described in Chapter 11. Don't forget to connect the motor wiring.

28 Wiring diagrams — general information

Since it isn't possible to include all wiring diagrams for every year covered by this manual, the following diagrams are those that are typical and most commonly needed.

Prior to troubleshooting any circuits, check the fuse and circuit breakers (if equipped) to make sure they're in good condition. Make sure the battery is properly charged and check the cable connections (Chapter 1).

When checking a circuit, make sure that all connectors are clean, with no broken or loose terminals. When unplugging a connector, do not pull on the wires. Pull only on the connector housings themselves.

Refer to the accompanying table for the wire color codes applicable to your vehicle.

12

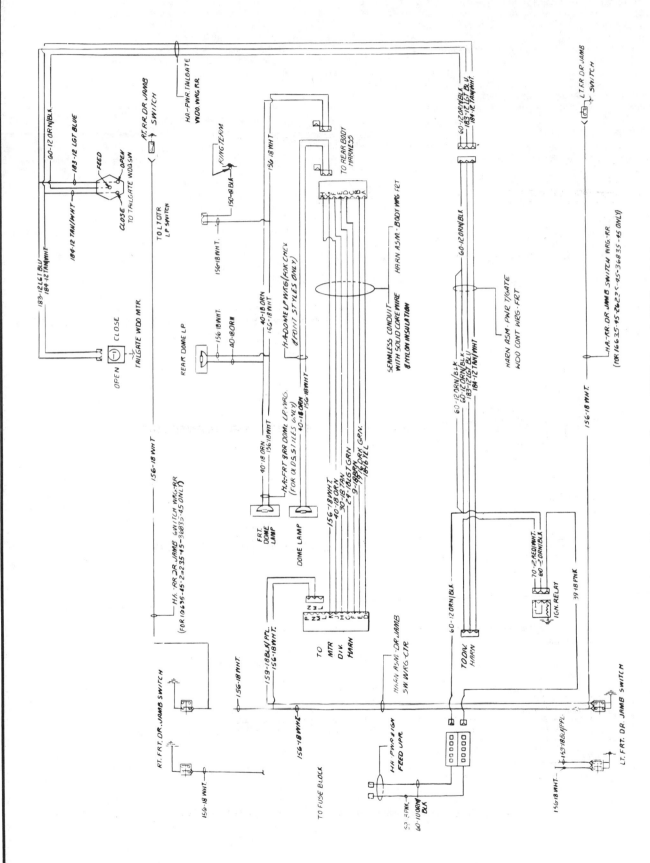

Typical front wiring harness wiring diagram (1970 through 1973 models)

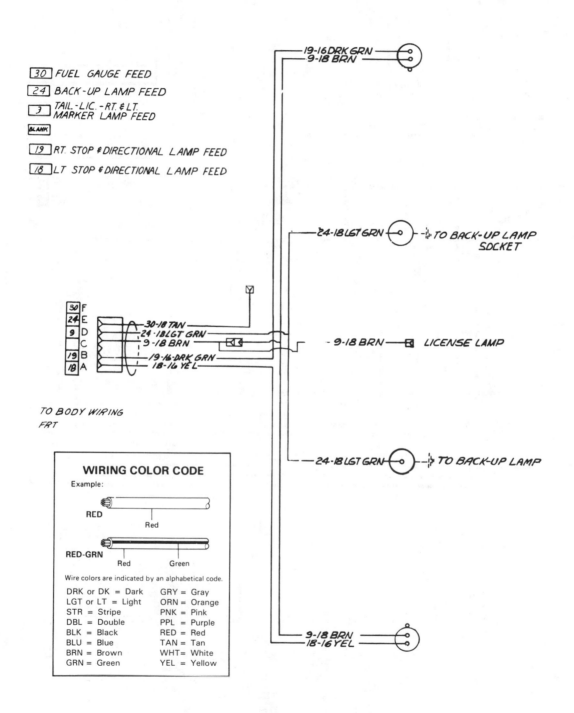

30 FUEL GAUGE FEED

24 BACK-UP LAMP FEED

3 TAIL-LIC.-RT. & LT.
MARKER LAMP FEED

BLANK

19 RT. STOP & DIRECTIONAL LAMP FEED

18 LT. STOP & DIRECTIONAL LAMP FEED

19-16 DRK GRN
9-18 BRN

24-18 LGT GRN — TO BACK-UP LAMP
SOCKET

30-18 TAN
24-18 LGT GRN
9-18 BRN — LICENSE LAMP
19-16 DRK GRN
18-16 YEL

30 F
24 E
9 D
19 B
18 A

TO BODY WIRING
FRT

24-18 LGT GRN — TO BACK-UP LAMP

9-18 BRN
18-16 YEL

WIRING COLOR CODE

Example:

RED
Red

RED-GRN
Red   Green

Wire colors are indicated by an alphabetical code.

DRK or DK = Dark   GRY = Gray
LGT or LT = Light   ORN = Orange
STR = Stripe   PNK = Pink
DBL = Double   PPL = Purple
BLK = Black   RED = Red
BLU = Blue   TAN = Tan
BRN = Brown   WHT = White
GRN = Green   YEL = Yellow

Typical rear wiring harness wiring diagram (1970 through 1973 models)

Typical electrical system diagram (1974 through 1976 models)

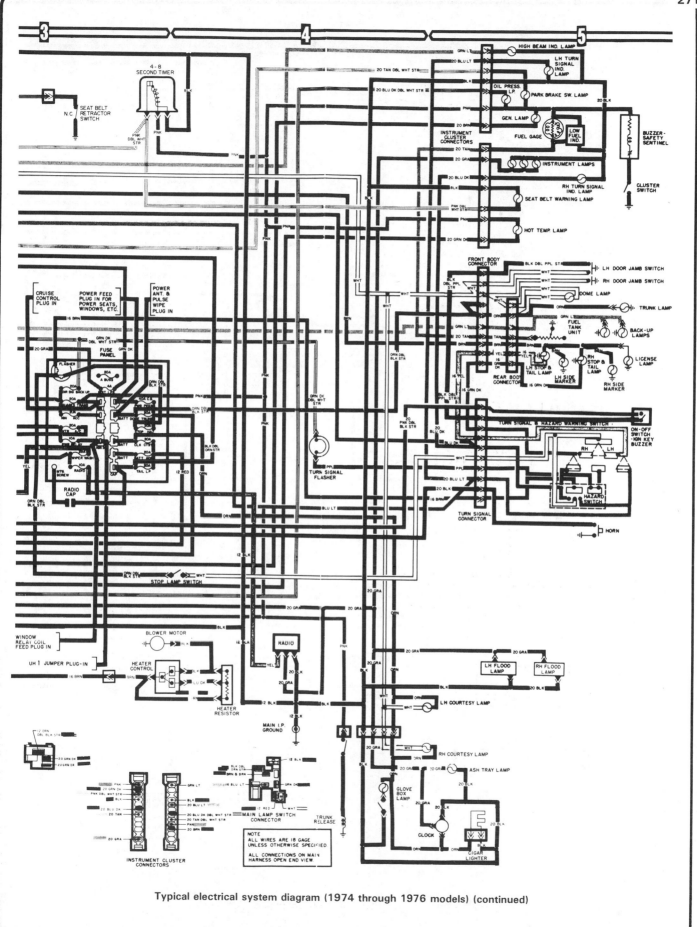

Typical electrical system diagram (1974 through 1976 models) (continued)

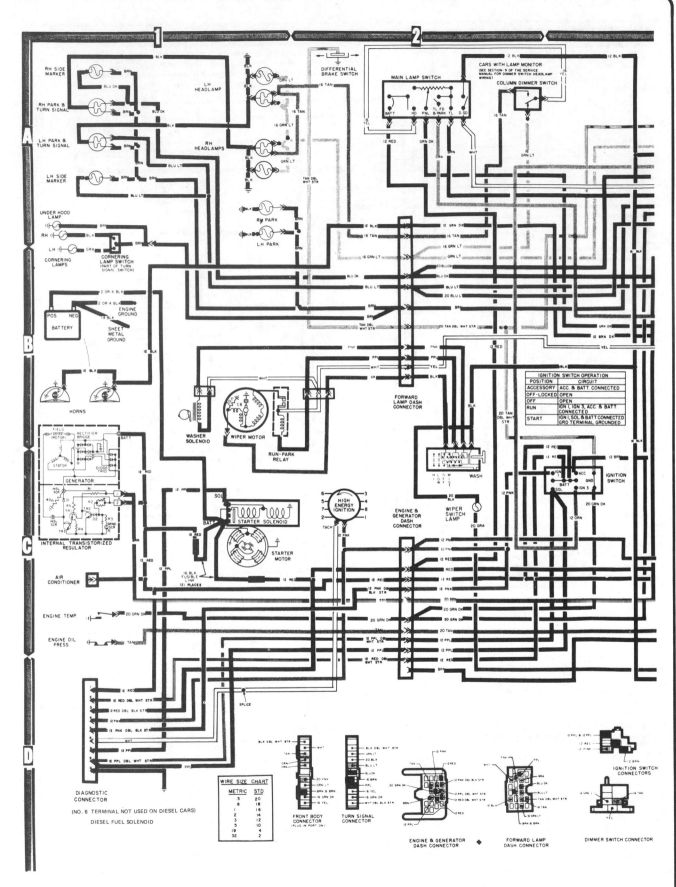

Typical electrical system diagram (1977 through 1979 models)

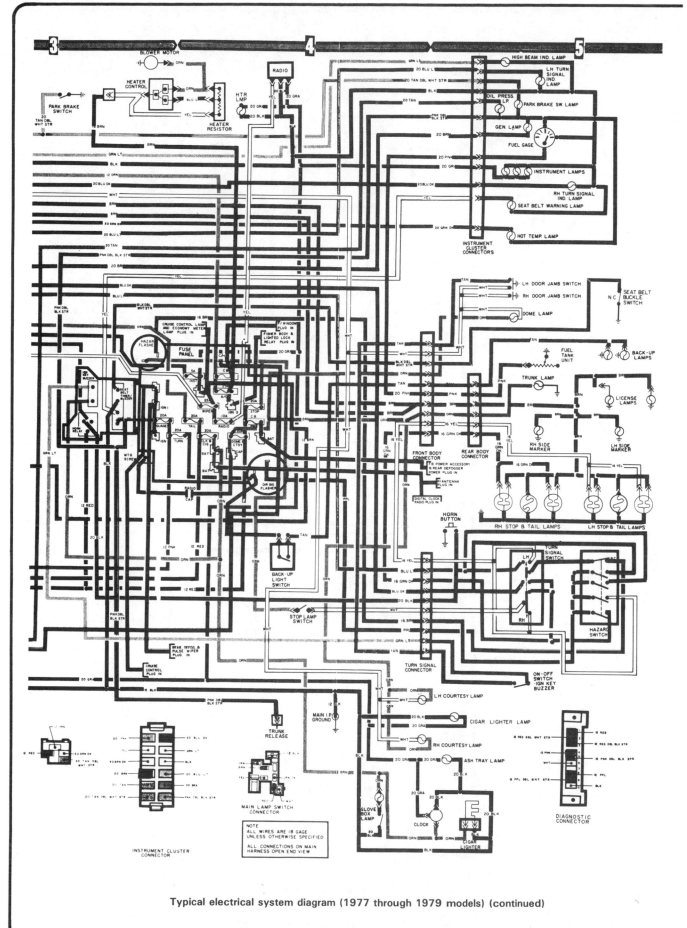

Typical electrical system diagram (1977 through 1979 models) (continued)

Typical power distribution wiring diagram (1980 through 1984 models)

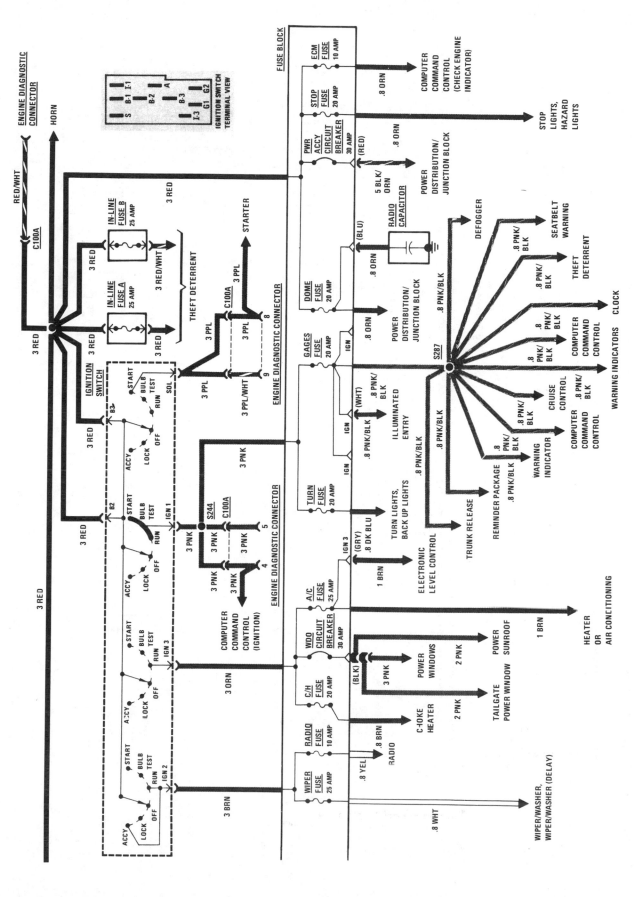

Typical power distribution wiring diagram (1980 through 1984 models) (continued)

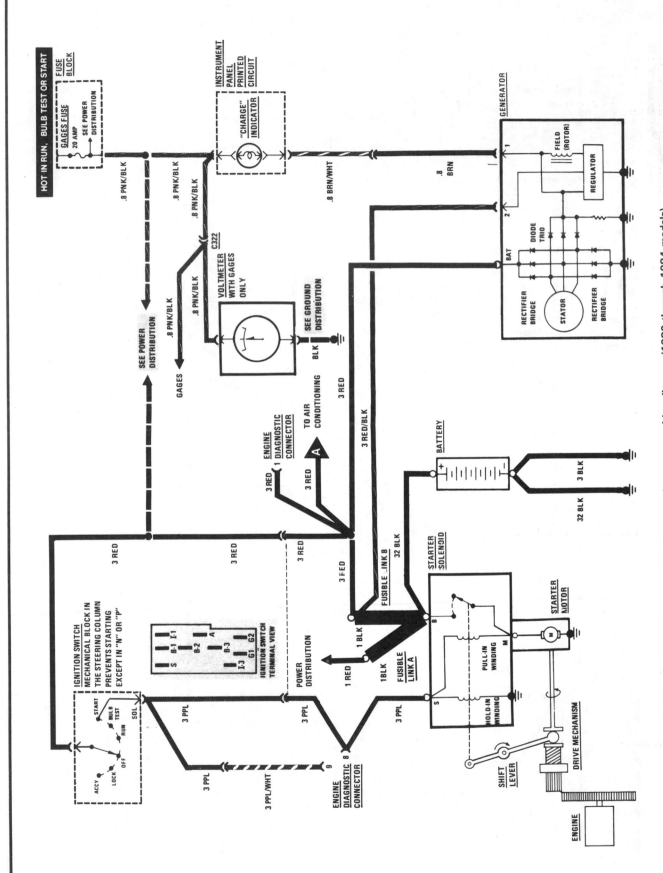

Typical V6 engine starting and charging system wiring diagram (1980 through 1984 models)

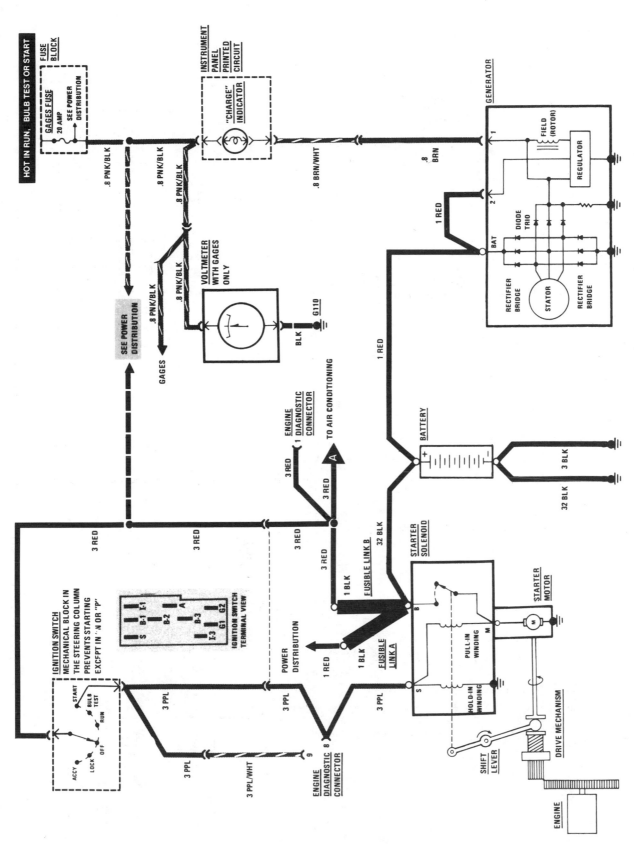

Typical V8 engine starting and charging system wiring diagram (1980 through 1984 models)

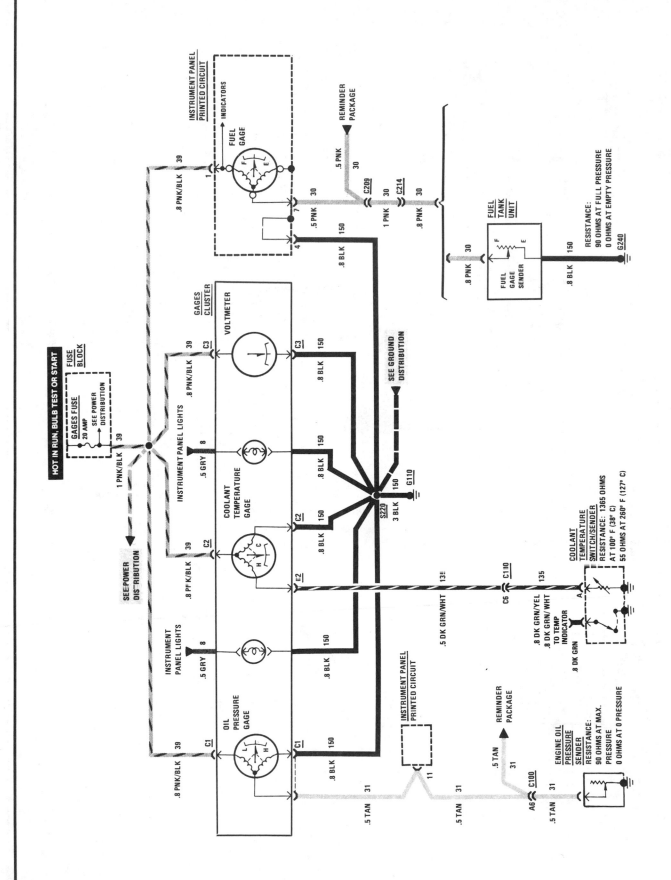

Typical instrument panel wiring diagram (1980 through 1984 models)

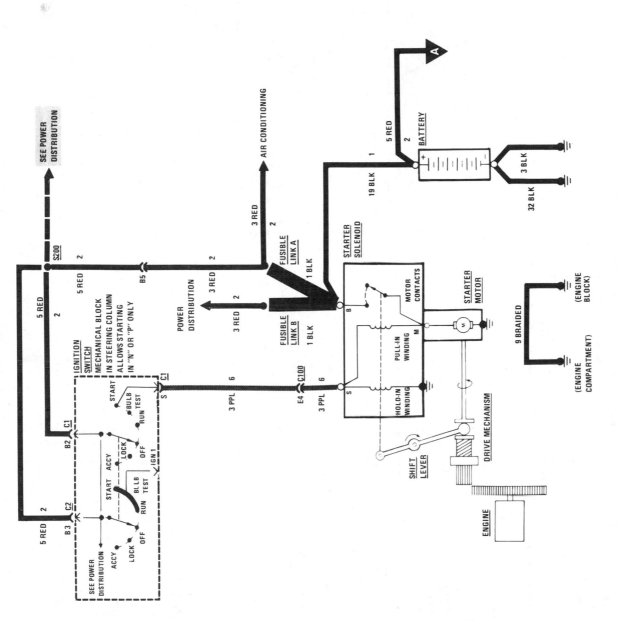

Typical charging system wiring diagram (1985-on)

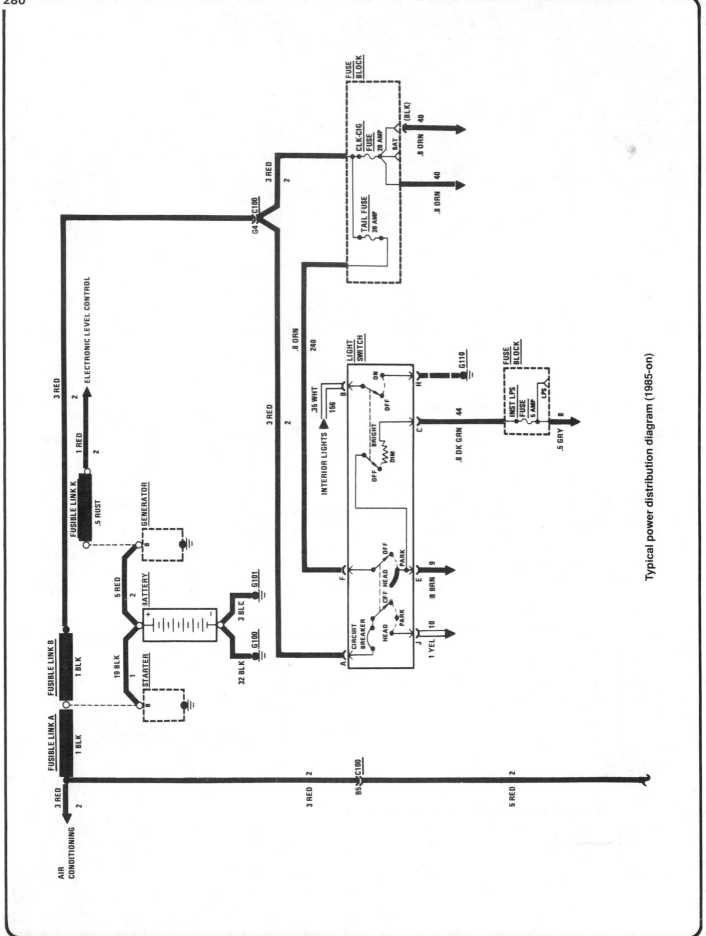

Typical power distribution diagram (1985-on)

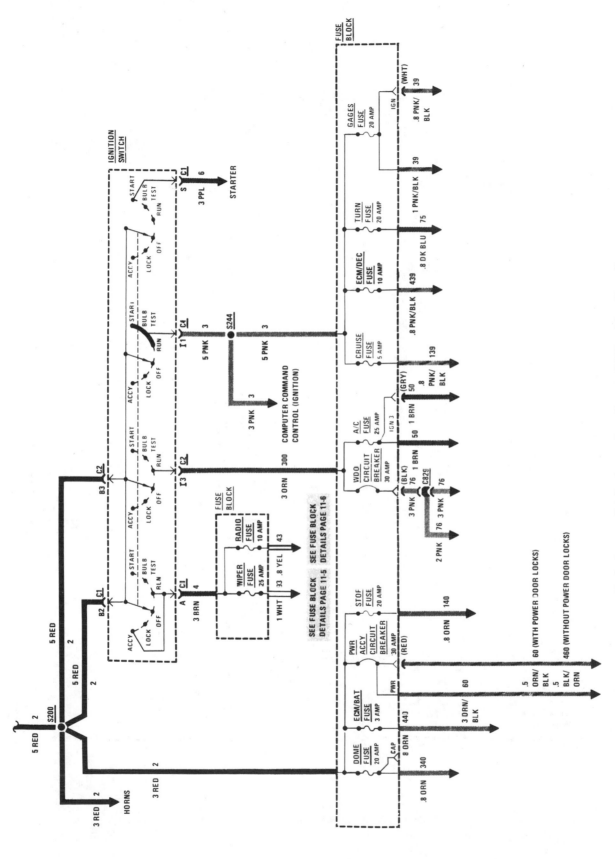

Typical power distribution system diagram (1985-on) (continued)

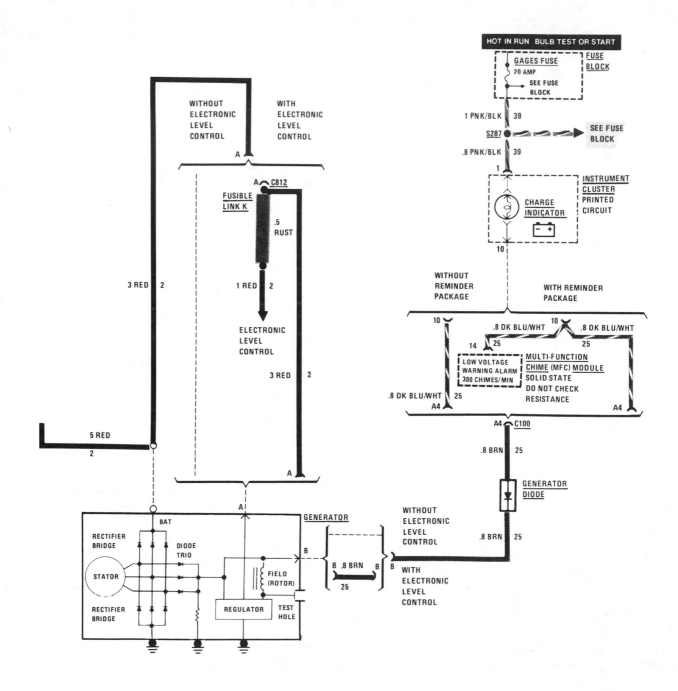

Typical starter system wiring diagram (1985-on)

Index

HAYNES AUTOMOTIVE MANUALS

NOTE: New manuals are added to this list on a periodic basis. If you do not see a listing for your vehicle, consult your local Haynes dealer for the latest product information.

ALFA-ROMEO
531   Alfa Romeo Sedan & Coupe '73 thru '80

AMC
    Jeep CJ – see JEEP (412)
694   Mid-size models, Concord, Hornet, Gremlin & Spirit '70 thru '83
934   (Renault) Alliance & Encore '83 thru '87

AUDI
615   4000 '80 thru '87
428   5000 '77 thru '83
1117   5000 '84 thru '88
207   Fox '73 thru '79

AUSTIN
049   Healey 100/6 & 3000 Roadster '56 thru '68
    Healey Sprite – see MG Midget (265)

BLMC
260   1100, 1300 & Austin America '62 thru '74
527   Mini '59 thru '69
*646   Mini '69 thru '88

BMW
276   320i all 4 cyl models '75 thru '83
632   528i & 530i '75 thru '80
240   1500 thru 2002 except Turbo '59 thru '77
348   2500, 2800, 3.0 & Bavaria '69 thru '76

BUICK
    Century (front wheel drive) – see GENERAL MOTORS A-Cars (829)
*1627   Buick, Oldsmobile & Pontiac Full-size (front wheel drive) '85 thru '90
    Buick Electra, LeSabre and Park Avenue; Oldsmobile Delta 88 Royale, Ninety Eight and Regency; Pontiac Bonneville
*1551   Buick Oldsmobile & Pontiac Full-size (Rear wheel drive)
    Buick Electra '70 thru '84, Estate '70 thru '90, LeSabre '70 thru '79
    Oldsmobile Custom Cruiser '70 thru '90, Delta 88 '70 thru '85, Ninety-eight '70 thru '84
    Pontiac Bonneville '70 thru '86, Catalina '70 thru '81, Grandville '70 thru '75, Parisienne '84 thru '86
627   Mid-size all rear-drive Regal & Century models with V6, V8 and Turbo '74 thru '87
    Regal – see GENERAL MOTORS (1671)
    Skyhawk – see GM J-Cars (766)
552   Skylark all X-car models '80 thru '85

CADILLAC
*751   Cadillac Rear Wheel Drive all gasoline models '70 thru '90
    Cimarron – see GM J-Cars (766)

CAPRI
296   2000 MK I Coupe '71 thru '75
283   2300 MK II Coupe '74 thru '78
205   2600 & 2800 V6 Coupe '71 thru '75
375   2800 Mk II V6 Coupe '75 thru '78
    Mercury Capri – see FORD Mustang (654)

CHEVROLET
*1477   Astro & GMC Safari Mini-vans '85 thru '90
554   Camaro V8 '70 thru '81
*866   Camaro '82 thru '90
    Cavalier – see GM J-Cars (766)
    Celebrity – see GM A-Cars (829)
625   Chevelle, Malibu & El Camino all V6 & V8 models '69 thru '87
449   Chevette & Pontiac T1000 '76 thru '87
550   Citation '80 thru '85
*1628   Corsica/Beretta '87 thru '90
274   Corvette all V8 models '68 thru '82
*1336   Corvette '84 thru '89
704   Full-size Sedans Caprice, Impala, Biscayne, Bel Air & Wagons, all V6 & V8 models '69 thru '90
    Lumina – see GENERAL MOTORS (1671)
319   Luv Pick-up all 2WD & 4WD '72 thru '82
626   Monte Carlo all V6, V8 & Turbo '70 thru '87
241   Nova all V8 models '69 thru '79
*1642   Nova & Geo Prizm front wheel drive '85 thru '90
*420   Pick-ups '67 thru '87 – Chevrolet & GMC, all V8 & in-line 6 cyl 2WD & 4WD '67 thru '87
*1664   Pick-ups '88 thru '90 – Chevrolet & GMC all full-size (C and K) models, '88 thru '90
*1727   Sprint & Geo Metro '85 thru '91
*831   S-10 & GMC S-15 Pick-ups '82 thru '90
*345   Vans – Chevrolet & GMC, V8 & in-line 6 cyl models '68 thru '89
208   Vega except Cosworth '70 thru '77

CHRYSLER
*1337   Chrysler & Plymouth Mid-size front wheel drive '82 thru '89
    K-Cars – see DODGE Aries (723)
    Laser – see DODGE Daytona (1140)

DATSUN
402   200SX '77 thru '79
647   200SX '80 thru '83
228   B-210 '73 thru '78
525   210 '78 thru '82

206   240Z, 260Z & 280Z Coupe & 2+2 '70 thru '78
563   280ZX Coupe & 2+2 '79 thru '83
    300ZX – see NISSAN (1137)
679   310 '78 thru '82
123   510 & PL521 Pick-up '68 thru '73
430   510 '78 thru '81
372   610 '72 thru '76
277   620 Series Pick-up '73 thru '79
    720 Series Pick-up – see NISSAN Pick-ups (771)
376   810/Maxima all gas models '77 thru '84
124   1200 '70 thru '73
368   F10 '76 thru '79
    Pulsar – see NISSAN (876)
    Sentra – see NISSAN (982)
    Stanza – see NISSAN (981)

DODGE
*723   Aries & Plymouth Reliant '81 thru '89
*1231   Caravan & Plymouth Voyager Mini-Vans '84 thru '89
699   Challenger & Plymouth Saporro '78 thru '83
236   Colt '71 thru '77
419   Colt (rear wheel drive) '77 thru '80
610   Colt & Plymouth Champ (front wheel drive) '78 thru '87
*556   D50 & Plymouth Arrow Pick-ups '79 thru '88
*1668   Dakota Pick-up all models '87 thru '90
234   Dart & Plymouth Valiant all 6 cyl models '67 thru '76
*1140   Daytona & Chrysler Laser '84 thru '89
*545   Omni & Plymouth Horizon '78 thru '90
*912   Pick-ups all full-size models '74 thru '90
*349   Vans – Dodge & Plymouth V8 & 6 cyl models '71 thru '89

FIAT
080   124 Sedan & Wagon all ohv & dohc models '66 thru '75
094   124 Sport Coupe & Spider '68 thru '78
310   131 & Brava '75 thru '81
479   Strada '79 thru '82
273   X1/9 '74 thru '80

FORD
*1476   Aerostar Mini-vans '86 thru '90
788   Bronco and Pick-ups '73 thru '79
*880   Bronco and Pick-ups '80 thru '90
014   Cortina MK II except Lotus '66 thru '70
295   Cortina MK III 1600 & 2000 ohc '70 thru '76
268   Courier Pick-up '72 thru '82
789   Escort & Mercury Lynx all models '81 thru '90
560   Fairmont & Mercury Zephyr all in-line & V8 models '78 thru '83
334   Fiesta '77 thru '80
754   Ford & Mercury Full-size, Ford LTD & Mercury Marquis ('75 thru '82); Ford Custom 500, Country Squire, Crown Victoria & Mercury Colony Park ('75 thru '87); Ford LTD Crown Victoria & Mercury Gran Marquis ('83 thru '87)
359   Granada & Mercury Monarch all in-line, 6 cyl & V8 models '75 thru '80
773   Ford & Mercury Mid-size, Ford Thunderbird & Mercury Cougar ('75 thru '82); Ford LTD & Mercury Marquis ('83 thru '86); Ford Torino, Gran Torino, Elite, Ranchero pick-ups, LTD II, Mercury Montego, Comet, XR-7 & Lincoln Versailles ('75 thru '86)
*654   Mustang & Mercury Capri all models including Turbo '79 thru '90
357   Mustang V8 '64-1/2 thru '73
231   Mustang II all 4 cyl, V6 & V8 models '74 thru '78
204   Pinto '70 thru '74
649   Pinto & Mercury Bobcat '75 thru '80
*1026   Ranger & Bronco II gasoline models '83 thru '89
*1421   Taurus & Mercury Sable '86 thru '90
*1418   Tempo & Mercury Topaz all gasoline models '84 thru '89
1338   Thunderbird & Mercury Cougar/XR7 '83 thru '88
*1725   Thunderbird & Mercury Cougar '89 thru '90
*344   Vans all V8 Econoline models '69 thru '90

GENERAL MOTORS
*829   A-Cars – Chevrolet Celebrity, Buick Century, Pontiac 6000 & Oldsmobile Cutlass Ciera '82 thru '90
*766   J-Cars – Chevrolet Cavalier, Pontiac J-2000, Oldsmobile Firenza, Buick Skyhawk & Cadillac Cimarron '82 thru '90
*1420   N-Cars – Buick Somerset '85 thru '87 Pontiac Grand Am and Oldsmobile Calais '85 thru '90; Buick Skylark '86 thru '90
*1671   GM: Buick Regal, Chevrolet Lumina, Oldsmobile Cutlass Supreme, Pontiac Grand Prix, all front wheel drive models '88 thru '90

GEO
    Metro – see CHEVROLET Sprint (1727)
    Tracker – see SUZUKI Samurai (1626)
    Prizm – see CHEVROLET Nova (1642)

GMC
    Safari – see CHEVROLET ASTRO (1477)
    Vans & Pick-ups – see CHEVROLET (420, 831, 345, 1664)

HONDA
138   360, 600 & Z Coupe '67 thru '75
351   Accord CVCC '76 thru '83
*1221   Accord '84 thru '89
160   Civic 1200 '73 thru '79
633   Civic 1300 & 1500 CVCC '80 thru '83
297   Civic 1500 CVCC '75 thru '79
*1227   Civic all models '84 thru '90
*601   Prelude CVCC '79 thru '89

HYUNDAI
*1552   Excel '86 thru '89

ISUZU
*1641   Trooper & Pick-up all gasoline models '81 thru '90

JAGUAR
098   MK I & II, 240 & 340 Sedans '55 thru '69
*242   XJ6 all 6 cyl models '68 thru '86
*478   XJ12 & XJS all 12 cyl models '72 thru '85
140   XK-E 3.8 & 4.2 all 6 cyl models '61 thru '72

JEEP
*1553   Cherokee, Comanche & Wagoneer Limited '84 thru '89
412   CJ '49 thru '86

LADA
*413   1200, 1300, 1500 & 1600 all models including Riva '74 thru '86

LAND ROVER
314   Series II, IIA, & III all 4 cyl gasoline models '58 thru '86
529   Diesel '58 thru '80

MAZDA
648   626 Sedan & Coupe (rear wheel drive) '79 thru '82
*1082   626 & MX-6 (front wheel drive) '83 thru '90
*267   B1600, B1800 & B2000 Pick-ups '72 thru '90
370   GLC Hatchback (rear wheel drive) '77 thru '83
757   GLC (front wheel drive) '81 thru '86
109   RX2 '71 thru '75
096   RX3 '72 thru '76
460   RX-7 '79 thru '85
*1419   RX-7 '86 thru '89

MERCEDES-BENZ
*1643   190 Series all 4-cyl. gasoline models '84 thru '88
346   230, 250 & 280 Sedan, Coupe & Roadster all 6 cyl sohc models '68 thru '72
983   280 123 Series all gasoline models '77 thru '81
698   350 & 450 Sedan, Coupe & Roadster '71 thru '80
697   Diesel 123 Series 200D, 220D, 240D, 240TD, 300D, 300CD, 300TD, 4- & 5-speed incl. Turbo '76 thru '85

MERCURY
See FORD Listing

MG
475   MGA '56 thru '62
111   MGB Roadster & GT Coupe '62 thru '80
265   MG Midget & Austin Healey Sprite Roadster '58 thru '80

MITSUBISHI
*1669   Cordia, Tredia, Galant, Precis & Mirage '83 thru '90
    Pick-up – see Dodge D-50 (556)

MORRIS
074   (Austin) Marina 1.8 '71 thru '80
024   Minor 1000 sedan & wagon '56 thru '71

NISSAN
1137   300ZX all Turbo & non-Turbo '84 thru '89
*1341   Maxima '85 thru '89
*771   Pick-ups/Pathfinder gas models '80 thru '88
*876   Pulsar '83 thru '86
*982   Sentra '82 thru '90
*981   Stanza '82 thru '90

OLDSMOBILE
    Custom Cruiser – see BUICK Full-size (1551)
658   Cutlass all standard gasoline V6 & V8 models '74 thru '88
    Cutlass Ciera – see GM A-Cars (829)
    Cutlass Supreme – see GM (1671)
    Firenza – see GM J-Cars (766)
    Ninety-eight – see BUICK Full-size (1551)
    Omega – see PONTIAC Phoenix & Omega (551)

PEUGEOT
161   504 all gasoline models '68 thru '79
663   504 all diesel models '74 thru '83

PLYMOUTH
425   Arrow '76 thru '80
    For all other PLYMOUTH titles, see DODGE listing.

PONTIAC
    T1000 – see CHEVROLET Chevette (449)
    J-2000 – see GM J-Cars (766)
    6000 – see GM A-Cars (829)

1232   Fiero '84 thru '88
555   Firebird all V8 models except Turbo '70 thru '81
*867   Firebird '82 thru '89
    Full-size Rear Wheel Drive – see Buick, Oldsmobile, Pontiac Full-size (1551)
    Grand Prix – see General Motors (1671)
551   Phoenix & Oldsmobile Omega all X-car models '80 thru '84

PORSCHE
*264   911 all Coupe & Targa models except Turbo '65 thru '89
239   914 all 4 cyl models '69 thru '76
397   924 including Turbo '76 thru '82
*1027   944 including Turbo '83 thru '89

RENAULT
141   5 Le Car '76 thru '83
079   8 & 10 with 58.4 cu in engines '62 thru '72
097   12 Saloon & Estate 1289 cc engines '70 thru '80
768   15 & 17 '73 thru '79
081   16 89.7 cu in & 95.5 cu in engines '65 thru '72
598   18i & Sportwagon '81 thru '86
    Alliance & Encore – see AMC (934)
984   Fuego '82 thru '85

ROVER
085   3500 & 3500S Sedan 215 cu in engines '68 thru '76
*365   3500 SDI V8 '76 thru '85

SAAB
198   95 & 96 V4 '66 thru '75
247   99 including Turbo '69 thru '80
*980   900 including Turbo '79 thru '88

SUBARU
237   1100, 1300, 1400 & 1600 '71 thru '79
*681   1600 & 1800 2WD & 4Wd '80 thru '89

SUZUKI
1626   Samurai/Sidekick and Geo Tracker '86 thru '89

TOYOTA
*1023   Camry '83 thru '90
150   Carina '71 thru '74
229   Celica ST, GT & liftback '71 thru '77
437   Celica '78 thru '81
*935   Celica except front-wheel drive and Supra '82 thru '85
680   Celica Supra '79 thru '81
1139   Celica Supra in-line 6-cylinder '82 thru '86
361   Corolla '75 thru '79
961   Corolla (rear wheel drive) '80 thru '87
*1025   Corolla (front wheel drive) '84 thru '91
*636   Corolla Tercel '80 thru '82
230   Corona & MK II all 4 cyl sohc models '69 thru '74
360   Corona '74 thru '82
*532   Cressida '78 thru '82
313   Land Cruiser '68 thru '82
200   MK II all 6 cyl models '72 thru '76
*1339   MR2 '85 thru '87
304   Pick-up '69 thru '78
*656   Pick-up '79 thru '90

TRIUMPH
112   GT6 & Vitesse '62 thru '74
113   Spitfire '62 thru '81
028   TR2, 3, 3A, & 4A Roadsters '52 thru '67
031   TR250 & 6 Roadsters '67 thru '76
322   TR7 '75 thru '81

VW
091   411 & 412 all 103 cu in models '68 thru '73
159   Beetle & Karmann Ghia all models '54 thru '79
238   Dasher all gasoline models '74 thru '81
*884   Rabbit, Jetta, Scirocco, & Pick-up all gasoline models '74 thru '89 & Convertible '80 thru '89
451   Rabbit, Jetta & Pick-up all diesel models '77 thru '84
082   Transporter 1600 '68 thru '79
226   Transporter 1700, 1800 & 2000 all models '72 thru '79
084   Type 3 1500 & 1600 '63 thru '73
1029   Vanagon all air-cooled models '80 thru '83

VOLVO
203   120, 130 Series & 1800 Sports '61 thru '73
129   140 Series '66 thru '74
244   164 '68 thru '75
*270   240 Series '74 thru '90
400   260 Series '75 thru '82
*1550   740 & 760 Series '82 thru '88

SPECIAL MANUALS
1479   Automotive Body Repair & Painting Manual
1654   Automotive Electrical Manual
1480   Automotive Heating & Air Conditioning Manual
1763   Ford Engine Overhaul Manual
482   Fuel Injection Manual
1666   Small Engine Repair Manual
299   SU Carburetors thru '88
393   Weber Carburetors thru '79
300   Zenith/Stromberg CD Carburetors thru '76

See your dealer for other available titles

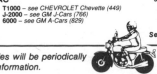

Over 100 Haynes motorcycle manuals also available   4-1-91

Listings shown with an asterisk (*) indicate model coverage as of this printing. These titles will be periodically updated to include later model years — consult your Haynes dealer for more information.

Haynes North America, Inc., P.O. Box 978, Newbury Park, CA 91320 • (818) 889-5400 • (805) 498-6703